'Fair value is a central notion in accounting practice, research and standard setting. This book, whose chapters are authored by top-notch accountants and academics, rolls over each of these dimensions to provide an authoritative and comprehensive analysis of the state-of-art and future developments in this area. I think it is a "must" for those interested in fair value accounting.'

Salvador Carmona, Rector, IE University, Spain.
Past President of the European Accounting Association
and past editor of the European Accounting Review

'Perhaps no issue in accounting has been as controversial as fair value. Written from the unique perspectives of leading scholars around the world, this collection explores its far-reaching implications for managers, regulators, and the stability of financial markets. An engaging and accessible foray into the complex world of fair value accounting.'

Karen Nelson, Texas Christian University, USA

T0330944

THE ROUTLEDGE COMPANION TO FAIR VALUE IN ACCOUNTING

The concept of 'fair value' marked a major departure from traditional cost accounting. In theory, under this approach a balance sheet better reflects the current value of assets and liabilities. Critics of fair value argue that it is less useful over longer time frames and prone to distortion by market inefficiencies resulting in pro-cyclicality in the financial system by exacerbating market swings.

Comprising contributions from a unique mixture of academics, standard-setters and practitioners, and edited by internationally recognized experts, this book, on a controversial and intensely debated topic, is a comprehensive reference source that

- examines the use of fair value in international financial reporting standards (IFRS) and the US standard SFAS 157 Fair Value Measurement, setting out the case for and against;
- looks at fair value from a number of different theoretical and practical perspectives, including a critical review of the merits and arguments against the use of fair value accounting;
- and explores fair value accounting in practice, involvement in the Great Financial Crisis, implications for managerial reporting discretion, compensation and investment.

This volume is an indispensable reference that is deserving of a place on the bookshelves of both libraries and all those working in, studying or researching the areas of international accounting, financial accounting and reporting.

Gilad Livne is Professor of Accounting at the University of Exeter, UK.

Garen Markarian is Chair of Financial Accounting at WHU, Vallendar, Germany.

ROUTLEDGE COMPANIONS IN BUSINESS, MANAGEMENT AND ACCOUNTING

Routledge Companions in Business, Management and Accounting are prestige reference works providing an overview of a whole subject area or sub-discipline. These books survey the state of the discipline including emerging and cutting-edge areas. Providing a comprehensive, up-to-date, definitive work of reference, Routledge Companions can be cited as an authoritative source on the subject.

A key aspect of these Routledge Companions is their international scope and relevance. Edited by an array of highly regarded scholars, these volumes also benefit from teams of contributors that reflect an international range of perspectives.

Individually, Routledge Companions in Business, Management and Accounting provide an impactful one-stop-shop resource for each theme covered. Collectively, they represent a comprehensive learning and research resource for researchers, postgraduate students and practitioners.

Published titles in this series include the following:

THE ROUTLEDGE COMPANION TO AIR TRANSPORT MANAGEMENT
Edited by Nigel Halpern and Anne Graham

THE ROUTLEDGE COMPANION TO THE GEOGRAPHY OF INTERNATIONAL BUSINESS
Edited by Jonathan Beaverstock, Gary Cook, Jennifer Johns,
Frank McDonald and Naresh Pandit

THE ROUTLEDGE COMPANION TO RISK, CRISIS AND SECURITY IN BUSINESS
Edited by Kurt J. Engemann

THE ROUTLEDGE COMPANION TO FAIR VALUE IN ACCOUNTING
Edited by Gilad Livne and Garen Markarian

For more information about this series, please visit: https://www.routledge.com/Routledge-Studies-in-Genocide-and-Crimes-against-Humanity/book-series/RSGCH

THE ROUTLEDGE COMPANION TO FAIR VALUE IN ACCOUNTING

Edited by
Gilad Livne and Garen Markarian

LONDON AND NEW YORK

First published 2018
by Routledge

2 Park Square, Milton Park, Abingdon, Oxfordshire OX14 4RN
52 Vanderbilt Avenue, New York, NY 10017

Routledge is an imprint of the Taylor & Francis Group, an informa business

First issued in paperback 2020

British Library Cataloguing-in-Publication Data
A catalogue record for this book is available from the British Library

Library of Congress Cataloging-in-Publication Data
Names: Livne, Gilad, editor. | Markarian, Garen, editor.
Title: The Routledge companion to fair value in accounting /
edited by Gilad Livne and Garen Markarian.
Other titles: Companion to fair value in accounting
Description: First Edition. | New York: Routledge, 2018. |
Series: Routledge companions in business, management and accounting |
Includes bibliographical references and index.
Identifiers: LCCN 2018002849| ISBN 9781138656505 (hardback) |
ISBN 9781315621876 (ebook)
Subjects: LCSH: Fair value—Accounting.
Classification: LCC HF5681.V3 R68 2018 | DDC 657/.7—dc23
LC record available at https://lccn.loc.gov/2018002849

ISBN: 978-1-138-65650-5 (hbk)
ISBN: 978-0-367-65613-3 (pbk)

Typeset in Bembo
by codeMantra

CONTENTS

Contents

CONTRIBUTORS

Amir Amel-Zadeh is Associate Professor of Accounting at Saïd Business School, University of Oxford. Among other topics, his research investigates accounting and regulatory issues at financial institutions, particularly in relation to fair value accounting. Amir's research has been published in leading journals such as *The Accounting Review, Review of Accounting Studies* and others. He has taught or consulted for the financial services industry in the USA, Europe, Asia and the Middle East and previously worked for Lehman Brothers in London. He received his PhD in Finance from the University of Cambridge.

Alan Ball is a former member of the financial stability unit, and senior advisor in the prudential policy division at the Bank of England, and co-chair of the Basel Committee of Banking Supervision working group on Disclosure. He has written extensively on market microstructure, systemic risks, and financial regulation.

Christof Beuselinck is Professor at IÉSEG School of Management (France) and Lille Économie et Management (LEM). His research specializes in the economic and governance outcomes of multinational corporate reporting. Christof has published in internationally peer-reviewed journals such as the *Review of Accounting Studies* and the *Journal of Corporate Finance*. He has been teaching on IFRS and related topics internationally and served as an associate member of the European Commission Sponsored INTACCT program on the effects of IFRS harmonization for European firms.

Yuri Biondi is tenured Senior Research Fellow of the National Center for Scientific Research of France (Cnrs – IRISSO) and Research Director at the Financial Regulation Research Lab (Labex ReFi), Paris, France. His research interests include economic theory, dynamic systems analysis as well as accounting theory and regulation. Further information is available at http://yuri.biondi.free.fr/.

Kay Blaufus is Professor of Business Taxation at Leibniz University Hannover, Germany. He is a certified tax advisor and received his PhD in 2005 from Freie Universität Berlin with a thesis on the economic effects of fair value accounting. His areas of expertise include tax accounting, behavioral taxation and tax compliance. His research has been published in

Contemporary Accounting Research, European Accounting Review, Journal of Economic Behavior & Organization and *Journal of Economic Psychology*.

John L. Campbell is Associate Professor and EY Faculty Fellow at the University of Georgia. He has written multiple research papers on the effectiveness of accounting information and, more generally, on derivative instruments. His work is informed by experience using (and accounting for) derivatives at a bank, a manufacturing firm and as a Big-4 auditor. He routinely interacts with members of the Financial Accounting Standards Board and the Securities and Exchange Commission on topics of interest to standard-setters.

Jun Chen is a professor of accounting at the School of Management of Zhejiang University. His research areas include auditing, earnings management, and corporate governance. His work has been published in a variety of academic and practitioner journals. He has served as an ad hoc reviewer for numerous journals and an independent board member for multiple listed companies in China. Jun Chen acknowledges financial support from the National Natural Science Foundation of China [grant number NSFC – 71572181].

Ester Chen is Head of Accountancy in the Accounting and Business Administration Department of the Peres Academic Center. She is also a Certified Public Accountant (Israel). In the past, Ester was the Head of the Professional Staff of ICPAI. Her research interests include accounting regulation, fair value accounting, tax avoidance, earnings management, corporate social responsibility, financial disclosure and venture capital.

Frank L. Clarke is Emeritus Professor of Accounting at the University of Newcastle; Honorary Professor of Accounting at the University of Sydney; and has held appointments at the Universities of Newcastle, Sydney, Glasgow, Canterbury (New Zealand) and Lancaster. He is a past editor and currently a consulting editor of *Abacus*. He is the author or joint author of nine books, numerous articles in refereed and business journals, is a frequent presenter at international conferences and is a contributor to the secular financial press (with Graeme W. Dean).

Jenna D'Adduzio is a PhD candidate at the University of Georgia. She researches topics of interest to standard-setters and, in particular, on derivative instruments (and cash flow hedges). She is interested in understanding how capital market participants price the information conveyed by firms' disclosures and how mandatory disclosure requirements affect the pricing of these disclosures.

Massimo De Buglio is Adjunct Professor of Accounting at Bocconi University – Milan. He has worked as a business consultant and chartered accountant. His area of expertise includes IAS/IFRS and Italian GAAP accounting, valuation and M&A. He is also a member of the statutory audit board in family and non-family firms.

Graeme W. Dean is Emeritus Professor of Accounting and formerly Head of Discipline of Accounting at The University of Sydney and has held visiting appointments at several overseas universities in Glasgow, Graz, Canterbury, Cardiff, Munich and Frankfurt. He was the sole editor (1994–2009) of *Abacus*, the fourth oldest and one of the leading Anglo-American accounting academic journals. Graeme has published several books and books of readings and nearly 50 refereed journal articles.

Jon Duchac is the Wayne Calloway Professor of Accounting at Wake Forest University. He has taught, researched and consulted on financial reporting issues affecting the financial services industry for more than two decades; working with the investment banking, equity research and corporate financial reporting groups at several large financial institutions. He has testified before the US House of Representatives, the Financial Accounting Standards Board and the Securities and Exchange Commission on a variety of financial reporting topics. In 2007, Jon was selected as a Fulbright Distinguished Chair at the Vienna School of Business and Economics.

Ilanit Gavious is Associate Professor of Accounting at the Guilford Glazer Faculty of Business and Management, Ben-Gurion University of the Negev. She serves as the Head of the MBA Program of Ben-Gurion University in Eilat. She also serves as a commissioner at the Israel Securities Authority (Israeli SEC). Ilanit is a certified public accountant. In the past, Ilanit served as Senior Accountant in a Big-4 accounting firm and in a leading commercial bank. Her research interests include fair valuations, earning management and corporate disclosure.

Thomas A. Gilliam is Assistant Professor with IE Business School and a former executive from Silicon Valley, where he worked with multinational technology companies including Silicon Graphics, Inc., LG Corp., Xerox Corp. and Telesensory Systems, Inc. At Silicon Graphics, he held the position of Director of Finance and Operations where he was responsible for the financial affairs of a 1.5-billion-dollar computer business. Thomas also managed and co-founded a 100-million-dollar data storage business.

Andrew Haldane is Chief Economist at the Bank of England. He is also Executive Director of Monetary Analysis, Research and Statistics. He is a member of the Bank's Monetary Policy Committee. He also has responsibility for research and statistics across the bank. Andrew has an Honorary Doctorate from the Open University, is Honorary Professor at University of Nottingham, a Visiting Fellow at Nuffield College, Oxford, a member of Economic Council of Royal Economic Society, a Fellow of the Academy of Social Sciences and a Member of Research and Policy Committee at NESTA. Andrew is the founder and Trustee of 'Pro Bono Economics', a charity that brokers economists into charitable projects and a Trustee of National Numeracy. Andrew has written extensively on domestic and international monetary and financial policy issues and has published over 150 articles and four books. In 2014, *Time* magazine named him one of the 100 most influential people in the world.

Uriel Haran is Senior Lecturer of Organizational Behavior at the Guilford Glazer Faculty of Business and Management, Ben-Gurion University of the Negev, and a member of the Center for Decision Making and Economic Psychology (DMEP). Uriel's expertise is in experimental behavioral research. His work focuses on issues of decision-making and behavioral ethics in interpersonal and managerial contexts.

Ronny K. Hofmann is Assistant Professor with IE Business School who has significant banking and audit experience. Working with Deloitte & Touche in their IFRS Centre of Excellence and as an assistant manager with KPMG, he specialized in the area financial institutions risk management (FIRM), audit financial services and accounting advisory. Ronny's focus was on providing reporting advice to audit and non-audit clients on a wide range of transactions, including M&As, IPOs and financial instrument valuations.

Martin Jacob is Professor of Business Taxation at WHU – Otto Beisheim School of Management. He received his PhD in 2010 from the University of Tübingen. His research focuses on the effects of taxation on investment and payout decisions, tax accounting as well as corporate tax avoidance. His research has been published in leading journals such as *Journal of Accounting and Economics*, *Journal of Accounting Research*, *Journal of Financial Economics* and *Review of Financial Studies*.

Kalin Kolev is Associate Professor of Accounting at Baruch College – CUNY, having previously served on the faculty of Yale School of Management. His research examines topics in financial accounting and reporting, financial reporting quality and fair value measurement being two of the focal points of his past and ongoing work.

Andrew Lennard is Director of Research at Financial Reporting Council, having joined in 1990, after qualifying as a chartered accountant with a major accounting firm. In addition to his contribution to the FRC, he has played a part in the development of the discussion of measurement in the conceptual frameworks of IPSASB and the IASB. He is a graduate of St Andrews University and a Fellow of the ICAEW.

Gilad Livne is Professor of Accounting at the University of Exeter Business School. Previously to joining Exeter, Gilad served on the faculties of the London Business School and Cass Business School. He received his PhD in accounting at the University of California, Berkeley. Gilad is also a CPA and worked as an auditor prior to pursuing his academic career. He has been a guest lecturer in several universities including HEC Paris, HEC Lausanne, NES Moscow, Bristol University and University of Lancaster Business School. He teaches financial accounting at all levels and has recently published a textbook on IFRS. His research is broadly within financial reporting and has been published in several accounting and finance journals. His research was covered in the FT and BBC as well as in other media. Gilad is a member of several editorial boards of accounting journals. He has also consulted analysts and bankers on accounting and reporting-related issues.

Michel Magnan is Professor and the Stephen Jarislowsky Chair in Corporate Governance at the John Molson School of Business of Concordia University. He is also Director of the Desjardins Center for Business Financing Innovation. He holds a PhD from the University of Washington (Seattle). His academic career spans over 30 years. His research and professional interests encompass financial statement analysis, governance, executive compensation, ethics and the environment and corporate disclosure. He was inducted into the Royal Society of Canada in 2014. He served as Chief Editor of *Contemporary Accounting Research* (CAR), one of the world's leading accounting academic journals, between 2007 and 2010. He is currently Consulting Editor of CAR and Associate Editor of European Accounting Review, Canadian Journal of Administrative Sciences and Revue française de gouvernance d'entreprise. He has been a member of the Canadian Accounting Standards Board (2011–2017). He is currently a Director and Chair of the Audit and Risk Management committee of Desjardins General Insurance Group, Canada's third largest property and casualty insurer, as well as a Director of the Institute for the Governance of Private and Public Organizations.

Garen Markarian holds the Chair of Financial Accounting at WHU – Otto Beisheim School of Management. As an international scholar specializing in corporate finance and governance, he has taught at IE Business School (Madrid), HEC (Paris), Bocconi (Milan), Concordia (Montreal),

Rice (Houston) and Case Western Reserve (Cleveland). Previously holding the position of First Regional Economic Officer for Western Asia at the United Nations, Garen has extensive experience in research on governance mechanisms, executive compensation, the banking crisis, stock markets and financial statements and valuation. His publications have received awards both from the American Finance Association and the American Accounting Association and were mentioned in the *Financial Times* and CFO magazine. Beforehand, he was a consultant for Standard & Poor's 'Society of Industry Leaders.' He is currently the academic director of the WHU risk management program partnered with the Stockholm School of Economics. Garen has earned a PhD from the Weatherhead School of Management at Case Western Reserve University.

Pietro Mazzola is Full Professor at IULM University, Milan and Adjunct Professor at Bocconi University, Milan. He received teaching and evaluation appointments from several Italian, European and US universities and worked as a strategic and accounting advisor for family and non-family firms. He is co-author of the Milan Stock Exchange listing guide on strategic planning.

Geoff Meeks is Emeritus Professor of Financial Accounting and Voluntary Director of Research at the University of Cambridge, Judge Business School. He has previously worked for Price Waterhouse, and Edinburgh University, as Director of Graduate Studies in Cambridge Economics, and as Acting Director of Judge Business School. One theme in his publications is the fragility of accounting numbers – especially those for financial assets and liabilities – in the face of market imperfections.

Vera Palea, PhD in finance and accounting at Bocconi University, is Associate Professor in Business Economics at the University of Torino. Her research focus is on the consistency of economic and financial regulations in the European Union with the EU socioeconomic model and constitutional setting. She is a member of international accounting research centers. She has published several papers in leading academic journals.

Antonio Parbonetti is Full Professor of Accounting at the University of Padova, Italy. He obtained his Doctorate in Business Administration from University of Pisa. During his PhD program, he was International Visiting Student at the Cardiff Business School and at the Case Western Reserve University (Cleveland). His research interests include board composition, CEO compensation, corporate governance and fair value accounting. He served for three years as a member of a supervisory board of a large bank under ECB supervision.

Ken Peasnel is Distinguished Professor of Accounting at Lancaster University Management School. He is the author of five books and over 100 articles, policy papers and official reports on various aspects of accounting and finance. Issues of income measurement and the valuation and recognition of assets and liabilities in financial statements have been major concerns of his research, going back into the mid-1970s and through to present day. His most recent work has focused primarily on issues concerning financial reporting in the banking industry, with particular reference to issues relating to the recognition of assets and liabilities and their basis of valuation, but it also includes studies of the value relevance to equity investors of accounting measurements that affect the majority of listed companies. He was the joint winner with his co-authors Wayne Landsman, Peter Pope and Shu Yeh of the American Accounting

Association Financial Accounting and Reporting Section 2008 Best Paper Award for their *Review of Accounting Studies* article, 'Which approach to accounting for employee stock options best reflects market pricing?'

Martin E. Persson is the J. J. Wettlaufer Faculty Fellow and Assistant Professor of Managerial Accounting and Control at the Ivey Business School, and his research is focused on the development of accounting thought. He is particularly interested in people, ideas and institutions from the 1900s as well as classical accounting theory and measurement issues. His research has been published in Emerald's book series *Development of Accounting Thought* and in *Abacus*, *Accounting Historians Journal*, *Accounting History* and *Meditari Accountancy Research*.

Arnt Verriest is Associate Professor of Accounting at EDHEC Business School in France and belongs to the Financial Analysis and Accounting Research Centre. He teaches financial statement analysis and advanced financial accounting in various graduate programs. His academic research focuses on fair value accounting in banks, international financial reporting standards (IFRS), corporate governance mechanisms in financial institutions and the design of syndicated loan agreements.

Yong Yu is an associate professor of accounting at the McCombs School of Business of the University of Texas at Austin. His research areas include financial analysts, institutional investors, and real effects of financial reporting and disclosure. His recent work has examined the economic consequences of mandatory IFRS adoption and the usefulness of fair value accounting for bank valuation.

PREFACE

We are very pleased to present this book to you. Putting this book together has been a massive challenge, and we have been gratefully assisted by the various contributors. We believe you will find here some original thoughts and perspectives brought to you by thinkers and experts in the field. Given the controversial nature of fair values, we strive to bring you differing points of view representing a balanced societal milieu. The Chief Economist of the Bank of England, a member of the British Financial Reporting Council, a member of the Canadian Accounting Standards Board, a retired CFO of an S&P 500 company and academicians from four continents bring many interesting and sometimes provocative points of view to this collection. We are infinitely grateful to them.

The book starts with a reflection on the economic crisis of 2008, a topic that is still very relevant as we write these words. In 'Does the usage of fair values increase systemic risks?', two prominent economists, drawing on their experiences, discuss improvements to fair value accounting so that it can better serve market processes going forward. This is followed by four parts. The first part covers issues related to standard-setting. The first chapter in this part, 'Fair value and the conceptual framework', discusses the fundamental building blocks as envisioned by theorists, politicians, practitioners and standard-setters in 'creating' fair value accounting. This is followed by two chapters, 'Fair value accounting: a standard-setting perspective' and 'Have the standard-setters gone too far, or not far enough, with fair value accounting?', which provide different points of view, one academic's and one practitioner's, with regard to the standard-setting process, the conflicts and the politicization of the process. The first part concludes with 'Shareholder value, financialization and accounting regulation: making sense of fair value adoption in the European Union', which discusses fair values as it is seen in the field from a political economist's point of view.

The book turns in the second part to explore how fair value accounting may affect perceptions of risk, with a particular focus on financial institutions. The first chapter, 'Measuring fair value when markets malfunction: evidence from the financial crisis', goes deeper into the technical specifics and builds upon the ideas put forth in the first chapter. 'Fair value accounting in financial institutions' zooms in on the role of fair value accounting where it probably matters the most. The final two chapters focus on how fair value accounting influences risk management: 'Bank risk management – and fair value accounting' discusses financial institutions and their usage of fair value accounting, while 'The use of fair value accounting in risk management in non-financial firms' looks at industrial companies.

Part III features some thoughts on the evolution in fair value including a historic perspective in 'The history of the fair value term and its measurements', which provides a most concise summary of fair value accounting, origins, uses and applications. The next chapter, 'The "fairness" of fair value accounting: marking-to-market, marking-to-model and financial reporting management', explores whether the introduction of fair value accounting has augmented the set of accounting choices that could be exploited by managers. 'Let the fox guard the henhouse: how relaxing the three-level fair value hierarchy increases the reliability of fair value estimates' expands on this question to explore behavioral aspects of fair value accounting.

Our final set of chapters present specialized topics of interest to those needing to build competency in specific issues. 'Fair value accounting – a manager's perspective' provides a perspective from internal accountants in industrial firms. 'Tax-related implications of fair value accounting' looks at taxes, while 'Fair value accounting and executive compensation' explores how fair values may affect compensation and managerial incentives. 'Fair value and the formation of financial market prices through ignorance and hazard' provides a unique philosophic point of view. The last two chapters, 'Fair values in China' and 'Fair values and family firms', close the book. The first discusses the usage of fair values in China – the next economic superpower if not already, and the last chapter deals with family firms. The latter presents the unique point of view of the thousands of entities, especially in Europe, that have differing motivations when it comes to the usage and presentation of fair value numbers, that is often lost in a world dominated by large publicly listed institutions.

We hope you enjoy reading these chapters!

Gilad Livne and Garen Markarian

PROLOGUE

A reflection

1

DOES THE USAGE OF FAIR VALUES INCREASE SYSTEMIC RISKS?

Alan Ball and Andrew Haldane

Introduction

In 2008, the global financial system experienced a dramatic thunderstorm. Lightning strikes threatened seizure in some financial markets and institutions, and, nearly a decade later, the rumbles of thunder are still discernable.

The debate on the causes and consequences of this perfect storm have been subject to considerable debate, but at the center of this storm is, on the face of it, a rather basic question: how should the instruments that make up the financial system be valued? So basic a question ought not to be a matter of life and death. But for a great many financial institutions during this crisis, it was precisely that.

The fundamental concept on which this debate hinges is fair value. Like beauty, its meaning lies in the eyes of the beholder. For some, the application of fair value principles risks exposing financial firms to the vagaries of markets. For others, ignoring the signals from financial markets risks creating a financial landscape that is anything but fair.

The fair value debate generates electricity in the usually static-free professions of accountancy and regulation. Bankers fulminate at the mere mention. Among Heads of State in some of the biggest countries in the world, accounting standards for derivatives have generated levels of fear and consternation usually reserved for non-financial weapons of mass destruction.

Three phases of fair value

So, what lies at the heart of this debate? It is well captured by Preston Delano, US Comptroller of the Currency:

> ...the soundness of the banking system depends upon the soundness of the country's business and industrial enterprises, and should not be measured by the precarious yardstick of current market quotations which often reflect speculative and not true appraisals of intrinsic worth.[1]

Delano was US Comptroller of the Currency in 1938. This provides a clue to the fact that the fair value debate is not a new one. To understand this debate, its origins and undulations, it is worth starting at the very beginning.

Although bookkeeping has far earlier antecedents, modern accountancy is believed to have begun in the Italian cities of Genoa, Venice and Florence in the 14th century. It is no coincidence that modern banking emerged at precisely the same time in precisely the same cities. Banks emerged to service rapidly expanding commercial companies, and double-entry bookkeeping became an essential means of recording and tracking who owed what to whom, oiling the wheels of finance.

It is no coincidence, too, that the first-known description of accountancy was provided by an Italian, Luca Pacioli, in the late 15th century.[2] Pacioli was not your typical accountant. A wandering Franciscan monk, tutor and mathematician, he was a friend, and sometimes collaborator, of Leonardo de Vinci. Although comfortably the less famous of the two, Pacioli is still known today as the father of modern accounting.

From those beginnings, double-entry bookkeeping began to spread north within Europe during the Middle Ages: to Germany in the 15th century, Spain and England in the 16th century and Scotland in the 17th century. By the late 18th century, Goethe had called double-entry 'among the finest inventions of the human mind'.[3] Some people are easily impressed. Despite that, the progress of double-entry was surprisingly slow. At the start of the 19th century, there were only 11 Londoners who listed their occupation as 'accomptants'.

The 19th century marked a turning point. In the UK, joint stock companies began to spring up. The Bankruptcy Act of 1831 gave accountants a role in winding-up enterprises, and the Companies Acts of 1844 and 1862 established a legal requirement for companies to register and file accounts. By the end of the century, audit practices were becoming established. The accountant's role was to provide a true and fair view of a company's assets and income, as protection for the state (to whom it paid taxes) and investors (to whom it paid dividends).

It was these concerns that led to the gradual emergence during the second half of the 19th century of fair value-based accounting conventions in the USA. From the late 19th century, banks' securities were carried at market values and their fixed assets at 'appraised values'. In other words, by the early 20th century, fair value principles were widely applied to companies in general and to banks in particular. In many respects, this period may have been the high-water mark for fair value principles.

In the USA, this first wave of the fair value debate ended in 1938.[4] The backdrop was inauspicious. The first phase of the Great Depression, between 1929 and 1933, saw the failure of a large number of US banks. Between 1933 and 1937, the US economy recovered somewhat, but by 1938, there were fears of a double dip. At the Fed's prompting, Franklin D Roosevelt called a convention comprising the US Treasury, the Federal Reserve Board, the Comptroller of the Currency and the Federal Deposit Insurance Corporation (FDIC). Its purpose was to determine what should be done with prudential standards to safeguard recovery.

This was no ordinary regulatory convention. Marriner S Eccles, Chairman of the Federal Reserve, called it 'guerrilla warfare'. In one corner were the regulators, the Comptroller of the Currency and the FDIC. Scarred by their regulatory experience, and fearing further bank failures, the Comptroller and the FDIC pushed for high prudential standards, including preservation of fair values for banks' assets. In the other corner was the Fed. Scarred by their monetary policy experience, and fearing a further collapse in lending, the Fed argued for laxer prudential standards and the abandonment of fair values. Battle commenced.

The tussle lasted two months, often played out in public through *The New York Times*. In the end, the Fed prevailed. On 26 June 1938, Franklin D Roosevelt announced (without so much as a hint of irony) the Uniform Agreement on Bank Supervisory Procedures. Banks' investment-grade assets were to be valued not at market values but at amortized cost. And banks' sub-investment-grade assets were to be valued at a long-run average of market prices. In the teeth of crisis, and in the interest of macroeconomic stability, the first phase of fair value had ended.

This pattern was to be repeated half a century later – the second wave of fair value. Historic cost accounting remained in the ascendancy in the USA from the 1940s right through to the early 1970s. But from the mid-1970s onward, accounting standard-setters began to embrace fair value measurement, first in the context of banks' portfolios of equities and other marketable securities.[5] By the late 1980s, there was widespread recognition that traditional accounting approaches were obscuring the real value of securities and derivatives.

US experience during the Savings and Loan crisis in the mid-1980s provided further impetus. Forbearance, including about the valuation of assets and liabilities, was widely believed to have been a cause of the buildup of problems among the thrifts.[6] In 1989, Congress passed the Financial Institutions Recovery, Reform and Enforcement Act, tightening valuation standards among banks and bringing them closer to fair values. In the same year, the International Accounting Standards Committee (IASC) commenced a project to assess the measurement and disclosure of financial instruments. These too were to suffer a setback.

By 1990, recession had taken hold in the USA, with lending contracting sharply. As in 1938, the US economy was suffering 'financial headwinds'. As in 1938, the Fed was quick to call for a relaxation of prudential and valuation standards to head off pressures on banks.[7] As in 1938, the upshot was a concerted move by the then-President, George H W Bush, relaxing examination and valuation standards.[8] For the second time, fair value had been returned to its box.

And so, to the present day – the third phase. By 2008, the ranks of 'accomptants' had swelled, with numbers of recognized accountants in the UK totaling over 275,000. Yet, the issues raised by the global financial crisis had loud echoes of 1938. Through the 1990s, the main international accounting standard-setters extended the boundaries of fair value. In the USA, this was given impetus by the Federal Deposit Insurance Corporation Improvement Act (FDICIA) in 1991. Widespread use of mark to market was a key ingredient of the prompt corrective action approach embodied in FDICIA.

From 1992, it became a requirement among US companies to disclose the fair value of all financial instruments in the notes to their accounts. Toward the end of the 1990s, this move was formalized with financial instruments (derivatives, equity and debt) being included explicitly in the accounts at fair value. In the USA, this followed the adoption of the Statement of Financial Accounting Standard 133 in June 1998. Elsewhere, it followed adoption of the IASC's International Accounting Standard 39 in January 2001.

The banking crisis brought that evolution to a halt. As pressures on banks' balance sheets intensified, subdued lending growth raised concerns that recovery may be retarded. A debate began internationally on rolling back fair value to arrest this downward trajectory. Once again, central bank governors, politicians, regulators and countries were prominent in their criticism of fair value, leading to fears that fair value was poised to enter the third dip on its roller-coaster journey.

Fair values and market prices

What have been the underlying forces leading fair value to be at first lauded, then questioned and periodically abandoned? At the heart of this is the vexed question of whether market prices are a true and fair assessment of value.

In theory, market prices ought to be a full and fair reflection of the present value of future cash flows on an asset. This is the fulcrum of the Efficient Markets Hypothesis (EMH). Market prices, if not perfect, are at least efficient aggregators of information – a one-stop shop for appraising value. This simplicity makes EMH a powerful theory. But its real power is its widespread application in practice. EMH has not just monopolized the finance textbooks; it has also dominated the dealing rooms.

If the EMH were to hold strictly, the fair value debate would be uncontentious. Marking of assets to market would be proper recognition of their economic value. In that financial utopia, the interests of accountants, investors and regulators would be perfectly aligned. Accountants would have a verifiable valuation yardstick, investors a true and fair view of their true worth and regulators an objective means of evaluating solvency. Fair value would serve treble duty.

In practice, the fair value debate is contentious and has been for at least a century. Through history, accountants, investors and regulators have not always sung in tune. Today, accountants are singing opera Pacioli-style and regulators are rapping at 300 words a minute, while investors are left to whistle. In part, this discord has been blamed on failures of EMH, 'the precarious yardstick of current market quotations'.

It should come as no surprise that fair value principles have faced their stiffest tests at times of crisis – the Great Depression during the previous century and the Great Recession during this. For it is at crisis time that EMH itself faces its stiffest test, perhaps none greater than recently. The heterodox British economist George Shackle observed: 'Valuation is expectation and expectation is imagination'.[9] Imagination, and thus valuation, is apt to run wild at the peak of the boom and trough of the bust.

These episodes of overactive imagination, or deviations from EMH, can be grouped roughly three ways. Each has an important potential bearing on financial stability and on the fair value debate:

- 'Excess volatility': Some of the earliest evidence against EMH focused on the tendency of asset prices to fluctuate more than could be justified by movements in fundamentals – so-called excess volatility. While early evidence focused on the behavior of equity prices, the same tests have now been applied to a wide range of asset markets, including corporate bonds, asset-backed securities and exchange rates.[10] There is overwhelming empirical evidence of excess volatility in asset prices.
- 'Medium-term misalignment': Excess volatility, while inconvenient, need not by itself severely distort the functioning of capital markets. Asset prices' signals might be noisy but correct on average. But there is emerging evidence of asset prices becoming persistently misaligned from fundamentals in a variety of markets including equity, residential and commercial property and corporate bonds.[11]
- 'Apparent arbitrage': A third aspect of the failure of EMH is evidence of seemingly pure arbitrage opportunities being sustained by market participants for lengthy periods. Unlike excess volatility and misalignment, these deviations from fundamentals represent riskless opportunities to make profits. They have been evident in past, and in particular in the present crisis.

Ultimately, the importance of these three features is an empirical question. Charts 1 and 2 plot the long-run behavior of the equity market, in the UK from the 1920s and in the USA from the 1860s. These long sweeps of history are revealing about patterns of misalignment and excess volatility. In each case, some metric of fundamentals is needed. A model-based measure of fundamentals is used, based on long-run average values of dividend growth discounted at a long-run average real interest rate.[12]

For the USA and UK, Charts 1 and 2 present persuasive evidence of both excess volatility and misalignment. On average over the sample, equity prices in the UK and USA are around twice as volatile as fundamentals. The average absolute deviation of UK and US equity prices from fundamentals has been over 20% and over 30% respectively. If anything, there is evidence of misalignments having increased. Average absolute misalignments have averaged almost 30% and 70% in the UK and USA since 1980.

These deviations from EMH are no less striking moving from financial to real assets. Since 1930, real property prices have been more than twice as volatile as typical measures of fundamentals. And real property prices have, in different countries, at times deviated significantly from measures of fundamentals over the same period.[13]

EMH predicts essentially a zero correlation in prices across time, as they follow the random walk of the homeward-bound drunk. This evidence paints a picture of excess volatility (in the short run) and slow mean reversion (in the long run). In other words, there is both positive (at short horizons) and negative (at longer horizons) serial correlation in market prices. This leaves EMH runover in both directions.

With a steely nerve and deep pockets, investors could make profits from exploiting these trends. But as Keynes remarked, the market can often remain irrational for longer than even a strong-willed investor can remain solvent. In other words, these are risky bets. The crisis also revealed, however, examples of bets that were, on the face of it, essentially riskless deviations from EMH or 'apparent arbitrage'.

Chart 3 considers the price of two, on the face of it, identical portfolios – an index of CDS contracts and an individually constructed portfolio of the same CDS contracts. On average, they ought to trade as one and the same. But for around a year from October 2008 onward, the spreads on these two portfolios differed by as much as 60 basis points. Even when transactions costs are taken into account, there were persistent and significant riskless profits on the table. Chart 4 looks at the difference between the two, again on the face of it, identical money market bets – forward rate-agreement spreads and forward rates implied by the LIBOR spreads, both of the same maturity. Over the exact same period, these differed by as much as 250 basis points.

So why were the bets not placed and the arbitrage opportunities exploited? First, money is needed to place even a riskless bet. That was the scarcest of commodities after the failure of Lehman Brothers in October 2008. Second, placing a bet also requires a trustworthy bookmaker. They too were thin on the ground in the midst of crisis. In their absence, arbitrage may be more 'apparent' than real. Market prices are likely to deviate from fundamentals due to liquidity and counterparty premia.

By way of illustration, Chart 5 provides a decomposition of the yield on sub-investment-grade corporate securities in the UK. By mid-2007 at the peak of the boom, the liquidity premium on these assets had pretty much been eliminated. By the end of 2008, this liquidity premium had risen by almost 2,500 basis points. As capital markets moved from flood to drought, market prices turned from rich to poor.

Fair value and financial stability

Against this backdrop, what are the potential financial stability implications of using market prices as a valuation yardstick? In roughly chronological order, three main arguments have been used in defense of marking to market. Broadly, these mirror the three historic phases of fair value, which follow.

Protecting shareholders

During the 19th and early 20th centuries, as joint stock companies sprang up, the key purpose of company accounts was to protect shareholders' interests. Like truth in the face of the
war, in the face of crisis, the financial accounts appear to have been the first casualty. During
the 19th century, the published accounts of Spanish banks became less frequent during episodes of crisis. Mussolini's Italian government of 1931 went one step further, suspending
publication of accounts by the banks to forestall panic.[14]

While less extreme, there is compelling evidence of British banks having massaged balance sheets from the late 19th century right up until the early 1970s, especially during crisis.
Typically, this involved the systematic undervaluation of assets to allow hidden reserves to be
carried on the balance sheet. The experience of UK banks in 1952 was typical. As the prices
of government securities fell sharply, the basis for valuation by banks was shifted from 'at or
below market value' to 'at or under cost'. This mirrored the Roosevelt and Bush forbearance
announcements of 1938 and 1990.

The motives for hidden reserves among UK banks were purportedly prudential, as protection against the 'excessive dividend expectations' of shareholders and as a cushion against
losses in crisis.[15] Although the Companies Act of 1947 prohibited the use of hidden reserves,
the banks were exempt from its provisions. But the writing was on the wall. Non-disclosure
by banks came under repeated fire during the 1960s. Sensing the inevitable, British banks 'voluntarily' decided to pursue full disclosure in 1969, in the interests of shareholder transparency
and protection, though there is evidence of hidden reserves persisting right up to the 1980s.

Those considerations remain relevant today. Market-based measures of banks' valuation
of its assets and liabilities, and the degree of uncertainty around it, remain elevated.[16] Confidence in banks' balance sheets has been shaken to the core and is unlikely to be restored by
a return to murky valuation and hidden reserves.

Gambling for resurrection

One special case of shareholder protection arises when management increase their risk-
taking incentives as the probability of failure rises. Such incentives are inbuilt in a world of
limited liability. But the ability to engage in such gambling for redemption depends importantly on the degree of information asymmetry between the shareholders and the manager.
The lower the transparency of the accounts, the greater the incentives and ability of management to bet the ranch.

This type of behavior is more likely among banks, given the intrinsically greater opacity
of their assets. Examples are legion. For example, in the run-up to the Savings and Loan crisis
in the USA, many thrifts financed long-term fixed-rate assets with variable rate deposits,
thereby running significant interest rate risk. This was a big gamble. But because it was dis-
guised in the accounts, neither regulators nor the thrifts themselves felt obliged to manage
this risk. As interest rates rose, the gamble failed, causing many thrifts to collapse. In response,
the Office of Thrift Supervision required fair values to be reported from the early 1990s.

Timely risk management

Perhaps the most recent of the arguments used to support fair values arises from its role as a
risk management device. Market prices, while noisy, offer timely signals. They are likely to
prompt early recognition and management of emerging risks and mistakes, by both regulators and the regulated. Sunlight can be an effective disinfectant.

In this regard, it is telling that more widespread marking to market accompanied regulatory efforts to improve prompt corrective action measures – for example, in the USA through FDICIA. Among market participants, the use of fair values and fleet-of-foot risk management techniques is widely felt to have contributed to the relative success of some firms during the course of the crisis. Lloyd Blankfein, CEO of Goldman Sachs, certainly appears to think so.[17]

For the prosecution, the main arguments also appear to be threefold. Essentially, these follow from the three commonly attributed failures of the EMH:

Excess volatility

If market prices exhibit greater volatility than warranted by fundamentals, this will be mirrored in the balance sheet footings and profits of entities marking their positions to market. This is far from a new phenomenon. Robert E Healy, the SEC's first Chief Accountant back in the early 1930s, lamented that firms 'can capitalise practically everything except the furnace ashes in the basement.'[18]

The impact of fair values on profits may have been even greater over recent decades. Banks' profits have become significantly more volatile over the past few decades, with the standard deviation of banks' return on equity trebling comparing the 40-year periods either side of 1970. There is also evidence of banks' equity prices having exhibited higher correlation as fair value principles have been extended.[19]

Consider a hypothetical experiment. Imagine banks in the UK had been required to mark their banking books to market over the period 1999–2008, in addition to their trading book. Market prices are used to proxy different categories of loan. For example, Residential Mortgage Backed Securities (RMBS) and covered bond prices are used to proxy mortgage loans. As with banks' trading books, all gains and losses arising on the banking book are assumed to flow directly to profits.

Chart 6 plots the path of UK banks' profits, both actual and simulated under the mark to market assumption. Simulated profits are around eight times more volatile. Between 2001 and 2006, UK banks' cumulative profits would have been around £100 billion higher than recorded profits, as the expected future returns to risky projects were brought forward. This would have been the 21st century equivalent of capitalizing the ashes in the blast furnace.

What goes around comes around. Hypothetical losses during 2008 would then have totaled in excess of £300 billion, as the risk from these projects was realized. The ashes in the furnace truly turned to dust. Had shareholders not already torn it out, this roller-coaster ride in profits would have been hair-raising. In this admittedly extreme case, it is questionable how much shareholder protection fair values would have delivered in practice.

Fundamental misalignment

A related but distinct issue arises when market prices deviate from their true values for a protracted period. Marking to market then runs the risk not just of unwarranted volatility, but also unjustifiable bankruptcy. Take a bank whose liabilities are perfectly maturity matched with its 10-year assets. So, there is no necessity for the bank to liquidate its assets to make good its liabilities as they fall due.

But the market price of the banks' assets might well embody a premium for instant liquidity – a liquidity premium. As Chart 5 indicates, at times of stress, these premia are large and overshoot, lowering asset prices below economic value. In this situation, a mark to market balance sheet may give a misleading impression of banks' worth. And if these distortions are large enough, fair values could even generate insolvency.

During this crisis, the precipitate rise in liquidity premia and fall in asset prices may have called into question the viability of many banks had their assets been fair-valued. Consider again the banking book of UK banks on a mark to market basis. Chart 7 shows the loss of value on this book, which would have peaked at over £400 billion during the early months of 2009. The total capital resources of UK banks at that time were around £280 billion. In other words, the UK banking system in aggregate would have been technically insolvent on a mark to market basis. The subsequent recovery in asset prices was almost as remarkable as the preceding fall. It meant UK banks were back in the black within a matter of months.

Liquidity and fire-sales

The act of marking to market may itself have a bearing on asset price dynamics. This arises because of its potential effects on banks' behavior. If swings in perceived solvency cause banks to sell assets, these fire sales may themselves add to downward pressures on asset prices. Under mark to market, these pressures are felt by all institutions, not just the seller. In effect, fire sales by one firm have negative externalities for all others. And as other banks adjust their own balance sheets in response, there is a risk the downward dynamic is perpetuated.

By acting in this way, marking to market has the potential to serve as an amplifier of stress in the financial system.[20] Other things equal, it could result in sharper and more severe asset price falls than in the past, accompanied by greater institutional stress. It could exaggerate excess volatility and misalignment. Marking to market may not just be a casualty of the failure of EMH; it may also be a cause.

Hyun Shin has likened the destabilizing dynamics of mark to market to the unstable oscillations of London's Millennium Bridge at the time it opened.[21] In finance, these adverse dynamics have a much longer historical pedigree. In their classic monetary history of the USA, Friedman and Schwartz assigned mark to market a key role in propagating banking failure during the Great Depression.[22] The evidence of such dynamics during the recent crisis is more mixed. Some studies have claimed this effect was limited to banks with large trading portfolios;[23] others that it has been significant and wide-ranging across the financial sector.[24]

Perhaps the truth lies somewhere in between, with some markets and institutions affected and others immune. Chart 8 plots commercial property values in the UK since 1920. There are five discernible boom-and-bust cycles in commercial property, signified by the dotted lines. Chart 9 looks at the cumulative falls in value during the bust. In four of the cases, the bust was similarly timed and sized. The exception is the bust of 2007–2008, where the fall in value has been both greater and faster. It is plausible that fire sales, aggravated in part by marking to market, may have contributed to this dynamic.

The fair value agenda

So how do these considerations relate to the debate on international accounting standards? At present, these stand at a crossroads. In the USA (through the Financial Accounting Standards Board (FASB)) and internationally (through the International Accounting Standards Board (IASB)), standard-setters are in the process of revising their treatment of financial instruments.

The IASB has agreed a new standard, IFRS9, which comes into force from 1 January 2018. One key dimension is valuation, where IFRS9 proposes a combination of amortized cost and fair values, with clear criteria to determine the suitability of assets for each category.

A second dimension is provisioning. The concern here is that the use of provisions based on incurred losses means that impairments are recognized too late, thereby contributing to pro-cyclicality of loan supply.[25] In response, the IASB's new standard will establish an 'expected loss' model for loans and receivables that focuses on the risk that a loan will default rather than whether a loss has been incurred. In the USA, FASB has also announced plans to make significant changes to its impairment model for most financial assets that are measured at amortized cost from an incurred model to a full-expected loss model.

Underlying both of these debates is a perceived tension between the needs of different stakeholders, in particular investors and regulators. So, what broad principles might frame accounting standards if the demands of these stakeholders are to be met? Using the framework outlined earlier, these principles might include the following.

The importance of a common measuring rod

Although the G20 committed FASB and the IASB to convergence of international accounting standards by June 2011, this was found to be unduly ambitious. It required not just a meeting of two minds but many, as there are perhaps more than 30 different accounting standards operating worldwide.

It could be argued that differences in accounting standards do little harm. Like foreign languages, we may learn to live, perhaps even love, them. Attempts to compel a common language might risk creating the accountancy equivalent of Esperanto. Unfortunately, the analogy is inexact. Banks are, by their nature, international; so too are investors in, and regulators of, banks. If all parties speak different languages at the same time, the result is likely to be noise rather than signal.

For banks, the noise to signal ratio has been particularly high during this crisis. Differences in accounting standards have contributed to this noise. In 2008, UK banks' assets would have been £2 trillion, or around 30%, larger under European IFRS than under US GAAP standards. These differences make problematic international comparisons of such rudimentary concepts as bank leverage. This in turn hinders investors' risk assessments and regulators' supervisory assessments.

A failure of efficient markets is not of itself a failure of fair value

It is commonly heard that the failure of EMH argues against fair value in favor of some alternative, such as amortized cost. The truth is more subtle than that. Deviation from EMH will cause both accounting measures to deliver distorted signals of value. Depending on the precise circumstances, either measure might deliver a more accurate measure of true economic value.

To see this, consider four scenarios. Consider first a bank making a single loan. In the first period, amortized cost and fair valuations of this loan will be equal. Expected cash flows will in both cases be discounted at the prevailing market discount rate. To the extent EMH is violated – for example, because the market discount rate is too low – both accounting concepts will result in asset overvaluation. Both concepts will be equally imprudent. In other words, credit cycles that cause failures of EMH contaminate bank asset valuations irrespective of the accounting convention.

Consider next a bank with a portfolio of two loans, one initiated when assets prices were priced correctly and the other when they were overvalued. In this situation, amortized costs and fair values will value the asset portfolio differently. Because market prices are applied to the whole asset stock, fair value will tend to result in greater recorded overvaluation. In other words, marking to market is more susceptible to valuation cycles than amortized cost.

Third, consider a situation where, having been overvalued, the market price of the second loan corrects back to equilibrium. Fair values now deliver the correct valuation of the entire asset portfolio. Amortized cost measures, meanwhile, will continue to give a misleadingly bullish account of the second loan's valuation, since this will be discounted at the artificially low discount rate used at initiation. In other words, in this set of circumstances, the tables are turned, with fair values giving a more accurate and prudent measure of valuation.

Finally, if instead of correcting to equilibrium, assume market prices overcorrect – say, because of an overshoot in illiquidity premia of the type witnessed during crisis – it is then no longer clear which valuation metric is preferable. Both will be inaccurate to some degree but in opposite directions – the amortized cost measure suggesting valuations that are 'too high', while fair value will suggest valuations that are 'too low'. The greater the initial misalignment in asset prices, and the smaller their subsequent overshoot, the greater the likelihood of fair values being preferred over amortized cost and vice versa. Ultimately, however, this is an empirical question.

In general terms, however, the point is clear: efficient markets are not necessary but may be sufficient to justify the use of fair value principles.

Better accounting for expected losses

What is clear from these examples is that there is a potential trade-off in the use of amortized cost versus fair value measures when market prices deviate from EMH. Both might give misleading signals, but in opposite directions. Recognizing the problems with either, is there a way of doing better than both?

Perhaps the simplest way of doing so would be to use both valuation metrics. There have already been suggestions that 'dual' accounts could be drawn up.[26] The upside of this approach is that it would give regulators and investors more information on which to base assessments. It releases stakeholders from the need to pick a winner. The downside is that both valuations may be inaccurate, with a lack of clarity about which ought to be used, for example, to judge bank solvency.

A more ambitious alternative would be to seek a more systemic and standardized valuation methodology in the first place, against which different approaches can be cross-checked. The key here would be to establish an objective measure of expected loss, less susceptible to the excess volatility of market prices but adept at picking up its timely signals. In the language of George Shackle, stricter valuation standards would help place some bounds on the expectations and imaginations of bankers.

One area where regulators have made moves to address perceived shortfalls in the accounting framework has been to introduce so-called prudent valuation adjustments[27] to banks' fair-valued positions. These adjustments aim to determine prudent values for all assets measured at fair value in banks' trading and banking books, stripping out much of the valuation uncertainty arising from the lack of observable market prices for many of these assets, and which leads to them being priced using management's own judgment or a bank's internal model.

Ultimately, however, this is a role in which neither accountants nor regulators are best placed to carry out. It would require a body with both expertise in valuation and objectivity. It would seek consistency and, as far as possible, accuracy in valuations across asset classes, institutions and countries. An International Valuation Standards Council (IVSC) already exists and issued new valuation standards in 2017.[28]

These valuation standards, however, focus more on business and real estate valuations, which are well developed, rather than on the valuation of financial instruments. The IVSC could add significant value by developing its nascent standards on the valuation of financial instruments. Accounting and regulation already have fora to support consistency of standards. During this crisis, valuation practices have been every bit as important. Perhaps they too need international recognition.

Business models matter, especially for banks

Accounting standards already reflect characteristics on the assets side of banks' balance sheet. For example, IASB standards require consideration of the cash flow characteristics of assets (for example, specified cash flows of interest and principal) and the intentions of the holder (for example, to collect the contractual cash flows). But for banks, the characteristics of their *liabilities* may be every bit as important as their assets. Indeed, at times of stress in funding markets, liability characteristics may be more important.

Consider, for example, a 10-year loan with regular interest payments that is intended to be held to maturity by a bank. These characteristics would justify the bank carrying the asset at amortized cost. But imagine this loan is funded with overnight loans. Whatever the intention, this liability structure would require early liquidation of the asset if funding were to dry up. In other words, the *ability* of a bank to hold assets to maturity may be as important as the *intention*.

The greater the maturity mismatch, the greater the likelihood of liability characteristics dominating asset intentions. In other words, the case for using fair values is greater when balance sheets are maturity mismatched. Or, put differently, precisely because market prices embody a liquidity premium, they could give a better view of the true asset position of a firm facing liquidity constraints. For institutions facing funding pressure, liquidity premia may be a legitimate measure of fundamentals.

And which companies' balance sheets are most subject to such maturity mismatch? Banks. It has been argued that banks ought to be protected from the vicissitudes of market prices. But, given their maturity transformation role, the case may actually be stronger for banks than for other types of both financial (such as insurance companies and pension funds) and non-financial firms. For some banks, this may be the accounting convention that best aligns the economic characteristics of both assets and liabilities.

It is interesting that there was evidence of financial markets making their own switch in valuation convention during the course of the crisis. As funding maturities shortened, the probability of asset liquidation rose. It became rational, then, for investors to begin valuing even banking book assets at market prices, as in Chart 7. For a time, this process appeared to generate its own downward dynamic, with shortening maturities and falling asset prices eroding the impliedly mark to market solvency position of banks in a liquidity/solvency loop.

Some have argued this downward dynamic itself justifies switching off fair values. But the perils of doing so are clear. Persisting with an inappropriate valuation metric may give an inaccurate picture of banks' true solvency positions. It will also reduce banks' incentives to adjust funding structures to guard against such a dynamic. It is precisely such risk management incentives that appear to explain the relative success of some firms, including Goldman Sachs, during this crisis. Therein may lie a lesson.

As a more radical option still, the UK Parliamentary Commission on Banking Standards suggested that banks should prepare a separate set of audited accounts for the regulator based on the regulatory, and not the accounting, framework. Although enhanced disclosures arising from the revised Basel Pillar 3 framework may have diminished the need for such accounts, an audited set of such accounts might provide some additional sunshine on the risks that banks run, which would be useful to investors.

Conclusion

The fortunes of fair value have waxed and waned historically, particularly at crisis time. So, it is no surprise that fair value is under attack today. We may be at yet another pivot point.

Now would be an unfortunate time to starve balance sheets of the sunlight provided by fair values. Blocking out the sun or, worse still, claiming it revolves around the earth will not serve banks or regulators well in the longer run. Restoring traditional accounting principles sounds desirable, provided the (Italian) values we import are Pacioli rather than Mussolini.

At the same time, it needs to be recognized that too much sunlight can scorch. That means applying appropriate filters to fair values, screening out their harmful rays. Rethinking valuation practices across firms, asset classes and countries, better to capture expected losses, is one important such filter. Recognizing the liability as well as asset characteristics of institutions may be another.

We need to ensure these changes do not erode fair value principles, as that would result in the baby being thrown out with the bathwater. Improving fair values ought to advantage both investors and regulators. It would protect fair value from lightning strikes when the next financial thunderstorm breaks.

APPENDIX

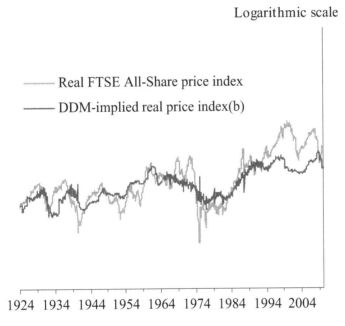

Logarithmic scale

——— Real FTSE All-Share price index

——— DDM-implied real price index(b)

1924 1934 1944 1954 1964 1974 1984 1994 2004

Chart 1 Real FTSE all-share price index and its fundamental-implied value[a][b]

Source: Global Financial Data and Bank calculations.

(a) For further details, see Shiller, R, 'From Efficient Markets Theory to Behavioral Finance', *Journal of Economic Perspectives* (2003).

(b) Assuming future real dividend growth rates and real discount rates equal to average values since 1923.

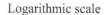

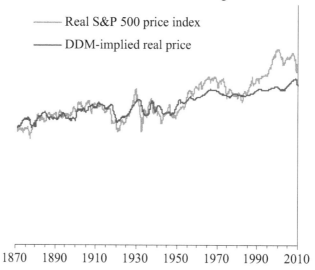

Chart 2 Real S&P 500 price index and its fundamental-implied value[a][b]

Source: www.irrationalexuberance.com.

(a) For further details, see Shiller, R, 'From Efficient Markets Theory to Behavioral Finance', *Journal of Economic Perspectives* (2003).

(b) Assuming real dividend growth rates and real discount rates equal to average values since 1923.

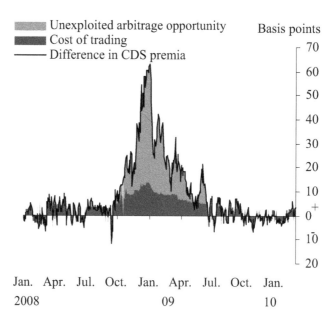

Chart 3 Price of CDS index versus basket of constituents

Sources: JP Morgan Chase & Co., Thomson Datastream and Bank calculations.

Chart 4   Forward sterling LIBOR spreads[a]

Sources: Bloomberg, British Bankers' Association and Bank calculations.

(a) Difference between forward sterling LIBOR rates calculated using the LIBOR curve and those implied by forward rate agreements.

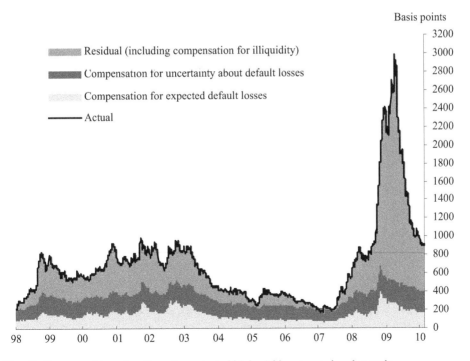

Chart 5   Decomposition of sterling-denominated high-yield corporate bond spreads

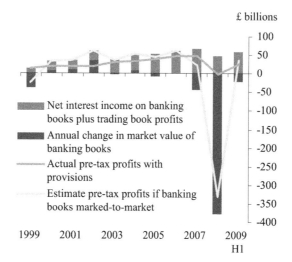

Chart 6   Major UK banks' profit with banking books marked to market[a]

Sources: Bank of England, Bloomberg, published accounts, UBS Delta, Merrill Lynch, JP Morgan and Bank calculations.

(a) The chart shows what major UK banks' profitability would have been if assets contained in the banking books were carried on a mark to market basis, using sensible proxies for the various exposures. For example, US RMBS are used to proxy the market value of US mortgage exposures. International exposure includes USA and Europe only. Peer groups include Barclays, RBS, Lloyds Group, HSBC, Santander Group and Northern Rock.

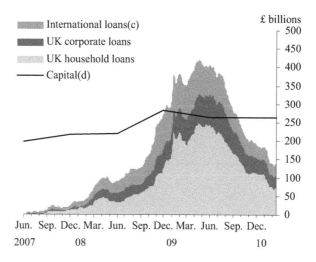

Chart 7   Market value discount to face value of major UK banks' loan books[a][b]

Sources: Bank of England, Bloomberg, published accounts, UBS Delta, Merrill Lynch, JP Morgan Chase & Co and Bank calculations.

(a) Based on the weekly moving average prices of traded instrument as proxies for market value of similar banking book exposures.

(b) Group companies of Barclays, HSBC, Lloyds Banking Group, Nationwide, Northern Rock, Royal Bank of Scotland and Banco Santander, with aggregate banking book exposures of £2.2 trillion.

(c) International exposures include the USA and Europe only.

(d) Held fixed from last reported data at end-2009 H1.

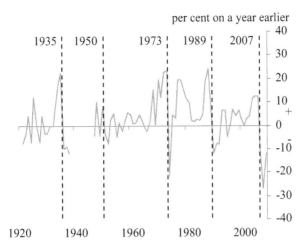

per cent on a year earlier

Chart 8 Long-run UK commercial property capital values[a]

Sources: Scott (1996), Intent Property Database and Bank calculations.

(a) The vertical dotted lines indicate the discernable at booms-and-busts. The attached labels indicate peak year.

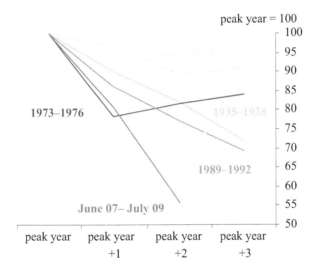

peak year = 100

Chart 9 UK commercial property value declines from cyclical peaks

Sources: Scott (1996), Intent Property Database and Bank calculations.

Notes

1 Revision in Bank Examination Procedure and in the Investment Securities Regulation of the Comptroller of the Currency, Federal Reserve Bulletin, July 1938, pages 563–564.
2 Pacioli (1494).
3 Goethe (1796).
4 Simonson and Hempel (1993) provide a fascinating account of this episode.
5 United States Securities and Exchange Commission (2008).
6 FDIC (1997).

7 In a letter to Richard Breeden, Chairman of the Securities and Exchange Commission, which refers back to the 1930s experience, then-Chairman Alan Greenspan notes 'that market value accounting raises a substantial number of significant issues that need to be resolved before considering the implementation of such an approach in whole or in part for banking organizations'. Alan Greenspan, 'Letter to Hon. Richard C. Breeden', Federal Reserve, 1 November 1990.

8 Simonson and Hempel (op. cit.).

9 Shackle (1972) quoted in Bronk (2009).

10 Shiller (1981).

11 Shiller (2005) and Smithers (2009).

12 Alternative metrics for fundamentals, such as cyclically adjusted price-earnings ratios or q, yield a broadly similar conclusion (Shiller 2005; Smithers 2009).

13 Shiller (2005).

14 James (1992).

15 Billings and Capie (2009).

16 Sarin and Summers (2016).

17 At Goldman Sachs, we calculate the fair value of our positions every day, because we would not know how to assess or manage risk if market prices were not reflected on our books. This approach provides an essential early warning system that is critical for risk managers and regulators. (Lloyd Blankfein, *Financial Times*, 13 October 2009).

18 Quoted in Seligman (2003).

19 Khan (2009).

20 For example, see Plantin et al. (2008) and Allen and Carletti (2007) for a theoretical exposition of these dynamics.

21 Strogatz (2005).

22 Under such circumstances, any runs on banks for whatever reason became to some extent self-justifying, whatever the quality of assets held by banks. Banks had to dump their assets on the market, which inevitably caused a decline in the market value of those assets and hence of the remaining assets they held. The impairment in the market value of assets held by banks, specifically their bond portfolios, was the most important source of impairment of capital leading to bank suspensions, rather than the default of specific loans or specific bond issues. (Friedman & Schwartz 1963).

23 For example, Laux and Leuz (2009).

24 For example, Wallison (2008).

25 For example, Turner (2010).

26 For example, FASB (2009).

27 Official Journal of the European Union – Commission Delegated Regulation (EU) 2016/101.

28 See www.ivsc.org/files/file/view/id/677.

References

Allen, F & Carletti, E 2007, "Market-to-market accounting and liquidity pricing", *Wharton Financial Institutions Centre Working Paper 06–15*.

Billings, M & Capie, F 2009, "Transparency and financial reporting in mid-20th century British banking", *Accounting Forum*, vol. 33, pp. 38–53.

Bronk, R 2009, *The romantic economist*, Cambridge University Press, Cambridge.

Federal Deposit Insurance Corporation 1997, *History of the eighties – lessons for the future*.

Financial Accounting Standards Board 2009, "Financial instrument: improvements to recognition and measurement", *Financial Statement Presentation of Financial Instruments*, 13 August 2009 *(Board meeting handout)*.

Friedman, M & Schwartz, AJ 1963, *A monetary history of the United States, 1867–1960,* Princeton University Press, Princeton, NJ.

Goethe, JW 1796, *Wilhelm Meisters Lehrjahre.*

James, H 1992, "Financial flows across frontiers during the interwar depression", *Economic History Review*, vol. 45, pp. 594–613.

Laux, C & Leuz, C 2009, "Did fair-value accounting contribute to the financial crisis?", *University of Chicago, Booth School of Business, Working Paper No.41.*

Khan, O 2009, "Does fair value accounting contribute to systemic risk in the banking industry?", *SSRN Working Paper No.1327596*.

Pacioli, L 1494, *Summa de Arithmetica, Geometria, Proportioni et Proportionalita*.

Plantin, G, Sapra, H & Shin, HS 2008, "Fair value accounting and financial stability", *University of Chicago Graduate School of Business Research Paper 08–15*.

Sarin, N & Summers, LH 2016, "Have big banks gotten safer?", *Brookings Papers on Economic Activity Fall 2016*.

Seligman, J 2003, *The transformation of Wall Street: a history of the securities and exchange commission and modern corporate finance*, 3rd edn, Aspen Publishers, New York.

Shackle, G 1972, *Epistemics and economics – a critique of economic critiques*, Transactions Publishers, New Brunswick, NJ.

Shiller, R 1981, "Do stock prices move too much to be justified by subsequent changes in dividends?", *American Economic Review*, vol. 71, no. 3, pp. 421–436.

Shiller, R 2005, *Irrational exuberance*, Princeton University Press, Princeton, NJ.

Simonson, DG & Hempel GH 1993, "Banking lessons from the past: the 1938 regulatory agreement interpreted", *Journal of Financial Services Research*, vol. 7, pp. 249–267.

Smithers, A 2009, *Wall Street revalued: imperfect markets and inept central bankers*, Wiley, Hoboken, NJ.

Strogatz, S 2005, *Explaining why the Millennium Bridge wobbled*, Science Daily. Available from: www.sciencedaily.com/releases/2005/11/051103080801.htm. [Accessed on 15 August 2017].

Turner, A 2010, *Banks are different: should accounting reflect that fact?* Speech given to the Institute of Chartered Accountants in England and Wales (ICAEW), London.

United States Securities and Exchange Commission 2008, *Report and recommendations pursuant to Section 133 of the Emergency Economic Stabilization Act of 2008: study on mark-to-market accounting*.

Wallison, PJ 2008, "Fair value accounting: a critique", *American Enterprise Institute for Public Policy Research*.

PART I

Standards and conceptual issues

2

FAIR VALUE AND THE CONCEPTUAL FRAMEWORK

Andrew Lennard

Introduction

How many paragraphs are there about fair value in the International Accounting Standards Board's (IASB) Conceptual Framework? I suspect many would be surprised that the correct answer is 'None'. Strictly speaking, the IASB's current Conceptual Framework is the one published in 2010 (IASB 2010). It took forward much unchanged material from the original 'Framework for the Preparation and Presentation of Financial Statements', which was originally published in 1989. So, the 2010 Framework continues to list the measurement bases that were set out in 1989 – historical cost, current cost, realizable (settlement) value and present value[1]. Fair value is not mentioned.

As is amply documented elsewhere in this volume, fair value is now used in several International Financial Reporting Standards (IFRS). One of the reasons that the IASB has been busy revising its Conceptual Framework is precisely because its thinking in developing standards has gone beyond that which was set out in 1989, and it needs to bring the Framework up to date. Unsurprisingly, fair value is discussed in both the IASB's Discussion Paper (IASB 2013) and the subsequent Exposure Draft of 2015 (IASB 2015) (hereafter, the Exposure Draft or 'the IASB's Exposure Draft').

The question that this chapter addresses is to what extent fair value should be reflected in the Conceptual Framework and how the Framework might provide guidance as to the circumstances in which it might contribute to the fulfilment of the objectives of financial reporting[2] as identified by the Framework. It may be too late to make a substantial impact on the IASB's current work on its Framework, but perhaps some thoughts might be useful for the next amplification or revision. In the meantime, the United States Financial Accounting Standards Board (FASB) is at the early stage of a project to revisit what its Framework says about measurement. This chapter may be pertinent to those efforts.

In order to maintain a focus on the principal theme – the role of fair value in accounting standard-setters' Conceptual Frameworks – some avenues that could be explored in greater depth are neglected in this chapter. In particular, fair value is not the only current measurement basis that might be used in financial statements: alternatives include current replacement cost[3] and value in use, and a comprehensive evaluation of their merits and demerits here would be a distraction. In addition, while the measurement of liabilities is clearly an important issue, much of the following discussion leaves liabilities in the background. This is not to suggest that the same principles should not apply to assets as to liabilities. Indeed – although liabilities give rise to the intriguing issue of an entity's own credit risk – it would seem that the same general principles should apply.[4] However, the key points are much clearer if considered in the context of assets.

For the purposes of this chapter, the definition of fair value given in the Exposure Draft (at paragraph 6.21) is adopted. It is

> The price that would be received to sell an asset, or paid to transfer a liability, in an orderly transaction between market participants at the measurement date.

This is identical to the definition given in IFRS 13 'Fair Value Measurement', and some references to that standard will be necessary, as it provides a much fuller appreciation of the IASB's understanding of the concept of 'fair value'.

Structure of this chapter

The plan of the remainder of this chapter is as follows.

- The next section reviews the nature of a Conceptual Framework, and what it can (and cannot) be expected to achieve. It also briefly summarizes the objective of financial reporting, which is particularly relevant to the selection of a measurement basis such as historical cost or fair value.
- The following section briefly explains why historical cost cannot be universally adopted in financial reporting, and hence why standard-setters need to identify alternatives such as fair value.
- The following section discusses a number of arguments that seek to establish the superiority of fair value. It argues that, at best, some are valid only in some circumstances, which suggests that the Conceptual Framework should address additional measurement bases and provide guidance as to how standard-setters should select the most appropriate basis in particular situations.
- A final section provides concluding comments.

About Conceptual Frameworks

To provide a context for the following discussion it is helpful to consider the nature of a Conceptual Framework, especially what can and cannot be expected of it. The following comments are, I believe, generally consistent with how the IASB and other accounting standard-setters view their Frameworks. They are also selective, in that they concentrate on aspects that are most relevant for present purposes.

The principal purpose of Conceptual Frameworks is to provide guidance to the standard-setter as to what considerations are relevant in the selection of accounting methods and disclosures that should be required in accounting standards. A Framework may make other important contributions, such as enhancing the dialogue between a standard-setter and its constituents, and assisting preparers in the selection of an accounting policy where standards are absent. Nevertheless, guiding standard-setters in the development of standards is the purpose on which this chapter focuses.

A Conceptual Framework requires a standard-setter to use rigorous thinking. It is insufficient to propose accounting practices that reflect the standard-setter's experience and inclinations without an examination of how what is proposed relates to the Framework. It is unimportant whether the thought process starts with the Framework or with received ideas, but it is important that consistency with the Framework is addressed at some point in the process.

This does not, however, imply that consistency with the Framework is the only relevant consideration. Standard-setters need to bear in mind the practical implications of their proposals. If, for example, adherence to the Framework would require a radical change from established practice, it might be unwise to suggest the approach that the Framework suggests. However, in such a case it would be necessary to document the rationale for the decisions. This should illuminate whether the proposal is made on pragmatic grounds or whether revisions to the Framework seem to be necessary.

If accounting standards are developed with due regard to a Framework, accounting standards will probably be more consistent than would otherwise be the case. Consistency of accounting standards is important because, if similar circumstances are reflected differently in financial statements, those statements are difficult to understand and interpret. Furthermore, inconsistency provides an opportunity for transactions to be structured so that they fall to be treated under the standard that provides a more flattering set of financial statements.

Questions and considerations that are properly considered in the creation of a Conceptual Framework ('conceptual issues') may be contrasted with those that are more appropriately considered in the development of accounting standards ('standards-level issues'). This distinction may sometimes be helpful, but can also be misleading. It suggests that there is a clear distinction between the abstract concepts addressed in the Framework and the practical realities that relate to the realm of standards. But constructed paradigms such as Conceptual Frameworks can be pitched at a variety of levels between the abstract and the practical. It is possible to set out a sparse theory of mechanics that, because it ignores friction, would suggest it is possible to construct a perpetual motion machine. Such a theory would not be useful to an engineer designing a machine that would work in the real world. On the other hand, if a theory is enriched to the extent that it reflects all the complexities of the real world it would be unmanageable – like a map that, to reflect every minute detail, is made as large as the territory it covers. Presumably architects designing moderately sized buildings implicitly assume that the world is flat.[5] As has been observed,

> the two questions to be asked of a set of assumptions in economics are: Are they tractable? and: Do they correspond with the real world?[6]

This wise observation clearly does not apply only to economics. An accounting standard-setter's Conceptual Framework needs to set out clear principles that provide a sense of direction for the setting of accounting standards that are capable of application in the real world. It must therefore recognize that, for example, there is not a single price for any asset: some markets are incomplete, and arbitrage[7] cannot be relied upon to ensure that identical assets are priced identically in different markets. Beaver and Demski (1979) demonstrate that accounting is straightforward if complete and perfect markets are assumed, but also uninformative, as they do not contain any information that is not already known.

On the other hand, the Framework should not be so complex that it will ineluctably lead to the 'correct' accounting solution for any issue. Setting such high expectations for the

Framework would make it excessively tortuous and ensure that it could never be completed. The aim must be for a Goldilocks framework – lean enough to enable rigorous thinking about accounting issues, but rich enough to have application in the real world.

In many walks of life standardization is useful. It is clearly handy that all electrical appliances within a country use the same type of plug, and a nuisance for travelers that this is not the case in different countries. In such a case, most of the benefits of standardization are achieved simply by requiring uniformity: provided the standard design is safe and otherwise serviceable, it would not seem to be important which of several possible designs is chosen. Nevertheless, there is an expectation of accounting standard-setters that they will seek to achieve more than mere uniformity – rather they will strive to ensure that their standards improve the quality of financial reporting. Hence another important contribution of a Conceptual Framework is to assist an accounting standard-setter to judge what counts as improvement, and hence why one accounting approach is to be preferred over another.

Conceptual Frameworks respond to this challenge by setting out the objectives of financial reporting. This is followed by identification of the qualitative characteristics – properties that information should have for it to contribute towards the objectives. In the IASB's Exposure Draft, these are relevance, faithful representation, comparability, verifiability, timeliness and understandability. The elements of financial statements – assets, liabilities, income and expenses – are then defined, followed by material on which elements should be recognized. Then we come to measurement.

It is clearly measurement that is engaged with here. Definitions of assets and liabilities and when they should be recognized can be left in the background. But to discuss what measurement bases should be used and in which circumstances, it is important to respect the objective of financial reporting.

The objective of financial reporting

The IASB's Exposure Draft identifies the objective of financial reporting as follows:

> The objective of general purpose financial reporting is to provide financial information about the reporting entity that is useful to existing and potential investors, lenders and other creditors in making decisions about providing resources to the entity. Those decisions involve buying, selling or holding equity and debt instruments, and providing or settling loans and other forms of credit.
>
> *(paragraph 1.2, footnotes omitted)*

The Exposure Draft notes that decisions by existing and potential investors about buying, selling or holding equity and debt instruments depend on the returns that they expect. It then goes on to observe that

> Investors', lenders' and other creditors' expectations about returns depend on their assessment of the amount, timing and uncertainty of (the prospects for) future net cash inflows to the entity and their assessment of management's stewardship of the entity's resources.
>
> *(paragraph 1.3)*

Whether the Conceptual Framework should identify an assessment of stewardship as part of the objectives of financial reporting, and if so, what status it should be given, has been the subject of much controversy, which cannot be reviewed here. Although my view is that it should have an important role[8], this chapter focuses on the decision-usefulness objective of financial reporting, which many – including some of those who would urge prominence for stewardship – regard as primary.

If the Framework is to provide useful guidance to standard-setters on the selection of a measurement basis, the challenge is to identify which basis will contribute best to the objective of financial reporting and in which circumstances that will hold. The term 'measurement basis' is used here in the same sense as in the Exposure Draft: that is, an identified feature of an item being measured, for example historical cost or fair value.

Historical cost

Historical cost is the most familiar measurement basis. It is often very simple and cost-effective to use. Life would be simpler both for accountants and for accounting theorists if historical cost could be universally adopted. However, there are many problems with such an approach. It will be sufficient to highlight three.

i   Historical cost reflects the conditions prevailing at the time of the acquisition of an asset. As prices and other economic circumstances change, it will not provide an informative or relevant depiction of the asset. Often this point is supported by reference to derivatives: a forward contract entered into for a cost of zero today may well be a large asset or liability tomorrow. But price changes have an important impact on non-financial assets, some of which are held for long periods. Moreover, even when the general level of price changes (as reported in headline reports of inflation) is modest, the price of specific assets, for example commodities, can change markedly.

ii   Over time an asset may change through consumption or obsolescence. Although various techniques (notably depreciation and impairment) are used to reflect such changes they are invariably subjective and may be imperfect.

iii   Sometimes, for example in a business combination, many assets are acquired in a single transaction. The cost of each asset cannot be ascertained except by a subjective allocation of the purchase price. Similarly, assets may sometimes be acquired as a result of a bargain purchase or, in the extreme, for no consideration as where an asset is donated to the entity. In such cases, historical cost will not provide useful information about the asset, and it may be necessary to use an alternative measurement basis, at least to provide a proxy for historical cost on initial recognition.

The advantages of historical cost are sufficiently great to ensure that it will continue to be widely used in financial reporting. Even when drawbacks of historical cost are manifest, alternative measurement bases have their own drawbacks, so in some cases none will be superior.

However, the drawbacks of historical cost are sufficiently clear so that the Framework must consider alternative measurement bases. By 'current measurement bases' I mean all measurement bases that have the objective of reflecting an attribute of the asset or liability as at the reporting date, in contrast to historical cost, which reflects the cost of the asset at an earlier date, usually the date of acquisition. Of course, historical cost may be adjusted to reflect, for example, consumption of the asset between the date of acquisition and the reporting date, but the amount at which the remaining, unconsumed, asset is reported is its historical cost. And, while there are alternatives, fair value seems to be the leading candidate.

Fair value

As noted above, the definition of fair value is

> The price that would be received to sell an asset, or paid to transfer a liability, in an orderly transaction between market participants at the measurement date.

Arguments that seek to establish the superiority of fair value, as defined are evaluated in the following.

Consistency with the definitions of elements

The argument that fair value is consistent with the way in which the Framework defines assets and liabilities was made in the Basis for Conclusions to SFAS No. 157 (reprinted in a Discussion Paper published by the IASB in 2006). It noted that the Framework defines assets in terms of future economic benefits (inflows) and liabilities in terms of future sacrifices of economic benefits (outflows). Because fair value reflects future inflows and outflows, it seems that it responds to these parts of the definition of elements.

The definitions of assets and liabilities attempt to set the boundaries of what is contained in financial statements – specifically in the statement of financial position, and income and expenses, representing changes in those same elements in the statement(s) of financial performance. They were never intended to prejudge the measurement bases that might be used for financial statements. If that had been the case, it is difficult to imagine how the definitions could ever have been accepted by those who believed that historical cost would continue to play a role in financial reporting. Historical cost accounting does not in any sense report the future inflows and outflows from assets and liabilities. Of course, if assets are written down for impairment, historical cost provides reassurance that future inflows are expected to be at least as great as their reported amounts, but typically, future net inflows will be expected to be greater. Similarly, liabilities are increased when they become onerous, and this provides confidence that the value of the future outflow will be no more than the reported amount – but it may be much less, as when performance obligations are reported at the amount of the consideration received from a customer, rather than the cost of fulfilment. Hence, cogent arguments for the superiority of fair value need to be based on a much more secure foundation than consistency with the definitions of assets and liabilities.

A market or an entity-specific perspective?

It has become common in standard-setting discussions to contrast 'entity-specific' and market measurement bases. Fair value is, of course, a market measurement basis. One of the advantages claimed for this is that entities that own identical assets should report them at identical amounts: this promotes comparability (one of the qualitative characteristics identified in the Exposure Draft) and any other answer detracts from it.

However, this is not always realistic. Imagine two companies that each own an aircraft: one is a profitable airline that uses the aircraft in its operations; the other is a bank that has acquired the aircraft following the default of a borrower. Should their aircraft, which are identical, be reported at identical mounts?

Suppose (not unreasonably) that, while the bank has a rich variety of skills, operating aircraft is not one of them. So, the bank can only gain economic benefit from the aircraft by selling it. It seems clear that the bank would have to report its aircraft at net selling price, but no one would object if the carrying amount in the airline's accounts (probably deprecated historical cost) was greater than net selling price.

This illustrates the point that different entities have different economic constraints and opportunities, and so the way in which they may exploit an asset varies. Consequently, the value of an asset is often different for different entities. It is an illusion to suppose that, for any given item of property, there is such a thing as its 'true value' independently of considering the perspective from which that value is being considered.

IFRS 13 – which, as we shall see, sometimes resorts to remarkable strategies to preserve the myth that fair value is derived purely from market information – concedes that value may not be the same for all entities. It requires that fair value should reflect a value on a market to which the entity has access. It explains it as follows:

> The entity must have access to the principal (or most advantageous) market at the mea-surement date. Because different entities (and businesses within those entities) with different activities may have access to different markets, the principal (or most advanta-geous) market for the same asset or liability might be different for different entities (and businesses within those entities). Therefore, the principal (or most advantageous) market (and thus, market participants) shall be considered from the perspective of the entity, thereby allowing for differences between and among entities with different activities.
>
> *(IFRS 13, paragraph 19)*

One of the Illustrative Examples provided in IFRS 13 (Example 7) demonstrates this. It addresses an interest rate swap entered into by a retail counterparty with a dealer that can access both the retail and the dealer market. The retail counterparty can only have regard to prices on the retail market, while the dealer would use prices from the dealer market. There-fore, the parties to the contract would report different amounts as 'fair value'. (Presumably, one party would report an asset and the other a liability, but the amounts, as well as the sign would differ.) Thus, IFRS 13 seems to accept the idea that for a measurement basis to be relevant it must reflect an opportunity that is available to the reporting entity. A price quoted on a market to which the entity has no access is not used to derive fair value.

On the other hand, insisting that measurement bases be relevant to the entity does not preclude the use of market-based values. In some circumstances, the market value will rep-resent precisely the economic constraints and opportunities that affect the entity's use of the asset. The IPSASB's Consultation Paper of 2010 'Measurement of Assets and Liabilities in Financial Statements' (IPSASB 2010) (which uses the term 'market value' rather than 'fair value') addressed this point as follows:

> Some question the relevance of market values where an asset is held for the long-term, for example where an equity investment is held to finance pension obligations. They argue that, in such a case, the short-term changes in value that are reported where a market value basis is used are not relevant to the entity's financial position and perfor-mance because the investment is primarily held with a view to the receipt of dividends and long-term capital appreciation, which are required to provide benefits many years in the future. Those who hold this view conclude that a fall (or indeed a rise) in market values is of no relevance, especially if expectations of future returns are unchanged.
>
> However, provided the entity is able to purchase a similar investment at the mar-ket price, that price represents the benefit, at the reporting date, of holding the asset.

The entity could secure the same prospective future dividend receipts and capital appreciation at the market price, so it would not be representationally faithful to report the value of the asset at an amount other than market price. Another way of making the point is to observe that the value of an equity investment is the same for all market participants because it offers all of them the potential of future dividends and capital appreciation, and all can acquire it at the market price. Thus, where an asset is traded on a deep and liquid market its value will be the same to all holders who have access to that market, and the objection that market values are not relevant to an entity that intends to hold an asset for the long-term cannot be sustained.

It might be concluded that the opposition between entity-specific and market values creates a false dilemma. Specifically, those who support fair values must acknowledge that it is relevant to consider whether the entity is able to access the market from which such values are derived. This apparently minor point has significant implications. One is that the argument that fair value ensures that identical assets are reported at identical amounts does not hold. But more generally, it opens the question of whether fair value should not be constrained, to reflect only economic opportunities that are available to the entity? On the other hand, so-called entity-specific values cannot be used to justify amounts in financial statements that disregard completely market conditions as they stand at the reporting date, as is shown by the example of the equity investment discussed in IPSASB (2010).

There is a definition of 'entity-specific value' in IAS 16 'Property, Plant and Equipment' and IAS 38 'Intangible Assets'. It is

> The present value of the cash flows an entity expects to arise from the continuing use of an asset and from its disposal at the end of its useful life or expects to incur when settling a liability.

This definition is similar to that of value in use, which is given in IAS 36 'Impairment of Assets', and repeated in the IASB's Exposure Draft (at paragraph 6.34). This seems to show that the concept has become established. However, the use of similar definitions for 'entity-specific' and 'value in use', which is one particular entity-specific measurement basis, cannot be expected to promote clarity of thought.

The definition has probably not endeared the idea of entity-specific values to those who attempt to develop high-quality accounting standards thoughtfully. The main problem is the notion of what 'an entity expects'. This gives the impression that, when required or permitted to use an entity-specific measurement basis, the entity is free to imagine whatever future cash flows it wishes and report the asset at the present value of those cash flows. (Of course, standards may contain checks on this, but the concept may seem clear.) Clearly financial statements should seek to represent the entity's financial position at the reporting date, rather than mere management expectations.

The term 'entity-specific' is deeply ingrained in the thinking of accountants so an attempt to change the meaning of the words is unlikely to succeed. However, much confusion could be avoided by discarding the term 'entity-specific', and replacing it with the term 'entity-relevant'. An entity-relevant measurement basis is one that reflects an economic opportunity that is available to the entity. With this vocabulary, we would be free to insist, reasonably enough, that all measurement bases are entity-relevant. And it would then be clear that entityrelevance is a desirable, indeed necessary, characteristic of any measurement basis used in financial statements. It would also be clear that there is no binary choice between entity-relevant values and fair values: in some cases, such as the equity investment discussed above, fair value will be entity-relevant.

'Entity-relevance' does not imply an extensive reliance on management intent. The relationship between the economic constraints and opportunities and management intent is somewhat subtle. After all, one might expect that in the majority of cases, management will intend to pursue the most profitable economic opportunity that they can. For this reason, management intent is often a helpful guide to the opportunities available to the entity. But this is not invariably the case. Suppose the fair value of an asset is clear[9], and it is also clear that it is greater than value in use. Management intends (for whatever reason) that it will retain and use the asset, and hence expects to realize value in use. Reporting the asset at any amount less than its fair value will not fairly represent the value of the asset. Management's decision to retain and use the asset implies a willingness to forego the receipt of fair value, and management ought rightly to be held account for that decision. This is why IAS 36 requires that impaired assets are written down to the higher of fair value and value in use, reflecting the fact that economically the impairment loss is limited by the asset's fair value.

It would not seem to be going too far to say that the value ascribed to an asset in financial statements should, conceptually, not be less than the value (at the reporting date) of the most profitable opportunity afforded by the entity's ownership of the asset. It must, of course, be acknowledged that it will often be difficult to identify what that opportunity is: this is one of the challenges of standard-setting.

An entity's opportunities and those of market participants

In the case of non-financial assets, IFRS 13 requires fair value to be assessed from the perspective of a market participant that can use the asset in its highest and best use (or can sell it to another that can) even if that is not the use intended by the entity (paragraph 30). This is entirely consistent with the 'most profitable opportunity' philosophy.

However, things get more puzzling when we learn that it is also assumed that our market participants will be able to use the asset with other complementary assets and liabilities and that those assets and liabilities will be available to them. This is a particularly important issue when entities own specialized assets[10] – that is, assets that are unlikely to find a buyer who could use them in the same way as the entity itself.

The issue was discussed in Statement of Financial Accounting Concepts (SFAC) No. 7 (FASB 2000), which played an important part in the development of standard-setters' thinking about fair value. It gave the example of an entity that intends to operate a property as a bowling alley while other market participants would use it as a parking lot. It seems reasonable to assume that our bowling alley entrepreneur would have to pay at least as much to acquire the property as would be paid by parking lot operators, and in addition, might have to incur the additional costs of installing machinery and facilities, which would have no value to a buyer that was interested in acquiring a property as a parking lot – it may indeed be that the price that such a buyer is prepared to pay is reduced to reflect the cost of removing the bowling alley apparatus. Thus, the fair value of the entity's bowling alley is less (probably considerably less) than the cost of acquiring it. If it were reported at fair value, all of the cost of investment in the bowling alley after the initial purchase of the property would be written off. SFAC No. 7 does not address why reporting such a loss would be informative or helpful. It does note (to paraphrase) that if the bowling alley venture is successful, and the alley is reported at fair value, the entity's subsequent reported earnings will be superior to those of a parking lot operator whose asset has a similar value (and, if the venture is unsuccessful its earnings will be inferior). However, one is left puzzled as to why it is easier or more helpful to compare the earnings of a bowling alley operator with those of a parking lot operator, rather than to assess them in the context of the costs of acquiring the property and installing the necessary improvements to operate a bowling alley.

IFRS 13 takes a different approach to this issue. Rather than contemplating a sale to a parking lot operator, it requires that fair value is estimated by considering a sale to another 'market participant' that is eager to operate bowling alleys. The rationale is explained in the Basis for Conclusions. It states:

> Some respondents to the exposure draft expressed concerns about using an exit price notion for specialised non-financial assets that have a significant value when used to-gether with other non-financial assets, for example in a production process, but have little value if sold for scrap to another market participant that does not have the com-plementary assets. They were concerned that an exit price would be based on that scrap value (particularly given the requirement to maximise the use of observable inputs, such as market prices) and would not reflect the value that an entity expects to generate by using the asset in its operations. However, IFRS 13 clarifies that this is not the case. In such situations, the scrap value for an individual asset would be irrelevant because the valuation premise assumes that the asset would be used in combination with other assets or with other assets and liabilities. Therefore, an exit price reflects the sale of the asset to a market participant that has, or can obtain, the complementary assets and the associated liabilities needed to use the specialised asset in its own operations. In effect, the market participant buyer steps into the shoes of the entity that holds that specialised asset.
>
> *(IFRS 13, paragraph BC78)*

The concerns raised by respondents seem valid. The response, however, is unsatisfactory. In some cases, it will be clear that the reality is that there is no other entity that would willingly buy and use the asset, so the 'market participant' that 'steps into the shoes of the entity that holds that specialized asset' is entirely hypothetical. How this relates to the requirement noted earlier that the entity must have access to the market from which fair value is derived is unclear: presumably, the entity must (hypothetically) have access to the (hypothetical) market. It is difficult to suppress the thought that this part of the technology of fair value may have been invented in order to enable the dogma that fair value, conceived in terms of market rather than entity-specific values, can always provide sensible measures for financial reporting.[11]

Exit values and entry values

During much of the evolution of fair value as used in accounting standards, the difference between exit values – the amount that would be received from sale of an asset – and entry values – the amount that an entity has (or perhaps would) pay to acquire an asset – was ne-glected. It was not mentioned, for example, in SFAC No. 7 (FASB 2000).

Some standard-setters denied that there was an important difference between exit and entry values. It was said, for example, that a transaction price represented one party's exit and another's entry. But this seemed to miss the point that the most relevant amount would be one that reflected the position of the entity: its own exit and entry prices may well be different from those of other entities. In any diverse economy, assets are regularly purchased from dealers by entities that cannot immediately resell them at the same amount, perhaps in part because purchasers will be warier of goods sold by random entities than those sold by established dealers. Edwards and Bell (1961)[12] make the point as follows:

> The terms on which a firm can buy and sell identical assets are often different. A firm may buy a new truck at one price but an immediate decision to sell may not return to the firm the full purchase price. The difference can be regarded as a payment for the additional selling and transfer services necessary to resell the truck to another final buyer, services which the firm itself is not equipped to furnish.
>
> *(page 76)*

As noted above, fair value is an exit value: it reflects the amount that would be received on sale of an asset or paid to transfer a liability.[13] It was also suggested above that the value ascribed to an asset in financial statements should, conceptually, not be less than the value of the most profitable opportunity afforded by the entity's ownership of the asset. The question that arises is how often and in what circumstances fair value meets this stipulation – and, perhaps, what alternative measurement bases might be considered in those cases where it does not.

The discussion is simplified by confining the consideration to two opportunities.[14]

- The entity may choose to sell the asset, in which case they will receive fair value; or
- The entity may choose to continue to use the asset in its operations and receive the return that is generated from that.

If the more profitable opportunity is to sell the asset, there is an obvious case for using fair value, as it will reflect the expected proceeds assuming that the entity maximizes its opportunities. In order to fully achieve this, however, it is of course necessary to deduct transaction costs – the costs that the entity would incur on such a sale. As noted above this is required by IAS 36.

If, however, the more profitable opportunity is to continue to use the asset in the entity's operations, fair value does not seem relevant. The entity will only sell the asset in unusual circumstances. An obvious example is a newly acquired item of plant. It is reasonable to assume that the entity paid the price to acquire the plant because it promises higher returns than the cost of acquisition. Thus, a fairer representation of the value of the asset to the entity would be given by the use of an entry value. In present practice, this will usually be historical cost, the drawbacks of which were noted above.

A measurement basis that avoids these drawbacks is current replacement cost, which reflects what it would cost the entity to buy an asset of equivalent service potential. There are, however, some disadvantages of replacement cost. One is that where current replacement cost is higher than historical cost it cannot be assumed that it is recoverable – the asset might be impaired.

It might be suggested that, where the most profitable opportunity is to continue to use the asset in the entity's operations, value in use should be used as the measurement basis. This would reflect all the returns that the entity expects the asset to provide. But although value in use may be the best available basis for measuring impaired assets (except when fair value less costs to sell is higher), there are serious objections to its use for other assets. It is highly subjective and anticipates future returns. If, as suggested above, an entity typically acquires an asset in the expectation of returns greater than cost, value in use will be greater than cost. So a profit will be reported merely as the result of purchasing an asset, and returns from operations will be correspondingly reduced. It would seem to provide a better basis for analysis to report the purchase of assets as giving rise to neither gain or loss and to charge the cost of using those assets (either in historical or current terms) against operations as they provide returns. Moreover, deprival value reasoning[15] suggests that value in use would overstate the value of the asset to the entity. Deprival value approaches measurement by asking what amount would fairly compensate the entity for loss of the asset, if that were to occur. If an asset that will contribute to future returns from operations is lost, the entity would not lose those returns but purchase a replacement asset. Hence, compensation equal to replacement cost would leave the entity in precisely the same position as it was before the loss of the asset.

The IASB seems to have recognized this point. Its Discussion Paper (IASB 2013) noted (in paragraph 6.50):

> An exit price is likely to be most relevant when an asset is held for sale because the exit price will reflect the likely proceeds from the sale. In contrast, use of an entry price (for example, replacement cost) might provide more relevant information when:
>
> a   assets are held for use rather than for sale; or
> b   exit prices are unavailable or do not reflect orderly transactions between willing buyers and sellers.
>
> Some existing Standards also use fair value less cost to sell for impairment adjustments or fair value plus transaction costs for initial measurement of assets (minus transaction costs for initial measurement of liabilities).

Similarly, the Exposure Draft notes that how an 'asset or liability contributes to future cash flows' is an important factor to consider when selecting a measurement basis (paragraph 6.54). However, it is not as explicit about the implications of this point as the Discussion Paper: perhaps this will be clarified in the final version of the new Framework.

The second point in the above quote from the Discussion Paper, which suggests that entry prices might be relevant when 'exit prices are unavailable or do not reflect orderly transactions between willing buyers and sellers', calls for further comment. It reflects part of the thinking of IFRS 13, which suggests that current replacement cost (an entry price) can be used to derive fair value (an exit price). This rather odd conclusion is justified on the grounds that

> The IASB noted that an entity's cost to replace an asset would equal the amount that a market participant buyer of that asset (that would use it similarly) would pay to acquire it (ie the entry price and the exit price would be equal in the same market). Thus, the IASB concluded that the cost approach is consistent with an exit price definition of fair value.
>
> *(paragraph BC141)*

One objection to this is that it assumes that all entities can replace assets at the same cost, which seems unlikely to be universally true. But even if that is overlooked, it is difficult to agree that our hypothetical purchaser would pay an amount as *great* as replacement cost: all that can reasonably be assumed is that they would not pay *more* than replacement cost. IFRS 13 itself reaches that conclusion when it notes that 'a market participant buyer would not pay more for an asset than the amount for which it could replace the service capacity of that asset' (paragraph B9).

There may be circumstances when fair value seems conceptually the right answer, but for pragmatic reasons replacement cost is used as a proxy. But it muddies our thinking if this is not clear, and the process is considered to provide fair value, rather than a proxy for it.

Much of the above discussion is most relevant to assets other than financial instruments. However, this is where many of the most difficult issues of measurement arise. For many kinds of financial instruments, the opportunities afforded are the same to any entity, or a large number of entities, and it may be reasoned that (leaving aside the issue of transaction costs, which may be important in some cases) fair value is an appropriate measurement basis. In particular, where markets are reasonably efficient, it is justifiable to assume that the value of future returns is the same as the current market value. Hence, it is unnecessary to consider what the most profitable opportunity is.

All future cash flows that are relevant to market participants

It was noted above that the IASB's Exposure Draft observes that existing and potential investors benefit from information that helps them assess the amount, timing and uncertainty of future cash flows. Fair value, based on the reasoning that markets efficiently reflect all available information, reflects all the available information that affects the amount, timing and uncertainty of future cash flows, so it is tempting to conclude that it is the ideal measurement basis – the one that can contribute the most to the fulfilment of the objective of financial statements.

But why do users of financial statements want to assess future cash flows? One obvious answer is that they wish to calculate the value of the entity, which is often done by discounting future cash flows. However, fair value information does not provide them with the inputs they need for such a calculation, rather it provides the result of that calculation. The fair value of an asset or a liability says almost nothing about the amount, timing and uncertainty of future cash flows, but only the value of future cash flows (as they would be assessed by market participants). Of course, fair value information can be accompanied by disclosures that give greater insight into future cash flows, but this is true of any measurement basis.

Penman (2007) suggests that

> Fair (market) values are a plus when value to the shareholders is determined solely by exposure to market price; that is, shareholder value is one-to-one with market prices.

Penman (2007), however, goes on to note that fair value does not provide useful information about businesses that add value by buying at input prices and selling at output prices. He notes that, for example,

> Raw material used in manufacturing does not get its value from a change in its exit market price, but as an input into a process that adds value to its market price by producing a product and selling it to customers; change in shareholder value is not one-to-one with the change in the market price of the input.

This raises an important difference between the information that is provided when fair value is used and that provided by entry values such as historical cost. Under fair value accounting, income and expenses are recognized when prices change, whether or not the asset is sold (or the liability transferred) at that price. Under entry value accounting, assets are held at entry value (usually, in practice, historical cost although current cost might also be considered) and profit is not reported until the goods are sold. Entry value accounting permits the financial statements to report the progress of the business and specifically to compare the revenues earned in a period with the costs incurred in obtaining it – in other words, the margin. Most investors in value-added businesses consider that information vital.

As Marshall and Lennard (2016) argue, consistently with Penman (2007), it follows that entry values are appropriate for the operating assets of businesses that obtain inputs from suppliers and employees and use those inputs to provide goods and services to customers from whom revenue is received.

Concluding comments

Whittington (2010, 2015) has given excellent overviews of the development of accounting standard-setters' thinking on measurement. One of the most striking, and welcome, features is that the search for a single ideal measurement basis that could be used universally in financial statements has been abandoned. It now seems to be widely (although, of course, not universally) accepted that a 'mixed measurement basis' – that is, the use of different measurement bases that provide the most relevant information in particular circumstances should be embraced rather than deprecated. The Exposure Draft puts it this way:

> Consideration of the objective of financial reporting, the qualitative characteristics of useful financial information and the cost constraint is likely to result in the selection of different measurement bases for different assets, liabilities and items of income and expense.
>
> *(paragraph 6.3)*

There is no doubt that fair value has a substantial role to play in the Conceptual Framework, especially for assets and liabilities that are traded on liquid markets and also, perhaps, for assets and liabilities that are similar to those that are widely traded. But fair value should not be considered the only current measurement basis: alternatives include value in use (which is addressed in the Exposure Draft) and current replacement cost, which receives only a cursory mention in the Exposure Draft, and on which the Basis for Conclusions observes, disheartingly, that 'the IASB would be unlikely to consider selecting current [replacement] cost as a measurement basis when developing future Standards' (paragraph BC6.23).

The Conceptual Framework should also provide direction as to which measurement basis should be selected in what circumstances. This is unlikely to be clear if 'market' and 'entity-specific' measures are assumed to be binary alternatives, and clear definitions of both terms are lacking. A promising avenue is to consider the most profitable opportunity available to the entity – whether it be through use (indicating an entry value) or sale (indicating an exit value). As we have seen the seed of this thought is set out in the Exposure Draft, but more specificity is necessary. The deprival value literature might be helpful in suggesting the guiding principles.

★★★★★

Acknowledgements

The views expressed in this paper are the personal views of the author, and do not represent official views of the FRC. He gratefully acknowledges, however, helpful comments from his colleagues at the FRC.

Notes

1 'Present value' corresponds to the measurement basis which is nowadays more usually described as 'value in use'. The change seems laudable as 'present value' confuses the significance of the measurement basis with how it is calculated.
2 For reasons that are mainly of historical interest, the Framework discusses the objectives of financial *reporting* rather than financial *statements*. This chapter, like IASB (2010) and the IASB's Exposure Draft, concentrates on the use of fair value in financial statements. In March 2018, after this Chapter was written, the IASB published a revised version of its Conceptual Framework.
3 Lennard (2010) discusses the role of replacement cost in financial statements.
4 See Lennard (2002) and IPSASB (2010).
5 An architect once told me, with pride, that the building he was working on was so large that the curvature of the earth had to be taken into account. This suggests that this is not the usual case.
6 Joan Robinson 'Economics is a serious subject' (1932) as quoted by Coase (1937).
7 Shleifer (2000) discusses the difficulties of arbitrage and why it may not be relied upon to secure efficient markets.
8 See Lennard (2007).
9 IAS 36 defines recoverable amount as the higher of an asset's fair value *less costs of disposal* and value in use, which is logical.
10 Barker and Schulte (2017) provide a conceptual critique and case study evidence on the difficulties of measuring specialised non-financial assets at fair value.
11 A parallel instance where IFRS 13 requires that the hypothetical transferee is assumed to be identical to the entity is in the treatment of non-performance risk, which is assumed to be the same before and after the transfer of the liability (paragraph 42). The Basis for Conclusions notes that 'such an assumption is unlikely to be realistic for an actual transaction' (paragraph BC94).
12 Whittington (2008) provides a helpful appreciation of the contribution of Edward and Bell (1961).
13 The Exposure Draft (like IFRS 13) does not allow fair value to be reduced by transaction costs—the costs that would be incurred if a sale were to take place. However, as we have noted, some standards (e.g. IAS 36) remedy this by using 'fair value less costs of disposal'.
14 The distinction between the two major opportunities is similar to that made in Marshall and Lennard (2016), who note that a similar distinction has been made by other authors, including Edward and Bell (1961), Penman (2007) and Botosan and Huffman (2015).
15 There is a large literature on deprival value. For a spirited defence see Macve (2010).

References

Barker, R & Schulte, S 2017, "Representing the market perspective: fair value measurement for non-financial assets", *Accounting, Organizations & Society*, vol. 56, pp. 55–67.
Beaver, WH & Demski, JS 1979, "The nature of income measurement", *The Accounting Review*, vol. 54, pp. 38–45.
Botosan, CA & Huffman, AA 2015, "Decision-useful asset measurement from a business valuation perspective", *Accounting Horizons*, vol. 29, no. 4, pp. 757–776.
Coase, RH 1937, "The nature of the firm", *Economica n.s.*, 4. Reprinted in Coase, RH 1988, *The firm, the market and the law*. The University of Chicago Press, Chicago, IL and London.
Edwards, EO & Bell, PW 1961, *The theory and measurement of business income*, University of California Press, Berkeley and Los Angeles, CA.
Financial Accounting Standards Board 2000, *Statement of financial accounting concepts No. 7 Using cash flow information and present value in accounting measurements*.
IFRS Red Bound Volume 2016a, IAS 16, *Property, plant and equipment*, IFRS Foundation.
IFRS Red Bound Volume 2016b, IAS 36, *Impairment of assets*, IFRS Foundation.
IFRS Red Bound Volume 2016c, IAS 38, *Intangible assets*, IFRS Foundation.
IFRS Red Bound Volume 2016d, IFRS 13, *Fair value measurement*, IFRS Foundation.
International Accounting Standards Board 2006, *Discussion paper: fair value measurements (includes Statement of Financial Accounting Standards No. 157 Fair Value Measurements)*.
International Accounting Standards Board 2010, *The conceptual framework for financial reporting*.
International Accounting Standards Board 2013, Discussion paper DP/2013/1. *A review of the conceptual framework for financial reporting*.

International Accounting Standards Board 2015, Exposure draft ED/2015/3. *Conceptual framework for financial reporting.*

International Public Sector Accounting Standards Board 2010, Consultation paper. *Conceptual framework for general purpose financial reporting by public sector entities: measurement of assets and liabilities in financial statements.*

Lennard, A 2002, *Liabilities and how to account for them: an exploratory essay*, Accounting Standards Board, London.

Lennard, A 2007, "Stewardship and the objectives of financial statements: a comment on IASB's preliminary views on an improved conceptual framework for financial reporting: the objective of financial reporting and qualitative characteristics of decision-useful financial reporting information", *Accounting in Europe*, vol. 4, no. 1, pp. 51–66.

Lennard, A 2010, "The case for entry values: a defence of replacement cost", *Abacus*, vol. 46, no. 1, pp. 97–103.

Macve, R 2010, "The case for deprival value", *Abacus*, vol. 46, no. 1, pp. 111–119.

Marshall, R & Lennard, A 2016, "The reporting of income and expense and the choice of measurement bases", *Accounting Horizons*, vol. 30, no. 4, pp. 499–510.

Penman, SH 2007, "Financial reporting quality: is fair value a plus or a minus?", *Accounting and Business Research* (Special Issue), pp. 33–44.

Shleifer, A 2000, *Inefficient markets: an introduction to behavioural finance*, Oxford University Press, Oxford and New York.

Whittington, G 2008, "What the 'old guys' can tell us: Edward and Bell's 'The theory and measurement of business income'", *The Irish Accounting Review*, vol. 15, no. 1, pp. 73–84.

Whittington, G 2010, "Measurement in financial reporting", *Abacus*, vol. 46, no. 1, pp. 104–110.

Whittington, G 2015, "Measurement in financial reporting: half a century of research and practice", *Abacus*, vol. 51, no. 4, pp. 549–571.

3

FAIR VALUE ACCOUNTING

A standard-setting perspective

Michel Magnan and Antonio Parbonetti

Introduction

In recent years, fair value accounting (FVA) has emerged as one of the key lenses by which standard-setters look at measurement, recognition and disclosure issues in financial reporting. The prevalence of FVA in contemporary financial reporting standard-setting is sometimes underappreciated since it applies either on a recurring or on a non-recurring basis. For instance, while the measurement of financial instruments relies on FVA on a continuous basis with fluctuations in value being directly reflected in comprehensive income, the reality is much more subtle for goodwill. At its initial recognition, goodwill reflects the differential between the fair value of the consideration paid for the acquisition of a business and the estimated fair values assigned to the various assets acquired and liabilities assumed as a result of the acquisition. However, following the transaction, the amount reported for goodwill does not change or evolve, except if and when there is impairment. In such a case, a valuation will be performed, and goodwill will be written down to an amount that approximates its current fair value. Hence, in the case of goodwill, FVA applies at specific times under particular, non-recurring, conditions.

The purpose of the chapter is to offer a standard-setter's perspective on FVA and to explore how and why it has evolved into a core underpinning of corporate financial reporting at the international level. More specifically, we review and analyze the following themes.

First, we intend to follow FVA through the ages as it went from being the standard-setter's whipping boy to its favorite son. Essentially, from a historical perspective, FVA went from being almost eliminated from financial reporting as standard-setting became formalized in the 1930s following the Great Depression to being a measurement method of choice in current-day standard-setting. We will focus on the key events and circumstances that drove its evolution in standard-setters' and regulators' minds. For instance, the high inflation that prevailed from the 1960s to the early 1980s led to renewed interest in measurement models, which reflected current costs or exit values (otherwise known as inflation accounting), with some standard-setters proposing alternative models to then prevailing historical cost-based accounting. While such interest waned in the 1980s, one may argue that it laid the conceptual foundations for the advent of FVA down the road. In parallel to such evolution, it must be noted that the standard-setters' landscape has greatly changed over the years. In the United States, a more or less free market for accounting standards was replaced by a more or less formal standard-setting institutional environment, with the federal government setting up the Securities & Exchange Commission in 1934 to oversee corporate reporting and the American Institute of Certified Public Accountants (AICPA) establishing the Committee on Accounting Procedure (CAP). The Committee was replaced by the Accounting Principles Board (APB), which eventually morphed into the Financial Accounting Standards Board (FASB), which is now independent from the accounting profession. At the international level, we have seen national standard-setting converging with the creation of the International Accounting Standards Committee in 1985 and its transformation into the International Accounting Standards Board (IASB) in 2000. The appearance and institutional transformations of standard-setters are relevant, as they imply that their constituencies, interests and views are subject to changes.

Second, we provide an overview of where and how FVA is now embedded in contemporary financial reporting. FVA underlies the measurement, recognition and/or disclosure dimensions of several standards, on a recurring or non-recurring manner. We will strive to develop a template as to FVA frames current financial reporting. In this regard, we will discuss also as to whether recognition or disclosure matter. Often, standard-setters have to decide if FVA information is disclosed or recognized, each approach having its advantages and inconveniences.

Third, in choosing a measurement model, standard-setters face several challenges and must trade off attributes such as relevance, reliability (faithful representativeness) and prudence. Furthermore, standard-setters must juggle with the several roles that accounting information play in the marketplace, either as a foundation for contracts (stewardship role) or as a source, one among others, of information for investment decision-making. Each of these roles requires different attributes from accounting information, but the frontier is sometimes fluid between these different roles and their accounting needs. For instance, it can be argued that historical cost-based accounting is more appropriate for financial reporting in a stewardship context. However, what is deemed to be historical cost is merely market value (or fair value) at the time of the original transaction, and what is different now is that standard-setters have moved beyond fair value at the time of a transaction to fair value without transactions. Historically, standard-setters have attempted to limit/constrain managerial discretion. Therefore, the focus was on (1) reliability, (2) income statement and (3) matching (transaction-based). However, as time passed, the focus shifted to (1) relevance, (2) balance sheet and (3) valuation away from transactions. We draw upon the conceptual, institutional and practical considerations that underlie standard-setters' decisions in this regard. For instance, the financial analysts' community, especially through its professional association, is now a key stakeholder in the standard-setting game. It must be noted that financial analysts typically support and encourage the reporting of market values. In contrast, regulators, especially prudential regulators, have been historically skeptical of FVA's merits. We thus analyze the dynamic institutional landscape that must have influenced standard-setters. Finally, we will conclude with some comments and observations as to how we perceive the standard-setting future with respect to FVA. As the Canadian philosopher Marshall McLuhan (1964) wrote in his book, 'the medium is the message'. The platform by which a message is conveyed, not the content it carries, is actually the key variable of interest in affecting society. This contrasts with some prior comments about accounting, and accountants, just being messengers, with respect to the role of FVA in the financial crisis (André et al. 2009; Magnan 2009).

Fair value accounting: from whipping boy to favorite son

Evolution in standard-setting institutions

To understand the mapping between accounting standard-setting and FVA, it is necessary to briefly review changes that have occurred in the institutions that underlie corporate financial reporting. In our view, the most important one was its formalization, with the United States leading the way in the wake of the 1929 Crash. The change was at two levels. At the federal government level, 1934 saw the creation of the Securities & Exchange Commission (SEC), with *both the power and responsibility for setting accounting and reporting standards for companies whose securities are publicly traded*. However, the SEC, a government appointed body, delegated the primary responsibility for setting accounting standards to the private sector.

Hence, at the level of the accounting profession, and in light of the SEC delegation of responsibility for accounting standard-setting, the American Institute of Accountants (predecessor to today's AICPA) created the CAP. Between 1938 and 1959, the CAP issued 51 *Accounting Research Bulletins (ARBs)*, which dealt with specific accounting and reporting problems. However, the lack of a conceptual framework for standard-setting ultimately led to its downfall. In 1959, the CAP was replaced by APB. The APB was still a creature of the AICPA and all its members belonged to the AICPA. From 1959 to 1973, the APB issued 31 *Accounting Principles Board Opinions (APBOs)* dealing with specific accounting and reporting issues, various *Interpretations,* and four *Statements.* Many *ARBs* and *APBOs* still represent authoritative GAAP as they have not been dropped or superseded. Ultimately, the APB failed for the same reason than the CAP, i.e. its inability to develop a conceptual framework for standard-setting. The APB was replaced in 1973 by the FASB and its supporting structure, most notably the Financial Accounting Foundation, which provides its funding. The FASB differs from its predecessor in several ways, the most relevant one being its membership, which represents various constituencies concerned with accounting standards, and its institutional independence from the accounting profession. Hence, the FASB represents a broad constituency of interest groups. One of the first tasks of the FASB was the development of a conceptual framework, which is now embedded in Statements of Financial Accounting Concepts (SFACs). The SFACs lay out the objectives, characteristics and other concepts that determine corporate financial reporting. Broadly speaking, the SFACs guide how standard-setters should create generally accepted accounting principles.

On the international scene, while national standard-setters still exist, emanating either from the private sector (e.g. United Kingdom, Canada) or from the state (e.g. France), there has been a trend toward convergence in financial reporting for listed entities. These efforts initially led to the creation of the International Accounting Standards Committee (IASC) in 1973, which goal was to develop global accounting standards. In 2001, the IASC restructured its governance and was replaced by the IASB as a global standard-setter. The IASB's objectives are (1) to develop a single set of high quality, understandable global accounting standards, (2) to promote the use of those standards and (3) to bring about the convergence of national accounting standards and international accounting standards. Similar to the FASB, the IASB's members represent different constituencies and interest groups. The IASB has also developed a conceptual framework, which is now under the last phase of a major overhaul. While initially conducted jointly with the FASB, the final versions will differ between the two standard-setters.

The institutionalization of accounting standard-setting does have profound implications as to the issues standard-setters tackle and how they resolve the challenges they face. First, as pointed out above, accounting standard-setting is now formally independent from the accounting profession and from its key constituencies, auditors and preparers, thus opening the doors to contrasting or differing viewpoints. Second, financial statement users, essentially financial analysts, bankers and portfolio managers, now have formal ways to provide input into the standard-setting process, including formal representation on standard-setting bodies and on their oversight organizations. Third, as standard-setting evolved from a practice-driven issue-specific activity steered by the accounting profession to a more formal process guided by an open consultation process and a conceptual framework, the balance may have shifted between principles deemed important by auditors (e.g. reliability, verifiability) to those considered important by users (e.g. relevance).

Fair value accounting: a brief history

Fair value is defined as '...the price that would be received to sell an asset or paid to transfer a liability in an orderly transaction between market participants at the measurement date...' (SFAS 157.5) (FASB 2006). FVA is neither a novel idea nor a new measurement method. In late 19th century and early 20th century, it was common for firms to report about their capital assets using appraised values, i.e. estimates of the net values at which the assets could be realized in the market (e.g. SEC 2008; Shearer 2010). Several economists also believed that the exit value, i.e. how much a firm would realize by selling an asset in the market, was the only appropriate basis to prepare financial statements (e.g. Diewart 2005).

However, by the 1930s, abusive valuation practices by some managers led to several fundamental changes in financial reporting.[1] Most importantly, as noted above, was the creation of the SEC, which was mandated by the US Congress to ensure that listed firms filed financial statements on a regular basis that *fully and fairly* disclosed the financial position and the earnings history of the registrant, applicant, or declarant, as the case may be (Pines 1965). In light of the vacuum as to what constituted proper financial reporting, the SEC took an active role in standard-setting by issuing its Accounting Series Releases (ASR), starting in 1937 with an ASR on the accounting treatment of losses resulting from the earlier revaluation of assets (typically in the 1920s). It is likely that the advent of a monitoring and enforcement authority such as the SEC, with an emphasis on ensuring that financials statement numbers are derived from formal and demonstrable methods, put a chill in the use of FVA by managers. Moreover, as financial statements were now required to be certified by a public accountant, or auditor, it is also more than likely that auditors were hesitant to certify fair value numbers.

In its first ARB published in September 1939 (CAP 1939), the CAP stated that corporate financial reporting needed to be approached from the perspective of buyers and sellers of securities, which, in their view, implied that

> Other phases have been increased recognition of the significance of the income statement, with a resulting increase in the importance attached to conservatism in the statement of income, and a tendency to restrict narrowly charges to earned surplus. The result of this emphasis upon the income statement is a tendency to regard the balance-sheet as the connecting link between successive income statements and as the vehicle for the distribution of charges and credits between them.
>
> *(p. 2)*

In that first ARB, the CAP also revealed that it was working on defining cost for fixed assets. Hence, as can be inferred from the SEC's stand and the CAP's first public announcement,

FVA was not going to continue as a popular practice. In fact, conservatism, historical cost and an emphasis on the income statement were emerging as the new basic foundations of corporate financial reporting.

FVA was kept as a default option in accounting for some assets (e.g. lower of cost of market). Nevertheless, FVA remained an attractive concept to many accounting theorists who formalized its appeal and form over the years. For instance, Staubus (1961), Chambers (1964) and Sterling (1970) argue for the use of exit values in financial reporting, i.e. the net realizable value for the asset. In that context, the advent of high inflation in the 1960s and 1970s renewed standard-setters' interest in a measurement model that reflected current values rather than historical cost. For instance, both the Canadian Institute of Chartered Accountants (CICA) and the FASB published standards that aimed to provide financial statement users with more current value information about underlying assets and liabilities (CICA Handbook Section 3510 in 1980; SFAS 33 in 1979). However, both standards were subsequently retrieved as inflation waned. The lack of a convergent view as to how to reflect the impact of inflation on financial statements' items and the challenges arising in terms of comparability, verifiability and uniformity also undermined interest for these standards.

FVA effectively reentered US firms' financial statements only in 1993 through SFAS 115 *Accounting for Certain Investments in Debt and Equity Securities*. Going beyond prior fair value disclosure requirements, SFAS 115 mandates that some securities be accounted for at their fair value, thus directly affecting a firm's balance sheet and income statement. The main rationale underlying SFAS 115 is the reduction of gains trading by financial institutions' managers, i.e. the ability to choose how and when unrealized securities portfolio gains are recognized into the income statement. Another potential motivation for SFAS 115 may have been the Savings & Loans (S&L) crisis. As interest rates shot up in the early 1980s, several S&L, essentially deposit-taking institutions offering long-term mortgages, ended up with severe discrepancies between the book values of their portfolio securities and their actual market value. While these S&L were economically insolvent, they were able to continue reporting as going concerns for a while with their securities at cost or amortized cost. Ultimately, their day of reckoning arrived but the crisis cost the US government more than $100 billion.[2] Moreover, the crisis raised concern as to the transparency of reporting for financial instruments (Linsmeier 2011). Other accounting pronouncements followed, reinforcing FVA's reach within financial statements, culminating with the enactment of SFAS 157 *Fair Value Measurements* in 2006. SFAS 157 formally defines fair value and frames its measurement and disclosure. The equivalent at the IASB is IFRS 13 Fair Value Measurement, which was issued in 2011.

While financial instruments are only one item among the many that firms report on their financial statements, with their use being concentrated in financial institutions, the reach and impact of the standard is probably greater that it appears at first sight. First, in today's economy, financial institutions, especially commercial banks, occupy a critical economic and social role, a fact that the 2007–2009 financial crisis clearly illustrated. In several markets, financial institutions are often the sector with the highest stock market capitalization. For example, the two largest stock market capitalizations in Canada are the Royal Bank of Canada and TD Canada Trust, another bank. Together, these two banks represent close to 10 per cent of Canada's total stock market capitalization. Second, investment entities such as pension plans, mutual funds or close-end funds also rely extensively on FVA and reach millions of investors. Third, even non-financial organizations now get extensively involved with financial instruments for their hedging or financing strategies. Finally, fair value measurement is also emerging in other sectors of the economy such as biological assets (IAS 41 – Agriculture) or real estate investment trusts (Haslam et al. 2015).

Fair value accounting: where is it in today's financial statements?

Background

FVA's reach into modern-day financial statements is quite extensive. Before detailing its extent, it may be useful to delve into the factors that led standard-setters to move away from the accounting principles that prevailed initially, such as conservatism, verifiability or reliability. Several explanations can be put forward as to what brought about that shift. We focus on two concurrent developments.

First, while symbolic in nature, the publication of the Statement of Financial Accounting Concept 1 (Objectives of Financial Reporting by Business Enterprises) by the FASB in November 1978 (FASB 1978) may have captured and reflected a deep shift in accounting thought. After more than 40 years of unsuccessful attempts by standard-setters to develop a conceptual framework, the publication of SFAC 1 can be deemed a momentous achievement. In our view, one aspect of SFAC 1 is particularly relevant and relates to the section about 'Information Useful in Assessing Cash Flow Prospects', especially paragraph 37:

> Financial reporting should provide information to help present and potential investors and creditors and other users in assessing the amounts, timing, and uncertainty of prospective cash receipts from dividends or interest and the proceeds from the sale, redemption, or maturity of securities or loans. The prospects for those cash receipts are affected by an enterprise's ability to generate enough cash to meet its obligations when due and its other cash operating needs, to reinvest in operations, and to pay cash dividends and may also be affected by perceptions of investors and creditors generally about that ability, which affect market prices of the enterprise's securities. *Thus, financial reporting should provide information to help investors, creditors, and others assess the amounts, timing, and uncertainty of prospective net cash inflows to the related enterprise* (emphasis is ours).

The focus on an enterprise's ability to generate future cash flows to meet its future needs, operating and investment-wise, and obligations implies that standard-setters must consider current or market values as finance theory informs us that they basically reflect discounted expected future cash flows. The concept is not a standard per se but represents a foundation upon which future standard-setting is performed and benchmarked.

Second, at about the same time, accounting academe was experiencing a dramatic transformation from an emphasis on normative/prescriptive research and measurement models to a focus on positive research (Watts & Zimmerman 1985). Building upon the recent developments in financial economics and finance, seminal work in the area includes Ball and Brown (1968) and Beaver (1968). The focus in accounting research thus moved toward showing that accounting information was relevant to investors, with relevance being defined as the ability of accounting numbers to affect stock markets (prices or trading volume). In that context, current earnings became viewed as a proxy for future earnings and cash flows. Therefore, releasing current earnings moved markets only to the extent that they contained new (unexpected) information about future earnings and cash flows. Moreover, the greater the association between balance sheet numbers and stock market prices, the greater the assumed relevance of such accounting information to investors. With these two premises, a plethora of studies attempted to show that certain accounting information or practices were either associated with stock market reactions or with stock market prices, thus showing their usefulness and relevance to investors. New generations of accounting academics were thus trained with a financial economics' perspective to the point that the majority of accounting studies being published worldwide now focuses on financial reporting issues using econometrics and other financial economics tools and concepts. The shift was initiated in the United States where what is now called capital markets research is now predominant. For these academics, the purpose of standard-setting is to provide investors with information that is relevant, with relevance being defined in terms of stock market value. Nevertheless, several alternative views are being put forward, one of which can be labeled either as contractual or as stewardship (e.g. Watts & Zuo 2016). However, their reach is not as dominant.

In the same vein, in its Conceptual Framework to financial statement, the IASC emphasized the importance of investors as main users of financial statement. Indeed, paragraph 10 of the Framework (1989) stated that 'as investors are providers of risk capital to the entity, the provision of financial statements that meet their needs will also meet most of the needs of other users that financial statements can satisfy'.

Fair value accounting in today's standards

While FVA is often associated with reporting for financial instruments, it must be pointed out that its reach is much more extensive that it appears. We now briefly review the standards for which fair value is the benchmark measurement mode.

At the time of transactions, we have already pointed out that historical cost does reflect in some sense the fair value of financing, goods or services being obtained, sold or acquired. However, beyond financial instruments, several standards refer to fair value. For instance, IFRS 3 (Business combinations) explicitly states that '...*all assets acquired and liabilities assumed in a business combination are measured at acquisition-date fair value*' (3.18). While the estimation of an acquisition's fair value can in itself be a challenge, especially in the case when consideration paid is in the form of securities issued by the acquirer, it is even more of an issue when we consider the underlying assets and liabilities, which in most cases do not have clearly defined and identifiable markets (e.g. input-production facilities in an integrated manufacturer, some intangible assets). SFAS 141 has a similar requirement.

Business combinations are one-off affairs. However, FVA is also pervasive in several standards that apply to ongoing transactions. For instance, one can argue that FVA is present or even underlies the standards pertaining to financial instruments (IFRS 9; SFAS 133 and subsequent amendments), share-based payments (IFRS 2; SFAS 123 and 148), non-current assets held for sale and discontinued operations (IFRS 5; SFAS 146), employee benefits (IAS 19, SFAS 106 and 112, among others that relate to employee post-retirement and post-employment benefits), changes in foreign exchange rates (IAS 21; SFAS 52) and retirement benefit plans (IAS 26; SFAS 158). Moreover, the recently enacted standards on revenue from contracts with customers (IFRS 15) specifies that "...*Where a contract has multiple performance obligations, an entity will allocate the transaction price to the performance obligations in the contract by reference to their relative standalone selling prices. [IFRS 15:74] If a standalone selling price is not directly observable, the entity will need to estimate it. IFRS 15 suggests various methods that might be used, including: [IFRS 15:79]*

Adjusted market assessment approach

One can easily argue that the above approach eerily resembles FVA. By bringing enterprises to break down revenues from certain contracts into their components, the standard forces management to engage in additional estimation and assessment work, thus pushing fair value down one level from the original contract into its components. Moreover fair value is allowed for tangible assets (IAS 16) and it is the preferred method of investment property (IAS 40), in addition to being used for biological assets (IAS 41).

In addition to what can be labeled a proactive FVA approach, several standards also embed an indirect or non-recurring form of FVA. For example, all impairment tests contained in standards for property, plant and equipment (IAS 16; ASC 360), goodwill (IFRS 3; SFAS 141), intangible assets (IAS 36, IAS 38), financial instruments at cost or amortized cost (e.g. loans) (IFRS 9, ASC 326) essentially imply the application of FVA principles and methods to assign new book values to these assets as a result of the impairment.

Hence, while it has been argued that there is no general will by standard-setters to push for a FVA agenda (e.g. Barth 2007), it must nevertheless be concluded that FVA is intricately associated with modern day financial statements, either on a proactive basis or on an indirect basis. Moreover, the obligation by standard-setters to justify new standards in reference to the conceptual framework, with its strong emphasis on future cash flows and user informational needs, further reinforces a potential tendency to view financial reporting as a mechanism to reflect fair values on the balance sheet. While reflecting fair values on the balance sheet does not necessarily imply that useful information is provided to estimate future earnings and cash flows (i.e. O'Brien 2009), the pressure from the financial analysts' community (CFA Institute) potentially further inflects standard-setters' positions, the alternative (historical cost) having lost its appeal on that count.

'Test driving' fair value accounting: a tale of three crises

Over the past few years, there has been a vigorous debate as to FVA's contribution, real or perceived, to the 2007–2009 financial crisis. While some argue that FVA was merely a messenger conveying relevant information to the markets (André et al. 2009), others point toward FVA's having a pro-cyclical impact on banks' financial condition or creating uncertainty in the marketplace with somewhat obscure valuation estimates (Allen & Carletti 2008). Our purpose in this chapter is not to review or discuss these various arguments and findings but to bring the debate to its core focus as it relates to standard-setters: which qualities or attributes does FVA bring to standard-setters as they consider and debate new accounting standards? One issue that clearly emerged from the crisis was the lack of sufficiently detailed guidance for the implementation of fair value measurement: while the principles underlying fair value measurement as reflected in SFAS 157 and IFRS 13 seem evident enough, the measurement of some types of financial assets, especially under unusual circumstances does appear to be problematic. For instance, on April 9, 2009, at the nadir of the financial crisis and under extreme pressures by several stakeholders, the FASB issued three final Staff Positions (FSPs) providing additional application guidance and enhancing disclosures regarding fair value measurements and impairments of securities:

- FSP FAS 157-4, *Determining Fair Value When the Volume and Level of Activity for the Asset or Liability Have Significantly Decreased and Identifying Transactions That Are Not Orderly*;
- FSP FAS 107-1 and APB 28-1, *Interim Disclosures about Fair Value of Financial Instruments*;
- FSP FAS 115-2 and FAS 124-2, *Recognition and Presentation of Other-Than-Temporary Impairments*.

As the Chair of the FASB stated at the time, 'The issuance of these final FSPs follows a period of intensive and extensive efforts by the FASB to gather input on our proposed guidance, …' (FASB 2009). In other words, the extreme market volatility that characterized the

2007–2009 period as well as the dearth of liquidity that followed the fall of Lehman Brothers in September 2008 highlighted the limitations and uncertainties surrounding fair value measurement and recognition standards, leading to difficulties for (and conflicts between) preparers, auditors and analysts.

The 2011 Greek crisis provides another illustration of the difficulties of mapping FVA principles into consistent numbers that reflect the underlying economic reality within a reasonable range of certainty.[3] In August 2011, the chair of the IASB, Hans Hoogervorst, issued a letter to the European Securities and Markets Authority highlighting problems in the way some European banks were accounting for their Greek government bond holdings. While the letter did not identify a country or bank, the Financial Times reported at the time that financial reporting by two French financial institutions, BNP Paribas and CNP Assurances, raised some concerns. Both firms had announced 21 per cent write-downs following the release of the details of the Greek bailout in July. In their view, the lack of reliable market prices for Greek government bonds because of their illiquidity did not provide a foundation for a mark to market valuation. Instead, both firms resorted to a 'mark to model' valuation. However, at the same time and facing the same market conditions, other banks and insurers relied directly on market prices and, accordingly, reported a larger impairment. For instance, Royal Bank of Scotland erased £733 million from the value of a £1.45 billion Greek government bond portfolio, a cut of 51 per cent. Furthermore, Mr. Hoogervorst challenged the justification for a 'mark to model' approach and also the valuations these produced. In his view,

> Although the level of trading activity in Greek government bonds has decreased, transactions are still taking place, it is hard to imagine that there are buyers willing to buy those bonds at the prices indicated… it is therefore difficult to justify that those models would meet the objective of a fair-value measurement.

Finally, the 2007 asset-backed commercial paper crisis in Canada provides another illustration of the challenges in using market values for financial reporting purposes under the aegis of FVA. Commercial paper has a long history in short-term corporate financing and essentially allows firms to borrow funds from investors by taking advantage of their unused bank lines of credit. However, in the decade preceding 2007, commercial paper morphed into a more sophisticated financial instrument as some originators essentially packaged various underlying financial assets (credit card receivables, commercial loans, mortgages, derivatives on loans or mortgages, etc.) into securities that got sold by some financial institutions and financial advisers to retail and institutional investors as a substitute to treasury bills. These asset-backed commercial papers were typically rated by credit rating agencies as investment grade (i.e. A or higher), in a way not dissimilar to mortgage-backed securities in the United States. Moreover, in the spirit of the more traditional commercial paper, these securities were in theory backed by bank lines of credit to provide liquidity. However, in the months leading to August 2007, concerns rose as to the quality of the underlying assets and some investors, who typically rolled over the security at maturity, demanded payment. However, the banks that had provided the lines of credit that were supposed to ensure liquidity in the market, did not allow issuers to draw down their lines of credit. The market essentially froze in August 2007 and, from that point in time, it became almost possible to trade on these securities. Eventually, the original securities got restructured but uncertainty reigned for several months as to the value and ultimate resolution of the issues. While executives of financial institutions that held such securities deemed most the underlying assets to be solvent, the application of FVA rules led to major write-downs. For instance, the Desjardins Group, a cooperative bank, ended up writing off around 50 per cent of the value of the asset-backed commercial paper it held at the end of 2007. However, as we write this chapter in 2017, it is estimated that the Desjardins Group will have recouped almost all of the value of its investment as most of the debtors ultimately repaid what they owed, a view that was consistent with management's perspective at the time but inconsistent with the market assessment!

These three events, the 2007–2009 financial crisis, the Greek crisis and the asset-backed commercial paper crisis, severely tested the robustness of the FVA model. Standard-setters reacted by developing further guidance. However, more importantly, they raised the issue as to the purpose of financial reporting and sharpened the debate as to the informational role of financial reporting and its use for prudential purposes. Moreover, in the case of the asset-backed commercial paper crisis, internal value estimates by management ended up being closer to the truth than market assessments: hence, while the write-down may have been prudent from a prudential perspective and consistent with mark-to-market FVA, it was actually deceptive if one takes a long term view.

Hence, for a standard-setter, these three crises also highlight that the merits and inconveniences of FVA are rather nuanced. On one hand, while some argue that FVA provides management with too much discretion in measurement and reporting (Watts 2003), especially in contexts where levels 2 and 3 inputs are used, it is also true that mark to market (level 1) is without mercy and quite straightforward and does not leave much leeway for management to make its case. On the other hand, market values can be quite volatile, much more so than the underlying intrinsic values. In addition, management may have information that investors or markets do not have access to regarding the value of underlying assets (Barth et al. 1998; Landsman 2007; Magnan et al. 2015). However, the use of mark to market does not easily allow managers to convey such information to investors in a credible way.

The standard-setter's dilemma

Challenges for setting accounting standards: The need for a template

In setting the scope of fair value, standard-setters face a trade-off between relevance and reliability. Given the underlying uncertainty of all business transactions, accounting information cannot be jointly fully relevant and reliable. Therefore, for a standard-setter deciding whether assets and liabilities have to be estimated at fair value requires addressing several challenges such as

1   Knowing to whom is financial reporting aimed at and understanding what the purported uses of financial reporting are,
2   Assessing the attributes/qualities for financial reporting that are deemed important in light of the intended use for the information and
3   Deciphering the potential institutional and market contexts that will underlie the financial reporting.

A conceptual framework for financial reporting tentatively provides a template for addressing these challenges. The conceptual frameworks, either at the international or at the US levels, are currently being revised but the IFRS exposure-draft issued in 2015 can help us ascertain the relative merits of alternative measurement models, including FVA.

In this context, it is useful to remind ourselves that, according to the IASB's draft conceptual framework,

> ...the objective of general purpose financial reporting is to provide financial information about the reporting entity that is <u>useful</u> to existing and potential investors, lenders and other creditors (users of financial statements) in making decisions about providing resources to the entity.[4]

Usefulness is understood to imply that the information is *relevant* and *faithfully represents* the underlying economic reality. The draft conceptual framework also states that financial information must be (1) helpful in assessing management's *stewardship* of the entity's resources, (2) determined with *prudence* in mind, i.e. the exercise of caution when making judgments under conditions of uncertainty, so that neutrality is achieved, a necessary condition for faithful representativeness (*emphasis added*). We now revisit these qualitative attributes of financial reporting with respect to FVA.

Fair value accounting and relevance

There is actually ambiguous evidence as to whether financial reporting based upon FVA is relevant. On one hand, there is a significant body of research suggesting that FVA-based information is deemed highly relevant by stock market investors (Magnan 2009). Such relevance appears conditional upon the type of fair value information being provided, with level 3 information (marked to model) being deemed less relevant than levels 1 and 2. A potential explanation for this finding is the lack of transparency regarding the underlying valuation models being used for level 3 fair value assets and liabilities. However, additional disclosure about the inputs being used to build models appears to compensate for such lack of initial transparency, assuming that it is deemed reliable (Chung et al. 2016).

On the other hand, the perspective of other stakeholders who have contractual claims against an entity, especially debtholders, is not as clear. It appears that financial information based upon FVA, such as IFRS relative to domestic accounting standards pre-2005 in Europe, is not viewed as being contractible to the same extent than historical cost based information. Examining the impact of IFRS adoption on the use of accounting covenants in debt contracts, Ball et al. (2015) observe that '*Overall, we conclude that IFRS rules sacrifice debt contracting usefulness to achieve other objectives, such as provision of accounting information relevant to valuation*'. Ball et al. (2015) explain this finding by pointing out that IFRS relies much more extensively on FVA than the domestic standards it replaced.

Hence, from a relevance perspective, one can conclude that FVA-based information is most likely useful to stock market investors in assessing firm value but does not appear to be as useful to other stakeholders who have fixed claims against a firm, such as debtholders. For standard-setters, this outcome poses a dilemma as shareholders and debtholders are the two constituencies that are closely identified as key users of financial statements. What are the conditions that underlie such contrasting views? We venture that faithful representativeness and prudence are two qualitative attributes of financial reporting, which may provide some clues.

Fair value accounting, faithful representativeness and prudence

As defined by the IASB in its conceptual framework project, financial information that faithfully represents economic phenomena has three characteristics: (1) it is complete, (2) it is neutral and (3) it is free from error. Prudence implies the exercise of caution when making judgments under conditions of uncertainty. In the view of the IASB, prudence is essential to ensure neutrality in financial information and, therefore, faithful representativeness. How does FVA score on both counts? Evidence pertaining to these attributes of FVA is rather scarce. However, it is possible to draw upon prior conceptual views and some empirical analyses to reach some conclusions. For instance, Milburn (2008) concludes that active, well-regulated, capital markets offer investors with a reasonable level of efficiency, thus providing a sound foundation for the use of FVA. However, such foundations are absent when considering assets measured using level 3 inputs, which are not based on real or observable market prices. For these types of assets, the use of FVA is less conceptually grounded and it is an open question as to whether the information being provided faithfully represents, in a prudent way, the underlying economic reality. Watts (2003), and several other observers, consider that under these conditions, FVA gives too much discretion to managers in the measurement and reporting of assets or liabilities.

Exploring the issue further, Plantin et al. (2008) show that FVA is likely to provide the best estimate of underlying values if securities being valued have short-term maturities, trade in liquid markets that are well-normalized and reflect intermediate or junior claims on an entity's underlying cash flows. In contrast, in settings where underlying assets have long maturities or trade infrequently or in markets lacking depth, estimates derived from FVA-based measurement are susceptible to induce artificial volatility and stray away from intrinsic values. In other words, under some conditions linked with the nature of the underlying assets (duration, priority in terms of cash flow) as well as with the market in which they can be traded (liquidity, regulation), FVA-based information will not properly reflect (faithfully represent) the economic values of such assets. Their arguments find echo in the work of Ramanna and Watts (2012) who argue, and find, that for firms subject to SFAS 142 (Goodwill and other intangible assets), the magnitude of goodwill impairments decreases as the proportion of unverifiable fair values increases. Their findings suggest that managers will avoid timely goodwill impairments under SFAS 142 when it is in their interest to do so, despite contrary market indications. Again, in such a case, reported numbers are not likely to faithfully represent the values of the underlying assets.

But how is it possible for audited numbers based on so-called fair values to misrepresent the underlying economic reality? An explanation put forward by Ramanna and Watts (2012) is that since for intangible assets or goodwill, fair value estimates essentially rely on managerial forecasts, which are unverifiable, the resulting reporting outcome is bound to be biased in a way that is consistent with managerial interests. A similar assessment can be made for level 3 fair value estimates. In other words, under conditions of measurement uncertainty, fair value estimates end up being less prudent, thus undermining their representational faithfulness.

Magnan et al. (2015) provide some additional clues regarding the robustness of fair value estimates under conditions of measurement uncertainty. Their results show that the greater the proportion of level 3 assets and liabilities on a bank's balance sheet, the more dispersed are analysts' forecasts, suggesting that level 3 fair value measurement confuses analysts more than it informs them. Hence, it can be inferred that fair value measurement at level 3, rather than being consistent with the objective of financial statements, which is to provide information useful to investors to estimate a firm's future cash flows, potentially impedes investors' efforts in this regard.

From our own experience with financial institutions, several factors underlie the potential confusion generated by level 3 numbers. First, and probably the most critical issue, is the choice of the valuation model. Several valuation models, based upon different assumptions, may be used to value any asset or liability. The selection of one instead of another can translate into different values, sometimes quite material. Existing accounting standards leave this issue rather open except in some specific contexts (e.g. stock options granted under compensation arrangements). For instance, alternative valuation methodologies are available to value embedded options contained in some securities. Second, assuming there is agreement on the selection of a particular model, the issue then arises as to the assumptions underlying the model: most valuation models are conceptually grounded in terms of expectations but, in practice, only the past is known and observable and thus serves as input, direct or indirect, to the model. Third, in most cases, valuation models typically require the development of forecasts or expectations about various variables. However, the underlying truth is in the beholder's eye! There is abundant research showing that even despite their best efforts, managers' and auditors' decisions and the resulting actions, such as forecasts, are susceptible to be influenced by unconscious biases (e.g. Milkman et al. 2009; M. Bazerman and colleagues have several papers on this issue, especially with respect to the ethics of decision-making).

Conclusions

Extant research provides two insights to standard-setters on the pros and cons of FVA. On one hand, FVA can provide information that is relevant, which faithfully represents the underlying economic reality, when markets are relatively efficient, liquid, well-regulated and when the assets/liabilities being reported about have relatively short or medium term durations with well-defined cash flow claims. Under these conditions, fair value-based numbers are useful to financial statement users, especially current and potential equity holders. On the other hand, FVA is potentially detrimental to certain stakeholders, especially debtholders but also equity holders, when there is much measurement uncertainty as it opens the door too wide to managerial discretion. While some level of managerial discretion, within tight standard and regulatory boundaries, can be helpful in enhancing the usefulness of FVA-based information, the opposite is true when managers cannot be held in check. In our view, these findings provide a template for standard-setters as to how they must consider the use of FVA in the development of new standards. Additional implementation guidance and careful thought about disclosure thus need to be explicitly considered under certain conditions of measurement uncertainty. Alternative measurement models need also to be seriously considered although it is a challenge to derive conceptually sound models.

In that regard, Lev and Gu (2016) make a cogent argument that the current accounting model is broken and that a new reporting framework is needed to reflect the new nature of firms and to address capital markets' informational needs. One of the points they raise is that the current financial reporting framework gives short drift to intangible assets, which now represent the bulk of the value of many firms. Their analysis points toward several weaknesses or gaps in the current mixed reporting model (i.e. mixing historical cost, fair value and other measurement models). They propose a new reporting model with more extensive disclosure and a focus on critical performance metrics. While what they propose is not per se FVA, it does include some of its elements, especially the prospective dimension, and may thus be subject to the same criticisms regarding the usefulness toward stakeholders other than stock market investors. Moreover, if the valuation of securities under level 3 fair value is subject to some criticisms and potential problems, it is even more the case for non-financial instrument assets. However, their book, and most of Lev's work in the past two decades, underline the point that standard-setters need to stand back from the current reporting model, including the current version of FVA, and adopt a fresh perspective. As such, it provides additional food for thought in the FVA debate and hints at issues that standard-setters should consider in the future if accounting standards are to retain their societal relevance and legitimacy. However, the informational needs to non-equity holders, especially debtholders, must be taken into consideration as well and standard-setters will need to successfully resolve the tension between these potentially divergent interests while keeping a unique set of standards, a perilous yet essential task.

As parting words, and to generate some further reflection, we would like to recall the phrase coined by Canadian philosopher Marshall McLuhan in his book *Understanding Media: The Extensions of Man* (1964; reprinted in 1994): 'the medium is the message'.[1] In this book, among other ideas, McLuhan proposes that a medium itself, i.e. the platform by which a message is conveyed, not the content it carries, is actually the key variable of interest. In other words, a medium affects society in which it is active not only by the content conveyed over the medium, but also by the medium's attributes. Does McLuhan's statement extend to FVA, which delivers a 'message' to society via the 'medium' of financial statements prepared by accountants under specific accounting standards? We raise the issue. In any case, it is interesting to contrast McLuhan's perspective with some prior comments about accounting, and accountants, just being messengers carrying a message with respect to the role of FVA in the financial crisis (André et al. 2009; Magnan 2009).

Notes

1 See Flesher, D. L. and T. Flesher, 1986, Ivar Kreuger's contribution to U.S. financial reporting, *The Accounting Review* 61 (3): 421–434. Cudahy, R.D. and W.D. Henderson. 2005. From Insull to Enron: Corporate (Re)Regulation After the Rise and Fall of Two Energy Icons. *Energy Law Journal* 26 (1), 35–110.
2 www.reuters.com/article/us-usa-subprime-bush-idUSB38105220070315.
3 www.ft.com/cms/s/0/9582fb8c-cfe9-11e0-a1de-00144feabdc0.html?siteedition=intl#axzz4 Gs0ltcXv.
4 IASB. 2015. Conceptual Framework for Financial Reporting. Exposure-Draft for comments. May. London.

References

Allen, F & Carletti, E 2008, "Mark-to-market accounting and liquidity pricing", *Journal of Accounting and Economics*, vol. 45 no. 2, pp. 358–378.
André, P, Cazavan-Jeny, A, Dick, W, Richard, C & Walton, P 2009, "Fair value accounting and the banking crisis in 2008: shooting the messenger", *Accounting in Europe*, vol. 6, no. 1, pp. 3–24.
Ball, R & Brown, P 1968, "An empirical evaluation of accounting income numbers", *Journal of Accounting Research*, vol. 6, no. 2, pp. 159–178.
Ball, R, Li, X & Shivakumar, L 2015, "Contractibility and transparency of financial statement information prepared under IFRS: evidence from debt contracts around IFRS adoption", *Journal of Accounting Research*, vol. 53, no. 5, pp. 915–963.
Barth, ME 2007, *Research, standard setting, and global financial reporting*, Now Publishers Inc, Delft.
Barth, ME, Clement, MB, Foster, G & Kasznik, R 1998, "Brand values and capital market valuation", *Review of Accounting Studies*, vol. 3, no. 1–2, pp. 41–68.
Beaver, WH 1968, "The information content of annual earnings announcements", *Journal of Accounting Research*, vol. 6, no. 2, pp. 67–92.
Chambers, RJ 1964, "Measurement and objectivity in accounting", *The Accounting Review*, vol. 39, no. 2, 264–274.
Chung, SG, Goh, BW, Ng, J & Yong, KO 2016, Voluntary fair value disclosures beyond SFAS 157's Three-level Estimates (May 1). Available from SSRN: http://ssrn.com/abstract=1335848 or http://dx.doi.org/10.2139/ssrn.1335848, accessed September 13, 2017. Forthcoming in *Review of Accounting Studies*.

Committee on Accounting Procedure 1939, General introduction and rules formerly adopted. September.

Financial Accounting Standards Board 1978, Statement of financial accounting concepts 1. Norwalk, CT.

FASB 2006, *Statement of Financial Accounting Standards 157, Fair Value Measurements.* FASB, Norwalk, CT.

Financial Accounting Standards Board 2009, News release: FASB issues final staff positions to improve guidance and disclosures on fair value measurements and impairments. Available from www.fasb.org/news/nr040909.shtml, accessed 9 August 2017.

Haslam, C, Tsitsianis, N, Andersson, T & Gleadle, P 2015, "December. Real Estate Investment Trusts (REITs): a new business model in the FTSE100", *Accounting Forum*, vol. 39, no. 4, pp. 239–248. Elsevier.

Landsman, WR 2007, "Is fair value accounting information relevant and reliable? Evidence from capital market research", *Accounting and Business Research*, vol. 37, sup 1, pp. 19–30.

Lev, B & Gu, F 2016, *The end of accounting and the path forward for investors and managers.* John Wiley & Sons, Hoboken, NJ.

Linsmeier, TJ 2011, "Financial reporting and financial crises: the case for measuring financial instruments at fair value in the financial statements", *Accounting Horizons*, vol. 25, no. 2, pp. 409–417.

Magnan, ML 2009, "Fair value accounting and the financial crisis: messenger or contributor?", *Accounting Perspectives*, vol. 8, no. 3, pp. 189–213.

Magnan, M, Menini, A & Parbonetti, A 2015, "Fair value accounting: information or confusion for financial markets?", *Review of Accounting Studies*, vol. 20, no. 1, pp. 559–591.

McLuhan, M 1994, *Understanding media: the extensions of man*, MIT Press, Boston, MA.

Milburn, JA 2008, "The relationship between fair value, market value, and efficient markets", *Accounting Perspectives*, vol. 7, no. 4, pp. 293–316.

Milkman, KL, Chugh, D & Bazerman, MH 2009, "How can decision making be improved?", *Perspectives on Psychological Science*, vol. 4, no. 4, pp. 379–383.

O'brien, PC 2009, "Changing the concepts to justify the standards", *Accounting Perspectives*, vol. 8, no. 4, pp. 263–275.

Pines, JA 1965, "The securities and exchange commission and accounting principles", *Law and Contemporary Problems*, vol. 30, no. 4, pp. 727–751.

Plantin, G, Sapra, H & Shin, HS 2008, "Marking-to-market: Panacea or Pandora's box?", *Journal of Accounting Research*, vol. 46, no. 2, pp. 435–460.

Ramanna, K & Watts, RL 2012, "Evidence on the use of unverifiable estimates in required goodwill impairment", *Review of Accounting Studies*, vol. 17, no. 4, pp. 749–780.

Shearer, J 2010, "Mark-to-market: delivering the financial crisis to your front door", *Ohio Northern Law Review*, vol. 36, pp. 236–261.

Staubus, GJ 1961, *A theory of accounting to investors.* Berkeley: University of California Press.

Sterling, RR 1970, *The theory of the measurement of enterprise income.* Lawrence: The University Press of Kansas.

U.S. Securities and Exchange Commission, Office of the Chief Accountant, Division of Corporation Finance, Report and Recommendations Pursuant to Section 133 of the Emergency Economic Stabilization Act of 2008: Study on Mark-to-Market Accounting, Washington DC, 2008. Available from www.sec.gov/news/studies/2008/marktomarket123008.pdf, accessed 7 August 2013.

Watts, RL 2003, "Conservatism in accounting part I: explanations and implications", *Accounting Horizons*, vol. 17, no. 3, pp. 207–221.

Watts, R & Zimmerman J 1985, *Positive accounting theory.* Prentice-Hall, New York.

Watts, RL & Zuo, L 2016, Understanding practice and institutions: a historical perspective. *Accounting Horizons*, vol. 30, no. 3, pp. 409–423.

4

HAVE THE STANDARD-SETTERS GONE TOO FAR, OR NOT FAR ENOUGH, WITH FAIR VALUE ACCOUNTING?

Ken Peasnell

> There are very few finance professionals who are without a strongly held viewpoint on the topic of fair value accounting. Some (mostly financial statement preparers and financial analysts) dread the day that IASB and FASB formally adopt a fair value basis of accounting. Others (primarily academicians and theoreticians) are counting the days until we get rid of historical cost accounting and move to a total fair value ('FV') basis.
>
> *(King, 2007, p. 24)*

The above remark was the opening statement that appeared in a leading practitioner's contribution to the 2007 edition of the present volume. It pithily summarizes a sentiment that could have appeared at any time in the past 40 years. When I started as a graduate student in the late 1960s, there was no standard-setting body in the UK. But it was certainly the case that leading accounting scholars had been actively debating for many years the merits of replacing historical cost accounting (HCA) with some version of current value accounting, and in those (rare) instances where practitioners had expressed views on the subject, they tended to strongly oppose such a change. The issue became pressing in the 1970s and 1980s with the inflation that occurred as a result of the breakup of the Bretton Woods system and the Organization of the Petroleum Exporting Countries' oil embargo, peaking at over 13% in the United States and over 20% in the UK and Japan. This earlier economic crisis led to the introduction of current cost accounting (CCA) in the UK and the mandating of similar disclosures in a number of other countries. The subject was then taken up again by accounting standard-setters in the closing years of the millennium in a completely different way, as a result of challenges posed by innovations in financial engineering, and subsequently was put to severe test as a result of the turmoil in asset prices that occurred during the 2007–2008 financial crisis.

In this chapter, I will step back a little and try to take a long view of this seemingly unending debate. I will argue that experience suggests that both camps have valid points to make, but they can be easily overstated. I will start with a brief summary of the experience with current value accounting in the 1980s to see what lessons it might suggest regarding the contemporary fair value accounting (FVA) debate. This is followed by an examination of FVA for financial instruments, how it was similar to and how it differed in important ways from CCA, and, in particular, how it is to be employed only in carefully delineated circumstances. I then give some examples of the application of fair value in other areas. I conclude from this analysis that FVA has been introduced as circumstances have arisen that suggest that it produces a superior result and not otherwise. Experience suggests that this piecemeal, problem-solving approach has been largely successful. The dread that King suggests practitioners have regarding the standard-setters' likely future actions is likely to be unwarranted. The mixed-attribute measurement approach is here to stay for the foreseeable future, with HCA remaining the main basis of measurement. The hopes of some theorists will continue to be dashed.

Current value accounting and accounting for inflation

Judged by its impact on teaching and practice, Paton and Littleton's 1940 textbook can reasonably be regarded as one of the most influential works ever written on accounting (Paton & Littleton 1940). Among other things, it provided clear arguments concerning the utility of HCA. A key feature of their analysis was the belief that the primary purpose of financial reporting was to measure business income, defined as '… the difference between costs (as efforts) and revenues (as accomplishments) for individual enterprises' (Paton & Littleton 1940, p. 16). This provided powerful intellectual support for the ban that the Securities and Exchange Commission (SEC) had introduced on the revaluation of assets in financial statements and prospectuses. The SEC's chief concern was that departures from historical cost would provide corporate managers with manifold opportunities to deceive investors. Objectivity was a key concern. HCA employs numbers that usually are grounded in real transactions and as such a strong case has been made by Ijiri (1975), Watts and Zimmerman (1986) and many others that they provide a better basis for use in contractual relationships between firms and managers, capital providers, tax authorities, tariff regulators and others. They certainly serve as a basis for determination of employee compensation, dividend distributions, interest payments, tax bills, prices charged to customers, etc. For accounting numbers to serve these contractual and distributional functions it is highly desirable, indeed arguably essential, that the numbers be 'hard' not 'soft'. It is an empirical issue whether historical cost numbers generally better meet this test than do current value alternatives, but clearly, they do in many (perhaps most) circumstances.

A related, but often overlooked, argument for making historical cost the basis of accounting is cost and speed of preparation. HCA numbers are derived directly from the records that enterprises need to keep simply to function. They have to have records of what they have received and what they have paid, who owes them money and who they owe money to, and how much. The usefulness of accounting depends not only on its relevance and reliability, but also on how timely reports can be produced and audited, and the cost of doing so. Incorporation of externally derived information is more challenging, particularly if the data needed are not readily to hand. The 'dread' that King attributes to many practitioners is doubtless grounded in such practical concerns.

Whether due to inertia or the power of such intellectual and practical arguments, historical cost generally has served as the basis for financial reporting by most business entities. However, exceptions were granted in many jurisdictions. For example, in the UK, companies had long been required in the Companies Acts to disclose the fair values of real estate where the current values of such assets had departed greatly from the reported carrying value, and they had the option to recognize them in the financial statements if it was deemed that doing so would better provide a true and fair view.

Historically, inflation posed the biggest challenge to the status quo – most notably over concerns that the use of historical costs could result in confiscatory taxation, pressure for the payment of wages or dividends or imposition of price controls that would erode the real value of a business's capital.[1] This came to a head in the 1970s and led, after much heated debate, to the introduction of some form of CCA in a number of countries, including in Australia, the USA and the UK. A critical issue that received much attention during these debates was whether it would be better (or at least sufficient) simply to adjust the historical cost numbers using an index of the change in the general level of prices – constant purchasing power accounting (CPP) – or whether it was better to incorporate into accounting the changes in relative prices. The latter was the path that was chosen in the UK. This opened up the thorny question of what is meant by 'current value'. Should it be what the asset could be sold for, or what it would cost to replace, or the present value (PV) of the benefits the enterprise expected to reap from owning it? In the UK, the standard that was eventually adopted, SSAP 16, employed a hybrid model known as 'value to the business' that required firms to publish, as supplements to the HCA statements, a balance sheet in which each asset is to be valued at current cost, defined as the lower of replacement cost (RC) and 'recoverable amount', the latter being the higher of the asset's PV and its net realizable value (NRV). In addition, a supplementary current cost income statement had to be presented in which costs of goods sold and depreciation were to be charged at current cost, and charges also made for the so-called 'monetary working capital adjustment' and the 'gearing adjustment'. In the USA, the FASB's solution was to issue SFAS 33 that required supplementary disclosures of the effects of inflation using both bases – the effects on reported income when cost of goods sold is measured using RC and the effects using historical costs adjusted to constant dollars (i.e. CPP) – and the full effects of changes in both relative and general price changes.[2] Business was happy with neither, and the standards were effectively discarded in both the UK and the USA when inflation abated.

During the period the standards remained in force, RC was the predominant basis used. One of the practical problems this posed was what was meant by replacement in the case of long-lived assets that might not readily (or sensibly) be replaced in their existing form. The conceptual solution offered was to base the calculation on the 'modern equivalent asset'. Thus, if one were to replace an existing asset by a much-improved one, RC would the price of the new version scaled down to reflect the inferior quality of the existing one, and then in the case of a wasting asset, to depreciate it to reflect its diminished remaining years of life. Needless to say, this requirement generally received little more than lip service, the task being implicitly outsourced to statisticians by relying on producer price indexes rather than actual market quotes – a task that is fraught with difficulty.[3]

For a modern audience, this raises an interesting question: why was RC preferred to NRV, which is the basis of the IASB's and FASB's extant FVA standards? The issue did indeed receive serious attention, in no small measure due to the formidable case that had long been mounted by Professor Raymond Chambers, one of the world's leading theoreticians who had been advocating a system of accounting that would value all assets at what they would fetch at the balance sheet date, incorporate all the resulting gains and losses in income and adjust equity for the changing value of money (Chambers 1966). One worrisome feature was that it could result in so-called day-one profit recognition if the business priced its finished goods inventory at what it could expect to get in its retail market. Thus, a store that bought wholesale and sold retail could immediately record its normal margin as a profit without waiting for completion of the irksome business of dealing with real customers. It could be argued, of course, NRV should be based on what the goods would fetch if sold back into the wholesale market. In this case, the firm would, unless it had cornered the market, report a 'day-one loss' because of the bid-ask spread. However, it is likely that day-one losses would have been greeted with much the same consternation as day-one profits – they simply flew in the face of how the businesses viewed their activities. These are at least assets for which markets exist. Chambers (1970) pointed out that application of exit price accounting would logically require assets for which there is no market, such as highly specialized assets and manufacturing work-in-progress inventory, to be written down to zero. For many critics, this ignores the operating and production processes that are needed to generate value, treating instead all businesses as though they were little more than investment funds that bought and sold assets. The debate at that time was focused on trading and manufacturing companies, something that needs to be remembered when considering FVA, where the concern has been in large measure about financial institutions (and treasury operations of major companies).

The 'deprival value' logic of CCA can be traced back at least as far as Bonbright (1937) and was subsequently developed as an accounting valuation algorithm by Wright (1965), Baxter (1975, 2003) and others. It is broad enough in conception to be able to encompass all sorts of business models. For an investment fund, the distinction between RC and NRV will be small if the assets it holds can be traded in markets where spreads are low, making the distinction between current cost and fair value as defined in FVA standards of possibly second-order importance (at least when compared to historical cost). For a manufacturing or retail firm, on the other hand, deprival might ordinarily be expected to result in the asset being replaced. Trading inventory is the obvious example, where 'deprival' that takes the form of a sale results in re-stocking (or bringing forward the time such re-stocking occurs). For a used durable asset, RC would be the cost of acquiring a new version of the asset adjusted downwards for its diminished service potential (or its second-hand price). However, except for industries where their prices are regulated by reference to the RCs of their assets,[4] few nonfinancial firms have reason to collect such data for day-to-day management purposes, and they tended to complain about the cost of having to do so for financial reporting. In the UK, the tax authorities dealt with corporate complaints about the tax effects of rising prices by introducing special allowances. Support for radical departure from the familiar HCA model diminished accordingly.

Another feature of the CCA debate was the muddled treatment of liabilities, which with hindsight seems curious because the one thing where inflation has a clear effect is that it erodes the value of claims that are fixed in money terms (particularly if the inflation was unanticipated and interest rates have risen as a result). The classic work of Edwards and Bell (1961) sets out very clearly, with worked examples, how specific price changes for both assets and liabilities can be recognized along with adjustments to reflect the effects of general price changes. Baxter (2003) explains how the concept of 'deprival' for assets has its counterpart notion of 'relief of a burden' for liabilities. In contrast, the monetary working capital and gearing adjustments required in SSAP 16 make little economic sense; their central feature being that they are defined in a way that ensures the reported CCA income number cannot exceed the HCA one.

The reason for devoting this much space to a failed attempt to introduce a form of current value accounting over 30 years ago is to provide a basis of comparison for the way the standard-setting community subsequently went about revisiting the issue in relation to accounting for financial instruments.

Accounting has generally changed in an incremental fashion. Specific issues, often posed by new business arrangements and innovative transactions, become difficult to accommodate within the existing structure. A good example of this was the growth of complex business groups in the late nineteenth and early twentieth centuries that led to the development of consolidated accounting techniques (Walker 2006). In the UK, group accounts were introduced as supplementary documents supporting the parent company statements. With the passage of time, the statements for the group came to be viewed as the primary statements, the parent company balance sheet now being reported as a supplement. Indeed, the most striking feature of the development of accounting has been the growth in supplementary disclosures. If these proved helpful then the next step has often been to incorporate them directly in to the measurement rules governing recognition. Often the changes involved specific transactions or events that required new measurement standards, but only for those matters, leaving the rest of the accounting structure unchanged. Pension accounting provides a clear example, one that also led to the introduction of further into the measurement process. In contrast, CCA involved changing practically everything, and as such had the potential to affect and disturb lots of different business arrangements. Push back was almost certain to occur, and it did.

I argue later that there are many ways in which fair values have become part of the disclosure and recognition process without encountering the full-blooded resistance of the business community that happened with CCA. I suggest this was so because the mooted changes did not impose large adaptation costs for many business entities, or where they did, the merits of at least part of the changes were widely accepted as obvious (e.g. the revaluation of real estate assets). The introduction of fair values for the measurement and recognition of financial instruments represents a middle ground in this spectrum: the response of financial institutions was often fierce, but it did not raise issues that turned the world upside down as far as most companies were concerned. Most importantly, for entities that were affected, it was becoming increasingly clear that changes had occurred that were poorly served by HCA.

FVA for financial instruments

The development of FVA has a tangled history in the sense that fair value has long been used to deal with a number of problematic areas. But the challenges that innovations in financial engineering in general, and derivatives in particular, have posed for accountants in the past two decades played a seminal role. Unlike many other assets, derivatives are highly leveraged claims, and as such can change value very quickly and by large amounts. For example, a forward contract that involves no exchange of cash at inception, and therefore has no historical cost, can quickly have a positive or negative economic value, and thus switch between being an asset and a liability. To complicate matters further, the derivative might be held for the express purpose of hedging an exposure of another asset or liability, suggesting that the relationship between the two needs to be considered as well. The approach the FASB adopted was first to issue SFAS 107 in 1991 that required supplementary disclosures about the fair values of these and other financial instruments. This was followed up in 1999 by SFAS 115 that required fair value for many types of debt and equity securities, and then a year later with SFAS 133 that required the same for all stand-alone derivatives.

Unlike with the earlier inflation accounting standards, these new standards had little or no impact on the many businesses that have few if any financial instruments. This is not the case for banks. Indeed, one of the major criticisms levelled at banks is that their accounting is opaque. There has always been a school of thought that banks *ought* to be opaque in order to discourage bank runs. Indeed, whereas the 1948 Companies Act prohibited companies from using secret reserves, banks were expressly exempted from this requirement. But a few important dissenters apart (e.g. Gorton 2014), this view no longer holds sway. Indeed, banks' annual reports contain voluminous amounts of data. The opaqueness that remains is a function of the sheer complexity of banking and modern financial engineering.[5] And to cap it all, banking is a highly regulated activity, one where the accounting numbers play an important role in bank regulation, e.g. in the determination of the leverage ratio and the Tier 1 risk-based capital ratio. Banks therefore have strong incentives to try to 'manage' their accounting numbers, either by cherry picking their way through the accounting or by devising new strategies or financial securities that exploit inconsistencies in the ways in which the accounting rules treat different kinds of financial instruments (Dye et al. 2015).

There are many different kinds of possible accounting arbitrage that banks can employ, if they are of a mind to do so, to take advantage of differences in the way economically equivalent portfolios of financial claims are treated for accounting purposes. For example, a credit default swap (CDS) derivative that is embedded in a credit-linked note is treated differently under IFRS 9 and IAS 39 than a free-standing CDS (Landsman & Peasnell 2013). Moreover, the fact that banks explicitly hedge many of their risks means that it is not sensible to treat the accounting for assets and liabilities separately. This is particularly true of the trading side of their operations, where net asset positions are routinely managed on a mark-to-mark basis. But prudential considerations require a bank to take account of how all its activities affect its overall risk position, using value-at-risk and other metrics, given the small amounts of equity cushions they have compared to businesses in other industries. Accounting for hedging activities poses particular difficulties when the accounting is based on a mixed-attribute model and explains why the FASB and IASB have been driven to include complex and seemingly arbitrary special treatments in the hedge accounting rules. It also suggests that the strategy they have followed of requiring large amounts of supplementary disclosures is understandable. This is particularly true when, on the one hand, existing measurement rules no longer appear to be capturing key aspects of a business's position or operations, but there are real concerns that changing the rules might make a bad situation worse. Medical students are taught the maxim that whatever you do, first do no harm. In these circumstances requiring supplementary disclosures could be argued to be the accounting standard-setters' way of trying to do good when there is a real danger of doing harm. The contrast with the CCA debate in the 1980s is noticeable, and suggests that important lessons were learned.

There are subtle (and sometimes important) differences in the definitions of fair value that have appeared in the standards, but these need not detain us here. Both SFAS 157 and IFRS 13 define it now as follows: Fair value is the price that would be received to sell an asset or paid to transfer a liability in an orderly transaction between market participants at the measurement date. It is an exit price, rather than the entry one favored in SFAS 33 and SSAP 16. This makes perfectly good sense for the assets and liabilities in a bank's held-for-trading (HFT) book, for that is how they are managed. But assets in a bank's banking books are not managed on this basis: these are the mortgage and other loans they make to customers, the normal expectation being that such loans and receivables (L&R) will be held to maturity (or earlier redemption).[6] Such assets are shown not at fair value, but rather at historical cost subject to loan-loss provisions. The third category is available-for-sale (AFS) financial assets; these also have to be measured at fair value. The key difference in the accounting for HFT securities and AFS assets is that the revaluation gains and losses on the former are to be included in income whereas those on the latter appear in other comprehensive income (OCI). Thus, the accounting treatments for the two polar cases, those in the HFT category and those in the L&R one, are designed to mirror the distinct ways they are managed by the banks.

The tricky case is the AFS category. One of the traditional criticisms levelled at HCA is that it provides opportunities to generate reported income by selective disposal of assets. On the other hand, including in income unrealized fair value gains and losses on debt securities that might in principle be sold at any time but in practice are usually held to maturity simply includes elements of income that cancel out through time; as such, it could be argued that this introduces misleading volatility. For banks, this is a non-trivial issue for two related reasons. Compared to almost any other type of business enterprise, banks have very little equity capital, and (as noted already) they are regulated by reference to adjusted accounting-based measures of equity capital. So volatility matters. Given the disputed status of AFS gains and losses, segregating them in OCI was a practical way for standard-setters to take account of key distinctions concerning how different bank assets and liabilities add value – through use or in exchange.[7] Nevertheless, the HFT/AFS distinction seems to be a cop-out that standard-setters deemed to be politically necessary at the time. The FASB effectively eliminated the distinction in 2016 as far equity securities were concerned: ASU 2016-01 now requires gains and losses on equity securities classified as AFS to be included in income. The IASB hasn't gone quite so far, settling instead in IFRS 9 to allow (but not require) firms to use the 'fair value option' (FVO) to include AFS gains and losses in profit or loss rather than OCI. It is difficult to conclude anything other than that both bodies would like to dispense with the HFT/AFS distinction, and FASB has actually done so as far as one type of investment is concerned.

FVA and the 2008 financial crisis

Many factors were blamed for the 2008 financial crisis, FVA being one of them. It was alleged that FVA exacerbated the business cycle: reporting fair value gains led to excessive lending during the good times, while subsequently reporting losses resulted in excessive contractions during the bad times.[8] The pressure to suspend FVA during the crisis was marked, the argument being that as the market for many assets had largely dried up, marking them to market was resulting in banks being forced into fire-sale disposals in order to protect their capital positions (American Bankers Association 2008).

The implicit assumption being made here is that FVA necessarily involves marking to market. However, this is not the case. In the relevant FASB and IASB standards, fair values are to be derived by reference to a tripartite hierarchy. At the top are level 1 measurements using prices from orderly transactions in active markets for assets that are identical to the ones being valued (essentially, marking to market). Fire sale prices do not qualify. If level 1 prices are not available, level 2 measurements based on (standard or own proprietary) models using observable inputs such as prices for similar assets or other market data such as interest rate yield curves or interest rate spreads (marking to model using market-based inputs). If level 2 measurements are not possible, then level 3 ones are to be used, which typically will be unobservable model assumptions (marking to model using non-market inputs). The objectivity of the measurements clearly declines as one moves down the hierarchy.

The criticism that was levelled at FVA during the financial crisis was that the measurements were based on fire-sale prices and that doing so resulted in larger asset write-downs than the underlying economics warranted. The problem with this argument is that proper application of the fair value hierarchy rules out using level 1 in circumstances where transactions are not derived from an orderly market, and clearly the market could not reasonably be judged to be orderly in the financial crisis.[9] This would mean that at best the values used would have to be level 2 or, more likely, level 3. Here, the more reasonable concern was that there might be a tendency for management to overstate fair values, not understate them. An investigation by the SEC revealed that the majority of the fair values reported on bank balance sheets at the time of the financial crisis were based on level 2 inputs (Securities and Exchange Commission 2008). Moreover, Badertscher et al. (2012) present evidence that shows that FVA had minimal effect on regulatory capital and only mixed evidence that banks sold securities in response to capital-depleting charges during the crisis, and these were economically insignificant. The title of their study unequivocally expresses the view that FVA was being treated as a 'very convenient scapegoat'.

Should FVA be restricted to level 1?

As Laux and Leuz (2010) point out, the strongest criticism that can be made of FVA is that it is at its best when measurements are based on level 1 and weakest when they are level 3. An equally important point to note is that, in practice, by far the largest component of most bank balance sheets consists of held-to-maturity mortgages and loan receivables that are measured at historical cost (Securities and Exchange Commission 2008). So has FVA gone too far? Might it be better to restrict the application of FVA to those securities that for which level 1 inputs are available?

Evidence of the practical difficulty of rolling back FVA to cover only those assets and liabilities that can be priced in deep and liquid markets is provided by the financial crisis itself. To see this, first suppose this was in fact done – in which case, FVA would be restricted to claims such as those for currencies, government bonds and the like. Next, consider another major unexpected economic shock occurs that completely unsettles prior expectations. David Vinlar, then CEO of Goldman Sachs, explained how market participants viewed the dramatic price changes that occurred during the 2008 financial crisis, expressed in statistical language: 'We were seeing things that were 25-standard deviation moves, several days in a row' (New York Times 2007). It has been pointed out that the probability of observing just one so-called 25-sigma event, if it were drawn from a standard normal distribution, would be akin to the odds on winning the UK National Lottery's £2.5 million prize 21 or 22 times in a row (O'Connor 2010).[10] In such uncertain market conditions, liquidity could (and did) disappear virtually overnight, making quoted bid and ask prices highly unreliable for valuation purposes, or indeed result in a complete absence of any price quotes (Easley & O'Hara 2010). This would pose a dilemma for accountants. If the alternative to level 1 was historical cost, should they write back the recognized fair value to historical cost, which for a derivative could be zero? Or should they simply not recognize any further gains or losses until the market stabilizes? Now the advantage of having levels 2 and 3 become clear. For in these circumstances, following the standards as currently written would suggest that they should move down the hierarchy to one of the two less objective categories – not a perfect solution, but better than the alternative. Or should this episode be regarded as a wakeup call and lead to an abandonment of all FVA so that the same problem won't arise again when the next market crash occurs?

To address this question, we have to return to the genesis of the FASB's and IASB's financial instruments projects. In particular, as already noted, the rapid growth in derivatives products posed a direct challenge to the traditional HCA model.[11] The one thing that the standard-setters have been firm about when faced with great pressures to row back on the application of FVA is that standalone derivatives must continue to be measured at fair value. Many derivatives are not traded in deep and liquid markets; indeed, most are traded over-the-counter. So they would seem to be obvious candidates for second thoughts on the suitability of fair values for financial reporting. And it is not as though the FASB didn't have prior warning. Benston (2006) argues that Enron was able to pad its reported earnings by using fair value estimates for its energy-delivery contracts and for its energy-trading dealings generally. A key feature of these derivatives was their long delivery dates, and these could only be valued using level 3 inputs in most cases. While commentators have pointed out that it is possible to adjust the standard models to deal with the known technical problems associated with the standard Black-Scholes model (e.g. Gupta et al. 2016), the mere fact that such complexities have to be addressed indicates the inherent subjectivity of the valuation process. However abandoning FVA for derivatives would unlikely to have improved matters. As Ryan (2007, p. xiii) observes,

> While not all financial instruments currently should be fair valued and errors in fair values will occur even for those that should, a desirable property of fair value accounting is that it corrects its mistakes over time, since financial instruments must be revalued each period based on current market conditions. In this regard, many of Enron's problems would simply have taken longer to uncover if its accounting were not based on fair value.

The counter-argument is that it might take a long time for the market to correct its mistakes in the case of long-dated derivatives. So the jury probably must remain out regarding Enron's use of FVA: hard cases make bad law. But more generally, it seems clear that the very nature of derivatives and the ways in which they are used by businesses to hedge positions suggest that there is no approach to measuring them that is better than fair value. And this provides the justification for having a tripartite hierarchy of methods.

As it is, there is not much evidence to indicate that financial institutions make much use of the latitude that levels 2 and 3 afford them to massage their numbers – or at least there is little evidence that investors think they do. One study found that bank equity was priced in the first three quarters of 2008 as though the market applied a discount to reported level 2 and 3 fair values relative to level 1 ones: a dollar of level 1, 2 and 3 fair values was priced at $0.96, $0.85 and $0.79, respectively (Song et al. 2010). However, a subsequent study found that the discount narrowed in the next three years as market conditions stabilized, such that in 2011 the relevant prices averaged $1.00, $0.95 and $0.88, respectively (Goh et al. 2015). It is therefore questionable whether the subjectivity of level 3 estimates is such a problem as to warrant abandoning them. Moreover, bearing in mind that most financial instruments that are recognized at fair value are based on level 2 inputs, the discounts would appear not to be out of line with what might be applied by equity investors to many other accounting estimates, such as loan-loss provisions.

So let's turn the question round: should the standard-setters go the whole hog and get rid of the L&R category, too, and require all financial instruments to be shown at fair value? Doing so would have the non-trivial benefit of greatly simplifying the rules governing hedge accounting.

The FASB gave serious consideration to this possibility, issuing a Proposed Accounting Standards Update on May 26, 2010 that would require all financial instruments, including L&R, to be shown on the balance sheet. The proposal stressed that the recognition of income and earnings per share would remain largely unchanged, '... because only changes arising from interest accruals, credit impairments, and realized gains and losses would be recognized in net income each reporting period'. The proposal was greeted warmly by the CFA Institute, who said they had polled their members and found that they supported the change by a two-to-one margin (CFA Institute, comment letter, September 30, 2010). But this was not the general reaction from the banking community. Indeed, Wells Fargo flatly contradicted the CFA Institute's position, writing:

> ... [W]e strongly oppose the expansion of fair value as the primary balance sheet measurement attribute for virtually all financial instruments. .... The feedback we have received from analysts and investors that follow Wells Fargo is consistent with the independent surveys performed by PricewaterhouseCoopers and Barclays, which indicate that the majority of investment professionals do not support fair value as the default model.
>
> *(Wells Fargo, comment letter, August 19, 2010; footnotes omitted)*

The L&R category comprises the great majority of most banks' financial instruments, and if they were required to be shown at fair value, then they would probably mostly have to be at level 3, given the absence of an active market for such assets. There are a variety of ways in which loan-loss provisions could possibly be determined under HCA, each with their advocates, and the FASB and the IASB failed to reach agreement on which was the best method.[12] However, be that as it may, level 3 fair values would presumably have to incorporate the banks' estimates of future loan losses, for there would be no way the expected cash flows could be derived from (nonexistent) market prices. In this case, the main difference between level 3 fair values and historical cost amounts would presumably be that the former would reflect discount rates updated to reflect changes in interest rates and credit spreads. As the FASB envisaged excluding interest rate changes from net income, the primary effect of moving to fair value would be on the amounts shown in the balance sheet. This would have a direct effect on a bank's regulatory Tier 1 and leverage ratios. Moreover, responses received by the FASB reveal that banks, the smaller ones in particular, argued that they foresaw operational problems in trying to fair value assets that they expected to hold for collection of interest and principal (e.g. see Patriot Bank of Georgia, comment letter, September, 16, 2010).

Embedded options

The Black-Scholes-Merton option pricing model shows how, under certain assumptions, the cash flow payoffs of complex financial claims like convertible or redeemable bonds can be expressed as aggregations of those of more primitive claims (Black and Scholes 1973; Merton 1973). This insight (and later refinements) has provided subsequent generations of financial engineers with the tools to develop new kinds of instruments and portfolio strategies capable of yielding any particular of future cash flow desired to manage risk. This in turn led the FASB to consider whether a fruitful way forward would be to decompose financial claims into more primitive components for valuation purposes. While drawing back from a wholesale application of the principle, it was decided to apply it in one particular area. SFAS 133 requires firms, with certain exceptions, to strip out derivatives embedded in a host financial instrument if the derivatives are not obviously related to that instrument and the instrument is not measured at fair value with gains and losses being reported in income. The intent was clear: to close down the possible loophole of allowing for derivatives to be reported at historical cost by 'hiding' it in an unrelated security that is recognized on this basis.

As always, the devil is in the details. Maintaining a dual valuation approach is open to the objection of the accounting failing to represent the underlying economics of the firm's activities. The FASB dealt with this problem in SFAS 155 by allowing firms irrevocably to choose at the time of first recognition of a hybrid instrument that would ordinarily be recognized at historical cost instead to fair value it and include subsequent gains and losses in income, thereby obviating the need to strip out the embedded instruments. The price of allowing firms to exercise this FVO is that it will inevitably result in similar firms accounting differently for similar instruments used in similar ways.

The financial crisis posed a particular challenge for the IASB because its standards were applicable to firms operating in countries exhibiting very different degrees of financial market development. Banks and politicians in Europe lobbied the IASB to relax the FVA rules set out in IAS 39. As a result, the IASB amended the standard to apply the FVO in the reverse direction by allowing them to elect to reclassify retroactively from HFT to AFS or to historical cost and for AFS to historical cost, thereby enabling them to avoid reporting substantial fair value losses and to significantly increase return on assets, return on equity, book value of equity and regulatory capital (Fiechter 2011; Paananen et al. 2012). This can be viewed as the IASB accepting that the liquidity crunch in 2008 was of such a magnitude as to require a response, albeit of a temporary nature. One may approve or lament such a move, but in these special circumstances it was probably inevitable. The extent to which European banks actually chose to avail themselves of this option depended on a variety of factors, including whether they were 'too important to fail' and therefore were less concerned about the damage fair losses might have on their regulatory capital (Fiechter et al. 2017).

Own credit risk gains and losses

It was noted earlier that financial instruments pose special issues not traditionally encountered by accountants – in particular, that some instruments can switch back and forth between being assets and liabilities, and that even those that cannot are generally managed to offset long and short positions. This naturally led to the conclusion that, where possible, the two should be treated symmetrically. Thus, SFAS 159 allows firms to use the FVO for matched financial assets and liabilities so that the gains and losses from both can be included in the income statement without having to comply with the complex hedge accounting rules that would otherwise be required under SFAS 133.[13] However, the extension of FVA to financial liabilities in general poses a difficulty for the standard-setters: doing so can result in liabilities appearing to diminish as the firm's underlying financial condition deteriorates. The results have been argued to be counterintuitive, gains being recognized when bad economic events occur, and as such are misleading and difficult to explain to investors (Lipe 2002; Chasteen & Ransom 2007).

Whether recognition of own credit risk gains and losses helps or hinders investors is an empirical question, the answer to which depends on whether financial statement users can figure out what is going on. The problem is likely to be aggravated by delays in the recognition of losses (gains) on the asset side of the balance sheet that gave rise to the fair value own-credit-risk gains (losses) the firm is reporting on its liabilities. Ideally, the two would be recognized at the same time and matched together in the income statement. But this would require all assets to be recognized at fair value, including assets that are not currently recognized at all (Fontes et al. 2017). However, it is important to understand that it is not a necessary condition that every own credit risk gain (loss) is associated with an economic loss (gain) on the firm's assets: the firm might simply change the composition of its asset portfolio such that it is less or more risky, without incurring any fair value gains and losses. So information on how the firm's risk has changed is of central importance to understanding what is going on.

Clearly, it would be a mistake for an investor to treat a reported own credit risk gain as unalloyed good news. At best, the equity investor can infer that the economic bad news that is driving the reported gain is being shared with other capital suppliers. The IASB's solution is to require such own credit risk gains and losses to be estimated and recognized separately from other fair value gains and losses. This is perhaps the best that can be done in the circumstances.

Other applications of FVA

There is an understandable tendency to see the issue in polar-opposite terms: pure HCA versus pure FVA. That is a mistake. FVA is not new; it didn't just arise with the CCA experiment, disappear and then emerge again with financial instruments. Fair values have always been part and parcel of HCA in practice. Fair values – I am using the term loosely here – play a variety of roles in HCA.

One role is that fair value is used to modify HCA in certain circumstances. The most well-known is the lower-of-cost-or-market rule for inventories and its application in impairment tests for other assets. This is usually rationalized as being due to a desire to be conservative. But there is a deeper reason, one that is at the heart of the logic of HCA, namely, that assets are costs that are to be matched against future benefits. But what if there are good reasons to suppose that the benefits one had hoped for at acquisition will not be realized? The rules that have been devised to write down the historical cost amount of an impaired asset to lower recoverable amount are scattered over many standards and have been developed at different times. But the principle of writing down the carrying value of an impaired asset has always been part of the HCA model, even if often it was applied very unevenly in practice.

Another key application of fair value is that it is needed sometimes actually to determine historical cost, notably in non-cash exchange transactions. The obvious example of this is accounting for business combinations. Fair value is used to determine the cost of the individual assets and the liabilities acquired, and, if the business was acquired by an exchange of shares, to impute the cost of the acquisition itself. The process can be very subjective, but few question this, because the alternative is – what?

A controversial application of this process is in accounting for employee stock options (ESOs). An estimate of the fair value of the ESO at grant date is needed if the historical cost of the benefit given to the employee is to be determined. However, if fair value has been used to determine cost, why not update it through time to the date it can be (or even is) exercised? After all, if an option lapses unexercised, the firm's current shareholders have incurred no cost. So why pretend they have? This makes accounting for ESOs such a conceptually difficult area.[14] Given the debate has also been highly politically charged – at least in the USA – one has to sympathize with the standard-setters.[15] But given the difficulties in getting this far, the prospects of any further change look slim and would probably depend on first changing the definition of a liability to include commitments to issue equity (Peasnell 2013).

One really attractive feature of the approach taken by the standard-setters is that it was decided to require firms to disclose not only the amount of ESO expense but also key parameters needed to assess the reliability of the estimates – in particular, the weighted exercise price of the options, stock-return volatility, risk-free rate and time to maturity of options issued during the year. This is particularly helpful if the user thinks that option expense is relevant but queries whether it has been measured properly. This is an important feature given the controversies as to the choice of an appropriate model – e.g. over whether models (such as Black-Scholes) created to value traded options are appropriate for fair valuing an

ESO, which is really a warrant, not an option, the name notwithstanding (Li & Wong 2005). The idea of backing up fair value measurements with supporting disclosures has been carried through into the accounting for financial instruments. In particular, firms are required to provide for their level 3 measurements a description of the valuation techniques used and quantitative information about significant unobservable inputs employed in those models.

Another area where FVA has been extensively applied is in accounting for defined-benefit retirement plans. The principle applied in the measurement of plan assets is fair value – which is hard to quarrel with, given that they are held expressly as an investment portfolio. Pension liabilities are much more problematic. After all, the concept of transferring the liability to a third party would be meaningless in jurisdictions where a firm is expressly forbidden to transfer pension liabilities to a third party. Moreover, if the definition of the fair value given earlier, namely, the price to be paid to transfer liabilities, were to be used, then it would have to be on the basis of assuming no service-based growth for continuing employees, for what investor would accept a commitment to a liability that the transferee could later increase at will? What we have in practice is an actuarially based calculation that uses PV principles. One can debate whether this is nothing more than the application of accrual accounting principles to be found elsewhere in HCA, mimicking market processes by discounting future cash flows – a relatively long-standing feature of many accrual procedures (Lovejoy et al. 1989). Again, the standard-setters deal with the subjectivity problem by requiring disclosures regarding key inputs.

Some applications of FVA are specific to certain industries. Investment properties have already been mentioned. IAS 41 requires fair value through profit and loss for biological assets and agricultural produce at point of harvest. In the former case, it is difficult to see how one could determine the historical cost of a new-borne animal other than by some kind of fair value approach.

One could go on, but probably enough has been said to make the point that fair values play a clear part in many aspects of accounting measurements in what are essentially HCA accounting systems. However, because they have grown up piecemeal, the approach to defining and determining fair value varies markedly from case to case. IFRS 13 was issued in 2011 to try to improve this state of affairs in two ways: first, by setting out in a single IFRS a definition of fair value and a framework for measuring it, and second, by requiring disclosures about the resultant measurements that would enable users to get better insight into their reliability. IFRS 13 applies when another standard requires or permits fair value measurements, with three exceptions – IFRS 2 share-based payment transactions, IAS 17 leasing transactions and measurements that are similar to but are not fair value. The IASB is to be commended for having started, at the time of writing, a post-implementation review of the effect that IFRS 13 has had upon financial reporting.

While applications of the use of fair value can be found throughout contemporary financial reporting, its incidence should not be exaggerated. A strong case can be (and has been) made against extending the application of fair values to assets that are managed in an operating process that does not envisage their being disposed of piecemeal through sale. In these situations what users seem to want are income measures that can enable them to evaluate the firm's success in creating value through their operations and deployment of these assets, the balance sheet values being treated as of strictly second-order importance for this purpose. If the firm needs to dispose of such assets, it is likely to sell them as complete business units, which will also be priced by potential buyers by reference to their projected operating incomes, because they can get a better price than can be obtained from selling the assets separately.[16] The standard-setters have wisely resisted the temptation to extend FVA into areas where fair values are likely to be hard to come by and of dubious relevance.

Concluding remarks

The main criticism that has always been levied at departures from historical cost that involve introducing fair values into the financial statements is that it involves counter-factual reasoning. In CCA, what would be the economic loss the firm would suffer if it were to be deprived of one of its assets? In FVA, how much might the firm expect to receive if it were to sell an asset? These are relatively easy questions to answer when there are deep and active markets for the assets in question. But where these are absent, it isn't. Subjectivity is thereby introduced into the measurement process, raising questions regarding the reliability of the numbers, especially if management has strong economic incentives to bias the results. However, conventional accrual accounting is not free of such problems either. A prime example of this would be estimates of the costs of dismantling North Sea oilrig platforms or decommissioning nuclear facilities. But accountants do it anyway because failure to make such provisions would result in even greater biases.

FVA provides clear examples of how the provision of supporting information that will help the reader get a handle on the reliability of the recognized amounts can go some way towards addressing the subjectivity problem. Some will object that doing so just burdens readers with more and more details. However, as the great economist Oskar Morgenstern pointed out more than half a century ago in a remarkable book, *The Accuracy of Economic Observations* (Morgenstern 1963), economists lag far behind physical scientists when it comes to alerting the reader to the reliability of their statistics. Morgenstern devotes a full chapter to the issue of the reliability of published accounting data. Accounting standard-setters have made great improvements in this regard, with the disclosures relating to value estimates in stock options and pensions providing prime examples.

Accounting employs a hybrid measurement system, and this is likely to continue in the future. Attempts to set out in the conceptual frameworks a single basis have not been successful. The primary reason is the (probably reasonable) fear that the choice of a single valuation basis, be it fair value or historical cost, would result in having to force hard cases into a box where the alternative might be more useful. Standard-setting is likely to continue in a piecemeal fashion, responding to new issues and challenges that cannot readily be dealt with by existing standards. Sometimes fair value might be the best attribute, other times it will not. It will continue to be a judgment call, and rightly so.

Notes

1 For an excellent account of the debates, going as far back as the late nineteenth century, see Tweedie and Whittington (1984) on the experience in Germany, France and The Netherlands between the world wars; the systems put forward by leading writers; and the attempts by the professional accountancy bodies and standard-setters to reach consensus on how to develop an appropriate standard.
2 The FASB subsequently issued in 1984 SFAS 82 that rescinded the requirement to disclose the effects using CPP.
3 A classic work on the complexities of index number construction is Allen (1975). The difficulties involved can be gauged from the manuals of the government statistical agencies – see, for example, Lukwell (2014).
4 For an analysis of the role of CCA in the regulation of utilities, see Whittington (1994). Johnstone (2003) examines and evaluates the complex economic issues involved in setting access tariffs paid to utilities to use their gas pipelines on the basis of the assets' depreciated RCs.
5 For those who doubt this, I suggest a quick glance through the pages of a modern financial engineering text, such as Hull (2012), should soon change their mind.

6 An important change to this banking book model that took place following deregulation in the latter part of the twentieth century was the increasing use banks made of securitization of loans and credit card receivables to finance their operations and manage their risks. Such transactions involved the transfer of these bank assets to so-called 'qualified' special purpose entities that were not required to be consolidated in the USA before the 2008 financial crisis. For further discussion, see Landsman and Peasnell (2013). The evidence suggests that investors regarded such transfers as secured financing rather than sales (Landsman et al. 2011).

7 For a recent general treatment of this issue, see Penman (2011).

8 For a theoretical analysis of how this might happen, see Plantin et al. (2008). Interestingly, over 60 years ago, Baxter (1955) argued that accounting could also exacerbate the trade cycle – though Baxter deemed HCA to be the culprit on this occasion.

9 One specific concern was that financial institutions were using ABX CDS indices to value subprime mortgage assets and these overstated default rates during the crisis. See Fender and Scheider (2009).

10 Financial economists have known for more than fifty years that the standard normal distribution is not a reasonable approximation of the behaviour of financial asset prices, which generally exhibit fatter tails, making extreme events much more likely in practice (Fama 1965). This is probably driven by the trading process itself (Roll 1984). Whether senior bank managers understood this is a different matter.

11 For further discussion, see Power (2010).

12 For further discussion of the issues surrounding loan-loan loss provisioning, see Hashim et al. (2016).

13 For evidence on how the adoption of SFAS 159 affected debt contracting, see Demerjian et al. (2016).

14 For theory and evidence on the relevance to equity pricing of the different ways of accounting for ESOs, see Landsman et al. (2006) and Barth et al. (2013). Landsman et al. (2011) empirically examine the problem posed by dilutive securities (of which ESOs are the most important example) in general for equity pricing.

15 As an example of the pressure the FASB faced, Steve Zeff has drawn my attention to the bill that was introduced by Senator Mike Enzi in November 2003. His proposed Stock Option Accounting Reform Act contained the following requirement: 'To the extent that an option pricing model, such as the Black-Scholes method or a binomial model, is used to determine the fair value of the option, the assumed volatility of the underlying stock shall be zero' (Paragraph 3A). Any option that has an exercise price equal to the stock price at date of issue – i.e. the usual case – would therefore have a zero fair value. Problem solved!

16 When the situation is reversed and the firm is acquiring a new business, the problem cannot be ducked, but the price paid for the business at least sets a constraint on what the total might be.

References

Allen, RDG 1975, *Index numbers in theory and practice*, Macmillan Press, Basingstoke.

American Bankers Association 2008, "Letter to SEC", September 23.

Barth, ME, Hodder, LD & Stubben, SR 2013, "Financial reporting for employee stock options: liabilities or equity", *Accounting Review of Accounting Studies*, vol. 18, pp. 642–682.

Badertscher, B, Burks, J & Easton P 2012, "A convenient scapegoat: fair value accounting by commercial banks during the financial crisis", *The Accounting Review*, vol. 87, no. 1, pp. 59–90.

Baxter, WT 1955, "The accountant's contribution to the trade cycle", *Economica*, New Series, vol. 2 no. 86, pp. 99–112.

Baxter, WT 1975, *Accounting values and inflation accounting*, McGraw-Hill, New York.

Baxter, WT 2003, *The case for deprival value*, Institute of Chartered Accountants of Scotland, Edinburgh.

Benston, GJ 2006, "Fair-value accounting: a cautionary tale from Enron", *Journal of Accounting and Public Policy*, vol. 25, pp. 465–484.

Black, F & Scholes, M 1973, "The pricing of options and corporate liabilities", *Journal of Political Economy*, vol. 81, pp. 637–659.

Bonbright, JC 1937, *The valuation of property*, McGraw Hill, New York.

Chambers, RJ 1966, *Accounting, evaluation and economic behavior*, Prentice-Hall, Englewood cliffs, NJ.

Chambers, RJ 1970, "Second thoughts on continuously contemporary accounting", *Abacus*, vol. 6, no. 1, pp. 39–55.

Chasteen, LG & Ransom, CR 2007, "Including credit standing in measuring the fair value of liabilities – let's pass this one to shareholders", *Accounting Horizons*, vol. 21, pp. 119–135.

Demerjian, PR, Donovan, J & Larson, CR 2016, "Fair value accounting and debt contracting: evidence from adoption of SFAS 159", *Journal of Accounting Research*, vol. 54, no. 4, pp. 1041–1076.

Dye, RA, Glover, JC & Sunder, S 2015, "Financial engineering and the arms race between accounting standard setter and preparers", *Accounting Horizons*, vol. 29, pp. 265–295.

Easley D and O'Hara M 2010, "Liquidity and valuation in an uncertain world", *Journal of Financial Economics*, vol. 97, pp. 1–11.

Edwards, EO & Bell, PW 1961, *The theory and measurement of business income*, University of California Press, Berkeley and Los Angles.

Fama, EF 1965, "The behavior of stock market prices", *Journal of Business*, vol. 38, pp. 34–105.

Fender, I & Scheider, M 2009, "The pricing of subprime mortgage risk in good times and bad: evidence from the ABX.HE indices", European Central Bank, May.

Fiechter, P 2011, "Reclassification of financial assets under IAS 39: impact on European banks' financial statements", *Accounting in Europe*, vol. 8, pp. 49–67.

Fiechter, P, Landsman, WR, Peasnell, K & Renders, A 2017, "The IFRS option to reclassify financial assets out of fair value in 2008: the roles played by regulatory capital and too-important-to-fail status", *Review of Accounting Studies*, vol. 22, no. 4, pp. 1698–1731.

Fontes, JC, Panaretou, A & Peasnell, K 2017, "The impact of fair value accounting for bank assets on information asymmetry and the moderating effect of own credit risk gains and losses", Working paper Lancaster University and Catolica University Lisbon.

Fontes, JC, Panaretou, A & Peasnell, KV 2018, The impact of fair value measurement for bank assets on information asymmetry and the moderating effect of own credit risk gains and losses. *The Accounting Review*.

Goh, BW, Li, D, Ng, J & Yong, KO 2015, "Market pricing of banks' fair value assets reported under SFAS 157 since the 2008 financial crisis", *Journal of Accounting and Public Policy*, vol. 34, pp. 129–145.

Gupta, NJ, Kurt, M & White, R 2016, "The Buffett critique: volatility and long-dated options", *Journal of Economics and Finance*, vol. 40, pp. 524–537.

Gorton, G 2014, "The development of opacity in U.S. banking", *Yale Journal on Regulation*, vol. 31, pp. 825–851.

Hashim, NAA, O'Hanlon, JF & Li, W 2016, "Expected-loss-based accounting for impairment of financial instruments: the FASB and IASB proposals 2009–2016", *Accounting in Europe*, vol. 13, no. 2, pp. 229–267.

Hull, JC 2012, *Risk management and financial institutions*, Wiley, Hoboken, NJ.

Ijiri, Y 1975, *Theory of accounting measurement*, American Accounting Association, Sarasota, FL.

Johnstone, D 2003, "Replacement cost asset valuation and regulation of energy infrastructure tariffs", *Abacus*, vol. 30, no. 1, pp. 1–41.

King, AM 2007, "What SFAS 157 does, and does not, accomplish", in *The Routledge companion to fair value and financial reporting*, ed P Walton, Routledge, London and New York.

Landsman, WR, Miller, BL, Peasnell, K & Yeh, S 2011, "Do investors understand really dirty surplus?", *The Accounting Review*, vol. 86, pp. 237–258.

Landsman, WR, Peasnell, K, Pope, PF & Yeh, S 2006, "Which approach to accounting for employee stock options best reflects market pricing?", *Review of Accounting Studies*, vol. 11, pp. 203–245.

Landsman, WR, Peasnell, K & Shakespeare, C 2008, "Are asset securitizations sales or loans?", *The Accounting Review*, vol. 83, pp. 1251–1272.

Landsman, WR & Peasnell, K 2013, "The changing landscape of banking and the challenges it poses for accounting and financial reporting", *Accounting Horizons*, vol. 27, pp. 757–773.

Laux, C & Leuz, C 2010, "Did fair-value accounting contribute to the financial crisis?", *Journal of Economic Perspectives*, vol. 24, pp. 93–118.

Li, F & Wong, MHF 2005, "Employee stock options, equity valuation, and the valuation of option grants using a warrant-pricing model", *Journal of Accounting Research*, vol. 43, pp. 97–131.

Lipe, RC 2002, "Fair valuing debt turns deteriorating credit quality into positive signals for Boston chicken", *Accounting Horizons*, vol. 16, pp. 169–181.

Lovejoy, C, Peasnell, K, Taylor, P & Talukdar, Y 1989, *Discounting in corporate financial reporting*, Institute of Chartered Accountants in England and Wales, London.

Lukwell, R 2014, *Producer price indices: methods and guidance*, Office for National Statistics, Kew.

Merton, R 1973, "The theory of rational option pricing", *Bell Journal of Economics and Management Science*, vol. 4, pp. 141–183.

Morgenstern, O 1963, *On the accuracy of economic observations*, Princeton University Press, Princeton, NJ.

New York Times 2007, "Goldman and investors to put $3 billion into fund", 14 August.

O'Connor, L 2010, "No tricks: the fabled 25 sigma event", blog 18 March 2010, Available from lukenotricks.blogspot.com/2010/03/fabled-25-sigma-event.html, access July 5, 2017.

Paananen, M, Renders, A & Shima, K 2012, "The amendment of IAS 39: determinants of reclassification behavior and capital market consequences", *Journal of Accounting, Auditing and Finance*, vol. 27, pp. 208–235.

Paton, WA & Littleton, AC 1940, *An introduction to corporate accounting standards*, American Accounting Association, Evanston, IL.

Peasnell, K 2013, "Discussion of 'financial reporting for employee stock options: liabilities or equity'?", *Accounting Review of Accounting Studies*, vol. 18, pp. 683–691.

Penman, S 2011, *Accounting for value*, Columbia University Press, New York.

Plantin, G, Sapra, H & Shin, HS 2008, "Marking-to-market: Panacea or Pandora's box?", *Journal of Accounting Research*, vol. 46, pp. 435–459.

Power, M 2010, "Fair value accounting, financial economics and the transformation of reliability", *Accounting and Business Research*, vol. 40, pp. 197–210.

Roll, R 1984, "Orange juice and the weather", *American Economic Review*, vol. 74, pp. 8601–8880.

Ryan, SG 2007, *Financial instruments and institutions: accounting and disclosure rules*, 2nd edn, Wiley, Hoboken, NJ.

Securities and Exchange Commission 2008, *Report and recommendations pursuant to Section 133 of the emergency economic stabilization act of 2008*, SEC, Washington DC.

Song, CJ, Thomas WB & Yi H 2010, "Value relevance of FAS No. 157 fair value hierarchy information and the impact of corporate governance mechanisms", *The Accounting Review*, vol. 85, pp. 1375–1410.

Tweedie, D & Whittington, G 1984, *The debate on inflation accounting*, Cambridge University Press, Cambridge.

Walker, RG 2006, *Consolidated statements: a history and analysis*, University of Sydney Press, Sydney.

Watts, RL & Zimmerman JL 1986, *Positive accounting theory*, Prentice Hall, Englewood Cliffs, NJ.

Whittington, G 1994, "Current cost accounting: its role in regulated utilities", *Fiscal Studies*, vol. 15, pp. 88–101.

Wright, FK 1965, "Depreciation and obsolescence in current value accounting", *Journal of Accounting Research*, vol. 3, pp. 167–181.

5

SHAREHOLDER VALUE, FINANCIALIZATION AND ACCOUNTING REGULATION

Making sense of fair value adoption in the European Union

Vera Palea

Introduction

This chapter discusses the causes and effects of adopting fair value accounting in the European Union by using a broader perspective that considers accounting within its wider socioeconomic context.

Many institutions and scholars argue that fair value accounting has significantly contributed to the financial market crisis that started in 2008 in the United States, exacerbating its severity for financial institutions all around the world (e.g. Allen & Carletti 2008; Banque de France 2008; Plantin et al. 2008). In Europe, the crisis has led to a major destruction of economic activities, dramatic job losses and a rise in inequality and poverty. Unemployment, especially among young people, has reached unprecedented levels, and welfare states have been constrained by low growth and stretched public finances (Draghi 2016).

Financial reporting is not a neutral, mechanical and objective process that simply measures the economic facts pertaining to a firm. It is rather a powerful practice that is embedded in an institutional context and shapes social and economic processes (Arnold 2009; Sikka 2015). It affects a great variety of stakeholders: not only firms, investors, bankers and auditors, but also ordinary citizens, employees and states, since financial information serves as a basis for determining a number of rights. It serves to set the limit for distributable profits, to elaborate public budget that social welfare is based on and to calculate taxes. To consider accounting standards independently of their social context, as accounting scholars sometimes do, is therefore inadequate.

Weber (1947) already pointed out that, to be useful, economic research must be significantly related to the legal, institutional and socioeconomic context. Along these lines, Galbraith (1987) noted that the economy should not have a purposeful life separated from politics. For the same reason, Bryan et al. (2012) suggest a more explicit political approach to understanding economics. Consistent with this view, this chapter adopts an alternative approach that looks at accounting within the broader institutional environment in which it operates. In doing so, it relies on an interdisciplinary approach that considers accounting policies within macro politics and economics. Specifically, this chapter focuses on the European Union (also EU hereafter) and sets the discussion on fair value accounting within the EU's constitutional setting. The constitutional setting of the EU is provided by the Lisbon Treaty (also 'Treaty' hereafter), which clearly defines the fundamental goals of the Union and the means whereby they can be achieved. The Treaty represents the political construct of the Union, setting the founding principles on which the EU has decided to build and shape its future. It therefore provides social science researchers with an important grid by which to examine economic policies in the EU, including International Financial Reporting Standards (IFRS) adoption.

Importantly, financial reporting regulation is one of the competences of the European Union, and, in fact, IFRS were mandated in the EU with European Regulation 1606/2002. According to legal hierarchy, the Lisbon Treaty comes first, and European regulations and directives have to comply with it (art. 2 TFUE). As a result, the Treaty's objectives have priority over regulation and directives' goals. Accordingly, IFRS in general and, more specifically, fair value adoption in the EU must be considered within the framework of the Lisbon Treaty.

The Treaty sets social market economy as one of the fundamental objectives of the European Union. Social market economy refers to an economic model that is quite different from free stock market-based capitalism.[1] A social market economy seeks to combine market freedom with equitable social development. Social welfare dominates, thereby public authorities can act and intervene whenever the market provides negative outcomes for society. There is general agreement that the Lisbon Treaty looked to the Rhenish variety of capitalism typical of Germany in setting the social market economy as a guiding principle for the European Union (Glossner 2014).

By adopting and extending fair value accounting as much as possible, IFRS instead institutionalize and spread the shareholder value maximization paradigm, typical of neoliberal economies, in the form of financial reporting practices (e.g. Jürgens et al. 2000; Nölke & Perry 2007), reinforcing the financialization process that led to the crisis.

Several warning signs indicate that the adoption of IFRS, which are shaped on the needs of stock market-based economies, has the potential of severely harming social market economies. From a balance sheet perspective, fair value accounting is likely to affect both the firms' real investments and capital provisions – that is, the assets and liabilities sides of financial reports. From the assets side, fair value accounting tends to push managers toward short-term strategies, with negative effects on capital allocation and economic growth. From the liabilities side, fair value accounting increases pro-cyclicality and, conceivably, contagion effects in the financial system, making it more prone to crisis, with adverse effects on stable firms' financing and growth. The lower the economic growth and the more fragile the economic system are, the more realizing an equitable social development becomes difficult.

The worldwide recession caused by the financial market crisis and excessive credit expansion has shown the fragility of stock market-based capitalism as an economic and political process, highlighting the need for alternative ways of doing business (European Commission 2015). By setting social market economy as a founding principle of the European Union, the Lisbon Treaty shows that there is more than one way of doing business. Nonetheless, unlike any other regulation, accounting regulation is almost uniform throughout all free market economies, and constantly expanding. While cultures, economic institutions and development history exert strong effects on national laws, financial reporting regulation defies diversity. Unlike other fields, there is no competition in financial reporting. Even the small differences between US GAAP and IFRS are in the process of disappearing due to the pressure to converge these systems. There is no other law or regulation that is similarly uniform throughout the world, with potentially disruptive effects on varieties of capitalism. This makes it sensible to open up a discussion that puts accounting regulation and rule-making under critical examination.

Along these lines, this chapter argues that researchers should definitely take into consideration the sociocultural features of the context under investigation. So far, mainstream research has analyzed the economic consequences of financial accounting by focusing foremost on the interests of shareholders, with no consideration of the socioeconomic characteristics of the society where financial reporting applies (e.g. Palea 2017). This chapter, instead, prefers a view of research aimed at social welfare, rather than focused on the needs of investors, and strongly embedded in its specific context. Accordingly, one important task for researchers would be to test economic events, policies and business models against the fundamental objectives of European society. This could enrich research, providing a wider set of intellectual tools for scholars, public discussion and, hopefully, social progress. It is at times of great uncertainty and changes, such as those in which we are living, that the advantages of new research modes could be appreciated. The chapter is structured as follows. The first section, 'The Political Economy of Fair Value Accounting', discusses the financialization process and the view of business underlying the ascent of fair value measurements, while the following section, 'Social Market Economy as a Founding Principle of the European Union', introduces the Lisbon Treaty as a framework for discussing IFRS and fair value adoption in the European Union. The section entitled 'Critical Issues in Adopting Fair Value Accounting in the European Union' highlights critical issues regarding fair value adoption in the EU that arise by examining IFRS using the grid of the Lisbon Treaty. The next section, 'Does Fair Value Accounting Fit for All Varieties of Capitalism?', discusses the suitability of fair value accounting for all varieties of capitalism, and the final section, 'Concluding Remarks', provides some concluding remarks. As a side note, the chapter also raises some fundamental questions about the potential for academics to conduct more socially engaged research, which deals with the EU's specific challenges, thus contributing effectively to the social and economic advancement of society.

The political economy of fair value accounting

In the last 40 years, worldwide economies have undergone profound transformations. The role of government has diminished, while that of the markets has increased. Economic transactions between countries have risen substantially, and domestic and international financial transactions have expanded at an exponential rate. In short, neoliberalism, globalization and financialization have been the key features of this changing landscape (Epstein 2005).

Specifically, the term financialization refers to an increasing importance of financial motives, financial markets, financial actors and financial institutions in the operation of economies (Epstein 2005). It has widely been used to designate such broad, interconnected but distinct phenomena as the globalization of financial markets, the rise of financial investment and incomes, the growing importance of the 'shareholder value maximization principle' in economic decisions and the changing structure of corporate governance, which have led to an economic, social and environmental embedding of finance in the system as a whole (e.g. Jürgens et al. 2000; Lazonick & O'Sullivan 2000; Duménil & Lévy 2004; Stockhammer 2004). The financialization process has been more apparent in Anglo-Saxon economies, where the United States and UK are the most representative cases (Brown et al. 2015), but equally other types of capitalism have been subject to the same process. The financialization process has also affected EU countries, although in a variety of historically and geographically related forms (e.g. Duménil & Lévy 2004; Alvarez 2015; Brown et al. 2015; Hein et al. 2016).

Specifically, a tight link exists between the ascent of the shareholder value maximization principle and the adoption of specific business practices including the publication of quarterly reports and the adoption of international accounting standards (e.g. Jürgens et al. 2000). A statement made by Piteco company (2015), which went public in 2015, is anecdotal in this respect: 'Shifting to the International Accounting Standards takes place a year earlier [...] if the Company should decide to share the net income of 2015 performance, adoption of IAS/IFRS will guarantee a distribution of a greater dividend' (Piteco 2015). Given the same fundamentals, IFRS adoption allows higher pay-out.

MacKenzie (2008) highlights the fundamental role played by economic theory in this process. Modigliani and Miller (1958), for instance, looked at the corporation from the 'outside', i.e. from the perspective of the investors and financial markets, and considered corporate's market maximization as the main priority of management. Accordingly, shareholder value maximization became a central feature of the corporate governance ideology, which spread across the whole private-sector (e.g. Lazonick & O'Sullivan 2000). Agency theory (Jensen & Meckling 1976) also provided an academic source of legitimacy for a greatly increased proportion of corporate executives' rewards in the form of stocks and stock options, with the specific purpose of aligning the shareholders' interest in maximizing returns and managers' objectives (Fligstein 1990).

There is no reason to think that financial economists saw themselves as acting politically in emphasizing shareholder value. Nonetheless, Van der Zwan (2014) notes that, for scholars in this body of work, shareholder value was not a neutral concept but an ideological construct that legitimized a far-reaching redistribution of wealth and power among shareholders, managers and workers. Financial economic theories became the cultural frame for economic actors and intrinsic parts of the economic. Paraphrasing Milton Friedman, economic models were an engine of inquiry, rather than a camera to reproduce empirical facts (MacKenzie 2008).

Likewise, accounting rule-making is deeply ideological (e.g. Cooper 2015; Ramanna 2015; Palea 2017). Different measurement systems correspond to different views of business in society as well as different notions of capital (Zhang & Andrew 2014; Cooper 2015). This, in turn, implies different levels of priority given to societal stakeholders.

The IASB includes existing and potential investors, creditors and lenders as primary users of financial reporting. The degree of the IASB's emphasis on securities markets, however, suggests a higher emphasis on structuring financial information according to the needs of equity investors (Palea 2015; Ramanna 2015). While other parties, such as regulators and members of the public other than investors, may find financial statements useful, these reports are not primarily considered for these other groups (IASB 2010 OB 10).

Critical research has highlighted how the IASB's focus on equity investors represents the institutionalization of the shareholder value maximization paradigm in the form of accounting standards (Lazonick & O'Sullivan 2000; MacKenzie 2008; Palea 2015). Indeed, the IASB's focus on investors reveals an elective affinity with the proprietary theory of the firm, according to which the firm is an exclusive vehicle for its proprietors to increase their wealth. Consistently, the IASB has over time increased the use of fair value, which is alleged to be essential for tailoring financial reporting to the information needs of investors (De Jager 2014; Zhang & Andrew 2014). Fair value accounting traces changes in the market value of assets (traded or estimated) and how they impact income and shareholder equity. Accounting is therefore done from the common shareholders' perspective, which is a balance sheet perspective, and firm performance, i.e. net income, is defined in terms of changes in the values of assets and liabilities (IASB 2010, 4.47). The prime objective of financial reporting is determining the owner's net worth (e.g. Van Mourik 2014).

If, on the one hand, the shareholder orientation has led standard-setters to increase fair value measurements, on the other hand, fair value accounting itself has acted as one vehicle through which short-termism takes the form of accounting practices (e.g. Nölke & Perry 2007; Cooper 2015; Palea 2015). The fair value definition provided by IFRS 13, *Fair Value Measurement*, is anecdotal in this respect. IFRS 13 defines fair value as an exit price – that is, a spot market price. IFRS 13 is the result of a joint project conducted by the IASB and the FASB, which, however, resulted in a passive alignment of the fair value definition, measurement and disclosure requirements to FAS 157. The market orientation in fair value definition is really pervasive: even at level 3 where 'data are unobservable', preparers of financial statements must simulate the existence of markets. As noted by Haslam et al. (2015), the definition of fair value as an exit price captures the 'modus operandi' of active capital markets, which tends to promote the vendibility of assets over the serviceability of these assets. Productivist culture, which focuses on technical efficiency and physical performance indicators, tend to be abandoned in favor of a monetary perspective of capital typical of financial markets (Müller 2014).

Social market economy as a founding principle of the European Union

As mentioned above, this chapter adopts a broader perspective that considers accounting within its socioeconomic context, and within the framework of the Lisbon Treaty on which the EU has decided to build and shape its future. According to the Treaty, social market economy is one of the fundamental objectives of the European Union. Art. 3 of the Treaty states that the European Union '*shall work for the sustainable development of Europe based on balanced economic growth and price stability, a highly competitive social market economy, aiming at full employment and social progress*'. Moreover, '*it shall combat social exclusion and discrimination, and shall promote social justice and protection*'.

As is clear, a social market economy represents a core value of the European Union. Social market economy refers to an economic model that is quite different from free stock market-based capitalism. The Lisbon Treaty, which came into effect in 2009, was the outcome of a long and lively democratic debate on the future of the Union that started in 2001 at the Laeken European Council and focused on what kind of economic and social model the European Union would pursue. The Lisbon Treaty goes beyond the Maastricht architecture of a simple economic and monetary union, establishing the basis for a new economic, political and social governance. For instance, it enshrined a Charter of Fundamental Rights into the European Union's constitutional order for the first time, thus establishing not only economic, but also political and social rights for citizens and residents of the European Union.

There is general agreement that the Lisbon Treaty looked to the Rhenish variety of capitalism in setting the social market economy as a guiding principle for the European Union (Glossner 2014). According to the literature, the Rhenish variety of capitalism refers to coordinated market economics (Hall & Soskice 2001), whereas the Anglo-Saxon variety refers to liberal market economics. These two models have been developed on the basis of the United States and Western Europe, while further models are of course necessary for other economies.

The defining characteristics of the Rhenish model typical of Germany and the Scandinavian Countries are the consensual – for the most part – relationship between labor and capital, the supporting role of the state, and the availability of patient capital provided by the bank system or internally generated funds. These characteristics have been key in developing a long-term perspective on economic decision-making, high skilled labor and quality products based on incremental innovation, each at the basis of post Second World War Germany's economic success (Hall & Soskice 2001; Perry & Nölke 2006). On the contrary, the Anglo-Saxon variety of capitalism is characterized by comparatively short-term employment, the predominance of financial markets for capital provision, an active market for corporate control, and more adversarial management-labor relations. Given these characteristics, the Anglo-Saxon business model is also called stock market-based capitalism.

As a matter of fact, the term 'social market economy' originates from the post-World War II period, when the shape of the 'New' Germany was being discussed. Social market economy theory was developed by the Freiburg School of economic thought, which was founded in the 1930s at the University of Freiburg, and received major contributions from scholars such as Eucken (1951), Röpke (1944) and Rüstow (1932). A social market economy seeks to combine market freedom with equitable social development. Social market economics shares with classical market liberalism the firm conviction that markets represent the best way to allocate scarce resources efficiently, while it shares with socialism the concern that markets do not necessarily create equal societies. As highlighted by Glossner (2014), social market economy is not intended as a dogmatic concept, but as a pragmatic one implying that conscious and measured state intervention is contingent on economic and social circumstances.

According to social market economics, a free market and private property are the most efficient means of economic coordination and of assuring a high dose of political freedom. However, as a free market does not always work properly, it should be monitored by public authorities who should act and intervene whenever the market provides negative outcomes for society. The social dimension is essential not only for society as a whole, but also for the market to work well. In fact, market efficiency and social justice do not represent a contradiction in terms, as is proven by Germany's post-World War II economic miracle.

In a social market economy, public authorities must set out the rules and the framework, acting as the referees that enforce the rules. A strong public authority does not assume a lot of tasks, but a power that keeps it independent from lobbies, for the sake of general interest (Glossner 2014). Consistently with this view, the Lisbon Treaty contains a 'social clause' requiring the European Union, in conducting its policy, to observe the principle of equality of its citizens, who shall receive equal attention from its institutions, bodies, offices and agencies. In order to promote good governance and ensure the participation of civil society, decisions shall be taken as openly and as closely as possible to citizens (art. 15 TFEU[2]). This should prevent the European institutions from being influenced by special interest groups. The Treaty also highlights the importance of social dialogue, which is one important pillar of social market economy (art. 152 TFEU). Social dialogue has indeed proved to be a valuable asset in the recent crisis: it is no mere coincidence that the best performing member states in terms of economic growth and job creation, such as Germany and Sweden, enjoy strong and institutionalized social dialogue between businesses and trade unions (Andor 2011).

Since the Lisbon Treaty represents the legal framework within which the European Union must act, financial reporting issues must be considered in this context. Along these lines, the potential effects of fair value accounting on society should be discussed in terms of its capability to match with the objectives of the Treaty. One important question therefore is whether an extensive use of fair value accounting is likely to hamper a social market economy.

Of course, this chapter does not provide definitive answers for such a complex question, yet it conducts a ground-clearing exercise designed to set the framework within which financial reporting regulation should be discussed in the European Union. It also encourages accounting scholars to focus on more contextualized research agenda, suggesting the need to test economic policies against the fundamental objectives of the European Union.

The European Regulation 1606/2002 mandating IFRS was issued in 2002 and became effective in 2005, before the Lisbon Treaty was signed. Now that it is in force, the Treaty provides us with the objectives of the European Union and its ideal economic and social model. It is therefore time we reconsidered the IFRS Regulation with regard to its consistency with the founding principles of the European Union.

Critical issues in adopting fair value accounting in the European Union

A thorough review of different research streams provides several warning signs with regard to the potential effects of fair value accounting on a social market economy, which is one of the founding principles of the European Union.

As mentioned above, the Conceptual Framework (2010) highlights that IFRS are developed and shaped on the needs of stock market-based capitalism. By adopting and extending fair value accounting as much as possible, IFRS indeed institutionalize and spread the shareholder value paradigm in the form of financial reporting practices (e.g. Jürgens et al. 2000; Nölke & Perry 2007), thus reinforcing the financialization process.

From a balance sheet perspective, fair value accounting is likely to affect both real investments and capital provisions of non-financial corporations, which represent the backbone of the EU's economy. From the asset side, fair value accounting is likely to push managers toward short-term strategies, with negative effects on capital allocation and thereby economic growth. From the liabilities side, fair value accounting increases pro-cyclicality and, conceivably, contagion effects in the financial system, making it more prone to crisis, with adverse effects on stable firms' financing and growth. As is clear, the lower the economic growth and the more fragile the economic system are, the more realizing an equitable social development becomes difficult.

Barlev and Haddad (2003) highlight how the definition of fair value as a spot market price provided by IFRS 13 reduces the enterprise's voice in favor of that of the market, making reporting of assets, liabilities and income independent of the manager's influence. When analyzing financial statements under IFRS, readers are now exposed to the 'market's voice'. Managers themselves are put under pressure to consider the firm as a portfolio of assets that must constantly be reconfigured and rationalized in order to maximize shareholder value and to demand that every corporate asset is put to its most profitable use as judged by market benchmarks. Since capital markets tend to take a more short-term perspective on profit, shareholder value orientation is likely to discourage long-term industrial strategies and to threaten economic growth (e.g. Lazonick & O'Sullivan 2000; Nölke & Perry 2007). Short-termism implicit in fair value measurement comes into conflict with the temporality of productive activity and its necessarily higher tolerance for uncertainty, which is quite a big issue for long-term investments in real economy, requiring time to yield results (e.g. Aglietta & Rebérioux 2005).

Empirical literature provides unequivocal evidence of the negative effects of shareholder value orientation on capital allocation (Duménil & Lévy 2004; Orhangazi 2008; Onaran et al. 2011; Alvarez 2015; Brown et al. 2015). Stockhammer (2004), among others, shows that an excessive focus on shareholder value reduces the rate of capital accumulation in the long term and undermines economic growth. Under the pressure of shareholder value, firms tend not to reinvest gains in their productive assets, but to distribute them to shareholders through dividend payouts and share buy-back (Lazonick & O'Sullivan 2000). Onaran et al. (2011) find a negative correlation between dividend and interest payments and real investment at a macro-level for US economy, while Orhangazi (2008) finds similar results at a firm-level. These results are also consistent with Duménil and Lévy (2004), Alvarez (2015) and Brown et al. (2015) for the EU setting.

Evidence also suggests that under the pressure of shareholders' focus on short-range returns, non-financial corporations' managers tend to increase financial investments at the expense of real investments, especially in times of upward market trends (e.g. Andersson et al. 2008). Alvarez (2015), among others, reports an increasing dependence on earnings through financial channels for French non-financial firms. These results are also consistent with Brown et al. (2015) for EU countries. Furthermore, most of these investments are financed with debt, which further increases corporate leverage and risk. Fair value measurement, by accruing holding gains for assets when markets inflate, is likely to reinforce this trend, with detrimental effects on long-term investments and capital accumulation (e.g. Nölke & Perry 2007; Palea 2015).

Furthermore, long-term investments in the European Union largely rely on bank financing. The financial system in Continental Europe has always been highly bank-oriented (Bank of Italy 2013),[3] mainly because the backbone of these economies is composed of small- and medium-sized manufacturing firms, which encounter greater difficulties in accessing bond markets than big corporates.

The European Central Bank (2004), the Banque de France (2008) and the International Monetary Fund (2009), among others, have raised several concerns on the pro-cyclical effects caused by fair value accounting on the banking system and thereby on firms' financing. There is general agreement that during the financial turmoil that started in 2007 fair value accounting caused a downward spiral in financial markets, which made the crisis more severe, amplifying the credit-crunch (e.g. Allen & Carletti 2008; Plantin et al. 2008). Allen and Carletti (2008) show that, when mark-to-market accounting applies, the balance sheets of financial institutions are driven by short-term market fluctuations that do not reflect their fundamentals. During financial crises, asset prices reflect the amount of liquidity available rather than the asset's future cash flows. Asset fair values may, consequently, fall below liabilities so that banks become insolvent, despite their capability to cover their commitments fully if allowed to continue until the assets mature. Likewise, Plantin et al. (2008) show that mark-to-market accounting injects an artificial volatility into financial statements, which, rather than reflecting underlying fundamentals, is purely a consequence of the accounting norms and distorts real decisions. Their analysis also suggests that the damage done by mark-to-market accounting is particularly severe for assets that are long-lived, illiquid and senior, which are exactly the attributes of the key balance sheet items of banks and insurance companies.

Likewise, Biondi and Giannoccolo (2015) show that fair value accounting leads to higher volatility and more instable financial systems than historical cost accounting. Stockhammer (2012) indeed reports that excessive volatility in asset prices heightens systemic risk and makes the economy prone to recurring crises.

Freixas and Tsomocos (2004) show that fair value accounting worsens the role of banks as institutions that smooth inter-temporal shocks. The weakening of bank balance sheets also heightens concerns over the future courses of some markets, the health of banks and, more broadly, the financial system, which results in several runs on banks (e.g. Allen et al. 2009).

Given the key role of banks in the economy, financial distress in the banking system exerts disruptive effects on real economy and employment. In this respect, Dell'Ariccia et al. (2008) report a correlation between bank distress and a decline in credit and GDP. Due to the financial system crisis in 2007–2009, economic activity declined significantly in the European Union and unemployment rose dramatically. All in all, the recent crisis has been the worst since the Great Depression (Allen et al. 2009).

Schwarz et al. (2015) points out that unequivocal evidence of fair value accounting's involvement in the financial crisis is provided by the decision taken by both the IASB and FASB to allow banks to reclassify, from the third quarter of 2008, certain non-derivative financial assets, which were measured at fair value, to amortized costs under certain circumstances. Fiechter (2011) reports that around one third of a sample of 219 European banks took up the reclassification option, which avoided substantial fair value losses. Similarly, Jarolim and Öppinger (2012) report that the reclassification option was used quite extensively by European banks and avoided recognition of losses of almost 900 million euros, on average, per bank. Many more banks could have run into substantial problems if accounting rules had not been amended at the peak of the crisis. Since the banking system does not just allocate, but also generates purchasing power, this is a sensitive issue that 'ties back to accounting as money' (De Jager 2014, p. 99).

Finally, some research shows that an excessive focus on investors' interest also leads to more conflictual relationships between enterprise managers, employees and other stakeholders. The IASB emphasizes the role of financial reporting in serving investors in capital markets, but investors in capital markets are not the only stakeholders of a firm. In many countries in Europe where a social market economy applies, shareholder wealth maximization has never been the only – or even the primary – goal of the board of directors. In the Rhenish variety of capitalism, companies have indeed been able to develop thanks to consensual corporate governance arrangements. In Germany, for instance, firms are legally required to pursue the interests of parties beyond the shareholders through a system of co-determination in which employees and shareholders in large corporations sit together on the supervisory board of the company. Austria, Denmark, Sweden, France and Luxembourg also have systems of governance that require some kind of co-determination. While the specific systems of governance in these countries vary widely, the inclusion of parties beyond shareholders is a common concern. As a result, workers play a prominent role and are regarded as important stakeholders in firms. For this reason, it is common to refer to the Rhenish variety of capitalism also as 'stakeholder capitalism'.

Recent research has however highlighted that industrial relations have significantly worsened due to shareholder value policies and short termism (Van der Zwan 2014). Evidence also documents that the shareholder value principle tends to make shareholders and managers rich to the detriment of workers (Lazonick & O'Sullivan 2000; Fligstein & Shin 2004). Taken as a whole, recent research shows a dramatic picture in which the pursuit of shareholder value is directly linked to a decline in working conditions and a rise in social inequality for large segments of the population (Van der Zwan 2014).

Does fair value accounting fit for all varieties of capitalism?

This being the context, one fundamental issue is whether IFRS and fair value accounting fit for all the varieties of capitalism. IFRS were mandated for consolidated financial statements of listed companies, with an option for member states to extend them to other reporting entities. Member states took up the option to extend the use of IFRS to different entities and financial statements in very different ways. A number of states, for instance, required IFRS for separate financial statements of all, or certain, types of listed firms, while others simply permitted their use (European Commission 2015 for a review). While compulsory use of IFRS was not widely extended to non-listed companies' separate financial statements, their use for consolidated financial statements was broadly permitted (European Commission 2015). As a result, an increasing number of non-listed companies have adopted IFRS over time (European Commission 2015). Some stakeholders and the IASB itself have repeatedly proposed to make IFRS mandatory for all non-listed companies in the EU in order to increase comparability of financial statements for investors in private equity or non-regulated markets (IASB 2009). Some others have proposed using a lighter version of IFRS, while another idea put forward was to align the European directives to IFRS (European Commission 2015). European directive 34/2013 has indeed made several steps toward IFRS. For instance, it makes explicit reference to IFRS for a definition of fair value. Although not explicitly, these changes seem to mark an underlying tendency to align domestic GAAP to IFRS and to extend, in actual fact, the latter to non-listed firms.

One of the purposes of Regulation 1606/2002 was to introduce a set of accounting rules that could be recognized at an international level. IFRS are currently required in more than 100 jurisdictions, although the European Union still remains the single biggest user of IFRS (European Commission 2015). Since 2002, the IASB and the FASB[4] have also engaged in a converging process for their standards with the purpose of ensuring a level playing field for companies on both sides of the Atlantic. Public support for a global set of accounting standards has also come from some international institutions, including the World Bank and the International Monetary Fund (European Commission 2015). Evidence, however, shows that, rather than converging, the process has consisted of a passive alignment of the IASB to FASB views. IFRS 13, Fair Value Measurement, is anecdotal in this respect: IFRS 13 is the result of a joint project between the IASB and FASB that, in actual fact, had led to the same fair value definition, measurement and disclosure provided by the US FAS 157.

Of course, a single set of global accounting standards would address the needs of international investors who incur costs and time in translating financial statements. However, as this chapter highlights, financial reporting is not just a matter for investors but yet a powerful practice that shapes social and economic processes. It serves as a basis for determining a number of rights and therefore affects a great variety of constituencies. As a result, a single set of global financial reporting standards, tailored, moreover, on the needs of stock market-based capitalism, represents a significant monopoly power that can harm the existing variety of capitalism and prevents alternative forms from evolving As outlined above, like the FASB, the IASB mainly focuses on investors and securities markets. Fair value accounting, too, is considered to be essential for tailoring financial reporting to the information needs of financial markets.

Proudhon (1846) used to say that 'the accountant is the true economist' to highlight that financial reporting is a powerful calculative practice that is embedded in an institutional context. The European Commission itself has acknowledged that 'accounting is not neutral' since it affects not only firms, investors, bankers and auditors, but also ordinary citizens, employees and states. In fact, financial information serves as a basis for determining both economic and social rights. It serves not only to set the limit for distributable profits and to calculate taxes but also to define the public budget to which social welfare is parametrized (Palea 2015).

Different measurement systems correspond to different views of business in society as well as to different notions of capital (Zhang & Andrew 2014; Cooper 2015). As mentioned above, fair value accounting represents the main difference between IFRS and domestic GAAP in the EU, which are based on European directives and set historical cost accounting as basic measurement criterion. It is widely recognized that historical cost accounting is closer to the entity view of the firm. This view grounds on the 'social institution' theory of the nature of the corporation, which considers the firm not only as a private association for the purpose of personal enrichment but also as a vehicle to serve some larger social good (e.g. Van Mourik 2014). All stakeholders are on the same level, and what counts is the generation of revenue from which to meet the claims of various stakeholders, from capital providers to tax authorities. Stewardship and social accountability are key, and financial reporting determines profit for distribution to the shareholders in a prudent and transparent way. Accordingly, financial reporting is more focused on determining efficiency through the matching of proceeds from operating activities with related efforts in terms of expenses, while less interested in valuation purposes (Paton & Littleton 1957).

Taken as a whole, the entity view of the firm seems more consistent with the founding principles of the European Union, where social welfare dominates and societal stakeholders are all on the same level. In social market democracies, equity investors are neither the main actors in the economy nor the primary users of financial statements. Social welfare dominates and a wide range of actors, including banks and employees, suppliers, customers, regulators and ordinary citizens, are considered as relevant stakeholders. The inclusion of parties beyond shareholders in corporate governance has always been a common concern in these democracies. Workers have played a prominent role and been regarded as important stakeholders in firms.

Along these lines, historical cost accounting pays more attention to the use-value aspect of capitalist production, keeping track of costs through the enterprises in a way that mirrors actual organizational and labor processes over time (Paton & Littleton 1957). The firm is seen as a production unit that is embedded into a socioeconomic environment with multiple social and economic long-term relations to workers, suppliers, customers and creditors. Again, this view of capital seems more consistent with the societal objectives of the EU. As Müller notes (2014), while fair value accounting is for the circuit of money capital, historical accounting better suits the circuit of industrial capital.

Indeed, the choice of full historical accounting made by national regulators for domestic GAAP prior to IFRS was consistent with the socioeconomic context in European social democracies, where banks were primarily concerned with ensuring the securities of their long-term loans to enterprises, and therefore took a relatively cautious view of the future, acknowledging its inherent uncertainty (e.g. Perry & Nölke 2006). A prudent valuation of assets reassured bankers that there was sufficient collateral to support their loans, and employees that the firm was solvent and stable over time. Evidence shows that conservative accounting standards based on the European directives combined with stakeholder corporate governance and bank financing have allowed companies in these countries to follow long-term strategies, such as investing heavily in human resource development. This has been crucial for gaining and maintaining a competitive advantage based on using highly skilled labor to produce high-quality, and often specialized, products (e.g. Lazonick & O'Sullivan 2000; Perry & Nölke 2006). Long-term strategies require stewardship, defined as accountability to all stakeholders, to be a primary objective of financial reporting and historical cost to be the relevant measurement basis.

Mandating IFRS in the European Union seems, instead, to go in the opposite direction. Taken as a whole, fundamental reasons question the consistency of Regulation 1606/2002, mandating IFRS in the European Union, and thereby fair value accounting, with the Lisbon Treaty.

Concluding remarks

By setting social market economy as a founding principle of the European Union, the Lisbon Treaty shows that there is more than one way of doing business. This chapter shows that mandating a single set of IFRS, designed to accommodate the needs of liberal stock market economies, for all the world is not neutral with respect to alternative forms of capitalism, and risks doing harm to these varieties.

Several warning signs indicate that the adoption of IFRS, which are shaped on stock market-based capitalism, runs the risk of severely harming social market economies. In addition, recent events have raised several doubts about unregulated free stock market capitalism being necessarily the best way to run economy. The worldwide recession caused by the financial market crisis and excessive credit expansion has indeed shown the fragility of stock market-based capitalism as an economic and political process, highlighting the need for alternative way of doing business (European Commission 2015). It is therefore at times of great uncertainty and change that the advantages of variety can be appreciated.

Unlike any other regulation, accounting regulation is almost uniform throughout all free market economies, and constantly expanding. While cultures, economic institutions, and development history exert strong effects on national laws, financial reporting regulation defies diversity. Differently from other fields, there is no competition on financial reporting. Even the small differences between US GAAP and IFRS are in the process of disappearing due to the pressure to converge these systems. There is no other law or regulation that is similarly uniform throughout the world, with potentially disruptive effects on varieties of capitalism. This makes it sensible to open up a discussion that puts accounting regulation and rule-making under critical examination.

By adopting a critical perspective, financial reporting should be large enough to accommodate different forms of capitalism and to let them compete on a level playing field. The optimal design of financial reporting regulation should depend on the institutional characteristics of the political and economic systems. For instance, the European directives, which regulated financial reporting for listed companies prior to IFRS adoption, have been successful in this respect. The European directives provided the same basic principles and a set of minimum accounting rules, but left member states some options that could be implemented in national law according to their diverse national historical and economic backgrounds, cultures and legislation. Given such flexibility, the implementation of the accounting directives into national law differed from country to country. Countries could choose between historical cost and fair value for evaluating certain assets. Countries from the Continental European Union required full historical cost accounting, while the UK, which is closer to stock market-based capitalism, allowed the use of fair value for some items.

The European directives have been able to conjugate unity and diversity effectively, guaranteeing the harmonization of financial disclosure, yet allowing countries to take into accounts the specific characteristics of their socioeconomic settings. A single set of global financial reporting standards, tailored, moreover, on the needs of stock market-based capitalism, instead represents a significant monopoly power that harms the existing variety of capitalism and prevents alternative forms from evolving.

Mandating IFRS in the European Union does not seem to be necessarily consistent with what the European constitutional setting has defined as public good. Short termism and shareholder orientation, for instance, are banned from the EU's conception of society. It goes beyond the scope of this chapter to elaborate specific proposals for the reformation of financial reporting in the European Union. What this chapter shows, however, is that there is much to gain from opening accounting discussion as well as standard-setting to their specific socioeconomic contexts. By the same token, European policy-makers should be made fully aware of the fact that accounting rule-making is a strong political process, rather than just a technical one, through which economic and social models can be affected profoundly. As discussed above, accounting rule-making is in fact deeply ideological: different accounting rules follow different views and ways of doing business (Zhang & Andrew 2014; Ramanna 2015; Palea 2017).

It has been noted that, by adopting IFRS, the European Union has dismantled financial reporting regulation under the control of the European Parliament, delegating it to the IASB. The IASB is a private, independent, British law organization over which it has no control (e.g. Gallhofer & Haslam 2007).[5] Many have already highlighted the huge power in the hands of IASB, which determines the way in which financial information is filtered and recorded in firms' financial statements (e.g. Palea 2015). Ramanna (2015) provides un-equivocal evidence of special-interest capture of the accounting rule-making process. For instance, he reports a close link between the increasing adoption of fair value measurement in financial reporting and the financial backgrounds of standard-setters. A vast majority of IASB's members have a strong background in the financial and auditing industries. Many come from securities and exchange commissions and international organizations (e.g. Iosco), which are fundamental institutions in stock market-based economies (Gallhofer & Haslam 2007; Nölke & Perry 2007). Several doubts can therefore be raised over the ability of the current process of accounting rule-making to generate rules able to accommodate different socioeconomic models. Since accounting serves not only to inform investors, but also to set the limit for distributable profits, to elaborate public budgets and for tax purposes, this is a key issue for business and society as a whole. According to the Treaty, European policy-makers should not look only at the consequences of financial reporting regulation for equity investors but at its overall economic and social impact. Recently, the European Union has become aware that *accounting policy choices have an impact on the public interest and so our choices in this area need to be carefully thought through* (European Commission 2013). Examples include links with prudential requirements for banks and insurance companies, as well as the rules applicable to the shadow banking system, the impact of long-term investments and access to financing for firms.

Taken as a whole, the founding principles of the Union suggest that the dominant para-digm of private self-regulation should be reoriented and that the imbalance of stakeholder groups in the standard-setting process should be fixed. While there has been a general trend for increasing privatization in recent years, the global financial crisis calls for this to be re-versed and for more democracy in supranational policy-making (e.g. Bengtsson 2011).

To conclude, the issues raised in this chapter require a research approach that takes into consideration the sociocultural features of the context under investigation. So far, main-stream research has analyzed the economic consequences of financial accounting by focusing foremost on the interests of shareholders, with no consideration of the socioeconomic char-acteristics of the society where financial reporting applies (e.g. Palea 2017).

On the contrary, this chapter prefers a view of research aimed at public good, rather than focused on the needs of investors, and strongly embedded in its specific context. Accord-ingly, it calls for a more well-rounded debate on the ability of the current financial reporting regulatory system to match with the European public good. Maystadt's report (2013) has started tackling this issue but much more research is required. As Einstein (1949) pointed out, 'science cannot create ends and, even less, instil them in human beings; science, at most, can supply the means by which to attain certain ends; outside of its scope are needed value judgments of all kinds'. Likewise, economic science can discuss the means by which to attain certain societal goals; but such goals must be democratically set by society. In this respect, the Lisbon Treaty represents the constitutional setting for the European Union and provides a definition of what has been intended by 'European public good' by the European community.

Given this context, one important task for researchers would be to test economic events, policies and business models against the fundamental objectives of European society. This could enrich research, providing a wider set of intellectual tools for scholars, public discussion and, hopefully, social progress. It is at times of great uncertainty and changes, such as those in which we are living, that the advantages of new modes of research can be appreciated.

Notes

1 Some may argue that so far European institutions have not done enough to reach these objectives and I do personally agree on this. However, this does not undermine the relevance of the European Union's ideals. In fact, ideals give rise to action even if they are not or cannot be enforced, since they inspire us to improve our institutions and behaviour. Moreover, after the fiscal compact and years of austerity, there is some evidence of important changes on the part of European institutions, which have started to look into industrial policies based on public intervention in order to foster, allegedly, a smart, sustainable and inclusive growth. The Juncker's Plan, for instance, goes exactly in this direction. Brexit has also represented a huge shock for the Union. This is, however, a good opportunity as well to rethink the future of the European Union and to discuss whether and how to fix it. For those believing that the integration process must go on tightening, even if just among a bunch of member states, the very progressive objectives of the EU set out by the Treaty – progressive in that social welfare dominates – represent an important reference.
2 TFEU is the acronym for "Treaty on the Functioning of the European Union".
3 In 2012 bank debts represented 31.4% of liabilities in the Euro-zone, in contrast to 14.2% in the United States (Bank of Italy 2013).
4 FASB stands for Financial Accounting Standards Board, which is the organisation responsible for setting accounting standards for public companies in the United States.
5 Many have blamed the European Parliament for having adopted Regulation 1606/2002 with the support of a large number of votes in favour (e.g. Biondi & Suzuki 2007). Several explanations could however be provided for this, one of them being that the Lisbon Treaty had not yet been signed at that time. At that time, there was not a clear idea of an economic and social model for the European Union.

References

Aglietta, M & Rebérioux, A 2005, *Corporate governance adrift: a critique of shareholder value*. The Saint-Gobain Centre for Economic Studies Series. Cheltenham, Edward Elgar.

Allen, F & Carletti, E 2008, "Should financial institutions mark to market?", *Banque de France, Financial Stability Review*, vol. 12, pp. 1–6.

Allen, F, Carletti, E & Babus, A 2009, "Financial crises: theory and evidence", *Annual Review of Financial Economics*, vol. 1, no. 1, pp. 97–116.

Alvarez, I 2015, "Financialization, non-financial corporations and income inequality: the case of France", *Socio-Economic Review*, vol. 13, no. 3, pp. 449–475.

Andersson, T, Haslam, C, Lee, E & Tsitsianis, N 2008, "Financialization directing strategy", *Accounting Forum*, vol. 32, no. 4, pp. 261–275.

Andor, L 2011, "Building a social market economy in the European Union", Press Releases Database Speech/11/965.

Arnold, PJ 2009, "Global financial crisis: the challenge to accounting research", *Accounting, Organizations and Society*, vol. 34, no. 6–7, pp. 803–809.

Banque de France 2008, *Financial stability review*, Available from doi://www.banque-france.fr/en/publications/financial-stability-review.html, accessed on May 3, 2017.

Bank of Italy 2013, *Annual report*. Available from www.bancaditalia.it, accessed on May 16, 2017.

Barlev, B & Haddad, JR 2003, "Fair value accounting and the management of the firm", *Critical Perspectives on Accounting*, vol. 14, no. 4, pp. 383–415.

Bengtsson, E 2011, "Repoliticalization of accounting standard setting—The IASB, the EU and the global financial crisis", *Critical Perspectives on Accounting*, vol. 22, no. 6, pp. 567–580.

Biondi, Y & Giannoccolo, P 2015, "Share price formation, market exuberance and financial stability under alternative accounting regimes", *Journal of Economic Interaction and Coordination*, vol. 10, pp. 333–329.

Biondi, Y & Suzuki, T 2007, "Socio-economic impact of international accounting standards: an international socio-economic review", *Socio-Economic Review*, vol. 5, no. 4, pp. 585–602.

Brown, J, Dillard, J & Hopper, T 2015, "Accounting, accountants and accountability regimes in pluralistic societies: taking multiple perspectives seriously", *Accounting, Auditing & Accountability Journal*, vol. 28, no. 5, pp. 626–650.

Bryan, D, Martin, R, Montgomerie, J & Williams, K 2012, "An important failure: knowledge limits and the financial crisis", *Economy and Society*, vol. 41, no. 3, pp. 299–315.

Cooper, C 2015, "Accounting for the fictitious: a marxist contribution to understanding accounting's roles in the financial crisis", *Critical Perspectives on Accounting*, vol. 30, pp. 63–82.

De Jager, P 2014, "Fair value accounting, fragile bank balance sheets and crisis: a model", *Accounting, Organizations and Society*, vol. 39, no. 2, pp. 97–116.

Dell'Ariccia, G, Detragiache, E & Rajan, R 2008, "The real effect of banking crises", *Journal of Financial Intermediation*, vol. 17, no. 1, pp. 89–112.

Draghi, M 2016, Reviving the spirit of De Gasperi: working together for an effective and inclusing Union.

Duménil, G & Lévy, D 2004, "The real and financial components of profitability (USA 1948–2000)", *Review of Radical Political Economics*, vol. 36, no. 1, pp. 82–110.

Einstein, A 1949, "Why socialism?", *Monthly Review*, vol. 1, pp. 9–15.

Epstein, GA 2005, *Financialization and the world economy*. Cheltenham Glos, Edward Elgar.

Eucken, W 1951, *Unser zeitalter der Misserfolge*, Mohr Siebeck, Tübingen.

European Central Bank 2004, April, Fair value accounting and financial stability. ECB Occasional Paper, no. 13.

European Commission 2013, Financial reporting obligations for limited liability companies (Accounting Directive). Memo/13/540.

European Commission 2015, *"Green" Paper: Building a Capital Markets Union*. COM 63 final.

ΓASB 2010, *Conceptual framework for financial reporting*.

Fiechter, P 2011, "Reclassification of financial assets under IAS 39: impact on European banks' financial statements", *Accounting in Europe*, vol. 8, no. 1, pp. 49–67.

Fligstein, N 1990, *The transformation of corporate control*, Harvard University Press, Cambridge, MA.

Fligstein, N & Shin, T 2004, "The shareholder value society: changes in working conditions and inequality in the U.S., 1975–2000" in *Social Inequality*, ed. K Neckerman, Russell Sage Foundation, New York.

Freixas, X & Tsomocos, D 2004, "Book vs. Fair value accounting in banking and intertemporal smoothing", working paper Pompeu Fabra University and Oxford University.

Galbraith, JK 1987, *A history of economics: the past as the present*, Hamilton, London.

Gallhofer, S & Haslam, J 2007, "Exploring social, political and economic dimensions of accounting in the global context: the International Accounting Standards Board and accounting disaggregation", *Socio-Economic Review*, vol. 5, no. 4, pp. 633–664.

Glossner, CL 2014, "The social market economy. Incipiency and topicality of an economic and social policy for a European community", *The Euro Atlantic Union Review*, vol. 1, pp. 53–62.

Hall, PA & Soskice, D 2001, *Varieties of capitalism*, Oxford University Press, Oxford.

Haslam, C, Tsitsianis, N, Hoinaru, R, Andersson, T & Katechos, G 2015, "Stress testing International Financial Reporting Standards (IFRS): accounting for stability and the public good in a financialized world", *Accounting, Economics and Law*, vol. 2, pp. 96–118.

Hein, E, Detzer, D & Dodig, N 2016, *Financialisation and the financial and economic crises. Country studies*, Berlin School of Economics and Law, Germany.

IASB 2009, IFRS for SMEs.

IASB 2010, Conceptual framework for financial reporting.

International Monetary Fund 2009, "Procyclicality and fair value accounting", working paper series, 39.

Jarolim, N & Öppinger, C 2012, "Fair value accounting in times of financial crisis. ACRN", *Journal of Finance and Risk Perspectives*, vol. 1, no. 1, pp. 67–90.

Jensen, MC & Meckling, WH 1976, "Theory of the firm: managerial behavior, agency costs and ownership structure", *Journal of Financial Economics*, vol. 3, no. 4, pp. 305–360.

Jürgens, J, Naumann, K & Rupp, J 2000, "Shareholder value in an adverse environment: the German case", *Economy and Society*, vol. 29, no. 1, pp. 54–79.

Lazonick, W & O'Sullivan, M 2000, "Maximizing shareholder value: a new ideology for corporate governance", *Economy and Society*, vol. 29, no. 1, pp. 13–35.

MacKenzie, D 2008, *An engine, not a camera. How financial models shape markets*, MIT Press, Cambridge.

Maystadt, P 2013, "Should IFRS standards be more "European"? Mission to reinforce the EU's contribution to the development of international accounting standards", report to the European Commission.

Modigliani, F & Miller, MH 1958, "The cost of capital, corporation finance and the theory of investment", *American Economic Review*, vol. 48, no. 3, pp. 261–297.

Müller, J 2014, "An accounting revolution? The financialisation of standard setting", *Critical Perspectives on Accounting*, vol. 25, pp. 539–557.

Nölke, A & Perry, J 2007, "The power of transnational private governance: financialization and the IASB", *Business and Politics*, vol. 9, no. 3, pp. 1–25.

Onaran, O, Stockhammer, E & Grafl, L 2011, "Financialisation, income distribution and aggregate demand in the USA", *Cambridge Journal of Economics*, vol. 35, no. 4, pp. 637–661.

Orhangazi, Ö 2008, "Financialisation and capital accumulation in the non-financial corporate sector: a theoretical and empirical investigation on the US economy: 1973–2003", *Cambridge Journal of Economics*, vol. 32, pp. 863–886.

Palea, V 2015, "The political economy of fair value reporting and the governance of the standards-setting process: critical issues and pitfalls from a European perspective", *Critical Perspectives on Accounting*, vol. 29, pp. 11–15.

Palea, V 2017, "Whither accounting research? A European view", *Critical Perspectives on Accounting*, vol. 42, pp. 59–73.

Paton, WA & Littleton, A 1957, *An introduction to corporate accounting standards*, American Accounting Association, Chicago, IL.

Perry, J & Nölke, A 2006, "The political economy of international accounting standards", *Review of International Political Economy*, vol. 13, no. 4, pp. 559–586.

Piteco 2015, Press release, September 15.

Plantin, G, Sapra, H & Hyun, SS 2008, "Marking-to-market: panacea or Pandora's box", *Journal of Accounting Research*, vol. 46, no. 2, pp. 435–460.

Proudhon, PJ 1846, *Système des contradictions économiques ou Philosophie de la misère*, Guillaumin et cie, Paris.

Ramanna, K 2015, *Political standards*, University of Chicago Press, Chicago, IL.

Röpke, W 1944, *Civitas Humana – Grundfragen der Gesellschafts-und Wirtschaftsordnung*, Erlenbach, Zurich.

Rüstow, A 1932, "Liberal intervention" in *Standard texts on the social market economy, two centuries of discussion*, eds W Stuetzel, C Watrin, H Willgerodt, K Hohmann & HF Wuensche, Stuttgart.

Schwarz, C, Karakitsos, P, Merriman, N & Studener, W 2015, "Why accounting matters: a Central Bank perspective", *Accounting, Economics and Law*, vol. 5, no. 1, pp. 1–42.

Sikka, P 2015, "The hand of accounting and accountancy firms in deepening income and wealth inequalities and the economic crisis: some evidence", *Critical Perspectives on Accounting*, vol. 30, pp. 46–62.

Stockhammer, E 2004, "Financialization and the slowdown of accumulation", *Cambridge Journal of Economics*, vol. 28, no. 5, pp. 719–741.

Stockhammer, E 2012, "Financialization, income distribution and the crisis'", *Investigacion Economica*, vol. LXXI, no. 279, pp. 39–70.

TFEU 2009, Treaty on the functioning of the European Union.

Van der Zwan, N 2014, "Making sense of financialization", *Socio-Economic Review*, vol. 12, no. 1, pp. 99–129.

Van Mourik, C 2014, "The equity theories and the IASB conceptual framework", *Accounting in Europe*, vol. 11, no. 2, pp. 219–233.

Weber, M 1947, *The theory of social and economic organizations*, Free Press, New York.

Zhang, Y & Andrew, J 2014, 'Financialisation and the conceptual framework", *Critical Perspectives on Accounting*, vol. 25, no. 1, pp. 17–26.

PART II

Fair value, risk and financial crisis

6

MEASURING FAIR VALUE WHEN MARKETS MALFUNCTION

Evidence from the financial crisis

Amir Amel-Zadeh and Geoff Meeks

Part of the impetus for fair value accounting – at least in banking – came from the experience of the US Savings and Loan Crisis (S&LC) in the 1980s through the early 1990s. Although the liabilities of the Savings and Loans institutions in aggregate exceeded their assets by as much as $100 billion on a fair value basis – leaving most institutions insolvent – their historic cost balance sheets disguised this deficit. In addition, rising interest rates caused average funding rates of the S&Ls to surpass the average return on their loan books, while under historic cost accounting the mounting losses were only recognized gradually in income (Enria et al. 2004). The historic cost accounting regime was blamed for concealing inefficiencies in the Savings and Loans institutions, and for contributing to the length and severity of the crisis, with detriment to stakeholders and taxpayers (Kane 1987, 1989; Michael 2004). Similarly, in the banking crisis in Japan in the mid-to-late 1990s, delayed loan loss provisioning and write-offs under the then prevailing historical cost regime was suggested to have contributed to the prolonged crisis, which – as was argued – would have resolved earlier under fair value accounting.

In turn, some have blamed the banking crisis of 2007, dubbed the Great Financial Crisis (GFC), on the 'new' fair value accounting rules introduced after the S&LC. For example, the American Bankers Association (2008) claimed the fair value regime led to capital being 'artificially eroded' and 'the [fair value] accounting formula is driving economic outcomes… and does not reflect economic reality'. This view has been challenged or qualified by, among others, Barth and Landsman (2010), Laux and Leuz (2010), Amel-Zadeh and Meeks (2013, 2015) and Amel-Zadeh et al. (2017).

In this chapter, we focus on just one aspect of fair value accounting in the GFC. We consider different ways of measuring fair value; and we use the experience of economies under stress, and where markets deviate significantly from textbook models of symmetric information and perfect competition, to trace some perverse economic consequences of measurement choices.

The International Accounting Standards Board's (IASB) fair value measurement standard, International Financial Reporting Standard (IFRS) 13, was developed as the GFC unfolded;[1] and it was issued in its aftermath. The standard prescribes a measurement hierarchy: quoted market prices ('level 1 inputs') are presumed to be the preferred basis for measuring assets or liabilities. Next in line are quoted market prices for similar assets or liabilities or other observable inputs ('level 2 inputs'). Preparers should resort to 'level 3 inputs', which might incorporate the entity's internal data and models, only if level 1 or level 2 inputs are unavailable.

Given the standard-setters' prescribed algorithm, our case material explores some consequences for the resulting fair value numbers of information asymmetry, agency problems and imperfect competition in markets for assets and liabilities; and some economic outcomes of employing those fair value measures. The cases are drawn from the banking crisis and its (continuing) aftermath for the wider economy. The discussion focuses particularly on banks' balance sheets and then on pension liabilities across all sectors.

The first section, 'The Accounting Standards', introduces the relevant sections of the accounting standards. The following section, 'The Collision of Two Trends in Standard-Setting', discusses the collision in the measurement rules between two trends in standard-setting: the trend toward fair values and the trend toward value-relevance (serving investment decisions) as an objective, rather than reliability (serving stewardship). The resulting tension helps to explain some otherwise puzzling aspects of the cases presented in the section entitled 'Fair Value and the Financial Crisis', where the markets generating prices for fair valuations have malfunctioned, with costly economic consequences. Information asymmetry is linked to the 'excess' volatility of level 1 security prices, in particular mortgage-backed securities (MBS), which triggered the banking crisis. It is linked to the freezing of certain financial markets, which led to the failure of at least one massive bank, which was balance sheet solvent according to fair value rules, resulting in massive negative externalities. And it is linked to the disparity between level 1 and level 3 valuations of pension fund liabilities, where, it turns out, the fair value algorithm has generated damaging economic outcomes. Then agent problems, which in the section, 'The Collision of Two Trends in Standard-Setting', influenced the valuation priorities in the fair value algorithm, are linked to the distortion of level 1 inputs because of the self-serving behavior of credit ratings agencies. Also, monopsonistic behavior by banks is identified as contributing to those pro-cyclical errors in credit ratings that distorted level 1 inputs. And, in the aftermath of the crisis, government exploited its monopsonistic power to rig financial markets, grossly distorting inputs to the fair valuation of pension liabilities. The final section, 'Fair Value and the Financial Crisis', gives some illustrations of the economic costs associated with these cases.

The accounting standards

US and international standard-setters intend fair values to be calculated using the prices at which an asset might be sold, or the liability transferred, in an orderly transaction between market participants. Both emphasize that fair value is a market-based and not entity-specific measurement, requiring firms to use 'the assumptions that market participants would use when pricing the asset or liability under current market conditions' (IFRS 13, IN9).

In the US fair value measurements were introduced in the early 1990s with SFAS 107 and SFAS 115 followed by their international counterparts with IAS 32 and IAS 39.[2] The definitions and measurement guidance for fair value were previously spread over various standards that required fair value measurements, which prompted both standard-setters, the FASB and the IASB, to subsequently clarify and provide application guidance on their proposed fair value measurement approaches in SFAS 157 and Accounting Standard Update (ASU) 2011-04 as well as IFRS 13.[3] Both have converged to outlining a three level hierarchy in measuring fair values.

IFRS 13, for example, prescribes that the valuation techniques used to measure fair value 'must maximize the use of relevant observable inputs and minimize the use of unobservable (non-public) inputs.' Level 1 inputs – quoted market prices – are seen as the primary evidence of fair value because they are assumed to be the most reliable; and, apart from exceptional circumstances, are to be used without adjustment whenever available (IFRS 13, 77). Second best are level 2 inputs – indirectly corroborated by market data: examples might be quoted prices for similar assets or liabilities in active markets, or quoted prices in markets that are not active (IFRS 13, 81). In the absence of such market data, preparers may resort to level 3 inputs, which could include the preparer's own internal data. An example would be projected cash flows, appropriately discounted.

During the financial crisis the FASB and the IASB responded (albeit differently) to concerns about the impact of fair valuation on banks' accounts (see below) by introducing modifications to the core regime. In October 2008 the IASB issued amendments to IAS 39 *Financial Instruments: Recognition and Measurement* and IAS 7 *Statement of Cash Flows* to permit reclassification of some financial instruments from asset categories specified by IAS 39 to be measured at fair value to those that were required to be measured at amortized cost (IASB 2008a). This allowed some predominantly illiquid assets that traded in thin markets at depressed prices to be recorded at amortized cost instead of at current (depressed) market value. Later that month the Board further issued guidance on measurement when markets become inactive, relaxing the requirement to use current market prices (IASB 2008b). This allowed management to apply judgment where the market inputs that are used are based on distressed markets. FASB followed a similar path, although the two boards have taken different views on which portions of bank's balance sheets should use level 1 prices. Specifically, FASB issued further guidance on the use of unobservable inputs when measuring fair values and modified requirements for other-than-temporary impairment losses.

The amendments came in response to difficulties financial institutions faced during the GFC in measuring complex (specifically debt) financial instruments using level 1, i.e. active market, inputs when those assets became thinly traded and often were part of distressed transactions.

The collision of two trends in standard-setting

At the same time as standard-setters have been moving toward fair values, they have also been shifting their priorities from serving the stewardship objective, where reliability is paramount, to informing investment, where value-relevance dominates. For example, Zeff's (2013) review of the objectives of accounting standard-setters quotes the AAA:

> The primary use of information in financial reports is for investment decisions (equity and debt).
>
> *(AAA 2007, commenting on FASB/IASB, 2006)*

Erb and Pelger (2015) chart the evolution over history of attitudes to reliability in pursuit of accountability, on the one hand, and relevance, on the other.[4] In the first decade of the IASB, Erb and Pelger document a shift in the approach of the standard-setters, relegating reliability (supporting stewardship) to a subordinate role, where investment decisions were the focus of interest and valuation usefulness the single objective (see also O'Connell 2007; Murphy et al. 2013). One Board member even described reliability as 'a stumbling block on the road to pushing fair value' (Erb & Pelger 2015, p. 31). A successful standard would yield data that are 'value-relevant', change investors' perception of prospective cash flows and so lead to timely changes in share price. This has become the prominent test of the effectiveness of accounting standards in market-based empirical accounting research (Barth et al. 2001; Holthausen & Watts 2001).

The standard-setters' shift toward an emphasis on value-relevance was supported by the accession of the efficient markets hypothesis as the prevailing paradigm in financial economics (Whitley 1986; Ravenscroft & Williams 2009). Under full informational efficiency market prices would not only be more value relevant, but at the same time also be considered most reliable. Market prices would serve as objective, indirect measures of value. That is, there would be no trade-off between reliability and relevance; and fair (market) values become the preferred choice for measuring assets.

In relation to this choice, are level 1 or level 3 inputs likely to be more informative to investors? It is a standard proposition in the strategy and finance literatures that manager-insiders will generally possess better information than investors about the value of their assets and liabilities (Bettis & Prahalad 1983; Myers & Majluf 1984). At first sight then it is puzzling that standard-setters should insist that quoted market prices should be used in preference to managers' better-informed estimates, and *without adjustment* for any superior information held by insider-preparers. Managers routinely make forward-looking assessments of uncertain cash flows for their own investment decisions and document these in management accounts. But when standard-setters have accorded priority to reliability it has been argued that unless the amount and timing of cash flows are known, managerial estimates are too subjective and the standard-setters are presumably concerned that managers will exploit their information advantage for their own benefit.[5]

Where incentives are not perfectly aligned and the integrity of disclosures is more difficult to assess – a feature of the forward-looking information underlying asset and liability measures – it has been suggested that managers may not always truthfully disclose private information (Crawford & Sobel 1982), but strategically bias their reporting (Rogers & Stocken 2005; Aboody et al. 2006; Bartov et al. 2007). The divergence of interests between manager and investor, agent and principal, was explored by Marris (1963), Jensen (1986), Mueller (1987) and others. Some discuss the desire of managers to run bigger firms, for power, prestige and pay (Hambrick & Finkelstein 1995); others emphasize the attractiveness for managers of the quiet life over higher shareholder returns (Hicks 1935, Cyert & March 1963).

Implicit in the standard-setters' priorities in prescribing fair value measurement rules is the view that the 'value-relevance' gains from incorporating manager's superior information in figures for assets and liabilities are exceeded by the agency costs associated with managers' exploiting their information advantage to their own ends, at the expense of shareholders – the traditional reliability/stewardship concern.

Another implicit assumption in the preference for level 1 fair values is that a functioning market for assets exist, i.e. markets are (at least for some assets) complete, the market price that results from a (hypothetical) transaction between buyer and seller represents the equilibrium outcome of demand and supply, and all market participants are price takers. Recurring financial crises, particularly the most recent one, have shown that markets can abruptly cease to function when liquidity dries up, often leaving just a few market participants who enjoy monopsonistic market powers, and that even in the most liquid markets asset prices might not be formed based on rational expectations. In the following section we explore implications for fair value measurements of these departures from ideal market conditions and discuss case evidence that highlights some of the resulting negative effects.

Fair value and the financial crisis

The formation of fair value prices in asymmetrically informed security markets

The tension between relevance and reliability when valuing assets is illustrated by the work of Nobel Laureate Shiller (2015). He contends that even in one of the deepest, most liquid of markets, that for company shares, the market systematically gets it wrong: in the latest version of his famous proposition, building on Keynes (1936), he supplies a wealth of evidence supporting his argument that the fluctuations in stock market prices are much greater than is warranted by the variation in subsequent cash flows – real dividends – which they are expected to reflect. This excess volatility of securities markets drives a wedge between level 1 valuations of assets (current market price) and potential level 3 valuations (discounted cash flows). If the latter, level 3 data, were reported accurately, they would more reliably reflect assets' value to a going concern, and be more relevant to investors' decisions, than the level 1 valuations prescribed by the standard-setters. Prior evidence suggests, however, that investors assign higher weight to banks' investment securities' values when these are actively traded compared to when they are based on model estimates (Barth 1994; Barth et al. 1996; Eccher et al. 1996).

In relation to the financial crisis, Ryan (2008) argues that the trigger for the GFC was a gross error by the securities market: 'underwriting in the [huge] subprime mortgage industry had been lax and losses on subprime mortgages would likely considerably exceed those expected by the market' (p. 1619).

It might have been expected that the information disadvantage of buyers in such markets would be mitigated by the activities of information intermediaries, such as the credit ratings agencies. But the US Financial Crisis Inquiry Commission (FCIC 2011) suggested that the agencies were conflicted, and misapplied their information and expertise, distorting the ratings that they issued, and which informed market prices. In 2007, for one of the three major agencies, half of its ratings income derived from MBS. The fee for rating MBS was as much as three times the fee for rating a corporate bond And, crucially, the fee was paid by the seller of the product, not by the buyer.

Tett (2010) explains the banks' exercise of monopsonistic power to distort the market:

> The banks…held the whip hand in a commercial sense. While in the corporate bond world, the agencies rated the bonds of thousands of companies and were not dependent on any one company for fees, these credit products were being produced by a much smaller circle of banks. These banks constantly threatened to boycott the agencies if they failed to produce the wished-for ratings, jeopardising the sizeable fees the agencies earned from the banks for their services.
>
> *(p. 119)[6]*

The FCIC (2011) describes a telling case. Kleros III, a CDO, owned $975m of mortgage-related securities, of which 45% were rated BBB or lower, 16% A and the rest higher than A. To fund these purchases, Kleros issued $1 billion of bonds to investors. Roughly 88% of these Kleros III bonds were AAA rated. The FCIC concluded:

> The three credit rating agencies were key enablers of the financial meltdown…Their ratings helped the market soar and their downgrades through 2007 and 2008 wreaked havoc across markets and firms.
>
> *(p. xxv)*

These examples then highlight how level 1 and level 2 inputs to fair values might be distorted even in deep and liquid markets when market sentiment, or in Shiller's words 'animal spirits', take over; or when a few market participants possess monopsonistic powers. The allocational effects of these distorted prices can further move level 1 prices away from level 3 valuations.

Level 3 inputs on the other hand can also be subject to asymmetric information problems as several cases of derivatives mis-valuations in over-the-counter markets have shown.[7] However, the empirical evidence on the reliability of level 3 estimates is mixed. On the one hand, investors seem to price level 3 assets at a discount compared to level 1 and 2 assets, in particular when information problems might be highest such as during financial crises or when corporate governance mechanisms are weak (Song et al. 2010; Goh et al. 2015). On the other hand, some evidence suggests that model-based fair value estimates are not valued materially differently by market participants (Venkatachalam 1996; Barth et al. 1998; Kolev 2009).

Buyers' and lenders' withdrawal from markets in the face of gross information asymmetry

Nobel Laureate Akerlof (1970) analyses the situation where information asymmetry, and consequent fear of being cheated, causes market failure:

> Consider a market in which goods are sold honestly or dishonestly: quality may be represented, or it may be misrepresented. The purchaser's problem, of course, is to identify quality. The presence of people in the market who are willing to offer inferior goods tends to drive the market out of existence…There may be potential buyers of good quality products and there may be potential sellers of such products in the appropriate price range; however, the presence of people who wish to pawn bad wares as good tends to drive out the legitimate business.
>
> *(p. 495)*

Akerlof's famous example is the market for second hand cars, and the problems of distinguishing 'peaches' from 'lemons'. But it is readily applicable to the market for securities, as Lev (1988) notes:

> At the extreme, suspecting gross information asymmetries, uninformed investors may quite rationally withdraw from trading…altogether…A massive withdrawal of uninformed investors from the market will…deprive the economy of the allocational and risk-sharing benefits of large and efficient capital markets.
>
> *(p. 7)*

The financial crisis saw just such a development as the problems with the mis-selling of MBS became clearer to investors. One example given by the FCIC was reported by Ralph Cioffi, who had been managing CDOs at Bear Stearns Asset Management:

> The REPO market, I mean it functioned fine up until one day it just didn't function.
>
> *(FCIC, 136)*

A notorious example of the collapse in market prices that would constitute level 1 inputs to fair valuation was the sale in the summer of 2008 by Merrill Lynch of its ABS CDO portfolio. This had a face value of $30.6 billion, but realized only $6.7 billion. This market transaction has obvious implications for the level 1 measure of such assets in other banks' balance sheets. And Amel-Zadeh and Meeks (2013) find that this market transaction did have a negative short-term effect on share prices for the banking sector overall at the time of the announcement. Anecdotal evidence also points to broker-dealers refusing to trade these illiquid securities upon clients' requests out of fear that market trades at low prices would feed into the valuations of similar assets on their own balance sheets.[8]

In the case of Lehman Brothers, such downgrading of asset values deprived it of a major source of finance, and drove it out of business because of cash flow insolvency. Lehman became trapped by the capital and term structure of its balance sheet: it relied heavily on short-term funding and high leverage (Zingales 2008). In contrast with commercial banks, as a broker-dealer it had no access to retail deposits and only limited access to liquidity from the Federal Reserve Bank. Just before its bankruptcy filing it faced collateral calls on its secured loans and was denied access to wholesale funds. Its assets exceeded its liabilities on the standard-setters' fair value rules, and it was compliant with prudential regulation (see Table 6.1). But the collateral value of the mostly illiquid and hard to value assets pledged for liquidity in repo markets required steep haircuts in the volatile markets described by Ryan and the FCIC – in the extreme case up to 100% for mortgage-related assets (i.e. these assets were not accepted as collateral any more – the situation described by Lev for extreme information asymmetry) (Gorton & Metrick 2012). Liquidity that was previously abundantly available froze. Lehman Brothers was cash flow insolvent and filed for bankruptcy.

Lehman's balance sheet at fair value immediately before the bankruptcy showed some $30 billion of tangible equity capital (Table 6.1). When the bankruptcy petition was submitted, it recorded assets of $639 billion against liabilities of $613 billion. And despite direct

Table 6.1 Balance sheet solvency of Lehman Brothers (filed for bankruptcy, 15 September 2008)

	$ billion
Panel A: Selected balance sheet items for Lehman Brothers, Q2, 2008 (31 August 2008)	
Assets	600.0
Liabilities	571.6
Tangible equity capital	29.3
Leverage ratios	
Total leverage	21.1x
Net leverage	10.6x

Note: $240bn of the assets and $142bn of the liabilities were reported at fair value (note 4 of the quarterly report)

Panel B: Selected balance sheet items for Lehman Brothers at the filing for Chapter 11 bankruptcy protection	
	$ billion
Assets	639
Liabilities	613

Panel C: Direct bankruptcy costs	
Legal costs (first 5 years) of administration	>3

Source: Lehman Brothers, Form 8-k, filed 10 September 2008; Financial Times, 12 September 2013.

bankruptcy costs (legal fees) that had exceeded $3 billion in the first five years of administration, and the attrition of receivables and expansion of payables that often follow bankruptcy (Meeks & Meeks 2009), creditors of at least Lehman's brokerage and European arms seemed set to recover all their money.[9]

Of course, if markets have ceased to function, the level 1 valuation, contemporaneous market price of an asset, is effectively zero. Level 3 valuations – the discounted sums the business might recover for their assets if orderly markets resumed – depended in this case on the monetary authorities fulfilling their historic role in liquidity crises as lender of last resort, restoring orderly markets. In Lehman's case they chose not to, leading to large bankruptcy costs and huge negative externalities (see below).

Externalities and unintended consequences in the aftermath of the crisis

Externalities

Externalities (uncompensated by-products) meant that the economic cost of the sector's crisis was far bigger than the bankruptcy costs for the banks' stakeholders. In Tett's (2010) words,

> ...millions of ordinary families, who never even knew that CDOs existed, far less deal with them, have suffered shattering financial blows.
>
> *(p. 300)*

The cost of government rescues and aid to the financial sector in response to the banking failures transformed the public finances in countries with large financial sectors. In the UK, funding the rescue program raised the ratio of government debt to GDP from some 40% to around 150% (IFS 2014). The tight fiscal policy adopted to meet the increased government interest payments has led to stagnant living standards. Whereas per capita incomes in the nine years leading up to the financial crisis had increased by 2% per year, they rose by only 2% in the whole of the subsequent nine years (IFS 2017). It has been estimated that for the world economy the total output loss will have summed to at least $60 trillion (Haldane 2010).

However, while fiscal policy has been tight in the UK, monetary policy has been extraordinarily loose, and this has had sometimes drastic unanticipated repercussions on companies' balance sheets associated with the standard-setters' fair value rules. In an attempt to stimulate the economy, central banks in the UK, USA (and, later, Continental Europe) drove down interest rates. In the UK they achieved this by exercising their monopoly right to print money, which was then used in an exercise of monopsony power to buy government securities, forcing their price up and their yield down.

Unintended consequences: level 3 inputs to company pension liabilities

Under International Accounting Standard 19, the net obligation of a company in respect of its defined benefit pension scheme was the market value of the scheme's accumulated assets minus the discounted value of the future pension obligations estimated at the balance sheet date. The key drivers of changes in the obligations figure for an illustrative company, British Telecom (BT), and the sensitivity in 2009–10 of the obligation to changes in each of its drivers are set out in Table 6.2, panel A. The liability would increase by one billion pounds if the scheme members' life expectancy rose by one year, or their salaries increased by an extra 1.25%, or the discount rate decreased by 0.016%. The resulting figure could be characterized

Table 6.2 BT: fair value of pension scheme liabilities

Panel A: Sensitivity of Level 3 fair value of scheme liabilities to different variables

Change in liability of 1 billion pounds associated with change of:
1 year in life expectancy of scheme members
1.25% in real salary of scheme members
0.016% in discount rate

Panel B: Discount rate and Level 3 fair value of scheme liabilities

Year	Discount rate (% real)	Attributed change in scheme liabilities (£ billion)
2008	3.24	
2009	3.84	−2.4
2010	1.83	9.5

Materiality Memorandum: 2010 equity = £15.8 billion

Panel C: Level 1 and Level 3 valuations of Scheme liabilities

	£ billion	Calculation (footnote)
Level 1	62.2	1
Level 3	43.3	2

Panel D: Net pension obligation

	£ billion
Level 3 value of defined benefit obligation	43.3
Fair value of plan assets	35.4
Net pension obligation	7.9

Source: British Telecommunications plc Annual Report 2010.
1 BT (2010) reports (p. 73) that the Scheme's assets of 35.4 billion pounds would buy from an insurance company a contract to pay 53% of the members' benefit entitlement. This implies that an insurance contract to pay all the obligations would cost 62.2 billion pounds.
2 BT (2010) shows Scheme assets as 35.4 billion pounds, 82% of Level 3 calculation of scheme obligations (43.3 billion pounds (p. 70)).

as a level 3 fair value estimate: it combines the company's modelling with market values for the discount rate, for which the Standard required firms to use the contemporaneous real AA corporate bond rate.

As bond rates tend to move together across the markets, the impact of the loose monetary policy of the UK government was reflected in corporate bond rates, and the resulting discount rates for the pension obligation are shown in Table 6.2, Panel B, alongside the respective change in liability attributed to the altered discount rate. The reduction of 2 percentage points in the assumed discount rate in 2010 added 9.5 billion pounds to the obligation (the small rise in the rate in the previous year having diminished the obligation by 2.4 billion pounds). As a guide to the materiality of this increase in the liability, the group's equity was reported as 15.8 billion pounds in March 2010.

Companies with large pension obligations relative to their assets and income have taken drastic steps to deal with the deficit. For example, Invensys, a very old-established British engineering firm with more than 16,000 employees was, according to Collins (2012) 'starting to look like a pension liability with a sideline in engineering'.[10] The deficit was cited as a major reason for its dismembering itself and selling the business piecemeal to overseas acquirers so as to discharge a pension liability that had been artificially swollen by the central bankers, who expected the interest rate reduction to be only temporary.[11]

Another development coinciding with the sharp increase in measured pension liabilities has been the freezing of defined benefit pension schemes by most employers: new employees have been excluded, and (often) existing members of schemes have been prevented from further increasing their future pension benefits.[12]

Incidentally, the valuation of pension obligations poses a further anomaly in assigning fair values. The fair value hierarchy would suggest that the preferred figure for the liability should be the price at which it could be transferred to a third party, for example an insurance company. It happens that the market for such transfers is thin;[13] but still, level 2 prices allow for an inactive market, and are deemed preferable in the Standard to Level 3 – mark to model – valuations. BT's accounts actually include in supplementary material in the notes an implied level 2 valuation: Table 6.2, Panel C suggests that it is implicit in the company's Annual Report that an insurance company would be willing to take over BT's pension liabilities for some 62 billion pounds, compared with the level 3 valuation – at 43 billion pounds much lower despite having been so inflated by the depressed discount rate. Given that the company's book equity was about 16 billion pounds, it is understandable that the management found the level 3 figure for the liability preferable to the level 2 total. But why should such a discrepancy arise? One possible explanation would focus on the difficulty of writing complete contracts, an issue explored by Nobel Laureate Hart (2016). One of the drivers of the liability of a defined benefit, final salary pension scheme is the pay of the employee upon retirement (see Table 6.2). If the insurance company had assumed responsibility for paying a pension based on whatever the employer ended up paying the employee at that point, the employer might see an advantage in manipulating final salaries at the expense of the insurer, who pays the pension bill. Perhaps the difference between level 2 and level 3 figures for BT reflects the difficulty of managing this risk through contracts, resulting in a risk premium if the pension liability is taken over by the insurer.

Concluding comments

We do not subscribe to the view that fair value accounting is to blame for the financial crisis. We have argued against that proposition elsewhere (Amel-Zadeh & Meeks 2013, 2015; Amel-Zadeh et al. 2017). And Admati and Hellwig (2013), the FCIC (2011) and Tett (2010) among others have documented the many failures in bank management that were primarily responsible for the crisis.

However, this chapter does point to a number of characteristics or consequences of the version of fair value accounting adopted, which were not always anticipated by the standard-setters, and can sometimes lead to misinterpretation of fair value numbers:

1   The insistence that, for reliability (verifiability) market prices be used whenever they are available, 'without adjustment' for information held by insider managements[14] runs

counter to the trend elsewhere in standard-setting, which has given priority to informing investment decisions over pursuing reliability/stewardship.

2   The embargo on using level 3 inputs – managers' information – if market prices are
available runs counter to the presumption in the finance literature that managers will
possess superior information to outsiders, and to the efforts in much of accounting to
secure the public release of such information.

3   The faith in market prices takes little account of the body of economics going back to
Keynes, and exemplified by Nobel Laureate Shiller, arguing that security prices commonly fail to reflect future cash flows.

4   Managers of the banks well understood Shiller's economics: they knew that market
prices of MBS were unwarranted, but they could not afford to miss out on the capital
gains, which would accrue if the speculative bubble continued to expand. As the CEO
of Citigroup, Charles Prince, remarked,

> As long as the music is playing, you've got to get up and dance. We're still dancing.
>
> *(FCIC 2011, p. 175)*

Citigroup subsequently wrote down its financial assets by $140 billion.[15]

5   The standard-setters had not taken on board the economics originating with Akerlof
(1970) that information asymmetry could cause markets to malfunction even to the
point where they disappear. Ryan (2008) concluded that the US fair value accounting
standard, FAS 157,

> does not contemplate the idea that information asymmetry between the current
> holder of a position and a potential purchaser or assumer of the position is so severe
> that markets break down altogether, as they have for so many subprime positions.
>
> *(p. 1626)*

6   It is puzzling that the Federal authorities did not recognize sooner that a market in a
state of panic could temporarily depress prices dramatically, and drive haircuts to 100%,
resulting in a liquidity crisis bankrupting even a firm that was balance sheet solvent (our
Lehman example); and it is puzzling that liquidity was not provided.

7   Distortions in fair value calculations have continued long after the crisis peaked. For
example, when governments subsequently pumped liquidity into the system, artificially
and temporarily depressing the interest rate, the fair values of pension fund liabilities
calculated using that interest rate were also artificially and temporarily inflated. This
had major adverse consequences for many companies' balance sheets and strategic decisions and for pension provision for company employees.

Notes

1   Although FASB's version, SFAS 157, was issued in 2006.
2   SFAS 107, *Disclosures about Fair Value of Financial Instruments*, became effective in 1993, and SFAS
115, *Accounting for Investments in Debt and Equity Securities*, became effective in 1994. The IASC/
IASB followed with IAS 32, *Financial Instruments: Presentation* in 1996 and IAS 39, *Financial Instruments: Recognition and Measurement*, in 2001.
3   SFAS 157, *Fair Value Measurements*, was introduced in 2006, ASU 2011-04, *Fair Value Measurement
(Topic 820):Amendments to Achieve Common Fair Value Measurement and Disclosure Requirements in
U.S. GAAP and IFRSs,* and IFRS 13, *Fair Value Measurement,* were issued in 2011.
4   Richer discussion of the evolution of different concepts of reliability, and their relation to different purposes of accounting, is provided by Erb and Pelger (2015), Lennard (2007), Power (2010)
and Whittington (2008a, 2008b). Zeff (2016) traces the debate leading to the landmark in this

evolution, the Trueblood Report, which marked a decisive shift in emphasis toward informing investors of future cash generating ability relative to reporting past events.

5 Even if managers truthfully estimate asset values, subjectivity and uncertainty can arise from the variability induced by different valuation methodologies, concerns about the validity of models and the volatility from changing input estimates.

6 Further supporting evidence is provided in the FCIC report. The report describes an interview during which an employee of Moody's ratings agency was asked if the investment banks ever threatened to withdraw their business if they didn't get their desired rating. The answer was: "Oh God, are you kidding? All the time. I mean that's routine. I mean they would threaten you all of the time…It's like, 'Well, next time, we're just going to go with Fitch and S&P'."

7 See for example the case of Deutsche Bank failing to write down a portfolio of Level 3 derivatives during the height of the financial crisis ("Deutsche Bank fined for misstating value of derivatives", FT.com available on www.ft.com/content/f9d4d8e8-03b2-11e5-b55e-00144feabdc0, last accessed on 19 March 2017; "Deutsche Bank to Pay $55 Million to Settle Derivatives Inquiry", New York Times Dealbook, available on www.nytimes.com/2015/05/27/business/dealbook/sec-says-deutsche-bank-misvalued-derivatives.html?_r=0, last accessed on 19 March 2017).

8 "Trade Now Could Cost Broker Later" New York Times June 20, 2008, available at www.nytimes.com/2008/06/20/business/20norris.html (last accessed on 19 March 2017), cited in Milbradt (2012).

9 See "Lehman 'zombie company' nears its end", Financial Times September 12, 2013 available at www.ft.com/content/48d4d7cc-1bb1-11e3-b678-00144feab7de (accessed on 17 March 2017); PwC, Lehman Brothers International (Europe) – In Administration, Joint Administrators' sixteenth progress report from 7 October 2016, available at www.pwc.co.uk/services/business-recovery/administrations/lehman/lehman-brothers-international-europe-in-administration-joint-administrators-sixteenth-progress-report-7-october-2016.html.

10 "Beware pension cosh hitting employers", Financial Times, November 30, 2012, available at www.ft.com/content/5656339c-3b00-11e2-bb32-00144feabdc0 (accessed on 29 March 2017).

11 "M&S and Invensys tackle pension deficits", Financial Times, November 28, 2012, available at www.ft.com/content/a3bcfc96-398f-11e2-85d3-00144feabdc0 (accessed on 29 March 2017).

12 See for example, "Closure looms for hundreds of defined benefit pension schemes" Financial Times, July 12, 2015, available at www.ft.com/content/afdb6442-2701-11e5-bd83-71cb60e8f08c (last accessed on 19 March 2017).

13 In the UK, following the government's pension liberalization measures, an alternative transfer mechanism presented itself: offering workers a cash lump sum to give up their final salary pension entitlement. Again the valuations rose dramatically with lower interest rates. The Financial Times reported transfer lump sum offers rising within a year from 20 times pension income to 35 times. "Breathtaking sums on offer for cashing final salary pensions", Financial Times, 6 June 2016, available at www.ft.com/content/54732558-5ae1-11e6-8d05-4eaa66292c32 (accessed on 29 March 2017).

14 Although IASB standards include impairment tests for downward adjustment – but typically to historical cost rather than current value.

15 As reported by Bloomberg in their Terminals under WDCI.

References

AAA 2007, "The FASB's conceptual framework for financial reporting: a critical analysis", *Accounting Horizons*, vol. 21, no. 2, pp. 229–238.

Aboody, D, Barth, ME & Kasznik, R 2006, "Do firms understate stock option-based compensation expense disclosed under FAS 123?", *Review of Accounting Studies*, vol. 11, pp. 429–461.

Admati, A & Hellwig, M 2013, *The bankers' new clothes*, Princeton University Press, Princeton, NJ.

Akerlof, G 1970, "The market for "lemons": quality uncertainty and the market mechanism", *The Quarterly Journal of Economics*, vol. 84, pp. 488–500.

Amel-Zadeh, A & Meeks, G 2013, "Bank failure, mark-to-market and the financial crisis", *Abacus*, vol. 49, pp. 308–339.

Amel-Zadeh, A & Meeks, G 2015, "Fair value and the great financial crisis" in *The Routledge companion to financial accounting theory*, ed S Jones, Routledge, Abingdon, UK.

Amel-Zadeh, A, Barth, ME & Landsman, WR 2017, "The contribution of bank regulation and fair value accounting to procyclical leverage", *Review of Accounting Studies*, vol. 22, no. 3, pp. 1423–1454.

American Bankers Association, ABA 2008. Letter to Robert H. Herz, Chairman, Financial Accounting Standards Board (November 13).

Barth, ME, Beaver, WH & Landsman, WR 1996, "Value-relevance of banks' fair value disclosures under FAS No. 107", *The Accounting Review*, vol. 71, pp. 513–537.

Barth, ME 1994, "Fair value accounting: evidence from investment securities and the market valuation of banks", *The Accounting Review*, vol. 69, pp. 1–25.

Barth, ME & Landsman, WR 2010, "How did financial reporting contribute to the financial crisis", *European Accounting Review*, vol. 19, pp. 399–423.

Barth, ME, Landsman, WR & Rendleman, RJ Jr. 1998, "Option pricing-based bond value estimates and a fundamental components approach to account for corporate debt", *The Accounting Review*, vol. 73, pp. 73–102.

Barth, ME, Beaver, W & Landsman, WR 2001, "The relevance of the value relevance literature for financial accounting standard setting: another view", *Journal of Accounting and Economics*, vol. 31, pp. 77–104.

Bartov, E, Mohanram, P & Nissim, D 2007, "Managerial discretion and the economic determinations of the disclosed volatility parameter for valuing ESOs", *Review of Accounting Studies*, vol. 12, pp. 155–179.

Bettis, RA & Prahalad, CK 1983, "The visible and the invisible hand: resource allocation in the industrial sector", *Strategic Management Journal*, vol. 4, pp. 27–43.

Crawford, VP & Sobel, J 1982, "Strategic information transmission", *Econometrica*, vol. 50, pp. 1431–1451.

Cyert, R & March, J 1963, *A behavioural theory of the firm*, Prentice Hall, Englewood Cliffs, NJ.

Eccher, EA, Ramesh, K & Thiagarajan, SR 1996, "Fair value disclosures by bank holding companies", *Journal of Accounting and Economics*, vol. 22, pp. 79–117.

Enria A, Cappiello, L, Dierick, F, Grittini, S, Haralambous, A, Maddaloni, A, Molitor, P, Pires, F & Poloni, P 2004, Fair value accounting and financial stability. European Central Bank Occasional Paper Series No 13, April 2004.

Erb, C & Pelger, C 2015, "'Twisting words'? A study of the construction and reconstruction of reliability in financial reporting standard-setting", *Accounting, Organizations and Society*, vol. 40, pp. 13–40.

FCIC 2011, The financial crisis inquiry report. January 2011. Available from www.gpo.gov/fdsys/pkg/GPO-FCIC/pdf/GPO-FCIC.pdf, accessed on May 30, 2017.

FASB 1991, Statement of Financial Accounting Standards 107, Disclosures about Fair Value of Financial Instruments, Norwalk, CT.

FASB 1993, Statement of Financial Accounting Standards 115, Accounting for Certain Investments in Debt and Equity Securities, Norwalk, CT.

FASB 2006, Statement of Financial Accounting Standards 157, Fair Value Measurements. Norwalk, CT.

FASB 2007, Statement of Financial Accounting Standards 159, The Fair Value Option for Financial Assets and Financial Liabilities, Norwalk, CT.

FASB 2009, FASB issues final staff positions to improve guidance and disclosures on fair value measurements and impairments, Press release, Norwalk, CT, April 9, www.fasb.org/news/nr040909.shtml, accessed on May 30, 2017.

Goh, BW, Li, D, Ng, J & Yong, KO 2015, "Market pricing of bank's fair value assets reported under SFAS 157 since the 2008 financial crisis", *Journal of Accounting and Public Policy*, vol. 34, pp. 129–145.

Gorton, G & Metrick, A 2012, "Securitized banking and the run on Repo", *Journal of Financial Economics*, vol. 104, pp. 425–451.

Haldane, A 2010, "Regulation or prohibition: the $100 billion question", *Journal of Regulation and Risk North Asia*, vol. 2, pp. 101–122.

Hambrick, DC & Finkelstein, S 1995, "The effects of ownership structure on conditions at the top: the case of CEO pay raises", *Strategic Management Journal*, vol. 16, pp. 175–193.

Hart, O 2016, Nobel lecture. Available from www.nobelprize.org/nobel_prizes/economic-sciences/laureates/2016/hart-lecture.html, accessed on May 30, 2017.

Hicks, J 1935, "The theory of monopoly", *Econometrica*, vol. 3, no. 1, pp. 1–20.

Holthausen, RW & Watts, RL 2001, "The relevance of the value relevance literature for financial accounting standard setting", *Journal of Accounting and Economics*, vol. 31, pp. 3–75.

Institute for Fiscal Studies (IFS) 2014, *Fiscal facts*. Available from www.ifs.org.uk/fiscalFacts/fiscal Aggregates, accessed on May 30, 2017.

Institute for Fiscal Studies (IFS) 2017, *Spring budget 2017*. Available from www.ifs.org.uk/events/1431, accessed on May 30, 2017.

IASB 2003a, International Accounting Standard 32, *Financial Instruments: Presentation*, London, UK.

IASB 2003b, International Accounting Standard 39, *Financial Instruments: Recognition and Measurement*, London, UK.

IASB 2008a, Reclassification of financial assets – Amendments to IAS 39 Financial Instruments: Recognition and Measurement and IFRS 7 Financial Instruments: Disclosures, Amendment to the Standards, London.

IASB 2008b, Measuring and disclosing the fair value of financial instruments in markets that are no longer active, IASB Expert Advisory Panel, London.

IASB 2011, IFRS 13 Fair Value Measurement, London, UK.

Jensen, M 1986, "Agency costs of free cash flow, corporate finance, and takeovers", *The American Economic Review*, vol. 76, pp. 323–329.

Kane, E 1987, "Dangers of capital forbearance: the case of the FSLIC and 'Zombie' S&Ls." *Contemporary Policy Issues*, vol. 5, no. 1, pp. 77–83.

Kane, E 1989, *The S&L mess: how did it happen?* Urban Institute Press, Washington, DC.

Keynes, JM 1936, *The general theory of employment, interest and money*, Palgrave Macmillan, London.

Kolev, K 2009, Do investors perceive marking-to-model as marking-to-myth? Early evidence from FAS 157 Disclosure, Working Paper.

Laux, C & Leuz, C 2009, "The crisis of fair-value accounting: making sense of the recent debate", *Accounting, Organizations and Society*, vol. 34, pp. 826–834.

Laux, C & Leuz, C 2010, "Did fair value accounting contribute to the financial crisis?" *Journal of Economic Perspectives (Winter)*, vol. 24, pp. 93–118.

Lennard, A 2007, "Stewardship and the objectives of financial statements: a comment on IASB's preliminary views on an improved conceptual framework for financial reporting: the objective of financial reporting and qualitative characteristics of decision-useful financial reporting information", *Accounting in Europe*, vol. 4, pp. 51–66.

Lev, B 1988, "Toward a theory of equitable and efficient accounting policy", *The Accounting Review*, vol. 63, pp. 1–22.

Marris, R 1963, *The economic theory of 'managerial' capitalism*, Macmillan, London.

Meeks, G & Meeks, JG 2009. "Self-fulfilling prophecies of failure: the endogenous balance sheets of distressed companies", *Abacus*, vol. 45, pp. 22–43.

Michael, I 2004, "Accounting and financial stability", *Financial Stability Review*, vol. 16, 118–128.

Milbradt, K 2012, "Level 3 assets: booking profits and concealing losses", *Review of Financial Studies*, vol. 25, pp. 55–95.

Mueller, DC 1987, *The corporation: growth, diversification and mergers*, Harwood Academic, New York.

Murphy, T, O'Connell, V & Ó hOgartaigh, C 2013, "Discourses surrounding the evolution of the IASB/FASB conceptual framework: what they reveal about the 'living law' of accounting", *Accounting, Organizations and Society*, vol. 38, pp. 72–91.

Myers, S & Majluf, N 1984, "Corporate financing and investment decisions when firms have information that investors do not have", *Journal of Financial Economics*, vol. 13, pp. 187–221.

O'Connell, V 2007, "Reflections on stewardship reporting", *Accounting Horizons*, vol. 21, no. 2, pp. 215–227.

Power, M 2010, "Fair value accounting, financial economics and the transformation of reliability", *Accounting and Business Research*, vol. 40, no. 3, pp. 197–210.

Ravenscroft, S & Williams, P 2009, "Making imaginary worlds real: the case of expensing employee stock options", *Accounting, Organizations and Society*, vol. 34, pp. 770–786.

Rogers, JL & Stocken, PC 2005, "Credibility of management forecasts", *The Accounting Review*, vol. 80, pp. 1233–1260.

Shiller, R 2015, *Irrational exuberance*, 3rd edn, Princeton University Press, Princeton, NJ.

Ryan, SG 2008, "Accounting in and for the subprime crisis", *The Accounting Review*, vol. 83, pp. 1605–1638.

Song, CJ, Thomas, WB & Yi, H 2010, "Value relevance of FAS No.157 fair value hierarchy information and the impact of corporate governance mechanisms", *The Accounting Review*, vol. 85, pp. 1375–1410.

Tett, G 2010, *Fool's gold*, Little Brown, London.

Venkatachalam, M 1996, "Value-relevance of banks' derivatives disclosures", *Journal of Accounting and Economics*, vol. 38, pp. 387–418.

Whitley, R 1986, "The transformation of business finance into financial economics: the roles of academic expansion and changes in U.S. capital markets", *Accounting, Organizations and Society*, vol. 11, pp. 171–192.

Whittington, G 2008a, "Harmonisation or discord? The critical role of the IASB conceptual framework review", *Journal of Accounting and Public Policy*, vol. 27, no. 6, pp. 495–502.

Whittington, G 2008b, "Fair value and the IASB/FASB conceptual framework project: an alternative view", *Abacus*, vol. 44, no. 2, pp. 139–168.

Wolfson, M & Epstein, G 2013, *The handbook of the political economy of financial crises*, Oxford University Press, Oxford, UK.

Zeff, SA 2013, "The objectives of financial reporting: a historical survey and analysis" *Accounting and Business Research*, vol. 43, no. 4, pp. 262–327.

Zeff, SA 2016, "The Trueblood Study Group on the objectives of financial statements (1971–73): a historical study", *Journal of Accounting and Public Policy*, vol. 35, pp. 134–161.

Zingales, L 2008, "Causes and effects of the Lehman brothers bankruptcy" Testimony before the Committee on Oversight and Government Reform, United States House of Representatives October 6, 2008.

7

FAIR VALUE ACCOUNTING IN FINANCIAL INSTITUTIONS

Christof Beuselinck and Arnt Verriest

Introduction

Over the last decades, standard-setters in the USA and Europe stressed ever more strongly that companies should 'mark-to-market' their financial assets and liabilities, instead of using historical cost. The underlying rationale for advocating this principle is that stakeholders are served better by economically relevant and timely indicators about a corporation's financial position and performance rather than having to rely on historical – and, hence, often outdated – figures. This practice of marking the financial instruments to the market value and account for any losses and revenues when these occur is called 'fair value accounting'. Many professional investors also felt changing to fair value accounting provides an opportunity for the accounting profession to catch up with changes in economic reality. Financial markets have become more volatile, leading to asset and liability values that constantly change. At the same time, financial markets have also become more sophisticated, and comparable prices are readily available more than ever before.

Banks were initially skeptical about the idea of fair valuing assets and liabilities. The primary reason for their concern was that it may introduce unnecessary volatility into a bank's financial statements. As a consequence of applying fair value accounting, many bank managers predicted a decrease in price-earnings multiples and an increase in the bank's cost of capital.[1] For instance, some of the largest French banks claimed that fair value accounting would threaten the stability of the entire banking environment, which has led to a European carve-out of the initial International Accounting Standard (IAS) on this matter (see IAS 39 exposure draft and comment letters). Despite this opposition, the general tendency applied by (international) accounting standard-setters was to proceed with the instalment of fair value accounting. Sir David Tweedie, former head of the International Accounting Standards Board (IASB), claimed that applying fair value to financial assets and liabilities would shift bank managers' attention to what they are actually doing with derivatives and other complex financial instruments.[2] Consequently, several efforts and concerted actions have been put in place to introduce and continue the use of fair value accounting. In this chapter, we demonstrate fair value disclosures and practices and shed light on how fair value is reflected in financial institutions' financial reports. Moreover, we provide an overview of prior research that has examined the usage of fair value numbers in our context.

This chapter is organized as follows. The first section, 'The Fair Value Debate', discusses important recent research findings on consequences of fair value accounting for banks and provides a comprehensive conclusion on the fair value debate. The following section, 'Types of Financial Assets and Liabilities', gives an overview of the different types of financial items. The section entitled 'Fair Value versus Amortized Cost' describes how fair value measurement differs from amortized cost accounting. The next section, 'Fair Value Assets and Liabilities: Illustrations and Examples', illustrates the different types of financial items by means of the financial statements of Hong Kong and Shanghai Banking Corporation Limited (HSBC), a large international bank. The section entitled 'Valuation of Financial Assets and Liabilities under Fair Value' explains in detail how these financial items are valued under fair value accounting. The following section, 'Fair Value Measurement: IFRS versus US GAAP', outlines differences in fair value accounting between International Financial Reporting Standards (IFRS) and US GAAP. The second to last section, 'Fair Value Assets in Practice: Large Sample Evidence', provides large sample evidence of the prevalence of fair value accounting in financial institutions. The final section, 'Concluding Remarks', concludes the chapter.

The fair value debate

The idea to marking values of assets or liabilities to the market price receives support as the market value of an asset or liability is more relevant than the historical cost (amortized over time, in many cases) at which it was purchased or obtained. The market price reflects the current transaction price unlike the historical cost amount. Proponents of fair value accounting argue that therefore market prices lead to more transparency and allow market participants to better gauge current firm risk, improving monitoring and investments decision efficiency.

However, it is important to understand that fair value accounting does not come without its deficiencies and potential negative side effects either. Most importantly, a first-order condition for the application of fair value accounting is the availability of market values. For traded stocks, this condition is usually met. However, for many other asset and liability classes, the prices at which a transaction takes place are not available or can be difficult to determine. Loans are a prime example. Loans comprise a very heterogeneous asset class for banks and usually do not trade in highly liquid markets. Many assets trade through the so-called over-the-counter (OTC) market in which prices arise through bargaining. Applying fair value accounting in these cases requires *estimating* the hypothetical price that would exist in case markets existed without frictions for such assets. As explained further in this chapter, these prices can be inferred from discount rates implied by transactions prices of related assets. This estimation exercise often proves to be very hard and tedious, as OTC markets typically lack liquidity. An inherent danger is that the opacity related to these estimations provides opportunity for bank managers to conceal true operational risks from investors.

An important view on this debate is provided by Plantin et al. (2008) who conceptualize a model that compares the effects of historical cost accounting with fair value accounting and its effects on financial stability. Historical cost measures are based on past transaction prices, which remain unaffected by more recent price signals. Therefore, historical cost measures do not incorporate the most recent fundamental value of the underlying assets or liabilities, possibly leading to inferior investment decisions. Fair value measures, or mark-to-market measures, overcome this price distortion by taking into account the signals provided by recent market prices. However, in doing so, fair values may also distort this information in extreme economic circumstances like when market values deviate substantially from their fundamental value. Hence, Plantin et al. (2008) state that (p. 88) 'The choice is between relying on obsolete information or the distorted version of current information. The ideal of having an undistorted, true picture of the fundamentals is unattainable'.

From the debate, one could conclude that fair value accounting is superior to historical cost accounting for assets trading in liquid markets, such as bonds and traded stocks. However, for less liquid and longer-term classes of assets and liabilities, such as bank loans, the benefits of fair value accounting should be outweighed by the harm caused by its potentially distorting effects. In sum, the implementation of fair value accounting for financial assets and liabilities requires thoughtful, rigorous and substantial investigation and attention.

As of today, there is no consensus whether a switch to fair value accounting informs outsiders better about inherent firm risk and future profitability than amortized cost accounting. The American Bankers Association (ABA), which is the largest industry trade group representing US commercial banks, argues for instance that amortized cost for non-traded financial instruments better represents the banks' business model than fair value (Laux and Leuz 2010) because subsequent changes in fair values are – by nature – only transitory and therefore are not value relevant for assets held-to-maturity. A neutral observer could conclude that this statement is broadly correct and only causes intermediary (i.e. before maturity) value estimates to be subject to unnecessary and extreme volatility, potentially misrepresenting inherent risk, especially when markets are getting under severe pressure. Others, like Laux and Leuz (2010), however, argue that having a possibility to mark-to-market financial instruments at fair values, and in cases when markets are destressed can reverse to historical cost concepts, is always better and more informative than not having this option.

The debate about an opportunistic versus pro-cyclical bias of fair value accounting started before the outbreak of the financial crisis. In 2007, the financial services sector had become a money-making instrument that contributed to over 40% of total corporate profits in the USA. One of the reasons was that some bankers became innovators in designing exotic financial derivative products – often in such a complex way that many managers and corporate directors were underestimating the inherent risk of the financial product. When a subsector in the economic system reaches such a size and trillions of dollars are at stake, it becomes obvious that corporations as well as politicians act stressfully when the system is trembling on its foundations. This situation severed during the months after March 17, 2008, when JP Morgan agreed to absorb Bear Stearns and when the US government decided to launch the largest public intervention in the nation's economic history because those giant banks in the financial industry were simply too big to fail. Now still, several years after the outbreak of the crisis, several questions remain important and ask for some further attention:

1   Does the application of fair value rules really induce more transparency in the underlying risks that financial institutions carried on their balance sheets?
2   Do global concerted efforts to install similar fair value treatments for financial assets and liabilities really improve comparability in the financial system?

In what follows below, we aim to summarize some answers to each of these important questions.

One. There is evidence that fair value accounting indeed brings more insights in financial risks; although not uniformly so. Blankespoor et al. (2011) show for a sample of US financial institutions that leverage measured using the fair values of financial instruments explains significantly more variation in bond yield spreads as well as subsequent bank failure than other (non-fair value) leverage ratios. Results like this confirm the general consensus view of professional experts like CFA Institute members who also label the fair value requirements as transparency improvements and contributors to investor understanding of financial institutions' risk. Also related to the use of fair value information by professional experts, Magnan et al. (2015) observe that analyst forecast dispersion increases after SFAS 157 suggesting that fair value reporting introduces more uncertainty. However, fair value measurement disclosure about level 2 instruments (i.e. instruments where prices are inferred from similar asset and liability classes) increases analyst forecast accuracy, suggesting that fair values accompanied with proper disclosures actually provide more and better information.[3] Note that one can cast doubt on the validity of this type of findings in times of crisis, such as during the global financial crisis, when banks were suffering from the pro-cyclical effects that fair value accounting had on firm value in times of inactive markets. Cheng (2012) observes that the additional accounting discretion that was allowed for Mortgage-Backed Securities (which was the epicenter of the financial crisis) actually resulted in reporting that was less associated with economic factors and firm-specific characteristics. However, he also finds that, even under the more flexible revised reporting standard, the mortgage-banking activities of the reporting entities are still well represented.

Two. Concerted initiatives to streamline fair value reporting globally did result in increased comparability. Although not uniformly. Two examples on concerted initiatives are worth mentioning here. One is the introduction of the fair value option in 2007 and the introduction of IFRS 13 in May 2013. These standards are an answer to the mixed measurement model of IAS 39, under which some financial instruments are measured at fair value through profit or loss and others are measured at amortized cost so that hedged positions may be measured on different valuation grounds. This potential 'accounting mismatch' induces synthetic earnings volatility. Fiechter (2011) studies the impact of this fair value option on the increased willingness of financial institutions to undo accounting volatility via the fair value option. For a sample of 222 banks located across 41 countries, he observes that earnings volatility of these banks is significantly lower in the post-introduction period of the fair value option than in the pre-introduction period. However, he also shows that the accounting mismatch is mainly driven by banks located in countries with strong regulatory quality.

In a study related to a post-implementation review of IFRS 13 (Fair Value Measurement) about the effectiveness of this standard concerning increased transparency and the level of consistency between this standard and its US counterpart standard SFAS 157, Plumlee et al. (2017) analyze stock price and financial statement data from financial institutions from 76 countries that used IFRS from 2009 to 2014 and from US financial institutions that used US GAAP from the same time period. The objective of their study was to observe (1) whether there is an increase in the consistency of reporting fair value assets after the adoption of IFRS13 compared to before its adoption and (2) whether reporting under IFRS 13 has resulted in increased comparability in the reporting of fair value assets and liabilities between IFRS and US GAAP. While the authors find some evidence that fair value reporting under the latest standard increased consistency in reported fair value assets across countries, they continue to observe important differences in the reporting of fair value liabilities and the relationship with these in explaining market values. Moreover, the increased consistency seems to be higher for non-EU countries and for non-G20 countries.

Finally, and related to the questions that were raised above, it has become clear that fair value accounting has been dominating the accounting standard-setters' agenda over the last decades and even moved to the epicenter of the political agenda. This illustrates the vast consequences that accounting and financial reporting decisions can have on the functioning of capital markets. Badertscher et al. (2012) find that fair value provisions only had a minor effect on bank's regulatory capital provisions and did not trigger massive 'asset fire sales' (i.e. the need to sell off assets because fair value accounting forced banks to impair several asset classes that much so that they were forced to sell some of them to satisfy collateral provisions). This evidence runs counter to claims that were often made around the outbreak of the financial crisis that fair value accounting worked in a pro-cyclical way in economic recessions. In a related study, Bisschof et al. (2017) investigate the involvement of US congresspersons in the fair value debate preceding the relaxation of fair value reporting around 2008. They find that especially politicians with a conservative ideology pushed for fair value relaxation as an alternative to government bailouts when fair value accounting started to get accused as the driver of the financial crisis. Later, however, when the potential design of the new accounting rules became more precise, politicians that were strongly involved in the political debate experienced larger benefits from their political connections with financial institutions resulting from the April 2009 relaxation. All in all, these findings are remarkable, but at the same time should not surprise us too much. Moreover, this insight nicely echoes that the financial sector had simply become 'too big to fail' and that several economic parties were trying to save their skin. No matter how complex and detailed the financial sector disclosures become, one should never expect to receive full transparency for granted and one not only needs to be financially literate but also cautious in interpreting the reported fair value numbers and additional disclosures.

Financial literacy about the reporting requirements cannot be discussed without taking note of various other forces coming into play such as corporate governance, financial regulation and managerial incentives. The fair value disclosure debate is no exception to this notion. The debate needs to be combined with a minimum of vigilance in interpretation of the application of the fair value rules to be properly informed.[4]

Types of financial assets and liabilities

This section discussed the different types of financial assets and liabilities that can be found on a bank's balance sheet. Two relevant standards within the IFRS framework speak to the recognition, measurement and disclosure of financial instruments: IAS 39 and IFRS 7.

IAS 39 Financial Instruments: Recognition and Measurement provides the requirements for the recognition and measurement of financial assets and liabilities. Financial instruments are initially recognized when an entity becomes a party to the contractual provision of the instrument, and are classified into different categories depending on the type of asset or liability. In turn, the type determines the subsequent measurement of the instrument, i.e. fair value or amortized cost. Special rules may apply to special types of instruments such as embedded derivatives and hedging instruments.

IFRS 7 Financial Instruments: Disclosures requires disclosure of information about the significance of financial instruments to an entity, and the nature and extent of risks initiating from those financial instruments, in both quantitative and qualitative terms. Specific disclosure requirements prevail for transferred financial assets and a number of other matters.

Financial instruments are contracts that give rise to a financial asset for one company and a financial liability or equity for another one. Financial instruments also include derivative instruments. Financial assets may include cash, contractual rights to receive an amount of cash or another financial asset from another party, contractual rights to exchange financial instruments with a third party and equity instruments from another company such as shares. Financial liabilities include contractual obligations to transfer cash to another party (such as the principal of a loan).

All financial instruments are initially recognized at fair value. On initial recognition, the fair value of a financial instrument is in general its transaction price, which is the fair value of the asset or liability given or received. The reporting of debt and equity securities of financial institutions usually classifies investments into four asset categories and two liability categories, as shown in Figure 7.1 (1) fair value assets, (2) loans and receivables, (3) held-to-maturity assets and (4) available-for-sale assets. For liabilities, there are (1) liabilities at fair value and (2) other liabilities.

Fair value assets (FVA) are further subdivided into those held-for-trading and financial assets designated at fair value. Held-for-trading assets are securities bought and held principally for the purpose of selling them in the short term. The intention of the holder of these assets is to realize a profit relating to short-term price movements. These assets are reported on a fair value basis. Changes in their value are recognized in the income statement through profit or loss. Therefore, this category is sometimes referred to as 'Fair Value Assets through Profit and Loss'. The FVA category consists of acquired debt and equity instruments such as equity stock, loans and receivables purchased with the intention to trade on them and trading derivatives. Often times, firms report a separate asset category for derivatives. Assets designated at fair value are also reported on a fair value basis. This item embodies contracts with embedded derivatives when the derivative must not be considered separately (e.g. contract to purchase oil at a price indexed to the gold price).

Loans and receivables (L&R) are assets that are not held for trading purposes. These assets are not quoted on an active market. Also, derivatives are never included in this category. They usually relate to instruments in which fixed or determinable payments are involved, such as commercial loans and mortgages. Loans are recognized when cash is transferred to a borrower and are derecognized when either the borrower repays its obligations or the loans are sold or when all the risks and rewards of ownership are

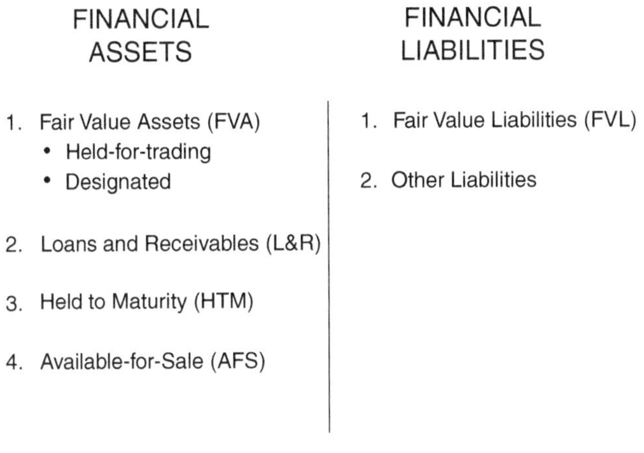

FINANCIAL ASSETS	FINANCIAL LIABILITIES

1. Fair Value Assets (FVA)
   • Held-for-trading
   • Designated
	1. Fair Value Liabilities (FVL)
	
	2. Other Liabilities

2. Loans and Receivables (L&R)	
3. Held to Maturity (HTM)	
4. Available-for-Sale (AFS)	

Figure 7.1 Types of financial assets and liabilities in financial institutions

transferred to another party. For many banks, the largest of part of their assets involves loans and receivables. Changes in the value of these asset items flow through the income statement.

Held-to-maturity (HTM) securities are debt and equity instruments for which the enterprise has the intent and ability to hold them to maturity. As with the previous item, this category usually involves securities in which fixed or determinable payments by the counterparty are involved and this category never includes derivatives. However, contrary to loans and receivables, HTM assets involve securities that are traded on an active market, such as corporate and sovereign bonds. Equity instruments are not included in this category, but fall under held-for-trading assets. HTM assets are measured at amortized cost.

Available-for-sale (AFS) securities are debt and equity products that are not classified as either held-to-maturity or trading securities. In other words, this is a residual category. Derivatives never enter this category. These may, for instance, involve loans that the company has originated but now wants to sell. AFS assets are recorded under fair value. Unlike the other categories, changes in the value of AFS assets do not flow through the income statement, but affect equity through other comprehensive income (OCI).

There are two categories of financial liabilities: liabilities at fair value and other liabilities. Fair value liabilities can also be subdivided into trading and fair value option liabilities. Trading liabilities, including derivatives when they have negative fair values, are measured at fair value. Changes in fair value are included in the income statement. All other (non-trading) financial liabilities are measured at amortized cost.

In sum, trading securities, AFS instruments and derivatives must always be reported at fair value on the balance sheet. Loans, receivables and HTM assets and liabilities are accounted for at amortized cost. However, HTM securities are subject to fair value adjustments when the fair value is lower than the value based on historical cost. In that case, impairment to the lower of the two is required. Impairment charges on HTM assets flow through the income statement. Changes in the value of financial instruments flow through profit and loss, with the exception of changes in the value of AFS assets that are recognized directly in equity. Figure 7.2 sums the accounting treatment for each financial asset class.

The prevailing standard IAS 39 *Financial Instruments: Recognition and Measurement* is to be replaced by IFRS 9 *Financial Instruments* as of 2018 onward. The IASB published the final version of IFRS 9 in July 2014. The new standard is effective for annual periods beginning on or after January 1, 2018 and an earlier adoption is permitted. The main objective of IFRS 9 is to make accounting for financial instruments simpler and more transparent, and

Category	Measurement	Recognition of changes in value	Impairment Test	Type of Assets
Assets held for trading	Fair value	Income statement (fair value fluctuations)	No	Quoted
Loans and receivables	Amortized cost	Income statement (amortization or impairment)	Yes	Unquoted
Assets held to maturity	Amortized cost	Income statement (amortization or impairment)	Yes	Quoted
Assets available for sale	Fair value	Equity (other comprehensive income)	Yes	Both

Figure 7.2 Accounting treatment of financial assets

simultaneously to amend the previous standard where deficiencies were notified. The main classification and measurement differences between IFRS 9 and IAS 39 can be summarized as follows:

- Under IAS 39, financial assets are classified as held for trading, loans and receivables, held to maturity and available for sale, which determine their measurement (see Figure 7.2). These are replaced in IFRS 9 with categories that reflect the measurement, namely (1) amortized cost, (2) fair value through the income statement (fair value through profit and loss or FVTPL) and (3) fair value through other comprehensive income (FVOCI).
- Under IFRS 9, financial assets are classified based on the contractual cash flow characteristics and the financial institution's business model for managing the asset, while IAS 39 classifies assets on specific definitions for each category. Overall, under IFRS 9, the classification requirements of financial assets are more *principles based* than under IAS 39.

Fair value versus amortized cost

Fair value measurement

The *fair value* of a financial instrument is the price or value that would be received by a party to sell an asset or would be paid to transfer a liability in an *orderly transaction* between market participants who are *independent* and *knowledgeable* about the underlying asset or liability. The fair value is the *exit price*, which is the price to sell an asset rather than the price to buy an asset. The exit price encompasses managerial forecasts of future cash flows related to assets or liabilities. Fair value valuation is a market-based valuation process and includes assumptions about future growth (potential) and risk factors among many other things that are potentially relevant to mark-to-market financial instruments. The intention of the owner of the asset to hold on to it, or to fulfil the liability is irrelevant in the context of fair value measurements. Since fair market values and replacement costs are based on estimates and opinions, the Financial and Accounting Standards Board (FASB) has decided to stick to the historical cost principle because it is more reliable and objective. In current years, the FASB as well as the IASB has become more open to fair value information.[5]

A fair value measurement consists of one or more *inputs*. These inputs are the assumptions market participants have when valuing financial instruments. The most reliable fair value input indicator is a quoted price from an active market. However, in many valuation exercises, there is no market price available. In those cases, financial institutions need to decide upon a valuation technique or model to estimate the fair value, in which they employ as most as they can observable and reliable inputs and minimize the use of unobservable inputs. These valuation inputs constitute the basis of the *fair value hierarchy*. This hierarchy categorizes fair value instruments in three groups, which are referred to as *levels*, based on the nature and reliability of their inputs: level 1 assets come about using inputs from quoted prices in active markets; level 2 assets arise from indirectly observable inputs from quoted prices of comparable items in active markets, identical items in inactive markets, or other market-related information; and level 3 asset values are determined using unobservable, firm-generated inputs. The categorization of a financial instrument within the valuation hierarchy is based on the lowest level of input that is significant to the fair value measurement. The next section, 'Fair Value Assets and Liabilities: Illustrations and Examples', describes the fair value process in greater detail.

Fair value accounting is applied by both financial and nonfinancial firms, but most prevalent for firms operating in financial services industries. In particular, commercial and investment banks, credit card companies, insurance companies and many other financial service providers are subject to fair value accounting regulations because these type of institutions typically hold on to large amount of financial assets and liabilities that they hold for investment purposes versus those that are available for sale. Many of the financial instruments held must be reported at fair value. Despite their relatively higher importance for financial than nonfinancial firms, fair value assets do not represent the majority of assets reported on the balance sheet for most publicly traded banks. The majority of bank assets are still accounted for under historical cost.

Amortized cost measurement

Financial assets and liabilities not measured at fair value are assessed at amortized cost. The amortized cost equals the acquisition cost minus the reimbursement of the principal minus any accumulated amortization of differences between acquisition cost and the amount to be reimbursed at maturity. The amortized cost is calculated according to the effective interest rate policy, at a rate that exactly converts the net present value of future expected cash flows to the initial net carrying value (also referred to as the IRR, or internal rate of return). As the aim of this chapter is to shed light on fair value accounting practices in financial institutions, we refer the reader to other sources for details regarding the accounting treatment and disclosure practices on assets measured at amortized cost. For example, such items accounted for using the amortized cost method can include commercial loans that are held to maturity.

Fair value assets and liabilities: illustrations and examples

To illustrate the different types of fair value assets and liabilities and fair value accounting disclosures and practices, extracts from the consolidated annual reports from HSBC are used throughout this section. HSBC is a major commercial bank headquartered in Hong Kong and is one of the most international banking and financial services organizations in the world. The bank employs over 250,000 people and has over 47 million customers worldwide. With a market capitalization of 129 billion USD in 2016, HSBC is the eighth largest bank in the world. In terms of assets, it is the fourth biggest. HSBC reports under IFRS and expresses its financial figures in millions of USD (m$). The consolidated balance sheet of HSBC looks as follows (Table 7.1).[6]

Similar to other financial institutions, HSBC distinguishes between four types of fair value assets: trading assets, financial assets designated at fair value, derivatives and financial investments that are available for sale. HSBC reports three types of liabilities that are reported under fair value: trading liabilities, financial liabilities designated at fair value and derivatives. The next section explains how these different types of financial assets and liabilities map into the four categories of financial assets and two categories of financial liabilities outlined in Section 'The Fair Value Debate'. The four types of fair value assets reported by HSBC look as follows:[7]

1   *Trading assets* (for an amount of 224,837 m$ or 9.3% of total assets)
2   *Financial assets designated at fair value* (23,852 m$ or 1% of total assets)
3   *Derivatives* (288,476 m$ or 12% of total assets)
4   *Financial investments: available for sale* (for 384,853 m$ or 16% of total assets).

Table 7.1 Balance sheet of HSBC

Assets	2015 (m$)	2015 (% of total assets)	2014 (m$)	2014 (% of total assets)	Fair value item?
Cash and balances at central banks	98,934	4.11	129,957	4.93	No
Items in the course of collection from other banks	5,768	0.24	4,927	0.19	No
Hong Kong Government certificates of indebtedness	28,410	1.18	27,674	1.05	No
Trading assets	224,837	9.33	304,193	11.55	Yes
Financial assets designated at fair value	23,852	0.99	29,037	1.10	Yes
Derivatives	288,476	11.97	345,008	13.10	Yes
Loans and advances to banks	90,401	3.75	112,149	4.26	No
Loans and advances to customers	924,454	38.36	974,660	37.00	No
Reverse repurchase agreements – non-trading	146,255	6.07	161,713	6.14	No
Financial investments	428,955	17.80	415,467	15.77	Partially
Assets held for sale	43,900	1.82	7,647	0.29	No
Prepayments, accrued income and other assets	54,398	2.26	67,529	2.56	No
Current tax assets	1,221	0.05	1,309	0.05	No
Interests in associates and joint ventures	19,139	0.79	18,181	0.69	No
Goodwill and intangible assets	24,605	1.02	27,577	1.05	No
Deferred tax assets	6,051	0.25	7,111	0.27	No
Total assets	2,409,656		2,634,139		

Liabilities					
Hong Kong currency notes in circulation	28,410	1.18	27,674	1.05	No
Deposits by banks	54,371	2.26	77,426	2.94	No
Customer accounts	1,289,586	53.52	1,350,642	51.27	No
Repurchase agreements – non-trading	80,400	3.34	107,432	4.08	No
Items in the course of transmission to other banks	5,638	0.23	5,990	0.23	No
Trading liabilities	141,614	5.88	190,572	7.23	Yes
Financial liabilities designated at fair value	66,408	2.76	76,153	2.89	Yes
Derivatives	281,071	11.66	340,669	12.93	Yes
Debt securities in issue	88,949	3.69	95,947	3.64	No
Liabilities of disposal groups held for sale	36,840	1.53	6,934	0.26	No
Accruals, deferred income and other liabilities	38,116	1.58	46,462	1.76	No
Current tax liabilities	783	0.03	1,213	0.05	No
Liabilities under insurance contracts	69,938	2.90	73,861	2.80	No
Provisions	5,552	0.23	4,998	0.19	No
Deferred tax liabilities	1,760	0.07	1,524	0.06	No
Subordinated liabilities	22,702	0.94	26,664	1.01	No
Total liabilities	2,212,138	91.80	2,434,161	92.41	No
Total equity	197,518	8.20	199,978	7.59	No
Total liabilities and equity	2,409,656		2,634,139		

The total amount of financial liabilities measured at fair value is 489,093 m$ (or 22% of total liabilities). Three types of fair value liabilities are being distinguished between at HSBC:

1   *Trading liabilities* (for an amount of 141,614 m$ or 6.4% of total liabilities)
2   *Financial liabilities designated at fair value* (66,408 m$ or 3%)
3   *Derivatives* (281,071 m$ or 12.7%).

The remaining financial assets and liabilities on HSBC's balance sheet are accounted for under amortized cost. In what follows, we go into detail on each of these categories of fair value assets and liabilities of HSBC.

Trading assets and liabilities

The fair value financial instruments 'Trading Assets' and 'Trading Liabilities' in the reports of HSBC fall into the category 'Fair value assets – subcategory 1: held-for-trading', described in Section 'The Fair Value Debate'. Financial assets and liabilities are recognized on a bank's balance sheet as held-for-trading if their main purpose is to be sold in the short term, or are part of a portfolio of financial assets that are managed together and for which there are indications that there has been profit-taking in the short run. Trading assets and liabilities for HSBC look as follows (Table 7.2).

Of a total amount of 224,837 m$ of trading assets (representing 9.3% of total assets), 173,358 m$ are trading securities measured at fair value (or 7.2% of total assets) and 51,479 m$ are trading loans and advances to banks and customers, which are also measured at fair value (or 2.1% of total assets). These loans are different from the loans that are held to maturity, which mount to 924,454 m$ (or 38.36% of total assets). The latter is the main category of assets excluded from fair value measurement, but instead is measured at amortized cost.

Table 7.2 HSBC trading assets

Trading assets (2015)	$m	% of trading assets
US Government	14,833	6.60
UK Government	10,177	4.53
Hong Kong Government	6,495	2.89
Other Government	48,567	21.60
Asset-backed securities	3,135	1.39
Corporate debt and other securities	23,660	10.52
Equity securities	66,491	29.57
Trading securities at fair value	*173,358*	*77.10*
Loans and advances to banks	22,303	9.92
Loans and advances to customers	29,176	12.98
Total	*224,837*	*100.00*
Trading liabilities (2015)	$m	% of trading liabilities
Deposits by banks	27,054	19.10
Customer accounts	40,208	28.39
Other debt securities in issue	30,525	21.56
Other liabilities	43,827	30.95
Total	*141,614*	*100.00*

Trading assets of HSBC include 106,867 m$ of debt securities and treasury bills and 66,491 m$ of equity securities. Further, HSBC discloses that a significant portion of their trading assets stem from debt securities issued by governments (80,072 m$, or 46% of fair value trading assets), mainly from the US government and related agencies, the UK government and the Hong Kong Government. Corporate debt securities (including corporate bonds) amount to 13.6% of fair value trading assets. HSBC recognizes any subsequent changes in the fair values of these assets and any interests received from them in the income statement under the item 'net trading income'. Further disclosures in the footnotes exhibit that the proportion of these fair value trading assets stemming from securities listed on a recognized stock exchange is about 80%. The remaining fifth of trading assets relate to equity and debt securities of unlisted entities. This additional disaggregation in the categorization of fair value trading assets per type is potentially relevant for investors assessing the bank's risk exposure. Trading liabilities for HSBC mount to 141,614 m$ in 2015, or 6.4% of total liabilities.

Financial assets and liabilities designated at fair value

The fair value financial instruments '*Financial assets and liabilities designated at fair value*' in the reports of HSBC fall into the category 'Fair value assets – subcategory 2: Designated (fair value option)', described in the section entitled 'The Fair Value Debate'. In accordance with accounting standards, financial instruments may be designated at fair value, with gains and losses taken to the income statement. Financial companies have the ability to make the fair value designation when holding the instruments at fair value reduces an accounting mismatch (caused by an offsetting liability or asset being held at fair value), or is managed by the bank on the basis of its fair value, or includes terms that have characteristics of derivatives. Financial assets and liabilities designated at fair value for HSBC are reported as follows for 2015 (Table 7.3).

Table 7.3 HSBC financial assets designated at fair value

Securities designated at fair value (2015)	$m	% of trading assets
US Government	145	0.61
UK Government	103	0.43
Hong Kong Government	33	0.14
Other Government	1,020	4.28
Asset-backed securities	25	0.10
Corporate debt and other securities	3,411	14.30
Equities	18,995	79.64
Loans and advances to banks and customers	120	0.50
Total	23,852	100.00
Securities designated at fair value (2015)	$m	% of trading liabilities
Deposits by banks	193	0.29
Liabilities to customers under investment contracts	6,027	9.08
Debt securities in issue	37,678	56.74
Subordinated liabilities	21,168	31.88
Preferred securities	1,342	2.02
Total	66,408	100.00

For HSBC, this item represents only a small fraction of total assets (23,852 $m or less than 1%). Financial liabilities designated at fair value represent 2.7% of the balance sheet. HSBC recognizes any future changes in the fair values of these assets in the income statement under a separate item called 'Net income from financial instruments designated at fair value'.

Derivatives

The fair value financial instruments '*Derivatives*' in the reports of HSBC fall into the category 'Fair value assets – subcategory 1: held-for-trading', described in the section entitled 'The Fair Value Debate'. Many large financial institutions have a substantial number of derivatives in their asset portfolio and report these instruments under a separate item. Their value is derived from the price of underlying assets and items including equity stocks, bonds, interest rates, commodities, foreign exchanges and credit spreads. Financial institutions structure and market derivative products to customers to enable them to take on operating risks, and to transfer, manage and eliminate these current and expected risks. Trading derivative activities include quoting bid and ask prices to market participants in order to generate revenues from spread and volume. Derivatives are recognized initially at fair value, and subsequently measured at fair value. In some occasions, fair values of derivatives are obtained from quoted market prices. However, most derivatives are valued using valuation techniques based on observable inputs (see the section entitled 'Fair Value Assets and Liabilities: Illustrations and Examples' for more details). Derivatives are classified as assets when their fair value is positive and as liabilities when their fair value is negative.

The most common types of derivatives at financial institutions are related to interest rates, foreign exchange rates, equities, credit and commodities. Interest rate derivatives include futures, interest rate and inflation swaps, swaptions (which are options granting its owner the right but not the obligation to enter into the underlying interest swap), caps, floors, inflation options and balance-guaranteed swaps. Foreign exchange derivatives include forward contracts, swaps and options related to foreign currency positions. Most of them are traded as OTC, or off-exchange, derivatives. Equity derivatives are derivatives linked to equity

Table 7.4 HSBC derivatives

	Assets				Liabilities			
	Trading	*Hedging*	*Total*	*Total*	*Trading*	*Hedging*	*Total*	*Total*
				% of total				*% of total*
	$m	*$m*	*$m*	*derivatives*	*$m*	*$m*	*$m*	*derivatives*
Foreign exchange	95,201	1,140	96,341	24.43	94,843	755	95,598	24.71
Interest rate	277,496	1,658	279,154	70.79	267,609	3,758	271,367	70.13
Equities	8,732	–	8,732	2.21	10,383	–	10,383	2.68
Credit	6,961	–	6,961	1.77	6,884	–	6,884	1.78
Commodity and other	3,148	–	3,148	0.80	2,699	–	2,699	0.70
Gross total fair values	391,538	2,798	394,336	100.00	382,418	4,513	386,931	100.00
Offset			−105,860	−26.85			−105,860	−27.36
Total			*288,476*	*73.15*			*281,071*	*72.64*

indices and single names. Credit derivatives are linked to the credit spread of an underlying entity, index or basket of entities through securitization. This category includes credit default swaps (CDSs). Commodity derivatives are exchange-traded and OTC derivatives based on underlying commodities such as metals, oil, agricultural products (wheat, corn, cocoa, etc.), power and natural gas. Derivative assets and liabilities for HSBC for 2015 look as follows (Table 7.4).

HSBC reports an amount of 288,476 $m of derivatives on its balance sheet or 11.66% of total assets. The majority of derivatives for HSBC stems from interest rate positions, followed by foreign exchange instruments. Equity, credit and commodities derivatives account for less than 5% of the total value. Most of the bank's derivative transactions associate with sales and trading activities. Offsetting, also known as netting, takes place when entities present their rights and obligations to each other as a net amount in their financial statements. The objective is to offset gains in one position with losses in another position. HSBC discloses substantial information on how it uses derivatives in order to manage market risks in other sections of the annual report.

Financial investments (available-for-sale)

The item 'Financial investments' in the reports of HSBC consists of both fair value assets and amortized cost assets. The fair value assets in this category belong to 'available-for-sale assets', described in the section entitled 'The Fair Value Debate'. Financial companies often disclose an item that classifies assets that are not derivatives and are not held for trading purposes or otherwise designated at fair value through profit or loss, or at amortized cost. Dividends and interest on these instruments are recognized in the income statement. On disposal, the cumulative gain or loss recognized in OCI is also included in net investment income. However, available-for-sale financial assets held at fair value have their capital gains and losses not included in the income statement, but in OCI (and, therefore, not affecting the bank's bottom-line net profit). HSBC classifies treasury bills, debt securities and equity securities intended to be held on a continuing basis, other than those designated at fair value, are classified as available-for-sale or held-to-maturity, all under the same item. Financial investments for HSBC look as follows for 2015 (Table 7.5a).

HSBC discloses carrying amounts (which are the amounts that appear in the balance sheet) and fair value amounts. For all available-for-sale items, the carrying amounts equal the fair value amounts as these instruments need to be measured at fair value. Held-to-maturity

Table 7.5 HSBC available-for-sale financial investments

Panel A

	Carrying amount		Fair value amount	
	m$	*%*	*m$*	*%*
Treasury and other bills – available-for-sale	104,551	24.37	104,551	24.31
Debt securities: available-for-sale	274,467	63.99	274,467	63.81
Debt securities: held–to–maturity	44,102	10.28	45,258	10.52
Equity securities	5,835	1.36	5,835	1.36
Total	*428,955*	*100.00*	*430,111*	*100.00*

assets are valued at amortized cost, which is why there are (albeit small) differences between the carrying amount and fair value amounts. Even though held-to-maturity debt securities are accounted for at amortized cost, HSBC discloses the fair value of these assets. HSBC further provides information how these financial assets would be valued if *all* of them would be accounted for using amortized cost versus if *all* of them would be valued at fair value (Table 7.5b).

Panel B

	Amortized cost		Fair value	
	m$	*%*	*m$*	*%*
US Treasury	61,585	14.48	61,779	14.36
US Government Agencies	22,910	5.39	22,843	5.31
US Government sponsored entities	10,365	2.44	10,627	2.47
UK Government	27,250	6.41	27,316	6.35
Hong Kong Government	53,676	12.62	53,674	12.48
Other Government	141,329	33.23	143,370	33.33
Asset-backed securities	14,239	3.35	13,375	3.11
Corporate debt	89,860	21.13	91,292	21.23
Equities	4,057	0.95	5,835	1.36
Total	*425,271*	*100.00*	*430,111*	*100.00*

We see that government securities stemming from the USA, UK and Hong Kong constitute the largest part. Most of these assets are available-for-sale and thus valued at fair value. One can notice only small differences between the carrying amount (428,955 m$), the total fair value amount (430,111 m$) of these assets and the total amortized cost amount (425,271 m$). The observed differences between amortized cost and fair value amounts allows one to conclude that most of the held-to-maturity assets (total of 44,102 m$) are corporate debt securities and equities. Finally, we note that, by construction, the actual carrying amount of financial investments on the balance sheet is in between the amortized cost and fair value amounts.

Valuation of financial assets and liabilities under fair value

This section outlines the main principles of fair value accounting. HSBC is again the focus bank to illustrate these principles. Fair value measures are made up of one or more inputs and classified in one of three levels according to the *nature* and *observability* of these inputs. Level 1 inputs are derived directly from quoted prices in active markets and considered most reliable. Level 2 inputs are observable inputs from quoted prices of comparable items in active markets, identical items in inactive markets or other market-related information. Level 3 inputs are unobservable inputs developed and estimated by management, and therefore often considered as least reliable. Further details are discussed below.

This categorization has significant consequences for disclosure practices. More disclosures are required for level 2 and especially level 3 fair value measurements. The categorization of a financial instrument within the valuation hierarchy is based on the lowest level of input that is 'significant' to the fair value measurement, as for many instruments multiple inputs are

Table 7.6 Level 1/2/3 fair value assets at HSBC

Assets (m$)	Level 1	Level 2	Level 3	Total
Trading assets	133,095	84,886	6,856	224,837
Financial assets designated at fair value	18,947	4,431	474	23,852
Derivatives	1,922	284,292	2,262	288,476
Financial investments available-for-sale	262,929	117,197	4,727	384,853
Total fair value assets	*416,893*	*490,806*	*14,319*	*922,018*
% of fair value assets	*45.22*	*53.23*	*1.55*	*100.00*
% of total assets	*17.30*	*20.37*	*0.59*	*38.26*

Liabilities (m$)	Level 1	Level 2	Level 3	Total
Trading liabilities	41,462	95,867	4,285	141,614
Financial liabilities designated at fair value	5,260	61,145	3	66,408
Derivatives	2,243	277,618	1,210	281,071
Total fair value liabilities	*48,965*	*434,630*	*5,498*	*489,093*
% of fair value liabilities	*10.01*	*88.86*	*1.12*	*100.00*
% of total liabilities	*2.21*	*19.65*	*0.25*	*22.11*

required to value them. Accounting standards do not provide guidance on how to determine 'significant'. The decision of whether an input is significant is a matter of judgment. The assessor is required to consider the relevance of the input in the overall fair value measurement and potential alternative assumptions for the input. For example, a fair value measurement cannot be classified as level 2 when it has multiple level 3 inputs that are all relevant to the measurement (even if their effects by coincidence happen to offset one another. HSBC sets out the financial instruments by fair value hierarchy as follows (Table 7.6).

Usually, firms provide a separate footnote on fair values of financial assets carried out at fair value. In the annual report of HSBC for 2015, this is footnote 13: '*Fair Values of Financial Instruments Carried at Fair Value*'. The total amount of assets that HSBC reports at fair value is 922,018 m$, or 38.3% of total assets. Level 1 assets represent 45.2% of fair value assets (17.3% of total assets), level 2 assets represent the biggest category and mount up to 53.2% (or 20.4% of total assets), while level 3 assets are relatively small with 1.6% of fair value assets (or 0.6% of total assets). As shown in the section entitled 'Fair Value Measurement: IFRS versus US GAAP', these proportions are similar to those of other large banks. Fair value liabilities are relatively smaller: total fair value liabilities are 22.1% of total liabilities with level 2 fair value liabilities as clearly the biggest category (88.9% of fair value liabilities, or 19.6% of total liabilities), with level 1 and level 3 liabilities being of smaller magnitude (2.21% and 0.25% of total liabilities, respectively).

Almost all derivative financial assets fall in the level 2 category (98.5% of all derivatives), while the majority of the trading assets (59.2%), financial assets designated at fair value (79.4%) and available-for-sale financial investments (68.3%) is valued based on level 1 inputs. Almost half (48%) of all level 3 assets are trading assets, 33% are available-for-sale investments, 16% are derivatives, 3% are financial assets designated at fair value. Relative to the overall amounts of each fair value asset type, 3% of HSBC's trading assets are level

3 fair value assets, 2% of financial assets designated at fair value are in the level 3 category, and only 1.2% and 0.8% of available-for-sale investments and derivatives are in level 3, respectively.

Level 1 financial instruments

Level 1 inputs are unadjusted, quoted market prices in active markets for identical assets and liabilities. Categorization into level 1 can only be obtained through using a quoted price in an active market for an identical asset or liability, without any adjustments. With a few narrow exceptions, level 1 inputs are required to be used whenever they are available, because the most reliable evidence of fair value is a quoted price in an active market. Level 1 investments and trading securities are those for which a quoted market price is available. Level 1 derivatives are those that are actively traded on an exchange and are valued by means of the exchange price.

What makes a market an 'active' market depends on the frequency of trading activities, the size of trading and the magnitude of the difference between the bid price and the offer price, among other characteristics. The bid price is the price a buyer is willing to pay for a security. The offer price (or ask price) is the price a seller is willing to sell the security for. The fair values of financial assets quoted in active markets are based on bid prices, and those for fair values of financial liabilities are based on offer prices. The fair value of the total holding of the bank equals the number of units multiplied by the quoted price.

Level 2 financial instruments

Level 2 inputs are established using observable inputs, but for which no identical asset or liability is traded on a market. In other words, level 2 are inputs other than quoted market prices that are observable for the asset or liability, either directly or indirectly. These include quoted prices for similar assets in active markets. Level 2 inputs may also stem from quoted prices for identical or similar assets or liabilities in inactive markets, and may also constitute inputs other than quoted prices that are observable for the asset (such as yield curves and exchange rates).

While the inputs to these models are considered reliable, the fair value estimation depends critically on the validity of the models used. The model inputs required to perform the necessary calculations include credit spreads, implied volatilities, correlations, exchange rates, interest yield curves and other observable market data. These concepts are explained in greater detail below in the section entitled 'Level 3 Financial Instruments'.

Loans and other investments and trading securities

The fair value of trading loans or a trading portfolio of lending agreements (e.g. residential mortgage loans, which are expected to be sold) is based on observable market prices (e.g. for mortgage-backed securities with similar collateral), broker quotes or market prices for similar instruments. The necessary adjustments are incorporated to these values to reflect differences in the quoted securities and the assets to be valued including portfolio composition and liquidity. Fair values of trading mortgage-backed (and asset-backed) securities usually come about using a combination of observable and specific unobservable inputs to estimate discounted cash flows.

Derivatives

Derivatives make up an important part of many banks' balance sheets. Most derivatives are classified as level 2 assets. For HSBC, derivatives account for 12% of their balance sheet in 2015. 98.5% of the asset derivatives are classified as level 2 assets. When market prices are available for nearly all of the term of the underlying derivative, its fair value will generally be classified as level 2 measurement. However, if market prices are not observable for part of the term, then it will likely lead to a level 3 classification. Unobservable model inputs are often determined by considering liquid market instruments and applying extrapolation techniques to match the appropriate risk profile.

The value of *interest rate* derivatives is assessed using interest rate yield curves whereby observable market data are used to construct the term structure of forward rates. Options are valued using volatilities implied from market observable inputs. These include interest rates, volatilities, correlations and others as appropriate. Inflation forward curves and interest rate yield curves may be extrapolated beyond observable inputs. Swaps are valued using cash flow models that calculate fair value based on loss projections, prepayment, recovery and discount rates. These parameters are determined by the underlying asset's performance.

The value of *foreign exchange* derivatives is determined by using standard option models. Input parameters include foreign exchange rates, their interest rates and volatilities, as well as interest rate volatilities. The valuations of *equity* derivatives, which are traded as OTC instruments, are determined using industry standard models. Input parameters include stock prices, dividends, volatilities, interest rates and, for multi-asset products, correlations.

Level 3 financial instruments

Level 3 inputs are unobservable estimates and often involve managerial judgment. Unobservable means that there are no reliable market data available from which to determine the value at which an arm's length transaction would be likely to happen. Accounting standards require additional disclosures for level 3 estimates as these involve a higher degree of subjectivity. A typical example of a level 3 instrument is a bank's equity investment in privately held companies. As there are no observable prices available for private companies, their fair value is necessarily based on unobservable inputs.

Fair value regulation mandates firms to disclose information that helps financial statement users to determine which assets and liabilities are measured at fair value on a recurring versus nonrecurring basis, which valuation models are employed and which inputs are used to develop the fair value measurements. For fair value estimates using unobservable inputs (level 3) firms must disclose the impact of the measurements on profit or OCI (see below in the section "Changes in Net Income versus Other Comprehensive Income"). The remainder of this section provides an overview of the most prominently used unobservable inputs in level 3 valuations, followed by an in-depth analysis of the level 3 assets and liabilities reported by HSBC.

Unobservable inputs used in level 3 valuations

The most prominently used unobservable inputs in the valuation of level 3 assets and liabilities are yields, credit spreads, prepayment rates, conditional default rates, volatilities, correlations, loan recovery rates and earnings multiples.

The *yield* is the interest rate employed in the model to discount future cash flows in a valuation computation. Ceteris paribus, an increase in the yield leads to a decrease in the fair value measure.

The *credit spread* is the mark-up above the market interest rate required before taking exposure to the credit risk of a financial instrument. The spread forms part of the denominator in discounted cash flow calculations. In case of mortgage-backed securities, yield and credit spread primarily reflect the underlying asset's risk. Inherent risk in mortgage-backed securities is determined by a borrower's creditworthiness, the loan-to-value ratio and the nature of the underlying property. For loans to corporations and public institutions, credit spreads primarily reflect the credit quality of the borrower. The higher a borrower's assessed risk level, the higher the spread. Higher spreads in general result in decreasing fair value estimates.

The *prepayment rate* is an estimate of the voluntary unscheduled repayments of the loan (or part of it) before the due date. They are important inputs in valuation models of asset-backed securities and securitization-linked derivatives. Prepayment speeds vary from portfolio to portfolio, potentially determined by the type of borrower, its location, the type of interest rate used in the contract (fixed or variable). Typically, higher probability of borrower delinquency is associated with lower prepayment rates.

Volatilities are measures of future variability in possible returns for an instrument or market price. Volatility is an especially important input in the pricing of options. The higher the volatility, the riskier the underlying asset and the more expensive the option. For instance, when the bank has a long position in an option, an increase in volatility will result in an increase in its fair value, and vice versa for a short position. Volatilities vary by underlying market price, strike price of the option and its maturity.

Correlations are measures of the association between two variables (e.g. how does the change in one market price relate to another price?). A positive correlation means that the two market prices move in the same direction. A negative correlation indicates that the prices move in opposite directions. Correlations range from −1 (perfectly negatively correlated) over zero (no association) to +1 (both prices move in exactly the same direction). As with volatilities, correlations are frequently used as inputs to price derivatives. They are also used to value complex instruments of which the payout depends on more than one market price. In many cases, same-instruments correlations are employed (e.g. the correlation between two equity prices) and in other cases cross-asset correlations are considered (e.g. commodity index rate – interest rate correlation). Financial institutions usually disclose a range with a minimum and maximum value between which correlations are likely to vary.

Loan recovery rate (also referred to as the loss severity, which is the opposite) is the expected amount of future losses that will be recovered when the loan is liquidated. Usually this amount is expressed as a percentage of the outstanding loan balance. A decrease in the recovery rate typically results in a decrease in the fair value of the loan.

Earnings multiples may exist in various forms. Widely used measures are multiples based on net income, revenues or earnings before interests, taxes, depreciation and amortization (EBITDA) in which case the input is often derived from a comparable company and subsequently used to estimate the company's value. An increase in the earnings multiple of the peer firm leads to an increase in the fair value.

Level 3 financial instruments for HSBC

Level 3 assets and liabilities for HSBC look as follows for 2015 (Table 7.7).

Table 7.7 Type of level 3 fair value assets and liabilities

$m	Assets					Liabilities			
	Available-for-sale	Held for trading	At fair value	Derivatives	Total	Held for trading	At fair value	Derivatives	Total
Private equity	3,443	55	453	.	3,951	35	.	.	35
Asset-backed securities	1,053	531	.	.	1,584	.	.	.	.
Loans held for securitization	.	30	.	.	30	.	.	.	.
Structured notes	.	4	.	.	4	4,250	.	.	4,250
Derivatives	.	.	.	2,262	2,262	.	.	1,210	1,210
Other portfolios	231	6,236	21	.	6,488	.	3	.	3
Total $m	4,727	6,856	474	2,262	14,319	4,285	3	1,210	5,498
% of level 3 instruments	33.01	47.88	3.31	15.80	100.00	77.94	0.05	22.01	100.00
% of total fair value instruments	0.51	0.74	0.05	0.25	1.55	0.88	0.00	0.25	1.12
% of total asset	0.20	0.28	0.02	0.09	0.59	0.18	0.00	0.05	0.23

Most of the financial assets that are valued with significant unobservable inputs stem from private equity investments, asset-back securities, loans, derivatives and held-for-trading portfolios. The majority of level 3 liabilities are structured notes and derivatives. Private equity and strategic investments of HSBC are mostly classified as available-for-sale and or not traded in an active market. Their values are based on the private equity company's financial health, risk exposure and future growth opportunities, but also on valuations for similar companies quoted in an active market or the price for which similar entities have been taken over. Asset-backed securities are associated with the cash flows of a pool of assets via securitization. This category includes residential mortgage and commercial backed securities. Structured notes are equity-related notes issued by HSBC providing the counterparty with a return tied to the performance of a certain equity portfolio. Unobservable inputs such as correlations between equity prices, interest rates and foreign exchange rates are required to value these notes. Most derivatives are classified as level 2 assets. However, for some derivative products, significant but unobservable inputs are required for its valuation. The next section provides further details on which unobservable inputs are used.

Unobservable inputs used in level 3 valuations for HSBC

HSBC provides the following information on the valuation technique, type of unobservable inputs and range of input values are employed for each type of level 3 financial instruments (Table 7.8).

Movements in level 3 valuations

TYPES OF MOVEMENTS

There are four reasons or sources of differences between beginning-of-the-year values of level 3 financial instruments and end-of-the-year values. A first reason is movements because

Table 7.8 The use of level 3 inputs

Nr.	Financial instrument type	Level 3 fair value: Assets	Valuation technique: Liabilities	Key unobservable inputs	Full range of inputs	Core range of inputs: Lower	Core range of inputs: Higher	Lower	Higher
1	Private equity	3,951	35	(No details disclosed)	(No details disclosed)	(No details disclosed)	(No details disclosed)		
2	Asset-backed securities	1,584				1%	6%	1%	6%
	– CLO/CDO	511		Discounted cash flow	Prepayment rate	3	147	54	117
	– Other ABS	1,073		Market proxy	Bid quotes				
3	Loans held for securitization	30		(No details disclosed)	(No details disclosed)	(No details disclosed)	(No details disclosed)		
4	Structured notes	4	4,250						
	– Equity-linked		3,719	Option model	Equity volatility	12%	72%	19%	43%
				Option model	Equity correlation	35%	93%	43%	79%
	– Fund-linked		13	Option model	Fund volatility	6%	8%	6%	8%
	– Foreign exchange-linked		166	Option model	FX volatility	5%	35%	5%	20%
	– Other notes	4	352	(No details disclosed)	(No details disclosed)				
5	Derivatives with monolines	196		Discounted cash flow	Credit spread	4%	4%	4%	4%
6	Other derivatives	2,066	1,210						
	– Interest rate derivatives								
	★ Securitization swaps	250	455	Discounted cash flow	Prepayment rate	0%	90%	14%	71%
	★ Long-dated swaptions	1,237	119	Option model	Interest rate volatility	3%	66%	20%	41%
	★ other	176	65	(No details disclosed)	(No details disclosed)				
	– FX derivatives	190	191	Option model	FX volatility	0.50%	35%	5%	14%
	– Equity derivatives	174	361	Option model	Equity volatility	8%	104%	18%	44%
	– Credit derivatives	39	19	(No details disclosed)	(No details disclosed)				
7	Other portfolios	6,488	3						
	– Structured certificates	4,434		Discounted cash flow	Credit volatility	2%	4%	2%	4%
	– Other	2,054	3	Market proxy	Bid quotes and others	70	124	100	123
	Total level 3 instruments	**14,319**	**5,498**						

Table 7.9 Accounting for changes in level 3 valuation

Panel A: Movement in level 3 assets and liabilities

	Assets					Liabilities			
$m	Available-for-sale	Held for trading	At fair value	Derivatives	Total level 3 assets	Held for trading	At fair value	Derivatives	Total level 3 liabilities
At 1 January 2015	4,988	6,468	726	2,924	15,106	6,139	–	1,907	8,046
Gains/(losses) recognized in profit or loss	−34	109	30	95	200	−573	−1	−209	−783
Gains/(losses) recognized in other comprehensive income	226	−192	−11	−126	−103	−118	−1	−64	−183
Purchases and new issuances	594	1,745	250	–	2,589	1,473	9	–	1,482
Sales	−757	−1,206	−50	–	−2,013	−66	−4	–	−70
Settlements	−32	−146	−135	−38	−351	−1,260	–	−241	−1,501
Transfers out of level 3	−1,471	−206	−336	−1,015	−3,028	−1,743	–	−283	−2,026
Transfers into level 3	1,213	284	–	422	1,919	433	–	100	533
At 31 December 2015	4,727	6,856	474	2,262	14,319	4,285	3	1,210	5,498

of purchases (and issuances) of new instruments. Second, values decrease when assets or liabilities have been sold during the year or have been subject to settlements. Third, existing assets and liabilities have been moved into or out of the level 3 category from other fair value categories. And finally, the inputs used to value level 3 financial instruments may have changed during the year affecting the value of the underlying instruments. For instance, increases in unemployment rates during the year may increase the expected default rates on loans, which will in turn decline the fair value. Some of these gains and losses flow through the income statement, while others are recognized in OCI. HSBC summarizes changes the fair value of level 3 instruments as follows (Table 7.9a).

Sales of level 3 assets and transfers out to other fair value categories are the main reasons why level 3 assets dropped in value, offset partially by the purchase of assets and transfer in the level 3 category. Settlements and transfers out of level 3 financial liabilities are mainly responsible for the decrease in level 3 liabilities in 2015.

CHANGES IN NET INCOME VERSUS OTHER COMPREHENSIVE INCOME

Most of the movements in equity flow through the firm's income statement, and therefore affect net income. Increases in equity (such as interest income or fees the bank receives from financial services) are recorded as revenues and decreases in equity (such as employee salaries and spending on advertises) are recorded as expenses. Subtracting expenses from revenues yields earnings, or net income, which is shown at the bottom of the income statement.

Comprehensive income is the difference between last year's equity and this year's equity, taking into account any dividend payments and stock issuances or repurchases. When all changes in equity are recorded for as either expenses or revenues in the income statement, comprehensive income equals net income. This is sometimes referred to as clean-surplus accounting.

However, some movements in equity do not flow through the income statement, but are recorded for as what is referred to as OCI. Next to the income statement, firms usually provide a detailed statement of comprehensive income. One important item that builds up to OCI for financial institutions are unrealized gains and losses on available-for-sale assets. Any changes in the value of available-for-sale portfolios and investments (which are typically much larger for financial firms than others) are not reported on the income statement and do not affect net income. However, at the time of sale, the difference between the proceeds from the sale and the original cost of the investment is recorded as a gain or loss on sale of available-for-sale securities. In this case, this is considered a realized gain or loss. Gains and losses from trading securities are included in the income statement. For HSBC, fair value changes in 2015 for HSBC of their level 3 financial instruments are reconciled as follows (Table 7.9b).

Panel B: Changes through net income versus OCI

$m	Assets				Liabilities		
	Available-for-sale	*Held for trading*	*At fair value*	*Derivatives*	*Held for trading*	*At fair value*	*Derivatives*
At 1 January 2015	4,988	6,468	726	2,924	6,139	–	1,907
Total gains/(losses) recognized in profit or loss	−34	109	30	95	−573	−1	−209
– trading income/ (expense) excluding net interest income	–	109	–	95	−573	–	−209
– net income from other financial instruments designated at fair value	–	–	30	–	–	−1	–
– gains less losses from financial investments	−269	–	–	–	–	–	–
– loan impairment charges and other credit risk provisions	235	–	–	–	–	–	–
Total gains/(losses) recognized in other comprehensive income	226	−192	−11	−126	−118	−1	−64
– available-for-sale investments: fair value gains	393	–	–	–	–	–	–

Panel B: Changes through net income versus OCI

$m	Assets				Liabilities		
	Available-for-sale	Held for trading	At fair value	Derivatives	Held for trading	At fair value	Derivatives
– cash flow hedges: fair value gains/ (losses)	–	–	–	−4	–	–	–
– exchange differences	−167	−192	−11	−122	−118	−1	−64
Other movements in level 3 assets	−453	471	−271	−631	−1,163	5	−424
At 31 December 2015	4,727	6,856	474	2,262	4,285	3	1,210

As can be seen in Table 7.9b, a large part of the changes in value of AFS assets does not flow through the income statement, but is recorded for as OCI. Changes in level 3 AFS stem from a loss of −34 m$ (recorded in net income) and a gain of 226 m$ (recognized in OCI). An interesting exercise for the reader is to reconcile disclosures in Table 7.9b with those from Table 7.9a.

Sensitivity of level 3 valuations

Unlike many other financial institutions, HSBC also discloses the effect of changes in significant unobservable assumptions to potential *alternative* scenarios. HSBC shows sensitivity analyses on level 3 instruments as follows (Table 7.10).

For each category of financial instruments reported at fair value, the bank shows the effect of favorable versus unfavorable changes. The banks states that 'the objective is to measure a range of fair values consistent with the application of a 95% confidence interval'. These estimates are based on deviations from the fair values measures reported on the balance sheet. The interpretation is as follows: the probability that the impact of favorable (unfavorable) changes in level 3 inputs has a positive (negative) effect on net profit of more than 394 m$ (269 m$) is less than 5%. Put differently, forecast errors in level 3 fair values are expected to remain within a range of −1.78% and +2.61% of total net profit. As comprehensive income is much smaller for HSBC in 2015, these percentages are much higher for potential deviations. We conclude from these disclosures that, despite the fact that level 3 fair values 'only' represent a small portion of a bank's assets and liabilities, measurement error in their valuations may have a significant (positive or negative) effect on earnings.

Evaluating the quality of fair value measures

A legitimate concern many investors have about fair value disclosures relates to the credibility of the fair value estimates. In particular, level 3 estimations are under scrutiny since these valuations are based on unobservable characteristics. Their estimation process is inherently more difficult and leaves ample room for managerial discretion. To mitigate these information issues and to reduce uncertainty, management may opt to voluntarily provide more information on the unobservable inputs.

Table 7.10 Sensitivity in level 3 valuation

	Reflected in profit or loss		Reflected in other comprehensive income	
m$	Favorable changes	Unfavorable changes	Favorable changes	Unfavorable changes
Derivatives, trading assets and trading liabilities	335	−215		
Financial assets and liabilities designated at fair value	24	−24		
Financial investments available-for-sale	35	−30	230	−243
Total effect	*394*	*−269*	*230*	*−243*
% of Net Profit	*2.61*	*−1.78*		
% of Comprehensive Income			*20.05*	*−21.19*

Several academic studies investigate the usefulness of the fair value estimates presented under the three-level hierarchy. Evidence of Kolev (2009) suggests that the more opaque level 3 fair value estimates are valued less by investors compared to the more transparent level 1 and level 2 estimates. Similarly, results from a study by Riedl and Serafeim (2011) suggest that banks with more opaque financial assets face a higher cost of capital. Song et al. (2010) show that the value relevance of fair value assets, and in particular for level 3 estimates, is higher for banks with stronger corporate governance. A more recent study of Chung et al. (2017) investigates voluntary fair value disclosures beyond the requirements in SFAS 157 and finds that banks with greater exposure to level 2 and level 3 assets provide more reliable disclosures, suggesting that managers disclose more information to reduce investors' concern about the reliability of more opaque fair value estimates.

In sum, these findings suggest that banks with higher levels of opaque assets face higher information asymmetry problems. Although these findings are important, one should see them in combination with our findings from the previous section. Level 3 assets are relatively small in size and they constitute a shrinking portion of the total balance sheet for the majority of banks. Level 3 assets are a potentially important risk indicator, but not always a crucial one. Scope Corporation AG, a Berlin-based rating agency specializing in banks, for instance, mentions that '*Overall, we consider that the presence of Level 3 assets in banks' balance sheets is generally not a concern, as these are justified in the context of the banks' normal operations*'.

Fair value measurement: IFRS versus US GAAP

The two main accounting standards that are applied worldwide are US GAAP and IFRS. The principles of fair value accounting under these two regimes are very similar. However, some (minor often) differences remain. Readers of financial statements are better off when being aware of them. The aim of this section is to summarize the main differences. For the reader interested in more detailed insights, please refer to FASB ASC Topic 820 and FASB No. 157 (*Fair Value Measurement*) for US GAAP guidance and IFRS 13 (*Fair Value Measurement*) for IFRS guidance. Convergence attempts are summarized in ASU 2011–04: *Amendments to achieve Common Fair Value Measurement and Disclosure Requirements in U.S. GAAP and IFRSs.*

A first difference between fair value measurements in US GAAP versus IFRS relates to the (non-)disclosure of recurring fair value measurements. Recurring fair value measurements relate to assets and liabilities that are categorized as fair valuable at the end of each reporting period, such as for trading assets. IFRS 13, para. 93 requires quantitative sensitivity information to be disclosed if input assumptions are changing, such as a change in mortality rate, risk exposure or customer retention rates. Specifically, IFRS 13 requires this disclosure independent of a firm's listing status. US GAAP only has this requirement for publicly listed entities, unlisted entities with total assets above 100 million USD and unlisted entities holding specific derivative instruments.

A second difference relates to the information disclosures in interim reports. Both US GAAP and IFRS require fair value disclosures of financial assets and liabilities in every interim financial report about (1) the fair value measurement and reasons for the measurement; (2) the level of the hierarchy in which the measurement is categorized; (3) the transfers between level 1 and level 2 categories (if any) as well as the reasons for these transfers; (4) a description of the valuation technique and inputs used for level 2 and 3 measurements; (5) if a change in the valuation technique has been made and, if so, the reasons for this change; (6) quantitative information about significant unobservable inputs for level 3 estimates and (7) a reconciliation of level 3 opening and closing balances. However, IFRS does not require disclosing information about nonfinancial assets and nonfinancial liabilities and for asset and liabilities classes that are not measured at fair value but for which fair values are disclosed.

A third difference that is worth noting relates to the practical technique for measuring fair value of loan receivables that do not belong to a homogenous category such as house/residence mortgages or credit card loans. This practical approach (also called entry-price technique) used under US GAAP to fair valuing the loan receivables can be based upon discounted future cash flows using the current rates at which similar loans would be made to similar clients with equal maturities. The standard technique that allows for fair valuing these types of heterogeneous loan receivables is not standard practice under IFRS 13.

Finally, interpretation differences exist with respect to hedging. In a hedging transaction the transaction price is an entry price, while fair value measurement is typically based on an exit price. In the situation where the derivative is subject to a bid-ask spread, both prices can be different. Under such conditions, US GAAP requires the recognition of day one gains and losses, even when the inputs to a fair value measurement are not observable. Under IFRS 13, the recognition of day one gains and losses is prohibited when the inputs to a fair value measurement are not observable and can be deferred under this condition. Many of the differences between US GAAP and IFRS will not materialize in substantial differences in valuation between reporting financial entities. The most relevant differences involve disclosure requirements, and not so much differences in how underlying values are obtained and estimated.

Fair value assets in practice: large sample evidence

In this section we provide a summary analysis of the importance of level 1/2/3 assets for all US banks in the period 2008–2015.[8] We compare the importance of fair value assets for all banks with that of the largest 100 and largest 10 US banks. Size is measured by total assets. Such an overview is insightful for different reasons. First, it can provide new evidence about the importance of bank asset classes' riskiness over time from a period that was still suffering from a financial crisis (2008–2009) toward an economic recovery period (2010 and later).

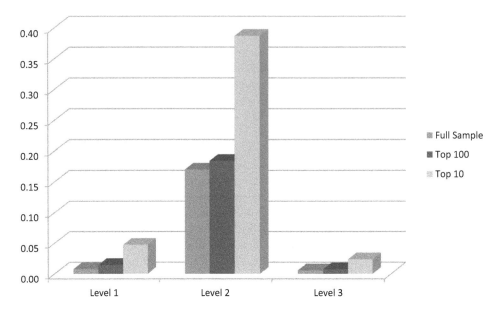

Figure 7.3   Level 1/2/3 assets (scaled by total assets)

Second, our analyses allow gaining further insights in the differences that are originated by bank size and consequently by a bank's business model. In particular, larger banks with a more significant wholesale and investment banking profile tend to have more level 3 assets compared to smaller banks with a more retail-oriented business model.

Figure 7.3 depicts the mean proportions of level 1/2/3 assets as a proportion to total assets. We employ three samples: a full sample of US bank observations for the period 2008–2015, including over 600 stock-listed banks and two subsamples based on bank size measured by total assets, where we focus on the top 100 and top 10 banks. Level 2 assets are by far the largest proportion of fair value assets on the balance sheet. The proportion is especially high for the subsample of top 10 US banks (37%). When including smaller banks, the average drops to 17%. With regard to the more risky and more opaque level 3 assets, again the highest proportions are observed for top 10 US banks. However, proportions here are nearly zero here for all banks (0.5% on average) and are never higher than 2.5% for top 10 US banks. A similar pattern is observed for level 1 assets although average are slightly higher: 1% for all banks; 1.5% for top 100 banks and about 4.5% for top 10 banks.

To gain a further understanding in the time series pattern of the different fair value asset classes over time we compare in Figure 7.4 the evolution for the top 100 compared to top 10 US banks. For level 1 assets, we observe a doubling of the proportion during the later crisis years (2008–2010) from about 3% to 6% and balances toward about 4.5% in the later years. For the sample of top 100 banks, the pattern is more stable and stays around 1.5% of total assets. These numbers suggest that large banks with significant exposure to investment banking activities considered rebalancing their risky assets toward the least opaque category.

For the proportion of level 2 assets, we observe a sharp decline for the largest banks from values close to 50% of total assets to about 30%. However, the proportion of level 2 assets remains considerably larger than the proportion is for smaller banks. The downward trend suggests that since the crisis banks are rebalancing their risky assets and that especially the largest banks are changing their underlying business model away from riskier asset categories.

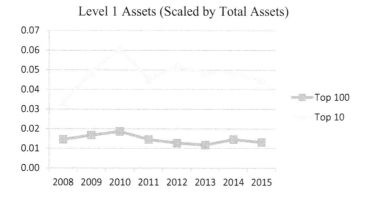

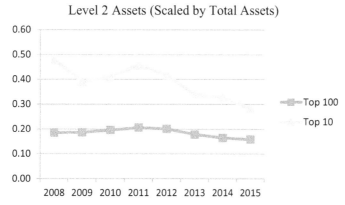

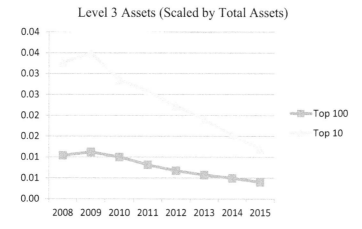

Figure 7.4 Level 1/2/3 assets over time

Finally, we observe that average for the proportion of level 3 assets for top 10 US banks was at its maximum during the crisis years (2009: 3.5%) and dropped afterwards to below 2%. In the last observation year, the value is close to 1% of total assets. For the top 100 sample, proportions were already around 1% in the crisis years and dropped to nearly zero in 2015. As such, the relative importance of level 3 assets has decreased over the last decade. The decrease is most pronounced for larger banks.

Concluding remarks

This chapter has outlined the objectives of fair value accounting of specific interest to financial institutions and discussed its main technical aspects. The fair value applications were studied by identifying the relevant sections in a real-life company case of HSBC but could have been illustrated by many other financial institutions as well. Apart from a technical description of the fair value implications of relevant accounting standards including IAS 39, IFRS 7, IFRS 9 and IFRS 13, we also reflected on a vital question that dominated several academic and professional debates about the usefulness of fair value accounting estimates for representing underlying bank risk. We assessed to what extent outsiders are better served with fair values compared to historical cost estimates. Finally, we have provided descriptive evidence on the importance of fair value assets for American banks and evidence on the evolution of fair value assets for the years 2008–2015.

An important conclusion from this chapter is that the treatment of fair value instruments received more intense and concrete guidance over the years as evidenced with the introduction of IFRS 9 and IFRS 13. The increased guidance and the demand for more transparency may lead to the impression that financial statement users are better informed about the inherent risks of bank activities, including credit risk. However, research insights warn us for the fact that more guidance does not automatically and unequivocally result in a more transparent reflection of underlying economic risks. Moreover, there is no incontestable evidence as of today that fair value accounting improves the accuracy or timeliness of the market's assessment of credit risk. As is the case with many accounting issues, the quality of fair value measures relies crucially on the intrinsic abilities and trustworthiness of the bank management. Users of financial statements require a high degree of financial literacy and an impassive mind to be able to accurately interpret fair value instruments in financial institutions.

Notes

1　E.g. "Shining a light on company accounts", The Economist Aug 16, 2001.
2　A derivative refers to a security class of which the price is a function of another underlying asset category, like stocks, bonds, interest rates, commodities, and exchange rates.
3　The classification into level 1, level 2 and level 3 instruments is treated in detail in the section entitled 'Valuation of Financial Assets and Liabilities under Fair Value'.
4　Further academic evidence on the fair value debate is summarized in the section entitled 'Evaluating the Quality of Fair Value Measures' after the details on the technicalities have been introduced.
5　Essential in the debate is the key position of the decision usefulness of financial reporting information where decision usefulness keeps the middle between the relevance and reliability principle in accounting. Supporters of fair value argue that fair values are more useful for decision makers than historical cost accounting, and a long list of academic research supports this claim. Refer to the section entitled 'Fair Value Assets in Practice: Large Sample Evidence' where this topic is discussed in more detail.
6　All numbers refer to the fiscal year 2015 unless mentioned otherwise.
7　These proportions for HSBC are similar to those reported by Livne et al. (2013) for a large sample of over 1,200 bank observations.
8　All data are retrieved from Compustat. Level 1/2/3 data are available as of 2008, since SFAS 157, the relevant standard under U.S. GAAP, became effective for fiscal periods after November 15, 2007.

References

Badertscher, B, Burks, J & Easton, P 2012, "A convenient scapegoat: fair value accounting by commercial Banks during the financial crisis", *The Accounting Review* vol. 87 no. 1, pp. 59–90.

Bisschof, J, Daske, H & Sextroh, C 2017, "Why did politicians intervene in the fair value debate? The role of ideology and special interests", Working Paper Mannheim University. 78 pages.

Blankespoor, E, Linsmeier, T, Petroni, K & Shakespeare, C 2011, "Fair value accounting for financial instruments: does it improve the association between bank leverage and credit risk?", *The Accounting Review* vol. 88, no. 4, pp. 1143–1177.

Cheng, K 2012, "Accounting discretion and fair value reporting: a study of US Banks' fair value reporting of mortgage-backed-securities", *Journal of Business Finance & Accounting*, vol. 39, nos. 5 and 6, pp. 531–566, June/July.

Chung, B, Goh, W, Ng, J & Yong, KO 2017, "Voluntary fair value disclosures beyond SFAS 157's three-level estimates. Forthcoming in *Review of Accounting Studies* vol. 22, no. 1, 430–468.

Fiechter, P 2011, "The effects of the fair value option under IAS 39 on the volatility of bank earnings", *Journal of International Accounting Research* vol. 10, no. 1, pp. 85–108.

Kolev, K 2009, "Do investors perceive marking-to-model as marking-to-myth? Early evidence from FAS 157 disclosure", Working paper.

Laux, C & Leuz, C 2010, "Did fair value accounting contribute to the financial crisis?", *Journal of Economic Perspectives*, vol. 24, no. 1, pp. 93–118.

Livne, G, Markarian, G, & Mironov, M 2013, "Investment horizon, risk, and compensation in the banking industry", *Journal of Banking and Finance* vol. 37, no. 9, pp. 3669–3680.

Magnan, M, Menini, A & Parbonetti, A 2015, "Fair value accounting: information or confusion for financial markets?", *Review of Accounting Studies* vol. 20, no. 1, pp. 559–591.

Plantin, G, Sapra, H & Shin, HS 2008, "Marking-to-market: panacea or Pandora's box?", Journal of Accounting Research, vol. 46, pp. 435–460.

Plumlee, M, Shakespeare, C & Lombardi Yohn, T 2017, "The impact of IFRS 13 on the comparability of fair values in financial reporting", Working Paper University of Michigan. 58 pages.

Riedl, EJ & Serafeim, G 2011, "Information risk and fair value: an examination of equity betas and bid-ask spreads", *Journal of Accounting Research*, vol. 49, pp. 1083–1122.

Song, CJ, Thomas, WB & Yi, H 2010, "Value relevance of FAS No. 157 fair value hierarchy information and the impact of corporate governance mechanisms", *The Accounting Review*, vol. 85, pp. 1375–1410.

The Economist, August 16, 2001, "Shining a light on company accounts".

8

BANK RISK MANAGEMENT – AND FAIR VALUE ACCOUNTING

Thomas A. Gilliam and Ronny K. Hofmann

Introduction

Financial institutions play an important role as an essential intermediary in the monetary system. From a macroeconomic perspective, we can view banks as the lifeblood of any economy as they provide funds, in the form of loans, to individuals and corporations. With these funds, firms invest in assets such as property, plant and equipment in order to generate a reasonable rate of return.[1] In addition to commercial banks, investment banks also participate in capital markets. In comparison to commercial banks, which manage cash deposit accounts, investment banks facilitate transactions that involve shares, bonds and derivatives as well as other investment vehicles. They also provide advice and other support to firms during initial public offerings as well as during seasoned equity offerings. Investors, creditors and regulators perceive the business model of investment banks as more risky than the regular deposit business of commercial banks. This is partly due to the volatile nature of the value of traded financial products. Although commercial and investment banks differ significantly with respect to their business models, this chapter addresses topics of equal importance to both types of banks.

In general, the business models of both commercial banks and investment banks are vulnerable to a variety of financial risks. Some of the most prominent exposures include interest rate risk, credit risk, operational risk, currency risk and liquidity risk. Although banks focus their asset and liability management skills on exploiting these market-inherent risks, they also need to hedge their risk exposures. A one-side approach that ignores risk exposures jeopardizes a bank's creditworthiness. In addition, as seen in the recent financial crisis, when a single bank fails, it can have ramifications across the banking industry. A contagion in the global banking sector could lead to instability and defaults of individual financial institutions that eventually spill over to the economy as a whole.

Interestingly, the objectives of regulatory oversight bodies and accounting standard-setters differ. Bank regulators set risk limits in the form of asset to equity ratios and other measures. The regulators also perform onsite audits and test asset quality. These actions are aimed at preventing banks from assuming excess risk that in turn could lead to failure. However, many market-related risks can be beyond the manager's control, so they build in an equity cushion. Bank executives are keenly aware of these restrictions and must adhere to them. In contrast, investors demand profits. The focus of accounting is to provide investors with information that is useful in allocating their investment dollars. Therefore, bank managers must balance the goal to maximize profits and minimize risk to a level that meets regulatory requirements. Fair value accounting requirements can add ambiguity to the decision-making process.[2]

International accounting rules also demand information about all major types of risks. The corresponding set of rules, International Financial Reporting Standard (IFRS) 7, which is applicable to both financial and non-financial institutions, mandates the disclosures with respect to financial instruments. These rules require financial institutions to provide both quantitative and qualitative information to support balance sheet and incomer statement figures, but they also need to provide insights on how management measures and mitigates risk exposures. IFRS 7 Paragraph 30 states:

> An entity shall disclose information that enables users of its financial statements to evaluate the nature and extent of risks arising from financial instruments to which the entity is exposed at the end of the reporting period.
>
> *(IFRS 7.30)*

With regard to risk disclosures, IFRS 7 requires information on market risks including interest rates exposures, credit risk and liquidity risk, and exchange rate risks by class of financial instrument. Besides the risk disclosure regime under international accounting rules, regulatory oversight bodies also demand, among other things, a detailed risk reporting. The Basel Committee on Bank Supervision for example provides uniform rules on minimum capital requirement and disclosures that inform about the capital adequacy of financial institutions.[3] From the perspective of their financial statements, both commercial and investment banks differ significantly from organizations involved in manufacturing or other industrial operations. In general, commercial banks advance the funds they receive from customer deposits to borrowers and in turn earn a profit on the spread between the interest they pay to depositors and the interest they receive from borrowers. Hence, typical borrowers recognize the received funds as a liability they must repay in the future. On the other hand, the banks recognize the loans they advance to their customers as assets they will collect in the future. In a simplistic way, we can look at the balance sheet of a financial institution as being just the mirror image to the one from a manufacturing corporation that borrows funds. However, this is not the only difference.

The balance sheet items of a bank are on average more complex than the typical manufacturing business. Complexity in this context refers to not only the nature of the assets and liabilities but also to the measurement difficulties that often arise. Financial products that are difficult to recognize and measure make up a large portion of the assets of a bank's balance sheet. For example, Deutsche Bank reported in its 2015 annual report the following assets: Financial assets at fair value through profit or loss, financial assets available for sale, equity method investments and loans. Financial institutions measure most of their assets at fair value.[4]

For manufacturing corporations, asset values often follow a cost allocation process (IAS 16 Property, Plant and Equipment), and thus, fair values can easily be determined.[5] In contrast, the accounting standards that prescribe the recognition and measurement of most assets held in a bank's balance sheet are reflected in IFRS 9 (IAS39), IFRS 7 and IAS 32. The rules in these standards are widely regarded as more complex than the rules in other standards that, for example, prescribing leases, inventory and business combination accounting.[6] For those reasons, regulators and others heavily criticized the accounting rules for financial instruments during the recent global financial crisis (GFC 2007–2009). For example, in a recent Financial Times article:[7]

> In good times, [these accounting rules] allowed the banks to mark ever more assets to market and book the profits that emerged—even if these were unrealized. Bad times brought the opposite incentive: banks squirrelled assets away into loan books. That allowed them to avoid realizing ugly losses or accounting for the higher risk that they might occur.

In this chapter, we discuss and highlight the importance of accounting rules for banks. In this context, we also discuss asset and liability risk management strategies for banks.[8] In particular, we explore the fair value accounting issues faced by financial institutions, the interdependency of bank risk and the value relevance of fair value gains/losses. We also cover dynamic loan loss provisioning, hedge accounting and embedded derivatives separation, as well as the need for regulatory disclosures that complement mandatory accounting rules such as IFRS and US Generally Accepted Accounting Principles (US GAAP). Finally, in the last section of this chapter we provide examples on how financial institutions address the mandatory disclosures requirements of both standard-setters and bank regulators.

Bank risk management – academic evidence and insights from practice

The preponderance of research in the banking sector focuses on understanding how managers exercise their discretion when reporting their firm's financial position and its performance. Lobo (2017) identifies four areas where managers use their discretion to manage or manipulate their financial reports: signaling, capital management, smoothing and risk taking. Signaling refers to situations in which managers enhance their institutions reported financial performance and its creditworthiness. Managers can accomplish these objectives through altering loan loss provisions to show the institution's capability of taking unexpected future losses in a more favorable light (Lobo & Yang 2001). Research in capital management investigates whether managers purposely alter loan loss provisions to fulfil minimum capital requirements set by banking sector oversight bodies (Lobo & Yang 2001). Their study concludes that managers do engage in these activities. Smoothing refers to incentives to manage net income by altering provisions that produces smooth predictable reported results when the actual underlying results suggest volatility. Toward this end, managers can inflate loan loss provisions to lower net income and save the excess provision for a rainy day when the need arises to report inflated profits. Similarly, managers can also use their discretion to alter loan loss provisions for risk management purposes (Lobo 2017). Beatty and Liao (2014) also discuss incentives behind research in the banking sector. In their in depth review, they refer to information asymmetry, delegated monitoring and equity capital and contrast bank regulation with debt contracting. For readers who desire a greater understanding of this line of research we recommend reading the Beatty and Liao (2014) study.

However, we caution that as former practitioners we view managerial manipulation of loan loss provisions as a more challenging task than these studies suggest. Managers who would intentionally manipulate loan loss provisions to meet their reporting objectives face steep challenges. The measurement of loan loss provisions follows strict and detailed procedures that firms must stipulate with their risk management documentation and procedures. Both the content of these procedures and compliance with them are subject to scrutiny. Both external auditors and bank regulatory units monitor all changes in assumptions and reasons for changing loan loss provisions. If loan loss provisions have been too high or low in preceding periods, banks must recalibrate their models and algorithms when assessing future provisions.

Another strand of bank-related risk management research focuses on bank regulatory metrics such as value-at-risk (Jorion, 1997, 2007). Value-at-risk measures the expected portfolio loss with a specified probability over a specified window (Linsmeier & Pearson 2000).[9,10] Although widely used by financial institutions, value-at-risk disclosures rely heavily on assumptions such as the statistical distribution of potential future values of market factors that need to be identified ex ante. Additionally, banks may choose between three different ways for measuring value-at-risk: historical simulations, the delta-normal method and Monte Carlo simulations. Jorion (2002) investigate whether the value-at-risk metric provides value-relevant information to investors and analysts. His results suggest that value-at-risk disclosures provide value-relevant information that investors can use to forecast an entities' trading revenues. Hence, investors may be able to evaluate the risks inherent in banks' trading portfolios.

From a practitioner point of view, managers do have the ability to fudge the underlying assumptions and to make self-serving alterations to the methods used for determining value-at-risk. The complexing of their models coupled with the simple fact that future events are unknown facilitate the insertion of managerial judgment. These attributes also make it difficult for auditors to challenge with any measure of confidence. Further, as former practitioners and current investors, value-at-risk disclosures seem to provide limited usefulness for predicting share price movements and returns.

Financial institutions and fair value accounting: a brief overview

Financial institutions make use of fair value accounting far more than manufacturing and service sector firms do. The Securities and Exchange Commission (SEC) reported that, on average, banks measure 31% of the assets reported on a bank balance sheet at fair value (Pozen 2009).[11] Under fair value accounting, banks record both assets and liabilities at current market values.

At first glance, fair values may lead investors and other stakeholders to believe the information about the value of a specific asset or liability is more precise. Nevertheless, IFRS 13 applies:

> ...to IFRS that require or permit fair value measurements or disclosures and provides a single IFRS framework for measuring fair value and requires disclosures about fair value measurement. The standard defines fair value on the basis of an 'exit price' notion and uses a 'fair value hierarchy', which results in a market-based, rather than entity-specific, measurement.[12]

Although IFRS 13 refers to an exit price, fair values can be determined through different valuation techniques that can be appropriate under specific circumstances and when sufficient data are available to measure fair value (IFRS 13 Paragraph 61).[13] Furthermore, IFRS 13 does not prescribe specific valuation techniques unless there is a quoted price in an active market (IFRS 13 Paragraph 63). Therefore, banks, with some types of assets included on their balance sheet, have discretion to choose favorable valuation techniques; among these techniques are quoted prices in an exchange market, depreciated replacement cost method, present value techniques, Black-Scholes-Merton model and multiples.

Depending on the valuation model used, discount rates determined and time horizon applied, banks are able to 'manage' the measurement of asset and liability values with some discretion or bias. Thus, the bank's investors and other stakeholders can fall prey to creative accounting. The sheer number of financial instruments coupled with the complexity and the number of the assumptions that institutions employ in their valuation models make it very difficult for auditors to verify values. Furthermore, if this type of manipulation is difficult for auditors to detect, it is all but impossible for financial analysts and regular investors to detect.

The rules governing fair value accounting for liabilities can present even more challenges than the rules for assets. As with assets, financial institutions are the main players that use fair values to measure liabilities. There are two reasons for this situation. First, for risk management purposes, banks fair value the hedged item, for example, a liability denominated in USD, and fair value the corresponding hedging instrument, using a forward contract on EUR/USD exchange rate. Since both financial instruments are fair valued, they offset movements with respect to the exchange rates. The financial institutions achieve hedging since both exchange rate movements offset each other and the income statement reflects this offsetting. Hence, through fair valuing liabilities, the financial statements report smoother income. Second, in comparison to corporations, banks are the market participants who are able to set fair values for liabilities, as this is part of their business model.

When banks hold trading securities that increase in price, they recognize the price increases through their income statement as unrealized gains.[14] Although these 'paper' gains represent hypothetical transactions, they increase the current period's income and, therefore, affect some financial performance ratios such as income quality or return on assets (ROA). The effects of fair value accounting for liabilities can be less intuitive. If the creditworthiness of a financial institution is impaired, then the probability of it paying back the full amount (principal) of its debt decreases. Therefore, the fair value of the liability also decreases, which in turn leads to reporting a gain on the income statement. To be clear, all else being equal, banks with impaired creditworthiness show higher net income and appear stronger simply because of their decline. Likewise, if the institution's credit worthiness improves, they record a loss. Financial institutions report gains when their creditworthiness declines and losses as it improves.

During the most recent global financial crisis, some analysts failed to understand these counterintuitive accounting rules. As a result, the stronger than expected financial results reported by some institutions with impaired credit ratings caught financial analysts by surprise. Part of the misleading nature of financial reporting for financial institutions during the crisis was a direct result of fair value accounting for liabilities.

If financial institutions reported their liabilities at historical costs, they would not record unrealized gains in situations where the firms' financial health is impaired. However, the use of historical cost would lead to other unintended consequences that could affect the credibility of reported income statement numbers. For example, if a bank that recognizes a liability denominated in USD at historical cost, hedges the foreign currency risk using forward or futures contracts, they would recognize the fair value changes in the derivative's value, but they would not record offsetting movements of the underlying liability that would continue to be valued at historical costs.

Even when financial institutions follow sound risk management strategies to reduce volatile financial performance, historical cost accounting can undermine their efforts by introducing more reporting volatility. No matter how successful a bank's actual risk reduction activities may be, historical cost accounting does not properly reflect these activities. Investors can consider the increased income volatility as risky although the bank 'de facto' reduces risk through the hedges associated with exchange rate fluctuations. In those instances, financial institutions can apply hedge accounting procedures: Fair value hedges, cash flow hedges and hedges of net investments in foreign operations.

Hedging and hedge accounting – a financial institution perspective

Hedging is a risk management strategy with the aim of limiting or offsetting losses from unexpected movements in prices, interest rates or exchange rates. Often, banks offset the volatility in prices with hedging instruments. Hedging instruments are often derivatives, such as forward and future contracts, interest rate swaps, currency swaps, options and credit default swaps.[15] By measuring both the hedged item and the hedging instrument at fair value through the income statement, an effective hedge relationship reduces income statement volatility. Nevertheless, IFRS and US GAAP follow the so-called mixed measurement model, where the balance sheet measures some items on at cost, some at historical costs and others at fair value. Consequently, a hedge relationship will not be effective if the measurement basis for the hedged item and the derivative differ. Even if management uses proper risk management strategies, in a case where the measurement basis differs, the income statement will reflect artificial volatility. So banks need accounting rules that provide the true and fair view to investors and other stakeholders. IFRS 9 introduces such a hedge accounting model and according to the International Accounting Standards Board (IASB) the aim is to

> more closely align accounting for hedging activities with a company's risk management strategies, and provides improved information about those strategies. Not all risk management activities are reflected in the financial statements through hedge accounting. The risk management activities represented by hedge accounting are those risks that management chooses to manage with financial instruments such as derivatives, and for which they elect to use hedge accounting.
>
> *(IASB – Investor Relations 2014)*

Both IFRS and US GAAP require fair value accounting through the income statement for stand-alone derivatives. Banks often use derivatives to mitigate unexpected price movements in the hedged item and they do not report the hedged items at fair value but the accounting for the hedging instruments deviates from the measurement basis of the hedged item. In the case of financial institutions, the hedged item can be measured at amortized costs (held-to-maturity investments), at fair value with changes in fair value recycled in other comprehensive income (OCI) (available-for-sale investments) or at (historical) costs (financial liabilities). Thus, the lack of synchronization with the timing of gains and losses between the hedged item and the hedging instrument introduces volatility into the income statement. Through fair value hedges, cash flow hedges and hedges of net investments in foreign operations, the timing and mismatch between price movements of the hedged item and hedging instrument gets eliminated, which ultimately reduces volatility in the income statement.

IFRS 9 does not require financial institutions as well as other corporations apply hedge accounting procedures, so they are free to adopt hedge accounting procedures voluntarily. IFRS 9 (6.1.3) states:

> An entity may choose to designate a hedging relationship between a hedging instrument and a hedged item.

In doing so, they need to compare the costs (disadvantages) with benefits (advantages) associated with the application of hedge accounting. Costs associated with hedge accounting relate to the formal designation and required documentation that is needed ex-ante to establishing the hedge relationship. Furthermore, the new standard IFRS 9, in contrast to IAS 39, also requires an elaboration on the sources of ineffectiveness, for example the financial institution's disclosure of the hedge ratio. In addition, firms have to provide information on the economic relationship between the hedged item and the hedging instrument. Managers need close monitoring of this relationship as it changes over time, to ensure the movements in the hedging instrument effectively offset movements in the hedged item.

With fair value hedges, it is the change in the fair value of a recognized asset or liability or an unrecognized firm commitment that banks hedge. The future change in fair value can represent a particular risk such as interest rate risk that affects the prices of the hedged item. This particular risk brings both price changes of the hedged item and the hedging instrument that the income statement combines, and should effectively offset each other. With unrecognized firm commitments, a bank records fair value adjustments for a particular risk although the hedged item is not yet recognized on the balance sheet. Again, such a fair value hedge achieves an offsetting affect in the income statement as the income statement recognizes both the hedged item and the portion that relates to the hedged risk and the hedging instrument in the same period.

In addition to fair value hedges, a financial institution can also designate so-called cash flow hedges. Instead of the volatility in fair values, the risk in a cash flow hedge relationship stems from the variability in cash flows. This situation is similar to fair value hedges on the variability in cash flows attributable to a specific risk, for example, interest rate risk. The hedged item in a cash flow hedge can be a recognized asset or liability, unrecognized firm commitment, or a highly probable forecast transaction. In a cash flow hedge, the fair value gains and losses on the hedging instrument that are effectively used to hedge the variability of the cash flows in the hedged item are booked into equity (cash flow hedge reserve). Therefore, this portion does not lead to volatility in the income statement. Rather, the overall equity will fluctuate through the effective portion in a cash flow hedge. Nevertheless, the bank recognizes the ineffective portion in the income statement. If the hedged item is a forecast transaction, the income statement recognizes the cumulative gain or loss that was recycled in equity at the time the forecast transaction resulted in the recognition of a financial asset or liability.

In contrast to fair value hedges, 'under-hedging' cannot occur with cash flow hedges. Ineffectiveness in a cash flow hedge cannot result from cumulative changes in the hedging instrument if these changes are less than the fair value changes of the expected cash flows of the hedged item.

Financial institutions that operate subsidiaries, affiliates and/or foreign operations use net investments in foreign operations.[16] The purpose of net investment hedges is to mitigate currency risk when translating net assets of foreign operations into the holding company's functional currency.[17] In order to mitigate a mismatch in the income statement, the balance sheet recognizes the foreign currency gains and losses on the hedging instrument directly in equity through OCI. Consequently, the bank records the exchange rate differences of the net investment and the hedging instrument together by 'parking' them in OCI until the institution disposes of the investment. When the institution disposes of the investment, it transfers the gains and losses from OCI to the income statement.

Institutions must also take into account the effectiveness of their hedges. IFRS 9 requires that the economic relationship between the hedged item and the hedging instrument not be impaired due to credit risk with either one.[18] Drastic changes in credit risk may lead to a large portion of the hedge relationship becoming ineffective. A bank manager could face negative consequences such as increases in income statement volatility that could result in the failure to meet specific benchmark ratios. Further, infusion of new capital through creditors and investors might prove impossible or bring about higher financing costs.

Dynamic risk management – macro hedging

Financial institutions price many financial assets and liabilities at fair value. Through level 1 and level 2 inputs, book values depend on market movements, such as interest rates and commodity prices. Therefore, market fluctuations appear on the balance sheet and the income statement of banks in a more prominent way in comparison to industrial companies. Due to this volatile nature of the financial industry's business, financial institutions use derivative contracts and hedging more often than firms in other industries do.

In 2014, Steve Cooper, a member of the IASB, discussed an accounting approach for dynamic risk management especially for financial institutions:[19]

> Dynamic management of interest rate risk is a critical component of a bank's ongoing risk management activities, and the fair value measurement of derivatives and the cost-based measurement of bank loans and deposits do not sit well together when the objective of holding those derivatives is to manage the interest rate risks (fluctuations in net interest income) of that business activity.

As mentioned earlier, some items on a bank's balance sheet are measured at fair value while others are measured with amortized costs. If banks hedge interest rate exposure with the use of derivatives, the different measurement approaches mandated under IFRS and US GAAP would not reflect the true and fair view of the transactions in the bank's financial statements and would not align with its internal risk management strategies. To improve hedge accounting rules, a 'potential new method of accounting for dynamic risk management' referred to as the Portfolio Revaluation Approach (PRA) has been proposed (IFRS – dynamic risk management – accounting in an age of complexity 2014). This approach is well suited for banks to manage a complete portfolio of loans and deposits and to re-evaluate them on a particular risk that derivative can mitigate. The income statement reports the risk-adjusted revaluation of the loan portfolio along with changes in value of the hedging instruments. Hence, this method helps mitigate income statement volatility, because the movements of the risk-adjusted revaluation of the portfolio and the price movements of the hedging instrument should offset each other.

Dynamic loan loss provisioning

Regulations require commercial banks to book loss reserves when they issue loans to their clients. As clients repay their loans, the loan loss reserves decrease. As they issue loans, they increase their reserves and as they collect the loans, they decrease their reserves. In theory, their reserves should cover losses that arise from a deteriorating loan portfolio. From a true and fair view perspective, loan loss reserves should be an adequate measure to reflect and cover potential losses in the loan portfolio.[20] Nevertheless, the accounting for deteriorating loan portfolios has been problematic. In the past, financial institutions exerted discretion when estimating amounts for their loan loss reserves or allowances. To the extent that the loan loss reserve is larger than their realized credit losses, the bank will be able to absorb more unexpected losses. On the other hand, if the estimated loan loss reserve is insufficient to cover realized losses, the bank's equity capital will deteriorate.[21] Furthermore, from a broader perspective, unreserved loan losses can pose a threat to the stability of the banking system.

In the past, IAS 39 required the use of a so-called incurred loan loss model. During the recent crisis, the incurred loan-loss model was criticized for delaying the recognition of credit losses and therefore delaying the dissemination of essential information about the financial health of the financial institutions. In too many cases, investors, regulators and other stakeholders grasped the truth about the bank's financial health after it was too late to take corrective action. The impairment rules mandated in IAS 39 create one reason for this situation. Under IAS 39, banks do not recognize credit losses until a specific credit loss occurs. This standard defines credit losses as follows:

A financial asset or a group of financial assets is impaired and impairment losses are incurred if, and only if, there is objective evidence of impairment as a result of one or more events that occurred after the initial recognition of the asset (a 'loss event') and that loss event (or events) has an impact on the estimated future cash flows of the financial asset or group of financial assets that can be reliably estimated. It may not be possible to identify a single, discrete event that caused the impairment. Rather the combined effect of several events may have caused the impairment. Losses expected as a result of future events, no matter how likely, are not recognized. Objective evidence that a financial asset or group of assets is impaired includes observable data that comes to the attention of the holder of the asset about the following loss events:

a   significant financial difficulty of the issuer or obligor;
b   a breach of contract, such as a default or delinquency in interest or principal payments;
c   the lender, for economic or legal reasons relating to the borrower's financial diffi-culty, granting to the borrower a concession that the lender would not otherwise consider;
d   it becoming probable that the borrower will enter bankruptcy or other financial reorganization;
e   the disappearance of an active market for that financial asset because of financial difficulties; or
f   observable data indicating that there is a measurable decrease in the estimated fu-ture cash flows from a group of financial assets since the initial recognition of those assets, although the decrease cannot yet be identified with the individual financial assets in the group.

[IAS 39 Paragraph 59]

Requiring lenders to wait until objective evidence of a credit loss occurrence can increase the credibility of the loss recognition because lenders cannot increase loss recognition by being overly conservative with their loan portfolio impairments estimates. Financial institutions may overestimate loan losses to create hidden reserves or 'cookie jars' that they can release in future times of turmoil in order to provide an enhanced picture of the financial performance and condition of the bank. Loan losses are directly booked in the income statement and reduce net income. Excessive conservatism in accounting also reduces the true and fair view and can distort forecasting accuracy of future earnings that often rely on historical accounting data. On the other hand, with conservatism, the overall stability of the financial system may be strengthened.

Through financial instruments and derivatives, banking institutions are interwoven and in-terdependent. As we have seen with the financial crisis, the default or even the potential default of just one major financial institution poses a threat to the entire global banking system. Banks could help prevent this contagion effect if they put into place more conservative accounting treatments to cover their exposure to future credit losses. By creating strong reserves when business is robust and when banks are making loans they make themselves stronger and better prepared to deal with a potential crisis – one that could very likely be beyond their control.

To overcome shortcomings of the incurred loan loss model, the IASB put forth a new model that it incorporated in the new standard – IFRS 9: Recognition and Measurement of Financial Instruments. In 2009, the IASB published an exposure draft called 'Financial Instruments: Amortized Cost and Impairment' that discusses an impairment model for fi-nancial instruments using amortized costs. The major change is its focus on expected losses rather than on incurred losses. If financial institutions record credit losses as they anticipate them, the income statement will report a more timely loss recognition and provide investors and other stakeholders with information about future potential losses.

Managing risks using the incurred loss model versus expected loss model

During the global financial crisis, standard-setters, regulators and investors grew concern about the precision and credibility of the disclosed loan impairments and reserves provided in the financial statements. IAS 39 mandated institutions to report loan losses applying the incurred loss model as briefly described above. Recall, with the incurred loss model, write-downs in the loan portfolio only occur when compelling evidence of an impairment exists. These rules prohibit institutions from exercising their managerial judgment, experience or discretion to record expected loan losses. On the other hand, by including expected losses in the impairment decision process, financial institutions can improve the reliability and timeliness of the information disclosed in the annual financial statements. For example, if management knows from experience that their borrowers will likely default on 5% of all loans they advance, they could provide the financial statement users with better information by recognizing a 5% loss at the time the loan funds are advanced. Certainly, the financial institutions take into account expected losses when pricing their loan packages. They use this information for their own internal decision-making but accounting rules prevent them from reporting the information to their investors. On the contrary, uncertainty stemming from the expect loss model may motivate managers to exert some discretion to artificially decrease or increase the impairments by being more or less conservative in their estimations. From a bank regulator view, an advantage of the use of the expected loss model during the GFC would have been that 'earlier recognition of loan losses could have potentially reduced the cyclical moves' at that time (EFRAG/FEE – Impairment of Financial Assets: The Expected Loss Model 2009). During the crisis, many observers blamed accounting practices for making the financial markets even more inactive and unstable as bad news reported in the financial statements on a piecemeal basis increased investor anxiety and reduced confidence in the markets even more.

The expected loss model embedded in IFRS 9 adjusts the objectives of the incurred loss model formerly included in IAS 39:

> The objective of the impairment requirements is to recognize lifetime expected credit losses for all financial instruments for which there have been significant increases in credit risk since initial recognition—whether assessed on an individual or collective basis—considering all reasonable and supportable information, including that which is forward-looking.
>
> *IFRS 9 Paragraph 5 (5.5.4)*

Expected credit losses will have an impact on the overall net income reported in the annual report. After the bank records the initial expected loss at the time they make the loan, the determination of significant increases in credit risk requires a comparison of the risk of a default at inception with the change in default risk at the reporting date. This task is inherently difficult and once done can be subject to debate. Managers can estimate the outcomes of future events but they cannot know the outcomes of future events. Nonetheless, managers can use forward-looking information to assess potential credit losses in a manner that indicates the bank should adjust the credit loss reserves in a favorable way. However, different information might indicate that the bank should adjust credit loss reserves in an unfavorable way. With a strategic choice of which information set to use for its credit loss assessment, the accounting adjustment can be subject to opportunistic manipulation. Therefore, auditors need to assess the economic environment of all related financial institutions as they monitor the credit risk movements in the loan portfolio. However, supplying more timely information about future credit risks brings costs. In addition to the challenges brought by uncertainty, a move from the incurred loss model to the expected loss model requires additional resources for both the financial institutions and the auditors.

With respect to the measurement of the credit losses, the IFRS 9 states:

> An entity shall measure expected credit losses of a financial instrument in a way that reflects:
> a   an unbiased and probability-weighted amount that is determined by evaluating a range of possible outcomes;
> b   the time value of money; and
> c   reasonable and supportable information that is available without undue cost or effort at the reporting date about past events, current conditions and forecasts of future economic conditions.
>
> *IFRS 9 Paragraph 5 (5.5.17)*

As we have seen, managers exert discretion when measuring credit risk changes. Initially, managers must specify the model for assessing credit risk losses. A decision needs to be made whether the focus is on 'specific idiosyncratic risk margins assumed by and priced in by credit institutions' or on 'expected cash flow fallouts at a homogeneous portfolio level, with or without instrument reclassifications among such portfolios' (*EFRAG/FEE 2009*). Therefore, the method for assessing credit risk losses may have an indirect impact on the overall performance of an institution. Investors may not make optimal resource allocation decisions when the evaluated firms use different approaches for credit risk assessment of their loan portfolio. Furthermore, the accounting and regulatory (Basel II) calculations of expected losses differ. Basel II requires one-year ahead information for the expected loss calculation whereas the expected loss model embedded in IFRS 9 requires information for the financial instrument up to maturity (*EFRAG/FEE 2009*).

Overall, the ISAB designed the expected loss model to provide more relevant and timely information to investors about potential credit losses. Banks report potential losses in the individual and homogenous portfolios 'earlier' under the expected loss model than they would under the incurred loss model. Nevertheless, the expected loss model requires additional human resources, information and models from the preparers who in turn must weigh costs and benefits of this new approach. Additionally, the introduction of managerial judgment with the expected loss model requires investors carefully compare the different approaches and information used in the calculation of the credit losses. Otherwise, an analysis of the performance of the loan portfolios of different financial institutions could lead to misleading conclusions.

Risk management and embedded derivatives

Financial Institutions routinely use derivative contracts to mitigate risk exposures as well as to speculate on a specific underlying index such as interest rates and betting that the index moves in the predicted direction.[22] If the derivative contract is freestanding, it is reported at fair value and changes to the fair value are directly booked into the income statement. If the derivative contract is used as hedging instrument, hedge accounting rules apply for the recognition and measurement of the derivative. Banks need to be aware of the accounting treatment these contracts cause as this may have adverse impacts on key financial ratios that are based on the balance sheet and income statement figures.

Besides freestanding derivatives and derivatives in a hedging relationship, these contracts can also be embedded into other financial and non-financial contracts. An embedded derivative is a component of a hybrid contract that also includes a non-derivative host contract – with the effect that some of the cash flows of the combined instrument vary in a way similar to a stand-alone derivative (IFRS 9 Paragraph 4.3). Embedded derivatives alter the cash flows of the host contract due to specific underlying metrics such as interest rates, financial instrument prices, commodity prices and foreign exchange rates. IAS 39 requires financial institutions to identify instruments that contain embedded derivatives, determine whether each embedded derivative is one that must be separated from the host instrument or one for which separation is prohibited, and if the embedded derivative is one that must be separated, determine its fair value. Banks, auditors and investors consider these rules overly complex and insufficient to support investors to assessments of the institutions financial well-being.

To address these issues IFRS 9 omits requirements that often led to an unfavorable cost-benefit analysis. For example, in contrast to IFRS 9, a hybrid financial asset that is measured now at FVTPL (fair value through the profit or loss statement) may previously have been separated into host contract and embedded derivative. In contrast to hybrid financial assets, hybrid financial liabilities are treated similar to IAS 39. If the derivative component is not closely related to the host contract, both IAS 39 and IFRS 9 demand separation. Overall, IFRS 9 requires the following:

> If a hybrid contract contains a host that is not an asset within the scope of this Standard, an embedded derivative shall be separated from the host and accounted for as a derivative under this Standard if, and only if:
>
> a   the economic characteristics and risks of the embedded derivative are not closely related to the economic characteristics and risks of the host,
>
> b   a separate instrument with the same terms as the embedded derivative would meet the definition of a derivative and
>
> c   the hybrid contract is not measured at fair value with changes in fair value recognized in profit or loss (i.e. a derivative that is embedded in a financial liability at fair value through profit or loss is not separated).
>
> *IFRS 9 Paragraph 4.3.3*

In the case of the separation of the host contract and derivative, the bank will account for the host contract in accordance with the appropriate standards. They will recognize the derivative at FVTPL. If the separation of the host contract and derivative were not mandated, the embedded derivative would alter the value of the whole instrument and investors could not comprehend the drivers of the value changes.

Disclosures of risk management practices

Financial statements provide useful information to assist actual and potential investors make capital allocation decisions.[23] Financial statements also help bring about a common view of the bank's financial condition and risk management practices, that actual and potential investors and creditors find useful, which leads to a reduction in information asymmetries between the principals (bank's investors) and the agents (bank's management).[24] Managers (agents) possess inside knowledge about their firm's operational and financial prospects. On the other hand, principles (bank's investors) who provide funding require information to evaluate how well their invested funds perform. To provide an information flow from the 'more knowledgeable' participants to the 'less knowledgeable' participants, non-financial institutions are required to publish periodic financial statements that inform their principles, as well as other external stakeholders, about the firm's financial position and performance. This form of communication helps reduce the information gap between in- and outsiders. Standard-setting bodies such as the IASB or the FASB mandate uniform accounting rules to provide external stakeholders with beneficial information. For example, SFAC No. 8 (US GAAP) states the following objective of general purpose financial reporting:

> OB2. "The objective of general purpose financial reporting is to provide financial information about the reporting entity that is useful to existing and potential investors, lenders, and other creditors in making decisions about providing resources to the entity. Those decisions involve buying, selling, or holding equity and debt instruments and providing or settling loans and other forms of credit."
>
> OB3. "Decisions by existing and potential investors about buying, selling, or holding equity and debt instruments depend on the returns that they expect from an investment in those instruments; for example, dividends, principal and interest payments, or market price increases. Similarly, decisions by existing and potential lenders and other creditors about providing or settling loans and other forms of credit depend on the principal and interest payments or other returns that they expect. Investors', lenders', and other creditors' expectations about returns depend on their assessment of the amount, timing, and uncertainty of is to provide financial information about the reporting entity that is useful to existing and potential investors, lenders, and other creditors in making decisions about providing resources to the entity. Those decisions involve buying, selling, or holding equity and debt instruments and providing or settling loans and other forms of credit."
>
> *(Source: FASB SFAC No.8)*

Academic studies often examine the value relevance of financial reporting information including disclosures that firms publish in their annual reports. Researchers use statistical regression analysis to verify whether specific information signals have an impact on share and bond prices. Over the past 60 years, research has shown that market prices of debt and equity instruments react in a predictable way to new financial reporting information (e.g. Ball & Brown 1968; Beaver 1968). Besides the function of providing relevant information to external stakeholders, accounting information also fulfils the so-called stewardship function. Here the focus is on how well manager-agents use the resources that creditors and investors provide. The need for oversight notwithstanding, the firm's managers and regulators must balance investors' information needs with the needs of management to keep proprietary information out of the hands of competitors.

In contrast to industrial corporations, financial institutions not only prepare financial reports that follow accounting rules but also fulfil extensive regulatory requirements pertaining to its financial condition. Regulatory reporting also targets insights into financial institutions' risk, financial leverage and liquidity positions.

To explain bank regulation, the different purposes and audiences, Danièle Nouy, Chair of the Supervisory Board of the European Central Bank (ECB), gave the following insights in a speech at the fourth ECB conference on accounting, financial reporting and corporate governance for central banks (*2014*):[25]

> Financial reporting forms the basis for various elements of prudential regulation. To take a single example, both the CRR capital ratios and the leverage ratio largely rely on

values derived from financial reporting. Moreover, several studies suggest that financial reporting information can influence the behavior of economic agents, in particular "short-termism" in management's decision-making. During the financial crisis, at least three accounting practices were cited as potentially obscuring the actual risks of banks and providing adverse incentives to banks:

1   the excessive use of fair value accounting,
2   the delayed recognition of credit losses or impairment charges and
3   the inadequate treatment for exposures to special purpose entities (SPEs).

Overall, accounting standard-setters, such as the IASB and FASB, predominantly focus their efforts on providing external stakeholders with reliable and value-relevant information concerning a firm's financial position and performance. By contrast, bank regulators put in place rules and regulations aimed at giving banks a sufficient cushion against unexpected losses that could ruin a financial institution and could ultimately affect the financial system as a whole. Therefore, the focus of bank regulators is on maintaining capital requirements including minimum capital ratios, and corporate governance mechanisms including additional reporting and disclosure requirements.[26] Disclosures include risk management information such as risk-weighted assets, credit risk exposures, securitization, operational risk, interest rate risk, liquidity risk and many others.

Financial reporting and risk management disclosures: illustrations

This section provides an illustration on how banks report their risk exposures and how they satisfy both regulatory and financial reporting obligations. Financial intuitions reporting under either US GAAP or IFRS disclose both mandatory accounting information and bank regulation information in their audited financial statements. To illustrate we use a recent Deutsche Bank disclosure.

In its 2016 financial report, Deutsche Bank reports under the 'Basis of Accounting' section that

> ...the Risk Report includes disclosures about the nature and the extent of risks arising from financial instruments as required by IFRS 7, "Financial Instruments: Disclosures"....

With regard to the bank regulatory disclosures it is mentioned that

> In addition, with respect to the table entitled "Transitional template for regulatory capital, RWA and capital ratios" set forth in the Risk Report within the section "Risk and Capital Performance: Capital and Leverage Ratio: Development of regulatory capital", the columns captioned "CRR/CRD 4" for each of December 31, 2016 and December 31, 2015 (but not the columns captioned "CRR/CRD 4 fully loaded") are also an integral part of the Consolidated Financial Statements, notwithstanding that they are not identified by bracketing in the margins. These disclosures are also audited.

The risk report of Deutsche Bank embedded in the 2016 financial report comprises approximately 100 pages capturing the following topics: 'Risk and Capital Overview'; 'Risk and Capital Framework'; 'Risk and Capital Management' including 'Risk Identification and Assessment', 'Credit Risk Management', 'Market Risk Management', 'Operational Risk' and 'Liquidity Risk Management'; and 'Risk and Capital Performance'.

In the 'Risk and Capital Overview', Deutsche Bank discloses the key risk metrics:

> The following selected key risk ratios and corresponding metrics form part of our holistic risk management across individual risk types. The Common Equity Tier 1 Ratio (CET 1), Internal Capital Adequacy Ratio (ICA), Leverage Ratio (LR), Liquidity Coverage Ratio (LCR), and Stressed Net Liquidity Position (SNLP) serve as high level metrics and are fully integrated across strategic planning, risk appetite framework, stress testing (except LCR), and recovery and resolution planning practices, which are reviewed and approved by our Management Board at least annually. The CET 1, LR, Leverage Exposure, LCR and Risk Weighted Assets ratios and metrics, which are **regulatory** defined, are based on the fully loaded rules under the Regulation (EU) No 575/2013 on prudential requirements for credit institutions and investment firms (Capital Requirements Regulation or "CRR") and the Directive 2013/36/EU on access to the activity of credit institutions and the prudential supervision of credit institutions and investment firms (Capital Requirements Directive 4 or "CRD 4"). ICA, Economic Capital and SNLP are Deutsche Bank specific internal risk metrics in addition to the above described regulatory metrics.

Deutsche Bank also discloses in a quantitative way the 'overall risk position as measured by the economic capital usage calculated for credit, market, operational and business risk'.

With regard to credit risk management, Deutsche Bank uses a so called credit risk framework. Credit risk, according to the 2016 Deutsche bank financial report,

> arises from all transactions where actual, contingent or potential claims against any counterparty, borrower, obligor or issuer (which we refer to collectively as "counterparties") exist, including those claims that we plan to distribute. These transactions are typically part of our traditional non-trading lending activities (such as loans and contingent liabilities). Additionally, traded bonds and debt securities form part of our direct trading activity with clients (such as OTC derivatives like foreign exchange forwards and Forward Rate Agreements). Carrying values of equity investments are also disclosed in our Credit Risk section. We manage the respective positions within our market risk and credit risk frameworks.

In its market risk framework section, Deutsche Bank states that

> The vast majority of our businesses are subject to market risk, defined as the potential for change in the market value of our trading and invested positions. Risk can arise from changes in interest rates, credit spreads, foreign exchange rates, equity prices, commodity prices and other relevant parameters, such as market volatility and market implied default probabilities.

Within the market risk section, Deutsche Bank also discloses its internally developed market risk models (Value-at-Risk – VaR). These models are rather sophisticated ones, as is apparent from the risk report:

> VaR is a quantitative measure of the potential loss (in value) of Fair Value positions due to market movements that will not be exceeded in a defined period of time and with a defined confidence level.
>
> Our value-at-risk for the trading businesses is based on our own internal model. In October 1998, the German Banking Supervisory Authority (now the BaFin) approved

our internal model for calculating the regulatory market risk capital for our general and specific market risks. Since then the model has been continually refined and approval has been maintained.

In addition to these risk types, the report also contains information on foreign exchange risk, credit spread risk in the banking book, investment risk and pension risk. Other major parts of the risk report include operational risk management, liquidity risk management, business (strategic) risk management and reputational risk management.

In a separate section, impaired loans and loan loss allowances are also qualitatively and quantitatively disclosed:

Impaired Loans

Credit Risk Management regularly assesses whether there is objective evidence that a loan or group of loans is impaired. A loan or group of loans is impaired and impairment losses are incurred if:

- there is objective evidence of impairment as a result of a loss event that occurred after the initial recognition of the asset and up to the balance sheet date ("a loss event"). When making our assessment we consider information on such events that is reasonably available up to the date the financial statements are authorized for issuance in line with the requirements of IAS 10;
- the loss event had an impact on the estimated future cash flows of the financial asset or the group of financial assets; and
- a reliable estimate of the loss amount can be made.

Credit Risk Management's loss assessments are subject to regular review in collaboration with Group Finance. The results of this review are reported to and approved by Group Finance and Risk Senior Management. For further details with regard to impaired loans please refer to Note 1 "Significant Accounting Policies and Critical Accounting Estimates".

Impairment Loss and Allowance for Loan Losses

If there is evidence of impairment the impairment loss is generally calculated on the basis of discounted expected cash flows using the original effective interest rate of the loan. If the terms of a loan are renegotiated or otherwise modified because of financial difficulties of the borrower without qualifying for de-recognition of the loan, the impairment loss is measured using the original effective interest rate before modification of terms. We reduce the carrying amount of the impaired loan by the use of an allowance account and recognize the amount of the loss in the consolidated statement of income as a component of the provision for credit losses. We record increases to our allowance for loan losses as an increase of the provision for loan losses in our income statement. Charge-offs reduce our allowance while recoveries, if any, are credited to the allowance account. If we determine that we no longer require allowances which we have previously established, we decrease our allowance and record the amount as a reduction of the provision for loan losses in our income statement. When it is considered that there is no realistic prospect of recovery and all collateral has been realized or transferred to us, the loan and any associated allowance for loan losses is charged off (i.e. the loan and the related allowance for loan losses are removed from the balance sheet).

Closing remarks

Bank risk management from a financial reporting and regulatory perspective is, by its very nature, a very complex topic. The business models of banks evolve quickly, presenting preparers, standard-setters and market authorities with constant challenges. Additional challenges arise as new and fast evolving financial instruments and other innovations where the banks hedge their risk exposures or speculate in order to achieve higher returns. This chapter briefly discusses and explains risk management and accounting topics that are especially relevant for banks and shows both the obstacles and challenges that market participants face. Bank risk management requires a sound understanding of the accounting for financial instruments, including hedge accounting, accounting for embedded derivatives, fair value accounting and accounting for loan losses. Further, this understanding is required to evaluate the financial position and performance of financial institutions. In addition to the mandated accounting rules, which are especially relevant for banks, the regulatory requirements put another burden on banks.

Overall, managers are able to exert discretion when preparing the financial reports of banks. Both the financial reporting and regulatory environment require interpretation and judgment. Managers must make assumptions for their valuation models and the information that flows into their valuation models, e.g. impairing loan losses. Therefore, investors must possess the knowhow to evaluate and analyze the quantitative information embedded in bank financial reports. Investors may also require qualitative information in the risk report to compare institutions among each other and over time. For example, to compare value-at-risk metrics requires an understanding of their underlying models. Analyzing banks is far more complex, on average, than valuing industrial corporations.

Banks provide the lifeblood of modern economies. Hence, it is crucial to understand how banks operate, how they manage their assets and liabilities and how the accounting system and bank regulatory system translate their transactions into meaningful numbers. However, the rules are fluid. Following the financial crisis, standard-setters now prefer expected loan loss models. Nevertheless, this may change again in the future.

Notes

1 Assets are resources that are controlled by an entity as a result of past events and from which future economic benefits are expected to flow to the entity (IAS 38 Paragraph 8). The required rate of return is the expected annual return earned by an asset. Value generation is achieved if the actual return is above the required rate of return.
2 Examples on how financial institutions meet both regulatory and reporting requirements is addressed at the end of this chapter in the section *"Financial Reporting and Risk Management Disclosures—Illustrations"*.
3 Minimal capital requirements refers to maintaining minimum capital ratios of regulatory capital over risk-weighted assets. Capital adequacy refers to minimum reserves of capital that a bank needs to hold in order to cover unexpected losses.
4 Financial instruments at fair value through profit or loss include trading assets, positive market values from derivative financial instruments and financial assets that are designated at fair value through profit or loss.
5 IAS 16 Property, Plant and Equipment outlines the accounting treatment for most types of property, plant and equipment. Property, plant and equipment is initially measured at its cost,

subsequently measured either using a cost or revaluation model, or depreciated so that its depreciable amount is allocated on a systematic basis over its useful life.

6 IFRS 9 Financial Instruments replaces IAS 39 Financial Instruments: Recognition and Measurement. The standard includes requirements for recognition and measurement, impairment, derecognition and general hedge accounting. The version of IFRS 9 issued in 2014 supersedes all previous versions and is mandatorily effective for periods beginning on or after 1 January 2018 with early adoption permitted (subject to local endorsement requirements). For a limited period, previous versions of IFRS 9 may be adopted early if not already done so provided the relevant date of initial application is before 1 February 2015. (Source: IASplus – Website)

7 "Banks Should Not Be Able To Game Accounting Rules", (Financial Times 2015).

8 Asset Liability Management (ALM) refers to the tools of a financial institution to navigate and control the mismatch between assets and liabilities that stem from underlying risk factors such as liquidity and interest rates.

9 Value-at-Risk is a measure of portfolio market risk and introduced as a standard metric by J.P. Morgan & Company in 1994 (Risk Metrics).

10 Dr Linsmeier served as an appointed member of the Financial Accounting Standards Board (FASB) from July 2006 to June 2016.

11 The U.S. Securities and Exchange Commission (SEC) is an independent, federal government agency responsible for protecting investors, maintaining fair and orderly functioning of securities markets and facilitating capital formation.

12 IFRS 13 describes three valuation approaches (see Paragraphs B5–B33 of IFRS 13): the market approach, the income approach and the cost approach.

13 IFRS 13 differentiates fair values into quoted prices (level 1), inputs other than quoted prices (level 2) and unobservable inputs (level 3). For more detail please refer to the chapter on managers' perspective and fair values.

14 Trading securities are investments in debt or equity that are actively in order to achieve short-term profits. In comparison, Available-for-sale financial assets (AFS) are any non-derivative financial assets designated on initial recognition as available for sale or any other instruments that the institution does not classify as (a) loans and receivables, (b) held-to-maturity investments or (c) financial assets at fair value through profit or loss. [IAS 39.9].

15 A derivative is a financial instrument between two or more parties whose value is dependent upon or derived from one or more underlying assets. Underlying assets are shares, interest rates (LIBOR/ EURIBOR), and commodities. There are two types of derivatives: (1) Over-the-counter contracts (OTC) and (2) exchange-traded contracts.

16 Foreign operations refer to an entity that is a subsidiary, associate, joint venture or branch of the reporting entity. Foreign operations base or conduct their activities in a country or currency other than those of the reporting entity.

17 Functional currency is the currency of the primary economic environment in which the entity operates. (IAS 21 Paragraph 8).

18 Credit risk is the risk that one party to a financial instrument will cause a financial loss for the other party by failing to discharge an obligation. (IFRS 7.A).

19 www.ifrs.org/-/media/feature/resources-for/investors/investor-perspectives/investor-perspective-apr-2014.pdf.

20 The IASB assumes the application of IFRS, with additional disclosure when necessary, will result in a fair value presentation of in the bank's financial statements. [IAS 1 Paragraph 15].

21 For an in-depth discussion on loan loss reserves see Wall and Koch (2000).

22 Derivatives are contracts between two or more parties whose value changes based on a specific underlying financial instrument, interest rate, index, or security price. Examples of derivatives include bonds, commodities, currencies, interest rates, market indexes, and equity shares.

23 In this context investors refers to anyone who provides or considers providing a firm with capital: actual equity investors, those considering investment, lenders, and vendors who extend credit.

24 In contract theory and economics, information asymmetry refers to a situation where interacting constituencies have a different level of information. For example, managers (agents) have more knowledge about the inner workings of the firm than outside investors (principal). As shareholders do not have the time and knowledge to manage a firm, they hire agents (managers) to improve the financial position and performance (increase shareholder value). In order to minimize the information asymmetries that exist between the principal and agent, firms are required to publish audited financial reports. In other words, inside information flows to third-parties.

25 www.bankingsupervision.europa.eu/press/speeches/date/2014/html/se140603.en.html.
26 The Basel Committee on Banking Supervision provides a forum for regular cooperation on banking supervisory matters. Its objective is to enhance understanding of key supervisory issues and improve the quality of banking supervision worldwide. (Website: Bank for International Settlements – www.bis.org/bcbs/).

References

Ball, R, Brown, P, 1968, "An empirical evaluation of accounting income numbers", *Journal of Accounting Research*, vol. 6, pp. 159–178.

Beatty, A & Liao, S 2014, "Financial accounting in the banking industry: a review of the empirical literature", *Journal Accounting and Economics*, vol. 58, no. (2–3), pp. 339–383.

Beaver, WH 1968, "The information content of annual earnings announcements", *Journal of Accounting Research*, vol. 6, pp. 67–92.

Cooper, S 2014, *Dynamic risk management—accounting in an age of complexity*. Investor perspectives. International Accounting Standards Board.

Deutsche Bank 2016, *Annual Report*.

European Central Bank (ECB) 2014, *Regulatory and financial reporting essential for effective banking supervision and financial stability*. Dinner Speech – Danièle Nouy. Fourth ECB conference on accounting, financial reporting and corporate governance for central banks.

European Financial Reporting Advisory Group (EFRAG) 2009, *Impairment of financial assets: the expected loss model*. Federation of European Accountants.

Financial Accounting Standards Board (FASB) 2010, *Conceptual framework for financial reporting*. Statement of Financial Accounting Concepts No. 8.

Financial Times 2015, *Banks should not be able to game accounting rules*.

International Accounting Standards Board (IASB) 2003a, *Financial instruments: presentation*. International Accounting Standard 32.

International Accounting Standards Board (IASB) 2003b, *Financial instruments: recognition and measurement*. International Accounting Standard 39.

International Accounting Standards Board (IASB) 2003c, *Presentation of financial statements*. International Accounting Standard 1.

International Accounting Standards Board (IASB) 2003d, *Property, plant and equipment*. International Accounting Standard 16.

International Accounting Standards Board (IASB) 2003e. *The effects of changes in foreign exchange rates*. International Accounting Standard 21.

International Accounting Standards Board (IASB) 2004, *Intangible assets*. International Accounting Standard 38.

International Accounting Standards Board (IASB) 2005. *Financial instruments: disclosures*. International Financial Reporting Standard 7.

International Accounting Standards Board (IASB) 2011. *Fair value measurement*. International Financial Reporting Standard 13.

International Accounting Standards Board (IASB) 2014. *Financial instruments*. International Financial Reporting Standard 9.

Jorion, P 1997, *Value-at-risk*, Irwin, New York.

Jorion, P (2002), "How informative are value at risk disclosure?", *The Accounting Review*, vol. 77, no. 4, pp. 911–931.

Jorion, P 2007, *Value-at-risk: the benchmark for controlling market risk*, 3rd edn, McGraw-Hill, New York.

Linsmeier, TJ & Pearson, ND 2000, "Value-at-risk", *Financial Analysts Journal*, vol. 56, no. 2, pp. 47–67.

Lobo, GJ 2017, "Accounting research in banking – a review", *China Journal of Accounting Research*, vol. 10, pp. 1–7.

Lobo, GJ & Yang, DH, 2001. "Bank managers' heterogeneous decisions on discretionary loan loss provisions", *Review of Quantitative Finance and Accounting*, vol. 16, no. 3, pp. 223–250.

Pozen, RC 2009, "Is it fair to blame fair value accounting for the financial crisis?", *Harvard Business Review*, vol. 87, pp. 84–92.

Wall, L & Koch, TW 2000, "Bank loan-loss accounting: a review of theoretical and empirical evidence", *Economic Review*, vol. 85, pp. 1–19.

9

THE USE OF FAIR VALUE ACCOUNTING IN RISK MANAGEMENT IN NON-FINANCIAL FIRMS

John L. Campbell, Jenna D'Adduzio and Jon Duchac

Introduction

Risk is the primary driver of value for any business. In order for a business to be profitable and create value, it must generate returns; and returns are compensation for the risks a business takes. Successful businesses are masters at carefully and consistently balancing risk and reward; extracting the most return for risks taken while avoiding risks for which the return is insufficient. As a result, sound risk management is an essential component to business success (i.e. in their risk management activities).

Over the last two decades, derivative financial instruments have emerged as an essential risk management tool, helping companies extract the most return for the risks taken. By 'hedging' with derivatives, managers are able to avoid risks that do not generate a sufficient return and focus on those opportunities (i.e. risks) that generate the greatest potential return. The financial reporting for derivatives and hedging activities is complex because (1) the decision to enter into a derivative contract is typically driven by an existing or potential risk exposure and (2) all derivatives are recorded on the balance sheet at their fair value. In some instances, as we will discuss, these underlying characteristics can lead to counterintuitive accounting outcomes.

In this chapter, we demystify the financial reporting for derivatives and hedging activities by discussing

- The economic motivations for hedging with derivatives,
- The accounting for derivatives and hedging,
- The financial statement analysis challenges that arise when firms hedge with derivatives and
- Techniques managers can employ to help users of the financial statements better map the accounting for derivatives into firm performance and value.

To summarize, firms undertake derivatives-hedging programs for a variety of macroeconomic, firm-specific and manager-specific reasons. Specifically, firms with business models that are sensitive to price changes that are outside of management's control (e.g. commodity prices, interest rates, foreign currency exchange rates) use derivatives to offset the effects of these price changes. In addition, firms use derivatives more often when they are large, have significant growth opportunities and face financing constraints. Finally, managers use derivatives more often when they have high levels of stock options and low levels of stock holdings.

The primary benefit of effective hedging programs is that the firm can reduce its earnings and cash flow volatilities. This reduction in volatility reduces a firm's cost of capital and raises its firm value. This reduction in volatility also helps the firm forecast and plan better for the future. In other words, any costs that firms incur by engaging in hedging activities are more than offset by a host of tangible benefits in the capital markets – a lower cost of borrowing, an enhanced ability to invest in profitable investment projects, lower taxes paid and an opportunity to make more informed operational decisions about the future.

Despite these significant benefits, the accounting for derivatives induces some complexity into the financial statements. Specifically, firms record derivatives at fair value at each balance sheet date, and record changes in fair value either as part of net income or part of shareholders' equity (excluded from net income). This accounting can lead to some financial statement analysis challenges when firms hedge items that are not currently reported on their financial statements. In these specific cases (known as 'cash flow hedges'), financial statement ratios related to leverage and profitability are misleading. We show how to adjust the ratios for the implications of derivative accounting. Furthermore, the unrealized gains/losses on cash flow hedges provide a firm-specific signal about the sensitivity of the firm's profits to recent price changes in underlying items (i.e. commodities, interest rates, foreign currencies) once the existing hedge protection expires and the firm is fully exposed to these price changes. Finally, we note that investors and analysts behave as if they do not anticipate this signal, and managers can help them better understand these issues with better disclosures. Overall, we discuss how firms can best maximize the significant benefits that hedging programs provide while minimizing the costs related to added financial statement complexity via better disclosures.

To focus our analysis, we limit our discussion to small-scale hedging activities for non-financial firms. While this is only a subset of potential applications, limiting the scope in this manner provides a parsimonious framework for illustrating the financial reporting challenges associated with derivatives hedging.

Derivatives and hedging

Derivatives

In mathematical calculus, a 'derivative' is defined as the change in some variable y given a change in some other variable x (i.e. dy/dx, or $\Delta y/\Delta x$). A financial derivative works in much the same way, in that the financial derivative's value is determined by (derived from) the change in value of some other instrument, called the **underlying**. In most cases, the value of the underlying is based on an underlying market variable; such as

- Rates (interest, foreign exchange),
- Prices (stock, commodity) or
- Indices (S&P 500, Dow Jones Industrial Average).

To convert the change in the applicable rate, price or index into a dollar value, derivative contracts multiply this change in value by an agreed upon amount of the underlying, called

Table 9.1 Commonly hedged items and their notional amounts

Underlying	Notional amount denominated in:
Gold	Ounces
Oil	Barrels
Common stock	Shares of stock
S&P index	250 units
Interest rates	Any predetermined amount of a specified currency on which interest payments are based
Foreign exchange rates	Any predetermined amount of a specified currency

the **notional amount** of the contract. For example, if a derivative contract is based on oil prices, the change in the price of oil must be multiplied by an amount of oil, defined in barrels, to determine the value of the derivative. In this case, the number of barrels of oil used in the calculation is the notional amount. It is called a 'notional' amount because this amount only exists for purposes of calculating the value of the derivative. Examples of various types of underlyings and associated notional amounts are shown in Table 9.1.

While the above table provides common denominations for notional amounts, derivative contracts can be written for any notional amount the two parties to the derivative contract agree upon.

Financial derivatives can be broadly categorized into one of four types: futures, forwards, options and swaps. There are both commonalities among and differences between these four types of derivatives. The most distinct commonality is that each type of derivative has two counterparties: a buyer and a seller. The responsibilities and rights of the buyer and seller of the derivative differ, however, depending on the type of instrument. The unique characteristics of each type of derivative are briefly outlined below:

Futures: A contract that creates (1) a notional commitment, (2) to buy or sell, (3) a standard quantity of a financial instrument (notional amount), (4) at a specified point in the future, (5) at a price determined in the present (futures price). One of the key features of a futures contract is that the contract is purchased and sold on an organized exchange, which requires that the contracts have a standard contract size. In a futures contract, the buyer has the obligation to buy in the future at the futures price, and the seller is obligated to sell in the future at the futures price. Thus, it is inevitable that one party (either the buyer or the seller) to the futures contract will experience gains, while the other party will experience equal, but opposite, losses.

Forwards: Similar to a futures contract, except that it is not traded on an exchange. As a result, forward contracts typically do not have a standard contract size.

Options: A contract between two parties that gives one party (the buyer) the right, but not the obligation, to buy or sell something from the other party (the seller) at a later date, at a price agreed upon at inception. In exchange for this right, the buyer pays the seller an amount at inception called the premium. There are two types of options: (1) the right to buy (or call) something from the other party (known as a 'call option') and (2) the right to sell (or put) something to the other party (known as a 'put option').

Swaps: A contract in which two parties agree to exchange financial instruments, rates or cash flows at some point in the future. Settlement is typically made in cash for the difference in value between the instruments, rates or cash flows.

Table 9.2 Key definitions related to derivatives

Initial net investment	The amount that a counterparty must pay to enter into a derivative contract. This amount is zero for symmetrical derivatives such as interest rate swaps, futures, and forwards. Option buyers must pay a premium at inception, while option sellers receive a premium at inception.
Settlement date	The date upon which the derivative contract terminates. On this date, the counterparties make their final payment under the derivative contract, which is called the Net Settlement Amount.
Net settlement amount	Derivatives typically settle in cash, rather than by transferring the underlying item. This is the amount of cash that is paid or received on the designated settlement date.
Notional amount	The predetermined amount of the unit-of-measure that is multiplied by the change in value in order to calculate the settlement amount of a derivative contract.
Underlying	The financial instrument upon which a derivative price is based.

Thus, each type of derivative contract has a unique structure that, in turn, determines its value. The key terms associated with derivative transactions are provided in Table 9.2.

To focus our analysis, we limit our discussion to cash settled futures contracts.[1] While futures contracts are defined in terms of purchasing or selling the underlying, most futures contracts are settled in cash for the difference between market price and the predetermined price of the underlying item at the expiration date.

Hedging with derivatives

Because a financial derivative's value is based on a market rate, price, flow or event, derivatives can be used to hedge the risk arising from changes in the market price of (1) income statement items or (2) existing assets and liabilities. This is accomplished by entering into a derivative contract whose value moves in the opposite direction of the firm's existing financial risk. For example, airlines might hedge against rising jet fuel prices by entering into a futures contract to buy jet fuel at a specified price at a specified point in the future. By doing this, the value of the derivative contract moves in tandem with fuel prices, offsetting the risk associated with rising jet fuel prices.

Benefits of hedging

Companies use derivative contracts to hedge the risks related to market-wide forces that are outside of managers' control, but are an inherent part of the business. These risks can take one of two forms: cash flow volatility (i.e. the volatility associated with existing or future cash flows resulting from the firm's transactions) or fair value volatility (i.e. the volatility associated with changes in the fair value of assets or liabilities). In this chapter, we focus on cash flow volatility.

The financial risks from cash flow volatility make it difficult for a company to create and adhere to budgets, plan and implement capital expenditures and initiate strategic investments; which ultimately increases the firm's cost of borrowing. In addition, investors typically consider a firm with lower cash flow volatility to be less risky, resulting in a lower cost of capital for the firm. Financial derivatives provide managers with a tool to reduce the firm's exposure to cash flow volatility.

Table 9.3 Items commonly hedged by industry

Industry	Hedged item
Airline/transportation	Fuel, oil, natural gas
All/general	Variable rate debt
Agriculture	Corn, wheat
Construction	Copper, brass, lead, steel
Gold mining	Gold
International firms with foreign sales or purchases	Foreign currency exchange rates (e.g. Euro, Yen, Singapore Dollar, Peso, Real, etc.)
Textile manufacturer	Cotton

Cash flow volatility outside of managers' control can arise from market-wide fluctuations in commodity prices, interest rates or foreign currency exchange rates. For example, commodity price fluctuations in key production inputs can make production planning and earnings forecasting difficult, as these price fluctuations can result in significant variation in actual cash flows for the firm. Managers therefore enter into derivative contracts to offset the volatility in the prices of the commodities the firm uses in production, thereby making cash flows more predictable. Managers generally choose to hedge risks with significant exposure for the firm. That is, they enter into derivative contracts for items or transactions that make up a significant part of the business. See Table 9.3 for examples of items commonly hedged in various industries.

Determinants of derivative use

As discussed in the previous section, the main reason firms enter into derivative contracts is to reduce the cash flow volatility associated with macroeconomic risks outside of managers' control. The industry in which a firm operates plays a significant role in determining a firm's derivative usage, as certain macroeconomic volatilities impact some industries more than others. For example, firms operating in the airline industry often use derivative contracts to hedge against volatility in jet fuel (i.e. oil) prices. Accordingly, academic research finds that firms operating in the utilities and the petroleum and natural gas industries tend to have the highest frequency of cash flow hedge use (e.g. Campbell 2015; Campbell et al. 2015; Campbell et al. 2017b), as these industries have inherently volatile macroeconomic environments where many of the input or output price fluctuations these firms face are outside of individual managers' control. Furthermore, a 1995 survey by Bodnar, Hayt and Marston finds that almost one-half (49%) of its survey respondents that use derivatives are firms operating in commodity-based industries (e.g. agriculture, refining and mining). Finally, the level of competition within an industry can determine the extent a firm is able to pass price fluctuations to its customers (e.g. Allayannis & Ihrig 2001), which also determines the extent a firm hedges its exposure to certain price fluctuations.

In addition to exposure to macroeconomic volatility, firm-specific characteristics also determine derivative use. Cash flow volatility can be costly for a firm as it can force a firm to forgo valuable investment opportunities and is associated with a higher cost of capital (Minton & Schrand 1999). There are several firm characteristics that are expected to make cash flow volatility relatively more costly for a firm, and thus these characteristics are expected to be associated with derivative use. Because internal financing is less costly than external financing, firms with valuable growth opportunities are more likely to use derivatives to reduce cash flow volatility, thereby ensuring they have cash available to pursue these investment opportunities (Myers & Majluf 1984; Froot et al. 1993; Nance et al. 1993; Geczy et al. 1997).

Volatile cash flows increase a firm's likelihood of financial distress, or bankruptcy. The more costly financial distress is for a firm (i.e. the more debt the firm has in its capital structure), the more it is expected to hedge to reduce cash flow volatility and thereby reduce the likelihood of incurring financial distress costs (Smith & Stulz 1985; Nance et al. 1993; Geczy et al. 1997; Haushalter 2000). Finally, because more volatile earnings (i.e. cash flows) are associated with higher taxes, firms can use derivatives to reduce taxable income volatility and therefore reduce taxes owed (Smith & Stulz 1985; Nance et al. 1993).[2] Additionally, firms can develop strategies to achieve favorable derivative taxation treatment under the current tax code, which can further reduce taxes owed.

The extent of a firm's exposure to a specific risk is also associated with derivative use, because the larger the firm's exposure to the risk, the larger its potential loss from that risk (Geczy et al. 1997; Haushalter 2000; Allayannis & Ofek 2001). For example, Geczy et al. (1997) show that firms are more likely to use foreign currency derivatives when they have more foreign income and/or foreign currency-denominated debt. Larger firms are also more likely to use derivatives, as hedging, including preparing the documentation required to qualify for hedge accounting treatment, is costly, and larger firms are expected to have greater returns to scale (Geczy et al. 1997; Bodnar et al. 1998).

Finally, manager-level incentives (i.e. managerial risk aversion) also determine derivative use. Because a manager's wealth is tied to firm value via stock compensation, a manager is expected to hedge to the extent that hedging increases firm value (i.e. stock price). The more sensitive a manager's wealth is to changes in the firm's stock price (i.e. the delta of a manager's stock options and holding portfolio), the more the firm is expected to hedge (Smith & Stulz 1985; Tufano 1996; Knopf et al. 2002). However, the more sensitive a manager's wealth is to the firm's stock price volatility (i.e. the vega of a manager's stock options and holding portfolio), the *less* the firm is expected to hedge (Smith & Stulz 1985; Tufano 1996; Knopf et al. 2002). This is because the value of stock options increases in the volatility of the underlying stock price.

See Table 9.4 for a summary of determinants of derivative use.

Once a firm makes the decision to use derivatives, it must decide on its hedging policy. A firm's hedging policy determines which risks to hedge and *how much* of the firm's exposure

Table 9.4 Derivative determinants

Derivative determinant	Description	Academic citation
Macroeconomic volatility	Fluctuations in commodity prices, interest rates, and foreign currency exchange rates are outside of the firm's control. Exposure to these risks is largely determined by industry and can be partially mitigated through hedging.	Bodnar et al. (1995), Allayannis and Ihrig (2001), Campbell (2015), Campbell et al. (2015) and Campbell, et al. (2017b)
Investment/growth opportunities	Firms with valuable growth opportunities can use derivatives to reduce cash flow volatility, allowing them to take on positive NPV projects as they become available.	Froot et al. (1993) and Geczy et al. (1997)

Derivative determinant	Description	Academic citation
Financial distress costs	Firms with high costs of financial distress (i.e. highly levered firms) use derivatives to reduce the likelihood of financial distress (i.e. bankruptcy) through lower cash flow volatility.	Smith and Stulz (1985), Nance et al. (1993), Geczy et al. (1997) and Haushalter (2000)
Taxes	Less volatile earnings (i.e. cash flows) are associated with lower taxes.	Smith and Stulz (1985) and Nance et al. (1993)
Extent of risk exposure	The greater a firm's exposure to a certain risk, the more likely it is to hedge that risk.	Geczy et al. (1997), Haushalter (2000) and Allayannis and Ofek (2001)
Firm size	Because hedging programmes can be costly to implement, larger firms are more likely to hedge due to greater returns to scale.	Nance et al. (1993), Geczy et al. (1997) and Bodnar et al. (1998)
Delta of managers' stock options and holding portfolio	The more closely a manager's wealth is tied to changes in stock prices, the more likely the manager is to hedge risks that may reduce the firm's stock price.	Smith and Stulz (1985), Tufano (1996) and Knopf et al. (2002)
Vega of managers' stock options and holding portfolio	The value of stock options is increasing in stock price volatility, which reduces a manager's incentive to hedge the risks that cause this volatility.	Smith and Stulz (1985), Tufano (1996) and Knopf et al. (2002)

to these risks to hedge. Generally, firms do not hedge 100% their risk exposures (Bodnar et al. 1998; Guay & Kothari 2003), likely due to costs associated with determining and implementing a hedging strategy (e.g. transaction costs; uncertainty regarding future price movement). However, firms usually hedge their risks on a rolling basis (Campbell 2015). For example, if an airline schedules flights nine months in advance, it may enter into a derivative contract to lock in a specific price at which it can purchase the jet fuel for these flights. The airline enters into the derivative contract because it knows that jet fuel prices are volatile and expected to move prior to the time the flight occurs. The derivative contract serves as a hedge against the expected jet fuel price movement, thereby reducing volatility in the firm's cash flows.[3] As the airline schedules each new wave of flights, it continuously enters into derivative contracts to offset any expected price movement for jet fuel that will be purchased at the time the flights occur.

ILLUSTRATIVE EXAMPLE

To illustrate the potential benefits of hedging, consider the case of a commercial airline, BDD Airlines, which is exposed to financial (price) risk associated with future jet fuel purchases. The airline expects to purchase 10 million gallons of jet fuel in early April to support the company's second quarter operations. On January 6 jet fuel is priced at 92.5 cents per gallon. Based on this price, the company projects second quarter net income of $4,000,000. However, if the price of jet fuel increases, the company's profitability decreases in direct proportion to the price increase. Tables 9.5 and 9.6 illustrate how an increase in jet fuel cost could impact second quarter net income.

Campbell, D'Adduzio and Duchac

Table 9.5 Example of derivative contract designed to hedge jet fuel

BDD Airlines
Projected and actual second quarter (Q2) fuel cost

	Projected, as of January 6	Actual: April 4
Projected Q2 fuel purchase (gallons)	10,000,000	10,000,000
Jet fuel spot price (per gallon)	$0.925	$1.040
Q2 fuel cost	$9,250,000	$10,400,000
Increase in fuel cost from projected		$1,150,000

Table 9.6 Example of derivative contract gain/loss on a firm's earnings

BDD Airlines
Projected and actual second quarter (Q2) net income

Projected Q2 net income (based on January 6 projected fuel price)	$4,000,000
Increase in fuel cost from projected	$1,150,000
Actual Q2 net income (based on April 4 actual fuel price)	$2,850,000

Table 9.7 Example of calculating a gain on a futures contract for heating oil

BDD Airlines
Gain from change in fair value of futures contract

	January 6	March 31
Spot price – heating oil	$1.100	$1.215
March heating oil futures price (lock-in price)	$1.100	$1.100
	$0.000	$0.115
Notional amount of futures contract (gallons)	10,000,000	10,000,000
Futures contract fair value	$0	$1,150,000
Gain on futures contract		$1,150,000

Because the price of jet fuel is a significant cost for the company, the airline may wish to reduce or eliminate the risk associated with changing prices by entering into an offsetting derivative contract. In this case, the company chooses to hedge this position by entering into a futures contract to buy 10 million gallons of heating oil futures at a futures price of $1.10 per gallon. Heating oil futures are used because they are more readily available than jet fuel futures, and the price of heating oil moves in parallel to the price of jet fuel. The futures contract (hedging instrument) settles at the end of business on March 31, and will serve as a hedge because the value of the futures contract (to buy) will move in the same direction of the price of jet fuel (hedged item). The calculation of the gain on the futures contracts is shown in Table 9.7.

The gain from the change in the fair value of the futures contract (hedging instrument) is used to offset the increased cost associated with rising jet fuel prices (hedged item). The combination of the hedging instrument and the hedged item effectively locks-in the price of jet fuel at the January 6 price as shown in Table 9.8.

Table 9.8 Example of futures contract gain/loss on a firm's earnings

BDD Airlines	
Hedged fuel cost	
Actual fuel cost (April 4) – unhedged ($1.04 per gallon × 10 million)	$10,400,000
Less: gain on futures contract (see Table 9.7)	($1,150,000)
Hedged fuel cost	$9,250,000

As the table illustrates, the increase in fuel cost associated with changes in the market price of jet fuel (hedged item) is offset by the gain on the futures contract (hedging instrument). Thus, the company has effectively offset (hedged) the risk associated with changes in the price of jet fuel.

This example illustrates a perfect, or 100%, hedge of BDD Airlines' exposure to jet fuel through the purchase of a futures contract. As a result, BDD Airlines' net income is the same as it would have been if it had purchased jet fuel at the January 6 spot price of $0.925 per gallon. In practice, however, a perfect hedge such as this is highly unusual for several reasons. First, economic conditions are hard to predict, and the firm may need to purchase more (or less) than 10,000,000 gallons of jet fuel. If so, the firm will either be under- or over-hedged by the difference between the notional amount of the derivative and the amount of the hedged item actually purchased. Second, changes in the price of heating oil may not perfectly correlate with changes in the price of jet fuel. Finally, as previously discussed, firms often intentionally hedge less than 100% of their forecasted purchase or sale commitments.

Hedging versus speculation

Companies use derivatives to hedge their exposure to financial risk when their business operations (and profits) are sensitive to changes in the price of an underlying rate (interest or foreign exchange), price (stock or commodity) or index (S&P 500 or Dow Jones Industrial Average). In these cases, the gains/losses on the derivative should largely offset the gains/losses from the underlying financial risk, reducing or **hedging** the firm's exposure to that risk. Alternatively, companies may elect to purchase derivatives for which they do not have an associated financial risk. That is, the firm has no risk to hedge. This might happen when firms have a strong belief about where rates/prices/indices are going to move in the future, and wish to make a bet on that prediction. In these cases, gains/losses on the derivative directly affect a firm's net income, and the firm is considered to be '*speculating*' about prices in the underlying item.

It is important to note that if a firm uses derivatives to offset or 'hedge' an existing risk exposure, they are not speculating. Consider the case of Delta Airlines, which was concerned that jet fuel prices might increase, and hedged a sizeable portion of its anticipated jet fuel purchases for the second quarter of 2016 with futures contracts. The futures contracts guaranteed that Delta could purchase fuel in the second quarter of 2016 at the price specified on the date the futures contracts were entered. In effect, the company was concerned that jet fuel prices would increase, and locked in the price they would have to pay for jet fuel in the second quarter of 2016 by hedging with a futures contract. In this particular case, jet fuel prices decreased, and the hedges moved into a loss position. To avoid larger potential losses on the futures contracts, Delta terminated the derivative contracts early, triggering the recognition of a loss on the difference between the contracted price and the current market value at the time of termination, or approximately $450 million.

A CNN Money article published on July 5, 2016 carried the title 'Delta loses $450 million bet on fuel prices'. Although the press may portray these transactions as 'bets', or speculation, in this case Delta was simply 'locking in' prices ahead of time. In doing so, Delta was able to remove the uncertainty and cash flow volatility associated with changes in jet fuel prices. Although the price did not move to the extent that Delta expected, they were not 'betting on', 'speculating on' or 'trying to make money off of' changes in jet fuel prices.

Accounting for derivatives and hedging

The accounting for derivatives is typically broken down into two broad categories, non-hedge accounting and hedge accounting. Unless a derivative instrument is specifically designated as an accounting hedge, and meets the criteria to qualify as an accounting hedge, it is classified as a non-hedging transaction for accounting purposes.[4]

Accounting for derivatives (non-hedge accounting)

Non-hedge accounting arises when a company enters into a derivatives contract, but does not designate the derivative as a hedge of an existing financial risk. In this case, (1) hedge accounting is **NOT** elected, and (2) the measurement basis for the derivative financial instrument is fair value. The derivative is reported on the balance sheet at its fair value, and any change in fair value during the period is reported on the income statement as a gain or loss.

To illustrate the financial statement effects of a derivative transaction without hedge accounting, consider our previous example with BDD Airlines. In this case, the company has entered into a futures contract to hedge its exposure to changes in the price of jet fuel. Because the contract settles on March 31, the gain from the futures contract is recorded during the first quarter (Q1) and is included in the calculation of Q1 net income. However, the fuel purchase does not occur until April 4 and is therefore included in the company's second quarter (Q2) earnings calculation (assuming the fuel is *used* to generate revenue in the second quarter). This creates a mismatch between the period in which the income statement effect of the futures contract (hedging instrument) is recorded and the period in which the income statement effect of the fuel cost (hedged item) is recorded. As shown in Table 9.9, the Q2 fuel cost will appear as if it is unhedged because the accounting system recognizes the gain of the futures contract (hedging instrument) in a different period (Q1) than it recognizes the fuel costs (hedged item; Q2). As a result, the second quarter earnings are subject to volatility associated with changes in the price of jet fuel, even though the fuel purchase is economically hedged by the futures contract.

Hedge accounting

To overcome the mismatch discussed above, accounting standards allow a company to elect **hedge accounting** for transactions in which a derivative financial instrument is used to hedge an existing financial risk. The primary benefit of hedge accounting is that it allows the company to align the financial reporting for the hedged item and the hedging instrument so that the income statement effects of the two items are captured in the same reporting period. In effect, the accounting system links the changes in the value of the hedged item with the changes in the value of the hedging instrument (derivative), so that they can offset one another in the same period on the income statement. This is accomplished by modifying the measurement basis of either (1) the hedged item (fair value hedge) or (2) the hedging instrument (cash flow hedge); thus, ensuring that the gain/loss on the derivative is reported in the same period as

Table 9.9 Example of derivatives gains/losses on earnings when hedge accounting is not used

	March 31 (End Q1)	April 4 (Q2)
BDD Airlines *Projected second quarter (Q2) fuel cost and net income* *The company does <u>not</u> use hedge accounting*		
Projected Q2 net income		$2,850,000
Gain (loss) on futures contract (from Table 9.7)	$1,150,000	
Net income (no hedge accounting)		$2,850,000

the income statement effects of the hedged item. By doing this, the financial statement effects of the hedged item and the hedging instrument are aligned in the financial statements. For this to occur, (1) the company must elect hedge accounting for the transaction, and (2) the hedging relationship must qualify as a hedge for financial reporting purposes.

The need for hedge accounting arises because of an inherent mismatch between either (1) the timing of the recognition of the derivative instrument and the hedged item, or (2) the measurement basis of the derivative instrument and the hedged item. As a result, there are two general categories of hedge accounting: fair value hedges and cash flow hedges. Each of these categories are discussed briefly below.

Fair value hedge

Fair value hedge accounting treatment can be elected when a derivative financial instrument is used to hedge (offset) the risk associated with changes in the fair value of an existing asset or liability that is already recognized on the firm's balance sheet, as well as for certain types of unrecognized firm commitments. In a fair value hedge, the hedged item has a measurement basis other than fair value, creating a mismatch with the hedging instrument that is reported at fair value. As a result, this type of hedging transaction can create income statement volatility despite the fact that the hedge is used to offset (reduce) an existing risk.

The volatility in this situation arises because of a difference in measurement bases between the hedged item (non-fair value) and the hedging instrument (fair value). To overcome this deficiency, fair value hedge accounting allows a company to modify (change) the measurement basis of the hedged item to fair value. By doing this, (1) the measurement basis of the hedged item and the hedging instrument become the same, and (2) the gain (loss) from the change in the FV of the hedged item and the loss (gain) from the change in FV of the hedging instrument offset one another on the income statement. This reduces volatility in earnings, which is consistent with the economic motivations for entering into the hedge.

The application of a fair value hedge is as follows. Suppose that on March 31, BDD Airlines borrows $100,000,000 5% bonds that pay interest semi-annually, requiring fixed interest payments of $2,500,000 every six months. The debt is issued at par. Therefore, the value of the debt is recorded on the balance sheet as a $100,000,000 liability on March 31. Because the bonds are recorded at amortized cost, the balance in the bond payable account remains constant at $100,000,000 for the life of the bonds.

BDD Airlines wants to convert its fixed rate debt into variable rate date. Therefore, on March 31 it enters into an interest rate swap derivative that provides for the company to receive a fixed interest rate of 5% every six months, and pay a variable interest rate (initially 4.5%) every six months, with the first swap payment occurring on the same date as the first interest payment on the bonds. The swap has a notional amount of $100,000,000, and has net settlement in cash for the difference between the interest rates on each interest payment date. These transactions are reflected in the first column of Table 9.10.

On September 30, BDD must make its first interest payment of $2.5 million on the bonds. In addition, BDD receives a net swap payment of $250,000 (i.e. the difference between the fixed rate and floating rate at the beginning of the swap period, or $100 million ★ (5–4.5%) / 2). Therefore, the net interest expense to BDD is $2.25 million, or the variable rate of 4.5%.

On the balance sheet, however, the interest rate swap must be recorded at fair value. On September 30, the variable rate of interest has decreased from 4.5% to 3.5%, creating a positive fair value of, say, $5,500,000.[5] When BDD records the change in the fair value of the interest rate swap (to $5,500,000 from $0), it creates a gain of $5.5 million. In the absence of hedge accounting, however, a mismatch occurs between the measurement basis of the interest rate swap (recorded at fair value) and the underlying hedged item (bonds payable, which are recorded at amortized cost). As a result, the gains (losses) from the derivative would introduce volatility into earnings, even though the swap is being used to hedge the bonds payable.

Table 9.10 Example of hedge accounting for a fair value hedge

	March 31 (End Q1)	September 30 (End Q3)
BDD Airlines *Projected third quarter (Q3) loan values – fair value hedge*		
Balance sheet impact		
Cash	$100,000,000	$100,000,000
Fair value hedge value (within other assets)	$0	$5,500,000
Total assets	$100,000,000	$105,500,000
Loan obligation	$100,000,000	$105,500,000
Total liabilities	$100,000,000	$105,500,000
Income statement impact		
Change in value of liability		
Loss due to increase in loan obligation		($5,500,000)
Gain due to increase in fair value hedge		$5,500,000
Net income effect of change in fair values		No change
Interest expense		
Interest payment on loan obligation (5%)		($2,500,000)
Interest received from fair value hedge (4.5%–5%)		250,000
Net interest expense – variable rate of 4.5%		($2,250,000)

By designating the interest rate swap as a fair value hedge, BDD can offset the earnings volatility created by the fair value adjustment to the interest rate swap. As mentioned earlier, fair value hedging allows a company to change the measurement basis of the hedged item to fair value. For BDD, this means that the company can modify (change) the measurement basis of the bond payable (hedged item) from amortized cost to fair value. In doing so, the gain (loss) arising from the change in the fair value of the bonds payable will offset the loss (gain) arising from the change in the fair value of the interest rate swap. When interest rates go down, the market value of its bond increases because the loan pays a higher rate than current market conditions. Because this is a perfect hedge, the gain (loss) resulting from the change in the fair value of the bonds will exactly offset the loss (gain) arising from the change in the fair value of the interest rate swap. Furthermore, because the gain (loss) from the derivative and the bonds completely offset, the income statement impact of the fair value changes is zero.

To summarize, firms can purchase derivatives that offset the financial statement impact of changes in the value of their assets or liabilities, and designate these derivatives as fair value hedges. Fair value hedges are recorded at fair value each balance sheet date, with changes in fair value going directly to the income statement. From a financial statement analysis standpoint, these derivatives are the easiest to interpret – the underlying asset/liability is recorded at fair value, the derivative position is recorded at fair value, and the income statement line items are perfectly offset.

Cash flow hedge

Cash flow hedge accounting treatment can be applied when a derivative financial instrument is used to hedge (offset) the variability in cash flows associated with an asset, liability or forecasted transaction. In this case, hedge accounting allows a company to modify the

Table 9.11 Example of hedge accounting for a cash flow hedge

	March 31 (End Q1)	April 4 (Q2)
BDD Airlines *Projected second quarter (Q2) fuel cost and net income – cash flow hedge*		
Balance sheet impact		
Jet fuel derivative value (within other assets)	$1,150,000[1]	$0
Accumulated other comprehensive income (within equity)	$1,150,000	$0[2]
Income statement impact		
Projected Q2 net income (unhedged, from Table 9.6)		$2,850,000
Reduction in fuel expense from releasing deferred gains from AOCI		$1,150,000
Net income (hedged)		$4,000,000

1 The derivative is settled for cash on March 31. As a result, the value of the derivative is converted into cash, and added to BDD airlines cash account at that time.
2 On April 4 the Accumulated Other Comprehensive Income Account is reduced (debited) by $1,150,000, bringing the account balance to zero. This debit is balanced by a $1,150,000 credit to fuel expense; reducing the total fuel cost to $9,250,000.

measurement basis of the hedging instrument (i.e. the derivative) to fair value, with changes in fair value captured in Accumulated Other Comprehensive Income (AOCI) until the period when the hedged item is reported in income. During the periods leading up to the period in which the hedged item is reported in earnings, any gains and losses on the derivative are accumulated (deferred) on the balance sheet in the equity account AOCI. When the hedged item is ultimately reported as part of earnings, the amount accumulated in AOCI is released into income and used to offset the income statement effects of the hedged item.

The application of a cash flow hedge to BDD Airlines is shown in Table 9.11.

As the example shows, the $1,150,000 gain on the futures contract is deferred in AOCI until the period in which fuel expense is recognized in the income statement. In the second quarter, when the purchase of the fuel occurs, the gain on the futures contract is removed from AOCI and recorded in earnings; thus offsetting the price of jet fuel, as illustrated below.

Fuel cost at market price ($1.04 per gallon × 10 million gallons)	$10,400,000
Gain on futures contract	1,150,000
Fuel cost (hedged)	$ 9,250,000

The net result is that fuel expense is reported in the Q2 income statement at the hedged price of $9,250,000 (10 million gallons × $.925 per gallon), rather than the market price of $10,400,000 ($1.04 × 10 million).

If the company had not used hedge accounting, (1) the $1,150,000 gain on the futures contract would have been reported in Q1 as other income, and (2) the fuel cost would be reported at $10,400,000 (the unhedged market price) on the date of purchase. Thus, without hedge accounting, there would be a considerable increase in the volatility of net income during all periods.

Financial statement and capital market consequences of derivatives accounting

Primary consequence of hedging: stock price reflects a 'hedging premium'

As discussed in the previous section, hedging with derivatives protects the firm from price movements in the underlying hedged item (i.e. the interest rate, commodity price, foreign exchange rate, etc.). By entering into a financial derivative, the firm's cash flows should be less volatile than if the firm had not hedged. When a firm experiences lower cash flow volatility, investors view the firm as less risky, and this reduces a firm's cost of capital, or discount rate.

A firm's stock price at time *t* is equal to its stream of expected future cash flows discounted back to time *t* using a discount rate that reflects the uncertainty of those cash flows. Because hedging activities reduce a firm's cash flow volatility and, thus, the uncertainty in its future cash flows, then – holding constant the level of expected future cash flows – the firm's stock price should increase. That is, all else equal, the stock price of a firm that commits to a hedging program should be higher than the stock price of a firm that does not hedge. This phenomenon has been documented in stock prices, and is known as the 'hedging premium'. This reduction in discount rate (i.e. firm risk) and corresponding increase in firm value is the most tangible and direct capital market benefit of a firm's hedging activities.

Findings in academic research support the existence of a 'hedging premium'. Guay (1999) and Allayannis et al. (2001) both show that risk exposure is lower for firms that use derivatives, which suggests that on average, firms effectively hedge risk exposure through derivative use. Furthermore, investors appear to view the reduction in risk exposure positively, as this reduction in risk is associated with an increase in firm value, i.e. a 'hedging premium' (Schrand 1997; Allayannis et al. 2001; Allayannis & Weston 2001; Wong 2001). Finally, recent evidence suggests that when firms use derivatives, they are more likely to issue management earnings guidance – a voluntary disclosure benefit related to derivatives usage (Campbell et al. 2017a).

Finally, it is important to note that the accounting treatment for cash flow hedges has undergone several changes over the past two decades. Prior to 1998, firms had the option to recognize derivative instruments on the balance sheet or instead, to disclose them in the footnotes to the financial statements. Ahmed et al. (2006) shows that investors value derivatives only when they are recognized as assets or liabilities on the balance sheet and *not* when they are disclosed in footnotes. Accordingly, current accounting standards require all derivative instruments to be recognized on the balance sheet.

Unique financial statement and capital market consequences of cash flow hedges

In addition to reducing the volatility of a firm's cash flows, derivatives designated as cash flow hedges (i.e. hedges of a forecasted purchase or sale denominated in a commodity price, interest rate or foreign exchange rate) have unique financial statement and capital market consequences. Recall that the need to modify the measurement basis of the derivative in a cash flow hedge arises from a timing difference between when the financial derivative (hedging instrument) and the hedged item are recorded in the firm's financial statements. The derivative (hedging instrument) is recorded when it is entered into and is subsequently adjusted to fair value on each balance sheet date, while the forecasted purchase or sale of the underlying hedged item is not recorded until the item is actually purchased or sold. In other words, there is a significant timing difference in the recognition of the two transactions in the firm's financial statements, resulting in only the derivative recognized on the firm's financial statements in the periods prior to the hedged transaction.

Consider the case of Southwest Airlines, which sells tickets to a flight taking place in nine months, but typically purchases jet fuel shortly before the flight takes place. If the cost of jet fuel increases after Southwest has sold tickets, Southwest faces a potential decline in profits. To protect itself from increases in jet fuel prices, Southwest purchases derivatives that increase in value as the cost of jet fuel increases. The derivative, in this case, is providing a hedge against increases in jet fuel prices.

This 'timing' problem applied to Southwest Airlines is illustrated in Figure 9.1. There are two items that must be accounted for (1) the purchase of jet fuel in nine months (at time $t = 9$) and (2) the derivative contract that locks in jet fuel prices today (from $t = 0$ through $t = 9$). At each balance sheet date from $t = 0$ through $t = 8$, Southwest records the derivative contract at fair value. At $t = 0$ the value of the hedge is an asset equal to the price Southwest paid for the jet fuel derivative (which is $0 if the derivative is a futures contract, and some nominal amount [i.e. a 'premium'] if the derivative is an option contract), and if jet fuel prices increase, then so does the value of the asset at each balance sheet date. That is, the derivative follows a fair value accounting model.

However, at time $t = 0$, the commitment to purchase jet fuel in nine months is not recorded on Southwest's balance sheet. Furthermore, subsequent changes in this potential future liability due to changes in jet fuel prices are also not recorded on the balance sheet

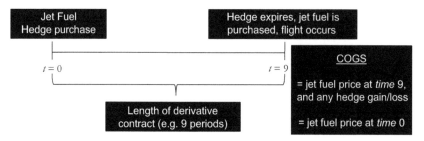

Figure 9.1   Illustration of the "timing" differences associated with cash flow hedges

because Southwest has not yet incurred a liability for financial reporting purposes. That is, the jet fuel purchase commitment follows a historical cost model and is not recorded until it is purchased.

This mismatch in accounting treatment for the hedge and the associated underlying transaction creates a 'timing' problem that can lead to investor confusion across time periods in at least two ways. First, balance sheet ratios are distorted because only half of the company's potential future transactions (i.e. the derivative portion) are recorded on the balance sheet up until the jet fuel purchase. We discuss this issue in detail in the next section, 'Implications of Cash Flow Hedge Amounts for Balance Sheet Ratios and Cost of Debt'. Second, the gains/losses on cash flow hedges serve as a signal about the firm's future profitability once the hedge protection expires. We discuss this issue in detail in the section entitled 'Implications of Cash Flow Hedge Amounts for Future Profitability'.

Implications of cash flow hedge amounts for balance sheet ratios and cost of debt

The hedge accounting treatment under US GAAP creates distortions for analyzing a firm's balance sheet because, prior to the forecasted purchase or sale, the balance sheet only tells half of the economic story because the underlying hedged transaction is neither recorded nor disclosed. Specifically, the derivative component is recorded on the balance sheet, but the associated forecasted purchase or sale in the underlying item is not recorded. Thus, balance sheet ratios focused on default risk (i.e. the leverage ratio) incorrectly contain assets and equity that do not reflect a firm's 'core' or 'fundamental' leverage position after the hedge protection expires.

Investors can correct the balance sheet for this hedge accounting distortion by removing the effect of the cash flow hedge (i.e. assets and their associated gains/losses in equity) when assessing a firm's 'core' or 'fundamental' leverage position.[6] At hedge inception, the firm pays cash and records a derivative asset (that, after considering transactions costs, locks in the firm's price on the underlying hedged item).[7] Subsequent changes in the value of the derivative create associated gains/losses in equity.[8] Thus, to remove the effects of cash flow hedging from a firm's balance sheet, investors should (1) subtract hedging gains from equity and asset amounts if the firm is in a net gain position on hedges or (2) add hedging losses to equity and asset amounts if the firm is in a net loss position on hedges. We illustrate this concept with Southwest Airlines.

If the price of the jet fuel increases, Southwest Airlines experiences an unrealized cash flow hedge gain recorded to shareholders' equity (i.e. AOCI), and the asset value of the derivatives contract increases. However, there is also an increase in the *future cost* of jet fuel (because it must be purchased at a now higher price), which is not recorded in the *current* period due to the cash flow hedge accounting rules described in the prior section. In other words, what appears as an 'asset' and 'equity' on Southwest Airlines' balance sheet has an equally offsetting and unrecorded 'liability'. Because the 'liability' is not recorded until the future jet fuel purchase occurs, for consistency investors should remove the offsetting hedging asset (and gain in equity) to correctly present the firm's balance sheet and leverage ratios.

For example, at December 31, 2005, Southwest Airlines had total assets of $14.0 billion, long-term debt of $2.5 billion, other liabilities of $4.8 billion and shareholders' equity of $6.7 billion. Included within equity are unrealized cash flow hedge gains of $0.9 billion, which are net of taxes of $0.6 billion (Southwest has a tax rate of 40.2% in 2005). Thus, included within assets is $1.5 billion of unrealized cash flow hedge gains that have equal and offsetting unrecorded liability amounts. To adjust for the effects of hedging gains on a firm's leverage ratio (i.e. long-term debt to assets), investors would need to remove $1.5 billion from the firms' assets, and thus the leverage ratio would be ($2.5 billion / $12.5 billion), or 0.20.[9] If instead investors fail to adjust for the fact that the recorded hedging gain is associated with an unrecorded forecasted jet fuel purchase, the leverage ratio would be ($2.5 billion / $14.0 billion), or 0.18. In other words, adjusting for the effects of hedging gains from equity causes the firm's debt to assets ratio to increase from 0.18 to 0.20, or 11.1%. See Table 9.12.

The same problem occurs if jet fuel prices decrease. In this case, Southwest Airlines experiences an unrealized cash flow hedge loss in shareholders' equity, and the asset value of the

Table 9.12 Illustration of cash flow hedge gain on balance sheet ratios

Southwest Airlines Illustration

Effects of unrealized cash flow hedge gain on balance sheet

As presented on balance sheet at December 31, 2005:

$$\frac{\text{Assets}}{\$\ 14.0} = \frac{\text{Long-term Debt}}{\$\ 2.5} + \frac{\text{Other Liabilities}}{\$\ 4.8} + \frac{\text{Equity}}{\$\ 6.7}$$

$$\frac{\text{Long-term Debt}}{\text{Assets}} = \frac{\$\ 2.5}{\$\ 14.0} = 0.18$$

After removing effects of unrealized cash flow hedge gain

$$\frac{\text{Assets}}{\$\ 14.0} = \frac{\text{Long-term Debt}}{\$\ 2.5} + \frac{\text{Other Liabilities}}{\$\ 4.8} + \frac{\text{Equity}}{\$\ 6.7}$$

$$\frac{-1.5}{\$\ 12.5} = \frac{}{\$\ 2.5} + \frac{-0.6^1}{\$\ 4.2} + \frac{-0.9}{\$\ 5.8}$$

$$\frac{\text{Long-term Debt}}{\text{Assets}} = \frac{\$\ 2.5}{\$\ 12.5} = 0.20$$

1 This amount relates to the deferred tax liability (DTL) associated with the hedging gain that is presented net-of-tax in AOCI. It does not affect the leverage ratio (calculated as long-term debt to total assets) because DTLs are not considered long-term debt. However, if instead the leverage ratio did include all liabilities (total liabilities to total assets), the inferences are unchanged. Specifically, the as-reported leverage ratio would be ($7.3 billion / $14.0 billion), or 0.52, while the adjusted leverage ratio would be ($6.7 billion / $12.5 billion), or 0.54.

derivatives contract decreases. However, because of accounting rules, there is also a decrease in an unrecorded 'liability' (from the commitment to purchase jet fuel at a now *lower* price). For consistency, investors should remove the effects of hedging on the firm's balance sheet by adding the hedging loss back to the firm's asset and equity balances.

At December 31, 2008, Southwest Airlines had total assets of $14.3 billion, long-term debt of $3.7 billion, other liabilities of $5.6 billion and shareholders' equity of $5.0 billion. Included within equity are unrealized cash flow hedge losses of $1.0 billion, which are net of taxes of $0.6 billion (Southwest has a tax rate of 38.5% in 2008). Thus, netted against assets is $1.6 billion of unrealized cash flow hedge losses that effectively reduced the firm's derivative assets to zero. However, this 'loss' is completely offset by a reduction in the amount of the future jet fuel purchase (i.e. an associated unrecorded liability amount). Thus, to undo the effects of hedging losses on a firm's leverage ratio (i.e. long-term debt to assets), investors would need to add $1.6 billion to the firm's assets, and thus the leverage ratio would be ($3.7 billion / $15.9 billion), or 0.23. If instead investors fail to adjust for the fact that the recorded hedging loss is associated with a lower price on an unrecorded forecasted jet fuel purchase, the leverage ratio would be ($3.7 billion / $14.3 billion), or 0.26. In other words, adjusting for the effects of hedging gains from equity causes the firm's debt to equity ratio to decrease from 0.26 to 0.23, or 11.5%. See Table 9.13.

Table 9.13 Illustration of cash flow hedge loss on balance sheet ratios

---

Southwest Airlines Illustration

Effects of cash flow hedge losses on balance sheet

As presented on balance sheet on December 31, 2008:

$$\frac{\text{Assets}}{\$\ \ 14.3} = \frac{\text{Long-term Debt}}{\$\ \ 3.7} + \frac{\text{Other Liabilities}}{\$\ \ 5.6} + \frac{\text{Equity}}{\$\ \ 5.0}$$

$$\frac{\text{Long-term Debt}}{\text{Assets}} = \frac{\$\ \ 3.7}{\$\ \ 14.3} = 0.26$$

After removing effects of unrealized cash flow hedge gain

$$\frac{\text{Assets}}{\$\ \ 14.3} = \frac{\text{Long-term Debt}}{\$\ \ 3.7} + \frac{\text{Other Liabilities}}{\$\ \ 5.6} + \frac{\text{Equity}}{\$\ \ 5.0}$$

$$\frac{+1.6}{\$\ \ 15.9} = \frac{}{\$\ \ 3.7} + \frac{0.6^1}{\$\ \ 6.2} + \frac{+1.0}{\$\ \ 6.0}$$

$$\frac{\text{Long-term Debt}}{\text{Assets}} = \frac{\$\ \ 3.7}{\$\ \ 15.9} = 0.23$$

---

1 This amount relates to the deferred tax asset associated with the hedging loss that is presented net-of-tax in AOCI (and that is netted against the firm's long-term deferred tax liability). It does not affect the leverage ratio (calculated as long-term debt to total assets) because deferred taxes are not considered long-term debt. However, if instead the leverage ratio did include all liabilities (total liabilities to total assets), the inferences are unchanged. Specifically, the as-reported leverage ratio would be ($9.3 billion / $14.3 billion), or 0.65, while the adjusted leverage ratio would be ($9.9 billion / $15.9 billion), or 0.62.

In sum, cash flow hedge accounting suffers from a timing problem where the gains/losses from the derivative are completely offset in the opposite direction once the forecasted purchase or sale occurs. This 'mismatch' in timing creates a problem for analyzing the balance sheet, because the balance sheet only tells half of the economic story. Therefore, for consistency, investors should remove the effects of changes in cash flow hedges (i.e. assets and their associated gains/losses in equity) when calculating balance sheet and leverage ratios.

Implications of cash flow hedge amounts for future profitability

In addition to having balance sheet implications, unrealized cash flow hedge gains/losses provide a signal about the firm's profitability. An unrealized gain on a cash flow hedge means that the price of the underlying hedged item (i.e. commodity price, interest rate or foreign exchange rate) moved in a direction that will hurt the firm's profits after the hedge protection expires. An unrealized loss means that the price of the underlying hedged item moved in a direction that will benefit the firm's profits after the hedge protection expires. As long as the price movement that created the gain or loss persists, the firm will be fully exposed to the new prices on the next purchase or sale that occurs – even if the firm is committed to buying derivatives to hedge its future transactions on a continuous (or rolling) basis. The reason is that as soon as the spot price of the underlying hedged item moves, the next hedge that the firm buys will be locking in the 'new' spot price. Therefore, although cash flow hedges protect the firm from volatility in cash flows, they do not protect the firm from long-term price shifts in the underlying hedged item as long as (1) the price movement that created the existing gain/loss does not revert back to the original price by the time the hedge expires (i.e. statistically, the underlying price follows a random walk where the best estimate for tomorrow's price is today's price), and (2) the firm does not have the ability to pass along input price changes to its customers in a real-time manner.[10] They only delay the impact. Academic research supports this description, showing that on average, unrealized gains/losses on cash flow hedges are negatively associated with future profitability (e.g. Campbell 2015; Campbell et al. 2015; Bratten et al. 2016; Campbell et al. 2017c).

To illustrate this point, consider the following example.[11] Suppose a firm has revenue of $4 and cost of goods sold (COGS) of $2. Revenue is constant over the next few years. The firm sells only one product. Taxes are ignored. During year t, the firm hedges its year $t+1$ inventory costs. After the hedge is in place and the current year's inventory is purchased, the price of inventory rises by $1, from $2 to $3. Therefore, in year t, the firm has a hedge gain of $1 in AOCI. However, because the firm purchased its inventory at $2, COGS is $2 in year t. In year $t+1$, the firm benefits from the hedge. It purchases inventory at the 'new' price of $3 but has the offsetting hedge gain of $1 being reclassified into the income statement. Thus COGS would again be $2. However, after year $t+1$, there is no hedge, so COGS is $3 in years $t+2$ and $t+3$. Therefore income is $2 in t and $t+1$ but $1 in years $t+2$ and $t+3$.[12] This scenario is illustrated graphically and through journal entries in Figure 9.2:

Investor response to cash flow hedge gains and losses

As just discussed, unrealized cash flow hedge gains/losses distort firms' balance sheet ratios and also serve as a signal that predicts future profitability. The natural question to ask is whether debt and equity investors understand these relationships, or if the timing problem

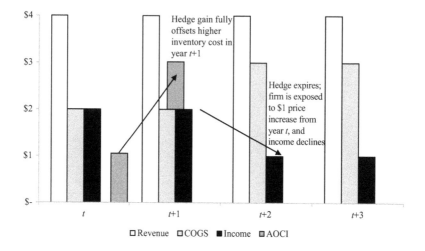

Figure 9.2   Effect of cash flow hedge gains/losses on future earnings

associated with cash flow hedge accounting rules leads to investor confusion. Academic research shows that only debt investors appear to understand the problem related to balance sheet ratios (Campbell et al. 2017b). That is, they adjust firms' cost of debt and equity for these relationships.

However, credit rating analysts, equity analysts and equity investors all fail to recognize the implications of unrealized cash flow hedge gains/losses on a firm's leverage ratio, as well as the fact that unrealized cash flow hedge gains serve as a signal that the firm's future profitability will decrease once the hedge protection expires, and unrealized cash flow hedge losses serve as a signal that the firm's future profitability will increase once the hedge protection expires. Specifically, unrealized cash flow hedge gains/losses predict future analyst forecast errors as well as stock market returns. For example, Campbell (2015) shows that a trading strategy where an investor buys firms with the largest unrealized hedging losses and sells short firms with the largest unrealized hedging gains, the investor will earn 8% returns a year over the following two years.[13]

Can firm disclosure help investors understand the financial statement impact of unrealized cash flow hedge gains/losses?

If managers provide detailed disclosures about the extent of their hedging relationships and the timing with which the hedge protection will expire, then all investors (debt and equity) will correctly price the information conveyed by cash flow hedge gains/losses. For example, Campbell et al. (2015) shows that if managers provide an earnings forecast that details the effects of the firm's risk management activities on future earnings, analysts and investors understand this information. Furthermore, Campbell et al. (2017c) show that during time periods after the FASB required firms to provide better disclosures about their risk management activities (FAS 161 in 2009), analysts and investors correctly price the information conveyed by cash flow hedge gains/losses.

Summary of capital market consequences of hedging

To summarize, the primary benefit of hedging is to reduce the firm's cash flow volatility. However, the accounting model for cash flow hedges leads to important implications for a firm's balance sheet ratios and future profitability. Managers can help investors and analysts understand these relationships with appropriate disclosures.

Conclusion

This chapter discusses the accounting for and financial statement interpretation of derivative financial instruments, an essential risk management tool that helps companies minimize risks and thus maximize their risk-return tradeoffs. By 'hedging' with derivatives, managers are able to avoid undesirable risks (that do not generate a sufficient return), and focus on the opportunities (risks) that generate the greatest potential return. The financial reporting for derivatives and hedging activities is complex because all derivatives are recorded on the balance sheet at fair value at each reporting date. In some instances, this can lead to counterintuitive accounting outcomes.

Firms can designate derivatives as either (1) fair value hedges, (2) cash flow hedges or (3) non-hedging derivatives. Fair value hedges are the easiest to interpret on financial statements. Cash flow hedges create problems as the balance sheet only conveys half of the economic story, and the gains/losses are inversely related to future profitability. Non-hedging derivatives often induce the most volatility on earnings, as their gains/losses go directly to net income without consideration of the timing of the economic transaction being hedged. In most cases, academic research finds that if investors are provided with sufficient disclosures regarding derivative transactions, they are able to efficiently understand and price the implications of these transactions in firms' stock prices and cost of capital.

Despite this added complexity to firms' financial statements, the benefits of hedging appear to more than offset the costs. The primary benefit of effective hedging programs is that the firm can reduce its earnings and cash flow volatilities. This reduction in volatility reduces a firm's cost of capital and raises its firm value. This reduction in volatility also helps the firm forecast and plan better for the future. In other words, any costs that firms incur by engaging in hedging activities is more than offset by a host of tangible benefits in the capital markets – a lower cost of borrowing, an enhanced ability to invest in profitable investment projects, lower taxes paid and an opportunity to make more informed operational decisions about the future.

Notes

1 Although we limit our discussion to futures contracts, the differences between futures contracts and the other contract types are not germane to our discussion.
2 This holds when a firm's effective marginal tax rate is a convex function of pre-tax firm value. See Smith and Stulz (1985) for additional detail.
3 An increase in jet fuel prices after the firm enters into a derivatives contract benefits the firm, as it has a contract to purchase jet fuel at the previous, lower price. However, it is also possible that jet fuel prices decrease after the firm enters into the contract. In this situation, the firm would have been better off not entering into the contract, although the firm cannot predict this outcome prior to entering into the derivative contract.
4 In addition to electing hedge accounting, the transaction must also qualify as a hedge for accounting purposes. A discussion of the qualification aspect of hedge accounting is outside the scope of this chapter.
5 The $5,500,000 amount is included for illustration purposes only. The actual calculation of the fair value of the interest rate swap is dependent on a number of additional variables, and is beyond the scope of this text.
6 If instead investors added back the changes in fair value on the unrecorded purchase or sale commitment, it would lead to the same effect on balance sheet ratios and default risk assessments (i.e. gains would increase default risk, and losses would decrease default risk). Because the commitment is *unrecorded*, but the cash flow hedge is recorded, we assume that the most appropriate adjustment is to remove the changes in fair value in the hedge position from the balance sheet.
7 If firms use options, forward, or futures contracts to hedge their risks the firm must pay cash up front for the derivative. If instead the firm uses an interest rate swap, there is no original cash payment for the derivative.
8 Derivative contracts can generally be converted to cash at any time because they are standardized (i.e. they trade on exchanges such as the Chicago Board of Trade) or can be otherwise sold to a third party that wants the associated risk.
9 We use debt to assets as our balance sheet ratio for assessing firm credit risk. We could just have easily used debt to equity, and the same relationships would exist.
10 Campbell (2015) provides evidence that after a shock to the price of an underlying hedged item (e.g. commodity prices, interest rates, foreign exchange rates), the new price (post-shock) does not fully revert back to the pre-shock level. Thus, the first hedge a firm buys "post-shock" will reflect, to some degree, the new price, which inevitably exposes the firm to the price volatility in the hedged item.
11 This example comes directly from Campbell et al. (2015).
12 This illustration assumes that inventory costs follow a random walk (and stay at $3 for the foreseeable future), that the firm only hedges in year *t*, and that it only hedges for the next year. Furthermore, even if the firm enters into hedges in year *t*+1, these hedges will lock the firm in to a $3 cost for its inventory and thus only protect the firm from *additional* cost increases beyond those experienced in year *t*.
13 For similar results, see also Makar et al. (2013), Campbell et al. (2015, 2017c).

References

Ahmed, A, Kilic, E & Lobo, G 2006, "Does recognition versus disclosure matter? Evidence from value-relevance of banks' recognized and disclosed derivative financial instruments", *The Accounting Review*, vol. 81, pp. 567–588.

Allayannis, G & Ihrig, J 2001, "Exposure and markups", *Review of Financial Studies*, vol. 14, pp. 805–835.

Allayannis, G & Ofek, E 2001, "Exchange rate exposure, hedging, and the use of foreign currency derivatives", *Journal of International Money and Finance*, vol. 20, pp. 273–296.

Allayannis, G & Weston, J 2001, "The use of foreign currency derivatives and firm market value", *The Review of Financial Studies*, vol. 14, pp. 243–276.

Allayannis, G, Ihrig, J & Weston, J 2001, "Exchange-rate hedging: financial versus operational strategies", *The American Economic Review*, vol. 91, pp. 391–395.

Bodnar, G, Hayt, G, Marston, R & Smithson, C 1995, "Wharton survey of derivatives usage by U.S. non-financial firms", *Financial Management*, vol. 24, pp. 104–114.

Bodnar, G, Hayt, G & Marston, R 1998, "Wharton survey of financial risk management by U.S. non-financial firms", *Financial Management*, vol. 27, pp. 70–91.

Bratten, B, Causholli, M & Khan, U 2016, "Usefulness of fair values for predicting banks' future earnings: evidence from other comprehensive income and its components", *Review of Accounting Studies*, vol. 21, pp. 280–315.

Campbell, J 2015, "The fair value of cash flow hedges, future profitability, and stock returns", *Contemporary Accounting Research*, vol. 32, pp. 243–279.

Campbell, J, Downes, J & Schwartz, Jr, W 2015, "Do sophisticated investors use the information provided by the fair value of cash flow hedges?", *Review of Accounting Studies*, vol. 20, no. 2, pp. 934–975.

Campbell, J, Cao, S Chang, H-S & Chiorean, R 2017a, "The effects of derivatives use on management forecast behavior", *Working paper*, University of Georgia, Georgia State University, Singapore Management University, and Lehigh University.

Campbell, J, D'Adduzio, J Downes, J & Utke, S 2017b, "Do investors adjust for balance sheet risk that should be "off balance sheet"? Evidence from cash flow hedges", *Working paper*, University of Georgia, University of Connecticut, and University of Nebraska.

Campbell, J, Khan, U & Pierce, S 2017c, "The effects of SFAS 161 on investor pricing of cash flow hedge fair values", *Working paper*, Columbia University, University of Georgia, and Florida State University.

Froot, K, Scharfstein, D & Stein J 1993, "Risk management: coordinating corporate investment and financing policies", *Journal of Finance*, vol. 48, pp. 1629–1658.

Geczy, C, Minton, B & Schrand, C 1997. "Why firms use currency derivatives", *Journal of Finance*, vol. 52, pp. 1323–1354.

Guay, W 1999, "The impact of derivatives on firm risk: an empirical examination of new derivative users", *Journal of Accounting and Economics*, vol. 26, pp. 319–351.

Guay, W & Kothari, SP 2003, "How much do firms hedge with derivatives?", *Journal of Financial Economics*, vol. 70, pp. 423–461.

Haushalter, D 2000, "Financing policy, basis risk, and corporate hedging: evidence from oil and gas producers", *Journal of Finance*, vol. 55, pp. 107–152.

Knopf, J, Nam, J & Thornton, J 2002, "The volatility and price sensitivities of managerial stock option portfolios and corporate hedging", *The Journal of Finance*, vol. 57, pp. 801–813.

Makar, S, Wang, L & Alam, P 2013, "The mixed attribute model in SFAS 133 cash flow hedge accounting: implications for market pricing", *Review of Accounting Studies*, vol. 18, pp. 66–94.

Minton, B & Schrand, C 1999, "The impact of cash flow volatility on discretionary investment and the costs of debt and equity financing", *Journal of Financial Economics*, vol. 54, pp. 423–460.

Myers, S & Majluf, N 1984, "Corporate financing and investment decisions when firms have information that investors do not have", *Journal of Financial Economics*, vol. 13, pp. 187–221.

Nance, D, Smith, C & Smithson, C 1993, "On the determinants of corporate hedging." *The Journal of Finance*, vol. 48, pp. 267–284.

Schrand, C 1997, "The association between stock-price interest rate sensitivity and disclosures about derivative instruments", *The Accounting Review*, vol. 72, pp. 87–109.

Smith, C & Stulz, R 1985, "The determinants of firms' hedging policies", *Journal of Financial and Quantitative Analysis*, vol. 20, pp. 391–405.

Tufano, P 1996, "Who manages risk? An empirical examination of risk management practices in the gold mining industry", *The Journal of Finance*, vol. 51, 1097–1137.

Wong, MHF 2001, "The association between SFAS No. 119 derivatives disclosures and the foreign exchange risk exposure of manufacturing firms", *Journal of Accounting Research*, vol. 38, pp. 387–417.

PART III

Development

10

THE HISTORY OF THE FAIR VALUE TERM AND ITS MEASUREMENTS

Martin E. Persson, Frank L. Clarke and Graeme W. Dean

Accounting is a discipline without any cohesive, unified theory of valuation (p. 131).[1]

Robert R. Sterling, 1967

Introduction

Robert R. Sterling, the founding Dean of the Jones Graduate School of Business at Rice University, made the above claim almost 50 years ago. West (2003) later explored this claim and its potential ramification for the public accounting profession in his book *Professionalism and Accounting Rules*, which won the American Accounting Association and the American Institute of Certified Public Accountants' Notable Contributions to Accounting Literature awards in 2008. In his book, West delivers a forceful argument that standard-setters have failed the accounting profession in their inability to develop a unified underlying theory of accounting valuation (he uses the more precise term of measurements). West predicts that this will eventually lead to the demise of the profession, a claim that several authors have subsequently investigated further and arrived at various conclusions (Lee 2013; Persson & Napier 2015; Persson et al. 2017).

Through a historical review, this chapter explores this lack of a unified theory of valuation in accounting standards related to fair value accounting and in particular the 2011 International Accounting Standards Board's *Fair Value Measurement* (International Financial Reporting Standard (IFRS) 13). Following a brief history of the term fair value, the second section traces the historical antecedents of the measurements currently used in fair value accounting. The former section traces the emergence of the term in legal precedents, its use in commerce generally and utility pricing in particular, its drift from these precedents to the accounting literature and its final drift in to financial accounting standards. The latter section is divided into three parts that correspond to the three levels of the fair value measurement hierarchy. Using this division, the latter section demonstrates how level 1 and 2 fair value measurements rose to prominence through accounting research in the 1960s, whereas the level 3 measurements emerged from a group of German foresters in the 1800s before being rediscovered in the fields of economics and accounting in the 1900s.

The result is a chapter that reaches back to the 1700s and stands in contrast to most prior research that has covered primarily the recent history of fair value accounting, as used by standard-setters, and its role in the 2007–2008 financial crisis (e.g. Laux & Leuz 2009). It extends the earlier work of Clarke (1980) and Dean and Clarke (2010a), in particular in our choice of separating out the historical developments of the fair value term from the historical developments of the measurements used in fair value accounting standards.

Fair value[2]

'Fair value' dates back to at least the late nineteenth century. Both sides of the Atlantic evidenced commercial dilemmas, sometimes involving fraud, pricing disputes, dividend determinations and concerns with the investment trust movement in the UK and the merger movement in the USA. In the case of the UK, the British author George Lisle refers to 'fair value' in his 1904 *Encyclopedia of Accounting* and the London accountant Francis W. Pixley used the term to describe market values as early as 1881:

> [As for] companies whose business depends on their periodically showing to their constituents and the public their sound and unquestionable financial position, … while … nothing could be more reprehensible than for directors of a bank to deceive their shareholders and the customers, by stating its securities at a value they know they do not possess, yet they would naturally, as competitors for public patronage, desire to set forth the assets at their fair market value, and to this the auditor cannot raise any objections.
>
> *(p. 130)*

In the USA, on the other hand, the court case of Smyth v. Ames (1898) was of particular importance. Commonly referred to as 'the maximum freight case', the US Supreme Court heard this case after an appeal from the Circuit Court for the District of Nebraska in 1897. The appellants in *Smyth v. Ames* were the Attorney General of Nebraska and his colleagues. The plaintiffs were a group of stockholders of the Union Pacific Railway Company who had sued the state government and all railway companies operating in Nebraska in July 1893.

The suit challenged the constitutionality of an act to regulate the rates charged on the local transportation of freight, known as the 'maximum rate bill', which had been passed by the state legislature and approved by the Governor earlier in April 1893. The stockholders argued that the act deprived the railroad companies of just compensation for their services. The Circuit Court had sided with the plaintiffs and the Supreme Court affirmed the lower court's decree upon appeal. This decision voided the maximum rate bill, came to define the constitutional limits of governments to set utility rates for the next four decades, and established that regulated companies had the right to earn a 'fair return' based on the fair value of the assets employed for public services (for more about this case, see Hall et al. 2005).

In their verdict, the Supreme Court defined fair value as

> [t]he basis of all calculations as to the reasonableness of rates to be charged by a corporation … under legislative sanction must be the fair value of the property being used by it for the convenience of the public. And in order to ascertain that value, [1] the original cost of construction, [2] the amount expended in permanent improvements, [3] the amount and market value of its bonds and stock, [4] the present as compared with the original cost of construction, [5] the probable earning capacity of the property under particular rates prescribed by statute, and [6] the sum required to meet operating

expenses, are all matters for consideration, and are to be given such weight as may be just and right in each case.

(Smyth v. Ames 1898, pp. 326–327)

Offering this definition, the court aimed to establish a fair value that would allow utility rates to be set at an amount that would enable regulated companies to recoup their initial investments, cover ongoing expenses, and earn a fair return for their stockholders (for more about this term from a legal perspective, see Hall et al. 2005). This marked a reversal of the tradition of public utilities to account for their assets in accordance with their original cost (Garfield & Lovejoy 1964), and the closest to this new notion in the accounting literature would have been the proposal of measuring assets in accordance with their 'replacement cost'. Hamilton had made such a suggestion in regard to the measurement of inventory as early as 1788:

> ... take an exact inventory of the goods on hand, as far as can be done; and affix a mod-
> erate value to each article, according to the current prices at the time; such a value as the
> owner would be willing to present to buy for.
>
> *(p. 285)*

This notion of replacement cost, however, had been fraught with ambiguity long before the maximum freight case. It had been defined in any number of ways in the literature, such as the current cost of an identical asset, the current cost of an equivalent asset, or the current cost of acquiring the service provided by the asset. This situation had one commentator lamenting that 'replacement cost ... means all things to all men (ICAS 1952, pp. 84–85)'.

The problem with the Supreme Court's definition of fair value was that it was even vaguer, though arguably broader, than the notion of replacement cost. In addition to its shared lack of measurement guidance, it employed a mix of past (items one and two), present (items three and four) and potential future transactions (items five and six) in order to arrive at some amount. Whereas the first four of these items could potentially be determined, one could only guess at the other two. The definition also gave no guidance as to the relative weighting of each of the six items, leading Clarke (1980) to conclude that this mixing of measurements made fair value '... neither wholly factual nor wholly conjectural; it was some kind of agglomeration of fact and fiction, without any specification of the proportions of each (p. 82)'.

The lack of guidance regarding the determination of fair value led to a period where the court often had to act as an arbiter in disputes about its computation (e.g. *Southwestern Tele. Co. v. Missouri* 1923).[3] During periods of falling prices, which had been the case during relevant period covering the Smyth v. Ames (1898) particulars (and for several decades prior), public utilities argued against the government for a heavier weighting of past transactions to maximize its rate base (e.g. the original cost of building a train station). These roles then reversed during periods of rising prices in the first few decades of the twentieth century, with the public utilities arguing for a heavier weighting of its most recent transactions (for more about this, see Goddard 1928). Similar to debates in the accounting literature on the measurement of replacement cost, the courts were in disagreement about whether this meant the current cost of an identical asset or one with similar capabilities. They were also in disagreement about how to account for the potential of price-level changes between the date of the court ruling and the later date of the construction or procurement of a replacement asset (Bonbright 1937).

Disputes over issues such as these continued until the mid-to-late 1930s, when the Supreme Court accepted the use of utilities' rates based on the historical cost of its assets as opposed to their fair value in two different cases (*California v. Pacific Gas & Electric Co.* 1938; *LA Gas & Electric Corp. v. California* 1933). Then, with the case of the *Federal Power Commission v. Hope Natural Gas Company* in 1944, the Supreme Court completely reversed their initial ruling in Smyth v. Ames (1898) and the fair value rule was abandoned by the courts (for more about this reversal, see Boer 1966).

Returning to the UK setting, we note that reference is made to *fair value* under the 'Balance Sheets' entry in the George Lisle's 1904 *Encyclopedia*. There, Lisle refers to the need to satisfy the overriding criterion that a '… balance sheet of a private or public concern be, as mentioned above, full and fair'. And later, in respect of the *Balance Sheet of a Bank,* 'all assets shall be stated at their 'fair value' and that liabilities be fully shown (pp. 207–208)'.

Lisle's *Encyclopedia* is presumably the product of concerns, throughout the latter half of the nineteenth century, about asset valuations emanating from unexpected company failures and sometime related frauds. Most notable of these would have been the Overend & Gurney collapse in the 1860s, the stock market imbroglios leading to the London Stock Exchange Commission of Inquiry in 1870, the ongoing dividend and asset valuation cases (e.g. Verner v. General and Commercial Investment Trust Ltd 1894) and the mainly British-financed mining boom-and-bust in Australia in the 1890s. Concerns of investors and legislators resulted in a review of the efficacy of the company law regime through the 1895 Davey Committee of Inquiry into the Companies Acts of 1862 through 1890. In those settings, there was much discussion in the submissions to the inquiry about full and fair accounts and the need for fair values (for some of this history, see Michie 1999).

Drift from legal precedents to the accounting literature

For space reasons, discussion in this section is limited to the US literature and relevant legal precedents. As mentioned above, the idea of measuring assets in accordance with their replacement cost or market value existed in the accounting literature prior to the Smyth v. Ames (1898) case (e.g. Hamilton 1788). Nonetheless, the legal precedents of the maximum freight case, subsequent disputes adjudicated in the courts and continued changes in general price-levels from the 1870s until the end of third decade of the twentieth century provided the impetus for increased discussion of fair value measurements in the form of some notion of replacement cost in the accounting literature.

This discussion took place in both professional (e.g. Chamberlain 1926; Hatfield 1927; Couchman 1928) and academic outlets (e.g. Paton 1918; Hull 1927; Rorem 1929). Significantly, many of the early supporters wielded considerable influence on the accounting discipline. Charles B. Couchman, for instance, was the Chairman of the Board of Examiners for the American Institute of Accountants and both Henry R. Hatfield and William A. Paton were prominent professors at the Universities of California Berkeley and Michigan, respectively.[4] This later became known as the 'appreciation debate', and a dedicated symposium was arranged to bring together various viewpoints, the proceedings of which were published in a special issue of *The Accounting Review* (Vol. 5, No. 1).

Clarke (1980, 1982) discusses those debates. In particular, he reveals that in the course of the appreciation debate, the idea of using replacement cost to measure the fair value of assets drifted from the context of public utilities to that of ordinary private companies. One of the underlying factors for this was the passing of the *Revenue Act of 1913*, which required *both* public utilities and private companies to reassess their assets in accordance with fair value for the calculation of depreciation.

The other underlying factor was the conflating of public utilities and ordinary private companies in the writings of early supporters of replacement cost. Paton (1918), for instance, addressed 'general commercial accounting' but used rulings from public utilities cases to make his point. He then made similar overtures in his seminal book, *Accounting Theory* (1922), which became the standard textbook on matters of accounting theory during this period (Gaffikin 2005).[5] Hull (1927) and Rorem (1929), on the other hand, drew on competitive pricing arguments from the economics literature, which actively downplayed the differences between public utilities and private companies. Clarke (1980) describes these activities as follows:

> ... the authors were breaking new ground. They were providing basic ideas about the financial effects of price changes and suggesting techniques of accounting that others could draw upon for guidance. For those ideas and techniques were being presented in a manner suggesting that they were backed up by the 'authority' of a large volume of case law and literature. They were, but with case law and literature relating specifically to the peculiar circumstances surrounding the setting of rates for the regulated utilities, not to the preparation of financial statements by the ordinary companies.
>
> *(p. 86)*

In addition to the passing of the *Revenue Act of 1913*, which applied the fair value idea to both public utilities and ordinary private companies, there were some good reasons why early supporters did not see the distinction between the two types of entities as important. Just as their counterpart in private companies, stockholders in privately held public utilities would expect a fair return on their invested capital. And, just as their counterpart in public utilities, private companies would have found it useful to consider the replacement cost of their assets when setting prices for their products and in budgeting for the future (for more about these arguments, see Hull 1927). It was commonalities such as these that led some authors to conclude that the two types of entities were so similar as to make a distinction between the two an impossible task (e.g. Farris & Sampson 1973).

As Clarke (1980) notes, however, the drift of the fair value notion from public utilities to ordinary private companies was not without problems. There is no evidence that there was any intention of the courts or public utilities for the fair value notion to drift into the financial reporting practices of private sector companies. In fact, the fair value notion remained a highly ambiguous one, even among public utilities, which is evidenced in 1944 with the Supreme Court's decision to recede their prior ruling in Smyth v. Ames (1898). This ambiguity only increased when accounting scholars applied it to private sector companies, which, unlike restricted public utilities, could adapt to changing market conditions and set their prices accordingly. The fair value notion's dependence on hypothetical prices, in the case of an estimated current, equivalent or future asset value, was also a stark departure from traditional financial reporting practices that were based on companies' actual transactions.

Drift from the accounting literature to standard-setting

When the Supreme Court decided to abandon the fair value term in 1944, there was little evidence that the appreciation debate had influenced financial reporting practices of private sector companies. Boer (1966) goes as far as to state that '... practicing accountants seem to have given it about as much attention as a ten-dollar mistake in the plant account (p. 97)'. As evidence of this, a survey of 208 corporations listed on the New York Stock Exchange showed that only a small fraction had ever adjusted the value of their assets either upward or downward (Fabricant 1936). Replacement cost, however, continued to be addressed in the literature through the 1940s (e.g. see Bradshaw 1948), primarily driven by the increase in the consumer price index due to the end of the Great Depression and manufacturing related to the Second World War.

In the 1960s, another corporate setting, takeovers, provided the catalyst to revisit the fair value term. This was the period of the conglomerate merger movement, and with the advent of these mergers there was pressure on the accounting profession to consider how to account properly for these new entities – namely to review the arguments underpinning the 'purchasing' v. 'pooling of interests' methods of accounting. In response, in 1970 the American Institute of Certified Public Accountants (AICPA) issued *Statement No. 4* stating that

> [f]air value is the approximation of exchange price in transfers in which money or money claims are not involved. Similar exchanges are used to approximate what the exchange price would have been if an exchange for money had not taken place.
>
> *(p. 72)*

The notion of selling price rather than replacement cost was clearly to the fore.

The International Accounting Standards Committee (IASC) eventually used the selling price form of fair value in the 1980s. The IASC issued *Accounting for Property, Plant and Equipment* (IAS 16) in 1982. The standard specified that the fair value of non-monetary assets had to be determined when those assets are used in an exchange for property, plant or equipment. It offered the following definition of the term: '[f]air value is the amount for which an asset could be exchanged between a knowledgeable, willing buyer and a knowledgeable, willing seller in an arm's length transaction (p. 6)'.

The IASC subsequently expanded the use of fair value to the accounting for such items as leases (IAS 17), government grants (IAS 20), business combinations (IAS 22) and retirement benefits (IAS 26) as well as certain cases of revenue recognition (IAS 18). Furthermore, with the issuance of *Financial Instruments: Recognition and Measurement* (IAS 39) in 1998, the committee eventually expanded the use of fair value to financial instruments.[6] In doing so, it broadened the previous definition of fair value to include liabilities and used the more generic term of 'parties' instead of buyer and seller.[7] Finally, in 2011, the International Accounting Standards Board (IASB), which had replaced the IASC in 2001, issued a separate standard, *Fair Value Measurements* (IFRS 13), which superseded all previous definitions of fair value accounting and offered a unified approach to its measurement. This new standard defined fair value as '… the price that would be received to sell an asset or paid to transfer a liability in an orderly transaction between market participants at the measurement date (p. 7)'.

The Financial Accounting Standards Board (FASB) soon followed the IASC in the use of the fair value term.[8] The board had been established in 1972, due to the failure of the AICPA to set adequate accounting standards on a timely basis (Zeff 1972), and in 1986, it had undertaken a project to address the accounting for financial instruments and off-balance sheet financing. The first standard of this project, FAS 105, was issued in 1990 and established disclosure requirements for financial instruments of this kind. The second standard, *Disclosures about Fair Value of Financial Instruments* (FAS 107), was issued the following year. The latter standard established that these financial instruments should be measured in accordance with their fair value and defined the process as follows:

... the fair value of a financial instrument is the amount at which the instrument could be exchanged in a current transaction between willing parties, other than in a forced or liquidation sale. If a quoted market price is available for an instrument, the fair value to be disclosed for that instrument is the product of the number of trading units of the instrument times that market price.

(p. 5)

Following the definition of the fair value process in FAS 107, and continued concerns about the measurement of financial institutions' holdings of financial instruments, the FASB issued *Accounting for Certain Investments in Debt and Equity Securities* (FAS 115) in 1993. FAS 115 extended the fair value measurement process to the treatment of some equity securities and all debt securities. In doing so, it also classified these securities into three categories: that is, securities held (1) to maturity, (2) for trading or (3) for sale.

The issuance of three more standards followed FAS 115. The first two, FAS 124 and FAS 133, were issued in 1995 and 1998, respectively, and extended the fair value measurement process to not-for-profit organizations and the accounting for derivative instruments and hedging activities. The third standard, *Fair Value Measurements* (FAS 157), was issued in 2006. Facing similar issues as the Supreme Court had in the 1940s after the maximum freight case, FAS 157, sought to clarify further the definition of the fair value term and introduced a hierarchy of measurement methods that companies should employ depending on their particular circumstances.[9]

The emergence of the fair value term in legal proceedings regarding public utilities in the late 1890s, the discussion of fair value measurements in terms of replacement costs in the accounting literature in the early 1920s, and the adoption of the term by accounting standard-setters in the 1980s has produced a rather precarious situation. First, because the drift took place over a 100-year span, there has been a failure for present parties to recognize the debates of the past. It is telling, for example, that the origin of the fair value term is not referenced in a single financial reporting standard. It is therefore also not surprising that the contemporary political struggle between banks and standard-setters on fair value measurements echo those between public utilities and the government at the turn of the twentieth century (Clarke & Dean 2009). Just as the public utilities in the past, the banks have switched allegiance depending on whether price-levels are increasing or decreasing. And, as Dean and Clarke (2010a) note, the outcome has been the politicization of accountancy '... with interested parties' special pleading ... producing pragmatism at the expense of logical and consistent reasoning (p. 191)'.

Second, the drift of the fair value term from the vastly different settings of public utilities, private sector companies and then primarily to the measurement of financial instruments resulted in it losing its original meaning entirely. When it drifted from court proceedings into the accounting literature, the Supreme Court's six proposed measurement factors were reduced to some notion of replacement cost. When it later drifted from the accounting literature into standard-setting, this notion of replacement cost was transformed into some form of a current exit price, perhaps due to a sense of false equivalence between replacement cost and current exit prices in the particular case of securities. In other words, the replacement cost tends to be close to the selling/acquisition price of the same securities but this is seldom true for other items. These are, of course, empirical questions but the point that we wish to make is that it is precisely insights such as these that have been lost in the disregard of the specific circumstances in which the fair value term has emerged.

The fair value measurements

As briefly mentioned in the previous section, the most current definition of fair value is '... the price that would be received to sell an asset or paid to transfer a liability in an orderly transaction between market participants at the measurement date (IASB 2011, p. 7)'. The inputs and techniques used to measure this current selling price (hereinafter the exit price) are categorized in accordance with a three-level hierarchy. The first level draws on actual prices from active markets of identical assets and liabilities, the second on prices of similar assets and liabilities and the third resorts to unobservable inputs to approximate an exit price. The fair value hierarchy prioritizes the first level, followed by the second level and then the third level, although the inputs and techniques in use can sometimes span several levels at once.

Whereas the fair value term dates back to the late 1890s, the antecedents of this fair value measurement system did not come from the subsequent discussions around replacement cost in the early 1920s. Instead, the system draws on ideas around measuring assets in accordance with their current exit price. Several authors, like Kenneth MacNeal (1939), had proposed exit (selling prices) to value certain assets such manufacturing stock, financial instruments, agriculture and livestock. Yet, systematic codification did not emerge in the Anglo-American accounting literature until the 1960s (later labelled the 'golden age of *a priori* research' by Nelson [1973]); it was driven in part by an increase in price-levels that started in the 1950s and culminated in the rampant inflation of the 1970s. This brought to the forefront concerns about the appropriate costs, prices and taxes under such conditions (for more about this period, see Persson 2013). And, in many ways, this debate was a re-emergence of ideas that originated in European, and in particular German, hyperinflation after the First World War (for more about some of this influence, see Clarke & Dean 1989). In the following three subsections, we trace these antecedents in regard to the inputs and techniques used in the three levels of the present fair value measurement hierarchy.

Level 1[10]

Fair value measurements should ideally be based on level 1 inputs, as these are deemed the most reliable in the fair value hierarchy. Being reliable, they are more easily audited. These '... inputs are quoted prices (unadjusted) in active markets for identical assets or liabilities that the entity can access at the measurement date (IASB 2011, p. 19)'. Furthermore, when an asset or liability is traded on multiple markets, one should use the 'principal' market or, in the absence of such a market, the one that gives the most 'advantageous' current exit price for the measurer. When level 1 inputs are available, however, there are only three exceptions to this measurement method. These are where (i) the individual exit price of a bundle of assets or liabilities is inaccessible, (ii) there is a discrepancy between the quoted price and the actual exit price of an item and (iii) prices are cross-matched between an entity's own liabilities/ equities and identical items traded as assets on active markets. In such situations, the entity might be forced to draw on level 2 and/or 3 inputs and/or measurement techniques.

The idea of measuring certain items in accordance with their current exit price has found occasional advocates for several centuries. In the case of measuring securities, in particular, the British accountant Pixley advocated for the use of historical cost on the balance sheet, but with an accompanying footnote that state '... the actual market value at the date on which the balance sheet is made out ... (p. 130)', as early as 1881. Robert H. Montgomery, the author of the first American auditing textbook, echoed these suggestions in regard to the measurement of securities in 1912. There are also similar examples from the courts. In the case of *Cannon v. Mills Co.* in 1928, for example, the Supreme Court of North Carolina ruled that '... it is necessary that the true value of the assets in cash, and not the mere book value, should be ascertained ... (p. 124)' for the determination and distribution of dividend.

In contrast to this particular treatment of securities, it has been suggested that the idea of measuring items *in general* in accordance with their market price, specifically current exit price, is much more recent and emerged during the golden age of *a priori* research in the 1960s (Gaffikin 1988). Chambers' 'Historical Cost – Tale of a False Creed' (1994) disagrees, drawing on evidence collected (and eventually published) in his *Thesaurus* (1995, see especially sections 540–49).

Edgar Edwards and Philip Bell proposed an accounting system based on a mix of inputs, one of them being current exit prices, in an influential book published in 1961.[11] It was Raymond J. Chambers (1966), however, who first published a comprehensive system of financial reporting based solely on the measurement of current exit prices. Chambers (1961) had some years earlier concluded that the function of accounting was to provide financial information about the reporting entity's ability to adapt to changes in its environment. This had led him to the measurement of current exit prices, which he argued was the sole monetary amount that was *always* relevant when evaluating the possibilities for adaption. For example, the current exit price is relevant when considering the procurement of new assets, the replacement of assets, or even the liquidation of the enterprise as a whole.

Ernest Weinwurm had been a major influence on Chambers' thinking that accounting measurements should draw exclusively on current exit prices as inputs.[12] Weinwurm was a Professor at DePaul University, deeply interested in the emerging field of scientific management, and an active member of the newly established Institute of Management Sciences. And, upon his urgings, Chambers had had spent considerable time reading up on the general literature on measurements (e.g. Chambers 1961). This excursion ultimately reinforced his earlier conclusion in favor of the sole use of current exit prices, as he had found that only this input would comply with the canons of measurements discussed in these readings. These canons dictated that any meaningful measurement system must be based on a common property (e.g. length, weight or contemporary prices), use a common scale (e.g. meters, kilograms or dollars) and only use a specified unit within that scale. As such, the conventional mixing of historical prices from previous periods, contemporary prices in the current period and hypothetical future prices through depreciation conventions was not mathematically sound. Regardless of the sophistication involved in its calculation, the result of such a system could be no better than the adding of meters and kilograms to derive a total figure (for more about these insights, see the preface to Chambers 1974).

Chambers' proposal for the use of current exit prices as the sole measurement input was first published in an article, 'Measurement in Accounting', in the *Journal of Accounting Research* in 1965. From his private correspondence, it appears that Chambers had begun writing the manuscript upon the return from a trip to tour universities in the USA in 1962; he completed it in 1963 and then distributed it to his colleagues in Australia and abroad.[13] The recipients included prominent individuals such as Charles Noyes, then the Editor of the *Journal of Accountancy*, Maurice Moonitz, Professor of Accounting at the University of California Berkeley, and Myron J. Gordon, who had developed the Dividend Discount Model at the Massachusetts Institute of Technology in the 1950s.[14]

The collective response to the article was one of enthusiasm and, with the establishment of both the function and measurement input of accounting, Chambers continued writing a book-length manuscript that he had begun around the same time as the article. This manuscript was eventually published under the title *Accounting, Evaluation & Economic Behavior*

(A, E&EB) in 1966. In this manuscript, he codified earlier writings to derive deductively a comprehensive accounting system, CoCoA, that recorded items in accordance with their current exit price to measure the entity's ability to adapt to changes in its environment at the reporting date. In correspondence with Stephen A. Zeff, he confided that he believed that it had the potential to raise a 'helluva storm' in the field of accounting.[15]

Chambers predictions proved accurate. A, E&EB became widely disseminated in both the practitioner (e.g. Dein 1966) and academic literatures (e.g. Solomons 1966), caused considerable debate (e.g. Larson & Schattke 1966), and found some strong advocates among Chambers' colleagues.[16] Sir Alexander Fitzgerald, the most senior accounting academic in Australia and Professor of Accounting at the University of Melbourne, felt that the manuscript's philosophical spirit, rigor of thought and distinction in expression were unmatched in the literature.[17] Robert R. Sterling similarly described the manuscript as flawless in logic, exceedingly thorough and irrefutable in its conclusion.[18] A third correspondent proclaimed that it would surely make Chambers '... one of the immortals of accounting'.[19]

Chambers would spend the remainder of his career advocating for the adoption of Co-CoA, with over 40 submissions to professional and public bodies, 250 presentations at various conferences and universities and 150 articles, books and monographs on the matter. These activities led to considerable esteem among contemporaries, over 25 academic recognitions, and even an induction into the Accounting Hall of Fame in 1991. During this period, exit prices also began to creep into some accounting standards for the revaluation of certain assets and the treatment of securities, primarily superannuation investments. There is no evidence, however, that Chambers' activities were the cause of this and there was no full-scale adoption of his proposal. The exception was a large-scale comparative financial reporting experiment in New Zealand in the 1970s, in which Chambers' proposal represented one of several methods under consideration (e.g. Craswell 1976). Chambers (1980) deliberated on this situation toward the end of his career, with the conclusion that

> [t]here is inevitably, and in every field, a gap in time between the development of an *art*, the development of theoretical *knowledge* and the impact of that knowledge on its related art or practice ... These gaps are no cause for alarm among those who appreciate the halting, vagrant and devious progress from ... art, through rationalization, to systematic knowledge and ultimately to ... practice ... To put things in perspective, may I remind you of some of the incidents in the history of science and technology ... [T]he following periods elapsed between the conception of the basic idea and its function—photography, 56 years; television, 63 years; antibiotics, 30 years; zip fasteners, 30 years; instant coffee, 22 years. In the light of this, it is perhaps understandable that the emergence of an agreed, serviceable form of accounting ... cannot be expected to occur speedily ...
>
> *(pp. 167–168)*

With the benefit of hindsight, it is now noteworthy that this passage indeed anticipated the current move to current exit prices in the form of level 1 fair values. With that said, however, it is worth mentioning again that there is no evidence that current standards were drawn from the writings of Chambers or his contemporaries from the golden age of *a priori* research in the 1960s (for some thoughts on the reasons behind this, see Persson & Napier 2014). Instead, it appears to be a matter of standard-setters arriving at similar conclusions but for its own reasons. There is not, for example, any recourse in current standard to the basics canons of measurements or ideas around adaptability, both of which formed the basis for Chambers' CoCoA.

Level 2

When level 1 inputs are unavailable, the FASB/IASB state that fair value measurements should ideally be based on level 2 inputs. These are observable inputs, other than quoted prices for identical assets and liabilities from level 1, such as (1) quoted prices for actively traded similar assets and liabilities, (2) quoted prices for non-actively traded similar or identical assets and liabilities and (3) a selection of market-corroborated prices. The latter can take into account factors such as the interest rate, yield curve, implied volatilities and credit spreads. Furthermore, when using (1) and (2) inputs, one can adjust for their relative condition and comparability and, when using (3) inputs, one can adjust for the volume or level of activity in the observed market. However, when these adjustments are deemed as 'significant', the inputs might be counted as a part of the third level of the fair value hierarchy (IASB 2011).

Similar to the case of current exit prices, Chambers was an early supporter of using items of similar kind to those held by the firm as proxies for current exit prices (i.e. the first category of level 2 inputs). At the time of writing A, E&EB (1966), his concern had been that it would have been too novel to suggest a zero balance for all items without an active market. In his own words:

> ... I suspect that I was intimidated by the novelty of the [exit] price idea which, to my knowledge, has no respectable antecedent in the literature. Perhaps, too, I was cowed by the possibility that a strict use of the [exit] price rule would entail the elimination of monetary representations of many assets.
>
> *(1970, p. 43)*

However, having argued that all measurements had to be based on a common property, scale and a specified unit within that scale, Chambers received considerable pushback from his detractors (e.g. Hendriksen 1967). The compromise to use similar items as proxies was not seen as an attempt to make his proposal more palpable but as a sleight of hand. This was particularly so with his suggestion to value inventories in accordance with their current entry price, which avoided the inclusion of unsold items in the adjusted net income but represented a stark departure from the uniform use of current exit prices.

In 'Second Thoughts on Continuously Contemporary Accounting', published in 1970, Chambers' responded to this criticism by admitting that he too had been the victim of accounting dogma in failing to dispose of the conventional revenue recognition principle when discussing inventories (i.e. the idea that one should not anticipate profits). Nonetheless, because of their criticism and further deliberation about the importance of adhering to the principles of measurement (following Weinwurm's promptings), he had now abandoned the use of proxies for the sole use of current exit prices and proposed the assignment of zero balances to those items without a resale market. He advocated for the use of a double account mechanism for reporting such items, accompanied by a detailed notation to indicate that the asset still had productive capacity (i.e. user value).

Besides being in agreement with the canons of measurements, this revision was consistent with Chambers' goal of measuring a firm's adaptability. The argument is that an item without a resale market cannot help the firm adapt and, rightly so, therefore should not be assigned a current exit price. Stated differently, a current exit price of zero is in and of itself valuable information and it is precisely this point that Dean and Clarke reiterated in a comment letter to FASB as recently as 2009:

For the owners of the particular item no market price simply means that the options regarding its use are limited – it may well be that it can be used to produce a revenue stream, it can be retired, allowed to sit idle, given away, but no market price means simply what it says – the item cannot be exchanged for cash, cannot generally be pledged as collateral for borrowing, cannot contribute directly to the fund to extinguish debts.

(pp. 2–3)

However, this conclusion, which is now attributed to what has become known as the 'Sydney School', is a point of departure from the evolution of the current fair value measurement standards, in which each iteration has expanded the use of alternative inputs when quoted market prices are unavailable (for more about this school of thought, see Clarke et al. 2010). One can only speculate that this trend comes from a similar reluctance among standard-setters to assign zero values to assets listed on the balance sheet, all of which would have been acquired with the goal of generating revenue.

Level 3[20]

When both level 1 and 2 inputs are unavailable, fair value measurements should be based on level 3 inputs. These are composed of unobservable inputs that act as proxies for the current exit price of assets held or liabilities owed. When determining what unobservable inputs to draw upon, the market participant should choose the best inputs available. This might include both internal and external inputs as well as the adjustment for any potential risk inherent in the inputs or the valuation technique employed (IASB 2011). The three most commonly advocated valuation techniques are the cost, market and income approach. Hypothetical current entry prices (i.e. the cost of replacement) are used as inputs in the cost approach, comparable items are used in the market approach and expected future cash flows are used in the income approach. A market participant might also draw on several of these approaches simultaneously.

As we have already traced the historical antecedents of current exit prices and market proxies for such prices in the earlier two sections, let us focus here on the historical development of the use of valuation techniques based on the income approach. As an early example, Jachomo Badoer, a Venetian merchant trading on the Black, Levantine, and Mediterranean seas, used valuation methods, based on expected future cash flows, in the absence of quoted market price in the 1400s (Peragallo 1938). These practices were later adopted by goldsmiths in London in the 1600s (De Roover 1948) and, as a contemporary example, the AICPA has also experimented with discounted cash flows as '… a valuation basis quantifying specific assets and liabilities or the enterprise as a whole … (1973, p. 41)' beginning in the 1970s. At the same time, the problems associated with valuation methods of this kind have also been documented in the literature. In the late 1920s, for instance, one author lamented that it was impossible to use discounted cash flows to value individual items as '… the earnings of a business are the joint products of all the assets, conditions and services which the business possesses and uses (Daines 1929, p. 98)'. Other criticisms of such methods are noted in Chambers' *Thesaurus* (1995, especially sections 552, 553).

Gane (1968) suggested that the first comprehensive system of using discounted future cash flows to derive a current exit price originated from a group of German foresters in the 1800s. In the process of determining the future value of their land, they were the first to develop several of the present value calculations employed today. This breakthrough in valuation, however, laid dormant until the 1900s when it was rediscovered by the prominent American economist Irving Fisher (1907), who erroneously credited John Rae (1834) with the original idea. In *The Rate of Interest*, Fisher re-established the principles of discounting future cash flows and argued for its universal application for the pricing of both debt and all income-generating assets (see pp. 10–11 in particular). John Bennet Canning adopted the approach in his 1929 *Economics of Accountancy*, describing the product as an 'indirect valuation'.

Nitzan and Bichler (2009) express Fisher's proposed relation between assets and debts and future cash flows as follows:

> ... a pecuniary asset, taken in its most general form, is merely a claim on earnings. In this sense, bonds, corporate shares, preferred stocks, mortgages, bank accounts, personal loans, or the registered ownership of an apartment block are simply different incarnations of the same thing: they are all income-generating entities.
>
> *(p. 156)*

Fisher's use of discounted future cash flows to derive hypothetical current exit prices initially generated minimal attention within the field of economics. Several commentators were rather skeptical of the universal application of present value calculations and quoted market prices were not readily available to evaluate Fisher's claims. For example, James C. Bonbright (1921), who brought the notion of deprival value into accounting (Baxter 2003), described the idea as both '... unsound in theory ... [and] vicious in its practical application (p. 482)'. As such, these types of calculations were initially limited to their use in the design, capital budgeting and pricing of public utilities. This situation remained throughout the 1940s, before Joel Dean (1951) reinvigorated the idea of using discounted cash flows in the 1950s and it reached general acceptance in the 1960s (e.g. Merrett & Sykes 1963).

As noted, Canning was the first to apply comprehensively Fisher's insight on using discounted cash flows to establish current exit prices in the field of accounting (Chambers picked up on this connection in two articles published in 1971 and 1979). *The Economics of Accountancy* had come about because Canning, a Professor of Economics, had been tasked with the development of an accounting course at Stanford University, and he had therefore set out to '... undertake a comprehensive study of accounting theory and practice from the point of view of the professional student of economics (p. iii)'. As evidenced in the acknowledgments to this study and in private correspondence, however, it turns out that Canning was not just a student of economics in general but of Fisher's work in particular.[21] The result was that a forceful argument in favor of the use of discounted cash flows as a valuation technique in accounting (see in particular 'Chapter XII: Indirect Valuation').

The Economics of Accountancy received very positive reviews in the accounting and economics literature (e.g. Beatty 1930; Meriam 1931). There was a sense that the work was pioneering in bridging both fields (for a contemporary perspective on its importance, see Beaver 2000). As Chambers (1979) points out, however, there is no evidence that those engaged in standard-setting noticed these ideas in the 1930s and there are no explicit references to it in current standards.

Instead, it was George J. Staubus who adopted similar ideas in his development of the 'investor decision-usefulness' criterion (and his maximum time-adjusted cash potential or MATACAP) in the 1950s, first in his doctoral dissertation at the University of Chicago and later in subsequent publications (for an edited compilation, see Staubus 2013). This decision-usefulness criterion later formed the basis of the IASB and FASB's conceptual frameworks and, eventually, led to the use of discounted future cash flows as one alternative valuation technique under the third level of the fair value hierarchy. In other words, the implicit claim here is that investors find the valuation that results to be more decision-useful than the assignment of a zero value to those items that lack a quoted market price. This is clearly in contrast with the conclusion of Chambers (1970) that it was more important to be consistent with the basic canons of measurement theory and report a zero balance, while having a narration to the accounts showing other information such as the expected discounted cash flows from using the asset.

Conclusion

After noting that in several countries 'fair value' has a long history, our focus was on its US origins. The chapter primarily traces the term through its emergence in legal precedents on public utilities in the late 1800s, its drift into the accounting literature in the early 1900s and its subsequent drift into financial accounting standards in the 1980s. Through this process, we showed that fair value had lost its original meaning, namely that of measuring the replacement cost of assets used by public utilities, and the politics that has been involved in its development. In recent decades, the selling price variant has dominated as standard-setters sought to mandate it for several types of monetary assets, like financial instruments. Drawing on the non-US origins, in particular the mainly European advocates of 'value to the owner', fair value has also become part of the impairment process related to valuing non-monetary (fixed) assets.

Separate from those historical developments, we then traced the historical antecedents of the fair value measurement system in accordance with its now mandated 'three levels'. We demonstrated how the first level, based on inputs from quoted market prices, had been alluded to in the late 1800s but did not emerge as part of a comprehensive accounting system until the golden period of *a priori* research in the 1960s, and especially the writings of Chambers (1966). The second level, based on quoted market prices of identical items to that being measured, emerged during this same period and from the same writer, although Chambers would in the 1970s abandon the use of proxies for non-monetary assets. Finally, we noted how the income approach, used in level 3 fair value measurements, emerged from a group of German foresters in the 1800s, was rediscovered in the economics literature in the early 1900s and drifted into the accounting literature in the late 1920s. As a caveat, however, standard-setters did not adopt these developments until much later when drawing on Staubus' decision-usefulness criterion.

With the preceding historical narrative in mind, it is easy to agree with Sterling's (1967) assessment that accounting is a discipline without a unified theory of valuation. The historical development of the fair value term and related measurement system is a complex one with ideas drawn from many disciplines and periods. What is more, these ideas were often not promulgated with accounting in mind and, consequently, their subsequent drift into the deliberations of standard-setters has tended to change their meaning. As Dean and Clarke (2010a) observe, this has led to a situation where '… history has been a curious victim … [and where] … a valuable resource has been overlooked (p. 190)'. We hope that this chapter has made inroads in filling this gap in the literature.

Notes

1 This and several subsequent historical quotes were retrieved from Chambers' *Accounting Thesaurus* (1995), which traces various interpretations of accounting concepts and terms through the past 500 years.

2 The reminder of the chapter draw heavily on the few studies that have examined fair value accounting (or some of its parts) from a historical perspective, in particular Clarke (1980) and Dean and Clarke (2010a).
3 For additional cases, see Chapter 11, 'The Rate Base: Cost or Value', in Bonbright (1961).
4 The American Institute of Accountants is the predecessor to the American Institute of Certified Public Accountants.
5 See in particular Chapter 18, 'Revaluation and Capital Maintenance', which demonstrate the use of replacement cost during periods of changes in specific and general prices.
6 Some investments are covered in IAS 25, which is the predecessor to IAS 39.
7 The IASB eventually phased out IAS 39 with its own standard, Financial Instruments (IFRS 9), which was issued in its entirety in 2014. This is also the case for most of IASC's earlier standards.
8 It is worth noting that the FASB has not always followed the IASC and later the IASB. IFRS 13, for instance, was issued in 2011 but derives much of its content from FAS 157, which was issued in 2006.
9 The IASB would come to use largely the same classification scheme and fair value hierarchy as FAS 115 and 157 in their own standard (IFRS 9 and 13). Interposed around this time was the work done by the Canadian Accounting Standards Board for the IASB.
10 This section draws on Dean (2007) who has already made the principle connection between Chambers' continuously contemporary accounting system (CoCoA) and fair value accounting, albeit noting several differences. Chambers was the foundation Professor of Accounting (1960) at the University of Sydney.
11 See Sprouse and Moonitz (1962) for another influential proposal based on mixed measurements and Persson et al. (2015) for more about the controversy that ensued after its publication.
12 The R. J. Chambers Archive at the University of Sydney (hereafter Chambers Archive) contains over 120 letters of correspondence between Chambers and Weinwurm. For more about this correspondence, see Dean and Clarke (2010b).
13 Material from the Chambers Archive: e.g. 10.USA P202/1/01154; 01168; and 2/08530.
14 Chambers Archive: 10.USA P202/1/01184; 07734; and 2/08609.
15 Chambers Archive: 10.USA P202/1/08198.
16 Chambers had review copies of A, E&EB sent to 47 journals, 24 prominent individuals, and the manuscript was eventually translated into both Japanese and Spanish (Chambers Archive: 10.USA P202/1/05805 and /3/09836).
17 Chambers Archive: 10.USA P202/3/09836.
18 Chambers Archive: 10.USA P202/1/01975.
19 Chambers Archive: 10.USA P202/1/02205.
20 This section draws heavily on Faulhaber and Baumol (1988) as well as Nitzan and Bichler (2009).
21 Irving Fisher Papers, Manuscript and Archives, Yale University: box 4, folder 48; box 7, folder 98; and box 8, folder 116.

References

AICPA 1973, *Objectives of financial statements (Study Group on the Objectives of Financial Statements)*, American Institute of Certified Public Accountants, New York.
Baxter, WT 2003, *The case for deprival value*, The Institute of Chartered Accountants of Scotland, Edinburgh.
Beatty, WC 1930, "The economics of accountancy: a critical analysis of accounting theory (Book Review)", *American Economic Review,* vol. 20, no. 1, p. 112.
Beaver, WH 2000, "Economics of accountancy: a critical analysis of accounting theory (Book Review)", *The Accounting Review,* vol. 75, no. 4, pp. 485–486.
Boer, G 1966, "Replacement cost: a historical look", *The Accounting Review,* vol. 41, no. 1, pp. 92–97.
Bonbright, JC 1921, "Earning power as a basis of corporate capitalization". *The Quarterly Journal of Economics,* vol. 35, no. 3, pp. 482–490.
Bonbright, JC 1937, *The valuation of property: a treatise on the appraisal of property for different legal purposes* vol. 1, McGraw-Hill Book Company, New York & London.
Bonbright, JC 1961, *Principles of public utility rates*, Columbia University Press, New York & London.
Bradshaw, TF (ed.) 1948, *Depreciation policy when price levels change: a source book of published opinions and information*, Controllership Foundation, New York.

Canning, JB 1929, *The economics of accountancy: a critical analysis of accounting theory*, Ronald Press Company, New York.

Cannon v. Mills Co., 195 N.C. 119 (Supreme Court of North Carolina 1928).

Chamberlain, HT 1926, "A discussion of surplus with reference to surplus available for dividends". *Journal of Accountancy,* vol. 41, no. 6, pp. 417–426.

Chambers, RJ 1961, *Towards a general theory of accounting*, Hyde Park Press, Adelaide, SA.

Chambers, RJ 1965, "Measurement in accounting". *Journal of Accounting Research,* vol. 3, no. 1, pp. 32–62.

Chambers, RJ 1966, *Accounting, evaluation and economic behaviour*, 1st edn, Prentice-Hall, Englewood Cliffs, NJ.

Chambers, RJ 1970, "Second thoughts on continuously contemporary accounting", *Abacus,* vol. 6, no. 1, pp. 39–55.

Chambers, RJ 1971, "Income and capital: Fisher's legacy", *Journal of Accounting Research,* vol. 9, no. 1, pp. 137–149.

Chambers, RJ 1974, *Accounting, evaluation and economic behaviour*, 2nd edn, Scholars Book Co, Houston, TX.

Chambers, RJ 1979, "Canning's the economics of accountancy–after 50 years", *The Accounting Review,* vol. 54, no. 4, pp. 764–775.

Chambers, RJ 1980, "The myths and the science of accounting", *Accounting, Organizations and Society,* vol. 5, no. 1, pp. 167–180.

Chambers, RJ 1994, "Historical cost–tale of a false creed. *Accounting Horizons,* vol. 8, no. 1, pp. 76–89.

Chambers, RJ 1995, *An accounting thesaurus: 500 years of accounting*, Pergamon, Oxford.

Churchman, CW 1961, *Prediction and optimal decision: philosophical issues of a science of values*, Prentice-Hall, Englewood Cliffs, NJ.

Clarke, FL 1980, "Inflation accounting and the accidents of history", *Abacus,* vol. 16, no. 2, pp. 79–99.

Clarke, FL 1982, *The tangled web of price variation accounting: the development of ideas underlying professional prescriptions in six countries*, Garland Publishing, New York & London.

Clarke, FL & Dean, GW 1989, "Conjectures on the influence of the 1920s Betriebswirtschaftslehre on Sweeney's Stabilized Accounting", *Accounting and Business Research,* vol. 19, no. 76, pp. 291–304.

Clarke, FL & Dean, GW 2009, "Toxic plan is nothing but humbug", The Australian Financial Review, p. 55.

Clarke, FL, Dean, GW & Wells, MC 2010, *The Sydney school of accounting: the chambers years*, Sydney University Press, Sydney.

Couchman, CB 1928 "Limitations of the present balance-sheet", *Journal of Accountancy,* vol. 46, no. 4, pp. 253–269.

Craswell, A 1976, *A manual on continuously contemporary accounting*, Times Commercial Printers, Hamilton, NZ.

Daines, HC 1929, "The changing objectives of accounting". *The Accounting Review,* vol. 4, no. 2, pp. 94–110.

De Roover, RA 1948, *The Medici Bank: its organization, management, operations and decline*, New York University Press, New York.

Dean, J 1951, *Capital budgeting: top-management policy on plant, equipment, and product development*, Columbia University Press, New York.

Dean, GW 2007, "IFRSs enter a fair value, exit price world?", *Abacus,* vol. 43, no. 2, pp. i–iv.

Dean, GW & Clarke, FL 2010a, Commentary: business Black Swans and the use and abuse of a notion. *Australian Accounting Review,* vol. 20, no. 2, pp. 185–194.

Dean, GW & Clarke, FL 2010b, "Ray chambers and Ernest Weinwurm - Scholars in unison on measurement in accounting", *Accounting Historians Journal,* vol. 37, no. 2, pp. 1–37.

Dein, RC 1966, Accounting, evaluation and economic behavior (Book review), *Journal of Accountancy,* vol. 122, no. 4, pp. 89–90.

Edwards, EO & Bell, PW 1961, *The theory and measurement of business income*, University of California Press, Oakland, CA.

Fabricant, S 1936 "Revaluations of fixed assets, 1925–1934" in *Revaluations of fixed assets, 1925–1934*, eds S. Fabricant, National Bureau of Economic Research, Cambridge, MA, pp. 1–12.

Farris, MT & Sampson, RJ 1973, *Public utilities: regulation, management and ownership*, Houghton Mifflin Company, Boston, MA.

FASB 1990a, *Disclosure of information about financial instruments with off-balance-sheet risk and financial instruments with concentrations of credit risks (FAS 105)*, Financial Accounting Standards Board, Norwalk, CT.

FASB 1990b, *Disclosures about fair value of financial instruments (FAS 107)*, Financial Accounting Standards Board, Norwalk, CT.

FASB 1993, *Accounting for certain investments in debt and equity securities (FAS 115)*, Financial Accounting Standards Board, Norwalk, CT.

FASB 1995, *Accounting for certain investments held by not-for-profit organizations (FAS 124)*, Financial Accounting Standards Board, Norwalk, CT.

FASB 1998, *Accounting for derivative instruments and hedging activities (FAS 133)*, Financial Accounting Standards Board, Norwalk, CT.

FASB 2006, *Fair value measurements (FAS 157)*, Financial Accounting Standards Board, Norwalk, CT.

Faulhaber, GR & Baumol, WJ 1988, "Economists as innovators: practical products of theoretical research", *Journal of Economic Literature*, vol. 26, no. 2, pp. 577–600.

Federal Power Commission v. Hope Natural Gas Co., 320 U.S. 591 (1944).

Fisher, I 1907, *The rate of interest: its nature, determination and relation to economic phenomena*, The MacMillan Company, New York.

Gaffikin, MJR 1988, "Legacy of the golden age: recent developments in the methodology of accounting", *Abacus*, vol. 24, no. 1, pp. 16–36.

Gaffikin, MJR 2005, "Creating a science of accounting: accounting theory to 1970". *Working Papers Series*. University of Wollongong.

Gane, M (ed.) 1968, *Martin Faustmann and the evolution of discounted cash flow*, Commonwealth Forestry Institute, Oxford.

Garfield, PJ & Lovejoy, WF 1964, *Public utility economics*, Prentice-Hall, Englewood Cliffs, NJ.

Goddard, EC 1928, "The problem of valuation. The evolution of cost of reproduction as the rate base", *Harvard Law Review*, vol. 41, no. 5, pp. 564–592.

Hall, KL, Ely, JW & Grossman, JB (eds) 2005, *The Oxford companion to the supreme court of the United States*, 2nd edn, Oxford University Press, Oxford.

Hamilton, R 1788, *An introduction to Merchandize*, 2nd edn, C. Elliot, T. Kay, & Co, London.

Hatfield, HR 1927, "What is the matter with accounting?", *Journal of Accountancy*, vol. 44, no. 4, pp. 267–279.

Hendriksen, ES 1967, "Accounting, evaluation and economic behavior (Book Review)", *The Journal of Business*, vol. 40, no. 2, pp. 211–213.

Hull, GL 1927, "Plant appraisals-their treatment in the accounts", *The Accounting Review*, vol. 2, no. 4, pp. 303–326.

IASC 1982a, *Accounting for leases (IAS 17)*, IASC Foundation, London.

IASC 1982b, *Accounting for property, plant and equipment (IAS 16)*, IASC Foundation, London.

IASC 1982c, *Revenue (IAS 18)*, IASC Foundation, London.

IASC 1983a, *Accounting for government grants and disclosure of government assistance (IAS 20)*, IASC Foundation, London.

IASC 1983b, *Business combinations (IAS 22)*, IASC Foundation, London.

IASC 1986, *Accounting for investments (IAS 25)*, IASC Foundation, London.

IASC 1987, *Accounting and reporting by retirement benefit plans (IAS 26)*, IASC Foundation, London.

IASC 1998, *Financial instruments: recognition and measurement (IAS 39)*, IASC Foundation, London.

IASB 2011, *Fair value measurement (IFRS 13)*, IFRS Foundation, London.

IASB 2014, *Financial instruments (IFRS 9)*, IFRS Foundation, London.

Institute of Chartered Accountants of Scotland (ed.) (1952), *Proceedings of the sixth international congress on accounting*, Gee Publishing, London.

Larson, K & Schattke, RW 1966, "Current cash equivalent, additivity, and financial action", *The Accounting Review*, vol. 41, no. 4, pp. 634–641.

Laux, C & Leuz, C 2009, "The crisis of fair-value accounting: making sense of the recent debate". *Accounting, Organizations and Society*, vol. 34, no. 6–7, pp. 826–834.

Lee, TA 2013, "Reflections on the origins of modern accounting", *Accounting History*, vol. 18, no. 2, pp. 141–161.

Lisle, G 1904, *Encyclopedia of accounting*, W. Green & Sons, Edinburgh.

Los Angeles Gas & Electric Corporation v. Railroad Commission of California, 289 U.S. 287 (1933).

MacNeal, K 1939, *Truth in accounting*, University of Pennsylvania Press, Philadelphia, PA.

McCardle v. Indianapolis Water Company, 272 400 (1926).

Meriam, RS 1931, "The economics of accountancy: a critical analysis of accounting theory (Book review)", *The Accounting Review*, vol. 6, no. 3, pp. 242–243.

Merrett, AJ & Sykes, A 1963 *The finance and analysis of capital projects*, Longmans, Green & Company, London.

Michie, RC 1999, *The London stock exchange: a history*, Oxford University Press, Oxford.

Montgomery, RH 1912, *Auditing theory and practice*, Ronald Press Company, New York.

Nelson, C 1973, "A priori research in accounting" in *Accounting research 1960–1970: a critical evaluation*, eds N Dopuch & L Revsine, Center for International Education and Research in Accounting, Urbana-Champaign, IL, pp. 3–19.

Nitzan, J & Bichler, S 2009, *Capital as power: a study of order and creorder*, Routledge, London and New York.

Paton, WA 1918, "The significance and treatment of appreciation in the accounts" in, *Twentieth annual report of the Michigan academy of science*, ed. GH Coons, University of Michigan, Ann Arbor, MI, pp. 35–49.

Paton, WA 1922, *Accounting theory: with special reference to the corporate enterprise*, Ronald Press Company, New York.

Peragallo, E 1938, *Origin and evolution of double entry bookkeeping: a study of Italian practice from the fourteenth century*, American Institute of Accountants Publishing Company, New York.

Persson, ME 2013, *The rise and fall of comprehensive accounting theories: R. J. Chambers and continuously contemporary accounting.* (PhD in Accounting), Royal Holloway University of London, London.

Persson, ME & Napier, CJ 2014, "The Australian accounting academic in the 1950s: R. J. Chambers and networks of accounting research", *Meditari Accountancy Research*, vol. 22, no. 1, pp. 54–76.

Persson, ME & Napier, CJ 2015, "R. J. Chambers and the AICPA's postulates and principles controversy: a case of vicarious action", *Accounting Historians Journal*, vol. 42, no. 2, pp. 101–132.

Persson, ME, Radcliffe, VS & Stein, M 2015, "Alvin R. Jennings: managing partner, policy-maker, and institute president", *Accounting Historians Journal*, vol. 42, no. 1, pp. 85–104.

Persson, ME, Radcliffe, VS & Stein, M 2017. "Elmer G. Beamer and the American institute of certified public accountants: the pursuit of a cognitive standard for the accounting profession", *Accounting History*, vol. 23, no. 1–2, pp. 71–92.

Pixley, FW 1881, *Auditors, their duties and responsibilities*, Effingham Wilson, London.

Rae, J 1834, *Statement of some new principles on the subject of political economy: exposing the fallacies of the system of free trade, and of some other Doctrines maintained in the wealth of nations*, Hilliard, Gray, and Co, Boston, MA.

Railroad Commission of California v. Pacific Gas & Electric Company, 302 388 (1938).

Revenue Act of 1913, 38, 114 Stat. (2013).

Rorem, CR 1929, "Replacement cost in accounting valuation", *The Accounting Review*, vol. 4, no. 3, pp. 167–174.

Smyth v. Ames, 169 U.S. 466 (1898).

Solomons, D 1966, "Accounting, evaluation and economic behavior (Book review)", *Abacus*, vol. 2, no. 2, pp. 205–209.

Southwestern Bell Telephone Company v. Public Service Commission of Missouri, 262 U.S. 276 (1923).

Sprouse, RT & Moonitz, M 1962, *A tentative set of broad accounting principles for business enterprises (Accounting Research Study No. 3)*, American Institute of Certified Public Accountants, New York.

Staubus, GJ (ed.) 2013, *The decision usefulness theory of accounting: a limited history*, Routledge, London and New York.

Sterling, RR 1967, "Conservatism: the fundamental principle of valuation in traditional accounting". *Abacus*, vol. 3, no. 2, pp. 109–132.

Verner v. General and Commercial Investment Trust Ltd, 2 Ch. 239 (1894).

West, B 2003, *Professionalism and accounting rules*, Routledge, New York & London.

Zeff, SA 1972, "Chronology of significant developments in the establishment of accounting principles in the United States 1926–1972", *Journal of Accounting Research*, vol. 10, no. 1, pp. 217–227.

11

THE 'FAIRNESS' OF FAIR VALUE ACCOUNTING

Marking-to-market, marking-to-model and financial reporting management

Kalin Kolev

[...] the marks are based on "unobservable" inputs reflecting a company's "own assumptions about the assumptions that market participants would use in pricing the asset or liability." Or, as I like to say, mark-to-make-believe. For instance, that dead horse that showed up in your backyard in Aspen last winter? Some math genius [...] has a model that says it's worth its weight in uranium – and climbing – just in time to beat analysts' earnings estimates for the quarter.

Errors will usually be honest, reflecting only the human tendency to take an optimistic view of one's commitments. But the parties to derivatives also have enormous incentives to cheat in accounting for them. Those who trade derivatives are usually paid (in whole or part) on "earnings" calculated by mark-to-market accounting. [...] In extreme cases, mark-to-model degenerates into what I would call mark-to-myth.

I came across these quotes in the midst of the Financial Crisis, while working on my dissertation. As I was interested in gaining an insight into the role of internally generated fair value estimates in the statement users' information sets, they struck a chord. The first is from a thought piece by Jonathan Weil (Bloomberg.com, October 29, 2007) and the second is from Warren Buffett, as part of the 2002 Berkshire Hathaway annual report. The outlets and the authors of the two pieces are intrinsically different; yet, both excerpts converge on the inherent vulnerability of ex ante unverifiable fair value estimates. More so, both emphasize the interaction between incentives of the reporting parties and the integrity of mark-to-model measurements. While clearly aimed at fair value estimates, at the time I could not help asking myself whether and how these claims differ at their core from the ones that have been made with respect to estimates embedded in an amortized historical cost accounting systems that play a primary role in International Financial Reporting Standards (IFRS) and US GAAP.

Fast-forward a decade. When I was offered an opportunity to share my thoughts on fair value accounting and earnings management in this book chapter, I found myself pondering the same question: all said and done, aren't fair value estimates just as much subject to noise and bias as accruals? And, isn't the likelihood and severity of the vulnerabilities attributed to fair value measurement as much a function of complexity, incentives and oversight as they are in the amortized historical cost setting?

On the surface, the answer appeared to be a resounding 'yes'. However, a deeper dive suggests a rich dimensionality to the problem, offering interesting parallels and contrasts.

Broadly speaking, the industry concentration of balance sheet components subject to fair value reporting, coupled with the inherent differences in the business model of financial and non-financial firms, industry-specific regulatory oversight and the mixed-attributes nature of fair value accounting, collectively introduce important counterpoints to the role of accruals and fair value estimates in financial reporting. In particular, financial institutions are asymmetrically exposed to (recurring) fair value measurement due to the nature of their operations. Since regulatory capital adequacy is critical to them, incentives to report strategically often relate to the balance sheet, rather than the income statement. As another example, the mixed attributes model currently in use allows for recognizing assets and liabilities at fair value, but the associated changes in value accrue to accumulated other comprehensive income rather than affect contemporaneous earnings. This separation of the balance sheet and income statement, in turn, opens the door to gains trading and strategic timing of write-downs. As a result, in an attempt to emphasize the richness of the fair value accounting – strategic reporting dynamic, I position the discussion relative to financial reporting management, rather than the more familiar and well-accepted concept of earnings management.

I start with the observation that the debate on the role of fair value in financial reporting is not new. However, the coincidence in the enactment of two accounting standards – one aimed at standardizing the definition of fair value and mandating additional disclosure on the observability of the measurement inputs and the other allowing the application of full fair value treatment to most financial instruments – and the recent Financial Crisis not only rekindled it, but also brought the polemic to the attention of the general public. Next, I expand on the choice to frame the discussion with respect to financial reporting, rather than earnings management, emphasizing that the scale and scope of fair value reporting renders balance sheet accounts as likely of a subject to bias as income statement accounts. I proceed with contrasting recurring and non-recurring fair value measurement, noting that the latter is a manifestation of conditional conservatism, a concept deeply ingrained in the historical cost accounting framework. I also note the role of incentives and oversight, highlighting that they are critical components for the existence and effect of reporting bias in the examined setting. The chapter concludes with the observation that while the volume of research on fair value accounting and financial reporting management is substantial, additional evidence is necessary to fully appreciate their interplay.

So, what is the big idea?

The debate on the role of fair value measurement in financial reporting has a rich history.[1] While providing a comprehensive timeline is outside the scope of this chapter, the Savings and Loan (S&L) crisis in the late 1980s and early 1990s and the collapse of Enron in 2001 deserve a mention as important inflection points in the recent past. The S&L crisis traces back to a series of interest rate increases. As the savings and loans associations, commonly known as 'thrifts', funded their operations primarily through customer deposits while providing long-term loans, they faced a duration mismatch, working against them in periods of increasing borrowing costs. When the Federal Reserve initiated interest rate increases in the late 1970s to fight off inflation, many thrifts felt the pressure, potentially becoming economically insolvent. However, the accounting procedures in place accomodated avoiding regulatory capital violations, allowing the thrifts to continue operating. In an effort to turn back fortunes, the troubled thrifts engaged in progressively risky investment strategies, magnifying the scale and eventual cost of the crisis.[2] In a way, the S&L crisis brought to focus the importance of understanding the fair values of a firm's holdings, which lead to the enactment of a series of standards aimed at expanding the role of fair value measurement and disclosure under US GAAP.[3,4]

In contrast, Enron became the poster child of marking-to-market gone wrong. Its energy business was built around trading energy swaps, which Enron accounted for at fair value. As deep and liquid markets for the contracts did not exist, determining the market value of the derivatives involved high level of discretion. In a company whose stock price depended on reporting profits, this offered a convenient means to engineer 'accounting performance'. Of course, the story is a lot more complicated than that, but, relevant to the discussion here, the unravelling of Enron served as a stepping stone for series of regulatory interventions and gained vocal support for calls to limit the role of fair value accounting in financial reporting.

As the S&L crisis and Enron examples highlight, the conversation on the role of fair value accounting is not static, with supporters and detractors having the upper hand at one point or another. Although the issue has remained of interest to regulators, practitioners and academics, as evidenced by the host of standards and related comment letters on the one hand, and prolific stream of research on the other, the recent Financial Crisis also brought the broad public into the debate. The cause for this (rather unusual) public interest in an accounting topic appears to be the coincidence of the enactment of SFAS 157, 'Fair value measurement', and SFAS 159, 'The fair value option for financial assets and financial liabilities', with the onset of the Crisis. SFAS 157, now part of ASC 820, standardizes the definition of 'fair value' and mandates the disclosure of a measurement hierarchy, and SFAS 159, now part of ASC 825, allows firms to adopt full fair value accounting for most financial instruments.[5] Interestingly, SFAS 159 offers means to expanding the role of fair value measurement in financial reporting, but it is SFAS 157, which is primarily a disclosure standard, that typically is portrayed as the 'villain'. While I found this counterintuitive for years, I am inclined to believe that a likely reason is the SFAS 157's mandate that firms identify the balance sheet components that are reported at values based on unobservable inputs, i.e. the 'dreaded' level 3. I make this conjecture because, although this disclosure does not have a first-order effect on the exposure of a firm's financials to fair value measurement, it may appear to provide a measure of the intensity of its reliance on managerial assumptions on the reported fair value estimates.

This brings the discussion back to the central question for the chapter: whether and how fair value accounting and financial reporting management interact. At its core, this question speaks to the decision-usefulness of fair value estimates, an issue underlying the ongoing debate on the role of fair value measurement in financial reporting. Indeed, both supporters and detractors of fair value accounting often call upon the notion of relevance and reliability to support their respective views.[6] While the specific arguments vary, they typically revolve around the idea that unless an estimate is sufficiently reliable, it cannot provide decision-useful information, despite how relevant it might be. Since financial reporting management introduces bias in the estimates, it affects their reliability, having a first-order effect on their decision-usefulness. In other words, the interaction between fair value measurement and financial reporting management construes an important dimension of the debate.

When deep and liquid markets for the respective asset exist, the opportunity to bias the reported fair value is limited; hence, the reliability of the estimate is seldom questioned in such cases. However, such markets do not exist for a number of asset classes, making managerial assumptions an important factor in fair value measurement. The estimates that depend on managerial assumptions are a convenient vehicle for communicating private information, ranking them high on the dimension of relevance. The inherent difficulty of verifying these assumptions, however, renders the resultant estimates vulnerable to both noise and bias, challenging their reliability. Thus, it comes as no surprise that a large part of the debate on fair value accounting focuses on the internally generated, mark-to-model, fair value estimates, where the relevance-reliability tension is most pronounced.

To be certain, this issue is not specific to fair value measurement. Rather, it relates to all estimates in accounting and mirrors closely arguments made with respect to accruals and earnings management. However, as I discuss next, I find that a separate examination of fair value measurement and financial reporting management is warranted, as business models, regulation and reporting standards interact to set fair value estimates apart as a unique setting. And, although extant research leaves little doubt that financial reporting management exists, as estimates play a major role, the jury is still out on the welfare effect of the practice. As such, this alternative setting to study the issue is a very welcome opportunity.

Why 'financial reporting management' rather than 'earnings management'?

Earnings is the most prominent and closely tracked universal corporate performance metric.[7] Leaning on the revenue recognition and matching principles under the amortized historical cost accounting framework, earnings purport to present a meaningful portrayal of a firm's performance during a period. As such, earnings play a key role in both valuation and contracting.[8] The metric's prominence, coupled with the flexibility inherent in accrual measurement and the discretion in generating and timing business transactions, offer both incentives and the means to manage reported earnings. Indeed, a plethora of evidence points to the existence of earnings management (e.g. Graham et al. 2005; Levitt 1998; the Sarbanes-Oxley Act), as the practice is one of the most researched and discussed accounting-related issues (as of the writing of this note a Google [Google Scholar] search for 'earnings management' yields over 400 thousand [70 thousand] results).

Most formal definitions of earnings management of which I am aware build on the notion that the practice reflects opportunism. One example is Healy and Wahlen (1999) who stipulate that

> Earnings management occurs when managers use judgment in financial reporting and in structuring transactions to alter financial reports to either mislead some stakeholders about the underlying economic performance of the company or to influence contractual outcomes that depend on reported accounting numbers.

> *(p. 368)*

A large literature adopts this view, noting that private benefits are a key driver for earnings management. However, another stream of research posits that managing earnings is a means to communicating private information (DeFond & Park 1997; Gunny 2010, among others). While the two literatures disagree on the ultimate role of earnings management, they converge on the idea that the practice is costly and firms make an active effort to achieve their earnings-related reporting objectives. Put differently, statement preparers and users perceive earnings to be a critical output of the accounting system, making earnings management an appropriate frame when thinking about strategic intervention in financial reporting in amortized historical cost regimes.

Under a fair value measurement regime, however, the focus shifts from the income statement to the balance sheet. In the (theoretical) case of full fair value accounting, the balance sheet serves as a summary statistic of firm value, as the income statement reflects the change in firm risk (e.g. Ronen 2008). The mixed-attributes model currently in use adds a layer of complexity since the periodic remeasurement of balance sheet components reported at fair value often bypasses contemporaneous earnings to be recognized as income in a future period (e.g. available-for-sale securities). This break in articulation between the balance sheet and the income statement opens the door to timing the release of the accumulated unrealized gains and losses as means to shaping reported earnings. However, while statement users do not ignore these releases, they often down-weight them relative to the core, recurring, components of income.[9] This effect is exacerbated in the case of non-recurring fair value measurement where balance sheet values recognized at amortized historical cost are written down to market value under one of the impairment rules.

Under current US GAAP, recurring fair value measurement applies predominantly to financial assets and liabilities. Although non-financial firms have expanded their holdings of financial instruments over the years (e.g. Duchin et al. 2017), the largest concentration remains among financial institutions. This, in turn, makes regulatory capital an important component of the 'fairness of fair value' discussion, once again emphasizing the role of the balance sheet. Moreover, as I note previously, the fair value hierarchy disclosure mandated by SFAS 157 highlights the observability of the inputs used in deriving the reported fair values. While this may appear benign on the surface, commentary suggests that some statement users perceive the concentration of level 3 holdings as a negative signal, prompting claims that firms engage in balance sheet shifting, strategically classifying their holdings among the FAS 157 level 1, level 2 and level 3 categories.[10]

To summarize, the concept of earnings management is familiar both within and outside academia, as the label is occasionally applied to strategic intervention in financial reporting not directly targeting GAAP income. However, in thinking about the practice in the fair value setting, the *earnings management* moniker downplays the complexity of the underlying dynamics, implicitly suggesting that the focus is strictly on the income statement.[11] For this reason, I deviate from convention and use the less familiar, but broader, *financial reporting management* label. To be certain, *financial reporting management* shares multiple characteristics with *earnings management*. Importantly, it also requires intent: whether it is used as means to communicate private information or reflects opportunism, it suggests that the involved party actively engages in the practice. Consistent with this notion, the subsequent discussion focuses on the possible drivers of bias in fair value accounting, largely ignoring issues pertaining to noise.[12]

Dimensions

Prior to discussing the specific ways in which financial reporting management and fair value measurement interact, it is worthwhile expanding on some of the issues briefly mentioned in the prior sections. In particular, knowledge of fair values is essential for the successful management of a company and is indispensable in assessing performance. The complexities involved with M&A activities, the amount of time MBA students spend thinking about net present value calculations and internal rates of return, and the staggering volume of research on valuation are few of the examples supporting this notion. However, since companies generate wealth through transforming inputs into value-added products and services, a common view is that recognizing the accretion of value at the time of sale is a sound reporting practice. Put differently, the amortized historical accounting system currently in place keeps the balance at historical cost, making earnings a summary statistic of firm value. As such, efforts of strategic intervention into financial reporting typically focus on earnings, as smoothing and meeting earnings targets are the most often discussed objectives. To achieve these objectives, firms can select from a large menu of tools, exercising discretion in accrual measurement and impairment testing, entering economic transactions, adjusting reported GAAP earnings and managing expectations, being among the most common ones. While different in nature, each of these tools is associated with economic costs and firms have been shown to exercise discretion in selecting among them.

Unlike non-financial assets, financial instruments are often not amenable to value enhancement by the entity that holds them (e.g. a single name stock, an index, or a mortgage-backed security). Indeed, these financial instruments often trade on active markets, and even when they do not, the current set of accounting rules requires that the respective fair value estimate be the price that would have obtained from such markets. In other words, they do not fit cleanly within the amortized historical cost framework, making them a prime candidate for fair value accounting. Thus, it does not come as a surprise that the debate on fair value accounting centers on financial instruments, placing emphasis on balance sheet measurement. By extension, this puts financial institutions in the spotlight: while non-financial firms often hold sizeable investment portfolios, tautologically, financial instruments are at the core of the financial institutions' business model. As such, most research on the characteristics of fair value accounting focuses on financial firms.[13]

Although recurring fair value measurement predominantly affects financial instruments, in practice, non-financial assets and liabilities are also subject to fair value measurement. Specifically, the series of 'lower-of-cost-or-market' rules embedded in the amortized historical cost framework require that balance sheet values are written down when evidence supports that the book value of the respective items exceeds its market value, as the effect is not likely to reverse in the near future. As a primary manifestation of the conditional conservatism principle, these rules impose fair value measurement on a non-recurring basis.[14] Importantly, while these mark-to-market revaluations affect contemporaneous earnings, they purport to reflect non-recurring income-decreasing adjustments. As such, statement users typically downweigh them relative to the core, operating, expenses; in fact, these charges are among the most common adjustments applied by firms and analysts in calculating non-GAAP earnings.

Financial instruments, including some that are reported at fair values on a recurring basis, are also subject to impairment testing. When the measurement basis is amortized historical cost, e.g. securities classified as held-to-maturity under SFAS 115, the treatment generally mirrors that of non-financial assets. At present, whether fair value measurement is considered recurring or non-recurring depends on the balance sheet treatment of the respective item. Thus, when the measurement basis is fair value, the effect derives from the mixed attributes model currently in use. In particular, when firms apply recurring fair value measurement for the balance sheet, but amortized historical cost for the income statement, the periodic revaluations bypass the latter, accruing instead to accumulated other comprehensive income. When there is evidence of non-temporary decline in value or of a firm's lack of willingness or ability to hold the security to maturity, the unrealized losses are released into earnings via an other-than-temporary-impairment charge. As noted earlier, this asymmetry between balance sheet and income statement treatments not only raises questions regarding the timing and magnitude of the impairment charges, but also opens the door to gains trading.

In thinking about the potential strategic application of fair value accounting, it is also important to consider the adoption optionality embedded in a number of the active accounting standards. While examples are abundant (e.g., SFAS 133/ASC 815 on derivatives and hedging and SFAS 156/ASC 860 on servicing of financial assets and liabilities), SFAS 115 deserves a mention as it gives companies a fair amount of flexibility in selecting the measurement basis for their holdings: from full fair value accounting (trading securities) to partial fair value accounting (available-for-sale) to amortized historical cost (held-to-maturity).[15] To be certain, the trend in accounting standards reveals a preference for expanding the role of full fair value measurement for financial instruments. SFAS 159 (ASC 825) serves as a case in point: the standard allows the adoption of full fair value accounting on an instrument-by-instrument basis for most financial instruments, with the intent of improving the alignment in accounting treatment among economically linked balance sheet components. However, the optionality in application, coupled with the common practice of allowing the adoption effect to bypass the income statement, adds the adoption and application of accounting standards to the menu of tools facilitating strategic reporting.

Finally, a discussion on strategic intervention would be incomplete without considering the forces that motivate the practice. Mirroring earlier comments, academic research, regulatory actions and practitioner commentary each indicates financial reporting management is costly, pointing to litigation, forgone investment opportunities, capital misallocation, restatements and managerial turnover as few of the many examples (Graham et al. 2005; Karpoff et al. 2008; Kedia and Philippon 2007, among many others). Thus, the reporting parties engage in the practice when the expected benefits exceed the expected costs. The benefits could be private or relate to the firm and its stakeholders, ranging from improving the informativeness of financial reports, to preventing a debt covenant violation, to avoiding triggering regulatory intervention, to beating the analysts' forecast or compensation targets, among others. Regardless whether the motivation is altruistic or opportunistic, firms will engage in the practice only if they have the means. As noted earlier, the fair value accounting framework offers a plethora of tools for strategic intervention into financial reporting. However, governance, or the system of checks in balances in place, acts as a break. Governance comes in many flavors, oversight by external and internal auditors, regulators, debt holders and large investors serving as examples. This interplay between incentives and oversight is not unique to fair value accounting. However, the richness of the setting and the complexities involved in working with mark-to-model estimates renders it an issue of notable importance.

But, even if the issue spurs intellectual curiosity, is it economically important? Turning to the SFAS 157 disclosures as summarized by Compustat, the average (median) US firm-year observation with assets reported at fair value and book value of equity exceeding one million, has 22 percent (10 percent) of its asset base marked to market. Contrasting financial and non-financial firms, the means (medians) are notably higher for the prior: 18 (5) percent versus 33 (21) percent. When the benchmark is owners' equity, the effect is even more pronounced: 114 (28) percent for the pooled sample, and 45 (13) versus 305 (158) percent for non-financial and financial firms, respectively. In other words, the answer appears to be a resounding 'yes'.

To recap, fair value accounting and financial reporting management interact at multiple levels, offering a unique setting to study the role of strategic intervention in financial reporting. Thus, while the overarching questions − is fair value accounting susceptible to financial reporting management and, if yes, is the effect net positive, negative or neutral (and to whom?) − may appear relatively unassuming, answering them requires nontrivial analysis. To this end, I dedicate the rest of the exposition to a deeper dive into the mechanisms and manifestations of the examined practices, structuring the discussion around recurring versus non-recurring fair value measurement.[16]

Recurring fair value measurement

Recurring fair value measurement requires a periodic updating of the values of the affected balance sheet components so they reflect current market pricing. As noted earlier, while prior accounting standards do not necessarily converge on the meaning of 'fair value', SFAS 157 fixes the concept as an exit value, i.e. the price that would obtain from transacting on an active market. When active markets do not exist, the pronouncement stipulates that the reported value should mimic what a hypothetical market would have provided. Similar to other ex ante unverifiable estimates in accounting, these mark-to-model valuations stand at the core of the relevance-reliability tension underlying in large part the debate on the role of fair value accounting in financial reporting.

One of the popular approaches to analyzing decision-usefulness of accounting data is through examining the partial association between the metrics of interest and stock price. Under this framework, a significant coefficient on the balance sheet components reported at fair value is interpreted as evidence that the estimate is relevant and sufficiently reliable, i.e. decision-useful.[17] The enactment of SFAS 157 allowed refining the analysis, making possible an explicit comparison among the mark-to-market (level 1), adjusted mark-to-market (level 2) and mark-to-model (level 3) measurements. In particular, level 3 estimates rely on material unobservable inputs, making them a prime vehicle for financial reporting management, should statement preparers choose to engage in the practice. As such, if opportunistic bias is suspected, the estimated level 3 coefficients should be lower than their level 1 or 2 counterparts. More so, as SFAS 157 equates fair value to exit price, an estimated coefficient of one emerges as a natural benchmark in assessing whether or not the estimates are unbiased.

Applying this value-relevance framework, early research finds evidence that the estimated coefficients on level 3 are both lower than the coefficients on level 1 estimates and lower than one, suggesting that equity investors discount firm-reported mark-to-model fair values (e.g., Goh et al. 2015; Song et al. 2010). On the surface, this evidence is consistent with assertions that investors perceive level 3 estimates as susceptible to opportunistic use in an effort to boost reported performance. Indeed, cross-sectional analyses indicate that the level 3 discount is deeper when firms face regulatory constraints or have weaker governance structure. However, additional analyses and subsequent research suggest that liquidity and research design issues are among a set of alternative explanations for these results (Goh et al. 2015, Lawrence et al. 2016, among others).[18]

My research on the perceived reliability of mark-to-model estimates aligns closer with the latter view (Kolev 2013). In this analysis, I examine a sample of S&P 1,500 financial institutions during the first three quarters of 2008, a period marked by a continuous escalation of the Financial Crisis. Similar to other studies using comparable samples, I find an economically and statistically lower level 3 coefficient than the respective level 1 and level 2 ones in price-level specifications. While also noting predictable attenuation in subsamples with poorer governance or low regulatory capital, the stock price–level 3 partial association remains statistically and economically significant across the board. However, when I move beyond the price-levels analysis, I find that the level 3 revaluations are not only significantly positively associated with contemporaneous returns, but in some specifications the estimated coefficients on the revaluation component is close to one.[19] This effect persists when the level 3 revaluation is partitioned between gains and losses, and realized versus unrealized net gains, among others. Finally, as additional analysis, I fail to find associations between the revaluation component of the change in level 3 and past or future returns. In other words, the findings fail to support that fair value measurement is used for opportunistic financial reporting management.

Evidence, of course, is not restricted to equity markets. As one example, Arora et al. (2014) analyze fair value estimates through the viewpoint of credit markets. In particular, the study examines the partial association between level 1, 2 and 3 estimates and credit default swap spread. Building on the model of Duffie and Lando (2001), which suggests that the term structure of debt instruments informs on information quality, the authors infer that reliability is a concern with fair value estimates, as the mark-to-model ones are especially vulnerable. As another example, Magnan et al. (2015) study the earnings forecasts of sell-side equity analysts, concluding that level 2 measurement corresponds to higher quality public and private information, whereas level 3 measurement has the opposite effect. As a third example, Ettredge et al. (2014) find that audit fees for US banks increase in the proportion of assets measured at fair value, as level 3 estimates are the primary driver. Finally, Altamuro and Zhang (2013) examine mortgage servicing rights, documenting that the ones classified as level 3 are better predictors of future servicing fees relative to their level 2 counterpart, concluding that managers use their information advantage to generate higher quality estimates when there are no active markets for the underlying asset.

A related literature examines how well fair value estimates inform on risk. As examples, Hodder et al. (2006) and Blankespoor et al. (2013) both find that marking-to-market improves the risk-relevance of financial reports. Riedl and Serafeim (2011) document that level 3 financial holdings have higher asset betas relative to those designated as level 1 or 2, adding to the debate.

To summarize, this stream of research offers conflicting evidence on the role of fair value measures in the statement users' information sets, as the challenge is especially pronounced with respect to internally generated estimates. In particular, while the evidence points to a possible strategic intervention in fair value measurement, opinions diverge on whether opportunism or efforts to improve the informativeness of financial reports motivate the practice.

The discussion thus far focuses primarily on the balance sheet. This should not come as a surprise as the concentration of financial assets and liabilities is highest among financial institutions, for whom regulatory capital management is of primary importance. However, income statement effects, which are the main focus of the classic earnings management literature, also play a role: similar to non-financial firms, the profitability of financial institutions is tracked by equity analysts and capital markets, and earning targets are important components of compensation contracts. As noted earlier, the mixed attributes model often results in a lag in the recognition of balance sheet fair value changes in earnings. This, in turn, raises questions on the possibility of gains trading and managing the timing of write-downs, both of which directly affect reported income. As I note in the next section, evidence supports that firms use both tools with non-financial assets. But, does the effect extend to financial instruments?

Not surprisingly, the answer appears to be 'it depends'. On the one hand, evidence supports that equity investors price both other-than-temporary-impairment charges and the realization of unrealized gains and losses generated through security sales (e.g. Badertscher et al. 2013; Dong et al. 2014), suggesting they are informative to statement users.[20] On the other hand, research indicates that management capitalizes on the flexibility inherent in fair value measurement to obtain private benefits. As an example, evidence supports a link between fair value measurement and CEO compensation (Dechow et al. 2010; Livne et al. 2011).[21]

While measurement takes the spotlight in the fair value conversation, the role of strategic application of the respective standards should not be ignored. As noted earlier, the fair value hierarchy disclosure mandated by SFAS 157 seems to have served as a key factor in re-igniting the debate. In particular, the mark-to-model, level 3, category houses estimates that depend on material unobservable inputs. As such, these estimates offer management a convenient tool for communicating private information, especially in times when markets are disrupted. However, the inherent difficulty in ex ante verifying the level 3 estimates also renders them subject to financial reporting manipulation. As such, classifying holdings among the SFAS 157 categories becomes a decision variable on its own, as firms trade off the benefits and costs associated with mark-to-model measurement and revealing the balance sheet concentration of illiquid holdings.[22] Evidence, again, is setting-specific. As noted earlier, Altamuro and Zhang (2013) document a cross-sectional variation in the classification of mortgage servicing rights between the SFAS 157 level 2 and level 3 categories, as the authors note that the information content of the level 3 estimates is superior to their level 2 counterparts. In contrast, studying a sample of insurance firms, Hanley et al. (2016) document that the classification of identical securities among the SFAS 157 categories is not uniform, as the deviations relate to financial reporting and regulatory objectives. And, Iselin and Nicoletti (2017) contrast samples of US public and private banks around the adoption of SFAS 157 to argue that firms strategically alter their portfolio composition and classification in an effort to avoid the disclosure of level 3 assets. More so, examining a sample of early adopter of SFAS 159, Henry (2009) notes that an important determinant of the choice to apply the full fair option early is the ability to transfer unrealized losses from accumulated other comprehensive income to retained earnings, bypassing the income statement.[23]

But, can firms get away with pushing the boundaries of fair value accounting? Both research and anecdotal examples suggest that the answer is 'not necessarily'. Returning to Henry (2009), the study notes that firms misapplying the standard rescinded or revised its adoption. More so, as noted throughout the discussion, auditors, regulators and market participants each provide discipline in the application of fair value accounting. To be certain, the notion that oversight is an important mechanism in financial accounting and reporting is well developed in the voluminous earnings management literature, so I will not elaborate further. However, I will reference the observations in Bens et al. (2015) that comment letters issued by the SEC mitigate the uncertainty associated with fair value measurements, and in Badia et al. (2017) that firms with high concentration of level 2 and 3 holdings report more conditionally conservative comprehensive income deriving from fair value measurement in an effort to mitigate the negative perception of mark-to-model estimates by statement users.

To sum up, similar to other estimates, fair value measures are susceptible to financial reporting management. While governance, in its many manifestations, provides discipline, whether firms use the flexibility embedded in the fair value accounting to improve the statements' informativeness or to gain private benefits remains an open question. And, although inroads are made to supplement the evidence through analysis of non-financial firms, research in the area remains focused predominantly on financial firms, leaving a material gap in understanding the fair value accounting-financial reporting management dynamics.

Non-recurring fair value measurement

The debate on the role of fair value measurement in financial reporting predictably focuses on financial instruments, and, by extension, financial services firms. Marking-to-market, however, is not limited to recurring measurement: M&A transactions, where the purchase price needs to be allocated over the net identifiable assets and goodwill, and calculating stock option expense serve as two of the many examples. Importantly, the amortized historical cost framework currently in use calls for regularly assessing the fair values of most non-financial components of the balance sheet, even if these fair value measurements are typically not recognized or disclosed. This derives from the requirement that assets are tested for impairment, as their value is written down when there is evidence that the book value exceeds the respective fair market value. When recognized, these write-downs flow through the income statement, decreasing net income for the period.

The impairment standards allow certain flexibility with respect to timing the recognition of the charge. More so, whereas active markets exist for certain asset classes (e.g. inventory), in many cases measurement relies on ex ante unverifiable assumptions, i.e. the magnitude of the recognized adjustment is susceptible to both noise and bias. And, while the incidence of an impairment aims to inform on material shocks to the firm, its magnitude is often down-weighted by statement users relative to the other components of income under the premise that it is non-recurring. Indeed, there charges are usually grouped within the *special items* category, which, while a component of net income, are among the main adjustments applied by managers and analysts in calculating non-GAAP earnings.[24] Thus, it should not come as a surprise that write-downs, which reflect non-recurring fair value measurements, present a convenient vehicle for financial reporting management.

To fix concepts, I turn to goodwill. Goodwill arises from M&A transactions when the consideration provided by the acquirer exceeds the fair value of the acquired net identifiable assets. Under the current set of accounting rules, goodwill is not amortized; instead, it is assessed for impairment periodically and written down as needed. Goodwill is notoriously difficult to value. As such, the incidence and magnitude of the impairment charges often become a subject of negotiation between management and providers of oversight. Starting with incidence, the recognition of a goodwill impairment implies that expected benefits from past M&A transactions will no longer accrue. Thus, such a charge frequently translates into negative shocks to the reporting firm's stock price and the human capital of its management team. In other words, firms have incentives to delay the recognition of goodwill impairment and evidence suggests they act on them (e.g. Ramanna and Watts 2012). When the charge is recognized, however, incentives shift to overstating the current period charge since this decreases the probability of a future write-down. As one example, Beatty and Weber (2006) use the enactment of SFAS 142 to examine the dynamic, demonstrating that firms are strategic in their choice of timing and intensity of goodwill impairments, as the effect is driven by financial reporting benefits and constrained by considerations related to valuation and contracting.

To be certain, the (potential) manifestation of strategic non-recurring fair value measurement is not restricted to goodwill. In fact, the incentives to engage in big bath accounting, i.e. writing down the value of a holding excessively, conditional on recognizing the charge, is even stronger for balance sheet components that can be used in gains trading at an opportune moment or are subject to periodic amortization or depreciation, as both offer means to boosting future reported income. Indeed, oversight mitigates concerns with respect to both timeliness and accuracy. However, the issue remains economically important: evidence suggests that, on average, one third of the Compustat-reported income-decreasing special items among US firms comprise recurring expenses shifted from the past, present, or the future (Cain et al. 2017).

The discussion here is purposefully concise. The literature on earnings management (not a typo) is broad in scope and large in size, and there are many excellent references for the interested reader. The evidence leaves little doubt that the practice exists, even if the jury is still out on whether the main driver is an attempt to improve the informativeness of financial reports or to obtain private benefits. Regardless of the motivation, however, many of the manifestations of earnings management relate to fair value measurement. Recognizing this offers broader insights into the characteristics of fair value measurement and its interplay with financial reporting management.

Concluding remarks

Estimates are an integral part of financial accounting, intended to improve the decision-usefulness of financial reports. However, their subjective nature renders them vulnerable to bias. This issue is exacerbated among mark-to-model estimates: although they offer a

convenient means for communicating private information, the inherent lack of *ex ante* vali-
dation makes them a convenient tool for an opportunistic intervention in financial reporting.
While regulators have advanced multiple projects aimed at improving the decision-usefulness
of fair value estimates and academic research has made significant progress in characterizing
the settings where these strategic interventions into financial reporting are likely to be dominated by efforts to obtain private benefits, the issue is far from resolved. As such, understanding the role of recurring and non-recurring fair value measurement in financial accounting
and reporting remains a work-in-progress.

Notes

1 The companion chapter by Ken Peasnell offers an excellent exposition on the issue. As noted
there, the work of the late Yuji Ijiry and Ray Chambers provides an eloquent presentation of the
arguments in support of historical cost and fair value accounting, respectively.
2 Curry and Shibut (2000), among others, offer an analysis of the causes and consequences of the
S&L crisis.
3 SFAS 107, 'Disclosures about fair value of financial instruments', and SFAS 115, 'Accounting for
certain investments in debt and equity securities', are two familiar examples.
4 To simplify the exposition, I focus on US GAAP and firms that follow them for financial reporting purposes. The majority of the arguments, however, generalize to IFRS and the domiciles that
conform to them.
5 SFAS 157 defines fair value as, '[...] the price that would be received to sell an asset or paid to
transfer a liability in an orderly transaction between market participants at the measurement date'
(p. 2), fixing the concept as an exit value, rather than, e.g. entry value or value-in-use.
6 The points of contention fueling the debate go beyond relevance and reliability. As examples, arguments have been made that fair value accounting exacerbates volatility, induces procyclicality,
and leads to downward spirals in asset values, as firms race to sell their holdings in expectation of
further declines in price driven by sales pressure (Allen & Carletti 2008; Plantin et al. 2008, among
others).
7 To be certain, non-financial metrics, such as new customer additions and churn, and comparable store sales, are closely monitored by statement users. Unlike earnings, however, these are
industry-specific, rather than market-wide.
8 Over the recent decades non-GAAP earnings, or GAAP earnings adjusted for components deemed
not representative of a firm's economic performance, have gained prominence. Here I use the term
'earnings' without distinguishing between GAAP and non-GAAP, relegating the discussion to a
subsequent section.
9 If these items were truly non-recurring, this would be a moot point. However, evidence suggests
that in many settings these items predict future earnings, cash flows, and returns (e.g. Cain et al.
2017), suggesting strategic play.
10 I revisit each of these points in the next section.
11 To be certain, fair value accounting is only one of many settings where this argument applies (e.g.
Livne & McNichols 2009, on true and fair overrides in the UK).
12 While self-evident, it is important to highlight that measuring fair values and classifying them
according to the SFAS 157 nomenclature requires significant judgment. As an example, current
accounting rules require firms to report to a point estimate. This estimate, however, derives from
a distribution of *ex ante* values. Similarly, whether an unobservable input is deemed material or a
market is considered insufficiently deep or liquid to warrant an adjustment to the market price of the
respective asset, i.e. whether the estimated is classified as levels 1, 2, or 3, often is discretionary. Thus,
similar to other estimates, noise is an inherent characteristic of the examined reporting practice.
13 I find this ironic as the research design in many empirical studies in accounting, some of my work
included, calls for the removal of financial institutions from the examined samples. Mirroring calls
to extend these analyses to financial firms, which comprise a large part of the economy, I think that
analyzing the issue with respect to non-financial firms is an important, yet largely overlooked, task.
14 I expand on the issue in a subsequent section.
15 This is not intended to imply that the pronouncements allow firms to be silent on the fair value of
the instruments for which they opt out of mark-to-market accounting. Indeed, current accounting

standards call for disclosure of the fair values of certain items reported at amortized historical cost (e.g. securities designated as held-to-maturity). Disclosure versus recognition provides an interesting experimental setting, as extant research demonstrates that both statement preparers and users treat estimates differently when they appear on the face of the financial statements rather than the footnotes. For the purposes of the exposition, however, I restrict the discussion to recognized fair values.

16 My objective is to provide a sketch of the role of financial reporting management in fair value accounting, rather than a comprehensive review of the literature. As such, the exposition emphasizes newer research and omits many excellent studies, while referencing work that is in a relatively early stage.

17 Barth et al. (2001) and Holthausen and Watts (2001) provide an informative overview of the pros and cons of value-relevance research.

18 The initial language in SFAS 157 stipulates that the reported value should not reflect a liquidity discount, i.e. it is set as *price × quantity*. Subsequent pronouncements, however, clarify that liquidity should be factored when generating the fair value estimate.

19 In addition to the valuation hierarchy disclosure, SFAS 157 also requires that firms reconcile the change in level 3 estimates during a period, identifying how much of the change is attributable to transfers between the three categories, net purchases, and revaluations.

20 Cantrell and Yust (2017) offer an interesting counter-point, conjecturing that firms strategically may opt out of selling securities to avoid triggering the recognition of other-than-temporary-impairment changes on the retained portion of the portfolio.

21 The accompanying chapter by Gilad Livne and Garen Markarian offers a discussion on the link between managerial compensation and fair value measurement.

22 While I focus on SFAS 157 for ease of exposition, this notion extends to other pronouncements. As one example, Hodder et al. (2002) argue that US banks deviated from the optimal allocation among the SFAS 115 categories – held-to-maturity, available-for-sale, and trading – when adopting the standard and note the 1995 FASB amnesty, which allowed firms to re-adopt SFAS 115.

23 This effect is not unique to the fair value setting: as one example, Beatty and Weber (2006) document a similar dynamic around the enactment of SFAS 142, 'Goodwill and other intangible assets'.

24 Special items refer to income statement components that are unusual or infrequent in nature, i.e. they are non-recurring. Non-GAAP earnings come in two flavors: *proforma*, or non-GAAP earnings as reported by the firm, and *street*, or non-GAAP earnings as assessed by analysts. While evidence suggests that analysts may exercise oversight over non-GAAP reporting, special items are among the items typically excluded by both parties. As such, to facilitate exposition, I use the non-GAAP moniker rather than distinguishing between the two flavors.

References

Allen, F & Carletti, E 2008, "Mark-to-market accounting and liquidity pricing", *Journal of Accounting and Economics*, vol. 45, no. 2, pp. 358–378.

Altamuro, J & Zhang, H 2013, "The financial reporting of fair value based on managerial inputs versus market inputs: evidence from mortgage servicing rights", *Review of Accounting Studies*, vol. 18, no. 3, pp. 833–858.

Arora, N, Richardson, S & Tuna, İ 2014, "Asset reliability and security prices: evidence from credit markets", *Review of Accounting Studies*, vol. 19, no. 1, pp. 363–395.

Badertscher, BA, Burks, JJ & Easton, PD 2013, "The market pricing of other-than-temporary impairments", *The Accounting Review*, vol. 89, no. 3, pp. 811–838.

Badia, M, Duro, M, Penalva, F & Ryan, S 2017, "Conditionally conservative fair value measurements", *Journal of Accounting and Economics*, vol. 63, no. 1, pp. 75–98.

Barth, ME, Beaver, WH & Landsman, WR 2001, "The relevance of the value relevance literature for financial accounting standard setting: another view", *Journal of Accounting and Economics*, vol. 31, no. 1, pp. 77–104.

Beatty, A & Weber, J 2006, "Accounting discretion in fair value estimates: an examination of SFAS 142 goodwill impairments", *Journal of Accounting Research*, vol. 44, no. 2, pp. 257–288.

Bens, DA, Cheng, M & Neamtiu, M 2015, "The impact of SEC disclosure monitoring on the uncertainty of fair value estimates", *The Accounting Review*, vol. 91, no. 2, pp. 349–375.

Blankespoor, E, Linsmeier, TJ, Petroni, KR & Shakespeare, C 2013, "Fair value accounting for financial instruments: does it improve the association between bank leverage and credit risk?", *The Accounting Review*, vol. 88, no. 4, pp. 1143–1177.

Cain, C, Kolev, KS & McVay, SE 2017, "Qualifying special items: an identification and examination of lower-quality versus higher-quality income-decreasing special items", *Working paper.*

Cantrell, BW & Yust, CG 2017, "Tainted portfolios: how accounting for other-than-temporary impairment restricts security sales", Working Paper.

Curry, T & Shibut, L 2000, "The cost of the savings and loan crisis: truth and consequences", *FDIC Banking Review,* vol. 13, no. 2, pp. 26–35.

DeFond, ML & Park, CW 1997, "Smoothing income in anticipation of future earnings", *Journal of Accounting and Economics,* vol. 23, no. 2, pp. 115–139.

Dechow, PM, Myers, L & Shakespeare, C 2010. "Fair value accounting and gains from asset securitization: a convenient earnings management tool with compensation side-benefits", *Journal of Accounting and Economics,* vol. 49, no. 1–2, pp. 2–25.

Dong, M, Ryan, S & Zhang, XJ 2014, "Preserving amortized costs within a fair-value-accounting framework: reclassification of gains and losses on available-for-sale securities upon realization", *Review of Accounting Studies,* vol. 19, no. 1, pp. 242–280.

Duchin, R, Gilbert, T, Harford, J & Hrdlicka, C 2017, Precautionary savings with risky assets: when cash is not cash, *The Journal of Finance,* vol. 72, no. 2, pp. 793–852.

Duffie, D & Lando, D 2001, "Term structures of credit spreads with incomplete accounting information", *Econometrica,* vol. 69, no. 3, pp. 633–664.

Ettredge, ML, Xu, Y & Yi, HS 2014, "Fair value measurements and audit fees: evidence from the banking industry", *Auditing: A Journal of Practice & Theory,* vol. 33, no. 3, pp. 33–58.

Goh, BW, Li, D, Ng, J & Yong, KO 2015, "Market pricing of banks' fair value assets reported under SFAS 157 since the 2008 financial crisis", *Journal of Accounting and Public Policy,* vol. 34, no. 2, pp. 129–145.

Graham, JR, Harvey, CR & Rajgopal, S 2005, "The economic implications of corporate financial reporting", *Journal of Accounting and Economics,* vol. 40, no. 1, pp. 3–73.

Gunny, KA 2010, "The relation between earnings management using real activities manipulation and future performance: evidence from meeting earnings benchmarks", *Contemporary Accounting Research,* vol. 27, no. 3, pp. 855–888.

Hanley, KW, Jagolinzer, AD & Nikolova, S 2016, "Strategic reporting of fair value estimate levels", *Working paper.*

Healy, PM & Wahlen, JM 1999, "A review of the earnings management literature and its implications for standard setting", *Accounting Horizons,* vol. 13, no. 4, pp. 365–383.

Henry, E 2009, "Early adoption of SFAS No. 159: lessons from games (almost) played", *Accounting Horizons,* vol. 23, no. 2, pp. 181–199.

Hodder, LD, Hopkins, PE & Wahlen, JM 2006, "Risk-relevance of fair-value income measures for commercial banks", *The Accounting Review,* vol. 81, no. 2, pp. 337–375.

Hodder, L, Kohlbeck, M & McAnally, ML 2002, "Accounting choices and risk management: SFAS No. 115 and U.S. bank holding companies", *Contemporary Accounting Research,* vol. 19, no. 2, pp. 225–270.

Holthausen, RW & Watts, RL 2001, "The relevance of the value-relevance literature for financial accounting standard setting", *Journal of Accounting and Economics,* vol. 31, no. 1, pp. 3–75.

Iselin, M & Nicoletti, A 2017, "The effects of SFAS 157 disclosures on investment decisions", *Journal of Accounting and Economics,* vol. 63, no. 2–3, pp. 404–427.

Karpoff, JM, Lee, DS & Martin, GS 2008, "The cost to firms of cooking the books". *Journal of Financial and Quantitative Analysis,* vol. 43, no. 3, pp. 581–611.

Kedia, S & Philippon, T 2007, "The economics of fraudulent accounting", *The Review of Financial Studies,* vol. 22, no. 6, pp. 2169–2199.

Kolev, KS 2013, "Do investors perceive marking-to-model as marking-to-myth? Early evidence from FAS 157 disclosure", *Working paper.*

Lawrence, A, Siriviriyakul, S & Sloan, RG 2016, "Who's the fairest of them all? Evidence from closed-end funds", *The Accounting Review,* vol. 91, no. 1, pp. 207–227.

Levitt, A 1998, "The numbers game", *The CPA Journal,* vol. 68, no. 12, p. 14.

Livne, G & McNichols, M 2009, "An empirical investigation of the true and fair override in the United Kingdom", *Journal of Business Finance & Accounting,* vol. 36, no. 1–2, pp. 1–30.

Livne, G, Markarian, G & Milne, A 2011, "Bankers' compensation and fair value accounting", *Journal of corporate finance,* vol. 17, no. 4, pp. 1096–1115.

Magnan, M, Menini, A & Parbonetti, A 2015, "Fair value accounting: information or confusion for financial markets?", *Review of Accounting Studies*, vol. 20, no. 1, pp. 559–591.

Plantin, G, Sapra, H & Shin, HS 2008, "Marking-to-market: panacea or Pandora's Box?", *Journal of Accounting Research*, vol. 46, no. 2, pp. 435–460.

Ramanna, K & Watts, RL 2012, "Evidence on the use of unverifiable estimates in required goodwill impairment", *Review of Accounting Studies*, vol. 17, no. 4, pp. 749–780.

Riedl, EJ & Serafeim, G 2011, "Information risk and fair values: an examination of equity betas", *Journal of Accounting Research*, vol. 49, no. 4, pp. 1083–1122.

Ronen, J 2008, "To fair value or not to fair value: a broader perspective", *Abacus*, vol. 44, no. 2, pp. 181–208.

Song, CJ, Thomas, WB & Yi, H 2010, "Value relevance of FAS No. 157 fair value hierarchy information and the impact of corporate governance mechanisms", *The Accounting Review*, vol. 85, no. 4, pp. 1375–1410.

12

LET THE FOX GUARD THE HENHOUSE

How relaxing the three-level fair value hierarchy increases the reliability of fair value estimates

Ester Chen, Ilanit Gavious and Uriel Haran

Introduction

The International Financial Reporting Standards (IFRS) have been developed to harmonize corporate accounting practices and to answer the need for high-quality standards that result in high-quality information, transparency and comparability in issuing financial reports.[1] One of the major changes introduced by the international standards has been the ability to recognize certain assets and liabilities at fair value. Unlike the US accounting standards (US GAAP) that permit the measurement of only financial instruments at fair value,[2] the IFRS allow the measurement of various financial statement items such as financial instruments, investment property, investment in subsidiaries and investment in associates and joint ventures at fair value.[3] As such, while fair value accounting in the USA is primarily relevant to financial institutions, fair value accounting in countries using IFRS affects firms in various industries.

To date, the accounting standards that provide a framework for the measurement of reporting elements at fair value (IFRS 13 and its corresponding US GAAP standard SFAS 157)[4] distinguish among three levels of inputs used to derive fair value estimates: level 1, reflecting observable inputs consisting of quoted prices in active markets for identical assets or liabilities; level 2, reflecting observable inputs other than quoted prices that are observable for the asset or liability, either directly or indirectly; and level 3, reflecting unobservable inputs. Given that level 1 consists of pure market-based inputs free from manipulation and estimation errors, they are regarded as providing objective fair valuations. Level 2 inputs should also yield relatively objective valuations, as they are mainly market-based. In contrast, level 3 inputs are firm-supplied, and, as such, are subject to managerial discretion.[5] Nevertheless, the level 3 inputs must be developed using the best information available at the time of valuation. Furthermore, due to their greater subjectivity, both IFRS 13 and SFAS 157 require expanded disclosures about level 3 measures.

The three-level hierarchy requires that a firm must measure fair values using level 1 inputs if available. If level 1 inputs are unavailable, then level 2 inputs may be used. Hence, level 3 measures are allowed only if neither level 1 nor level 2 inputs are available. The standards are clear in that the valuation technique the entity uses must maximize the use of relevant *observable* inputs and minimize the use of unobservable inputs.

One of the items allowed to be measured and reported at fair value in accordance with IFRS is a *significant influence* investment in an entity (e.g. holding 20% or more of the voting power of the investee) held by an investment entity. In accordance with IAS 28 *Investments in Associates and Joint Ventures*, investment entities[6] present their investments in other entities at fair value in the financial statements in accordance with IFRS 13's definition of, and framework for measuring, fair value.[7] Even when the investment entity obtains control of another entity, it is required to measure the investment in its subsidiary at fair value, rather than consolidate it in its financial statements (IFRS 10 *Consolidated Financial Statements*). This chapter calls into question the appropriateness of the three-level hierarchy as defined by IFRS 13 for the fair value measurement of a significant influence investment (including control) in an entity whose shares are traded on the exchange. It is highly likely that level 1 fair values – in this case, the investment's quoted price on the exchange – do *not* capture the fair value for a market participant as defined by the accounting standard itself. As per the definition of a market participant in IFRS 13, the fair value of such an investment should reflect the price that a potential buyer would pay for *all* of the shares being held by the current parent company. Thus, the fair value of an investment in another entity with significant influence (i.e. an investment held with strategic intent as part of a long-term view) should incorporate elements such as premium controls and synergy expectations. Such elements are obviously not taken into account by the marginal investor trading shares on the exchange.

The evidence presented in the extant literature examining market premiums in sale transactions of significant influence investments,[8] as well as more recent data extracted from the markets that use IFRS, further highlight the unsuitability of the three-level hierarchy for such investments. Based on a recent study by Chung et al. (2017) showing that firms using external and independent pricing of their level 3 fair values enhance the latter's credibility, we suggest that the three-level hierarchy can be relaxed in the case discussed above conditional on the firm's use of external and independent pricing. Specifically, we suggest allowing investment entities to recognize level 3 fair values of significant influence investments in their financial statements provided that (1) fair values have been estimated by an independent pricing service vendor (say, a broker, an analyst or an investment manager), rather than using an internal appraiser within the firm, and (2) the investment entity discloses the level 1 values in the notes to the investment.

Notwithstanding the greater reliability that investors associate with external versus internal value estimations, we contend that the setting of accounting standards should not be based on the premise that firms are likely to take advantage of flexibility in financial measurement and reporting rules to misstate reported values. Empirical studies examining the impact of greater flexibility in reporting rules on firms' reporting quality provide support for our argument (e.g. Barth et al. 2008; Atwood et al. 2010; Blaylock et al. 2012; Zeghal et al. 2012; Watrin et al. 2014). Whereas conventional wisdom states that stronger constraints curb the managers' ability and motivation to engage in manipulative financial reporting, empirical findings suggest the opposite. This phenomenon can be explained by behavioral theories of motivation. By merging psychological and accounting theories, we suggest that relaxing external constraints on the managers' reporting discretion increases their level of autonomy over and ownership of their reports and curbs feelings of defiance, resulting in higher quality reporting. Our suggestion is based on research in social psychology and organizational behavior, which shows that environments characterized by greater individual autonomy are associated with greater trust and organizational commitment, and, consequently, with higher quality performance (e.g. Deci et al. 1989; Ryan & Deci 2000; Moller et al. 2006). Controlling systems, on the other hand, often prompt defiance rather than compliance, motivating managers to do the opposite of what the policy demands (Moller et al. 2006). Similarly, when the constraints put forth by the three-level hierarchy are relaxed, the managers' decision-making power with respect to financial reporting is increased, and, hence, their sense of autonomy and control over their work, which may lead to higher quality reporting, is then under greater constraint. The behavioral insights gathered in this chapter are of particular relevance to accounting standard-setters who face the task of choosing the optimal (fair value) measurement and reporting rules for restraining opportunistic reporting by firms and encouraging them to adhere to higher ethical standards over time.

Background

The international accounting standard that provides a framework for the measurement of reporting elements at fair value is IFRS 13, *Fair Value Measurement*. Its corresponding US GAAP standard is SFAS 157, *Fair Value Measurement*. The two standards, IFRS 13 and SFAS 157, are virtually identical.[9] Their purpose is to define fair value, create a unified framework for measuring fair value and broaden the required disclosure regarding fair value measurement. However, given that US GAAP permits the measurement of only financial instruments at fair value, SFAS 157 is primarily relevant to financial institutions given their substantial exposure to financial instruments, many of which must be reported at fair value (e.g. Riedl & Serafeim 2011). In contrast, the IFRS allows the measurement of other financial statement items as well, including investment in associates and joint ventures – our item of interest – at fair value. We thus, henceforth, refer to IFRS 13 in our discussion.

IFRS 13 defines fair value as 'the price that would be received to sell an asset or paid to transfer a liability in an orderly transaction between market participants at the measurement date'. Fair value measurement under IFRS 13 assumes that a transaction to sell an asset or to transfer a liability takes place in the principal market or, in the absence of a principal market, in the most advantageous market. The principal market is the market with the greatest volume and level of activity for the asset or liability. The most advantageous market is the market that maximizes the amount that would be received to sell the asset or minimizes the amount that would be paid to transfer the liability, after considering transaction costs and transport costs. Consistent with rational economic behavior, it would be reasonable to assume that the principal market in which an entity actually transacts would be the most advantageous market. Given that there might be buyers and sellers who are willing to pay high prices and deal outside the principal market, the most advantageous market may not be the principal market. However, an entity may assume that the principal market is the most advantageous market provided that the entity can access the principal market.

IFRS 13 does not mandate the use of a particular valuation technique(s) but sets out a principle requiring an entity to determine a valuation technique that is 'appropriate in the circumstances' for which sufficient data are available and for which the use of relevant observable inputs is maximized. The standard discusses three widely used valuation techniques: (1) the market approach, (2) the cost approach and (3) the income approach.[10] Furthermore, it defines a three-level categorization of the fair value measurement hierarchy. This hierarchy is determined based on the source of the inputs used to evaluate the fair value, such that the input used with the highest-level ranking (1 [quoted input], 2 [unquoted input but observable] or 3 [unobservable]) determines the level in which the asset or liability is classified. Specifically, level 1 inputs are quoted prices (unadjusted) in active markets for identical assets or liabilities. Level 2 inputs are inputs other than the quoted prices included within level 1 that are observable for the asset or liability, either directly or indirectly. Such inputs include quoted prices for similar assets or liabilities in active markets, quoted prices for identical or similar assets or liabilities in markets that are not active, inputs other than quoted prices that are observable for the asset or liability (such as interest rates, implied volatility for the shares and a price to customers in a retail market or a price to retailers in a wholesale market), and market-corroborated inputs. Level 3 inputs are unobservable inputs for the asset or liability. These inputs are firm-developed using the best information available at the time of valuation.[11] Moreover, the standard requires that the firm disclose additional information regarding level 3, over and above the disclosure requirements for levels 1 and 2. This requirement is due to the asymmetric information gap between the firm's management and the users of the firm's financial statements that results from the use of unobservable inputs for developing level 3 fair value measurements.

IFRS 13 is clear in that the valuation technique the entity uses must maximize the use of relevant observable inputs and minimize the use of unobservable inputs. Unobservable inputs are developed using the best information available about the assumptions that market participants would use when pricing the asset or liability. In other words, unobservable inputs reflect the reporting entity's own view about the assumptions that market participants would use. Thus, if a quoted price is available for a specific asset, this price must be used instead of the entity's assumption about the price. Concurrently, the standard requires that, in a fair value measurement, an entity considers the assumptions that a market participant, acting in their economic best interest, would use when pricing the asset or liability. Market participants are defined as having all of the following characteristics: being independent of the reporting entity (that is, they are not related parties), being knowledgeable, having a reasonable understanding about the asset or liability and the transaction based on all available information, including information that might be obtained through due diligence efforts that are usual and customary; being able to engage in transactions of the asset or liability and being willing to engage in such transactions (that is, they are motivated but not forced or otherwise compelled to do so). Thus, the standard requires the entity to put itself in the place of a market participant and exclude any entity-specific factors that might impact the price that the entity is willing to accept in the sale of an asset or be paid in the transfer of a liability. The entity must consider the extent to which a market participant would take all of the relevant characteristics of the asset being measured into account (e.g. restrictions on the sale or use of the asset) when pricing the asset on the measurement date.[12]

The unsuitability of the three-level hierarchy for valuing a significant influence investment in an entity

In its preference for quoted prices in active markets (e.g. the stock price on the exchange), IFRS 13 puts the greatest weight on objectivity, even if the objective number does not capture fair value under the assumptions of a market participant as per the standard's own definition. In addition, in this preference, the standard assumes that the market is efficient and, in the case of tradable securities, that the marginal investor on the exchange represents a market participant with sufficient knowledge and expertise to determine the fair value of a security. Moreover, if the tradable securities represent a significant influence investment in an entity, in its preference for quoted prices in active markets the standard effectively assumes that the marginal investor on the exchange represents a market participant with sufficient knowledge and expertise to determine the fair value had s/he bought *all of the shares* from the current investor. Obviously, this is not always the case. According to Palea and Maino (2013), IFRS 13's fair value hierarchy (levels 1, 2 and 3) results in assets being presented according to their liquidation value, which does not suit investments made by going concerns. Palea and Maino (2013) have questioned the appropriateness of fair value as defined by IFRS 13 for private equities. They contend that market-based rather than entity-specific fair value measurement fails to consider the financial instrument's liquidity and the investors' horizons, which are key to private equity valuation. Employing fair value estimates based on market and transaction multiples (level 2 in the standard's fair value hierarchy), Palea and Maino reveal that, as conjectured, market-based valuation techniques do not provide a faithful representation of the economic value of the underlying asset, in their case – private equity.

However, the irrelevance of the market-based valuation documented is not confined only to privately held investments for which a quoted price for the original assets is absent, but also applies to investments in publicly traded equity.[13] In particular, it applies to the measurement of the fair value of a significant influence investment in another entity (e.g. holding 20% or more of the voting power of the investee) whose shares are traded on the exchange (we will refer to all of them as 'investments' for short).[14] In accordance with IAS 28 *Investments in Associates and Joint Ventures*, entities that are investors with joint control of, or significant influence over, an investee (associate or joint venture) are generally required to apply the equity method when accounting for their significant influence investments in other entities. An exception for this requirement is when the investor is an *investment entity*. As per IAS 28, investment entities (e.g. venture capital organizations, mutual funds, unit trusts, investment-linked insurance funds and alike)[15] present their investments in other entities at fair value (rather than the equity method) in the financial statements in accordance with IFRS 13's definition of, and framework for measuring, fair value. Moreover, as per IFRS 10 *Consolidated Financial Statements*, investment entities are exempted from the requirement to consolidate their subsidiaries when they obtain control of another entity. Instead, as determined for significant influence investments in general, investment entities are required to measure an investment in a subsidiary at fair value through profit or loss.[16] As indicated, while level 1 fair values are the most objective measure, whether the investment's quoted price on the exchange is an appropriate measure of fair value for a market participant as defined by the accounting standard is questionable at best.

An investment in another entity with significant influence is held with strategic intent as part of a long-term investment devoted to exploiting business opportunities, commercial or entrepreneurial relationships, or other types of synergies. For such an investment, which is not being held for trading, quoted prices on the exchange most likely do not capture fair values. As stated, in accordance with the definition of a market participant in IFRS 13, the fair value of such an investment should reflect the price that a potential buyer would pay for all of the shares being held by the current parent company. A question thus arises: Shouldn't the fair valuation of such an investment incorporate premium controls as well as synergy expectations and other positive factors (e.g. increased competitive power) taken into account by a potential buyer? Such a potential buyer is obviously not represented by the marginal investor trading shares on the exchange. Hence, IFRS 13's preference for a $P \star Q$ measurement, where P is the quoted price on the exchange and Q is the number of shares outstanding, may lead to biased measures of fair values.[17]

Indeed, the accounting and finance literatures dealing with market premiums in transactions involving the sale of a significant influence investment in another entity document premiums ranging from 20% to over 100% above the pre-offer stock price on the exchange (e.g. Comment & Jarrell 1987; DeAngelo 1990; Brigham & Gapenski 1996; Pratt 2001). In Table 12.1, we provide specific examples from recent sale transactions that took place in

Table 12.1 Market premiums in significant influence sale transactions by investment entities

Transaction date	Voting power sold (%)	Sale price	Pre-offer market value	Discrepancy between sale price and pre-offer market value (%)
November 2016	22	107 million NIS	84 million NIS	27
December 2016	100	1,480 million NIS	861 million NIS	72

Israel, where IFRS have been mandatory since 2008 for companies listed on the Tel Aviv Stock Exchange (TASE). In the two transactions displayed, an investment entity (as per the definition of IAS 28) sold a significant influence investment in another entity outside the exchange. In one transaction, 22% of the voting power in the investee was sold for a price 27% higher than the pre-offer market value. In another transaction, another investment entity sold 100% of its voting power in an investee. In this transaction the market premium was 72% over the pre-offer market value.[18] The results displayed in Table 12.1 do not change significantly if instead of the share price on the day prior to the initial offer, we take the average share price during the five to ninety trading days prior to the offer.

Information about the transactions was obtained from the immediate reports submitted by the companies to the Tel Aviv Stock Exchange (TASE), the Israeli Securities Authority (ISA) and the press regarding the transaction. These reports are required by law and have to be filed with the authorities immediately following significant events concerning the transactions. We obtained the market value of the companies' shares from the *Bloomberg Professional* database. During November-December 2016, the FX rate was in the range of 3.787–3.876 NIS (new Israeli shekels) per $1 US.

A proposed adjustment to the fair value hierarchy in case of a significant influence investment in an entity

We acknowledge that investors may value market quoted prices more than they do firm-supplied inputs due to information risk, inherent estimation errors and suspicion of a reporting bias.[19] Riedl and Serafeim (2011) show that equity betas increase monotonically across levels 1, 2, and 3 in the fair value hierarchy, reflecting the higher information risk of fair values that are based on unobservable inputs for their estimation compared to those that are based on observable inputs. Magnan et al. (2016) draw similar inferences for the firm's cost of debt. Studies further document that level 3 fair values have lower value relevance than level 1 and level 2 fair values (Kolev 2009; Song et al. 2010; Goh 2015).[20] Nevertheless, the most recent study examining both the information risk and the value relevance of the three-level fair value hierarchy shows that the provision of reliability disclosures *reduces* the information risk and *increases* the value relevance of level 3 estimates (Chung et al. 2017). Chung et al. (2017) examined three types of reliability disclosures provided voluntarily by firms in their 10-K reports: (1) a discussion of how external and independent pricing of the fair value estimates were obtained, (2) a discussion about the proper classification of the fair value estimates in accordance with the three-level hierarchy and (3) a discussion of assurances made of management responsibility for the reliability of the fair value estimates. Chung et al. found that, among the three types of disclosures, the provision of discussions of the external and independent pricing, and of the proper classification, of fair value estimates enhance the credibility of, and thus reduce investors' uncertainty about, the more opaque – level 3 – estimates. Thus, for firms that obtained external fair value pricing from an independent pricing service vendor (say, a broker, an analyst or an investment manager), rather than using an internal appraiser within the firm (e.g. an internal risk department), investors regarded the level 3 fair values as less biased and more accurate. This reduction in the information risk of level 3 measures improved their market pricing (Chung et al. 2017).[21]

Given the inherent bias caused by using market quoted prices in the case of significant influence investments in other entities, we call for a reconsideration of the three-level hierarchy, as defined in IFRS 13, for such investments. Other valuation techniques (such as discounted cash flows (DCF)) may provide a measure that is closer to the fair value of the investment as captured by the bids of potential buyers. This is particularly true if the firm obtained external and independent pricing of its investment. According to Chung et al. (2017), investors take seriously the disclosure of a firm that it has used such pricing and '...do not simply regard them as boilerplate or "cheap talk" from management' (p. 434). Our proposal is further supported by prior studies showing that transactions taking place outside the exchange, where a significant influence in the investee is being sold, are usually executed at a price closer to (or similar to) an expert valuation than to the stock market value (e.g. Comment and Jarrell 1987; DeAngelo 1990; Brigham & Gapenski 1996; Pratt 2001; Elnathan et al. 2010).[22]

We thus suggest allowing investment entities to recognize level 3 fair values of significant influence investments in their financial statements provided that (1) fair values have been estimated by an independent pricing service vendor (say, a broker, an analyst or an investment manager), rather than using an internal appraiser within the firm, and (2) the investment entity discloses the level 1 values in the notes to the investment.

Predictions of managers' reporting behavior under a relaxed reporting policy

Notwithstanding the greater reliability that investors associate with external versus internal value estimations, we contend that relaxing the fair value hierarchy does not necessarily imply that companies would exploit the ability to present significant influence investments in other entities based on unobservable inputs to intentionally bias the valuation results. The setting of accounting standards should not be based on the premise that firms are likely to take advantage of flexibility in financial measurement and reporting rules to misstate values. Empirical findings in the extant accounting literature challenge this conventional wisdom.

Empirical evidence of managers' restrained reporting behavior under a relaxed reporting policy

Take as an example the greater flexibility allowed by IFRS, such as the ability to recognize unrealized revaluation earnings arising from various items. This greater flexibility has drawn academic attention to the firms' incentives to take advantage of this flexibility to manipulate earnings. Various studies examined whether the adoption of IFRS enhanced the scope for earnings management[23] in the adopting countries (for example, Van Tendeloo & Vanstraelen 2005; Barth et al. 2008; Jeanjean & Stolowy 2008; Zeghal et al. 2012; Ahmed et al. 2013). These studies by and large indicate that earnings quality (earnings management) is either unchanged or higher (lower) under IFRS. Moreover, the evidence reveals that the adoption of IFRS is associated with *more* timely loss recognition and *more* value relevance of reported earnings (e.g. Barth et al. 2008; Zeghal et al. 2012; Ahmed et al. 2013; Elbarky et al. 2017).

As another example, take the greater flexibility in financial reporting (particularly in reporting earnings) allowed by a non-conformity between the accounting and the tax rules. The growing gap between reports of book earnings (the income statement) and taxable earnings (the tax return) has catalyzed a debate among researchers and regulators regarding the effectiveness of book-tax conformity (BTC)[24] in curbing opportunistic or low-quality financial reporting.[25] Conventional wisdom states that less conformity or similarity between these rules facilitates manipulative reporting by managers. Of course, the motivation for self-presentation in each type of report is different: to their shareholders, managers generally want to paint a rosy picture of high earnings; when dealing with the IRS, however, it is in the firm's best interest to claim poverty. The fact that the rules governing each type of report are not identical allows managers to exercise flexibility in their earnings reports. Specifically, different rules enable firms to inflate book earnings upward without affecting taxable earnings (e.g. Phillips et al. 2003; Hanlon 2005), deflate taxable earnings downward without affecting book earnings (e.g. Weisbach 2002; McGill & Outslay 2004), or even inflate book earnings *and* deflate taxable earnings in the same reporting period (e.g. Frank et al. 2009). However, recent empirical findings challenge this assumption, showing that less conformity is associated with a higher, not lower, quality of financial reports (i.e. more truthful reporting; e.g. Atwood et al. 2010; Blaylock et al. 2012; Watrin et al. 2014).

Markedly, the studies to date do not provide an explanation for the positive relationships found between greater flexibility in financial reporting and reporting quality. Why do managers forgo taking full advantage of their ability to manipulate reported numbers, even when greater flexibility in the reporting rules allows them to do so? We seek to identify the behavioral underpinnings of the increased compliance exhibited by managers under looser restrictions. By merging psychological and accounting theories, we suggest that relaxing external constraints on managers' reporting discretion increases their level of autonomy over and ownership of their reports and curbs feelings of defiance, resulting in higher quality reporting.

Psychological underpinnings of managers' restrained reporting behavior under a relaxed reporting policy

Prior studies of managers' financial reporting have naturally been limited to accounting and related fields. To our knowledge, this chapter is the first one to incorporate insights from behavioral research in an attempt to explain the phenomenon described above.

Self-Determination Theory and the role of motivation in regulating behavior

Early research on motivation (e.g. White 1959) distinguished between two basic types of motivation. *Intrinsic motivation* is defined as the engagement in an activity for the enjoyment of the activity itself. Conversely, *extrinsic motivation* describes the engagement in an activity in order to attain some external reward, or to alleviate an external pressure. The two sources of motivation can complement each other, but may also contradict and undermine one another. Extrinsic motivation has typically been portrayed as the less effective of the two. When a behavior is extrinsically motivated, it is externally regulated and engaged in with the intention of obtaining a desired consequence or avoiding an undesired one. Thus, the person performs the behavior only when it is instrumental to those ends. However, some extrinsic factors can facilitate intrinsic motivation processes. The Self-Determination Theory (SDT, Deci & Ryan 1985) posits a controlled-to-autonomous continuum to describe the degree to which an external regulation has been internalized (Gagné & Deci 2005). The autonomously motivated person feels a sense of choice and volition and fully endorses his or her own actions or decisions (Ryan 1995). In contrast, to be controlled is to be pressured to act in a certain way, or to perceive an external locus of causality for one's actions.[26]

Self-Determination Theory, and the autonomy construct in particular, is a powerful predictor of the ability to regulate behavior. In work organizations, support for greater managerial autonomy is associated with increased job satisfaction among employees, more trust in corporate management and a higher quality of employee performance (Deci et al. 1989). Furthermore, training managers in supervisory styles that support autonomy results in increasing these measures among employees.

Studies examining the autonomy-control continuum in regulatory policies suggest that while controlling approaches to regulation can have immediate effects on behavior, they also have a number of serious limitations. Their effects typically do not last long, and the behaviors they aim to enforce are not sustained over time (Rupp & Williams 2011). In addition, stringent external control may sometimes prompt defiance rather than compliance, leading people to do the opposite of what the policy demands simply because the policy demands it (Moller et al. 2006). SDT has been applied in particular to the study of the trust between regulators and regulatees as an effective compliance mechanism in regulatory relations (Braithwaite & Makkai 1994; Murphy 2004; Murphy et al. 2009). Six (2012) commented that the public at times appears to want the state to assume that regulatees cannot be trusted. Empirical findings, however, have challenged the view of trust and control as mutually exclusive, the existence of one being at the expense of the other. Rather, the two may be applied simultaneously and may even reinforce each other by encouraging a moral commitment and sense of civic responsibility among the regulated actors (Tyler 1990; Das & Teng 1998; Mollering 2005; Weibel 2007). These findings are consistent with SDT, which emphasizes the importance of the regulatees' internalizing the regulators' objectives in achieving compliance.

Predictions of Self-Determination Theory regarding reporting quality under a relaxed fair value hierarchy

The three-level fair value hierarchy is designed to deter reporting aggressiveness by giving managers very little leeway in conveying information. By being so strict and limiting, this type of policy is a classic example of a controlling regulatory mechanism. In addition to restricting managers' flexibility in conveying financial information, a strict hierarchy sends a message to managers that their work is under close scrutiny. Thus, despite the advantages of added control, the fair value hierarchy might also have the disadvantages of controlling regulatory mechanisms, such as the dependence on maintaining reward and punishment contingencies and the increased motivation for defiant acts.

Relaxing the fair value hierarchy, as proposed in this chapter, may have several implications. First, relaxing the constraints put on managers may allow them to experience higher levels of control over and ownership of their own work. This change typically increases the stake people feel they have in their product. Providing managers, for whom high-quality reporting constitutes a display of professional skill, with the legal means to do so may increase their sense of autonomy. Second, greater flexibility in reporting provides managers with a greater degree of choice than they enjoy under a strict reporting rule. Research shows that the experience of greater choice, for example, by having control over one's own work, increases the likelihood of internalizing behavioral regulation (Moller et al. 2006). Finally, increasing the managers' autonomy and decision-making power may significantly reduce their motivation to defy the regulations (Murphy et al. 2009). Hence, increasing managers' flexibility in conveying information to their stakeholders effectively reduces their motivation to exploit the policy's limitations.

In sum, the theoretical arguments and empirical findings discussed above suggest that reducing the regulatory constraints on managers' reporting behavior (in our case, relaxing the fair value hierarchy) might provide them with the opportunity to engage in accounting manipulation (in our case, manipulating the estimated fair value). However, it might also prompt them, by way of increased autonomy, to exhibit greater restraint and maintain a higher quality of reporting.

Concluding remarks

In this chapter, we call for a reconsideration of the fair value measurement of a significant influence investment in an entity, where the investee's shares are traded on the exchange and the investor is an investment entity, as defined in IFRS 13. Currently, the IASB conducts a post-implementation review (PIR) whereby reconsiderations take place regarding the fair value measurements of assets. By using psychological and accounting theories, we suggest that the three-level hierarchy can be relaxed in the case of a significant influence investment in an entity, conditional on the investor's use of external and independent pricing. We utilize several social psychology and organizational theories of motivation as well as empirical studies in the accounting literature examining the impact of greater flexibility in reporting rules on firms' reporting quality to support our suggestion. Thus, counterintuitive as it may seem, we maintain that allowing the fox to guard the henhouse will improve everyone's outcomes.

Notes

1 See, for example, Ashbaugh and Pincus (2001); Barth et al. (2008); Daske et al. (2008).
2 FASB Statements No. 115 *Accounting for Certain Investments in Debt and Equity Securities* (1993), FASB Statements No. 133 *Accounting for Derivative Instruments and Hedging Activities* (1998), and FASB Statements No. 159 *The Fair Value Option for Financial Assets and Financial Liabilities* (2007).
3 IAS No. 39 *Financial Instruments: Recognition and Measurement* (as revised in 2005), to be replaced by IFRS 9 *Financial Instruments*; IAS No. 40 *Investment Property* (as revised in 2005); IAS No. 27 *Consolidated and Separate Financial Statements* (as revised in 2005); IAS No. 28 *Investment in Associates and Joint Ventures* (as revised in 2005); IFRS 11 *Joint Arrangements* (2011).
4 International Financial Reporting Standards (IFRS 13), *Fair Value Measurement* (IASB 2011), effective 2013 (with early adoption allowed); Statement of Financial Accounting Standards (SFAS) 157, *Fair Value Measurements* (FASB 2006), effective 2008 (with early adoption allowed for 2007).
5 The level 3 inputs must be developed using the best information available at the time of valuation.
6 Investment entities, as per IAS 28, include venture capital organizations, mutual funds, unit trusts and similar entities including investment-linked insurance funds.
7 All other entities that are investors with joint control of, or significant influence over, an investee (associate or joint venture) must apply the equity method when accounting for their significant influence investments in other entities.
8 See, for example, Pratt (2001); Brigham and Gapenski (1996); DeAngelo (1990).
9 A careful examination of the international standard (IFRS 13) and the corresponding US GAAP standard (SFAS 157) shows that the two are identical with the exception of one requirement that appears in IFRS 13 [paragraph 93(h) (ii)] and not required by SFAS 157. This excess requirement determines that, for financial assets and financial liabilities, if changing one or more of the unobservable inputs to reflect reasonably possible alternative assumptions would change the fair value significantly, an entity shall state that fact and disclose the effect of those changes.
10 Valuation techniques should be applied consistently from one period to the next.
11 Using this three-level categorization hierarchy, the standard broadens the purpose of the disclosure beyond the former disclosure requirements. The firm is required to provide separate disclosures

for assets and liabilities measured at fair value on a recurring or non-recurring basis and to specify in which of the three levels (1, 2 or 3) the asset or liability is being measured. It also requires that for assets and liabilities not measured at fair value, but for which the fair value is disclosed, the firm must provide the levels (1, 2 or 3) in which the assets or liabilities were classified and other information.

12 For example, the extent to which restrictions on the sale or use of the asset should be reflected in its fair value depends a great deal on where the source of the restriction comes from and whether or not the restriction is separable from the asset (Deloitte. Clearly IFRS. Summary guidance and practical tips for *IFRS 13* – Fair Value Measurement. www2.deloitte.com/content/dam/Deloitte/ca/Documents/audit/ca-en-audit-clearly-ifrs-fair-value-measurement-ifrs-13.pdf.)

13 Note that Palea and Maino (2013) conducted their empirical analysis on randomly selected listed companies that they assumed to be private.

14 If the entity is traded on multiple equity exchanges, the entity should document which particular market price is used and what process was followed to determine the appropriate market to use for determining fair value.

15 IFRS 10 *Consolidated Financial Statements* supplements the definition of an investment entity by indicating that the latter is an entity that

> (a) obtains funds from one or more investors for the purpose of providing those investor(s) with investment management services; (b) commits to its investor(s) that its business purpose is to invest funds solely for returns from capital appreciation, investment income, or both, and (c) measures and evaluates the performance of substantially all of its investments on a fair value basis.

16 An exception for the exemption from consolidation is where that subsidiary provides services that relate to the investment entity's investment activities.

17 Note that, on the acquisition date, the investor recognizes the investment on the balance sheet at cost. This cost is generally higher than the quoted value on the exchange because, when buying a significant influence in another entity, the payment is likely to include control premiums or payments for other potential benefits and/or synergies. As such, in the subsequent financial statements the investor will probably have to recognize a loss from the revaluation of this investment to the exchange quoted value.

18 Recall that investment entities do not consolidate their subsidiaries. Rather, they are required to measure an investment in a subsidiary at fair value through profit or loss.

19 Fair values obtained by valuation techniques could entail unintentional and/or intentional estimation errors (Barth 2004; Benston 2006, 2008).

20 Kolev (2009) and Goh et al. (2015) find that L2 and L3 estimates are valued similarly by investors.

21 It should be noted that, for long-lived tangible assets (mainly real estate) there is a debate in the literature over the reliability and value relevance of revaluations conducted by independent appraisers, compared to internal appraisers. For UK investment property firms, Dietrich et al. (2000) and Muller and Riedl (2002) find evidence consistent with external appraisers providing less biased (more accurate) estimates, resulting in reduced information asymmetry across traders. In contrast, for a sample of Australian firms, Barth and Clinch (1998) find no evidence for a difference in the value-relevance of revaluations conducted by external versus internal appraisers.

22 According to DeAngelo (1990), a company's market value differs from its intrinsic value because the former is based on market assessment of managers' inside information, and not on the actual inside information that managers have; hence the need for independent expert valuations. However, according to DeAngelo (1990) there is a snag. Some claim that these experts are 'rubber stamps' to a price already determined by the company's directors. Such expert valuations conducted by, e.g. financial analysts or investment banks, are generally commissioned as part of the process required for the execution of transactions that take place outside the exchange. The academic and practitioner literatures indicate that fair valuations conducted by financial experts for such transactions usually consider different methodologies (generally between two and seven valuation methods), with the DCF, also called the 'field football' method, often receiving significant weight. Importantly, courts of law accept any valuation method that the financial and business community recognizes (https://cdn-media.web-view.net/i/3fzza2dd/.pdf). In our two examples of recent transactions displayed in Table 12.1, as well as in other non-tabulated transactions, the valuation was consistently based on a weighted average of values obtained from different methodologies. The DCF methodology got a significant weight in the calculation, but it was not the only one taken into account.

23 Earnings manipulation or earnings management refers to techniques that managers deliberately employ to achieve a desired level of reported earnings (e.g. Healy & Whalen 1999).
24 The degree of similarity between the rules governing book earnings (reported to shareholders) and taxable earnings (reported to the IRS) is called book-tax conformity, or BTC.
25 This debate took off in the late 1990s. See, for example, evidence presented in the US Treasury tax return analysis of large corporations (1999) (US Department of the Treasury 1999); Sullivan (1999); Plesko (2000); Manzon and Plesko (2002); Desai (2003); Plesko and Shumofsky (2004) and Hanlon et al. (2005). In most IFRS adopting countries, the gap between the tax and the accounting rules has increased following the adoption, because these countries generally took the approach of maintaining local GAAP for tax purposes (e.g. Australia, New Zealand, Germany, Russia, China, Israel, etc. Only Canada allowed but did not mandate the use of IFRS for tax purposes, where local GAAP is still used to report taxes. See Chen & Gavious 2017).
26 The distinction between autonomous and controlled motivation is not synonymous with the intrinsic versus extrinsic distinction. Extrinsically motivated behaviors vary widely in the level of autonomy that accompanies them; some motivational processes represent high levels of autonomy, whereas others are characterized as more controlling (Ryan & Connell 1989). When the extrinsic motivation for a behavior revolves only around external reward and punishment contingencies, it is referred to as 'external regulation'. In contrast, 'introjected regulation' occurs when internal, self-esteem-based contingencies drive behavior. When people enjoy the highest level of autonomy, they identify with the importance of the behavior and integrate it with their sense of self. This state is defined as 'identified regulation' (Moller et al. 2006). When people experience threats of punishment, surveillance, deadlines, controlling evaluations, goal imposition, and pressure to win a competition, their sense of autonomy is diminished (Ryan & Deci 2000). Autonomous extrinsic motivation occurs in environments with fewer controlling rewards or punishments, enabling people to identify with the importance of the behavior, integrate it with their sense of self and internalize the extrinsic motivation into personally endorsed values (Deci et al. 1999).

References

Ahmed, K, Chalmers, K & Khlif, H 2013, "A meta-analysis of IFRS adoption effects", *International Journal of Accounting*, vol. 48, no. 2, pp. 173–217.

Ashbaugh, H &Pincus, M 2001, "Domestic accounting standards, international accounting standards, and the predictability of earnings", *Journal of Accounting Research*, vol. 39, no. 3, pp. 417–434.

Atwood, TJ, Drake, MS & Myers, LA 2010, "Book-tax conformity, earnings persistence and the association between earnings and cash flows", *Journal of Accounting and Economics*, vol. 50, no. 1, pp. 111–125.

Barth, ME 2004, "Fair values and financial statement volatility" in, *The market discipline across countries and industries*, eds C Borio, WC Hunter, GG Kaufman & K Tsatsaronis, MIT Press, Cambridge, pp. 323–35.

Barth, ME & Clinch, G 1998, "Revalued financial, tangible, and intangible assets: associations with share prices and non-market-based value estimates", *Journal of Accounting Research*, vol. 36, (Suppl.), pp. 199–233.

Barth, ME, Landsman, W & Lang, M 2008, "International accounting standards and accounting quality", *Journal of Accounting Research*, vol. 46, pp. 467–498.

Benston, GJ 2006, "Fair-value accounting: a cautionary tale from Enron", *Journal of Accounting and Public Policy*, vol. 25, pp. 465–84.

Benston, GJ 2008, "The shortcomings of fair-value accounting described in SFAS 157", *Journal of Accounting and Public Policy*, vol. 27, pp. 101–114.

Blaylock, B, Shevlin, T & Wilson, R 2012, "Tax avoidance, large positive temporary book-tax differences and earnings persistence", *The Accounting Review*, vol. 87, no. 1, pp. 91–120.

Boggiano, AK, Flink, C, Shields, A, Seelbach, A & Barrett, M 1993, "Use of techniques promoting students' self-determination: effects on students' analytic problem-solving skills", *Motivation and Emotion*, vol. 17, no. 4, pp. 319–336. doi:10.1007/BF00992323

Braithwaite, J & Makkai, T 1994, "Trust and compliance", *Policing and Society*, vol. 4, no. 1, pp. 1–12.

Brigham, EF & Gapenski, LC 1996, *Intermediate financial management*, 5th edn, The Dryden Press, Orlando, Florida.

Chen, E & Gavious, I 2017, "The roles of book-tax conformity and tax enforcement in regulating tax reporting behavior following International Financial Reporting Standards adoption". *Accounting and Finance*, vol. 57, no. 3, pp. 681–699.

Chung, SG, Goh, BW, Ng, J & Yong, KO 2017, "Voluntary fair value disclosures beyond SFAS 157's three-level estimates", *Review of Accounting Studies*, vol. 22, no. 1, pp. 430–468.

Comment, R & Jarrell, GA 1987, "Two-tier and negotiated tender offers: the imprisonment of the free-riding shareholder", *Journal of Financial Economics*, vol. 19, no. 2, pp. 283–310.

Das, TK & Teng, BS 1998, "Between trust and control: developing confidence in partner cooperation in alliances", *The Academy of Management Review*, vol. 23, no. 3, pp. 491–512. doi:10.2307/259291

Daske, H, Hail, L, Leuz, C & Verdi, R 2008, "Mandatory IFRS reporting around the world: early evidence on the economic consequences", *Journal of Accounting Research*, vol. 46, no. 5, pp. 1085–1142.

DeAngelo, LE 1990, "Equity valuation and corporate control", *The Accounting Review*, vol. 65, no. 1, 93–112.

Deci, EL & Ryan, RM 1985, *Intrinsic motivation and self-determination in human behaviour*, Plenum Press, New York.

Deci, EL, Connell, JP & Ryan, RM 1989, "Self-determination in a work organization", *Journal of Applied Psychology*, vol. 74, no. 4, pp. 580–590. doi:10.1037//0021–9010.74.4.580

Deci, EL, Koestner, R & Ryan, RM 1999, "A meta-analytic review of experiments examining the effects of extrinsic rewards on intrinsic motivation", *Psychological Bulletin*, vol. 125, no. 6, pp. 627–668.

Desai, MA 2003, "The divergence between book and tax income" in *Tax policy and the economy*, vol. 17, ed. JM Poterba,, MIT Press, Cambridge, MA, pp. 169–206.

Dietrich, JR, Harris, MS & Muller KA, III., 2000, "The reliability of investment property fair value estimates", *Journal of Accounting and Economics*, vol. 30, pp. 125–58.

Elbarky, AE, Nwachukwu, JC, Abdou, HA & Elshandidy, T 2017, "Comparative evidence on the value relevance of IFRS-based accounting information in Germany and the UK", *Journal of International Accounting, Auditing and Taxation*, vol. 28, pp. 10–30.

Elnathan, D, Gavious, I & Hauser, S 2010, "An analysis of private versus public firm valuations and the contribution of financial experts", *The International Journal of Accounting*, vol. 45, no. 4, pp. 387–412.

Flink, C, Boggiano, AK & Barrett, M 1990, "Controlling teaching strategies: undermining children's self-determination and performance", *Journal of Personality and Social Psychology*, vol. 59, no. 5, pp. 916–924. doi:10.1037//0022–3514.59.5.916

Frank, MM, Lynch, LJ & Rego, SO 2009, "Tax reporting aggressiveness and its relation to aggressive financial reporting", *The Accounting Review*, vol. 84, no. 2, pp. 467–496.

Gagné, M & Deci, EL 2005, "Self determination theory and work motivation", *Journal of Organizational Behavior*, vol. 26, pp. 331–362.

Goh, B, Li, D, Ng, J & Yong, KO 2015, "Market Pricing of Banks' fair value assets reported under SFAS 157 during the 2008 economic crisis", *Journal of Accounting and Public Policy*, vol. 34, no. 2, pp. 129–145.

Hanlon, M 2005, "The persistence and pricing of earnings, accruals, and cash flows when firms have large book-tax differences", *The Accounting Review*, vol. 80, no. 1, pp. 137–166.

Hanlon, M, Laplante, S & Shevlin, T 2005, "Evidence for the possible information loss of conforming book income and taxable income", *Journal of Law and Economics*, vol. 48, pp. 407–442.

Healy, PM & Whalen, JM 1999, "A review of the earnings management literature and its implications for standard setting", *Accounting Horizons*, vol. 13, no. 4, pp. 365–383.

Jeanjean, T & Stolowy, H 2008, "Do accounting standards matter? An exploratory analysis of earnings management before and after IFRS adoption", *Journal of Accounting and Public Policy*, vol. 27, no. 6, pp. 480–494.

Kolev, K 2009, "Do investors perceive marking-to-model as marking-to-myth? Early evidence from FAS No. 157 disclosure", *Working paper*, New York University.

Magnan, M, Wang, H & Shi, Y 2016, "Fair value accounting and the cost of debt", *Working paper*, Concordia University, Montreal.

Manzon, GB & Plesko, GA 2002, "The relation between financial and tax reporting measures of income", *Tax Law Review*, vol. 55, pp. 175–214.

McGill, G & Outslay, E 2004, "Lost in translation: detecting tax shelter activity in financial statements", *National Tax Journal*, vol. 57, no. 3, pp. 739–756.

Moller, AC, Ryan, RM & Deci, EL 2006, "Self-determination theory and public policy: improving the quality of consumer decisions without using coercion", *Journal of Public Policy and Marketing*, vol. 25, no. 1, pp. 104–116.

Mollering, G 2005, "The trust/control duality: an integrative perspective on positive expectations of others", *International Sociology*, vol. 20, no. 3, pp. 283–305. doi:10.1177/0268580905055478

Muller, K & Riedl, E 2002, "External monitoring of property appraisal estimates and information asymmetry", *Journal of Accounting Research*, vol. 40, no. 3, pp. 865–881.

Murphy, K 2004, "The role of trust in nurturing compliance: a study of accused tax avoiders", *Law and Human Behavior*, vol. 28, no. 2, pp. 187–209.

Murphy, K, Tyler, TR & Curtis, A 2009, "Nurturing regulatory compliance: is procedural justice effective when people question the legitimacy of the law?", *Regulation and Governance*, vol. 3, no. 1, pp. 1–26. doi:10.1111/j.1748-5991.2009.01043.x

Palea, V & Maino, R 2013, "Private equity fair value measurement: a critical perspective on IFRS 13", *Australian Accounting Review*, vol. 23, no. 3, pp. 264–278.

Phillips, J, Pincus, M & Rego, S 2003, "Earnings management: new evidence based on deferred tax expense", *The Accounting Review*, vol. 78, pp. 491–521.

Plesko, GA 2000, "Evidence and theory on corporate tax shelters", Proceedings of the Ninety-Second Annual Conference, National Tax Association – Tax Institute of America, Washington D.C., pp. 367–371.

Plesko, GA & Shumofsky, N 2004, Reconciling Corporations' book and taxable income, 1995–2001, *SOI Bulletin*, (Winter 2004–2005), US Government Printing Office, Washington DC, pp. 103–108.

Pratt, SP 2001, *Business valuation discounts and premiums*, John Wiley & Sons Inc, New York, NY.

Riedl, EJ & Serafeim, G 2011, "Information risk and fair values: an examination of equity betas", *Journal of Accounting Research*, vol. 49, no. 4, pp. 1083–1122.

Rupp, D & Williams, C 2011, "The efficacy of regulation as a function of psychological fit: reexamining the hard law/soft law continuum", *Theoretical Inquiries in Law*, vol. 12, no. 2, pp. 581–602.

Ryan, RM 1995, "Psychological needs and the facilitation of integrative processes", *Journal of Personality*, vol. 63, no. 3, pp. 397–427.

Ryan, RM & Connell, JP 1989, "Perceived locus of causality and internalization: examining reasons for acting in two domains", *Journal of Personality and Social Psychology*, vol. 57, no. 5, pp. 749–761.

Ryan, RM & Deci, EL 2000, "Intrinsic and extrinsic motivations: classic definitions and new directions", *Contemporary Educational Psychology*, vol. 25, no. 1, pp. 54–67. doi:10.1006/ceps.1999.1020

Six, F 2012, "Trust in regulatory relations: how new insights from trust research improve regulation theory", *Public Management Review*, vol. 15, pp. 1–20.

Song, CJ, Thomas, WB & Yi, H 2010, "Value relevance of FAS No. 157 fair value hierarchy information and the impact of corporate governance mechanisms", *Accounting Review*, vol. 85, no. 4, pp. 1375–1410.

Sullivan, M 1999, "Shelter fallout? Corporate taxes down, profits up", *Tax Notes*, vol. 84, no. 5, (Aug 2), pp. 653–657.

Tyler, TR 1990, *Why people obey the law*, Yale University Press, New Haven.

US Department of the Treasury 1999, *The problem of corporate tax shelters: discussion, analysis and legislative proposals*. U.S. Government Press, Washington, D.C.

Van Tendeloo, B & Vanstraelen, A 2005, "Earnings management under German GAAP versus IFRS", *The European Accounting Review*, vol. 14, pp. 155–180.

Vansteenkiste, M, Sierens, E, Soenens, B, Luyckx, K & Lens, W 2009, "Motivational profiles from a self-determination perspective: the quality of motivation matters", *Journal of Educational Psychology*, vol. 101, no. 3, pp. 671–688. doi:10.1037/a0015083

Watrin, C, Nadine, E & Thomsen, M 2014, "Book-tax conformity and earnings management: insights from European one- and two-book systems", *The Journal of the American Taxation Association*, vol. 36, no. 2, pp. 55–89.

Weibel, A 2007, "Formal control and trustworthiness: shall the twain never meet?", Group and Organization Management, vol. 32, no. 4, pp. 500–517. doi:10.1177/1059601106293961

Weisbach, DA 2002, "Ten truths about tax shelters", *Tax Law Review*, vol. 55, pp. 215–253.

White, RW 1959, "Motivation reconsidered: the concept of competence", *Psychological Review*, vol. 66, no. 5, pp. 297–333. doi:10.1037/h0040934

Zeghal, D, Chtourou, SM & Fourati, YM 2012, "The effect of mandatory adoption of IFRS on earnings quality: evidence from the European Union", *Journal of International Accounting Research*, vol. 11, No. 2, (Fall), pp. 1–25.

PART IV

Specific topics

13

FAIR VALUE ACCOUNTING
A manager's perspective

Thomas A. Gilliam and Ronny K. Hofmann

Introduction

This chapter provides a former executive's insights into key issues surrounding the use of historical cost accounting versus the use of fair value accounting. Like all managers, as Senior Director of Finance and Operations of a 1.5 billion dollar multinational computer business, my job was to make and to implement decisions. That is what managers do. Managers often make important decisions based on how they project their decisions will affect financial reporting results.[1] In some circumstances, fair value accounting provides the best decision support while in other circumstances historical cost accounting provides the best decision support. In my experience, ideal circumstances where the manager faces straightforward decisions are rare. As a financial executive, I made decisions in the mist of ambiguity that often did not lend themselves to textbook solutions. Therefore, the goal of this chapter is to provide insights about the pros and cons of the two different accounting treatments within a variety of settings so that individual decision-makers can make the best accounting choices for their business.

Since this chapter presents the manger's perspective as a decision-maker, it focuses on issues related to both external and internal reporting. For external reporting purposes, we address issues related to raising capital through public markets as well as through private commercial lenders. These topics naturally extend into stock market expectations, reporting quality and earnings volatility. For our discussion on internal reporting issues, we cover internal controls, internal reporting and decision support.

As a Chief Accounting Officer, I found the expense of development, implementation and maintenance of accounting systems favored the use of historical cost systems. Historical cost systems are less complex; can often be maintained by lower-level, non-professional staff; and much of the accounting can be automated, e.g. depreciation schedules. On the other hand, with fair value accounting systems, there must be personnel and processes in place to determine fair values. Under Statement of Financial Accounting Standards (SFAS) 157, 'Fair Value Measurements', and International Financial Reporting Standards (IFRS) 13, 'Fair Value Measurement', consistency and comparability in fair value measurements use a fair value hierarchy. The valuation aspects of tiers 1, 2 and 3 can be very complex, which demands even higher levels of expertise – levels of expertise that bring even higher costs.

Further, US GAAP and IFRS require most firms to employ third parties to fulfil their valuation criteria. Whether the added cost justifies the use of fair value accounting varies by circumstance.

Executives must also consider how the two accounting methodologies affect internal controls. Executives are required by the various Sarbanes Oxley Act (SOX) (2002) laws around the world to maintain internal controls, and they can incur substantial penalties if they fail to do so. When I worked in Silicon Valley, managers felt a constant tension between meeting reporting expectations, such as steady predictable growth, and maintaining tight internal controls. The absence of tight controls makes it easier for managers to inject bias judgments into the accounting process. Historical cost accounting strengthens controls because it is more rule-bound and less subject to bias. On the other hand, fair value accounting often requires numerous judgments in the form of estimates that managers can use to manipulate results, e.g. the disgraceful demise of Enron and Arthur Anderson.

Raising capital is at the heart of external reporting. As a Senior Manager, with several technology companies, I saw firsthand how managers strive to meet market expectations. When we met the market's expectations, we attracted capital, and we enhanced our own reputations in Silicon Valley.

Historical cost accounting often provides smoother more predictable accounting results than fair value accounting provides. For example, the cost of fixed assets can be material and can help determine whether the firm meets its earnings target. Managers using straight-line depreciation can easily predict the cost associated with changing fixed asset values.[2] However, fair value accounting that in many cases is arguably more accurate is often unpredictable and out of management's control. Managers can seek to manage their business according to their budgets, but their budgets cannot accurately predict market changes in asset value that introduce volatility. Likewise, firms seeking capital from private sources such as commercial lenders must also be concerned about predictability. Commercial lenders demand predictable results, and they use assets as collateral. If the value of assets is unpredictable, then they offer less value as collateral.

Managers have more freedom with internal reporting. Beyond maintaining internal controls, regulators do not limit their choices. My goal as an executive was to have an internal reporting system in place that would lead to the best decisions. Because managers have little control over fair value fluctuations, fair value often comes up short as a measurement tool. On the other hand, firms that use hedging strategies that can be critical to their success, particularly firms that consume large quantities of commodities or multinational companies with transactions in foreign currencies, can benefit from fair value accounting. Fair value accounting can reduce firm risk and volatility if managers align their hedge strategies with fair value accounting rules.

Background

Managers have a fiduciary responsibility to both protect their firm's assets and employ them in a manner that provides equity investors with maximum returns on their invested capital.[3] Financial reporting is a fundamental aspect of management's fiduciary responsibilities. The purpose of financial reporting is to provide those who provide capital or who are considering doing so with information to make informed investment decisions. Strong financial performance attracts capital but when financial statements reflect poor performance, the firm can experience a loss of capital. Therefore, decisions impacting financial statements are important.[4]

While the primary purpose of financial reporting is to provide actual and potential investors with useful information for decision-making, financial statements can also reflect the quality of management's stewardship. Consequently, managers are motivated to meet financial reporting goals by more than the financial markets.[5] In order to advance their careers, managers strive to achieve financial performance that reflects well on their job performance. Regardless of motives, it is clear that financial reporting influences managerial decision-making.[6]

The profit and loss statements (income statements) generally receive the most attention by management, financial analysts, equity investors and those contemplating equity investment. The focus on income statements can easily be seen with the market's reaction to quarterly earnings announcements. Firms typically announce their revenue, earnings and little other information before filing a complete set of financial statements with regulators. Balance sheet items are rarely discussed during earnings announcements – hence the term earnings announcement. In other words, the balance sheet often takes a backseat to the income statement. Consequently, it is easy to overlook the importance that managers place on the balance sheet.[7] Yet, managerial oversight of items such as accounts receivable and inventory are crucial to their company's financial performance. Striking the right credit and collection balance with the company's customers can help maximize sales and minimize bad debt expenses. Similarly, the value of excess inventory can decline rapidly and result in large write-offs if not managed well.

Academic studies show that the financial markets respond to a firm's earnings announcements, but comparatively not as much to the subsequent release of its financial statements, which implies that balance sheet information is of lesser importance. Of course, such conclusions depend on the nature of the business; for example, financial institutions are vastly different compared to non-financial firms and as such they are often studied separately when investigating the capital market effects of accounting-related issues. It is also worthwhile to note that financial institutions measure most balance sheet items using fair value accounting so they have ample incentives to circumvent fair value accounting rules. The emphasis placed on the income statement though could lead one to believe that managers have little incentive to be concerned with balance sheet accounting issues that in many cases is where fair value accounting has the greatest impact.[8]

The importance of the income statement notwithstanding, managers have a strong interest in their balance sheets and in accounting policies that affect the manner in which their balance sheets are reported. This managerial focus is driven, in part, by the relationship between the balance sheet and the income statement. Through traditional accounting, changes in balance sheet values are captured by the income statement and Other Comprehensive Income (OCI). Though we should point out that income-generating activities that are reported on the income statement often drive balance sheet changes. In the simplest terms, the more profit a firm makes the more equity increases and vice versa.

With traditional accounting (non-fair value accounting), a firm's profit can either be defined as the sum of its balance sheet changes or as the earnings reported on its income statement. Obviously, it is easier to draw conclusions about the firm's performance from the income statement, and since the two statements are easily reconciled under traditional accounting, the income statement garners more attention. Over time, these relationships have changed and the connection between the income statement and the balance sheet has become less straightforward. In particular, OCI has had an increasingly larger impact on the firms' equity. For example, IFRS (IAS 16 Property, Plant and Equipment) allows firms to revalue their fixed assets with changes in the value reported in OCI. Under US GAAP, this choice between the historical cost model and revaluation is not allowed. Hence, for many international companies, their fair value adjustments go through OCI and do not directly impact earnings. Arguably, when companies record gains and losses through OCI, it is trans-parent to investors as they can simply combine OCI with net income. Yet, the evidence sug-gests that this doesn't happen as intensely and as frequently as it should. The focus has been, and still is, on earnings, oftentimes sidestepping valuable information in OCI. We are not able to pinpoint the exact reasons as to why this happens, perhaps investor inattention, lack of sophistication, etc.[9] As a financial executive in the computer industry, I participated in numerous earnings conference calls where we tried to answer analyst's questions. It seemed that the analysts were often fixated on how the announced numbers varied from their own forecast. In many cases, they had their own definitions for earnings that seemed to change routinely with circumstance. Their questions rarely strayed from topics that affected their definition of earnings. Also, as a manager and as an investor, it was easy to view OCI as consisting of items that were not germane to the core business, i.e. I could not dominate my industry by focusing on OCI.

With traditional historical accounting, the adjustment managers make to the value of their assets flow through the income statements. Three of the largest non-cash assets for many firms are accounts receivable, inventory, and property plant and equipment. Under the rules of traditional accounting current assets are recorded at the lower of cost or net realiz-able value. And, under IFRS, accounts receivables fall under IFRS Financial Instruments. IFRS 9 (2014) requires an entity to recognize a loss allowance for expected credit losses on different types of receivables while property plant and equipment are depreciated over time.[10] The costs are charged to the income statement and directly reduce profits. These are costs that management, largely, have control over. For example, accounts receivable is reduced to realizable value to account for the estimated amounts that cannot be collected. These uncollected amounts can be directly associated with the firm's credit policies. If managers freely issue credit in an effort to increase sales then their income statements will also reflect the higher costs associated with those actions.

In a manner similar to accounts receivable, managers have control over their inventory policies. They can carry lean inventories and risk losing sales or carry large inventories to facilitate sales and risk exposure to inventory obsolescence. While inventory write-downs to realizable value can be a result of poor management or a downturn in the economy by having the costs reflected on the income statement, investors can judge the efficacy of managements' decision-making. Accounting for changes in the value of property, plant and equipment is usually more simplistic. It is assumed that the property's value will decline to a residual value over its useful life.[11] With real property being an exception, the value of prop-erty, plant and equipment is written down based on time or use.

Under traditional accounting rules, balance sheet adjustments are made in one direction – down. These rules are driven by the use of prudence or the concept of conservatism. Simply put, conservatism dictates that accounting conventions and judgments error on the side of understating balance sheet values. Also, under IFRS and US GAAP both physical and intan-gible assets can be subjected to impairment tests. Once an asset is written down, it cannot be written back up when conditions reverse. However, there are actions that managers can take to mitigate the one-way effects of traditional accounting. For example, with property, plant and equipment the useful life can be increased. It is noteworthy though that not all firms report the expanded write-down period in the notes of the financial statements. Hence, this change in deprecation may not be visible to investors. Firms that do not provide these dis-closures may do so for the purpose of hiding its effect on earnings, i.e. mangers could choose to let investors assume the positive impact on earnings was a result of good management and not a mere accounting change. As a financial executive, I preferred a boilerplate approach to disclosures that tended to be limited to reoccurring items unless they were of sufficient magnitude. In addition, if the firms do not to disclose changes in their depreciation schedules, they could force analysts to use dated information that could lead to inflating certain ratios. On the other hand, reserves for accounts receivable and inventory can be reduced, which has the same effect as writing them 'up'. These actions go through the income statement. Investors and other readers of the financial statements can see effects of changing the value of these assets reflected on the income statement.

Fundamental considerations with fair value accounting

The initial issues a manager encounters when implementing fair value accounting are often very basic, but nonetheless important. Accounting is expensive and journal entries do not record themselves so people may have to be hired and trained to put fair value accounting into practice. Beyond the base accounting issues, there must be personnel and processes in place to determine fair values. The valuation aspects of tiers 1, 2 and 3 can be very complex, which demands even higher levels of expertise – levels of expertise that bring even higher costs. Under SFAS 157, 'Fair Value Measurements', and IFRS 13, 'Fair Value Measurement', consistency and comparability in fair value measurements are introduced through a fair value hierarchy. This hierarchy distinguishes between quoted prices in active markets for identical assets or liabilities that the entity can access at the measurement date and inputs other than quoted market prices that are observable (directly or indirectly) or not observable at all (IFRS paragraphs 76 and 81). Costs can also be incurred to ensure fair value accounting standards are met in accordance with regulations and to this end, internal controls must be developed, implemented and maintained. Finally, firms must keep records to provide an audit trail for the firm's outside auditors. Outside auditors must also perform additional work that brings additional costs. The external audit costs can also be inflated if the outside auditors require additional expertise to evaluate fair values when the valuation process is complex such as when asset-pricing models are employed.[12] In short, expanding the firm's accounting activities to include fair value accounting can be an expensive proposition.

In contrast with fair value accounting, traditional or historical cost accounting systems are less complex and therefore less expensive to maintain. With traditional accounting, the recording of transactions is straightforward. For the purchase of property, plant and equipment, an accounting clerk can simply debit assets and credit liabilities for the actual costs at the time of the transaction. Recording the subsequent changes in asset values is also simple. The use of standard accounting lives for large categories of assets coupled with straight-line depreciation permits valuation changes to be recorded automatically using basic accounting software programs. Assets such as accounts receivable and inventory are more complex, but under traditional accounting, they too are often reduced to a formula. For example, firms can use a standard aging of the receivables and apply fixed percentages to each age category to estimate the unrealizable amount. Similarly, companies can streamline the process for recording inventory and, while subject to review, much of the initial work can be automated or completed by lower level clerical personnel.

Since higher costs are associated with fair value accounting, managers need to weigh the costs against the benefits to be received. Increased costs can mean that the firm may need to spend more on accounting and less on activities that contributes more directly to the firm's growth. While this notion is not trivial, it is not the most important consideration a manager has to consider. The manner in which fair value accounting affects the firms reporting and its decision-making can be far more important factors.

Internal controls and reporting quality

For external reporting, firms are subject to regulations such as GAAP, IFRS, and other government regulations. Government regulations also require managers to maintain internal controls. Both fair value and traditional accounting methods pose internal control challenges. In many cases the challenges brought about by one methodology can be mitigated by use of the other. In other words, while fair value accounting can be used to curb some accounting abuses, fair value accounting can also introduce the opportunity for new abuses.

Throughout my career as a manager and later as an executive, I strived to report smooth and predictable earnings growth – a common goal across every industry where I worked. This is in contrast with the objective of international accounting standards to provide 'a true and fair view' of the financial position and performance of a respective firm. Nevertheless, it is in the interest of managers to show less volatile earnings to outside stakeholders because investors view volatility as risk. Regulations can play a role in creating or mitigating earnings volatility. For example, earnings reporting under IFRS and US GAAP are often more volatile than earnings reporting produced under German, Italian and French GAAPs. Managerial decision-making also plays a role in determining earnings volatility. In many cases, managers are willing to make long-term economic sacrifices in order to meet short-term reporting objectives.[13] Before the advent of fair value, accounting managers could use the sale of liquid investments as a vehicle to help achieve their reporting goals. Under traditional accounting rules where companies held liquid assets at historical costs, there was a built-in assumption that the true underlying value of those assets remained unchanged. Historical cost accounting ignores real changes in the value of assets so that companies can accumulate unrecognized gains and losses over time. This circumstance provides a setting for abusive accounting practices.

To help smooth reported earnings, managers can simply choose to liquidate assets for the purpose of recognizing gains or losses as needed. For example, assume a firm holds a portfolio of equity investments in various firms that have been accumulated over time. Some of those equity positions will likely increase in value while others decline. Assume further that the firm is just short of its earnings goal. Managers could merely go through the firm's equity portfolio and choose to sell the instruments that will bring about the needed profit. Since the funds can often be reinvested, the cash flow implications are often irrelevant. Likewise if the firm is having an exceptional year, they can choose to sell financial instruments that have accumulated unrecognized losses. This type of downward earnings management can serve to clean up the balance sheet by removing assets that represent future losses and by lowering earnings expectations so that they are more achievable going forward.[14]

Arguably investors and analysts should be able to see through management attempts to mislead them with smooth reported earnings that are achieved through the sale of liquid assets. However, managerial conversion of unrealized gains (losses) to actual gains (losses) to meet their reporting objectives has been well documented (Bartov 1993). Such actions are often designed to fool investors and other stakeholders into thinking that the firm has met its earnings target through ordinary business practices (as opposed to timing the sale of assets) when in fact it has not. While the practice of timing asset sales is not illegal per se, it is illegal when managers seek to fool investors. So, the question of misleading comes down to one of intentions. It is inherently hard to implement internal control to address the subtleties of 'intentions'. Indeed, it is all but impossible to do so.

It should also be noted that the timing of liquid asset sales for reporting purposes is not necessarily without costs. When assets are sold for this purpose, they are not chosen based on their long-term outlook but rather on the basis of the short-term accounting that will materialize. Real long-term economic benefits can be sacrificed to achieve short-term reporting goals. To the extent that investors are fooled, they incur costs as well. However, one easy way to address this practice is the use of fair value accounting.

The use of fair value accounting makes the practice of timing liquid asset sales to meet reporting objectives unworkable. Fair value accounting recognizes gains and losses as the value of the assets change. Therefore, managers cannot simply choose to time the sale of an asset that has a book value far below (above) its market value in order to recognize a gain (loss) as desired. The ability of fair value accounting to curb such practices is often cited by practitioners in discussions about the benefits of fair value accounting.

Nevertheless, the use of fair value accounting is not a cure all for misleading reporting practices that can take advantage of changing values with the firms' assets and liabilities. As fair value accounting introduces additional complexity to the accounting process, it also opens the door for new accounting abuses. Complexity and managerial judgment are introduced when there is an absence of an active market for the assets subject to fair value adjustments. Without an active market, it can be difficult for both managers and outside auditors to determine the true fair value for the firm's assets. If markets are relatively inactive, managers are able to use more discretion with fair value measurement than they are allowed when using models that make use of observable and unobservable input parameters. In addition, studies have shown that when managerial judgment is introduced to the accounting process, managers often use their discretion to sway estimates in the direction of their reporting biases, e.g. inflating or deflating estimates for expense accruals. Likewise, managers can use their discretion to influence the determination of fair values for assets that rely on models and appraisals that contain multiple variables. Models that are more complex often rely on more assumptions that in turn can open the door for managerial bias. Unfortunately, this is one of many techniques employed by Enron, an energy company with a large swathe of assets held at fair value – one extreme instance that brought our profession into disrepute, a large public outcry, and a myriad of what many considered knee-jerk reactions by a group of politicians that led to a large body of excessive regulations.

Even when there are active markets for the firm's assets that allow managers to determine fair values in a straightforward manner that can subsequently be verified by outside auditors, there are still opportunities for abuse. Managers can apply judgment with the classifications of assets that in turn can influence how earnings are reported. Changes in fair value of assets held for trading have a direct income statement affect while changes in fair value of assets available-for-sale escape the income statement until they are liquidated.[15] Hence, managers can shift assets from one classification to another. However, this practice is often constrained because outside auditors will not stand idly by as asset classifications shift back and forth to help meet earnings targets. But the practice of shifting asset classifications can be employed sparingly. Another form of accounting abuse can occur when managers engage in the practice of selling assets held for trading then buy back those assets only to account for them as available-for-sale assets. To curtail this practice, new IFRS rules no longer allow this type of sale buy back arrangement and the category available-for-sale assets is no longer allowed. Hence, changes of fair values will no longer be 'recycled' in OCI.

When a firm employs fair value accounting for their assets, they can still use a different category for its liabilities. Industrial corporations tend not to fair value their liabilities while it is common practice for financial institutions to fair value both assets and liabilities.[16] And, there are parallels between using fair value accounting for assets and using it for liabilities. Some liabilities have active markets so that they can easily be valued internally and subsequently verified by outside auditors. Bonds, certain short commercial loans and some other short-term liabilities tend to fall into this category. As with assets, though, many liabilities require sophisticated models that inherently rely on managerial judgment. Liabilities without active markets include items such as long-term contracts that call for payments in a different currency, or the estimated costs of a global product recall, or the cost of environmental cleanup, and of course pensions. In a manner similar to asset valuations to help obtain a desired reporting result, managers also have opportunities to introduce judgment into the valuation process for liabilities. Especially the discretion to disentangle the liability and equity components of compound instruments because they are so complex. By carefully adjusting liability contracts, managers' can alter leverage ratios. Therefore, additional internal controls are also required for the liability side of the balance sheet.

With either traditional accounting or fair value accounting, the firm's internal controls and its external auditors must guard against earnings management behaviors. While accounting research has examined the use of liquid asset sales to meet with earnings targets, we are not aware of any big scandals surrounding this type of reporting abuse. This statement is not to imply that the practice is acceptable but rather to suggest that it is not clear whether investors are in fact fooled. After all, the alleged offenders reported the asset sales. And, of course, intention is hard to prove. The same thing cannot be said about other abuses with application of fair value accounting.

One of the largest accounting scandals the world has witnessed is associated, at least in part, with fair value accounting. Enron Corp., once the darling of Wall Street, who brought about the largest accounting scandal in modern history, took advantage of fair value accounting rules to fool investors. At the time the scandal broke, based on the market value of their stock, Enron Corp. was the seventh largest company listed on the New York Stock Exchange (NYSE). In the years preceding the scandal, Enron reported unprecedented growth in its profits. Financial analysts during the time seemed unable to explain how the company made money yet they consistently issued strong buy recommendations. While Enron generated tremendous profits, it paid very little in taxes and its profits did not generate cash flows. Instead, Enron's cash flows were derived from a myriad of financial schemes.

It was not fair market value accounting alone that was used to perpetuate Enron's fraud, but without their mark to market practices, their accounting schemes would not have succeeded. To make matters worse, Enron was so large that it could manipulate the market prices of its assets. Enron was in the unique position to create shortages of the products it sold under contract that in turn drove up prices as set by contractual arrangements that it held with state and municipal governments along with other large institutions.[17] Enron also made use of accounting loopholes in the form of Special Purpose Entities (SPEs) to hide its liabilities. Enron's downfall began with a whistleblower, Sharon Watkins, who questioned not only the SPEs but also the mark to market accounting practices that Enron employed to advance its fraud.[18]

The amounts of money and greed were so immense that Enron was able use multi-million dollar underwriting deals to create bias among financial analysts' who seemed content to marvel at the mysterious ways in which Enron generated its huge profits. It was the analysts' job to find out how Enron's generated its earnings, but they failed to do so. How could a company report enormous profits that no one seemed to understand, have no tax bill, and no operating cash flow? These and other basic questions were never addressed. In a similar manner, Enron paid off its accounting firm, Arthur Anderson, with lucrative consulting contracts.[19] Consulting contracts were so large that Anderson did not feel they could afford to lose them. As a result, Anderson shirked it duties as auditors and became complicit in the fraud. In addition to turning a blind eye to Enron's accounting practices Anderson was eventually caught shredding documents at 3 o'clock in the morning. By the end, Arthur Anderson closed in disgrace and Enron collapsed because of pressure from its lenders, the providers of its capital. As a result, lives were ruined, families broken up, people lost their life savings and jobs, some of the culprits went to prison and some died through suicide. By the end, the whole world knew what mark-to-market meant. It was no longer just an accounting term associated with fair value accounting.

Following the shameful actions of Enron and of many other companies that came to light during that time, the United States passed the Sarbanes Oxley Act (SOX) that was intended to curb such practices. The law took aim at financial analysts, auditing firms and executives by putting into place regulations aimed at improving the integrity of financial reporting for publicly held companies. Many other countries followed suit with their own versions of SOX. New regulations governing fair value accounting followed.

Consequently, managers complied with the law and incurred the significant costs associated with implementing SOX. These costs included implementing a well-documented system of internal controls, which could pass third party scrutiny, changing the members of the board of directors and incurring additional audit costs. In many cases, such procedures affected virtually every aspect of the business. Managers had to take these actions not because they were seen as prudent but simply because it was the law. In the United States, implementing the law even inferred that managers have a good attitude and embraced the changes.[20]

However, the association of accounting scandals with fair value accounting did not end. Indeed, it seemed to be only just the beginning. According to a study conducted by the US Securities and Exchange Commission (SEC) at the time of the global financial crisis, 31% of banking assets in the United States alone were subject to fair value accounting (SEC 2008). Financial lending institutions did well as the housing bubble expanded. Their loan portfolios (assets) expanded at previously unheard of rates. When the housing market bubble burst, the financial institutions assets were written down (marked down to market). This was problematic for the lenders because in many cases the loans were still performing. But their loans were under-collateralized and there was no longer a market to sell or package their loan portfolios.[21]

Banks often act as lending retailers putting together loan portfolios, managing the loans, i.e. collecting the payments, and then selling the assets to investors. Once the bubble burst, the investors disappeared meaning there was no market for their assets – the assets were essentially frozen. Many write-downs were taken even though the loans were still performing – simply because the market was frozen. Under traditional accounting rules, the bank would have reserved for non-performing loans, but not taken the large write-downs that are associated with global financial crisis.[22]

In summary, fair value accounting bolsters the need for strong internal controls over asset sales. For example, with fair value accounting as the market value of assets change gains and losses accrue and thus eliminate the practice of timing asset sales to meet reporting targets. However, we have also seen where the use of fair value accounting resulted in unintended consequences. Therefore, while fair value accounting enhances internal controls over asset sales, it simultaneously creates the need for new internal controls to guard against abusive practices.

Capital markets and earnings volatility

Managers believe that both investors and lenders want to see smooth predictable earnings growth. Managers strive to meet the market's expectations by minimizing earnings volatility. Consequently, managers make decisions aimed toward producing smooth predictable growth. The daily financial press provides an abundance of evidence that the financial markets respond to earnings announcement surprises. Several academic studies also confirm this observation and find that the magnitude as well as the source of surprises also influence how the financial markets react.[23]

Not surprisingly, managers also see smooth earnings reports as being indicative of good management. The very nature of their jobs brings about this perspective in large part. It is the manager's job to generate sales growth through new product development and expand market share. It is the manager's job to control spending, and it is the manager's job to invest wisely when procuring the firm's assets. Managers also want reporting systems that are reflective of their efforts.

Our previous discussion about internal controls addressed some of the nefarious methods managers have employed to shore up earnings and to avoid negative earnings surprises. Beyond the knowledge required to institute adequate internal controls, most managers have little interest in the means of trickery to achieve reporting goals. So, in the absence of malfeasance, we evaluate how fair value accounting compares with historical cost accounting in providing managers with financial reporting that delivers more predictable results and that are also more indicative of managerial performance.

Historical cost accounting appears to provide managers with more control than that which fair value accounting provides. When managers acquire assets either through the issuance of credit sales (e.g. accounts receivable) or the purchase of goods and services for resale, they know what the costs are and they know that those costs are unlikely to change in the normal course of business. Further, when costs do change, such as in the case of writing down receivables or inventories to their net realizable value, the write-down is often predicated by sub-optimal decision-making on the part of management. Therefore, in this sense, management has control. They can avoid high bad debt costs with more prudent credit policies. Similarly, when investments are held at historical cost, managers have complete control. The value on the books is the value they chose when purchasing the assets.

In contrast, fair values that are based on market values are more volatile almost by definition. For example, one merely has to look at the financial news for a few minutes before seeing that key financial indexes have changed in value since the day begun, since the week begun, or how they have rebound since the last week. Prices fluctuate by the minute. Efficient market theory notwithstanding, it is hard to understand how the value of an asset can increase by $X\%$ in the morning and decline in value by the end of the day then start the next day with a higher opening price. Yet, this description is more typical than it is exceptional of how financial and commodity markets operate.

When accounting rules force adjustments of the value of a firm's assets according to the short-term whims of the market, it is hard for managers to feel responsible. This statement is particularly true when delegating authority and accountability within the organization. This circumstance presents a dilemma. On the one hand, if decision-makers purchase assets for investment purposes, it makes little sense to sit idly by as the assets decline in value while pretending under the rules of historical cost accounting that the decision-maker's acquisition is whole. Similarly, the firm may not want to wait until they realize gains to reward decision-makers whose purchases have increased steadily in value. On the other hand, evaluating the decision under fair value accounting on the last day of the reporting period can be problematic. Arguably, the value of information content from this 'snap shot point of view' can be questionable, especially if the asset was worth more the day before and rebounds the following day. To the manager, it can seem more like a game of chance where the market penalizes sound long-term decision-making because of short-term market volatility.

It is important to note, that while the continuous recording of changes in asset value can create volatility from quarter to quarter, such record keeping can mitigate large shocks when assets are sold. For example, if an investment increases or decreases 5% over several periods under historical cost accounting, the firm would recognize the entire gain (loss) at the time of sale. While under fair value accounting, the assets' increase in value would be recognized during each of the periods in which it accrued gains (losses). In addition, while the quarterly recognition of value changes may not represent a steady increase over time, it will nevertheless better capture gains that occur over time.

In summary, managers strive to control the business in a manner that produces steady predictable results. As managers we understood that stability represents sound management and that stability a variety of stakeholders. In many cases, managers are directly responsible for changes in the value of assets because of their decision-making. Fair value accounting removes some of the control managers have over the valuations of their assets. On the other hand, fair value accounting also provides a more realistic presentation of the balance sheet. In this sense, investors may gain better insight into the firm's intrinsic value, but lose some insight about management's stewardship.

Borrowing is different

Reading the financial press it is easy to come away with the impression that the three most important data items contained in financial reports are earnings, earnings and earnings. It frequently seems that when analysts venture into more depth about a firm's reporting, it often has to do with how earnings are measured or what it is that constitutes earnings, e.g. 'street earnings' EBITA, earnings before tax, net income, etc. Or the analysts may delve a little deeper into the income statement by evaluating such things as sales volume, gross margins, research and/or advertising expenditures. There is no doubt that these things are important as research shows the markets respond to earnings announcements even when very little other useful information is available. Typically, though, only earnings and revenues are included in earnings announcements.[24]

The market for commercial loans is clearly different. When managers pursue capital in the form of commercial loans, they know their lender has a different perspective than their stockholders. On the one hand, commercial lenders are not fixated on reported earnings. On the other hand, in the long run losses are unsustainable and they are not looking to subsidize money-losing enterprises. In the end, for managers seeking commercial credit, the task is to convince their lender that their firm has the means to repay all funds advanced along with its accrued interest.

Managers can have two primary sources of funds available for loan repayment. The first, and most important potential source of repayment, comes from the firm's cash flow. Accrued earning cannot pay the bills. So bankers perform an in depth review of the client's cash flows both backward and forward-looking. Logically they would like the cash flows to be derived from earnings but that is hardly the most important consideration. The challenge for the manager is to show the lender how cash flows will be generated in order to pay the loan obligations.

The second potential source of repayment comes from the strength of the firm's balance sheet. Lenders have a priority over equity investors on claims on the firm's assets. For example, in the United States, secured lenders take priority over everyone except for employees (payroll) and the Internal Revenue Service. Not surprisingly, lenders prefer to receive their payments from cash flows generated by the day-to-day business and not by liquidating a firm's assets. When lenders foreclose, assets often prove hard to sell and doing so can often adversely affect the communities in which they do business.

Still, every manager knows that to secure a commercial loan, they need the capacity to repay the loan, i.e. cash flow and they may need the collateral to secure the loan. Under historical cost accounting conventions, establishing the value of the firm's assets can be a difficult task. Firms that have held assets for a long period may have a book value substantially below market value due to inflation alone. For example, excluding the recent housing crisis, real estate has traditionally increased in value over time. Accounting conservatism can also contribute to larger reserves being taken against accounts receivable and inventory than might be taken using one's best estimate.[25] And, of course, there is a risk to the lender that the value of firm's assets are overstated, but this risk is minimized under both traditional accounting and fair value accounting conventions.

While commercial bankers tend to be experts at reading and interpreting balance sheets, they also tend to review them through very conservative glasses. Despite a lender's sophistication with balance sheets, it is inherently difficult for a manager to try to explain why the assets on the balance sheet are really worth more than their recorded value. In short, to advance a loan application, the banker needs sufficient cash flows and a strong balance sheet to present to their loan committees. Furthermore, it is the manager's job to provide the necessary evidence and supporting arguments.

Commercial loan packages are inherently complex including both historical financial statements and forward-looking pro forma financial statements. Long complicated stories about how a business is in better financial condition than what is reported in the financial statements only muddies the waters. The fact that the package includes so much information about the future, which is built on assumptions that are always subject to challenge, makes it all the more important to have financial statements that accurately represent the business.

The use of fair value accounting can be particularly helpful for use in balance sheet presentations for commercial loan packages. As much as commercial lenders rely on balance sheets, as presented, they know that historical cost will have little meaning if they are forced to foreclose on collateralized assets. For this reason there can be a reluctance in the banking community to acknowledge that historical costs tend to understate values. The application of fair value accounting can remove analytical distractions such as trying to determine the true value of assets when using historical accounting procedures. Consequently both the manager and the banker are free to focus on future projections and not interpreting the value of past events.[26]

Finally, commercial lenders are interested in the firm's equity as suggested by one banker's lament, '*I don't want to own more of your company than you and your investors do*'.[27] Simply put, lenders generally do not want to be the primary source of financing. There are exceptions and in some countries such as Germany, debt financing can be more pervasive than equity financing. But a simple test for the lender is to compare the funds being sought by the manager with the amount of equity on the balance sheet. Along these lines, it is also worthwhile to note that absent extraordinary circumstances, lenders will not advance funds to be used for dividends.[28] Indeed many governments prohibit dividends in excess of accumulated earnings. Equity is important to bankers.

Since fair value accounting tends to bolster the value of assets over what would otherwise be reported with historical costs, its application can help the manager overcome a simple but basic loan limit that is often placed on loan applications. But as with so many other business situations, fair value accounting can be seen as a double-edged sword. Many fair value adjustments typically go through OCI. Excluding the impact on equity of changes in asset values from operating income tends to serve the needs managers have to meet the demands of equity investors. But commercial bankers focus on the balance sheet. When equity is volatile, a lender's projections of equity tend to be conservative, which in turn can translate into lower loan caps. Still, fair value accounting provides more advantages than it does disadvantages during the loan application process.

Just as managers have to report financial results to equity investors and reap the rewards or suffer the consequences of their firm's performance relative to investor expectations, they must also meet the demands of their lenders. Commercial lenders often write numerous performance covenants into their loan agreements. While the manager and the loan officer negotiate covenants up front, the lender does not expect them to be broken or renegotiated later.[29] Some covenants are very basic. For example, banks will rarely issue loans to fund dividends. Also, relying on a strong balance sheet at the time of the loan, the covenants usually contain requirements that a strong balance sheet be maintained. This objective is usually spelled out in the form of ratios. Covenant examples can include debt-to-equity ratios, current ratios, quick ratios, accounts receivable aging specifications, inventory turns, minimum cash balances and many, many more than can easily be violated if the balance sheet is not actively managed. Managers cannot afford to violate their covenants. The penalties for doing so are harsh for the firm as well as for the manager's own reputation among commercial lenders.

In summary, for managers seeking debt capital infusions, fair value accounting establishes more realistic values for their collateralized assets. In turn, this reporting aspect allows managers and commercial loan officers to put together more streamlined loan packages. The loan packages are more streamlined in part because there is a simpler story for loan committees than talking about 'what the numbers really mean or how much the assets are really worth'. Lending proposals are subject to rigorous review by loan committees and once approved loans are subject to monitoring by auditors and regulators. Everyone is happier when the balance sheet is purported to mean what it says versus attempts at trying to interpret an analysis of asset values when traditional accounting is used. This upfront advantage is not without costs though. Because of the inherent volatility associated with fair value accounting, managers face additional challenges in meeting covenants that are in the form of maintaining asset and liability ratios. In order to avoid breaking covenants due to changes in market values, managers must be more conservative in how they manage their businesses that in turn creates an added cost.

Operating decisions and strategies

Both managers and investors dislike uncertainty. Managers' aversion to uncertainty stems in large part due to the kinds of problems it inserts into the planning process and to the actual implementation of their operating plans. To facilitate a stable operating environment, managers strive to produce smooth predictable results even when the nature of business is not necessarily conducive to achieving this goal. To this end, managers often take actions to reduce uncertainty especially when it can be done without jeopardizing core business strategies. As has been seen, the use of fair value accounting can bring more volatility to financial reporting than would be the case under traditional historical cost accounting. As a result, the outcome of managerial decisions can hinge on the method of accounting they employ. In particular, as previously described the implementation of fair value accounting can lead to more volatility for both earnings and asset values. From a managerial perspective, volatility represents risk. This type of risk is in addition to the normal risks managers are expected to take in both their operating and strategic decision-making. Managers must balance their risk taking and the added risk of volatility brought about by fair value accounting can lead some managers to more conservative business practices that are not necessarily in the firm's best interest.[30]

The simple notion that accounting choices can influence operating decisions suggests that the use of fair value accounting may result in sub-optimal decision-making. Of course, just the opposite could hold true where the use of fair value accounting could lead to an improvement in decision-making. It is important to understand how decisions can be influenced by the use of different accounting conventions. Even the most mundane decisions can be influenced by the presence or absence of fair value accounting.

Frequently companies carry their cash reserves in the form of actual cash in bank checking accounts and in the form of safe liquid interest-bearing instruments. This common sense practice provides firms with a small return while still providing a safety net of readily accessible cash. However, the use of fair value accounting can introduce a discontinuity between the underlying business activity and the financial reporting of that activity. As interest rates rise and fall, which they do on a daily basis, the fair value of interest-bearing instruments fluctuate. For cash reserves, fair value accounting is negligible; nevertheless, if a firm uses interesting-bearing instruments and the option to fair value those instruments, the financial statements will show the impact. Therefore, managers face a risk of writing down otherwise safe interest-bearing instruments, even though when there is little likelihood of realizing a loss. Managers may choose to forgo interest income to avoid short-term financial reporting risks. Obviously, this type of decision-making is sub-optimal when viewed through a long-term lens. Managers can reduce risk by hedging interest-bearing instrument through interest-rate swaps. Nevertheless, many small firms do not have the expertise to use derivatives. Additionally, firms may incur additional costs as hedge accounting rules are complex and most businesses may need to hire third-party consulting firms to overcome the lack of expertise. Overall, such a risk management strategy may increase costs that do not justify the benefits. Mangers should make these types of hedging decisions based on a cost benefit analysis.

The reporting impact of fair value accounting can negatively affect business decisions. For example, with many business transactions, a seller cannot simply pass along the effects of fluctuating costs to its customers through an endless series of price changes. Ordering in advance to secure both supplies and predictable prices is a basic practice that also mitigates earnings volatility.

However, in many circumstances firms are not in a position to pre-order goods and services with locked in prices. The more a company's costs drive its prices the more risk the company incurs. With clouded costs projections it is difficult for a company to get its pricing right. The apparel industry provides a good illustration of how cost-related risks can impact business.

Levi Strauss & Co of San Francisco 'is a $4 billion a year apparel manufacturer'. In this capacity, they are one of the world's largest buyers of cotton. Cotton prices change daily. This circumstance means that when a retailer orders a shipment of blue jeans, Levi Strauss & Co.'s management cannot know what the actual cost of filling the order will be. The situation is problematic for two reasons.

First, the denim jean business is very competitive. Levi Strauss & Co. competes with Old Navy, Gap Inc., Wrangler, Lee Jeans, Zara, Hugo Boss and a host of others. It is very difficult for them to simultaneously offer their most competitive pricing and to maintain their gross margins when the cost of their primary material is unknown. Of course their competition has the same problem but that fact or knowledge does not facilitate their decision-making. Second, with locked in selling prices and the resulting fluctuating gross margins, it is difficult to plan and commit to investments in the company's infrastructure and its property plant and equipment.

Hedging strategies can provide a usual tool for companies such as Levi Strauss & Co. to offset fluctuations in the costs of their planned future purchases. These companies can employ what is known as a 'long hedge' to secure a purchase price for a supply of cotton that they intent to acquire at some specified date in the future. To implement the long hedge, companies purchase enough cotton futures to cover the amount of cotton that they predict will be required to meet their forecasted cotton demand. If the price of cotton goes up, the additional costs will be offset with the profits from settling the cotton futures contract. Conversely, if the price of cotton falls the company will lose money on its long hedge but that loss will be offset by lower actual purchase prices for its cotton. The risk of commodity price fluctuation is mitigated for the cost of the hedge instruments. Essentially, it works like an insurance policy that protects against costs fluctuations.

We use Levi Strauss & Co. and the apparel industry's cotton purchases to illustrate this type of hedging but many other industries use it as well. Industries such as the airlines (fuel), automotive (steel), tires (rubber), building (lumber & steel) and many others who commit to selling prices either formally or informally when their costs are subject to almost certain change. These kinds of risks are not part of a company's core business but rather a function of the environment in which they operate, i.e. these are operating risks.[31] Hedging offers these industries a cost-effective way to minimize this type of market risk.

Commodity price fluctuation is not only on the cost side of the transaction but can also manifest on the selling side when prices are determined by the market. In some businesses such as agriculture, mining, drilling and other commodity type businesses customers accept the fact that their costs will fluctuate with the various markets. Indeed, the price of a barrel of oil is reported daily on most cable news channels. So while businesses dealing in commodities have little if any control over prices, their customers do accept this condition. However, when the selling firm has steady predictable costs in an industry such as drilling for oil and fluctuating prices that it can charge its customers, the result can be volatile earnings.

Companies that sell commodities can also use hedging strategies to combat earnings volatility that is driven by selling price fluctuations. To protect against selling price risks, these companies can employ a 'short hedge'. With a short hedge, companies can effectively secure a selling price for the product they will deliver at future dates. Systematically this strategy works the same, as a long hedge except it is the selling price that is protected. When the commodity price rises (drops), the value of the hedge drops (rises). Consequently, the selling company can use gains or losses from settling its hedge contract to offset gains or losses brought about by changes in its selling prices.

Another source of earnings volatility can be created by currency fluctuations. In the global economy, it is common to purchase products in the currency of the selling country, which can be different from the reporting currency. When companies place advance orders for products at a fixed price in a foreign currency, they face risk that it will require more of their reporting currency to complete the purchase due to currency fluctuations. Companies can use currency hedges to guard against this type of risk. And, as in the cases of hedging illustrated above, if the hedge derivative is well matched with the underlying business activity it will mitigate or eliminate currency translation-related risks.

Hedge accounting rules allow the firm to match the gains and losses from the hedge instrument to offset the impact of cost fluctuations in the items being hedged. For managers, this accounting is ideal. The accounting matches the underlying economic activity by reporting the effect of the hedge strategy to control volatility. But hedge accounting rules can be tricky with the application of fair value accounting to hedge derivatives under the rules of IFRS, and US GAAP.

In order to use hedge accounting, the firm must align the hedge with the hedging item in a highly correlated manner. Often times this does not match the way firms execute hedging strategies. For example, just as a firm may choose to only partially ensure an asset, the firm may choose to only partially hedge. Also, the firm may not be under contract to purchase products but rather purchases are driven from an internal plan or forecast for product purchases that may constantly be revised throughout the operating period. In the case of commodities, they may order materials as needed at spot prices. And earlier when they set prices for finished goods, they may have purchased long hedges to help offset cost fluctuations without a clear picture of the quantities or timing involved. The purchases and the hedges may not be sufficiently correlated to meet hedge accounting rules.

When the hedge is not highly correlated with the underlying activity, which can often be hard to achieve, fair value accounting rules require the hedging company to record gains and losses on the hedge derivatives based on spot prices of the last day of each reporting period. This action undermines the purpose of hedging and renders the hedging strategy useless from a financial reporting perspective.[32]

Consequently, managers who employ hedge strategies face two paths. First, managers must determine whether they qualify for hedge accounting, i.e. can they ensure a highly correlated hedge strategy. If they do not qualify for hedge accounting, then managers must choose whether to proceed with a hedging strategy aimed at generating cash flows that are more predictable even though earnings volatility may increase. Alternatively, instead of using hedge accounting rules, managers can use fair value for both the hedging instrument and the hedged item. One advantage is that firms are not required to use hedge accounting rules, but they can achieve a similar result. On the other hand, managers have to fair value their financial instruments. Normal accounting principles apply to the hedged item. The hedging derivative instrument is measured at fair value each period, but the effective portion of the change in fair value is deferred in OCI and presented within equity.

If managers decide to fair value both the hedged item and the hedging instrument, they may reveal proprietary information about their business strategies and global expansion objectives that investors and competitors can identify. If the hedged items are reported at historical cost, it is less transparent and therefore more difficult to attach a fair value to the firm's assets. Additionally, although the hedging instrument is measured at fair value, the effective portion of the cash flow hedge is parked in OCI and only later reported in the income statement. For managers this means that inaccuracies in the risk management strategies will be shown in the income statement. Investors may be able to analyze the sophistication and quality of a firm's risk management through the disclosures of the effective and ineffective portion that needs to be disclosed under IFRS and US GAAP. In contrast, if a firm uses fair values for both hedged items and hedging instruments, it is nearly impossible to analyze whether the movements in the income statement stem from ineffective risk management procedures.

Internal reporting

Accounting rules promulgated under GAAP and IFRS are designed to provide investors and lenders with the necessary information to make informed decisions. For internal accounting purposes, managers must grapple with ambiguity based on their firms unique needs and circumstances. While obtaining capital is essential for a firm's success, often, the larger challenge for managers is putting the capital to work. Managers allocate capital to their internal projects or to their operating divisions in much the same manner as investors and lenders choose where to invest their capital. Managers are expected to manage their businesses in a manner that grows capital. For middle to large size organizations, this can be an enormously complex task involving the coordination of marketing a myriad of products, operating in multiple countries, using multiple currencies, managing people from differing cultures and abiding by a labyrinth of regulations.

Internal financial reporting provides managers with a critical set of tools to help allocate resources and to manage and control the activities of their organizations. The importance of external financial reporting notwithstanding, managers typically devote far more resources to internal financial reporting than they do to external reporting. While this disparity in resource allocation might be viewed as an indicator of the relative importance of internal reporting over external reporting, that would be wrong. External reporting typically occurs on a quarterly basis, while internal reporting is often a daily event. Moreover, much of what is contained in a firm's external reports can be garnered from its internal reporting, i.e. there is often a strong link between internal and external reporting.

Internal reporting is also more resource consuming because it is more detailed. Rules of external reporting recognize the need to protect proprietary information whereas the same rules do not apply to internal accounting. Internal reporting, while far more extensive than external reporting, is not subject to the rules and regulations promulgated by regulators.[33] Rather than relying on regulation to dictate internal reporting polices, managers rely on such factors as the trade-off between costs and benefits. With this scenario, the costs are the costs of producing the accounting information and the benefits are the value associated with improved decision-making. Internal accounting policies are designed to support optimal decision-making. Funds are expended for better information only when better information will result in improving decisions to the point that doing so will offer benefits that more than cover the costs of providing the additional reporting information.

Beyond decision support, internal financial reporting also provides a feedback mechanism that allows managers to monitor the financial effects of implementing their decisions. Typically firms have many levels of management that are responsible for decisions and/ or activities that can be accompanied by significant financial consequences. Firms use internal reporting, often with comparisons to budgets, to hold mangers responsible for the implementation of their decisions. Through this mechanism they can reward the profitable decision-makers and address problems associated with poor decision-making.

Fair value accounting is often not seen as meaningful for internal accounting purposes. This perspective can be problematic if for no other reason than because it further distances external accounting from internal accounting. This means that when managers evaluate the financial effectiveness of their pending decisions, the benefits that materialize may not necessarily turn into benefits that managers can report externally. A major challenge for managers is to ensure that the internal reporting system is easily tied to external reporting results. Firms do not want to have a system in place where all the managers can be successful in meeting their targets while the firm fails to meet its target. There needs to be a coming together of the two reporting systems.

One way firms manage to bring the internal and external systems together is by breaking down responsibility for the financial results. For example, the firm might choose to employ income statement accounting for each major product line with a general manager assigned to each one. These statements could then be summed to equal the external reports. Likewise, the firm could use geographical reporting or whatever business segments fit its operating models. But, at the end of the day, the sum of all the parts needs to equal that which is reported externally.

Managers must decide whether to use fair value accounting for internal reporting purposes. While the question of whether to use fair value accounting for external reporting is
often dictated by regulators or external users, managers must make the decision about how
to employ fair value accounting for internal reporting. The question of whether to use fair
value accounting for internal reporting is best answered by analyzing its impact on internal
decision-making.

Just as investors can judge firms by return on capital, so too managers can judge a firm's
divisions, products or even individual projects based on returns. For internal measurement
purposes, managers often look at a project's or a division's return on assets. By dividing operating profits by assets, managers obtain a comparative measure, across operations that may
vary significantly in scope and size. Companies also use return on sales as a performance
measure. While this measure brings comparability to otherwise unique activities, it does not
capture profitability in a manner that can be easily matched to capital market expectations at
the firm level. When a firm is seeking to optimize investor returns and it is looking at returns
on assets across a range of businesses within the firm, it is better able to see which internal
organizations are contributing the most (or least) to its profit objectives.[34]

One caveat to judging operating divisions and the managers that run them with return on
assets is that it implies that the managers have a high level of influence on both the returns
and the amount of assets deployed. In general, managers have a high level of control over
the assets they employ. This reasoning stems in large part from the simple fact that managers
procure assets, i.e. it takes affirmative action on the part of the managers to deploy assets.
In contrast to asset acquisition, earnings reflect how well managers use the assets that they
have acquired. When asset values are subject to market swings, interpreting results using the
return on assets measure becomes more complex.

With historical costs, it is much easier to hold managers throughout the organization
responsible for changes in asset values. This is because changes in value are largely either
controllable or predictable. When managers increase the value of the asset they employ, it is
through conscience acquisition, i.e. they decide that they need more assets to run their division properly. Similarly, managers choose the optimal time to retire or sell assets that are no
longer providing best use. Moreover, with devaluation, because most firms use straight-line
depreciation, managers can easily foresee asset depreciation in a predictable manner that directly impacts the income statement. As an executive, my managers were required to include
a depreciation schedule with their budget submissions.

Distributing responsibility throughout the organization for financial results provides
management with more power or leverage as well as with more control. In addition, distributed responsibility among managers is associated with best management practices. Consequently, there are strong arguments in favor of ignoring fluctuations in the market value of
assets in determining performance internally.

Using fair value reporting for external reporting and using traditional historical cost accounting for internal reporting and decision-making is not without cost though. Companies
must maintain two sets of records and be content with internal results that do not line up
with external results. While companies maintain separate records for internal reporting because of the amount of detail and other reasons discussed above, the more differences there
are between the two systems, the more costs that are incurred and the harder it is to bridge
the differing sets of results.

Another argument against the use of fair value accounting for internal purposes comes
about because managers often make short-term tactical decisions that should line up with
long-term strategic objectives. Companies rarely plan on long-term growth in their assets

market value as a way to achieve market success. Consequently if managers see short-term market volatility as a risk factor, then they could be driven to more conservative decision-making that would be out of sync with the company' overall objectives. A good internal measurement system aligns reporting to reflect how well managers meet short- and long-term objectives.

On the other hand, there are advantages to using fair value accounting internally. When the firm uses fair value accounting for its external reporting, its internal use provides alignment between the two reporting systems. This alignment means that managers throughout the organization will be making decisions in a manner that is consistent with external reporting goals. Doing so can help avoid the phenomenon where middle level managers achieve success while the firm fails. Also, despite the inherent volatility that fair value accounting brings, it does tend to bring about a greater awareness of the true value of assets that are being employed. This latter point can be crucial when evaluating new or on-going projects based on return on assets employed.

Conclusion

Ambiguity, ambiguity and ambiguity – three of the most difficult factors that I came across making executive level decisions. In some circumstances, the benefits derived from the use of fair value accounting far exceed the benefits associated with historical accounting, while in other circumstances just the opposite conclusion held. These types of ideal circumstances where the manager's decision is straightforward rarely present themselves. As a financial executive, I made decisions in the mist of ambiguity that often did not lend themselves to mechanical decision-making. Therefore, in this chapter we provide insights about the pros and cons of the two different accounting treatments using a variety of setting so that the individual decision-maker can adopt the optimal accounting practices given their circumstances.

Since this chapter presents the mangers perspective, which is a decision-making perspective, it focuses not only on external reporting issues but also on the myriad of issues that mangers face when developing internal accounting systems. For external reporting purposes, we discuss issues related to raising equity capital through public markets as well as private capital through commercial lenders. From there these topics extend into market expectations, reporting quality, earnings and internal reporting.

As a chief accounting officer, I found cost to be one aspect of the two accounting methods that favored the use historic cost accounting. Historical cost systems are less complex and can often be maintained by clerical staff, and much of the accounting can be automated, e.g. depreciation schedules. On the other hand, with fair value cost accounting there must be personnel and processes in place to determine fair values. The valuation aspects of tiers 1, 2 and 3 can be very complex, which demands even higher levels of expertise – levels of expertise that bring even higher costs. Under SFAS 157, 'Fair Value Measurements', and IFRS 13, 'Fair Value Measurement', introduce consistency and comparability in fair value measurements through a fair value hierarchy. Whether the added cost justifies the use of fair value accounting varies by circumstance.

Very little is straightforward in choosing which accounting methodology is best for a particular organization. For internal purposes, a firm may choose to use multiple methods of internal accounting to support different decisions. As a chief accounting officer, at one of my last companies, I developed and maintained separate accounting systems for tax, external reporting and duel internal accounting systems.

Notes

1 This statement holds for most accounting choices a chief accounting officer makes. However, the scope of this chapter is limited to comparing the use fair value accounting with the use of traditional accounting.

2 We choose property, plant, and equipment to illustrate this point because it is the clearest example. Nevertheless, we could evaluate the balance sheet item by item starting with current assets such as accounts receivable and draw the same conclusion. We discuss the phenomena more in the main text of the chapter.

3 Financial Accounting Standards Board. 1978. Statement of Accounting Concepts No. 1.

4 The reader should note that in recent years the responsibility of the firm has expanded to include a duty to all stakeholders. Stakeholders are often defined as anyone who has an interest in the firm. This broad definition can include such people as employees, people who live in proximity to the business, people who live in the environment the business can affect, and advocates for many other social responsibilities. In this chapter we focus on the more traditional managerial responsibilities. We do this not because traditional responsibilities are more important but rather because the topic of fair value accounting is not well suited to addressing issues surrounding social responsibility.

5 See the Graham et al. (2005) survey of Chief Financial Officers for a more information about management's reporting incentives.

6 See Roychowdhury (2006) for illustrations of managerial decision-making motivated by meeting financial reporting targets.

7 Through clean surplus accounting no adjustments to equity are made through transactions involving hedge accounting, pension adjustments, unrealized gains and losses from the available-for-sale portfolio and foreign currency translation, and revaluations of property, plant and equipment.

8 Some transactions lead to movements in other comprehensive income (OCI) which is shown within equity in the balance sheet. Hence, if investors believe that specific value movements are value relevant, they will extract this information when the annual reports are released and combine this information with the net income that might have been announced before the release of the balance sheet.

9 See Barton et al. (2010) for more information about how investors value different earnings measures.

10 The International Accounting Standards Board (IASB) changed the requirements of IAS 39 which followed a so called 'incurred loss' model. During the recent financial crisis in 2007/2008 it was recognized that many credit losses were reported too late which mislead investors. Credit losses were only reported when objective evidence of impairment was available. The new IFRS 9 incorporates a more forward-looking measure of credit losses. Hence, firms are encouraged to use discretion and measure expected losses in order to have a timelier picture of the credit risk position inherent in the portfolio.

11 As mentioned earlier, for property, plant and equipment IFRS permit the use of a so-called revaluation model that is not allowed under US GAPP rules.

12 In some circumstances, auditors face complex fair value measurements and do not have the know-how or resources to provide a true and fair view. As an executive in the semi-conductor and computer industry, I was also responsible for 'field upgrades' either as part of a marketing program, a product upgrade or maintenance. Field upgrades consists of such things as installing faster processors in computers at the customer's site. I experienced a situation where our newest state of the art computers were catching fire. Unfortunately, we did not learn of the problem until after a large quantity of high-end computers shipped. It was also yearend. I had at least a hundred estimates from experts such as design engineering, manufacturing, technical marketing, purchasing, field engineering, internal financial analysts, and my own estimates. No one knew how much it would cost; the auditors had no ability to evaluate the cost beyond looking at our calculations and making their own judgement about reasonableness and materiality.

13 See Graham et al. (2005) for the complete survey results of CEOs and CFOs.

14 See Bartov (1993) for more information about and evidence of this practice.

15 Assets held for sale are generally assets that are held long term. Such assets can include long term investments as well as things such as abandoned property. On the other hand, assets held for trading are generally held short-term and often include liquid assets.

16 Through fair valuing both sides of the balance sheet's movements, assets and liabilities achieve a natural hedge. Ideally, managers mitigate risk through business transactions that have offsetting movements and use hedging to manage the residual risk.

17 Subsequent investigations found that Enron actually shut down power plants causing black outs during peak periods in order to manipulate prices under contractual obligations.

18 Sharon Watkins was a Vice President at Enron with an accounting background who is often cited as the whistleblower who brought to light Enron's practices. She subsequently testified before congressional hearings in the United States.

19 At the time was one of the five largest accounting firms in the world.

20 'Tone at the top' has been a corner stone of internal control systems since the passage of the Sarbanes Oxley Act in 2001.

21 According to a report of the ECB ('Fair Value Accounting in the Banking Sector'):

> Instruments held in the trading book are valued at market prices. A profit and/or loss arising from the revaluation of trading book instruments is recognized in the profit and loss account. The accounting rules for the trading book thereby take all market risks (i.e. price risk, interest rate risk, foreign exchange risk and liquidity risk) into account. Banking book instruments, by contrast, are carried in the balance sheet at the lower of historical cost and market value. Whereas a loss on a banking book instrument is transferred to the profit and loss account, unrealized gains are not recognized and can therefore become hidden reserves in the balance sheet.

22 The purpose of this discussion about the global financial crisis is to offer a managerial perspective about untended consequences associated with fair value accounting. The reader should know that there is much debate about the role of fair value accounting in helping to bring about the financial crisis. Obviously the housing bubble, lending practices at the time, and many other economic factors led to the financial crisis. But the fact that fair value accounting is so often mentioned in these discussions suggests that we would be remiss not to discuss it in this chapter.

23 For a more detailed discussions on the market response to earnings announcement see: Ertimur et al. (2003), Ghosh et al. (2005), Jegadeesh and Livnat (2006), Callen et al. (2008) and Kama (2009).

24 Jegadeesh and Livnat (2006) note that 95% of the firms they sample report earnings and revenues in preliminary earnings announcements, making reported earnings and revenue publicly available relatively early while other important financial information are not available to the public until SEC filings become available.

25 See Jackson and Liu (2010) for a discussion on the how conservatism leads firms to build larger and larger accounts receivable reserves over time. The larger reserves reduce the realizable value relative to the face value even when accounts are being collected at a fairly constant rate.

26 Note: we do not devote space to discuss balance sheet liabilities in the context of securing capital in the form of debt. Obviously, lenders want to understand the borrowers other obligations. Typically, liabilities that are coming due during the loan term are accounted for in the cash flow projections.

27 Janice M. Smith, former senior executive in charge of commercial lending at BNP Paribas.

28 In recent years, firms have accumulated offshore cash, i.e. profits earned abroad and subject to taxation if the cash is returned home. This was a topic of debate during the 2016 presidential campaign in the United States. Lenders have advanced cash for dividends when there was cash reserves abroad that could be used to secure the loans. But this practice is the exception and it is created by asymmetric global taxation policies.

29 When managers foresee that they are in danger of breaking a covenant, they would then be expected to contact the bank up front and then the term would be renegotiated before the covenant is broken. Naturally, bankers do not like this and, if it came without penalty, firms would have no incentive to meet their covenants when they could be so easily renegotiated. Therefore renegotiated covenants often come with higher interest rates or some other method of compensating the bank and penalizing the borrower all the while maintaining the guise that the terms of the loan have been met.

30 See the Graham et al. (2005) survey of Chief Financial Officers for a more information about management's reporting incentives.

31 When we speak of core business risk, we are referring to decisions related to such things as new product offering, strategic pricing, marketing strategies, etc. This includes the kinds of decisions

where management must decide whether to invest or whether to look to other projects for opportunities, but not inherent risks.

32 This type of hedge can still serve to mitigate cash flow volatility.

33 It should be noted that while managers have a great deal of freedom to design their internal reporting systems and their decision support algorithms in the way that they see fit there are some restrictions. However, SOX laws (and managers' implicit fiduciary responsibilities) require managers to maintain internal controls. Internal reporting is a key component of any internal control system. Hence, some consideration of external reporting requirements may necessarily influence the design of internal reporting systems.

34 We discuss return on assets here because it is so popular among companies. The fact that total assets does not equate to equity can be addressed by reducing the assets associated with a division by the amount of liabilities that are associated with its activities. This practice is often referred to as return on net assets. Because of the added costs and sometimes ambiguity that can be associated with allocating liabilities, total assets are often chosen instead of net assets. For very large or independent divisions, subsidiaries, or conglomerates where separate records are mandated for other reasons then net assets can be easily used as a performance metric.

References

Barton, J, Hansen, TB & Pownall, G 2010, "Which performance measures do investors around the world value the most—and why?", *The Accounting Review*, vol. 85, no. 3, pp. 753–789.

Bartov, E 1993, "The timing of asset sales and earnings manipulation", *The Accounting Review*, vol. 68, no. 4, pp. 840–855.

Callen, JL, Robb, SWG & Segal, D 2008, "Revenue manipulation and restatements by loss firms", *Auditing: A Journal of Practice and Theory*, vol. 27, no. 2, pp. 1–29.

Ertimur, Y, Livnat, J & Martikainen, M 2003, "Differential market reactions to revenue and expense surprises", *Review of Accounting Studies*, vol. 8, pp. 185–211.

European Central Bank (ECB), *Fair value accounting in the banking sector.* Available from: www.ecb. europa.eu/pub/pdf/other/notefairvalueacc011108en.pdf?f569946e5cb4b13adaf9cb70e935ffb1. Accessed on 14 March 2018.

Financial Accounting Standards Board 1978, *Statement of Accounting Concepts No. 1.*

Ghosh, E, Gu, Z & Jain, PC 2005, "Sustained earnings and revenue growth, earnings quality, and earnings response coefficients", *Review of Accounting Studies*, vol. 10, pp. 33–57.

Graham, J, Harvey, R & Rajgopal, S 2005, "The economic implications of corporate financial reporting", *Journal of Accounting and Economics*, vol. 40, pp. 3–73.

International Financial Reporting Standard (IFRS) 9 2014, *Financial instruments,* International Accounting Standards Board, London.

Jackson, S & Liu, X 2010, "The allowance for uncollectible accounts, conservatism, and earnings management", *Journal of Accounting Research*, vol. 48, no. 3, 565–601.

Jegadeesh, N & Livnat, J 2006, "Revenue surprises and stock returns", *Journal of Accounting and Economics*, vol. 41, pp. 147–171.

Kama, I 2009, "On the market reaction to revenue and earnings surprises", *Journal of Business Finance and Accounting*, vol. 36, no. 1–2, pp. 31–50.

Roychowdhury, S 2006, "Earnings management through real activities manipulation", *Journal of Accounting & Economics*, vol. 42, no. 3, pp. 335–370.

Sarbanes Oxley Act (SOX) 2001, *The United States Congress.*

Sarbanes Oxley Act (SOX) 2002, http://legcounsel.house.gov/Comps/Sarbanes-oxley%20Act%20 Of%202002.pdf. Accessed on 12 March 2018.

Securities and Exchange Commission (SEC) 2008, *Report and recommendations pursuant to Section 133 of the Emergency Economic Stabilization Act of 2008: study on mark-to-market accounting.*

Smith, JM 2015, former Senior Vice President BNP Paribas.

14

TAX-RELATED IMPLICATIONS OF FAIR VALUE ACCOUNTING

Kay Blaufus and Martin Jacob

Introduction

Fair value accounting has received considerable attention by standard-setters, policy-makers and academic research (see, for example, the other chapters in this companion) over the past years. However, policy-makers and scholars have directed limited attention to the implications of fair value accounting for taxation. One potential reason is that due to a lack of book-tax conformity as, for example, in the United States, the discussion on fair value accounting for financial reporting can be led without considering tax consequences. In this chapter, we aim to fill this gap by discussing potential effects of defining taxable income based on fair value accounting, or fair value taxation.

We first provide an overview of existing tax systems in Europe and the United States and the use of fair value elements for tax purposes. Tax accounting is generally based on historical cost measurement rather than on fair value accounting. However, there are several countries that have implemented elements of fair value accounting, in particular for banks, in their respective tax code. For example, financial assets and liabilities held for trading are valued at fair value, and unrealized revaluation profits are subject to corporate income tax in the Czech Republic, Denmark, Finland, France, Hungary, Italy, Portugal, Slovakia, Slovenia, Spain, Sweden and the United Kingdom. However, the use of fair values in taxation is rather limited to some few specific cases and tax base elements.

Next, we discuss potential costs and benefits of implementing fair value taxation. First, according to a theory (Samuelson, 1964; Johansson, 1969), a tax system that defines taxable income on economic profits – or more broadly on fair values – ensures that the tax system does not distort investment decisions. Any distortion of investment decisions represents a welfare loss that could be reduced by fair value taxation. In this chapter, we provide two examples of such decisions – investment decisions of firms and capital gains realization decisions – that are distorted by historical cost accounting but that are not distorted by fair value accounting. We provide some suggestive empirical evidence for this conjecture.

We acknowledge, however, there might be some challenges when introducing fair value accounting for tax purposes, in particular with respect to tax compliance. Fair values are already used for tax purposes such as company valuation or asset valuation for estate taxes, wealth taxes or inheritance tax purposes. Hence, extending the use of fair value accounting

to income taxes is feasible. On the other hand, there are arguments that fair value accounting for income tax purposes substantially increases compliance costs, as fair values cannot be
easily determined for non-traded assets. Ambiguous fair value measurements might provide
managers with the opportunity to manage tax profits in order to save taxes. Hence, fair value
accounting for income tax purposes might be prone to tax avoidance.

We further discuss other potential costs of introducing fair value taxation from a societal
perspective, such as the volatility of tax revenues and the cyclicity of fair value taxation. Prior
research highlights a potential pro-cyclicality and increasing revenue volatility as drawbacks
of fair value taxation (Sole et al. 2009; Keen et al. 2010). In contrast, we demonstrate that
fair value taxation might also decrease the volatility of corporate tax revenues and could lead
to a counter-cyclical taxation of firms. Hence, when in economic downturns, firms might
have to pay taxes even though historical cost accounting would lead to negative income. We
show some evidence in favor of this prediction. Another drawback of fair value taxation is
that firms and individuals might have to pay taxes on unrealized profits, which may cause
them to sell assets to finance the tax liability. Empirical evidence on this issue is missing. We
present a theoretical solution to this liquidity-related concern.

Taken together, our chapter provides an overview of costs and benefits of fair value taxation. We acknowledge that it is beyond the scope of this chapter to quantify costs and
benefits and to compare them. We cannot reliably gauge the overall economic consequences
of introducing fair value accounting to define taxable income, which would depend on a
particular country's contextual underpinnings. In order to derive policy implications, more
research on the effect of fair value taxation on investment decisions, tax avoidance, tax compliance and tax revenues is necessary to weigh the potential costs and benefits of using fair
values to define taxable income for corporate tax and personal income tax purposes.

Fair value taxation in the United States and the European Union

While fair value accounting has gained increasing importance in financial accounting, this
trend did not yet fully spill over to tax accounting. As we demonstrate in Table 14.1, tax
accounting is predominantly based on historical cost measurement rather than on fair value
accounting.[1] Nevertheless, financial accounting income is used as a starting point to determine the corporate tax base in all EU countries. Either IFRS or National GAAP are used
as basis for taxable income. In some countries, for example Ireland, Italy and the United
Kingdom, corporations are allowed to choose whether they use IFRS or National GAAP
for financial and tax accounting. In contrast, the United States strictly separates financial and
tax accounting.

In all countries, taxable corporate income determination follows the accrual principle.
Transactions and events are recognized when they occur and not when cash is received.
Only in Denmark, the Netherlands and the United States, general revenue recognition criteria are codified by tax law or follow tax practice. The other countries follow financial
accounting recognition rules. As a general rule, in all countries profits and losses are to be
recognized only when realized. There are, however, small differences across countries regarding the point in time when a profit from the sale of goods is assumed to be realized. For
example, in Belgium, Denmark and Poland, revenue may be recognized upon execution of
a sales contract.

With respect to fair value accounting, there are several countries that provide exceptions
from the general realization principle. These exceptions mainly concern financial assets and
liabilities held for trading. In the Czech Republic, Denmark, Finland, France, Hungary,

Table 14.1 Determination of the corporate income tax base in the European Union and the United States

Country	Starting point	Revenue recognition and realization dates for the sale of goods	Taxation of unrealized profits: Financial assets and liabilities held for trading	Taxation of unrealized profits: Other revaluation gains	Lower of cost and market (Stock items and work-in-progress)	Exceptional depreciation: Individually depreciable assets	Exceptional depreciation: Assets not subject to depreciation	Specific tax rules for banks
Austria	National GAAP	Delivery/Transfer of Economic Ownership	Not Taxable	Not Taxable	Applied (other[a])	Permitted	Permitted	No
Belgium	National GAAP	Prior to Delivery (Possible), Delivery/Transfer of Economic Ownership	Not Taxable	Capital Gains on Stock Items and Work-in-progress are Taxable	Applied (other[a])	Prohibited	Permitted	Mark-to-market taxation of financial trading assets possible
Bulgaria	IFRS	Delivery/Transfer of Economic Ownership	Not Taxable	Not Taxable	Not Applied	Prohibited	Prohibited	Mark-to-market taxation of financial fixed and trading assets
Cyprus	IFRS	Delivery/Transfer of Economic Ownership	Not Taxable	Not Taxable	Applied (net realizable value)	Prohibited	Prohibited	No
Czech Republic	National GAAP	Delivery/Transfer of Economic Ownership	Taxable	Not Taxable	Not Applied	Prohibited	Permitted	No
Denmark	National GAAP	Prior to Delivery (Possible), Delivery/Transfer of Economic Ownership	Taxable	Not Taxable	Applied (net realizable value)	Prohibited	Prohibited	No
Finland	National GAAP	Delivery/Transfer of Economic Ownership	Taxable	Not Taxable	Applied (net realizable value)	Permitted	Permitted	Mark-to-market taxation of financial trading assets
France	National GAAP	Delivery/Transfer of Economic Ownership	Taxable	Taxable (exceptions for intangible assets)	Applied (net realizable value)	Permitted	Permitted	No
Greece	Optional (National GAAP or IFRS)	Delivery/Transfer of Economic Ownership	Not Taxable	Revaluation Gains of Land and Buildings are Taxable	Applied (other[a])	Prohibited	Prohibited	No

(Continued)

| Country | Starting point | Revenue recognition and realization dates for the sale of goods | Taxation of unrealized profits | | Lower of cost and market (Stock items and work-in-progress) | Exceptional depreciation | | Specific tax rules for banks |
			Financial assets and liabilities held for trading	Other revaluation gains		Individually depreciable assets	Assets not subject to depreciation	
Hungary	National GAAP	Delivery/Transfer of Economic Ownership	Taxable	Not Taxable	Applied (other²)	Permitted	Permitted	No
Ireland	Optional (National GAAP or IFRS)	Delivery/Transfer of Economic Ownership	Not Taxable	Not Taxable	Applied (net realizable value)	Prohibited	Prohibited	No
Italy	Optional (National GAAP or IFRS)	Delivery/Transfer of Economic Ownership	For IFRS Adopters: taxable when recorded in the P&L	Not Taxable	Applied (net realizable value)	Prohibited	Prohibited	No
Lithuania	Optional (National GAAP or IFRS)	Delivery/Transfer of Economic Ownership	Not Taxable	Not Taxable	Not Applied	Prohibited	Prohibited	No
Luxembourg	National GAAP	Delivery/Transfer of Economic Ownership	Not Taxable	Not Taxable	Applied (other²)	Permitted	Permitted	No
Latvia	National GAAP	Delivery/Transfer of Economic Ownership	Not Taxable	Not Taxable	Not Applied	Prohibited	Prohibited	No
Malta	IFRS	Delivery/Transfer of Economic Ownership	Not Taxable	Not Taxable	Not Applied	Prohibited	Prohibited	No
Netherlands	National GAAP	Delivery/Transfer of Economic Ownership	Not Taxable	Not Taxable	Applied (other²)	Permitted	Permitted	No
Poland	Optional (National GAAP or IFRS)	Prior to and after delivery (Possible), Delivery/Transfer of Economic Ownership	Not Taxable	Not Taxable	Not Applied	Prohibited	Prohibited	No

Country	Accounting Standard	Realization	Revaluation (asset)	Revaluation gains of some biological assets	Lower of cost or market			Mark-to-market
Portugal	IFRS	Delivery/Transfer of Economic Ownership	Taxable	Revaluation gains of some biological assets are taxable	Applied (other)[1]	Prohibited	Prohibited	No
Romania	National GAAP	Delivery/Transfer of Economic Ownership	Not Taxable	Not Taxable	Not Applied	Prohibited	Prohibited	No
Slovakia	National GAAP	Delivery/Transfer of Economic Ownership	Taxable	Not Taxable	Not Applied	Prohibited	Prohibited	No
Slovenia	Optional (National GAAP or IFRS)	Delivery/Transfer of Economic Ownership	Taxable	Not Taxable	Applied (other)[1]	Prohibited	Permitted	No
Spain	National GAAP	Delivery/Transfer of Economic Ownership	Taxable	Not Taxable	Applied (net realizable value)	Permitted	Permitted	No
Sweden	Optional (National GAAP or IFRS)	Delivery/Transfer of Economic Ownership	Taxable	Not Taxable	Applied (other)[1]	Permitted	Prohibited	Mark-to-market taxation of financial fixed and trading assets
United Kingdom	Optional (National GAAP or IFRS)	Delivery/Transfer of Economic Ownership	Taxable	Not Taxable	Applied (net realizable value)	Prohibited	Prohibited	No
United States of America	Autonomous Tax Law	Delivery/Transfer of Economic Ownership	Not Taxable	Not Taxable	Applied (other)[1]	Prohibited	Prohibited	Mark-to-market taxation for dealers in securities

Sources: Spengel, C., & Zöllkau, Y. (Eds.). (2012). Common Corporate Tax Base (CC (C) TB) and determination of taxable income: An international comparison. Springer Science & Business Media. Commission Staff Working Paper Impact Assessment accompanying the document Proposal for a Council Directive on a common system of financial transaction tax and amending Directive 2008/7/EC. We do not present information on corporations in Estonia as they are subject only to a flat-rate tax on distributed profits including transactions that are considered hidden profit distribution. Estonia uses IFRS as a starting point. If unrealized gains are distributed, then these are subject to tax upon distribution.

1 Write down to replacement costs determined by reference to the procurement market or other deviations from net realizable value.

Italy, Portugal, Slovakia, Slovenia, Spain, Sweden and the United Kingdom financial assets and liabilities held for trading are measured at fair value and unrealized revaluation profits are subject to corporate income tax. Moreover, unrealized revaluation gains from depreciable and other financial assets are subject to corporate income tax in France; unrealized gains on stock items and work-in-progress increase taxable corporate income in Belgium; Greece taxes unrealized revaluation gains concerning land and buildings. Hence, there are some tax base elements for which fair value accounting is already implemented.

In contrast to the treatment of unrealized gains, the recognition of unrealized losses concerning stock items and work-in-progress for tax purposes is a general rule in the United States in and the majority of the EU countries. With the exception of Bulgaria, Czech Republic, Lithuania, Latvia, Malta, Poland, Romania and Slovakia, all other countries apply the lower-of-cost-and-market principle for corporate income tax purposes. However, there are differences with respect to the determination of the lower fair value. Further, fixed assets that have permanently decreased in fair value are usually subject to extraordinary write-downs in financial accounting. However, for tax purposes the majority of countries prohibit extraordinary write-downs.

Finally, some countries have implemented specific tax rules for financial assets held by banks. Belgium, Bulgaria, Finland, Germany and Sweden allow or even prescribe fair value taxation for some financial assets of banks. Similarly, in the United States, there are specific rules regarding mark-to-market taxation for dealers in securities (26 U.S. Code § 475).

In sum, while historical cost measurement dominates tax accounting, there are important exceptions in several countries that allow or prescribe fair value taxation for some financial assets. In line with this, Article 21 of the proposed Council Directive on a Common Corporate Tax Base (COM (2016) 685) for the taxation of the EU-wide activities of multinationals suggests that financial assets and liabilities held for trading have to be valued at market value for corporate income tax purposes. For a simple guide, in Table 14.1 we tabulate the determination of the corporate income tax base in the European Union and the United States.

The effect of fair value taxation on investment decisions

Fair value taxation and investment neutral taxation

The primary role of the income tax system is to achieve a desired revenue and redistribution level in a way that minimizes the costs of the tax system. These costs comprise compliance costs of the taxpayers, administration costs and economic distortions. Economic distortions occur when individuals and corporations respond to taxation by changing their real behavior. For example, if a firm reduces its investments due to an increasing tax rate, this, generally, leads to a welfare loss that is not compensated by the additional tax revenues (excess burden). A tax system that does not affect firms' and individuals' choices and behavior is called a neutral tax system. Under neutral tax systems there is no excess burden and there is no incentive to devote socially wasteful time or resources on tax planning.

Many accounting and economics researchers have studied the neutrality properties of different tax systems. The determination of the tax base through fair value accounting that is directly related to a neutral tax system is called the Johansson-Samuelson Tax after its early proponents.[2] This tax system is comprehensive in that it includes company profits and personal interest income where interest on debt and true economic depreciation are deductible. This tax system has been interpreted as the theoretical benchmark underlying the income tax systems employed in the OECD countries (Howitt & Sinn 1989). The link to fair value accounting is that the depreciation allowance for such a tax is calculated as the difference between the fair value of the assets at the beginning and at the end of the period.

We demonstrate that fair value taxation according to Johansson-Samuelson does not distort investment decisions. According to IFRS 13 and FASB ASC Topic 820 fair value is the price that would be received by selling an asset or paid to transfer a liability in an orderly transaction between market participants. If we make simplifying assumptions of a perfect capital market in which the interest rate on borrowing equals the interest rate on saving, with rational subjects and risk-free cash flows, the market price, and, thus, the fair value, equals the present value of an asset. Let FV_t denote the fair value of an investment project that is financed with equity in point of time t. With a uniform tax rate τ, risk-free cash flows from the investment CF, and the interest rate i, we obtain the following equation for the fair value in a point of time $t \leq T$, with T denoting the end of the planning horizon for this investment:[3]

$$FV_t = \frac{CF_{t+1} + FV_{t+1} - \tau\left(CF_{t+1} - \left(FV_t - FV_{t+1}\right)\right)}{1 + i(1-\tau)}. \tag{1}$$

The fair value is calculated by discounting after-tax cash flows with the after-tax interest rate. The taxable income from the investment in $t+1$ is calculated as the difference between the cash flows and the economic depreciation: $CF_{t+1} - \left(FV_t - FV_{t+1}\right)$. Note that the economic depreciation is the difference between the project's fair value at the beginning and at the end of the period. The net present value (NPV) of an investment is not subject to tax. That is, in the Johansson (1969) and Samuelson (1964) tax, the difference between the initial investment expenditures and the fair value of the project in $t = 0$ is tax-exempt. Multiplying equation (1) with $\left(1 + i(1-\tau)\right)$ and subtracting τFV_t leads to

$$FV_t(1+i)(1-\tau) = CF_{t+1}(1-\tau) + FV_{t+1}(1-\tau). \tag{2}$$

After dividing both sides of Equation (2) by $(1-\tau)$ and solving to FV_t, we obtain

$$FV_t = \frac{CF_{t+1} + FV_{t+1}}{(1+i)}. \tag{3}$$

From equation (3), it becomes obvious that the pre-tax fair value of the investment is not affected by taxes if we assume that tax depreciations are based on fair value accounting and that the NPV remains tax-exempt. We can either discount pre-tax cash flows using the pre-tax interest rate as discount rate equation (3) or we discount after-tax cash flows with the after-tax interest rate [equation (1)]. As long as we assume that pre-tax cash flows and pre-tax interest rate are not affected by taxation, we obtain the same fair value irrespective whether taxes are considered or neglected. The intuition for this result is that real investment projects are taxed the same way as capital market investments. Hence, taxes do not discriminate between these two investment alternatives. This can be seen if one rearranges equation (3) to $CF_{t+1} - \left(FV_t - FV_{t+1}\right) = iFV_t$; the tax base for real investments is equal to the interest rate times the asset's fair value at the beginning of the period. This exactly matches the tax base calculation for capital market investments. The following numerical example illustrates the neutrality:

In the example of Table 14.2, we show that the NPV of the investment is not affected by a taxation that is based on fair value accounting. Thus, decision-makers could neglect taxes

Table 14.2 Net present value and fair value taxation

Panel A: Without taxes

Year t	0	1	2	Net Present Value (i = 5%)
Cash flow	−100,000.00	70,000.00	50,000.00	12,018.14

Panel B: Fair value taxation

Year t	0	1	2	Net Present Value (i = 5%)
Cash flow	−100,000.00	70,000.00	50,000.00	
Fair value of the investment	112,018.14	47,619.05	0.00	
Economic depreciation	0.00	64,399.09	47,619.05	
Tax base (Cash flow minus depreciation)	0.00	5,600.91	2,380.95	
Tax payments (τ = 40%)	0.00	2,240.36	952.38	
After-tax cash flow	−100,000.00	67,759.64	49,047.62	**12,018.14**

Notes: Panel A (B) of this table displays the calculation of the net present value without any taxes (with fair value taxation according to Johansson/Samuelson). The investment expenditure amounts to 100,000 and the planning horizon for this investment is two years. Discounting the pre-tax cash flows with a pre-tax interest rate of 5% leads to a fair value of the investment amounting to 112,018 (Panel A). Thus, the net present value without taxes is 112,018 − 100,000 = 12,018. In Panel B a fair value tax with a tax rate of 40% is considered, that is, after-tax cash flows are discounted with the after-tax interest rate of 0.05 − 0.05 × 0.4 = 3%. Taxes on the investment income in t > 0 are calculated as 40% × (cash flows − economic depreciation). Note that the immediate increase in FV in t = 0 (the NPV amounting to 12,018) is tax-exempt under the Johansson/Samuelson tax.

when making their investment decisions. Hence, a tax system that defines taxable income based on fair values does not distort investment decisions. In addition, the pre-tax fair value of an investment is not affected by taxation as the NPV remains tax-exempt under the Johansson/Samuelson tax system.

Importantly, the investment neutrality also holds, if the NPV itself is subject to a tax. Suppose the investment must be capitalized and measured at fair value in t = 0. This would lead to a taxable gain amounting to the NPV. In the example of Table 14.2, this would mean that the asset's account is debited for 112,018.14, the cash account is credited for 100,000, and the profit and loss account is credited for 12,018.14. In this case, NPV after and before taxes would differ. In the example of Table 14.2, the investor would have to pay additional taxes of 12,018.14 × 0.4 = 4,807.26 reducing the NPV after taxes to 7,210.88. Nevertheless, since the NPV after taxes is simply the pre-tax NPV multiplied with (1−τ), fair value taxation does not change the rank order of investment alternatives. Investors could still neglect taxes when making their investment decisions. The investment neutrality of fair value taxation also holds under time-variant tax rates, if tax rates differ across individuals, or if cash flows are risky and investors are risk-neutral.[4]

In contrast, if one uses standard historical cost accounting as the basis for taxation, taxes usually affect the fair value of investments in a way that investment decisions may be distorted and, thus, lead to an excess burden and tax planning costs. This is illustrated in Table 14.3. Historical cost accounting uses the acquisition or purchase price as basis for the calculation of depreciation rates; the historical costs are simply allocated over the useful life of the asset. In the example of Table 14.3, we assume that the investment does not need to be capitalized for tax purposes. That is, the investment expenditure reduces the taxable income in $t = 0$ and leads to a tax refund. If we compare NPV before and after taxes, we find that historical cost taxation may lead to an overinvestment because the NPV after taxes is positive while it is negative before taxes.[5]

Table 14.3 Net present value and historical cost taxation

Panel A: Without taxes

Year t	0	1	2	Net present value ($i = 5\%$)
Cash flow	−100,000.00	70,000.00	35,000.00	**−1,587.30**

Panel B: Historical cost taxation: cash accounting

Year t	0	1	2	Net present value ($i = 5\%$)
Cash flow	−100,000.00	70,000.00	35,000.00	
Depreciation	0.00	0.00	0.00	
Tax base (cash flow minus depreciation)	−100,000.00	70,000.00	35,000.00	
Tax payments ($\tau = 40\%$)	−40,000.00	28,000.00	14,000.00	
After-tax cash flow	−60,000.00	42,000.00	21,000.00	**571.21**

Panel C: Historical cost taxation: straight-line depreciation

Year t	0	1	2	Net present value ($i = 5\%$)
Cash flow	−100,000.00	70,000.00	35,000.00	
Depreciation	0.00	50,000.00	50,000.00	
Tax base (cash flow minus depreciation)	0.00	20,000.00	−15,000.00	
Tax payments ($\tau = 40\%$)	0.00	8,000.00	−6,000.00	
After-tax cash flow	−100,000.00	62,000.00	41,000.00	**−1,159.4**

Notes: Panel A (B) of this table displays the calculation of the net present value without any taxes (with historical cost taxation). Panel C uses straight-line depreciation. The investment expenditure amounts to 100,000 and the planning horizon for this investment is two years. Discounting the pre-tax cash flows with a pre-tax interest rate of 5%, leads to a fair value of the investment amounting to 98,412.70 (Panel A). Thus, the net present value without taxes is 98,412.70 − 100,000 = −1,587.30 and the investment project would be rejected in a world without taxes. In Panel B a historical cost tax with a tax rate of 40% is considered. The investment expenditure is assumed to be immediately deductible from the tax base, which leads to a tax refund amounting to 40% × 100,000 = 40,000 in $t = 0$. After-tax cash flows are discounted with the after-tax interest rate of 0.05 − 0.05 × 0.4 = 3%. The resulting net present value is positive, so that investors would make this investment. In this case, taxes induce an overinvestment.

When we assume straight-line depreciation, the result changes. Instead of immediately writing off the asset, the expenses are now realized in $t = 1$ and $t = 2$. While after-tax cash flows in these two years increase, the initial after-tax cash flow in $t = 0$ decreases. Overall, the NPV of the investment declines and becomes negative. Firms will not invest in this project and the tendency to overinvest declines relative to cash accounting.

Taken together, the simple example shows that the tax accounting system – cash versus accrual versus fair value accounting – can have a significant impact on investment decisions. In tax systems that are closer to fair value accounting, we would expect less deviations from the pre-tax optimal investment level. However, empirical evidence on this conjecture is rare.

Empirical evidence

In this subsection, we take a first attempt at testing the hypothesis that moving toward fair value accounting leads to less over- or underinvestment. We acknowledge that this section should be seen as first step at providing empirical evidence consistent with this hypothesis. We do not have the setting to provide causal evidence. We leave this for future research.

There are two main empirical issues when testing whether the accounting system, e.g. cash versus accrual accounting, distorts investments decisions. First, one needs a suitable proxy for the accounting system. Second, one needs a measure of the extent to which investment decisions are distorted.

As a proxy for accrual accounting for tax purposes, we use the *Tax Accrual Index* by Goncharov and Jacob (2014). They construct an index that measures the extent to which cash versus accrual accounting is used for tax purposes. To map the tax systems of 26 countries, Goncharov and Jacob (2014) collect information on the tax treatment of noncurrent intangible assets, noncurrent tangible assets, inventory valuation and provisioning. A higher (lower) value of their index score indicates more use of accrual (cash) accounting. Given that accrual accounting is closer to fair value accounting than cash accounting, we use their index in our empirical analysis and interpret a higher value of the *Tax Accrual Index* as a move toward fair value taxation.

To measure the extent to which investment decisions are distorted, we rely on prior literature measuring over- and underinvestment (see, e.g. Biddle et al. 2009; Cheng et al. 2013). Following Biddle et al. (2009), we start by estimating a firm-specific model of investment with a proxy for investment opportunities as the independent variable. We use *Sales Growth* from $t-1$ to t as Biddle et al. (2009). The dependent variable *Inv* is defined as capital expenditures over lagged total assets. The actual model is

$$Inv_{i,t} = \beta_0 + \beta_1 \times Sales\ Growth_{i,t} + \varepsilon_{i,t}. \tag{4}$$

We run equation (4) for each country-industry-year based on Fama and French 12-industry classifications. We use all industry-years with at least 30 observations for the respective industry in a given country-year. We use public firm data from Compustat Global over the period 1999–2013. We then rerun the test with private firm data from Amadeus using data from 2005 to 2013.

The residuals form these regressions are a proxy for the deviation from expected investment (Biddle et al. 2009). We then define a dummy variable *DEVIATION* to capture a large deviation from expected investment in each country-industry-year. We set *DEVIATION* equal to one if the residual is at least one standard deviation above or below zero, i.e. above or below the average residual. In the final step, we calculate the percentage of firms in a country over the sample period with over- or underinvestment using private and public firm data.

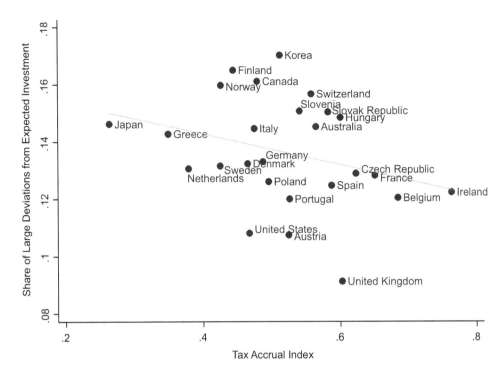

Figure 14.1   Accrual accounting and over-/underinvestment

Figure 14.1 is a simple scatter plot where the *Tax Accrual Index* is displayed on the *x*-axis. The *y*-axis summarizes the percentage of firms that have a large deviation (*DEVIATION* = 1) from expected investment over the sample period for both, public and private firms. For example, our results indicate that in the Netherlands, about 13% of firms have either large positive deviations (overinvestment) or large negative deviations (underinvestment) from expected investments. Importantly for our argument, we observe a negative association between the tax accrual index and large deviations from expected investments. That is, as countries define the tax base more on accrual versus cash basis, firms appear to have smaller deviations from expected investments. The line in Figure 14.1 represents this negative correlation. The corresponding slope coefficient amounts to −0.054 and is statistically significant at the 5% level (t-stat = 2.60).

In Figure 14.2, we now split deviations from expected investment into over- and underinvestment. The example above has shown that cash accounting can induce overinvestment as a negative pre-tax NPV turned out to be positive after tax. While we could, of course, twist the numerical example easily in a way that accrual accounting may lead to underinvestment, cash versus accrual accounting generally leads to higher NPVs after tax. Hence, we would expect to observe more overinvestment if the tax base is more defined on a cash basis.

This is exactly what we observe in Figure 14.2. The observed correlation in Figure 14.1 is driven by overinvestment. The fraction of firms overinvesting is negatively correlated with the tax accrual index. The corresponding slope coefficient is −0.049 and is statistically significant at the 1% level (t-stat = 3.76). In contrast, there is no correlation between underinvestment and the tax accrual index.

Taken together, this section provides some indications that fair value accounting might be related to investment decisions. Consistent with the theoretical arguments, our findings suggest that moving toward fair value accounting to define taxable income is related to lower

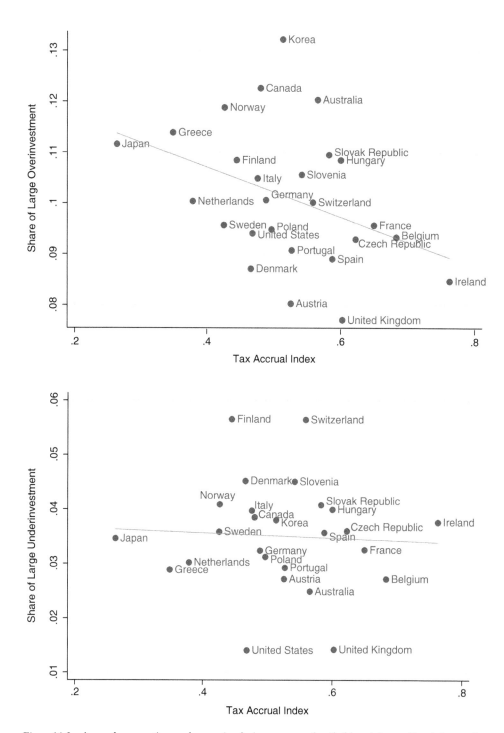

Figure 14.2 Accrual accounting and over-/underinvestment: detailed breakdown. Panel A: overinvestment and Panel B: underinvestment

deviations from expected investment or less over- and underinvestment. However, we also note that we provide correlations and not a causal link. Future research needs to exploit settings where the potential link between fair value taxation and investment distortion can be tested rigorously.

Fair value taxation and capital gains realization decisions

Fair value taxation versus historical cost accounting has also implications for the decision to realize accrued capital gains. We can illustrate the decision to realize capital gains under historical cost accounting using a simple two-period model based on Auerbach (1991).[6] There is no uncertainty in our example. We assume that an investor has invested 1 and has accrued a capital gain, denoted g. The investor now decides whether to immediately sell the asset and thereby realizing the capital gain (*Sell*) or hold the asset (*Hold*). If the investor sells the asset, he or she reinvests at a rate of return i. If he or she holds the asset, the investor realizes a return of r. Both returns r and i as well as capital gains are taxed at a uniform rate τ. We can now compare the final wealth W for both strategies. If the investor sells the asset and invests at the rate i, the investor realizes the following final wealth:

$$W^{Sell} = \left[1 + g(1-\tau)\right] \times \left[1 + i(1-\tau)\right]. \tag{5}$$

The first part, $\left[1 + g(1-\tau)\right]$, represents the amount that is reinvested after paying the tax on the realized gain g in the first year. The second part, $\left[1 + i(1-\tau)\right]$, is the after-tax return that is earned on the reinvestment,

In contrast, if the investor holds the asset, he or she realizes the following final value:

$$W^{Hold} = \left[1 + g\right] \times \left[1 + r\right] - \tau\left[\left(1 + g\right) \times \left(1 + r\right) - 1\right]. \tag{6}$$

In this case, the investor is able to defer the tax on the initial gain g without interest to the second period. Consider the case where $r = i$. In a world without taxes, the investor is indifferent between holding or selling the asset as he or she realizes exactly the same wealth (which is equal to [1+g] × [1+r]). However, taxation upon realization, i.e. historical cost accounting-based taxation, leads to a deviation. The investor has an incentive to hold the asset because he or she realizes higher wealth when holding the stock until the second year ($W^{Sell} < W^{Hold}$).

This is the well-known lock-in effect. The lock-in effect has been shown in other theoretical studies, e.g. Constantinides (1983, 1984), Ball (1984), Auerbach (1991), Klein (1998, 1999), Dammon et al. (2001), Poterba (2002) or Shackelford and Verrecchia (2002). The existence of the lock-in effect has also been shown in several empirical studies examining investor responses. For example, there is empirical evidence that corporate taxes on capital gains and also on dividend income affect the volume of M&A deals, the likelihood of M&A Deals, and also the premium (see, e.g. Huizinga & Voget 2009; Huizinga et al. 2012, Feld et al. 2016). Moreover, Reese (1998) uses a sample of IPOs to document that the qualification for long-term capital gains for personal tax purposes and thus a reduced capital gains tax rate affects trading volume and stock returns. Likewise, Seida and Wempe (2000) using stock market data show that trading volumes are consistent with a tax-induced trading model as outlined, for example, by Constantinides (1983, 1984). Further, some studies are able to use microdata to observe capital gains realization decisions at the individual level.

Ivkovic et al. (2005) use data by a large discount brokerage house and show that trading decisions are tax-motivated. Jacob (2013) uses German income tax data and documents that the likelihood to realize gains (loss) decreases (increases) with the personal income tax rate. Exploiting a panel of Swedish individuals over several decades, Jacob (2018) shows that individuals' capital gains realization decisions are highly sensitive to capital gains taxes and, further, to temporary tax incentives created by progressive taxation.

Overall, these studies and the arguments above indicate that a realization-based capital gains taxation based on historical costs leads to distortions of the holding-selling decision. In case of gains, capital gains taxation induces investors to hold assets longer (lock-in effect). In case of losses, investors hold their assets for a shorter period of time (lock-out effect). Both effects represent a tax-induced distortion and thus a welfare loss.

These distortions can be removed if fair value taxation of unrealized gains is implemented. To illustrate this, let us reconsider the simple two-period example from above. Fair value taxation would not change the final wealth in the selling case. The investor still realizes:

$$W^{Sell,\ FV} = \left[1 + g(1-\tau)\right] \times \left[1 + i(1-\tau)\right].$$ (7)

There is, however, a change in the case of holding the asset. In case of fair value taxation, the accrued capital gain g would be immediately taxed leading to a cash outflow of $\tau \times g$ in the first period. Assuming that the tax is financed by short-selling the asset, the investor's reinvestment is reduced to $1 + g(1-\tau)$. This leads to a final wealth of

$$W^{Hold,FV} = \left[1 + g(1-\tau)\right] \times \left[1 + r(1-\tau)\right].$$ (8)

As a result, the decision to hold or sell the asset is driven only by the rate of returns r and i. Put differently, the optimal decision before tax is also the optimal decision after tax. Capital gains taxation based on fair value accounting when gains accrue does not distort the timing of capital gains realization decisions. Hence, the welfare losses from distorting trading decisions created by historical cost accounting could be avoided by taxing fair values.

Potential issues of fair value taxation

Fair value taxation and tax compliance

In the next step, we subsequently, discuss potential costs of fair value taxation. We start with discussing tax compliance and tax avoidance. On the positive side, fair value taxation of financial derivatives has often been proposed as an instrument to combat corporate tax avoidance.[7] Donohoe (2015b) documents significant corporate tax savings from financial derivatives. He finds a 4.4 percentage point reduction in three-year cash effective tax rates after a corporation initiates a derivate program. Currently, under historical cost taxation, firms can exploit the ambiguity in financial derivatives' taxation because not all economically equivalent transactions are taxed in the same manner, the correct tax treatment of novel financial products is indeterminable, and the tax treatment of transaction partners is sometimes asymmetric (Donohoe 2015a, 2015b). Moreover, firms can to some extent selectively realize losses to offset gains. Using fair value taxation for financial derivatives and for the underlying assets could theoretically reduce these avoidance opportunities.

One drawback of fair value taxation is that fair values cannot always be determined in a reliable manner. For so-called level 1 assets, where fair value measurement is based on observable data from active markets, management's opportunities to manipulate the fair value are limited. In contrast, for complex financial instruments or other intangible assets, one must often rely on management assumptions regarding future cash flows because observable market data do not exist. In this case, fair values could be manipulated and are difficult to verify (Benston 2008). Indeed, there is some evidence from financial accounting studies that banks manage the fair value of loans (Nissim 2003), and loan loss provisions (Bernard et al. 1995). Further, managers exercise discretion with fair values of reported property (Dietrich et al. 2000), and managers have considerable discretion to determine both the timing and the amount of write-downs (Beatty & Weber 2006; Hilton & O'brien 2009).

In addition, prior literature demonstrates that multinational firms shift profits to low-tax countries by manipulating the price of assets in intercompany transactions (Bernard et al. 2006; Klassen et al. 2017). Similar to fair value measurement, tax law requires assets that are traded in intragroup transactions to be valued at arm's length market prices. However, in practice, the ambiguity regarding the determination of this market price gives firms the opportunity to manage their profits. To limit these mispricing strategies, tax administrations worldwide introduced high documentation requirements, which have increased tax compliance costs for firms significantly. Because of the ambiguity in fair value measurement, some tax researchers argue that 'the objectivity of fair values is not always sufficient for taxation in order to guarantee equality' and it is thus 'obvious that they are not appropriate for taxation' (e.g. Eberhartinger & Klostermann 2007).

However, this argumentation ignores that fair values are already used for corporate tax purposes in many areas, e.g. in the case of in-kind capital contributions, dividends in kind, firm reorganizations, or transfer pricing. In these cases, fair values are required and if these are readily available from financial accounting, this certainly reduces compliance costs. Moreover, if the fair value measurements from financial accounting would be relevant for tax purposes, this could reduce the incentives for tax avoidance as suggested by empirical evidence from the book-tax conformity studies (e.g. Atwood et al. 2012; Tang 2015). Moreover, the valuation of assets is also relevant in many other tax settings, for example, when valuing companies or assets for inheritance or wealth tax purposes.

Taken together, the effects of fair value taxation on tax compliance are theoretically ambiguous. On the one hand, fair value taxation may reduce firms' tax avoidance opportunities (e.g. using financial derivatives); on the other hand, ambiguous fair value measurements might provide managers with the opportunity to manage tax profits in order to save taxes. Future empirical tax research should investigate which of both effects dominates.

Fair value taxation and liquidity restrictions

A potential difficulty is that taxation on fair market value induces tax payments when profits accrue and not when they are realized. As we have seen in the example of capital gains realizations in the section entitled 'Fair Value Taxation and Capital Gains Realization Decisions', the investor needs to pay a tax even if the gain is not realized. Financially constrained firms or investors might thus not be able to pay the tax liability as profits accrue. One consequence would be that firms or individuals sell assets to finance the accruing liability. Such fire sales have downsides. For example, prior literature shows that when trading against financially distressed investors, the firm or investor providing liquidity earns significant positive returns (see, e.g. Andrade & Kaplan 1998 or Coval & Stafford 2007). These positive returns come at the cost of the distressed investors.

Auerbach (1991) proposes a solution to this liquidity-related issue, namely a retrospective capital gains taxation. He shows that a realization-based taxation with a taxation of the realized gain and on the interest on the accrued, unrealized gain is equivalent to an immediate tax on the fair value. Intuitively speaking, his suggestion of a retrospective taxation implies that the tax liability is based on fair value accounting. However, the actual tax payment is postponed and compounded with interest. It is paid when the asset is actually sold. Such a system would ensure that holding decisions are not affected by taxes and that financially distressed investors and firms do not need to sell assets in order to finance tax liabilities.

We acknowledge that this debate is rather theoretical. The extent to which firms and investors really need to sell assets in order to finance tax payments is an empirical question. To the best of our knowledge, there is no empirical evidence to support this view or reject it. Future research may exploit a setting around the implementation of fair value accounting for tax purposes as we have outlined in the section entitled 'Fair Value Taxation in the United States and the European Union'. Exploiting law changes, one could test whether there are increased fire sales of assets of financially constrained firms relative to unconstrained firms around the introduction of fair value accounting. Moreover, one could use such a setting to further assess the potential downsides of introducing fair value accounting as basis for taxable income.

Fair value taxation and the volatility of tax revenues

Despite the advantages of fewer economic distortions, there is the argument that increased use of fair value taxation may increase the volatility of revenue. For example, Keen et al. (2010: p. 41) argue that '[i]ncreased use of marking to market (fair value accounting) in taxing financial institutions may increase the volatility of revenue'. As corporate tax revenues are already the most volatile tax revenue source in most governments' portfolios (Felix 2008), increased volatility of corporate tax revenues might be an issue and, hence, a reason not to implement fair value accounting for tax purposes.

Let us reconsider this argument in two ways. First, we use a very simple numerical example. In $t = 0$, we invest 1,200 in a project generating cash flows of 450 in $t = 1$, $t = 2$ and $t = 3$. We then calculate the profit based on (1) cash flow taxation, (2) accrual accounting with straight line depreciation and (3) fair value taxation as discussed in the section entitled 'Fair Value Taxation and Investment Neutral Taxation'. Table 14.4 presents the respective revenues, depreciation, book/fair value and the resulting profit.

In Panel A (*Cash Accounting*), the profit is equal to the cash flows and thus substantially more volatile than under *Accrual Accounting* assuming straight-line depreciation (Panel B). While both accounting systems lead to the same level of profits over time, the actual standard deviation of profits, i.e. taxable income is reduced from 714 to about 22 in our example. In Panel C, we illustrate fair value taxation. For this purpose, we first calculate the fair value in each point in time assuming an interest rate of 3%. Given the change in fair values, we then obtain the profit based on fair values. In contrast to the argument put forward by Keen et al. (2010), our example illustrates that relative to historical cost accounting, fair value accounting can actually lead to *less* volatile revenues. This argument is consistent with the role of accruals alleviating matching problems between cash flows and profits (e.g. Dechow 1994; Dechow et al. 1998). However, these results need to be interpreted with caution because (a) we need to assume that there is perfect foresight and (b) our simplified example assumes a time-invariant discount rate: Profits in a fair value accounting tax system may vary as interest rates become more volatile.

Table 14.4 Volatility of Profits under different accounting systems

Panel A: Cash accounting

Year	0	1	2	3	
Revenues		450.00	450.00	450.00	
Investment	−1,200.00				
Depreciation	1,200.00				**Std. Dev**
Profit	−1,200.00	450.00	450.00	450.00	**714.47**

Panel B: Accrual accounting

Year	0	1	2	3	
Revenues		450.00	450.00	450.00	
Investment	−1,200.00				
Book value	1,200.00	800.00	400.00	0.00	
Depreciation	0.00	400.00	400.00	400.00	**Std. Dev**
Profit	0.00	50.00	50.00	50.00	**21.65**

Panel C: Fair value accounting (i = 3%)

Year	0	1	2	3	
Revenues	0.00	450.00	450.00	450.00	
Investment	−1,200.00				
Fair value	1,272.88	861.06	436.89	0.00	
Depreciation	0.00	411.81	424.17	436.89	**Std. Dev**
Profits	0.00	38.19	25.83	13.11	**14.23**

To demonstrate empirically that moving from cash accounting to accrual accounting is related to less volatile tax revenues, we follow Goncharov and Jacob (2014) and rerun the analysis of their Figure 14.1 where they show that the *Tax Accrual Index* is negatively associated with the volatility of tax revenues. We replicate their figure and extend the sample period to include the most recent years. For this purpose, we collect corporate tax revenue data from the OECD to obtain tax revenue data over the period 1997–2014. We then calculate the standard deviation of corporate tax revenues (scaled by GDP) for each country. Figure 14.3 presents a scatter plot of the standard deviation of tax revenues (y-axis) and the tax accrual index (x-axis). Consistent with the findings in Goncharov and Jacob (2014), the volatility of tax revenues declines as the tax base is defined more on an accrual vis-à-vis cash basis.

However, there is one potential downside of moving to fair value accounting for tax purposes, again, assuming that there is perfect foresight, i.e. forward-looking provisioning. While smoothing profits, fair value accounting could lead to a more counter-cyclical taxation under this assumption.[8] To illustrate this, a 10-period investment has been used in Table 14.5. The profit based on fair value accounting is very smooth and does not spike in years with the highest revenues (years 2, 3, 9 and 10). Moreover, in years with 0 cash flow, the profits are positive. Hence, the firm would have to pay taxes even though there are zero cash flows. While such a countercyclical tax might be desirable for governments, the issue

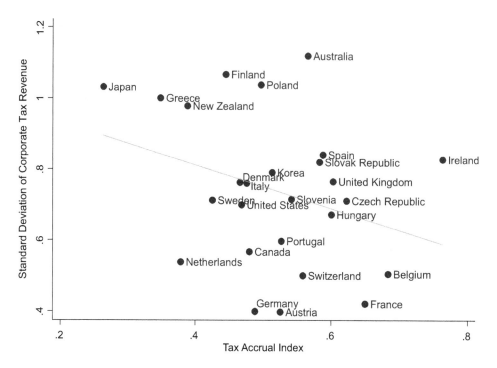

Figure 14.3 Volatility of tax revenues and tax accounting

Table 14.5 Cyclicality of profits under fair value accounting ($i = 3\%$)

Year	0	1	2	3	4	5	6	7	8	9	10
Revenues	−2,000	200	400	600	200	100	0	0	100	400	500
Fair value	2,142	2,006	1,666	1,116	950	878	905	932	860	485	
Depreciation		136	340	550	167	72	−26	−27	72	374	485
Profits		64	60	50	33	28	26	27	28	26	15

from the last section of potential fire sales comes up again. Hence, policy-makers face a trade-off between smoother tax revenues while potentially charging corporate taxes from firms in economic downturns when defining taxable income based on fair value accounting.

The effect of taxes on fair values

In the previous sections, we discussed potential consequences of defining a fair value-related tax base. However, since tax payments reduce after-tax cash flows, taxes potentially have value implications. To be more precise, the fair value might be affected by taxes. Hence, one needs to consider the fair value implications of taxes.

Regarding the effect of taxes on fair value measurement, the accounting standard-setters simply state that 'assumptions about cash flows and discount rates should be internally consistent. (...) after-tax cash flows should be discounted using an after-tax discount rate. Pre-tax cash flows should be discounted at a rate consistent with those cash flows' (ASC 820-10-55–6, IFRS 13.B14). It seems as if the standard-setters consider both approaches as equivalent.

However, the theoretical discussion in the section entitled 'Fair Value Taxation and Investment Neutral Taxation' has shown that both approaches only lead to the same results if the tax system is a Johansson-Samuelson tax system using fair value taxation. In contrast, real-world income taxes mostly use historical cost accounting (see the section entitled 'Fair Value Taxation in the United States and the European Union'). One should, therefore, expect that income taxes affect an asset's fair value. Surprisingly, little is known empirically about the effects of corporate income taxes on asset prices. In contrast, there is evidence on the impact of investor-level taxes on stock prices (see also the review by Hanlon & Heitzman 2010). In general, these studies provide evidence of dividend and capital gains tax capitalization (see, e.g. Dai et al. 2008). For example, Lang and Shackelford (2000) show that the 1997 capital gains tax reduction affected stock prices. Furthermore, Auerbach and Hassett (2006) or Sikes and Verrecchia (2015) find that the dividend tax rate cut of The Jobs and Growth Tax Relief Act of 2003 significantly increases stock prices. Li et al. (2016) find that IPO offer prices decrease in long-term capital gains taxes. In light of this evidence, accounting setters might rethink their recommendations regarding the consideration of taxes in fair value measurements.

Conclusion

This chapter provides an overview over potential consequences of using fair values to define taxable income for corporate tax and personal income tax purposes. On the one hand, there might be benefits from defining taxable income based on fair values. First, a fair value-based tax system theoretically ensures that taxes do not distort investment and capital gain realization decisions. Second, there are at least in theory, less tax avoidance opportunities when the corporate tax base is defined on a fair value basis. On the other hand, there might be some challenges when introducing fair value accounting for tax purposes, in particular, with respect to tax compliance (managerial manipulations of fair value estimates) and the risk of liquidity-induced fire sales.

Future research should use this chapter as a starting point for empirical and theoretical analyses on fair value accounting for tax purposes. There is very limited empirical and also theoretical evidence on the economic consequences on investment behavior, tax avoidance or tax compliance. In order to derive policy implications, more research is necessary. Based on the current state of the literature, we cannot reliably weigh the potential costs and benefits of using fair values to define taxable income for corporate tax and personal income tax purposes. We look forward to reading studies on this issue in the coming years.

Notes

1 For a detailed description of the determination of the corporate tax base in the EU and US see Spengel and Zöllkau (2012).
2 Johansson (1969) and Samuelson (1964).
3 After T, no future cash flows result from this investment, such that $FV_T = 0$ regardless whether we consider taxes or not.
4 See, for example, Fane (1987) and Niemann (1999). With imperfect loss offsets, however, fair value taxation could lead to an underinvestment in risky investment projects (Becker & Steinhoff 2014).
5 However, historical cost taxation could also induce underinvestment. If one modifies the example of Table 14.3 so that the cash flow in $t = 2$ amounts to 37,000 and assumes depreciation rates according to the straight-line method, the net present value before taxes would be positive while it would become negative after taxes.
6 Alternatively, one could also use a model building on Constantinides (1983). One would reach similar conclusions with his approach.

7 See, for example, the proposed 'Modernization of Derivatives Tax Act of 2016' from Senate Finance Committee Ranking Member Ron Wyden. www.finance.senate.gov/download/moda-leg-text.
8 In contrast, prior research mainly discusses a potential procyclicality of fair value accounting, for example, Sole et al. (2009).

References

Andrade, G & Kaplan, SN 1998, "How costly is financial (Not Economic) distress? Evidence from highly leveraged transactions that became distressed", *Journal of Finance*, vol. 53, no. 5, pp. 1443–1493.

Atwood, TJ, Drake, MS, Myers, JN & Myers, LA 2012, "Home country tax system characteristics and corporate tax avoidance: international evidence", *The Accounting Review*, vol. 87, no. 6, pp. 1831–1860.

Auerbach, AJ 1991, "Retrospective capital gains taxation", *American Economic Review*, vol. 81, no. 1, pp. 167–178.

Auerbach, AJ & Hassett, KA 2006, "Dividend taxes and firm valuation: new evidence", *American Economic Review*, vol. 96, no. 2, pp. 119–123.

Ball, R 1984, "The natural taxation of capital gains and losses when income is taxed", *Journal of Banking and Finance*, vol. 8, no. 3, pp. 471–481.

Beatty, A & Weber, J 2006, "Accounting discretion in fair value estimates: an examination of SFAS 142 goodwill impairments", *Journal of Accounting Research*, vol. 44, no. 2, pp. 257–288.

Becker, J & Steinhoff, M 2014, "Tax accounting principles and corporate risk-taking", *Economics Letters*, vol. 125, no. 1, pp. 79–81.

Benston, GJ 2008, "The shortcomings of fair-value accounting described in SFAS 157", *Journal of Accounting and Public Policy*, vol. 27, no. 2, pp. 101–114.

Bernard, VL, Merton, RC & Palepu, KG 1995, "Mark-to-market accounting for banks and thrifts: lessons from the Danish experience", *Journal of Accounting Research*, vol. 33, no. 1, pp. 1–32.

Bernard, AB, Jensen, JB & Schott, PK 2006, "Transfer pricing by US-based multinational firms (No. w12493)", National Bureau of Economic Research.

Biddle, GC, Hilary, G & Verdi, RS 2009, "How does financial reporting quality relate to investment efficiency?", *Journal of Accounting and Economics*, vol. 48, no. 2–3, pp. 112–131.

Cheng, M, Dhaliwal, D & Zhang, Y 2013, "Does investment efficiency improve after the disclosure of material weaknesses in internal control over financial reporting?", *Journal of Accounting and Economics*, vol. 56, no. 1, pp. 1–18.

Constantinides, GM 1983, "Capital market equilibrium with personal taxes", *Econometrica*, vol. 51, no. 3, pp. 611–636.

Constantinides, GM 1984, "Optimal stock trading with personal taxes: implications for prices and the abnormal January Returns", *Journal of Financial Economics*, vol. 13, no. 1, pp. 65–89.

Coval, J & Stafford, E 2007, "Asset fire sales (and purchases) in equity markets", *Journal of Financial Economics*, vol. 86, no. 2, pp. 479–512.

Dai, Z, Maydew, E, Shackelford, DA & Zhang, HH 2008, "Capital gains taxes and asset prices: capitalization or lock-in?", *Journal of Finance*, vol. 63, no. 2, pp. 709–742.

Dammon, RM, Spatt, CS & Zhang, HH 2001, "Optimal consumption and investment with capital gains taxes", *Review of Financial Studies*, vol. 14, no. 3, pp. 583–616.

Dechow, PM 1994, "Accounting earnings and cash flows as measures of firm performance: the role of accounting accruals", *Journal of Accounting and Economics*, vol. 18, no. 1, pp. 3–42.

Dechow, PM, Kothari, SP & Watts, RL 1998, "The relation between earnings and cash flows", *Journal of accounting and Economics*, vol. 25, no. 2, pp. 133–168.

Dietrich, JR, Harris, MS & Muller, KA 2000, "The reliability of investment property fair value estimates", *Journal of Accounting and Economics*, vol. 30, no. 2, pp. 125–158.

Donohoe, MP 2015a, "Financial derivatives in corporate tax avoidance: a conceptual perspective", *The Journal of the American Taxation Association*, vol. 37, no. 1, pp. 37–68.

Donohoe, MP 2015b, "The economic effects of financial derivatives on corporate tax avoidance", *Journal of Accounting and Economics*, vol. 59, no. 1, pp. 1–24.

Eberhartinger, E & Klostermann, M 2007, "What if IFRS were a tax base? New empirical evidence from an Austrian perspective", *Accounting in Europe*, vol. 4, no. 2, pp. 141–168.

Fane, G 1987, "Neutral taxation under uncertainty", *Journal of Public Economics*, vol. 33, no. 1, pp. 95–105.

Feld, LP, Ruf, M, Scheuering, U, Schreiber, U & Voget, J 2016, "Repatriation taxes and outbound M&A", *Journal of Public Economics*, vol. 139, pp. 13–27.

Felix, RA 2008, "The growth and volatility of state tax revenue sources in the Tenth District", *Economic Review-Federal Reserve Bank of Kansas City*, vol. 93, no. 3, p. 63.

Goncharov, I & Jacob, M 2014, "Why do countries mandate accrual accounting for tax purposes?", *Journal of Accounting Research*, vol. 52, no. 5, pp. 1127–1163

Hanlon, M & Heitzman, S 2010, "A review of tax research", *Journal of Accounting and Economics*, vol. 50, no. 2–3, pp. 127–178.

Hilton, AS & O'brien, PC 2009, "Inco Ltd.: market value, fair value, and management discretion", *Journal of Accounting Research*, vol. 47, no. 1, pp. 179–211.

Howitt, P & Sinn, HW 1989, "Gradual reforms of capital income taxation", *The American Economic Review*, vol. 79, pp. 106–124.

Huizinga, H & Voget, J 2009, "International taxation and the direction and volume of cross-border M&As", *Journal of Finance*, vol. 64, no. 3, pp. 1217–1249.

Huizinga, H, Voget, J & Wagner, W 2012, "Who bears the burden of international taxation? Evidence from cross-border M&As", *Journal of International Economics*, vol. 88, no. 1, pp. 186–197.

Ivkovic, Z, Poterba, JM & Weisbenner, S 2005, "Tax-motivated trading by individual investors", *American Economic Review*, vol. 95, no. 5, pp. 1605–1630.

Jacob, M 2013, "Capital gains taxes and the realization of capital gains and losses – evidence from German income tax data", *FinanzArchiv/Public Finance Analysis*, vol. 69, no. 1, pp. 30–56.

Jacob, M 2018, "Tax regimes and capital gains realizations". *European Accounting Review*, vol. 27, no. 1, pp. 1–21.

Johansson, SE 1969, "Income taxes and investment decisions", *The Swedish Journal of Economics*, vol. 71, no. 2, pp. 104–110.

Keen, M, Klemm, A & Perry, V 2010, "Culprit, accomplice, or bystander? Tax policy and the shaping of the crisis" in *Taxation and the financial crisis* eds J Alworth & G Arachi, European Tax Policy Form/Institute for Fiscal Studies Conference.

Klassen, KJ, Lisowsky, P & Mescall, D 2017, "Transfer pricing: Strategies, practices, and tax minimization", *Contemporary Accounting Research*, vol. 34, no. 1, pp. 455–493.

Klein, P 1998, "The capital gain lock-in effect with short sales constraints", *Journal of Banking and Finance*, vol. 22, no. 12, pp. 1533–1558.

Klein, P 1999, "The capital gain lock-in effect and equilibrium returns", *Journal of Public Economics*, vol. 71, no. 3, pp. 355–378.

Lang, MH & Shackelford, DA 2000, "Capitalization of capital gains taxes: evidence from stock price reactions to the 1997 rate reduction", *Journal of Public Economics*, vol. 76, no. 1, pp. 69–85.

Li, OZ, Lin, Y & Robinson, JR 2016, "The effect of capital gains taxes on the initial pricing and underpricing of IPOs", *Journal of Accounting and Economics*, vol. 61, no. 2–3, pp. 465–485.

Niemann, R 1999, "Neutral taxation under uncertainty–a real options approach", *FinanzArchiv/Public Finance Analysis*, vol. 56, no. 1, pp. 51–66.

Nissim, D 2003, "Reliability of banks' fair value disclosure for loans", *Review of Quantitative Finance and Accounting*, vol. 20, no. 4, pp. 355–384.

Poterba, JM 2002, "Taxation, risk-taking, and household portfolio behavior", *Handbook of Public Economics*, vol. 3, pp. 1109–1171.

Reese, WA 1998, "Capital gains taxation and stock market activity: evidence from IPOs", *Journal of Finance*, vol. 53, no. 5, pp. 1799–1819.

Samuelson, PA 1964, "Tax deductibility of economic depreciation to insure invariant valuations", *The Journal of Political Economy*, vol. 72, no. 6, pp. 604–606.

Seida, JA & Wempe, WF 2000, "Do capital gain tax rate increases affect individual investors' trading decisions?", *Journal of Accounting and Economics*, vol. 30, no. 1, pp. 33–57.

Shackelford, DA & Verrecchia, RE 2002, "Intertemporal tax discontinuities", *Journal of Accounting Research*, vol. 40, no. 1, pp. 205–222.

Sikes, SA & Verrecchia, RE 2015, "Dividend tax capitalization and liquidity", *Review of Accounting Studies*, vol. 20, no. 4, pp. 1334–1372.

Sole, J, Novoa, A & Scarlata, JG 2009, *Procyclicality and fair value accounting,* vol. 9, Washington, DC, International Monetary Fund. www.imf.org/en/About

Spengel, C & Zöllkau, Y (eds) 2012, *Common Corporate Tax Base (CC (C) TB) and determination of taxable income: An international comparison.* Heidelberg, Springer Science & Business Media.

Tang, TY 2015, "Does book-tax conformity deter opportunistic book and tax reporting? An international analysis", *European Accounting Review*, vol. 24, no. 3, pp. 441–469.

15

FAIR VALUE ACCOUNTING AND EXECUTIVE COMPENSATION

Gilad Livne and Garen Markarian

Overview

In this chapter, we discuss the relation between fair value measures reported in the financial statements and executive compensation. We start with a brief discussion of the broader issue of the compensation relevance of accounting numbers, and other non-accounting measures. Here we present the desired properties of a measure that make it compensation relevant. We next review the literature and the evidence on whether fair value measures are associated with executive compensation. We then go on to discuss how compensation expense itself may be fair valued. This is the case when employees, top executives in particular, are paid with options and restricted stocks (RS).

Until the great financial crisis of 2007–2009, the question of whether accounting-based performance measures that are affected by fair value accounting are compensation relevant largely escaped public and academic scrutiny. Public attention to bankers' compensation since the crisis has naturally intensified with some observers claiming that managers awarded themselves healthy pay based on speculative and yet-to-materialize profits. Because fair value accounting allows the booking of gains before cash is received, a particular concern has been the claw-back problem that is implicated with fair value accounting. Specifically, rewarding bankers for booking unrealized gains exposes shareholders to the risk that managers are rewarded upfront, but shareholders are left to bear the risk that these gains would fail to materialize. If unrealized earnings turn into real losses, shareholders may not be able to claw back past compensation. Although this problem was highlighted in banks, it is general in nature and extends beyond the financial sector.

Fair value accounting also affects the measurement of employee compensation expense, and this has probably been even more controversial. This is so because employees, particularly top management, are awarded equity instruments as part of their overall compensation package. We present a brief history of the debate and politics of the accounting for equity-based compensation because its adoption in the 2000s was met with great resistance. We then examine what is the information content of fair value compensation and also summarize research that looks into fair value compensation expense. We proceed to look at trends in executive pay over the recent period, and we conclude this chapter by looking at pay-related disclosures.

Theoretical arguments as to whether fair value performance measures should be compensation relevant

The essence of the agency problem faced by shareholders is that the actions and managerial qualities of the incumbent manager are not directly observable. As a result, compensation contracts cannot be written on variables that cannot be effectively monitored. Yet, shareholders wish to incentivize the manager to exert more effort and take on risky projects that can bring greater returns to shareholders and higher pay to the manager, even though managers may be risk-averse. This may be achieved by writing a compensation contract that is linked to observable *proxies* of effort and talent. In theory, any verifiable measure can be included, as long as it is believed to be correlated with the unobservable effort. For example, if greater effort leads to better earnings, then it stands to reason that earnings can be regarded as compensation relevant.

More generally, performance measures that are used in compensation contracts improve contract efficiency (i.e. increase shareholders' returns) if they are more sensitive to effort. That is, if the underlying measure is more highly correlated with the level of effort exerted by the manager (Banker & Datar 1989). Another useful property of a performance measure is its accuracy. Less accurate measures capture effort more poorly. In addition, a higher degree of inaccuracy would lead to greater variability in compensation. To the extent that managers are risk-averse, greater variability implies a greater compensation risk that is unrelated to effort and to desired outcomes. Compensation risk is required to motivate the manager to exert effort that leads to uncertain outcomes. This is best understood from the insight that with fixed salary, by definition, pay is unrelated to performance, and the manager will shirk. Nevertheless, if shareholders wish managers to assume a larger risk, they need to increase the incentive levels. This leads to two outcomes: higher effort and hopefully higher payoffs to both managers and shareholders. However, the higher the incentive levels and the higher the ultimate pay to the manager, the less of the payoffs is left to shareholders. Crucially, and for an efficient contract, shareholders need to provide incentive levels that maximize effort/outcomes minus the cost of incentives, at the margin.

Alternatively, compensation contracts may limit, or eliminate altogether, penalties for under-performance. For example, failure to meet performance targets may entitle the manager to the fixed salary element only, but no cash will be paid back by the manager to the firm. Rewarding managers through employee stock options (ESOs) also limits downside risk in compensation because in the worst case scenario (i.e. when share price is low owing to poor performance), the manager does not exercise the options, and this is costless.

One advantage of historical cost-based earnings is that they are easier to verify and are less volatile than fair value measures, especially when the latter are not directly observable (e.g. level 3 of fair value). The higher level of verifiability stems from the fact that recorded figures are objectively observed – for example a supplier's invoice or an invoice issued to a customer. The greater the verifiability, the lower the measurement risk. However, earnings are mostly historic and backward looking, and so fail to reflect effort in growth-related future-oriented investments. This problem is aggravated with conservative accounting, whereby current investment is either expensed or is not reflected in the income statement. A prime example of this is the cost of Research and Development (R&D). Accounting rules largely do not allow capitalization of these costs, although R&D efforts create economic assets (think of the pharmaceutical industry). Given that earnings are often depressed due to future-oriented investments, tying compensation to earnings can hinder such activities. There are a couple of possible solutions to this problem. The first is to defer compensation until the income from the R&D investment is realized. One drawback of this solution is that it may take a long time for the resultant cash flows to materialize. The longer it takes, the lower the present value of any compensation that is tied to this income stream. Hence the incentive for a manger to invest is smaller. Another issue is that with high labor mobility, the incumbent manager may work for another firm when the cash flow materializes. If the incumbent CEO is not entitled to compensation following the job change, the incentive to invest is again reduced.

Another solution to the problem of historical cost accounting is to rely on an estimate of the future benefits for current compensation purposes. However, this estimate is essentially a fair value estimate that is prone to bias, manipulations, inaccuracy and high variability.[1] An alternative forward-looking measure that is used in practice is the firm's share prices and/or returns. Firms typically use share prices as a performance measure in addition to earnings. This is naturally applicable for companies whose shares are publicly listed, and less applicable to other organizations. The logic here rests with the idea that the price of a traded security incorporates investors' expectations about future cash flows. In doing so, the compensation contract relies on observable prices. This is a prime example of using fair values (in this case, market value) in compensation contracts.

Should earnings and prices enter the compensation contract with an equal weight? More broadly, should several performance measures be used and with which weights? The answer to this question is provided by analytical research (e.g. Holmstrom 1979; Banker & Datar 1989). Although the insights gained from theory are not always simple to implement, the general idea is simple enough to be applicable. Because underlying effort is not observable, each performance measure is a noisy signal about the true value and its weight in the contract should be inversely related to its measurement noise. All performance measures should be used as long as they are not perfectly correlated. The weight of each performance measure (i.e. each signal) is assessed by its ratio of information to noise. The greater the information element, the more accurate is the signal. The implication is that a more accurate signal should attract a higher compensation weight. Boards therefore need to assess the relevance of fair value measures that may be used in compensation contracts and how accurate they are. This, in turn, should affect their relative importance.

The association between fair valued income items and executive compensation

Fair value accounting advances the timing of recognition of gains and losses. Since compensation schemes typically protect managers from incurring penalties when they fail to meet performance targets, an important issue that boards need to address is how to design compensation contracts that mitigate against the claw-back problem that arises when unrealized gains are recorded. In academic jargon the claw-back problem is also known as the ex-post settling up problem. Some empirical evidence pertaining to this pay design issue is provided in Leone et al. (2006). They examine the relation between stock returns – a common performance measure in compensation contracts – and cash pay. Although this relation does not speak directly to the relation of unrealized fair value gains with executive pay, share prices, like fair value accounting, are forward looking and so anticipate future gains (or losses). Leone et al. (2006) find that cash pay is not as sensitive to positive stock returns as to negative stock returns. This suggests that boards design pay contract to mitigate against the ex-post settling up problem.

Fair value accounting features in several accounting contexts, as other chapters in this book illustrate. However, the academic research has not extensively examined the link between the specific fair value contexts and executive compensation. Therefore, this is an area that invites future research. Nevertheless, we discuss below a few studies that examine particular contexts. The first is Shalev et al. (2013) who look at the relation between earnings-based compensation and recognition of goodwill arising on acquisition of control in other firms. Fair value accounting plays an important role here because goodwill is an accounting artefact that is defined as the difference between the price paid for the target firm and the fair value of its net assets. There is a negative relation between the amount of goodwill recognized and the fair value allocation of the purchase price to the net assets of the target firm. For example, if a greater portion of the purchase price is allocated to depreciable property plant and equipment (PPE), a smaller portion is allocated to goodwill, which is *not* subsequently amortized. A consequence of this is that following the acquisition, consolidated income is reduced by a higher depreciation expense the more is allocated to PPE. Shalev et al. (2013) therefore conjecture that increasing earnings-based cash compensation increases the incentive of managers to allocate a greater portion of the purchase price to goodwill. Equity-based compensation, in contrast, is more sensitive to overstating goodwill because the adverse effect of share price to subsequent announcements of goodwill impairments. Using a sample of 320 acquisitions during 2001–2008, Shalev et al. (2013) find that a greater cash bonus intensity is associated with higher amount of goodwill recognized. The conclusion from this study is that managers use fair value accounting to allocate lower amounts to target assets such as PPE and inventory when their performance is rewarded by cash bonus than when performance is rewarded with equity instruments.

Another interesting context where fair values play a role is in determining securitization gains and losses. Specifically, a firm can sell a large portion of its receivables to a third party in return for immediate cash injection. A small portion of the original receivables is typically retained by the selling firm and this should be assessed at fair value. Importantly, managers determine the fair value of the remaining portion, and can influence this value through, among other factors, selecting the appropriate discount rate. 'Smart' packaging of receivables with different credit risks by investment banks often results in a sale price that, once combined with the fair value of the remaining portion, exceeds the original carrying value of the original balance of the receivables. As a result, the receivables-selling firm recognizes a gain. Dechow et al. (2010) investigate whether boards exclude this gain when compensating managers because of the discretion involved in their calculations. However, they find that such fair value gains are positively associated with total compensation. Both Dechow et al. (2010) and Shalev et al. (2013) therefore suggest that fair values are compensation relevant, and that boards do not adjust income numbers for the effect of fair value estimates or opportunistic behavior on part of managers.

These two studies focus on compensation-motivated managerial discretion that influences fair value estimates. It may be argued that the effects of discretion on fair value gains (and losses) should be removed from the earnings measure that is the basis for compensation. By the same token, perhaps fair values that are based on objective measures should enter compensation contracts. Recall that even if observed market prices are not biased, relating market-based measures to compensation is prone to the ex-post settling up problem. Livne et al. (2011) examine this question using a sample of holding banks in a period before clawback provisions were introduced. The focus on banks is motivated by the fact that their balances sheets comprise mostly financial instruments. Livne et al. (2011) further exploit the fact that several financial institutions report trading assets and assets available for sale (AFS) securities that are routinely marked-to-market. In particular, changes in the market value of trading assets are taken to the income statement and are reported as trading income. They do not find that trading income is associated with CEO compensation, after controlling for the intensity of trading assets on the balance sheet. Because the trading assets reported on the balance sheet embed unrealized profits, the incremental explanatory power for trading income, if any, should stem from realized profits that are recognized in income. Therefore, this result is surprising because it suggests that reported trading income is not compensation relevant even though it relates to objectively observed prices. Yet, Livne et al. (2011) find that the intensity of trading assets is positively related to compensation. Since trading assets are speculative in nature, their findings suggest that compensation schemes in banks encouraged risk-taking and exposed banks to the claw-back problem.

A brief history of accounting for equity-based compensation

Younger managers may take profit sharing plans, stock options or share payments as an entitlement. Yet, compensation schemes that include anything other than a simple salary is a relatively recent phenomenon. In 1987, Michael Schuster warned in the Sloan Management Review of the drawbacks of profit-sharing systems (Schuster 1987). On the other hand, in the same year, the Journal of Labor Economics published an article advocating a two-part compensation system composed of a salary and a merit-based bonus because it decreases employee turnover (Blakemore et al. 1987). In fact, a number of profit-sharing programs at US factories appeared in the 1940s and even earlier. Procter and Gamble introduced employee stock ownership in the late 19th century. The earliest allegations of executive greed appeared in *Fortune* magazine, in 1939, when they reported President Roosevelt's call to cap salaries of top executives. An analysis by the National Bureau of Economic Research shows that one-third of large US companies used stock option systems for top executives in the 1950s (Brownstein & Panner 1992).

Despite early examples of profit-sharing and share-based compensation, the practice became fashionable only much later. It was the US automotive industry in the 1980s, which was falling behind in quality and efficiency, which started to implement Japanese-imported compensation systems that reward factory productivity.

Before we turn to discuss what we learn from the literature about executive compensation, stock options and accounting using fair values, it will be useful to review the reporting requirement regarding ESOs and RS from a historic perspective. In the USA, until the Financial Accounting Standard Board (FASB) issued a revision to SFAS 12 in 2004 (FASB 2004), granting of options to employees did not involve any accounting recognition in the financial statements,[2] unless the exercise price was below the share price. Therefore, most companies issuing ESO set the exercise price equal to the share price on grant day at that time.

It took some time for standard-setters to require fair value measurement for equity-based compensation owing to a stiff opposition mainly from executives and the big accounting firms (Murphy 2011). The FASB made the decision to expense the fair value of equity-based compensation instruments already in 1992, but was forced by the SEC and Congress to cancel it. A compromise was struck later when the FASB issued SFAS 123, which offered the option to expense options, but did not require it. Nevertheless, companies were required to provide additional disclosure about the value of options granted to employees. In the early 2000s, following a string of accounting scandals and increasing pressure from investors, the FASB issued a revision to SFAS 123. This revision, SFAS 123 (Revised) introduced for the first time the *requirement* to expense the value of equity-based instruments that are used for compensation. About the same time the IASB issued IFRS 2 – Share Based Payments (IASB 2004) – with similar requirements.

Fair valued compensation expense

As explained above, fair value accounting affects the wage bill reported in income statements owing to the use of ESOs and other equity instruments. Current rules [IFRS 2 and SFAS 123 (Revised)] require that the fair value of ESOs granted during the year is taken as salary expense over the vesting period against an equal increase in equity.[3] The rationale is that employment costs exist whether an employee is paid cash or options. Alternatively, options issued free to employees have an opportunity cost that is the cash the company could have raised by issuing the options on the open market.[4] Note that each year's income takes a portion of the initial fair value estimate as an expense. This effectively implies there is an off balance sheet asset, representing future benefits that arise to the employer from the employee owing to improved productivity, which is gradually amortized to zero until the options expire. Landsman et al. (2006) discuss the validity of the required method, and highlight two possible alternatives. The first is to fully recognize an ESO asset and increase equity by the fair value of the options granted upfront. Following this, the asset is amortized over the vesting period. While this results in similar income numbers as the required method, the balance of equity is higher until the options are exercised (or expire). A second alternative is to recognize an ESO asset, as in the first alternative, but balance it against a liability. Following initial recognition, Landsman et al. (2006) suggest that the liability is fair valued annually and the fair value adjustments are taken to income. Landsman et al. (2006) provide evidence indicating that the second alternative exhibits greater association with market value of the firm than the current method or the first alternative. This implies that investors disagree with the balancing of the compensation expense against equity because they regard it as a liability (whose value may change over time).

The fair value of ESO is typically measured using the Black-Scholes (1973) model. But what does this value represent? To the extent that ESOs better align employee incentives with shareholders' interest, one would expect a positive association between the fair value of ESOs and future performance metrics. If, in contrast, powerful managers design options plans to their personal benefit (see Bebchuk et al. 2002), the fair value represents the value of rent extraction (that is, unfair pay). Hanlon et al. (2003) examine this question and conclude that poor governance is not associated with Black-Scholes ESO values. Moreover, they find that these fair values have a predictive ability for future profit margins. They therefore conclude that the fair value represents net future benefits that arise to shareholders from the alignment of employee incentives with shareholders' interest.

Top executives receive in addition to ESO RS, which is also measured at fair value. Several papers report that RS-based compensation has increased in popularity in recent years while ESOs lost ground (Carter et al. 2007; Irving et al. 2011; Murphy 2011; Skantz 2012).[5] This may have been caused by equalizing the accounting treatment of ESO to RS under SFAS 123 (Revised), whereby the fair value (in the case of RS the fair value corresponds to the share price) is spread over the vesting period. It is also possible that the preference for RS stems from the difference in benefits they confer to employees. Specifically, this form of compensation entitles the employee to receive shares at the end of the vesting period in addition to dividends that are paid out during that period. Thus, RS may be preferred by the employee over ESO because it ensures a monetary reward by the end of the vesting period regardless of the stock price (options are valuable only if the stock price exceeds the exercise price) and, in addition, any dividend paid. Given the beneficial terms of RS to the recipient, it is questionable if it represents future net benefits to the firm, arising from better alignment of benefits, or whether it corresponds to employee rent extraction. Irving et al. (2011) explore this question in the context of RS awarded to top executives. Consistent with Hanlon et al. (2003), Irving et al. find that the fair value of ESO is positively related to market value of equity. However, in contrast to Hanlon et al., they find the fair value of RS is negatively related to the market value of equity. This is consistent with the rent extraction hypothesis for RS, given the premise that they are awarded excessively.

In interpreting the results reported for the increased popularity of RS, we note that just before SFAS 123 (Revised) was promulgated, there was another important regulatory change that may have influenced compensation practices. Since June 2003, the SEC has required shareholders' approval of equity-based compensation plans. Ng et al. (2011) report that following the new SEC rule, equity-based compensation declined to 50% from 60% of total compensation, while cash compensation increased from 40% to 50%. While Ng et al. (2011) attribute this change to SEC regulation, it is possible that the change in accounting rules also reduced firms' appetite for equity-based compensation.

Executive pay and the pay-for-performance relation

One of the powerful lessons of economics is that incentives matter, and how firms pay managers and employees affects their productivity, loyalty to the employer and due care to other employees, stakeholders and society. In today's labor market, CEO compensation has increased exponentially over the last three decades, entirely due to the rise of option grants (Hall & Murphy 2003) and RS holdings (Carter et al. 2007). A desirable facet of providing compensation with stock options or RS (i.e. equity pay) is that it ties a manager's compensation to observable firm specific signals (i.e. prices). Hence, stock prices have a direct link to a manager's yearly pay, through its effects on the fair values of a manager's holdings. At its most basic level, good contracts ensure that CEOs do not become wealthy at the expense of shareholders. They both get wealthy together at the same time because the compensation incentives work well for both.

We already mentioned the seminal work by Holmstrom (1979), which motivates the use of observable signals that inform about CEO decisions. These observables include ROA, stock returns, market share, patent approvals, new product launches and so on. Moreover, such observables enable labor and capital markets to monitor and discipline managers (Shleifer & Vishny 1997). Reading through the compensation section in proxies of various firms, it can be seen that compensation is (normally) awarded upon achieving pre-determined strategic goals as discussed above.

Nevertheless, an intriguing question is whether the use of stock options and RS leads to a tighter pay-for-performance relation or is it another form of rent extraction? The answer depends on whom you ask, and much has been written on the topic. On the one hand, as discussed above, tying compensation to stock prices links two items measured at fair value (stock prices and equity pay). On the hand, the manager may get to benefit from general market conditions rather than her own actions. If the recent bull market run of the past eight years is any indication, many got wealthy due to exogenous luck and not due to strategic effort. One way to deal with this is by filtering out general price trends from managerial compensation, for example, by reference to a peer group (i.e. indexing pay).[6] In an influential series of papers, Lucien Bebchuk of Harvard has argued that this is hard to achieve because executives have the power to exert influence on their own pay, leading to rent extraction (see Bebchuk & Fried 2004; Bebchuk, 2009). Hence, the suspicion is that RS and options are awarded for easy-to-meet performance targets, the peer group is opportunistically selected or that a relative performance evaluation is not used.

A large number of studies argue that relative performance evaluation does not often enter compensation contracts (e.g. Janakiraman et al. 1992; Garen 1994). Several explanations have been put forward, including the notion that CEO effectiveness is correlated with industry-wide patterns as a whole, the favorable accounting treatment of options that are not indexed and that indexing pay is useless given that CEOs can trade the index (Core et al. 2003). Hence, in sum, although the use of fair values in compensation may enhance the pay for performance relation, there is significant gaming of the system leading to inefficiencies in setting pay, which often is coupled with excessive pay.

Trends in executive pay

In prior sections we discuss how managerial compensation relates to fair values in the balance sheet and income statement. In this section we discuss changes in compensation patterns given that these have ramifications for risk-taking activity and financial reporting. There has been a large shift in executive pay structures in the USA over the past 20 years and hence for the role that fair values play in measuring executive pay. Below we examine the pay of both bankers, and industrial firms. These changes in compensation have strong ramifications for risk taking, for enhancing the relation between pay and performance, and for improving governance and transparency. Given that the compensation between banks and industrial firms are different, we examine these separately.

To look at trends in compensation patterns, we select data from Compustat's Execucomp database. We look at yearly option pay, bonuses, RS and total compensation. Figure 15.1 shows the structure of pay arrangements at US banks and non-banks in the period 2000–2014. We start our analysis in 2000 since that is the year where bank deregulation was already in full force. We include only banks that are present throughout the 15 year time period to show a balanced view on pay evolution. This of course induces a survivorship bias since banks that got merged or failed are not included (but if we include those also, general patterns do not change).

The depicted patterns in pay show a number of interesting developments. CEO compensation has almost doubled in the past 15 years. There is a predictable dip in the year 2009, but by 2010 it had already recovered to pre-crisis levels. Currently, compensation is at an all-time high of $6 million for the median CEO, a full 25% increase over 2006. Bonuses were on average zero in 2009, but are back to pre-crisis levels. The two main changes, though, are in the utilization of restricted shares and stock options. The usage of stock option exhibited a predictable decrease post-2002 when the SEC mandated their expensing starting June 15, 2005. The subprime crisis put the final nail in the stock options' coffin, and its risk-taking features. Specifically, the median US bank stopped using them altogether. Interestingly, the use of stock options had a rise-and-fall in the US banking system, but has been more stable in industrials. Only a third of banks used options in 1995, rising to 90% in the 2000 period. Recently, stock options declined yearly, 2009 had roughly a 50% utilization rate and in 2014 only 35% of banks used them (hence the median is a zero starting 2009). Consistent with the explanation above about the attractiveness of RS, stock options now have been phased out since 2007. Compensation at industrial firms also shows an evolutionary pattern. Part due to regulation, i.e. accounting rules mandating the expensing of stock options affecting both banks and non-banks or mandating the deferring the compensation for bankers. Patterns also changed in part because society learned that initial pay arrangements that were low on pay-for-performance, or were a result of powerful executives setting their own pay, yielding unintended consequences.

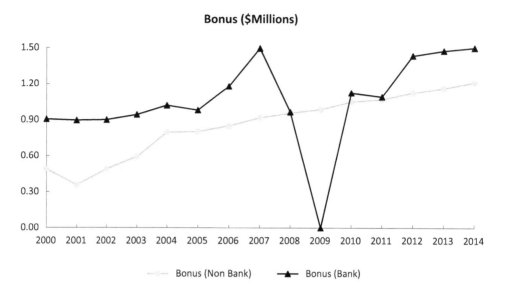

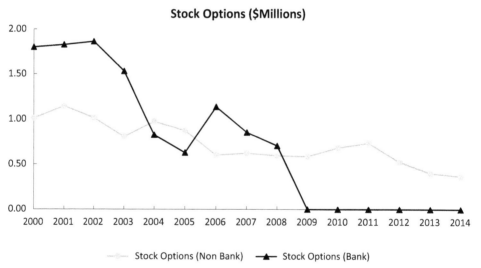

Figure 15.1 CEO compensation patterns of US Banks vs. Non-Banks: 2000–2014

It has been the case that, historically speaking, compensation in banking is less incentivized as compared to industrials (Houston & James 1995), with a lower proportion of options that incentivize risk taking. This trend has been changing since the deregulations of the 1980s, including the Gramm-Leach-Bliley Act (1999), which permitted banks to enter into insurance and investment banking, and saw a noted shift in compensation patterns toward pay for performance. The main takeaway from Figure 15.1 is that key pay-for-performance measures show similar incentivization levels. Yet, recent banker pay is geared less for risk-taking (less options), but cash bonuses are significantly larger.

A fundamental concern with options-based pay is that it can cause a claw-back problem if options are exercised prior to a (expected) fall in the share price. As such, a large number of companies have implemented wide-ranging programs to forfeit gains to managers, if such gains are found to be illicit ex-poste. For example, Visa Inc., when hiring J.P. Morgan's head of consumer-banking division in 2013, provided a generous portion of options – accompanied with vague and far reaching claw-back terms in the employment contract, filed with the SEC, an excerpt of which we provide below:

> *you also will be subject to the Visa Inc. Clawback Policy (the "Policy"). This Policy allows the board of directors to recoup any excess incentive compensation paid to members of the executive leadership team if the financial results on which the awards were based are materially restated due to fraud, intentional misconduct or gross negligence of the executive.*[7]

A number of studies have examined such claw-back provisions. Datta and Jia (2013) examine the valuation consequences of voluntary adoptions of claw-back provisions. Given that claw-back provisions are expected to enhance financial reporting quality, they find that firms experience a positive stock price increase after the adoption of such provisions. In a similar vein, Chan et al. (2012) find that claw-back provisions are associated with lower audit fees and faster audit completions. Although evidence on the consequences of claw back are yet preliminary, the Dodd-Frank act (2010) has proposed making claw-back provisions a legal requirement for all publicly held firms – something that has yet to be finalized by the current Republican administration (and might never will!).

Compensation and related disclosures

Given the perceived benefits of transparency, capital markets in recent years have demanded more and better information about compensation. Proxy statements and annual reports contain compensation information that now look vastly different than even 20 years ago. Since the start of securities regulations in 1934, the SEC had mandated the disclosure of compensation given to high ranking executives. These rules were further revised in 1992, to include a formalization, tabular representation and a discussion of incentive compensation by the compensation committee (Lo 2003). Similar trends have taken place elsewhere. At the heart of this global trend in regulation is a quest to improve transparency: who is compensated, on what basis and what are the incentive features? Disclosures enable various stakeholders to properly evaluate whether compensation is adequate, that it links to performance, and claw-back features deter scrupulous behavior.

Exogenously mandating disclosure systems may not eliminate opacity (Fisch 2009). Nevertheless, Craighead et al. (2004) argue that mandated compensation disclosures improve governance, as it permits shareholders to set rewards for executives that are consistent with investor objectives (see also Brickley et al. 1994). Zeckhauser and Pound (1990) also argue that compensation disclosures, which improve governance, enable shareholders to exert pressure on the board/CEO.

Although the principle that more transparency is innocuous, the role of information in setting and analyzing pay is complex. First, shareholders have cognitive limitations when processing outcomes that are fully determined by the manager. It has been repeatedly shown that managers have the incentive, and ability, to obfuscate information. A long line of research has indicated that managers can manipulate both financial and non-financial information, over varying time horizons (see Dechow et al. 1995; Dechow & Dichev 2002; Bergstresser & Philippon 2006). Second, even if the manager does not altogether intentionally mislead, shareholders do not have access to the same information set regarding products, markets and capital investments. Managers are reluctant to disclose proprietary information, much of information is historic in nature and future-oriented information is biased and uncertain. Third, to the extent that shareholders face a diverse set of incentives, investment horizons and information needs, providing uniform prescriptions on compensation disclosures may not suit all stakeholders.

These limitations notwithstanding, it is clear that better disclosure of compensation arrangements, including disclosure of fair value-based compensation, enhances monitoring and performance. Does it also work the other way around? That is, does increasing the weight of equity-based compensation in total compensation motivate managers to make better disclosures about firm performance? Nagar et al. (2003) examine this question. They observe that contracting on disclosure quality and activity is very difficult. This is unfortunate because obfuscation of private information increases managers' private control benefits. Nagar et al. (2003) then argue, and provide evidence consistent with, if managers are rewarded compensation that is based on share prices, they will have a greater incentive to disclose information that, in turn, informs price formation.

We next turn to illustrate some examples of pay disclosures in practice. In Figure 15.2, we provide an extract from Tesco's annual report for 2015, which illustrates some of the issues we have discussed. The drive to link compensation with performance is evident in that up to 80% of pay is linked to performance targets. Nevertheless, some of these targets are measured using traditional accounting measures such as sales and profits. The equity-based rewards come in the form of deferred share bonus and performance share plan (PSP). The PSP is 70% based on total shareholders' return (TSR), which implies that equity-based compensation is largely tied to share price performance. However, TSR is based on *relative* share price performance and the benchmark group can be selected opportunistically. In Tesco's case the benchmark group is a '*bespoke* group of FTSE 100 consumer business and services companies' (emphasis added). This illustrates the difficulty analysts and other users may face at trying to predict, or analyse, compensation elements that are fair valued.

How much did Tesco recognize in its income statement for share-based pay, and is it related to performance? Tesco discloses that '[t]he fair value of employee share option plans

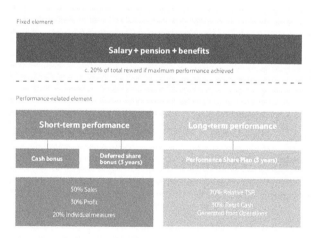

Figure 15.2 Tesco's compensation structure
Source: Tesco's annual report 2015 (p. 48).

is calculated at the grant date using the Black-Scholes model. The resulting cost is charged to the Group Income Statement over the vesting period'. In Note 4 Tesco reveals that in 2015 share-based pay was £144m vs. £81m in the previous year. Share-based payment has increased significantly year-on-year; however, Tesco reported a very large loss in 2015 (a loss of £5,766m, to be precise) while in the previous year it reported a profit of £970m. Though Tesco has implemented claw-back provisions, it is not clear what their effect was in 2015.

Tesco's pay-related disclosures are relatively simple and straightforward. In contrast, Goldman's proxy statement on compensation runs on pages 33–63 for the May 2016 annual meeting, while in comparison, it was a mere 9 pages in 2007. The 2007 proxy included no material on how bonuses are determined, no claw-back provisions and roughly 50% of awards vested immediately. The length of the total proxy document now is 104 pages compared to 50 in 2007. Morgan Stanley's procedures are almost identical to Goldman's, now their proxy runs at 96 pages, compared to 64 pages in 2007.[8] The compensation section of the proxy runs from page 24 to 56 while it was 19 pages a few years earlier. It is an open question whether the enhanced disclosure is more informative or is used to conceal the big picture.

Conclusions

The review we conduct in this chapter suggests several conclusions. First, boards use income as a performance measure in compensation decisions, but do not make any adjustments for unrealized gains or losses that stem from the application of fair value accounting. Second, the regulatory shift to require equity-based compensation to be recognized as an expense changed the reward mix between options and RS. As options lost their accounting 'appeal', more RS has been issued following the promulgation of SFAS 123 (Revised). We believe that another contributing factor to this trend is that managers prefer RS to options because the monetary rewards are more secure. Third, findings of prior research suggest that the fair value of ESO corresponds to the alignment of employee incentives with shareholders' interest. In contrast, the fair value of RS seems to represent rent extraction by managers. Fourth, while there is more information about executive pay, and in particular, equity-based pay, it is not clear that the lengthy reporting is more useful to various stakeholders. Notwithstanding the 'wealth' of information, it may remain hard for outsiders to have a good understanding as to how fair value estimates affect compensation levels.

Notes

1 See the accompanying chapter by Kalin Kolev, for a discussion of financial reporting management in the context of fair value accounting.
2 This is now called FASB ASC Topic 718 – Stock Compensation. The previous no-expense-recognition were promulgated in APB 25 and SFAS 123.
3 Note that the overall effect on equity is zero because retaining the expense is offset against the increase to equity.
4 A limitation of this argument, however, is that options issued to employees may create incentives on part of the employees to work harder for the benefit of the shareholders. This incentive effect may, or may not, be impounded in the fair value of ESO. However, options trading in public exchanges clearly lack this feature and hence should not have the same fair value.
5 See also our Figure 15.1 and related discussion.
6 The normal practice of stock options is that the payoffs to the manager are determined by the current stock price (S), minus a strike price (X) which is the stock price on the grant date a few years earlier. Proponents of indexing argue that this provides payoffs to a manager when general market conditions are positive (such as in boom markets). They argue that indexing options, where X is

replaced by a moving benchmark, such as the S&P 500, filters out market wide trends that are not due to managerial effort.

7 Source: SEC website, www.sec.gov/Archives/edgar/data/1403161/000119312513232521/d543134 dex992.htm, accessed on September 15, 2017.

8 This pattern of increased disclosures about pay has become the norm even at the international level. HSBC now has 32 pages dedicated to pay, while it had only 7 pages in 2007. UBS now has a dedicated compensation report that runs for 56 pages, while Deutsche Bank has one similar that runs 41 pages. UBS also links CEO pay to bank security/soundness, as 15% of compensation is tied to leverage ratios and regulatory capital requirements.

References

Bebchuk, LA 2009, *Pay without performance: the unfulfilled promise of executive compensation*, Harvard Business Press, Cambridge, MA.

Bebchuk, LA, Fried, JM & Walker DI 2002, "Managerial power and rent extraction in the design of executive compensation", *University of Chicago Law Review*, vol. 69, pp. 751–846.

Bebchuk, LA & Fried, JM 2004, *Pay without performance*, Harvard University Press, Cambridge, MA.

Bergstresser, D & Philippon, T 2006, "CEO incentives and earnings management", *Journal of Financial Economics*, vol. 80, pp. 511–529.

Banker, R & Datar, S 1989, "Sensitivity, precision, and linear aggregation of signals for performance evaluation", *Journal of Accounting Research*, vol. 27, pp. 21–39.

Black, F & Scholes, M 1973, "The pricing of options and corporate liabilities", *Journal of Political Economy*, vol. 81, no. 3, pp. 637–654.

Blakemore, AE, Low, SA & Ormiston, MB 1987, "Employment bonuses and labor turnover", *Journal of Labor Economics*, vol. 5, no. 4, Part 2, pp. S124–S135.

Brownstein, AR & Panner, MJ 1992, "Who should set CEO pay? The press? Congress? Shareholders?", *Harvard Business Review*, vol. 70, no. 3, pp. 28–38.

Brickley, JA, Lease, CR & Smith, CW 1994, "Corporate voting: evidence from charter amendment proposals", *Journal of Corporate Finance*, vol. 1, no. 1, pp. 5–31.

Carter, M, Lynch, L & Tuna, I 2007, "The role of accounting in the design of CEO equity compensation", *The Accounting Review*, vol. 82, no. 2, pp. 327–357.

Chan, LH, Kevin, CW, Chen, TY & Yangxin Y 2012, "The effects of firm-initiated clawback provisions on earnings quality and auditor behaviour", *Journal of Accounting and Economics*, vol. 54, no. 2–3, pp. 180–196.

Core, J, Guay, W & Verrecchia, R 2003, "Price versus non-price performance measures in optimal CEO compensation contracts", *The Accounting Review*, vol. 78, pp. 957–981

Craighead, JA, Magnan, ML & Thorne, L 2004, "The impact of mandated disclosure on performance-based CEO compensation", *Contemporary Accounting Research*, vol. 21, no. 2, pp. 369–398.

Datta, MI & Jia, Y 2013, "Valuation consequences of clawback provisions", *The Accounting Review*, vol. 88, no. 1, pp. 171–198.

Dechow, P & Dichev, I 2002, "The quality of accruals and earnings", *The Accounting Review*, vol. 77, no. S–1, pp. 35–59.

Dechow, P, Sloan, R & Sweeney, A 1995, "Detecting earnings management", *The Accounting Review*, vol. 70, pp. 193–226.

Dechow, P, Myers, L & Shakespeare, C 2010, "Fair value accounting and gains from asset securitizations: a convenient earnings management tool with compensation side-benefits", *Journal of Accounting and Economics*, vol. 49, pp. 2–25.

Financial Accounting Standards Board (FASB) 2004, Share-based payment. Statement No. 123. Revised December 2004. FASB, Norwalk, CT.

Fisch, JE 2009, "Top cop or regulatory flop? The SEC at 75", *Virginia Law Review*, vol. 95, no. 4, pp. 785–823.

Garen, JE 1994, "Executive compensation and principal-agent theory", *Journal of Political Economy*, vol. 102, no. 6, pp. 1175–1199.

Hall, B & Murphy, K 2003, "The trouble with stock options", *Journal of Economic Perspectives*, vol. 17, no. 3, pp. 49–70.

Hanlon, M, Rajgopal, S & Shevlin, T 2003, "Are executive stock options associated with future earnings?", *Journal of Accounting and Economics*, vol. 36, pp. 3–43.

Holmstrom, B 1979, "Moral hazard and observability", *Bell Journal of Economics*, vol. 10, pp. 74–91.

Houston, JF & James, C 1995, "CEO compensation and bank risk: is compensation in banking struc-tured to promote risk taking?", *Journal of Monetary Economics*, vol. 36, no. 2, pp. 405–431.

International Accounting Standards Board (IASB) 2004, IIFRS 2 RS 2 share-based payment, London.

Irving, JH, Landsman, WR & Lindsey, BP 2011, "The valuation differences between stock option and restricted stock grants for US firms", *Journal of Business Finance & Accounting*, vol. 38, no. 3–4, pp. 395–412.

Janakiraman, SN, Lambert, RA & Larcker, DF 1992, "An empirical investigation of the relative per-formance evaluation hypothesis", *Journal of Accounting Research*, vol. 30, no. 1, pp. 53–69.

Landsman, WR, Peasnell, KV, Pope, PF & Yeh, S 2006, "Which approach to accounting for em-ployee stock options best reflects market pricing?", *Review of Accounting Studies*, vol. 11, no. 2–3, pp. 203–245.

Leone, AJ, Wu, JS & Zimmerman, JL 2006, "Asymmetric sensitivity of CEO cash compensation to stock returns" *Journal of Accounting and Economics*, vol. 42, no. 1–2, pp. 167–192.

Livne, G, Markarian, G & Milne, A 2011, "Bankers' compensation and fair value accounting", *Journal of Corporate Finance*, vol. 17, no. 4, pp. 1096–1115.

Lo, Kin 2003, "Economic consequences of regulated changes in disclosure: the case of executive com-pensation", *Journal of Accounting and Economics*, vol. 35, no. 3, pp. 285–314.

Murphy, KJ 2011, The politics of pay: a legislative history of executive compensation (August 24, 2011). Marshall School of Business Working Paper No. FBE 01.11. Available at SSRN: https://ssrn.com/abstract=1916358 or http://dx.doi.org/10.2139/ssrn.1916358.

Nagar, V, Nanda, D & Wysocki, P 2003, "Discretionary disclosure and stock-based incentives", *Journal of Accounting and Economics*, vol. 34, pp. 283–309.

Ng, L, Sibilkov, V, Wang, Q & Zaiats, N 2011, "Does shareholder approval requirement of equity compensation plans matter?", *Journal of Corporate Finance*, vol. 17, no. 5, pp. 1510–1530.

Shleifer, A & Vishny, R 1997, "A survey of corporate governance", *Journal of Finance*, vol. 52, pp. 737–783.

Schuster, M 1987, "Gain sharing: do it right the first time", *Sloan Management Review*, vol. 28, Winter, pp. 17–25.

Shalev, RON, Zhang, IX & Zhang, Y 2013, "CEO compensation and fair value accounting: evidence from purchase price allocation", *Journal of Accounting Research*, vol. 51, no. 4, pp. 819–854.

Skantz, TR 2012, "CEO pay, managerial power, and SFAS 123 (R)", *The Accounting Review*, vol. 87, no. 6, pp. 2151–2179.

Zeckhauser, RJ & Pound. J 1990, Are large shareholders effective monitors? An investigation of share ownership and corporate performance, in *Appearing in Asymmetric information, corporate finance, and investment*, ed. R. Glenn Hubbard, University of Chicago Press, Chicago, IL, 149–180.

16

FAIR VALUE AND THE FORMATION OF FINANCIAL MARKET PRICES THROUGH IGNORANCE AND HAZARD

Yuri Biondi

Introduction

Fair value refers to current values as the backbones of accounting measurements. Current value reference follows the efficient financial market hypothesis, which bases upon an equilibrium approach. The latter defines the efficient pricing under ideal conditions, establishing the benchmark for actual pricing. By construction, equilibrium abstracts away from realization and from the financial market investment process, which occur through periods. Equilibrium does assume the existence of efficient market prices, scoping out all the details concerning their formation through ignorance and hazard.

This chapter develops a dynamic systems analysis to the financial system that generates financial market clearing prices over time and circumstances. This systemic approach relaxes the efficient financial market hypothesis by introducing two essential details about price formation. On the one hand, there is timely provision and treatment of firm-specific information; on the other hand, there is the market clearing price fixing that aggregates and assures the ongoing matching between market orders, which may depend on that information.

Under this systemic approach, each price time series becomes unique and dependent on conditions situated in space and time. Statistical tests may be conducted to infer regularities and properties from the pricing performance of each financial system. According to simulation analysis over a large set of circumstances, fair value regimes increase market volatility and market exuberance with inefficient economic allocation effects, although the correlation of accounting information with the market price series is improved. Accounting information provision does result in playing a better role when it provides a fundamental signal that remains independent from financial market price dynamics.

The rest of the chapter is organized as follows. "The fair value revolution" introduces the fair value revolution, which has been featured in the accounting world in recent decades. "Fair value and the efficient financial market hypothesis" clarifies the relation between fair value and the efficient financial market hypothesis. "Fair value and the formation of financial market prices over time and circumstances" introduces a dynamic systems analytical approach, which relaxes its unrealistic assumptions framed by equilibrium. This systemic approach offers an alternative view based upon the alternative concept of the financial system. "Comparative assessment of fair value and historical cost accounting regimes" summarizes main findings derived from dynamic systems analysis. A summary of the main argument concludes.

The fair value revolution

In recent decades, accounting has undertaken a fair value revolution. On the one hand, accounting academia has been importing concepts and methods from financial economics. On the other hand, International and US accounting standards-setters have been promoting and enforcing fair (current) values as the backbone of their accounting basis. Current values refer to current market prices to determine accounting measurements at the specific time of financial statement preparation. Absent actual market prices of reference, some comparable transactions or forecast mathematical models are applied to mimic what those market prices could be.

Several explanations have been provided for this revolution, as well as several arguments to endorse or criticize it (see Biondi 2011b providing further references). This chapter develops a constructive critique that addresses the theoretical roots of fair value in the efficient financial market hypothesis. Our driving idea is that the latter framework abstracts away from time and realization. When the hazard of realization through time is considered, fair value loses its imaginary foundations. By relaxing the efficient financial market hypothesis, this chapter develops a dynamic systems analysis to comparatively assess fair value regimes against historical cost accounting regimes.

Fair value and the efficient financial market hypothesis

The financial market price formation process involves interactions and exchanges between investors, who aim to buy and selling securities traded on the financial market of reference. The efficient financial market hypothesis develops an elegant mathematical model that exploits some properties of equilibrium prices. Equilibrium is assumed by construction, and those properties are empirically tested through econometric methods. According to this frame of analysis, an efficient financial market does fully and correctly integrate into its current price any new information that affects the fundamental value of the traded security. Investors are expected to develop rational forecasts of future prices. Given rational expectations, all foreseeable information is already incorporated into the current price. Only unexpected information is then assumed to have an impact on the market price trough time. Accordingly, the current price is the best predictor of future prices, and the price time series behaves as a random walk through time. As Fama (1995, p. 4) argues, 'in an efficient market at any point in time the actual price of a security will be a good estimate of its intrinsic value. [...] Although uncertainty concerning intrinsic values will remain, actual prices of securities will wander randomly about their intrinsic values'. Formally:

$$p_t = E_t\{p_{t+1} \mid I_t\} \sim N(\bar{p}, \sigma_\varepsilon) \text{ where } I_t = \varepsilon_t \rightarrow iid \ N(0, \sigma_\varepsilon)$$

The efficient financial market hypothesis does not address the formation of market clearing prices through ignorance and hazard (see Malkiel 2003; Shiller 2003; Biondi 2011a; "Fair value and the formation of financial market prices over time and circumstances" provides further literature review). Its framework does not specify whether and how equilibrium prices can be attained over time and circumstances (Shubik 2007). As a matter of fact, the market clearing pricing depends on both (i) the provision and treatment of firm-specific information, and (ii) an aggregating market price fixing that assures the matching between market orders, which may depend on that information.

Concerning epistemic conditions (point i above), some have imagined that the fundamental value exists, and can be correctly known by at least some informed investors, who

act as arbitrageurs between ongoing market prices and that fundamental value. Those investors would make illusory (or temporarily) profits while driving the market price toward its
fundamental benchmark through the very impact of their trades. Others have imagined that
every investor can observe the fundamental value with noise. This noise can be progressively
eliminated by emergent information that is extracted from evolving market prices. Hayek
(1945) further argued that no investor observes the fundamental value, but the market pricing assures its emergent collective discovery. In sum, market price opinions $E_{i,t}$ expressed
by investor i at time t are imagined to be fixed around the universal value F_t of reference.
Tentatively, these interpretations may be formalized in one of the following ways:

$$p_t = \overline{F}$$

$$\lim_{t \to \infty} p_t = \overline{F}$$

$$E_{i,t}\{p_{t+1} \mid F_t\} = p_t - \theta_{i,t}(\overline{F} - p_t)$$

$$E_{i,t}\{p_{t+1} \mid I_t\} = I_{i,t} \sim N(\overline{F_t}, \sigma_\varepsilon)$$

Concerning the market mechanism (point ii above), the efficient financial market hypothesis does not specify how the market price fixing process aggregates market orders based on
evolving investor opinions. However, its frame of analysis implies that market prices fluctuate randomly over time (no serial correlation between p_{t+1} and p_t) as if they were extracted
from a normal distribution (Samuelson 1965, 1973). Formally:

$$p_t \sim N(\overline{F_t}, \sigma_\varepsilon)$$

As a matter of principle, accounting plays no role in this framework, since the current market
price provides sufficient information to invest and trade on financial markets. At best, accounting is assumed to follow the market pricing, incorporating the most updated market evaluation
into financial reports (Kothari 2001; Biondi 2015). Fair value subsumes this market perspective
in a conceptual framework for accounting. Fair value bases accounting upon market-based
measurements of a portfolio of independent elements that are defined as assets and liabilities,
that is, positive and negative stocks of corporate worth at some arbitrary point of time. Accordingly, the market reference assures these measurements to be relevant, timely and objective.

Fair value and the formation of financial market prices over time and circumstances

The fair value basis of accounting abstracts away from realization. The market prices are assumed to exist and to comply with conditions derived from equilibrium in the financial mar-
ket(s). The quality of accounting information is assessed through the correlation with these
imagined prices. The actual price formation through time and circumstances is neglected.

However, contrary to old-fashioned notions of scientific measurement of natural phenomena, accounting 'measurement' interacts with the phenomena that are measured. This
interaction takes place through ignorance and hazard. One problem with equilibrium is that
it neglects this interaction. And it is in the context of this temporal interaction that accounting becomes relevant in the financial market investment process.

By construction, equilibrium prices are supposed to be fixed before trade takes place. Price formation is then ignored. But it is through market price formation that accounting signals of corporate performance become relevant, since accounting provides firm-specific fundamental information F_t that assists investors in developing those priors that they interpret to base their market orders upon.

By construction, equilibrium prices – as implied by efficient markets – scope out arbitrage opportunities. This implies that price change over time cannot be exploited to make profits. However, the very existence of active market trading (and Securities Exchanges) enables investors to speculate on ongoing market price changes, $(p_t - p_{t-1})$. The IASB (2010, OB3)'s conceptual framework includes 'market price increases' among returns that investors expect from an investment.

Empirical evidence from actual financial markets clearly shows that statistical properties derived from equilibrium are not respected by actual series of market prices and market returns (defined as the relative change of market prices over time, $(p_t - p_{t-1}) / p_{t-1}$). Both series show fait tails in their distributions and short-term correlations over time (see Mantegna & Stanley 2000, providing further references). Contrary to the efficient financial market hypothesis, these series are not normally distributed.

Theoretical limitations and empirical evidence invite to amend the equilibrium frame of analysis, relaxing the efficient financial market hypothesis. Equilibrium approaches depend on a reductionist modelling strategy that assumes ideal properties for the market price time series, implying the correct and timely alignment between market price and fundamental value over time (Cutler et al. 1989; Fama 1991, 1998; McQueen & Roley 1993; Fair 2002). This strategy neglects specific conditions of information provision and diffusion, as well as the market clearing pricing microstructure.

From a theoretical perspective, Grossman and Stiglitz (1980) show the impossibility of a perfect informationally efficient market, since informed investors would not have incentives to trade, preventing their privileged information to be translated into market prices. Accordingly, market clearing prices cannot be formed if market is informationally efficient. A large body of literature explores this finding, investigating whether and which configurations for information diffusion and market microstructure do trigger informational efficiency or inefficiency (see Biondi & Righi 2017, reviewing further references). Another large body of accounting literature explores the relationship of accounting information provision with the financial market dynamics (Kothari 2001; Arnold 2009; Biondi & Giannoccolo 2015, reviewing further references).

Drawing upon these literature bodies, an extended framework may aim to comprehend the accounting role in the formation of financial market prices over time. In a series of articles (Biondi et al. 2012; Biondi & Bensimhon 2013; Biondi 2015; Biondi & Giannoccolo 2015; Biondi & Righi 2016, 2017), we have been developing a financial dynamic systems analysis that expands upon the received framework to include both the fundamental information provision F_t and the market price change in profit opportunities. According to our systemic approach, investor opinions $E_{i,t}$ include both elements as follows:

$$E_{i,t}\{p_{t+1}\} = p_t + \alpha_{i,t}(p_t - p_{t-1}) - \beta_{i,t}(E_{i,t-1}\{p_t\} - p_t) + \gamma_{i,t}I_{i,t}\{F_t\}$$

From our financial system perspective, investors consider the current price, the price change, the revision of their forecast error and their interpretation of the fundamental signal of reference, to form their opinion on the next future price. Investor market orders are based upon their evolving opinion. The market aggregation mechanism rules over these market orders that every investor may post to the market agency at each trading period. This financial market investment process occurs through ignorance and hazard. In particular, the clearing price p_t that is fixed at period t interacts with the further investor opinions $E_{i,t}$ trough time and circumstances.

Contrary to an equilibrium approach, investors do not trade in a vacuum. Market clearing prices are not assumed under ideal conditions, but they are actually formed through the ongoing aggregation of market orders posted by investors. These orders are submitted to the hazard of realization. Clearing market prices do realize in circumstances that are located in space and time. Their realization is affected by evolving behavioral and institutional conditions. On the behavioral side, the realization depends on the ongoing opinions $E_{i,t}$ and related market trading strategies by interacting heterogeneous investors. On the institutional side, the realization depends on both the market aggregation mechanism – which transforms individual market orders into clearing market prices p_t – and the provision and treatment of fundamental information F_t on the ongoing financial performance and position of the reporting entity whose securities are traded.

Under these evolving conditions, the market agency aggregates and clears trade orders posted by heterogeneous investors. Each market price provides a realization that does the following: send back a collective signal to trading investors, challenge their opinions and make them gain or lose from their market bets. When time and realization are introduced, each market price series follows its own unique trajectory over time and circumstances. A statistical analysis of various series may extract regularities and infer properties on the financial system behavior.

From this systemic perspective, an equilibrium situation where the price is fixed or short-time stationary becomes a cornerstone of limited interest. To be tested empirically, the equilibrium price series must be assumed and thus compared with realized price series; however, the generating conditions of this realization remain out of experimental control. This setting makes it impossible to comparatively assess each price series under the actual conditions that generate it. To overcome this limitation, we design artificial financial markets and perform comparative analysis through simulation and experiment. These methods enable to observe each artificial market price series under its specific conditions that are under experimental control.

Comparative assessment of fair value and historical cost accounting regimes

Our financial system approach provides an analytical model of the formation of financial market prices over time. Step-by-step realizations generate feedbacks and loops over space and time. This model is capable to reproduce relevant stylized facts concerning financial market dynamics, including fait tails in distributions and short-term correlations over time in the series of financial market prices and returns.

By calibrating this model through simulation and experiment, we design artificial financial systems and perform comparative assessment of alternative accounting models of reference, according to a dualistic perspective that opposes current value (fair value) regimes to historical cost accounting regimes (Anthony 2004; Biondi 2011b). Alternative accounting models are introduced by reshaping the functional form of the fundamental information provision F_t. Generally speaking, fair value regimes provide a fundamental signal that is linked to the market price dynamics, while historical cost accounting regimes provide a fundamental signal that remains independent from the market price series. On this basis, we test the financial system performance under each regime according to a large set of possible circumstances denoted by the parameter space. Main findings concern the impact of fair value on market volatility, market exuberance, investor wealth distribution and accounting information quality.

Market volatility refers to the statistical distribution of market prices. It can be measured either as the price standard deviation over the mean price, or through other measures of market price series dispersion. According to our dynamic systems analysis, volatility and dispersion are materially and significantly increased in market price series generated under fair value regimes, relative to historical cost accounting regimes. At the same time, market liquidity is endogenously decreased under the former regimes.

While volatility involves univariate statistical tests, market 'exuberance' (Shiller 2003), 'vagary' (Biondi & Righi 2016) and 'errancy' (Biondi & Righi 2017) point to bivariate tests of the joint movement between market price series p_t and fundamental signal series F_t. This assessment asks whether and to which extent the market price series shows excess distance from some available estimation of the fundamental performance of reference. Experimental and simulation findings show that fair value regimes worsen the alignment between market clearing price series and the fundamental signal series of reference over time. Therefore the incorporation of firm-specific information becomes haphazard while the movement of the market price series becomes erratic. The market price is no longer a reliable estimate of the fundamental performance of the business firm through time and circumstances.

According to these findings for volatility and exuberance, the market pricing dynamics appears to produce dysfunctional effects under fair value regimes. This intuition is confirmed by testing their impact on the economic allocation of resources. Fair value regimes do increase the inter-individual dispersion of investor revenue and wealth, worsening the allocative efficiency of financial market investment process (Biondi & Bensimhon 2013).

Although fair value regimes result in the worsening of the financial system performance concerning volatility, exuberance and allocative efficiency, this does not imply that their widespread measure of accounting quality is worsened. According to our findings, covariance measures between p_t and F_t are increased by fair value regimes relative to historical cost regimes (Biondi & Righi 2016). Therefore, the accounting information follows better the market series under fair value regimes where the financial system shows decreased performance, while the accounting information is more independent from the market series under historical cost regimes where the financial system performance improves.

Concluding remarks

In recent decades, accounting standards-setters and academics have been advocating and enforcing a fair value revolution, seeking to make accounting information dependent on the markets of reference and more aligned with the financial market pricing.

This conceptual framework does fundamentally transplant the efficient financial market hypothesis into accounting. Accounting is then assumed to take information from the markets of reference. In fact, this framework abstracts away from realization, although the formation of financial market prices factually occurs through ignorance and hazard.

Our financial dynamic systems analysis relaxes this hypothesis by introducing realization throughout periods. Every investor takes decisions and posts orders according to the available information at each time period t. Investor opinions and bets are thus submitted to the hazard of realization, as well as to the evolving conditions of financial market investment process that occurs through time and circumstances.

When this process is considered, fair value regimes result in a worsening of the financial system performance. In particular, market volatility and market exuberance are increased with inefficient economic allocation effects, although the correlation between accounting information and the market price series is improved.

Therefore, accounting information provision appears to play a better role when it provides an accounting lighthouse that remains independent from the market pricing dynamics, offering an outside benchmark to financial market participants confronted with ignorance and hazard.

These findings invite us to reconsider the importance of realization in the conceptual framework of accounting. Accounting may then play its specific role in view to manage and govern the ongoing enterprise entity over time (going concern), while providing firm-specific information for the markets, and not from them.

Acknowledgments

Yuri Biondi is tenured senior research fellow of the National Center for Scientific Research of France (Cnrs – IRISSO, University Paris Dauphine PSL), and research director at the Financial Regulation Research Lab (Labex ReFi), Paris, France. I wish thanking Garen Markarian for his kind invitation to contribute and both book editors for their comments and suggestions on a previous version of this chapter. Usual disclaimer applies.

References

Anthony RN 2004, *Rethinking the rules of financial accounting: examining the rules for accurate financial reporting*, McGraw Hill Professional, New York.

Arnold, PJ 2009, "Global financial crisis: the challenge to accounting research", *Accounting, Organizations and Society*, vol. 34, pp. 803–809.

Biondi Y 2011a "Disagreement-based trading and speculation: implications for financial regulation and economic theory", *Accounting, Economics and Law: A Convivium*, vol. 1, no. 1. doi:10.2202/2152-2820.1017

Biondi Y 2011b, "The pure logic of accounting: a critique of the fair value revolution", *Accounting, Economics and Law: A Convivium*, vol. 1, no. 1. doi:10.2202/2152-2820.1018

Biondi, Y 2015, "Accounting and the formation of share market prices over time: a mathematical institutional economic analysis through simulation and experiment", *Applied Economics*, vol. 47, no. 34–35, pp. 3651–3672. doi:10.1080/00036846.2015.1021461

Biondi, Y & Bensimhon, L 2013, "Financial bubbles, common knowledge and alternative accounting regimes: an experimental analysis of artificial spot security markets", *Accounting for or from the Market?' The Japanese Accounting Review*, vol. 3, pp. 21–59. doi:10.11640/tjar.3.2013.02

Biondi, Y & Giannoccolo, P 2015, "Share price formation, market exuberance and financial stability under alternative accounting regimes", *Journal of Economic Interaction and Coordination*, vol. 10, no. 2, October, pp. 333–362. doi:10.1007/s11403-014-0131-7

Biondi, Y & Righi, S 2016, "What does the financial market pricing do? A simulation analysis with a view to systemic volatility, exuberance and vagary", *Journal of Economic Interaction and Coordination*, vol. 11, no. 2, October, pp. 175–203. doi:10.1007/s11403-015-0159-3

Biondi, Y & Righi, S 2017, "Much ado about making money: the impact of disclosure, news and rumors over the formation of security market prices over time", *Journal of Economic Interaction and Coordination*, Forthcoming. doi:10.1007/s11403-017-0201-8

Biondi, Y, Giannoccolo, P, & Galam, S 2012, "Formation of share market prices under heterogeneous beliefs and common knowledge", *Physica A: Statistical Mechanics and its Applications*, vol. 391, no. 22, pp. 5532–5545.

Cutler, DM, Poterba, JM, & Summers, LH 1989, "What moves stock prices?", *The Journal of Portfolio Management*, vol. 15, no. 3, pp. 4–12.

Fair, RC 2002, "Events that shook the market", *The Journal of Business*, vol. 75, no. 4, pp. 713–731.

Fama, EF 1991, "Efficient capital markets: II", *The Journal of Finance*, vol. 46, no. 5, pp. 1575–1617.

Fama, EF 1995, "Random walks in stock market prices", *Financial Analysts Journal*, vol. 51, no. 1, pp. 75–80.

Fama, EF 1998, "Market efficiency, long-term returns, and behavioral finance", *Journal of Financial Economics*, vol. 49, no. 3, pp. 283–306.

Grossman, SJ & Stiglitz, JE 1980, "On the impossibility of informationally efficient markets", *American Economic Review*, vol. 70, no. 3, pp. 393–408.

Hayek, FA 1945, "The use of knowledge in society", *American Economic Review*, vol. 35, no. 4, pp. 519–530.

IASB – International Accounting Standards Board 2010, The Conceptual Framework for Financial Reporting. London.

Kothari, S 2001 "Capital markets research in accounting", *Journal of Accounting and Economics*, vol. 31, pp. 105–231.

Malkiel, BG 2003, "The efficient market hypothesis and its critics", *Journal of Economic Perspectives*, vol. 17, no. 1, Winter, pp. 59–82.

Mantegna, RN & Stanley, HE 2000, *An introduction to econophysics. Correlations and complexity in finance*, Cambridge University Press, Cambridge, UK.

McQueen, G & Roley, VV 1993, "Stock prices, news, and business conditions", *Review of Financial Studies*, vol. 6, no. 3, pp. 683–707.

Samuelson, PA 1965, "Proof that properly anticipated prices fluctuate randomly", *Industrial Management Review*, vol. 6, no. 2, pp. 41–49.

Samuelson, PA 1973, "Proof that properly discounted present values of assets vibrate randomly", *The Bell Journal of Economics and Management Science*, vol. 4, no. 2, pp. 369–374.

Shiller, RJ 2003, "From efficient markets theory to behavioral finance", *Journal of Economic Perspectives*, vol. 17, no. 1, pp. 83–104.

Shubik, M 2007, "Accounting and its relationship to general equilibrium theory", in *The firm as an entity: implications for economics, accounting and the law*, eds Y, Biondi, A, Canziani, & T, Kirat, Routledge, London and New York.

17

FAIR VALUE ACCOUNTING

China experience

Jun Chen and Yong Yu

Introduction

The phenomenal economic growth of China over the past three decades represents one of the greatest economic success stories in modern times. Since initiating its economic reforms in 1979, China has been among the world's fastest-growing economies, with real gross domestic product (GDP) growing about 10% through 2016, and is now the world's largest economy on a purchasing-power parity basis. To accommodate its economic transition, China has been constantly reforming its accounting system, transforming it from the former Soviet Union model designed for a centrally planned economy to the Western accounting model that serves a market economy. This reform culminated in 2006 with China's adoption of International Financial Reporting Standards (IFRS)-based new accounting standards.

Fair value accounting, which originated in mature market-based economies as a tool to provide better information that facilitates arm's length transactions, offers an interesting lens to observe the institutional factors that determine the outcomes of China's accounting reforms. As detailed in the next section, fair value measurement was first introduced into China Accounting Standards (CAS) in 1998, but this early experiment lasted only for about two years and was terminated in 2001 due to the widespread abuse of fair value measurement as a convenient way to manipulate earnings. After being discarded for about six years, fair value accounting was reintroduced into the new IFRS-based CAS in 2006 with a much more extensive use as a measurement basis. Chinese standard-setters have expressed optimism that the implementation of fair value accounting can improve companies' financial reporting quality and provide more useful information to financial statement users for their decision-making.

However, this optimistic view seems to have underestimated the degree of challenge involved in implementing fair value measurement in China's unique institutional environment. Despite the tremendous economic growth and the remarkable progress in moving toward a market-based economy, the market institutions that are critical to the successful implementation of fair value accounting are still weak or lacking in China. China's fundamental political-economic institution, characterized as a 'regionally decentralized authoritative system' by Xu (2011), shares the basic framework with the top-down bureaucracy that prevailed over China's extremely long imperial history. This system centralizes political power in the central government, enabling it to keep control of local bureaucrats, key economic resources, ideology and the media, and, at the same time, decentralizes economic activities in the local governments, allowing them to run the self-contained regional economies and compete with each other for delivering GDP growth. While many view this system as a key factor contributing to China's economic successes, others have been concerned that it may have impeded the establishment of market institutions that are necessary for achieving stable and sustainable economic development over the long run.

China's unique institutional environment has raised serious questions about the comparability with the Western accounting standards such as fair value measurement. Perhaps the most important challenge for fair value accounting in China is the weak incentives or even disincentives of Chinese-listed companies to provide high-quality financial information. It is well recognized that managers' reporting incentives, rather than accounting standards, have a first-order effect on reporting outcomes (e.g. Ball et al. 2000, 2003; Burgstahler et al. 2006). However, the government's close control of economic resources and business activities and the lack of the rule of law have substantially reduced demand for high-quality financial information and thereby managers' incentives to provide such information (Piotroski & Wong 2012). Further, given the underdeveloped capital markets, meaningful market prices are rarely available for assets and liabilities, affording managers much discretion in making fair value estimates. This discretion, coupled with the lack of effective monitoring and managers' and controlling shareholders' strong incentives to manipulate earnings, is likely to result in considerable measurement error in fair value estimates. Therefore, the apparent incompatibility between China's institutional environments and fair value measurement has cast serious doubt on the quality of fair value numbers provided by Chinese-listed companies.

This doubt appears to be supported by the findings from existing studies that we review in this chapter.[1] Overall, these studies provide preliminary evidence that fair values provided by Chinese-listed companies provide little value-relevant information to equity investors, reduce the usefulness of earnings for compensation contracting with company executives and provide opportunities and incentives for managers to manipulate financial reports. However, we note that the existing evidence is far from conclusive, and substantially more research is needed to draw any definite inferences about the role of fair value measurement in China. Further, a number of potentially interesting questions related to fair value accounting in China have been unexplored.

The next section discusses the evolution of fair value measurement in CAS. The following section, 'Fair Value Accounting and China's Institutional Environment', highlights the key challenges posed by China's unique institutional environment for financial reporting in general and fair value measurement in particular. Then the section entitled 'Extant Literature on Fair Value Accounting in China' reviews prior studies examining the usefulness of fair values provided by Chinese-listed companies. The final section, 'Conclusion', concludes with some suggestions for future research opportunities that may further our understanding of the role fair value measurement can play in China.

Evolution of fair value measurement in China accounting standards

CAS have been constantly changed by the government to facilitate the transition from a central planned economy to a market economy. Accounting practices prior to the initiation of economic reforms were largely borrowed from the Soviet Union and served the needs of the government to run a centrally planned economy. China's accounting system was drastically reformed in 1992, which marked the starting of adopting a Western accounting system that presumably better serves a market economy. The history of fair value measurement in CAS after the 1992 reform can be roughly divided into four stages: 1992–1997, during which historical cost was the dominant measurement basis; 1998–2000, which witnessed the initial introduction of fair value measurement; 2001–2006, marked by the prohibition of fair value measurement; and 2007–present, when fair value was reintroduced along with the essential adoption of IFRS and became relatively commonly used as a measurement basis, especially, for financial instruments.

The historical cost stage: 1992–1997

China's sweeping economic reforms in state-owned enterprises, taxation and budgeting systems, foreign capital and investment, special economic zones, etc. over the 1980s resulted in fundamental shifts in the economic structure of the country. The Shanghai Stock Exchange and Shenzhen Stock Exchange were established in 1990 and 1991, and the China Securities Regulatory Commission (CSRC) was formed in 1992. Not surprisingly, these radical regime changes generated strong demand for a set of accounting standards that could better serve the transitional economy.

In 1992, the Chinese Ministry of Finance initiated China's first accounting standards – *The Accounting Standards for Business Enterprises* (ASBE). This set of standards was largely based on the Western accounting model and resulted in a fundamental change in companies' reporting practices. The standards were further expanded to include 13 industry-specific accounting rules. The standards mandated that all assets and liabilities be measured on the historical cost basis. The dominance of historical cost measurement was in line with Chinese standard-setters' goal for financial reporting during this early stage of China's transition. In this stage, state-owned enterprises (SOEs) controlled by the government comprised virtually the whole economy, and capital markets just started to emerge and develop. The accounting standards were thus shaped more by the need for financial reports to facilitate capital preservation. The overall goal of financial reporting was mainly to enhance accountability and stewardship rather than provide useful information to outside investors for valuation purposes (Allen et al. 2005).

The initial introduction stage: 1998–2000

With the rapid economic growth and the fast development of capital markets in the 1990s, the historical cost-based accounting systems were increasingly criticized for failing to provide relevant information on companies' performance and financial conditions. For example, it was well recognized that companies' balance sheets contained countless uncollectible receivables and overvalued assets while omitting large amounts of unrealized investment gains. Meanwhile, the rapid emergence of new financial instruments amplified the weakness of historical costs in providing timely information on the value of these instruments. The theoretical advantages of fair value accounting in incorporating relevant information in a timely manner began to draw attention and gain support from various parties (Lu 2006). Many scholars in China started to propose that fair value could potentially provide an alternative, better measurement basis for assets and liabilities. Moreover, the adoption of fair value measurement by the international community over this time period also helped Chinese standard-setters realize potential benefits of fair value measurement.

In 1998, fair value measurement was introduced into CAS on debt restructuring, and then investment and non-monetary transactions, with fair value defined as the price for which an asset could be exchanged or a liability could be settled between willing parties in an arm's length transaction. The standards on debt restructurings and investments require all transactions involving non-monetary assets to be measured at fair value with the difference between fair value and book value recognized as part of current income. The standards on non-monetary transactions further differentiate between exchanges among similar versus different types of non-monetary assets. For the former, assets received should be recognized using the book value of assets surrendered, but if the fair value of assets surrendered is lower than the book value, then the fair value should be used to recognize assets received and the difference between the fair value and book value of assets surrendered should be recognized as losses for the current period. For the latter, assets received should be recognized using its own fair value and the difference between the book value of assets received and the book value of assets surrendered should be recognized as gains or losses for the current period. However, if the fair value of assets received cannot be reliably determined, assets received should be recognized using the fair value of assets surrendered and the difference between the fair value and the book value of assets surrendered should be recognized as gains or losses for the current period. If neither assets received nor assets surrendered can be reliably fair valued, assets received should be recognized using the book value of assets surrendered with no gain or loss recorded.

This initial application of fair value measurement, however, did not achieve the objective of improving the transparency of financial reporting. Rather, fair value measurement required by the new standards was found to be commonly used by management and controlling shareholders of Chinese-listed companies as a convenient tool to manipulate earnings via profit-increasing asset reclassification or revaluation (e.g. Peng & Bewley 2010). Further, standard-setters' intended benefits of fair value measurement were not observed in data. Tests of the relation between accounting numbers and stock prices by Eccher and Healy (2000) reveal evidence consistent with the prior standards based solely on historical costs actually providing more value-relevant information to equity investors than the new standards incorporating fair value measurement (see also Lin & Chen 2005). The mounting evidence on fair value-related manipulations eventually prompted Chinese standard-setters to reevaluate the desirability of adopting fair value accounting in China and led to their decision to essentially prohibit fair value measurement only two years after the initial introduction.

The prohibition stage: 2001–2006

In January 2001, the Chinese Ministry of Finance revised CAS on debt restructurings, non-monetary transactions and investments, largely discarding the use of fair value measurement and switching back to historical cost conventions. For example, the revised standards on investments eliminate fair value measurement and require companies to use the book value of non-monetary assets to recognize the initial investment on balance sheets. The revised standards on non-monetary transactions also no longer distinguish between exchanges among similar versus different types of assets and mandate the use of book value as the measurement basis.

It is worth noting that although Chinese standard-setters largely prohibited fair value measurement during this period, they did not throw it out completely. The revised standards on debt restructuring and non-monetary transactions still retain the definition of fair value and some limited applications of fair value measurement (though associated fair value changes are not allowed to go into current income). Additionally, tax codes continue to use fair value measurement. For example, Order No. 6 Article 4 of the State Administration of Taxation stipulates that when the debtor use non-monetary assets to pay off debt, unless mandated otherwise by corporate restructuring or liquidation rules, the tax base should be determined partially by the fair value of the non-monetary assets and the difference between the fair value and the book value should be recognized as gains or losses for tax purposes.

The discarding of fair value measurement, however, did not significantly reduce earnings manipulation by Chinese-listed companies, which were found to continue to cook their books through a variety of other ways. This observation helped standard-setters and scholars to realize that the fundamental driver for earnings manipulation by Chinese-listed companies may not be fair value measurement or some other accounting treatments, but the institutional environment in China. As such, the prohibition of fair value measurement wouldn't curb manipulation, but reduced the comparability of Chinese-listed companies' financial reports with their foreign peers' and increased transaction costs of conducting international trades.

With this recognition built over time and the further development of economic cooperation and exchange with foreign countries, fair value accounting was gradually viewed as a necessary step to attract foreign investments, promote domestic companies in foreign markets, and lower transactions costs. The demand for fair value measurement became especially pronounced when China committed to opening its domestic accounting market as part of the terms of joining the WTO in 2001 and when the existing accounting standards apparently hindered the improvement of China's international status (e.g. lack of fair value accounting was one stated reason for the European Union to deny China's market economy status in 2004). Thus, it is not surprising for Chinese standard-setters to bring back and expand fair value measurement in its new, IFRS-based accounting standards.

The IFRS stage: 2007 to present

In February 2006, Chinese Ministry of Finance issued new CAS that essentially adopted IFRS, which became effective for all listed companies on the Shanghai and Shenzhen stock exchanges at the beginning of 2007. One of the most important changes brought by the new CAS is the expanded use of fair value measurement for balance sheet items and the recognition of fair value changes in income. Eight out of the 15 major changes mandated by the switch to IFRS are fair value accounting related (Deloitte Touche Tohmatsu 2006), and 25 out of the 38 standards mandate or allow for the use of fair value measurement (Peng & Bewley 2010). To date, the direct or indirect use of fair value measurement is required by 17 out of 41 issued standards (41%), especially CAS 22 (Financial Instruments Recognition and Measurement), which requires the initial recognition of financial assets and liabilities to be based on fair value, CAS 23 (Transfer of financial assets), which requires the realized fair value gains or losses of financial assets to be recognized as current income, and CAS 37 (Financial Instrument), which explicitly requires a table presentation of fair value changes and disclosure of certain related information.

The promulgation of the CAS, especially the reintroduction of fair value measurement with more extensive use, marked a significant progress in converging CAS with IFRS. However, in terms of fair value measurement, some differences remain between CAS and IFRS. For example, IFRS 9 requires the recognition of fair value changes for financial liabilities arising from a company's own credit risk changes in other comprehensive income, while CAS 37 recognizes these fair value changes in current period's income. Similarly, for available-for-sale (AFS) securities, IFRS 9 requires fair value measurement with fair value changes recognized in other comprehensive income, but CAS 37 allows for the recognition of fair value changes in earnings. As another example, differing from IFRS, CAS stipulate that 'historical cost be used generally for measuring accounting items' (ASBE: Basic Standard, Article 43) and fair value be used as the measurement basis for specified assets such as real estate investments and non-monetary asset exchanges under appropriate economic and market conditions.

The definition of fair value was also revised in 2014. In ASBE No. 39 – Measurement of Fair Value, fair value is re-defined as the price that would be received to sell an asset or paid to transfer a liability in an orderly transaction between market participants at the measurement date. Compared to the prior definition, the new definition reflects several notable changes. First, it clarifies the nature of the transaction and the market participants. Compared to 'an arm's length transaction' in the previous definition, the term 'an orderly transaction' is more specific, stressing common or usual market transactions rather than forced transactions such as liquidation or fire sales. The term 'market participants' also puts more emphasis on market factors in that the transaction should be conducted between market players with appropriate conditions. The highlight of the market condition is consistent with Chinese standard-setters' goal of improving the transparency and quality of fair value measurement in China. Second, the new definition explicitly uses exit prices to define fair value, whereas the previous definition does not clearly define the price for which an asset is exchanged or a liability is settled. Third, the new definition makes it clear that fair value should reflect the market conditions at the measurement date rather than past or future trading conditions. Overall, the new definition of fair value is clearer and more practicable, and generally consistent with that of the Financial Accounting Standard Board (FASB) and the International Accounting Standard Board (IASB).

Extant research has found some evidence consistent with the adoption of IFRS-based CAS benefiting at least some Chinese-listed companies. Chen et al. (2017) document evidence that equity investors perceived the adoption of the IFRS-based CAS to be beneficial for certain Chinese-listed companies, with the benefit depending on the companies' reporting incentives. Following the approach of Armstrong et al. (2010) and Chen et al. (2017) examine market reactions around seven events that indicated an increased possibility of adopting IFRS in China. Their test sample includes Chinese-listed companies issuing only A-shares (shares in Renminbi issued primarily for domestic investors), which reported under old CAS prior to the adoption and switched to the new IFRS-based CAS afterward. Their control sample includes Chinese-listed companies issuing both A-shares and B-shares (shares in US dollars or Hong Kong dollars issued primarily for foreign investors), which already reported under IFRS prior to the adoption and thus was presumably not affected by the adoption. They find a positive reaction to the events for the test sample relative to the control sample. However, this positive reaction was not evenly distributed, but was more pronounced among companies that were not state-owned (non-SOEs), which generally rely more on external funds from investors, than SOEs, which tend to have privileged access to funds and resources from the state.

Liu et al. (2011) examine changes in value relevance and earnings management of accounting numbers for a sample of 870 Chinese-listed firms over 2005–2008 to provide evidence on the effect of IFRS adoption on Chinese firms' reporting quality. They report a decrease in earnings management (measured by earnings smoothing and timely loss recognition) and an increase in value relevance of earnings and book value (measured by both prices and returns models based on Ohlson's (1995) framework) after the adoption. They also find this improvement is smaller for firms audited by large auditors, which they argue should have reported high-quality reports already prior to the adoption and thus experience less improvement. Overall, these findings are consistent with the large body of evidence on IFRS adoption from other countries, emphasizing that simply mandating a better set of standards may not result in any real change in firms' financial reporting and the consequences of IFRS adoption are determined by adopting firms' reporting incentives (e.g. Daske et al. 2008, 2013; Byard et al. 2011; De George et al. 2016; Leuz and Wysocki 2016).

Fair value accounting and China's institutional environment

Accounting practices in China are shaped by its unique institutional environment. Xu (2011) characterizes China's fundamental political-economic institution as a 'regionally decentralized authoritative system' that combines a high degree of both political centralization and economic decentralization. The basic pillars of this system are not new – they originated from the long-lived, top-down imperial bureaucracy that prevailed and evolved over the long history of China. On one hand, political power is highly centralized in this system. The central government delegates power to local (provincial, municipal and county) governments, appoints and removes local bureaucrats, commands key economic sectors like banking and telecommunications, and retain tight control of ideology and the media. The political centralization ensures that the central government can direct and monitor local officials and motivate them to fulfil given tasks and compete with each other to deliver better set performance measures (GDP growth). On the other hand, economic activities are highly decentralized to the local levels. Regions are relatively self-contained in terms of economic and governmental functions. Local officials run the regional economy by controlling and allocating major resources (e.g. local governments essentially own land and most SOEs and influence the allocation of financial and energy resources), providing public services, and implementing reforms, policies, regulations and laws within their jurisdictions. While this top-down bureaucratic institution may facilitate the past economic development, especially in the early stage of the transition from the planned economy, many have expressed concerns that it has contributed to the thorny socioeconomic problems China faces today and has remained perhaps the biggest challenge for establishing market institutions regarded as critical for the stability and sustainability of future development over the long run (Xu 2015).

It has been well recognized in the literature that managers' reporting incentives rather than accounting standards have a first-order effect on reporting outcomes (e.g. Ball et al. 2000, 2003; Burgstahler et al. 2006). Thus, the biggest challenge for financial reporting in general and fair value accounting in particular is that China's regionally decentralized authoritative system weakens and sometimes even distorts reporting incentives of mangers of Chinese-listed companies. More specifically, the government's control of economic resources and business activities and the lack of the rule of law diminish potential financial statement users' demand for high-quality financial information and managers' and controlling shareholders' incentive to provide such information (Piotroski & Wong 2012).

The functioning of the regionally decentralized authoritative system in China requires the government to keep control of economic resources and business activities. One important control mechanism is state ownership of enterprises. Despite China's privatization effort since the 1990s, the majority of companies listed on the two stock exchanges are still SOEs with the controlling shareholder being the central or local governments and the top executives being government bureaucrats rather than professional managers. The state ownership substantially reduces demand for high-quality external reports. SOEs generally have privileged access to bank and equity financing, tax breaks and other government subsidies, diminishing management's incentives to provide high-quality accounting information to external investors to lower the cost of capital. SOEs' government owners also reply more on direct access to management and political networks rather than financial reports to evaluate and monitor management. Further, SOEs typically operate within a large 'family' of state-owned entities controlled by the same government bureau, and the related-party nature of their business transactions within the 'family' diminishes the contracting need for financial reports. Additionally, Piotroski and Wong (2012) argue that domestic investors perceive state ownership as an implicit bailout commitment from the government and thus demand less public information on SOEs' financial conditions.

Beside state ownership, the government also has close control of financial markets and key economic resources such as land and energy. The allocation of these resources is heavily in-fluenced by political forces, and companies' political connections play a key role in obtaining these resources. As an example, the large Chinese banks are all state-owned and they supply virtually all bank loans for Chinese-listed companies. The banks tend to give preferential treatments to SOEs, and their lending decisions are often influenced by government' political agendas and borrowers' political connections rather than borrowers' performance and financial conditions (Fan et al. 2008). Chinese banks also tend to monitor borrowers directly based on information they collect through political networks and other private channels rather than efficient contracts based on financial reports. As a result, creditors have weak demand for fi-nancial reporting quality, and borrowers have little incentive to supply it. Further, this resource allocation system can even motivate managers to deliberately lower the quality of financial reports. One such motivation is to conceal the suboptimal resource allocation based on political connections and the expropriation through related party transactions (Jian & Wong 2010; Jiang et al. 2010). Another motivation is to meet regulatory thresholds that are based on accounting numbers (e.g. Chen & Yuan 2004; Haw et al. 2005). For instance, the equity financing through the two stock exchanges is tightly controlled by the CSRC, which is in charge of selecting firms for listing and share offerings. Given their limited resources, it is virtually impossible for the CSRC to gather and analyze each applying company. As a result, the CSRC relies on bright line rules based on accounting information such as accounting losses or return on equity for the important listing and offering decisions. These rules create powerful incentives for Chinese companies, state controlled and privately owned alike, to manipulate financial reports.

The regionally decentralized authoritative system has also inevitably resulted in the lack of the rule of law and the weak protection of property rights. An independent court system is central to protecting investors' property rights. Yet local and state courts in China are controlled by their respective governments, who are also the owners of SOEs. Therefore, it should surprise no one that the courts will rule in favor of the government and SOEs in disputes involving private parties. Given the high risk of being expropriated by insiders and the ineffective legal protection of minority investors, domestic investors have weak incen-tives to make long-term investment in the listed companies and to monitor management, which in turn lead to low valuation and contracting demand for financial reports. To survive and thrive in this system, private entrepreneurs must build, maintain and expand political connections with government bureaucrats through benefit exchanges or simply bribery and corruption (e.g. Fan et al. 2007; Hung et al. 2015). The political connections further terrify minority investors and deter them from investing in and monitoring the company, contrib-uting to the concentration of ownership in those private companies. Fan and Wong (2002) note that this concentrated ownership structure also benefits the entrepreneurs by facilitat-ing their relationship building activities with the bureaucrats. The concentrated ownership structure and the lack of monitoring by outside investors lower the costs of manipulating financial reports to conceal their expropriation activities.

In sum, China's unique institutional environment substantially lowers managers' reporting incentives to provide high-quality financial reports including fair value information. This problem is perhaps more severe for fair value measurement because of the lack of well-functioning capital markets in China. Market prices for identical and similar assets and liabilities arguably provide the most reliable inputs into fair value estimates. The lack of liquid markets and the prevalence of related party transactions in China mean that more of fair values must be estimated by managers using unverifiable assumptions and models. This mark-to-model or market-to-myth measurement increases the inherent difficulty of estimating fair values, and perhaps more importantly, interacts with management's strong earnings manipulation incentives to render the resulting fair value estimates lower quality or even misleading.

Extant literature on fair value accounting in China

Extant literature on fair value accounting in China has largely focused on examining the valuation and contracting usefulness of fair values provided by Chinese-listed companies and managerial manipulation of earnings through fair value estimates. Some other studies have also touched upon the effects of fair value measurement on auditors and management's voluntary disclosures. We discuss them in detail below.

Valuation usefulness of fair values

One primary goal of adopting fair value accounting in China is to provide equity investors more transparent information for valuating a company. Yet existing studies examining the value relevance of fair values have provided little evidence in support of the valuation usefulness of fair values from Chinese-listed companies.

Early studies compare value relevance of financial reports under CAS versus international accounting standards (IAS) in the pre-IFRS-adoption regime. While these studies do not directly examine fair values, they shed light on the valuation usefulness of fair values in that fair value measurement constitutes a significant difference between CAS and IAS prior to the convergence in 2007. Eccher and Healy (2000) examine a sample of 83 Chinese companies listing both A-shares and B-shares over the period of 1992–1997. Prior to 1998, Chinese companies were allowed to list multiple classes of shares, and reporting standards varied with the share class listed, with firms listing A (B) shares providing reports under CAS (IAS). Thus, the companies listing both A- and B-shares provide an opportunity to observe the accounting numbers prepared under CAS and IAS by the same companies. Eccher and Healy (2000) find no difference in the ability of accounting accruals reported under CAS versus IAS to explain future cash flows. They further find that CAS and IAS earnings have a similar association with stock returns for B shares (issued for international investors), but CAS earnings have a higher association with stock returns for A shares (issued for domestic investors). They argue that the result from A share returns can be driven by language barrier for domestic investors or their fixation on CAS earnings, while the result from the predictive value of accruals and the association with B share returns can be due to the lack of institutions that can effectively enforce accounting standards and monitor managers' reporting practices. Lin and Chen (2005) conduct a similar comparison using a sample over 1995–2000, and report that CAS earnings and book value provide more value-relevant information for valuing A-shares and B-shares. They do not examine the underlying drivers for the failure of IAS reports to provide more value-relevant information to equity investors.

In a more recent study, Qu and Zhang (2015) examine the value relevance of fair values under the new, IFRS-based CAS. Following Collins et al. (1997), they use the Ohlson (1995) model and use the explanatory power of earnings and book value for stock prices to gauge value relevance of financial reports. They first compare the change in the value relevance from the pre-adoption (2001–2006) window to the post-adoption window (2007–2010). They focus on 58 Chinese-listed companies from four sectors (financial, real estate, mining and farming-forestry-fishery) that they argue are most likely to measure assets and liabilities based on fair value. They manually collect fair value adjustment data and classify these firms into 43 FV-applied companies (defined as firms that used fair value measurement) and 15 non-FV-applied companies. They find no improvement in the value relevance of financial reports, combined or on a separate basis, for the FV-applied companies relative to the non-FV-applied companies. Rather, they find a relative decrease in the value relevance in some specifications for the FV-applied companies. Further, they examine whether fair value adjustments (for trading, AFS and held-to-maturity securities) in these industries are incrementally value relevant by testing their relation with stock prices after controlling for pre-adjustment book value and earnings. They find no evidence that these fair value adjustments convey incremental information to equity investors. The authors allude to China's lack of well-developed market mechanisms as well as qualified accounting professionals as reasons why fair values do not seem to provide value-relevant information to equity investors.

Contracting usefulness of fair values

Another primary goal of financial reporting is to provide useful information that facilitates contracting (e.g. Watts & Zimmerman 1986; Bushman et al. 2006; Kothari et al. 2010). Public equities and bonds account for a relatively small component of corporate financing in China, while bank loans remain a dominant financing source for Chinese companies. As such, understanding the role of fair values in debt contracts is particularly important. Further, given the weak investor protection in China, compensation contacts have been viewed by some scholars as a potential way to align managers' interests with shareholders (e.g. Ke et al. 2012; Chen et al. 2013). Given the use of accounting performance measures in these contracts, fair values can possibly enhance the efficiency of the contracts.

Shao et al. (2012) examine the relation between recognized fair value gains and losses and cash compensation of executives (the Chairman of the board, CEO and CFO) for 1,148 firm-years from Chinese-listed companies. They find an overall positive relation between the two, consistent with fair values providing useful inputs into executive compensation contracts. They further find that the sensitivity of cash compensation to fair value changes is asymmetric: fair value gains have a bigger effect in increasing compensation but fair value losses have a smaller effect in reducing compensation. The authors hypothesize that the asymmetric sensitivity can result from managers' opportunistic use of fair value changes to extract higher pay rather than any efficient contract design. Consistent with this hypothesis, the authors find that the asymmetric sensitivity to fair value gains versus losses increases with their measures of managerial power.

Ke et al. (2016) examine changes in managerial pay-for-performance sensitivity for SOEs around the adoption of the new IFRS-based standards in 2007. A key design feature of their study is to differentiate between central-government-controlled and local-government-controlled SOEs. They predict and find that central-government-controlled SOEs are more likely to link CEOs' pay to performance because they have a relatively stronger incentive to maximize shareholder value. Using local-government-controlled SOEs as a control group, they document a decrease in pay-for-performance sensitivity for central-government-controlled SOEs after the adoption of the new standards. Further, using the presence of fair value gains or losses from trading and AFS securities to identify firms with more reliance on fair value accounting, they find that the decrease in the pay-for-performance sensitivity is more pronounced for firms relying more on fair value measurement. Overall, their results are consistent with the adoption of the new standards reducing the usefulness of earnings for executive compensation contracts, at least partly due to the expanded use of fair value measurement in the new standards.

Ball et al. (2015) contend that fair values can reduce the value of accounting numbers in debt contacts because fair value gains and losses are transitory and will likely reverse before debt maturity and they do not capture the amount of the principal and interest borrowers have to pay. Given the heavy reliance of Chinese-listed companies on bank loans and the unique ownership structure of SOEs, it seems important to understand whether and how fair values influence the use of accounting numbers in debt contracts between Chinese-listed companies, SOEs and non-SOEs, and state-controlled banks. However, we are unaware of any prior study directly examining the role of fair values in debt contracts in China. The closest study is perhaps Yuan et al. (2013), who find that the relation between the amount of new debt and accounting profitability decreases after China's adoption of IFRS-based new standards in 2007. They interpret this result as evidence consistent with fair value accounting reducing the usefulness of earnings for debt contracts. However, they do not directly link the change in the debt-profitability relation to fair value gains or losses, so it is difficult to attribute the pre- and post-adoption change they document to fair value accounting per se.

Fair value accounting and earnings manipulation

Fair value measurement affords managers considerable discretion. This discretion is even greater for Chinese-listed companies, because of the lack of liquid markets for identical or comparable assets and the weak internal and external monitoring of managers. Therefore, China provides a particularly powerful setting to examine managers' earnings manipulation through fair value estimates, which can be a potential explanation for the findings of fair values conveying little useful information for either valuation or contracting purposes.

He et al. (2012) study unintended consequences of China's adoption of IFRS-based CAS in 2007, focusing on the implementation of new fair value accounting rules for trading securities and debt restructuring. In contrast to the lower of cost or market rule under the old standards, the new CAS require that trading securities be measured at fair value and fair value changes included in income, with the intention to enhance the transparency on these trading securities. However, examining 786 firm-years from Chinese-listed companies over 2007–2008 that reported fair value changes in trading securities, He et al. (2012) find that companies with negative fair value changes in trading securities are more likely to offset this fair value loss by selectively selling AFS securities for a gain, and this strategic selling behavior is more pronounced among firms with stronger incentives to avoid reporting losses.

Further, the new CAS require firms to recognize the value of exchanged nonfinancial assets during debt restructurings at fair value (rather than at book value under the old CAS) with the gains included in income. He et al. (2012) argue that because the market prices for those nonfinancial assets are generally unavailable and the debtors and creditors are often related parties, the fair value accounting for debt restructurings under the new CAS provide more opportunities for manipulating earnings. To test this expectation, the authors examine 423 firm-years over 2007–2008 that reported gains from debt restructurings. They find that abnormal gains from debt restructuring increase systematically with the strength of managers' loss-avoidance incentives. Additionally, they also find that the estimated manipulation also varies with the regional institutional environment and firm-level corporate governance in a predicted manner. Overall, they conclude that fair value accounting may not provide intended benefits in China, where the reliance of government regulations, the lack of active markets and the prevalence of related party transactions provide managers incentives and opportunities to abuse fair value accounting to manipulate earnings.

Yang et al. (2017) provide survey evidence on practitioners' views on the usefulness of fair value versus historical cost measurement in China and the challenges for implementing fair value measurement in the process of accounting convergence. They gained access to senior financial managers of 45 Chinese-listed companies located in one province through personal networks and received survey responses from 33 firms. Regarding historical cost versus fair value accounting as the measurement basis, surveyed managers expressed clear preferences for historical cost, as evidenced by their general agreement that 'all assets and liabilities should be reported at historical cost, with fair value information presented in the notes'. Regarding potential benefits of fair value accounting for financial reporting, surveyed managers generally agree that the implementation of fair value accounting increased the financial statement comparability between Chinese and international companies, but disagree that fair value accounting has resulted in an improvement in either transparency or credibility of Chinese companies' financial reports. Further, echoing He et al.'s (2012) findings, surveyed managers believe that the implementation of fair value accounting has led to unintended opportunistic earnings management behaviors, with 24 out of 33 agreeing that 'fair value accounting provides Chinese companies with more opportunities than historical cost accounting for earnings management'.

Other studies related to fair values

Several studies argue that fair value measurement mandated by the new IFRS-based CAS can change auditors' risk assessment and thereby audit fees they charge clients. However, none of these studies provide direct evidence in support of this argument. Specifically, Zhu and Sun (2012) argue that fair values can convey useful information to auditors on client firms' market risk – the potential impacts of changes in market prices of assets on the client firms' operations – and this market risk information can increase auditors' assessment of the expected audit risk and thereby the fees they charge. They find that the 2007 adoption of the IFRS-based CAS is associated with an increase in audit fees for a sample of 802 non-financial Chinese-listed companies. Habib (2015) argues that the lack of liquid markets and the greater managerial discretion combine to increase the difficulty auditors face with regard to managers' fair value estimates, and as a result, auditors have to spend more time in completing their audit work. Consistent with this expectation, he finds an increase in the audit report lag (the period between the fiscal year-end and the audit report date) among Chinese-listed companies after the 2007 adoption of the IFRS-based CAS. However, it is important to note that neither Zhu and Sun (2012) nor Habib (2015) directly link the observed changes around the adoption (audit fees or audit report lag) to the application of fair value accounting. Thus, given the numerous other changes brought by the adoption, their results cannot be definitely attributed to fair value accounting per se.

Li and Luo (2016) examine the relation between fair value accounting and corporate disclosures as captured by the frequency of management forecasts. They argue that fair value measurement can increase management forecast frequency because (1) fair value accounting increases information asymmetry, so managers have incentives to issue more forecasts to mitigate this adverse effect and (2) the regulation in China requires firms to provide forecasts prior to announcements of large changes in earnings or losses, so fair value accounting increases earnings volatility and thereby the likelihood that managers need to release forecasts prior to announcements. Consistent with their expectation, they find an increase in management forecast frequency around the adoption of the IFRS-based CAS. However, like the aforementioned studies on fair value accounting and auditor behaviors, the adoption includes numerous other accounting standard changes and occurred with other economic shocks, so it is unclear whether we can attribute this forecast frequency increase to the fair value-related components of the adoption only.

Conclusion

This chapter reviews the extant literature on fair value accounting in China. We first provide a discussion of the evolution of fair value measurement in China. This discussion highlights that the increasing demand for fair value accounting arises from China's continuing transition toward a market economy and development of capital markets. We then highlight the challenges China's unique institutional environment poses for implementing fair value measurement, focusing on the effect of China's 'regionally decentralized authoritative system' on weakening or even distorting managers' reporting incentives. We note that the lack of active markets has also exacerbated the difficulty of applying fair value accounting in China and given managers more opportunities to abuse fair value estimates. We next review the extant studies on fair value accounting in China, which have largely focused on the usefulness of fair values provided by Chinese-listed companies for valuation and contracting purposes and managers' manipulation of earning through fair value estimates. Overall, these studies have provided some preliminary evidence that fair values provided by Chinese-listed companies convey little useful information for equity valuation or for compensation contracting with company executives and that fair value estimates are used by managers to manipulate earnings to extract rents. These findings are obviously at odds with Chinese standard-setters' intended benefits for adopting fair value accounting, but consistent with the concern on the incompatibility between fair value accounting and China's institutional environment.

However, we stress that the extant evidence is preliminary and much more research should be conducted before we can draw any meaningful conclusions on the role of fair value accounting in China. First, future research can expand the type of fair value estimates examined. We note that the extant research has largely focused on securities. Future research can examine fair values of other financial instruments or non-financial assets. In this regard, we note that financial firms can provide a particularly powerful setting. Since financial instruments constitute a large portion of financial firms' balance sheets, such firms provide a unique setting to test both the incremental value relevance of various types of financial instruments simultaneously and the relative value relevance of fair value-based versus historical cost-based financial reports (especially balance sheets). In addition, with the rapid development of insurance and secures industries and the accelerated emergency of new financial instruments in China, studies examining fair values from such industries can have timely and important implications for regulators and investors.

Second, future research can expand the scope of research questions examined. Extant research has largely focused on the usefulness of fair values for valuation and compensation contracting. As discussed above, there is little research on the role of fair values in debt contracting. This omission seems surprising given that bank loans are the primary funds for Chinese companies. For example, future research can examine whether and how debt contracts from state-owned and non-state-owned financial institutions incorporate or adjust for fair value information from borrowers. Future research can also examine the use of fair value accounting by various groups of market participants such as sell-side analysts and institutional investors. Do they react to fair values? If fair value estimates reflect managerial manipulation, do they see through the manipulation and gain an information advantage over individual investors? Along this line, it also seems interesting to examine how the government responds to fair values provided by SOEs and private enterprises. For instance, when local governments or tax authorities evaluate the performance of a company, how do they use fair value gains or losses? More specifically, do they make any adjustments to the company reported numbers, especially when these numbers are manipulated? Do their treatments of fair value information vary between SOEs they control and other non-SOEs?

Third, future research can go deeper to examine how managerial incentives to manipulate earnings and governance mechanisms influence the quality of fair value estimates. The extant research has focused on the loss-avoidance incentives arising from the regulations based on accounting profits. Future research can explore the incentives arising from their ownership structure, share listings, related party transactions, executives' career concerns, political connections, product market competition, etc. Take ownership structure as an example. Will ownership by private parties such as foreign investors mitigate the abuse of fair value estimates? If so, through what mechanisms? Along this line, will cross-listing shares in a foreign country with stronger investor protection discipline managers' fair value estimates? More broadly, do new corporate governance mechanisms recently adopted by increasing numbers of Chinese-listed companies have any impact on the quality of fair values? Overall, we believe that fair value accounting in China continues to provide a fruitful setting that researchers can explore to increase our understanding how financial reporting is shaped by unique institutional factors of a major economy of the world.

Note

1   This review focuses primarily on the papers published on US journals. Papers published on Chinese journals are generally not included. See Lu (2006) for a review of the studies on Chinese Journals.

References

Allen, F, Qian, J & Qian, M 2005, "Law, finance, and economic growth in China", *Journal of financial economics*, vol. 77, no. 1, pp. 57–116.

Armstrong, CS, Barth, ME, Jagolinzer, AD & Riedl, EJ 2010, "Market reaction to the adoption of IFRS in Europe", *The Accounting Review*, vol. 85, no. 1, pp. 31–61.

Ball, R, Kothari, SP & Robin, A 2000, "The effect of international institutional factors on properties of accounting earnings", *Journal of Accounting & Economics*, vol. 29, pp. 1–51.

Ball, R, Robin, A & Wu, JS 2003, "Incentives versus standards: properties of accounting income in four east Asian countries", *Journal of Accounting & Economics*, vol. 36, no. 1–3, pp. 235–270.

Ball, R, Li, X & Shivakumar, L 2015, "Contractibility and transparency of financial statement information prepared under IFRS: evidence from debt contracts around IFRS adoption", *Journal of Accounting Research*, vol. 53, no. 5, pp. 915–963.

Burgstahler, D, Hail, L & Leuz, C 2006, "The importance of reporting incentives: earnings management in European private and public firms", *The Accounting Review*, vol. 81, no. 5, pp. 983–1016.

Bushman, R, Engel, E & Smith, A 2006, "An analysis of the relation between the stewardship and valuation roles of earnings", *Journal of Accounting Research*, vol. 44, no. 1, pp. 53–83.

Byard, D, Li, Y & Yu, Y 2011, "The effect of mandatory IFRS adoption on financial analysts' information environment", *Journal of Accounting Research*, vol. 49, pp. 69–96.

Chen, KC & Yuan, H 2004, "Earnings management and capital resource allocation: evidence from China's accounting-based regulation of rights issues", *The Accounting Review*, vol. 79, no. 3, pp. 645–665.

Chen, Z, Guan, Y & Ke, B 2013, "Are stock option grants to directors of state-controlled Chinese firms listed in Hong Kong genuine compensation?", *The Accounting Review*, vol. 88, no. 5, pp. 1547–1574.

Chen, C, Lee, E, Lobo, G & Zhu, J 2017, "Who benefits from IFRS convergence in China?", *Journal of Accounting, Auditing & Finance*, forthcoming.

Collins, D, Maydew, E & Weiss, I 1997, "Changes in the value-relevance of earnings and book values over the past forty years", *Journal of Accounting & Economics*, vol. 24, pp. 39–67.

Daske, H, Hail, L, Leuz, C & Verdi, R 2008, "Mandatory IFRS reporting around the world: early evidence on the economic consequences", *Journal of Accounting Research*, vol. 46, pp. 1085–1142.

Daske, H, Hail, L, Leuz, C & Verdi, R 2013, "Adopting a label: heterogeneity in the economic consequences around IAS/IFRS adoptions", *Journal of Accounting Research*, vol. 51, pp. 495–547.

De George, E, Li, X & Shivakumar, L 2016, "A review of the IFRS adoption literature", *Review of Accounting Studies*, vol. 21, pp. 898–1004.

Deloitte Touche Tohmatsu 2006, China's new accounting standards: a comparison with current PRC GAAP and IFRS. Available from: www.iasplus.com/en/publications/china/other/pub1136 (accessed on March 18, 2018).

Eccher, E & Healy, P 2000, The role of international accounting standards in transitional economies: a study of the People's Republic of China. *Working paper.*

Fan, J & Wong, TJ 2002, "Corporate ownership structure and the informativeness of accounting earnings in East Asia", *Journal of Accounting and Economics*, vol. 33, no. 3, pp. 401–425.

Fan, J, Wong, TJ & Zhang, T 2007, "Politically connected CEOs, corporate governance, and Post-IPO performance of China's newly partially privatized firms", *Journal of Financial Economics*, vol. 84, no. 2, pp. 330–357.

Fan, J, Rui, M & Zhao, M 2008, "Public governance and corporate finance: evidence from corruption cases", *Journal of Comparative Economics*, vol. 36, no. 3, pp. 343–364.

Habib, A 2015, "The new Chinese accounting standards and audit report lag", *International Journal of Auditing*, vol. 19, no. 1, pp. 1–14.

Haw, I, Qi, D, Wu, D & Wu, W 2005, "Market consequences of earnings management in response to security regulations in China", *Contemporary Accounting Research*, vol. 22, no. 1, pp. 95–140.

He, X, Wong, TJ & Young, D 2012, Challenges for implementation of fair value accounting in emerging markets: evidence from China", *Contemporary Accounting Research*, vol. 29, no. 2, pp. 538–562.

Hung, M, Wong, TJ & Zhang, F 2015, "The value of political ties versus market credibility: evidence from corporate scandals in China", *Contemporary Accounting Research*, vol. 32, no. 4, pp. 1641–1675.

Jian, M & Wong, TJ 2010, "Propping through related party transactions", *Review of Accounting Studies*, vol. 15, no. 1, pp. 70–105.

Jiang, G, Lee, CM & Yue, H 2010, "Tunneling through intercorporate loans: the China experience", *Journal of Financial Economics*, vol. 98, no. 1, pp. 1–20.

Ke, B, Rui, O & Yu, W 2012, "Hong Kong stock listing and the sensitivity of managerial compensation to firm performance in state-controlled Chinese firms", *Review of Accounting Studies*, vol. 17, no. 1, pp. 166–188.

Ke, B, Li, Y & Yuan, H 2016, "The substantial convergence of Chinese accounting standards with IFRS and the managerial pay-for-accounting performance sensitivity of publicly listed Chinese firms", *Journal of Accounting and Public Policy*, vol. 35, no. 6, pp. 567–591.

Kothari, SP, Ramanna, K & Skinner, D 2010, "Implications for GAAP from an analysis of positive research in accounting", *Journal of Accounting and Economics*, vol. 50, no. 2, pp. 246–286.

Leuz, C & Wysocki, P 2016, "The economics of disclosure and financial reporting regulation: evidence and suggestions for future research", *Journal of Accounting Research*, vol. 54, no. 2, pp. 525–621.

Li, X & Luo, T 2016, "The impact of fair value accounting on corporate disclosure", *China Accounting and Finance Review*, vol. 18, no. 4, pp. 36–74.

Lin, ZJ & Chen, F 2005, "Value relevance of international accounting standards harmonization: evidence from A- and B-share markets in China", *Journal of International Accounting, Auditing and Taxation*, vol. 14, no. 2, pp. 79–103.

Liu, C, Yao, L, Hu, N & Liu, L 2011, "The impact of IFRS on accounting quality in a regulated market: an empirical study of China", *Journal of Accounting, Auditing & Finance*, vol. 26, no. 4, pp. 659–676.

Lu, X 2006, "A review of the international application and empirical research on fair value accounting", *Accounting Research* (In Chinese), vol. 4, pp. 81–85.

Ohlson, J 1995, "Earnings, book values, and dividends in security valuation", *Contemporary Accounting Research*, vol. 11, pp. 661–688.

Peng, S & Bewley, K 2010, "Adaptability to fair value accounting in an emerging economy: a case study of China's IFRS convergence", *Accounting, Auditing & Accountability Journal*, vol. 23, pp. 982–1011.

Piotroski, J & Wong, TJ 2012, "Institutions and information environment of Chinese listed firms" in *Capitalizing China*, eds, Joseph Fan and Randall Morck. University of Chicago Press, Chicago, IL, pp. 201–248.

Qu, X & Zhang, G 2015, "Value-relevance of earnings and book value over the institutional transition in China: the suitability of fair value accounting in this emerging market", *International Journal of Accounting*, vol. 50, pp. 195–223.

Shao, R, Chen, C & Mao, X 2012, "Profits and losses from changes in fair value, executive cash compensation and managerial power: evidence from A-share listed companies in China", *China Journal of Accounting Research*, vol. 5, no. 4, pp. 269–292.

Watts, RL & Zimmerman, JL 1986, *Positive accounting theory.* Prentice-Hall, Englewood Cliffs, NJ.

Xu, C 2011, "The fundamental institutions of China's reforms and development", *Journal of Economic Literature*, vol. 49, no. 4, pp. 1076–1151.

Xu, C 2015, "China's political-economic institutions and development", *Cato Journal*, vol. 35, no. 3, pp. 525–548.

Yang, H, Clark, C, Wu, C & Farley, A 2017, "Insights from accounting practitioners on China's convergence with IFRS", *Australian Accounting Review*, forthcoming.

Yuan, H, Li, Y, Lou, F & Zhang, Y 2013, "New Chinese accounting standards and the usefulness of accounting information in debt contracts", *China Accounting and Finance Review*, vol. 15, no. 1, pp. 85–144.

Zhu, K & Sun, H 2012, "The reform of accounting standards and audit pricing", *China Journal of Accounting Research*, vol. 5, no. 2, pp. 187–198.

18

FAIR VALUE ACCOUNTING AND FAMILY FIRMS

Pietro Mazzola and Massimo De Buglio

Introduction

Extant research offers two different insights on the pros and cons of fair value accounting (e.g. Barth 1994; Landsman 2007; Barth & Landsman 2010; Laux & Leuz 2010). While fair value accounting can provide useful and relevant information to current and potential equity holders, it also leaves some level of managerial discretion that may be detrimental to information reporting quality. These findings call for more fine-grained research to understand whether and to what extent firm and market characteristics can directly affect fair value accounting or moderate the relationship between fair value accounting and financial reporting quality.

The purpose of this chapter is to provide some insights on the possible impact of family firm status on the use of fair value accounting and on its measurement reliability. We believe that exploring fair value accounting use and reliability in the context of family firms is an internationally relevant topic for several reasons.

Family firms are the dominant form of organization across the globe, in emerging as well as in established economies (Bertrand & Schoar 2006). Although there is still some debate surrounding the appropriate definition of family firms, they still represent a majority, even when a rather narrow definition is used.

Accounting studies have only recently started investigating the accounting and reporting behaviors of family firms. Overall, they argue and find that not only the level of ownership concentration or insider ownership, but also the nature of the dominant shareholder influence accounting practices, thus suggesting significant differences in the accounting practices of family firms compared to non-family firms (e.g. Wang 2006; Ali et al. 2007; Chen et al. 2008; Salvato & Moores 2010; Prencipe et al. 2014; etc.). The majority of existing studies explore the effect of family firm status on financial accounting and reporting issues. In particular, these studies examine whether family firms are more or less prone to accruals and real earnings management than non-family firms, and whether family owners and managers prefer less or more public disclosure than non-family firms.

Overall, these studies provide evidence consistent with two competing views: the first posits higher earnings quality reported by family firms, while the second predicts lower quality. On the one hand, some scholars emphasize the tendency of family owners to use their power to divert firm resources to pursue non-economic goals, even at the expense of firm profitability (e.g. Bertrand & Schoar 2006; Schulze et al. 2003). Conversely, other scholars see family owners as highly committed investors with strong economic interest in increasing the firm's profits to preserve the firm's wealth-generating capabilities in the long run (e.g. Anderson & Reeb 2003; Le Breton-Miller & Miller 2006). According to the former view, based on the *alignment hypothesis*, family involvement in ownership and management is positively related to financial reporting quality, since the reduction of agency conflicts between owners and managers reduces managers' incentives to report accounting information that deviates from the firm's underlying economic performance. According to the latter view, based on the *entrenchment hypothesis*, family involvement in ownership and management is negatively related to earnings quality, since concentrated ownership, beyond a certain threshold, increases owner-owner agency problems and the risk of wealth expropriation by controlling owners at the expense of minority shareholders.

Faced with the competing theoretical arguments, some scholars conclude that the influence of family ownership on firm behavior and performance is ultimately an empirical issue (e.g. Anderson & Reeb 2003). However, prior studies also show empirical indeterminacy. With some exceptions, supporting evidence for the alignment hypothesis is usually reported in studies based on research settings where family ownership is lower and where the legal and enforcement systems are stronger. Instead, the entrenchment hypothesis finds support, again with a few exceptions, in studies focused on research settings where family involvement in ownership and management is higher and where the legal and enforcement systems are weaker (Salvato & Moores 2010).

This theoretical and empirical indeterminacy calls for more fine-grained research on how the characteristics of such an important form of organization, family firms, affects accounting and reporting practices. To the best of our knowledge, the impact of a family firm status on fair value measurement reliability has not been directly investigated thus far, although there is some evidence of an indirect application of fair value accounting in the context of family firms, i.e. the adoption of fair value logics and methods in the context of impairment tests (Greco et al. 2015).

The remainder of this chapter is structured as follows. In the next section, we briefly recall some key features of fair value accounting. The aim of this section is not to provide a new view or specific insights on the definition of fair value or fair value measurement, but to recall some of the underlying aspects and logics that enable us to formulate some propositions on the relationship between family firms and fair value accounting. Understanding this relationship requires recalling that in the fair value view (Whittington 2008), a '*short-term orientation*' implicitly prevails as a direct consequence of the assumption of market price as a reference point; the measurement process refers to the '*market selling (exit) price*' and to the '*market perspective*'. Furthermore, *stewardship is not a distinctive objective of financial statements*, although its needs may be met incidentally. As we shall discuss in the section entitled 'Fair Value Accounting Use and Reliability in Family Firms', these features appear to be highly inconsistent with some idiosyncratic elements of family firms.

In the following section, 'Family Firms: Definition and Key Characteristics', we briefly recall some of the fundamental characteristics of family firms. As in the previous section, the specific aim is not to provide a new view on the functioning of family firms, but rather to evoke certain aspects that enable a more in-depth understanding of the relationship between family firms and the quality of fair value accounting. To this end, it would seem useful to first recall the definition of family firm, or, rather, the criteria generally used to identify family firms, and subsequently indicate, also based on the definition criteria, certain key features of family firms and their way of functioning relevant to the analysis of the relationship between family firms and fair value accounting. In particular, in the third section, we report that in family firms, owner and management decisions are characterized by a *long-term orientation (LTO)*, defined as the tendency to prioritize the long-range implications and impact of decisions and actions that come to fruition after an extended time period. *Exit strategies are often perceived as a failure* with respect to the desire to extend family control to the next generation. The business unit and family unit interplay *gives rise to a unique bundle of resources and capabilities* that affect family firm performance. Family owners may pursue *heterogeneous sets of goals that include non-economic as well as economic goals*. Finally, prior studies show that, in the analysis of family firms, *stewardship theory is largely adopted as an alternative framework*.

In the fourth section, we build on the principal features relative to fair value accounting and family firms, and provide three preliminary insights. Comparing the findings from the two previous sections, we first argue that there may be a cultural lack of fit between some of the most relevant idiosyncratic features of family firms and the fair value view. In light of such lack of fit, we suggest that family firm status may restrict the use of fair value accounting, concurring to discourage the voluntary adoption of international accounting standards for private family firms and leading public family firms to use the fair value approach only in circumstances where using other accounting methods is not permitted.

A second insight concerns the traditional operating models adopted by family firms and their potential recourse to transactions for which IAS/IFRS mandate the disclosure or recognition of accounting amounts using fair values. Drawing on prior studies, we argue that the strategic and financial models of family firms can reduce the number of these types of transactions.

Finally, we elaborate on the potential impact of family firm status on the usefulness of its fair value accounting-based information. Based on the two alternative views used in accounting literature to examine the impact of family firm status on earnings management and disclosure policies, it could be argued that family firm status may both enhance and reduce the reliability of fair value measurement. However, arguments supporting the potential positive effect of family firm status on fair value measurement can be drawn integrating prior studies on impairment tests for goodwill and intangible assets (a process that implies the application of the fair value approach), and the impact of founding family ownership on accounting conservatism and on real earnings management. The first literature stream suggests that the alignment of owner-manager interests is particularly relevant in explaining the delay in impairment loss recognition (Ramanna & Watts 2012), while the still-limited empirical evidence shows that the family firms' specific structure and set of priorities positively affect the reliability of long-lived asset write-offs (Greco et al. 2015). The second stream emphasizes that family owners have both the incentives and the ability to implement conservative financial reporting (Chen et al. 2014), and use fewer real earnings management practices (Achleitner et al. 2014). Based on the converging arguments of these prior theoretical views and empirical evidence, we suggest that the specific set of priorities and preferences of family firm status can positively affect the reliability of fair value accounting.

The final section, 'Conclusions', concludes by highlighting the contributions and the limitations of this chapter as well as directions for future research.

Fair value accounting

In the following, we briefly recall some key features of fair value accounting and some of the underlying aspects and logics that will later enable us to formulate some insights on the relationship between family firms and the quality of fair value accounting.

The definition of fair value is laid down in both US GAAP and in IAS/IFRS. FASB and IASB dedicate a specific accounting standard to the issue of fair value accounting, respectively, SFAS 157, Fair Value Measurements, and IFRS 13, Fair Value Measurement. Since the contents of the two standards and the terminology the two standard setters use are very similar, in this chapter, we refer to the international accounting standards, also given their application within the EU and their greater dissemination and global relevance.

IFRS 13 defines fair value as '*the price that would be received to sell an asset or paid to transfer a liability in an orderly transaction between market participants at the measurement date*'.[1]

Under IFRS, fair value accounting is most frequently used for financial assets and financial liabilities (IAS 39, Financial Instruments: Recognition and Measurement, which will be replaced in the coming years by the new IFRS 9, Financial Instruments). However, fair value accounting is pervasive in other standards, on a recurring or a non-recurring basis (Landsman 2007). For example, the disclosure or recognition of accounting amounts using fair value is mandatory for all assets acquired and liabilities assumed in a business combination (IFRS 3, Business Combinations), shared-based payments (IFRS 2, Share-based Payment), employee benefits (IAS 19, Employee Benefits), biological assets and agricultural produce (IAS 41, Agriculture), revenues from contracts with customers (IAS 18, Revenue, which will be replaced in the coming years by IFRS 15, Revenue from Contracts with Customers) and leases (IAS 17, Leases, which will be replaced in the coming years by the new IFRS 16, Leases). In addition, fair value is an allowed option for the measurement of tangible assets, such as property, plants and equipment (IAS 16, Property, Plant and Equipment), intangible assets (IAS 38, Intangible Assets) and investment property (IAS 40, Investment Property). Finally, some transactions require indirect or non-recurring forms of fair value measurement (Magnan & Parbonetti 2018). This is the case of impairment tests for property, plants and equipment (IAS 16), goodwill and intangible assets (IAS 36, Impairment of Assets), financial instruments at cost or amortized cost (IAS 39 and new IFRS 9), non-current assets held for sale and discontinued operations (IFRS 5, Non-current Assets Held for Sale and Discontinued Operations).

The almost universal adoption by standard setters of fair value accounting (Magnan 2009) and its pervasive reach was preceded and followed by an intense and still ongoing debate among academics and practitioners regarding its relevance, reliability and pro-cyclicality (e.g. Barth 1994; Ronen 2008; Whittington 2008; Laux & Leuz 2010). For the specific purpose of this chapter, however, we focus on five key features that could help in better understanding the relationship between fair value accounting and family firms: the emphasis on the concept of exit price, the emphasis on the current market situation, the adoption of a market perspective, the accessory role of stewardship in the fair value approach and the switch from present shareholders to current and potential investors and creditors as users of reference of general-purpose financial statements.

The emphasis on the concept of exit price

While the previous IAS 32 fair value definition as '*the amount for which an asset could be exchanged, or a liability settled, between knowledgeable, willing parties in an arm's length transaction*' did not specifically clarify whether fair value is intended as an exit price, entry price or mid-price, following the introduction of IFRS 13, it is now clear that fair value is an exit price. As explained in paragraphs 36–45 of the Basis for Conclusions, the definition of fair value in IFRS 13 as an exit price is not in itself a controversial issue. In developing the revised definition of fair value, the IASB concluded that the exit price is always a relevant definition of fair value for assets and liabilities, regardless of whether an entity intends to use or sell the asset and fulfil the liability or transfer it to another party.

The emphasis on the current market situation

Fair value is estimated according to the current and ordinary conditions at the time of the transaction and on a standalone basis, thus considering only synergies that would be available to the generic market participants. Although the fair value of an asset and a liability embodies expectations about future cash flows, fair value measurement implicitly adopts a short-term horizon through the incorporation of current and ordinary conditions at the time of the transaction. In paragraph 24, IFRS 13 clarifies that

> [...] the objective of a fair value measurement in both cases is the same – to estimate the price at which an orderly transaction to sell the asset or to transfer the liability would take place between market participants *at the measurement date under current market conditions* (i.e., an exit price at the measurement date from the perspective of a market participant that holds the asset or owes the liability).
>
> *(emphasis added)*[2]

While it is true in principle that the values expressed in the context of efficient markets should also reflect the long-term flow expectations, they cannot fail to be affected by the short-term dynamics of the market and its volatility.

The adoption of a market perspective

IFRS 13 requires that the fair value measurement of a non-financial asset must take into account the perspective of a market participant that can use the asset in its highest and best use or sell it to another market participant that would use the asset in its highest and best use, hence, even if an entity may not actively intend to use an acquired non-financial asset or use the asset according to its highest and best use.[3] This is entirely consistent with idea that fair value accounting should reflect the 'most profitable opportunity' philosophy (Lennard 2018). It also follows that if a non-financial asset generates greater value when used in combination with other assets, liabilities, resources or complementary factors, its fair value must be determined by assuming that such assets, liabilities, resources or complementary factors are available to the market operators, even if such use does not represent that carried out by the company conducting the valuation.

The accessory role of stewardship in the fair value approach

In the fair value view of the IAS/IFRS, the basic objective of the financial statement is its stakeholder decision-usefulness, rather than monitoring the management's responsibility in managing the company with respect to the interests of stakeholders (Ronen 2008; Abdel-Khalik 2011). According to the fair value view, the information needs for assessing stewardship are consistent with the information needs for decision-making and 'could be subsumed within the general objective of decision usefulness' (Whittington 2008).

As we will try to highlight in the fourth section, 'Fair Value Accounting Use and Reliability in Family Firms', of this chapter, we believe that most of these features, which are quite distant from the prevailing logic and approach of family owners and affiliated managers, could lead to a lack of a cultural fit between fair value accounting and family firms.

Family firms: definition and key characteristics

In the following, we recall some key characteristics of family firms. As in the previous section, the objective is not to provide a new view of the functioning of family firms, but to evoke certain aspects that allow formulating preliminary considerations on the relationship between family firms and fair value accounting. In particular, we first recall the definition of family firm, or, rather, the criteria generally used to identify family firms, and subsequently indicate, also based on these criteria, certain key characteristics of family firms and their way of functioning, which, as explained in the section entitled 'Fair Value Accounting Use and Reliability in Family Firms', are relevant to the analysis of the relationship between family firms and fair value accounting.

The definition of family firm: a still open question

Even today, the identification of family firms is an issue debated in literature. In general terms, family firms are identified by using different and sometimes complementary approaches to arrive at a more general definition and establish a link between family involvement and the distinctive behaviors of family firms. Scholars introduced the components of involvement approach and the essence approach (Chrisman et al. 2005), later integrated with the family identity approach (Zellweger et al. 2010).

According to the components of involvement approach, family firms should be identified based on the degree of involvement of the family and related family power in directing the firm's goals, principal strategic decisions and actions. According to a more traditional approach, this influence may be exerted primarily through the ownership concentration in the hands of one or a few families. While in the case of private firms, ownership control is exercised through a majority stake in publicly listed family firms, control can also be exercised through a significant minority stake (e.g. Anderson & Reeb 2003; Villalonga & Amit 2006). Family influence can also be exerted thanks to family involvement in the top management team and in the governance bodies. The underlying explanation here is that ownership identifies only the potential ability to exercise influence, which can only really be achieved through entrepreneurial or managerial leadership. Hence, precisely family involvement in management can offer much in the way of explaining family firm behavior (e.g. Steier 2003; Villalonga & Amit 2006). These two versions of the influence approach to family firm definition overlook the possible existence of other dimensions of family influence. To overcome this possible limitation, family business literature began using a more articulated version of this approach based on the identification of multiple drivers of family influence (Astrachan et al. 2002).

According to some researchers, involvement does not necessarily translate into significant influence on the firm's and the management's behavior. To overcome the limitations of the components of involvement approach, the essence approach proposes that the identification of family firms should be sought precisely in the behaviors put in place by the members who control the firm and that produce distinctiveness in their behaviors. According to the essence approach, what matters for the identification of family firms is identifying the perspective and vision with which the firm is managed. The essence approach claims a firm can be defined as a family firm when the controlling family shows a transgenerational vision for the business and family members may provide financial support through outside sources of income, emotional support through encouragement, and instrumental support through knowledge and the family firm's human capital (Danes et al. 2009).

Finally, it has been observed that not all family firms recognize themselves as such. In many cases and for various reasons, the firm leaders do not identify their own company as a family firm, despite the presence of high ownership concentration (and vice versa). This has led some scholars to emphasize the importance of the firm's self-perception in identifying a business as a family firm (Zellweger et al. 2010). The overlap of family and business systems and the family's involvement contribute to creating a unique and particular identity in family firms: family firm members are likely to view their firm as an extension of their family.

Although at times the use of these criteria translates into a dichotomous approach to the definition of family firm, there is growing agreement among researchers and practitioners that there is no such clear distinction between family and non-family firms (Astrachan et al. 2002), and that family firms are heterogeneous in various aspects that should be carefully taken into consideration as antecedents or moderators of family firm behavior.

The characteristics of family firms and their traditional management choices

As also emerges from the analysis of the family firm definition criteria, these firms are characterized by specific key features, some of which are relevant to understanding the relationship between family firms and fair value accounting. Although for convenience such features are kept separate, in reality they tend to interact. For example, the overlap between the owners' and managers' role affects the LTO of family firms, which in turn also depends on the presence of non-financial goals that stem from, among others, the initial overlap between the family and the business, and so forth.

There is general agreement among scholars and practitioners that one key feature of family firms is the interaction of partly incompatible subsystems: the family unit, the business entity and the individual family members (Tagiuri & Davis 1996; Habbershon et al. 2003). This interaction creates unique systemic conditions and constituencies that affect the behavior and the performance outcomes of the family business social system. According to some scholars (e.g. Habbershon et al. 2003), the interplay of the three subsystems – business unit, family unit and individual unit – gives rise to a bundle of resources called familiness that is unique to the family firm: according to this view, familiness is an idiosyncratic resource that can be developed into superior performance.

In any case, the simultaneous presence of multiple roles of owner family members – owner, manager and family member – plays a pivotal role in shaping the particular set of priorities, preferences and problems that characterize family firms, and influences the choice of the appropriate theoretical framework.

From an agency theoretical standpoint, family firms represent a particular empirical setting. According to the agency framework (Jensen & Meckling 1976), family firms should have less significant owner-manager agency problems because, in this type of organization, there is often a certain overlap between owners and managers whose interests are therefore more aligned. In addition, due to the family members' long-term presence in the firm, their knowledge of the family business, and their intention to preserve the family name, controlling families may monitor firms more effectively (Wang 2006). However, family firms may be characterized by potentially more significant owner-owner agency problems, given the powerful position of controlling family executives vs. minority non-influential owners, who may be either members of the same family or outsiders. According to this competing view, family members can leverage their leadership positions and their information advantage to adopt opportunistic behaviors at the expense of other shareholders (e.g. Schulze et al. 2003; Fan & Wong 2002). In addition, opportunistic behaviors may not be discovered by the governance bodies given the controlling family's ability to exert direct or indirect influence over these. The presence of these two potentially conflicting effects leads to ex ante uncertainty of the family firm's accounting practices and disclosure behaviors.

Given their specific features, family firms have also been studied from other theoretical perspectives. For example, stewardship theory has been largely adopted as an alternative framework to analyze family firms (Corbetta & Salvato 2004; Miller & Le Breton-Miller 2006). Stewardship theory posits that some leaders and executives are not simply self-serving economic individuals, but often act for the benefit of the organization and are committed to making it succeed, even at personal sacrifice. Scholars argue that these attitudes are especially prevalent among family business leaders who are either family members or emotionally linked to the family. The stewardship perspective provides complementary arguments to the view that family-controlled firms are typically characterized by a close and long-term relationship between managers and the controlling family, which reduces managerial incentives for the adoption of opportunistic behavior also in terms of accounting and reporting practices (Prencipe et al. 2011).

Relative to non-family businesses, family firms are known to favor non-economic goals requiring a long-term perspective. Moving from this premise, some scholars (Gomez-Mejia et al. 2007) developed a new theoretical perspective, the socioemotional wealth (SEW) model, which has been largely adopted in studying family firm behavior. The SEW model suggests that family firms are typically motivated by, and committed to, the preservation of their SEW, which refers to non-financial aspects. According to this model, gains or losses in SEW represent the pivotal frame of reference that family-controlled firms use to make major strategic choices and to select their accounting and disclosure practices (Gomez-Mejia et al. 2014).

Another idiosyncratic element of family firms directly influenced by the specific characteristics of this type of organization is the time horizon typically taken as reference by owners and managers in their decision-making. Compared to non-family firms, senior executives of family firms tend to have longer tenures and greater interest in their firm's long-running performance (Le Breton-Miller & Miller 2006). Indeed, researchers highlight that family firms can be driven by a multi-generation investment horizon and by the desire to build a lasting family legacy. Such concerns give many family businesses a LTO, defined as the tendency to prioritize the long-range implications and impact of decisions and actions that come to fruition after an extended time period (Lumpkin et al. 2010: 245). This prioritization also implies lower attention to the fluctuations in the results and the value of assets held in the near term, and concurs to explain the adoption of less aggressive accounting and reporting practices (e.g. Wang 2006; Chen et al. 2014).

According to some researchers, family firms are associated with greater caution and a type of conservative behavior in strategic, financial and accounting terms. For example, family firms with a strong inclination to preserve wealth may be unwilling to invest in R&D projects with uncertain outcomes or risk capital to expand operations; family businesses concerned about their legacy may forego opportunities they perceive as risky or competitively aggressive for fear of damaging their reputation. In addition, family firms may see an increase in financial debt as a potential risk for the business and the family wealth, thus preferring to maintain zero-leverage.

One last important element that is worthy of mention in relation to family firms is the markedly negative connotation given to exit strategies. In fact, these are typically perceived as a very difficult event, a failure that endangers the firm's continuity, especially when owners are deeply emotionally involved in the business and when it is part of the family firm's historic roots. This negative view of exit strategies derives from the specific characteristics of family firms thus far observed: the overlap between the firm and the family, the high level of emotional attachment to the historic roots of the firm, the desire to continue the business and to extend its control to the next generation. In a family firm context, when the emotional logic prevails over the business logic, exit options can be undermined, whereas family owners and affiliated managers can behave very much like traditional investors when exit strategies do not concern the family firm's historic business (e.g. Zellweger et al. 2012; DeTienne & Chirico 2013).

Fair value accounting use and reliability in family firms

In this section, we build on the principal features related to fair value accounting and family firms, in part comparing the observations from the two previous sections, in part drawing on previous theoretical and empirical studies to develop some preliminary insights on the impact of family firm status on fair value accounting use and reliability.

Fair value accounting and family firms: are they on the same page?

In the sections entitled 'Fair Value Accounting' and 'Family Firms: Definition and Key Characteristics', we highlighted some of the significant characteristics of fair value accounting on the one hand and family firms on the other. The comparison between these elements – briefly summarized in Table 18.1 – enables grasping the strong cultural inconsistency between the logics and perspectives that characterize these two worlds. On some important aspects, fair value accounting and family firms do not only speak different languages, but are even incompatible.

While the exit price represents the uncontroversial reference criterion for fair value accounting, exiting is a prospect distant from the typical logic of family firms, in view of the involvement of family members in the management team, the strong emotional bond between the controlling family and the firm, and the desire to pass on the business or assets owned to the next generation. According to family business scholars, an important reference point in framing strategic and accounting decisions is preserving the ability to exercise family influence, perpetuating the family dynasty and the family's identification with the firm. Since exit decisions can be perceived as a devastating cause of SEW loss, we argue that it can be culturally difficult for family managers and owners to be involved in valuation processes aimed at establishing the exit price of an asset or a business.

Equally inconsistent is the temporal perspective that characterizes fair value accounting and directs the behavior of family firms. Reference to the long term is an essential aspect of the culture of family businesses, and a value that typically guides their business decisions and allocation of financial resources, while fair value accounting incorporates the short-term market dynamics, drawing the attention of managers and shareholders to the current market situation and short-term price fluctuations. Since family firms, in their daily work and in their strategic choices, are characterized by the 'the tendency to prioritize the long-range implications and impact of decisions and actions that come to fruition after an extended time

Table 18.1 The inconsistency between the main characteristics of fair value accounting and family firms

Key features and logics	Fair value accounting	Family firms
Exit option	Fair value is an exit price.	Exit is perceived as a difficult event. Low likelihood of family exit choice for financial reasons or for short-term purposes.
Time horizon	Although market prices should in principle reflect true fundamental values, fair value accounting brings with it short-term market fluctuations.	One of the characteristics of family firms is long-term orientation (long-term priority over short-term fluctuations). In many cases, family businesses are managed in a transgenerational logic.
Firm (subjective) vs. market (objective) approach	Highest and best use of assets, assuming they have all the complementary resources and factors.	Family firms often make specific use of assets that also takes into account non-financial goals. The interplay of business unit, family unit, and individual unit gives rise to a bundle of resources called familiness that is unique to the family firm.
Stewardship	Stewardship is not a distinctive objective of financial statements, although its needs may be met incidentally.	Stewardship attitude is especially prevalent among family business leaders who are either family members or emotionally linked to the family.

period' (Lumpkin et al. 2010: 245), family managers and owners may be uncomfortable with adopting and employing an accounting view that reflects a concern with the more immediate consequences of decisions and actions involving near-term time horizons and directs the decision-makers' focus on present conditions and opportunities for short-term financial gain.

Even the 'most profitable opportunity' philosophy seems to be inconsistent with two relevant family firm idiosyncratic features: the presence and importance of non-financial goals and familiness, which is a distinctive and unique resource arising from the interaction between the business system; the family system; and the unit system. With regard to the first aspect, family owners and managers, in their decision-making on the use of different assets, frequently refer to the existence of non-economic goals (e.g. establishing positive relationships with key stakeholders, such as employees and the local community, brand consolidation, and more generally, the conservation and development of SEW) and not just economic-goals. The importance assumed by non-economic goals in family firms seems inconsistent with the strict adoption of the most profitable opportunity philosophy of the fair value approach. With respect to the second aspect, to be noted is that family firms are also characterized by the presence of a bundle of idiosyncratic resources and capabilities that explains the nature of family influence on performance outcomes. Therefore, in the case of family firms, the various non-financial assets are jointly used with this bundle of unique and distinctive resources. In the perspective of family owners and managers, it may therefore be difficult to understand the fair value measurement hypothesis according to which 'an exit price reflects the sale of the asset to a market participant that has or can obtain the complementary assets and the associated liabilities needed to use the specialized asset in its own operations' (IFRS 13, § BC78).

A final inconsistency could be represented by the different emphasis on stewardship: in fair value accounting, stewardship is not a distinctive objective of financial statements, although its needs may be met incidentally. However, in family firms, stewardship is one of the most widely used perspectives to explain the behavior and choices of managers. Thus, typically assuming the perspective of stewards in managing the firm and in the relationship with various stakeholders, managers may be uncomfortable with accounting approaches that *'do not do well in serving the stewardship function, as they do not properly measure the managers' ability to create value for shareholders'* (Ronen 2008: 186).

Overall, this diversity of perspectives and logics could create the lack of a cultural fit between fair value accounting and family firms. We argue that this inconsistency of the fair value approach with the logics and values that guide the behavior and choices of family firms may restrict their use of fair value accounting. In the case of unlisted family firms, this lack of cultural fit could discourage the voluntary adoption of international accounting standards, which necessarily involve using this approach in valuating certain items. In the case of IAS/IFRS adoption – such as for listed family firms – the same lack of cultural fit could lead family firms to use the fair value approach only in circumstances where other accounting methods are not permitted.

Box 1 reports anecdotal evidence on the adoption of fair value accounting in the case of five firms listed on the Milan Stock Exchange. These companies are characterized by family involvement in ownership and in governance bodies, and have been identified as listed family firms in many studies. While these companies operate in different industries and are characterized by different size and age, they show a common trait in explaining their approach to fair value accounting.

Box 1: Examples of listed family firms' approach to fair value accounting

A   Davide Campari-Milano S.p.A., the parent company of the Campari Group, is a family firm listed on the Italian Stock Exchange since 2001. The Group is one of the largest players in the global spirits industry, with a portfolio of over 50 premium brands (e.g. Aperol, Campari, Grand Marnier). Group net sales were €1,726.5 million in 2016; in the same year, Group EBITDA was €372.1 million.

    In its Annual Report, the firm states: *'the accounts were prepared on a cost basis, taking into account, where appropriate, any value adjustments, except for balance sheet items that, according to the IFRS, must be recognised at fair value, such as financial derivatives, biological assets and new acquisitions, and except in cases where the IFRS allow a different valuation criterion to be used'* (see Davide Campari-Milano S.p.A. Annual Report at 31 December 2016, p. 82).

B Brunello Cucinelli S.p.A., the parent company of the homonyms Group, is a family firm listed on the Italian Stock Exchange since 2012. The Group's product range focuses on a single fashion brand, Brunello Cucinelli, internationally recognized as an example of absolute luxury, combining exclusive 'Made in Italy' features with the ability to innovate and identify new trends. In 2016, revenues from sales and services amounted to €457.0 million and EBITDA was €76.7 million.

In its Annual Report, the firm states: '*the consolidated financial statements have been prepared based on a historical cost basis, except in the case of derivatives and available-for-sale financial assets which are recognised at fair value*' (see Brunello Cucinelli Annual Financial Report – Consolidated Financial Statements at 31 December 2016, p. 76).

C Danieli & C. Officine Meccaniche S.p.A., the parent company of the Danieli Group, is a family firm listed on the Italian Stock Exchange since 1984. The Group produces and installs innovative machinery and plants worldwide for the iron and steel industry and the non-ferrous metals sector. At 30 June 2016, the Group's revenues amounted to €2,508.4 million with EBITDA of €211.4 million euro.

In its Annual Report, the firm states: '*the consolidated financial statements have been prepared on the historical cost principle, except for derivative financial instruments and available-for-sale financial assets, which have been recorded at fair value; investments in associates and joint ventures, valued by the equity method; and construction contracts, recognised according to the percentage of completion method*' (see Danieli Annual Report at 30 June 2016, p. 50).

D ERG S.p.A., the parent company of the ERG Group, is a family firm listed on the Italian Stock Exchange since 1997. In 2016, the ERG Group completed a profound transformation from leading Italian private oil operator to leading independent operator in the generation of energy from renewable sources (wind, thermoelectric, and hydroelectric), At 31 December 2016, the Group's revenues from ordinary operations amounted to €1,025 million with EBITDA of €455 million euro.

In its Annual Report, the firm states: '*the Consolidated Financial Statements, expressed in thousands of euros, were prepared under the general historical cost principle, with the exception of financial assets available for sale, financial assets held for trading and derivative instruments, which were measured at fair value*' (see ERG Annual Report as at 31 December 2016, p. 195).

E Buzzi Unicem S.p.A. is a family firm listed on the Italian Stock Exchange since 1999. The parent company and its subsidiaries manufacture, distribute, and sell cement, ready-mix concrete and aggregates. In 2016, consolidated sales revenue amounted to €2,669.3 million and consolidated EBITDA was €550.6 million.

In its Annual Report, the firm states: '*the consolidated financial statements have been prepared under the historical cost convention, as modified by the revaluation of available-for-sale financial assets and financial assets/liabilities (including derivative instruments) at fair value through profit or loss, as well as on the going concern basis*' (see Buzzi Unicem Annual Report 2016, p. 62).

The lesser need to use fair value accounting in family firms

A second consideration regarding the relationship between fair value accounting and family firms concerns the fact that, due to their key features, the operating model adopted could lead to a lesser recourse to transactions for which IAS/IFRS mandate disclosure or recognition of accounting amounts using fair value. In Table 18.2, we briefly illustrate some

Table 18.2 Items and transactions for which fair value accounting is required and their relevance within the traditional operating model of family firms

Accounting standard	Transactions/items	Relevance for the traditional family firm model
IFRS 3	PPA	Less recourse to external growth.
IFRS 2	Equity based incentives	Lower level of professionalization and less management shareholding. Long-term relationships based on emotional involvement.
IFRS 9	Derivatives and financial instruments	Limited use of leverage and lower level of financial sophistication.
IFRS 5	Assets (disposal group) held for sale and discontinued operations	Lower propensity to exit or sell business lines.
IFRS 15	Revenue from contracts with customers	Family firms are often active in traditional manufacturing sectors.

transactions/items for which fair value accounting is required and their possible limited relevance or incoherence with the system of values and typical operating model of family firms.

According to IFRS 3, all assets and liabilities assumed in a business combination must be measured at their fair value at the acquisition date. Family firms, as well as non-family firms, sometimes engage in acquisitions to pursue their financial goals. However, in the case of family firms, acquisition and the subsequent integration of processes may not only jeopardize their economic performance, but may also generate a number of negative effects on the non-economic objectives pursued by this type of firm. In the perspective of family mangers and shareholders, the financial resources needed for an acquisition could weaken family control or increase firm financial risk. In addition, the post-acquisition integration process could have destructive effects on the acquirer's well-established social networks, on the community of long-time employees and on the family firm's identity. In fact, family firms engage less frequently, compared to non-family firms, in acquisitions and these, among other things, are smaller in scale (Miller et al. 2010; Gomez-Mejia et al. 2015). Based on this evidence, we suggest that family firms could make less recourse to the fair value measurement required by the application of IFRS 3.

Fair value accounting is required by IFRS 2 for recognizing equity-based incentive systems. Although these instruments generally find extensive application among listed companies, including family firms, it can be argued that this type of incentive system may be less common in family firms for three fundamental reasons. First, one of the elements that characterize family businesses is the presence of family members in the top management team (TMT). If these managers are also owners of more or less significant amounts of capital, shareholders may expect that the use of equity-based incentive systems is not required to ensure full alignment between the interests of the TMT and those of the owners. At the same time, family managers, if they already have a significant part of their wealth invested in the family firm's shares with a long-term perspective, could have an interest in increasing the share of their incentives system not paid through the equity-based system. Second, one of the weaknesses of family firms is the lesser ability to attract qualified and specialized managers. In the case of family firms, this element may also, *ceteris paribus*, limit recourse to equity-based incentive systems. In addition, researchers report that in family firms external managers may over time show greater commitment and identification with the firm and are willing to accept lower pay levels in exchange for higher job security (Gomez-Mejia et al. 2003; Sraer & Thesmar 2007). In summary, it is possible that family firms, *ceteris paribus*, make less recourse to the fair value measurement required by the application of IFRS 2.

An intriguing context for fair value adoption in family firms concerns the application of IAS 39 and the new IFRS 9 (derivatives and financial instruments). The literature suggests that family owners tend to be more risk averse than non-family owners (Naldi et al. 2007) resulting in more caution in their strategic and financial decisions. Therefore, family firms could be characterized by the less speculative use of derivatives and, more generally, by less complex financials tools for which the initial fair value may significantly differ from the nominal value of the debt. In broader terms, however, literature reports conflicting theoretical arguments and empirical evidence on family firm use of financial leverage. From a theoretical point of view, it has been observed that the desire to maintain family control can lead to its greater use, *ceteris paribus*. Conversely, the opposite has also been suggested: since indebtedness poses a greater risk to the firm and to SEW, family firms are more reluctant to accept high levels of leverage. From an empirical point of view, the evidence is conflicting: for example, studying US public firms, Strebulaev and Yang (2013) find that family firms are more likely to pursue zero-leverage policies, while Anderson and Reeb (2003) find that family firms utilize more leverage. Even assuming that family firms make use of financial leverage, we argue that due to their risk aversion and lower level of professionalization in the TMT, *ceteris paribus*, they make less use of fair value measurements required by the application of IAS 39 and the new IFRS 9.

IFRS 5 specifies the accounting for non-current assets and disposal group held for sale and requires fair value to be considered in their measurements. However, the recognition and measurement of assets (and even more of the disposal group) held for sale is the consequence of a strategic or a financial choice that can be inconsistent with the family firm's non-financial goals and can produce a significant amount of loss in the family firm's SEW. Since decision-makers in family firms managed in a transgenerational perspective will see exit as a failure rather than a source of opportunity to improve firm performance, we argue that the need to use IFRS 5 can be lower for family firms.

Finally, as regards the application of IFRS 15 on revenues for contracts with customers, this would seem to find greater application in certain specific industries that do not have a large presence of family firms. In fact, given the strengths and weaknesses typical of family firms, their presence tends to be higher in service sectors – where family firms can leverage the uniqueness of their network, mutual trust and long-term relationships – and in manufacturing sectors characterized by a lesser need for capital (Villalonga & Amit 2006).

In summary, the key features of family firms may result in their adoption of business models, financial and organizational strategies that involve a limited number of those transactions/items that typically require the application of fair value accounting.

Fair value accounting discretion and accounting quality: the potential moderating role of family firms

Fair value accounting is deemed to enhance the comparability of financial statements, provide relevant information that faithfully represents the underlying economic reality and increase the quality of financial reporting to the benefit of investors and the functioning of financial markets. However, fair value accounting allows considerable room for managerial discretion and judgment in addition to the use of private information, thus leaving managers substantial leeway to apply earnings management techniques.

Recent literature argues and finds that reporting incentives at the firm level dominate accounting standards in determining accounting quality (Christensen et al. 2015) and that the role of managers' incentives is particularly relevant in explaining cross-sectional variation of financial reporting practices related to assets with unverifiable and non-auditable valuations (Ramanna & Watts 2012).

Notwithstanding their lack of cultural fit with the fair value view, after the mandatory adoption of IFRS for listed firms, public family firms must adopt IFRS and develop fair value measures. A steadily growing number of studies show that the particular set of priorities and risk preferences of family firms influence their accounting and reporting practices, thus implicitly highlighting the opportunity to investigate the interplay between family firms and fair value measurement.

Broadly speaking, the two alternative views used in accounting literature to predict and explain the impact of family firm status on earnings management and disclosure policies could also be used to assess the potential impact of family firm status on fair value measurement. Indeed, drawing on extant literature, it could be argued that if the alignment hypothesis prevails, family managers' interest in the long-term viability of the firm and their concern over firm reputation should positively moderate the relationship between the use of fair value measures and accounting quality. Conversely, if the entrenchment hypothesis prevails, it could be argued that the controlling family's interest in concealing firm performance and leveraging its information advantage to the detriment of shareholders should negatively moderate the same relationship.

However, no accounting study has directly elaborated on this relationship nor empirically and directly examined whether family firm priorities and preferences affect the quality of their fair value measures. Nevertheless, we believe some insights on the potential effect of family firm status on fair value measures can be indirectly drawn from studies that investigate impairment tests for goodwill and intangible assets, i.e. a process that implies the application of the fair value approach.

The fair value of goodwill is difficult to verify and audit, since this is also a function of the management's future strategic decisions and operational actions. As such, managerial discretion in estimating the current fair value of goodwill is greater than for most other asset classes. Ramanna and Watts (2012) investigate managers' implementation of the goodwill impairment test in a sample of firms with market indications of goodwill impairment, searching for antecedents of the delay in recognizing goodwill impairment in the accounts. They find support for the hypothesis that the decision to delay goodwill losses is driven by manager' incentives, including their interest in increasing their compensation and in shielding their reputation from the implications of a goodwill write-off. This finding supports the expectation that the reliability of the fair value measurement could be positively influenced in family firms where the alignment effect prevails over the entrenchment effect (and vice versa). Indeed, according to the alignment hypothesis, family influence reduces managers' incentives to report accounting information that deviates from the underlying economic reality. Supporting evidence of an alignment effect on the faithfulness of fair value estimation in the impairment test is reported in a study examining accounting behavior in relation to long-lived asset write-offs in a sample of firms listed on the Italian Stock Exchange (Greco et al. 2015). Building on these studies and the still-limited empirical evidence, it could be argued that when the alignment effect prevails, compared to non-family firms, family firm status can positively affect the quality of fair value measures.

Additional support for the potential existence of a positive effect of family firm status on fair value measurement could be drawn from – always taking as reference the studies relating to the use of fair value in impairment tests – the theoretical considerations and the empirical evidence of recent studies that examine, on the one hand, the impact of mandatory IFRS adoption on conditional conservatism in Europe (Andre et al. 2015) and, on the other, the impact of founding family ownership on accounting conservatism (Chen et al. 2014). André and colleagues document an overall decline in the degree of conditional conservatism following IFRS introduction, which is more pronounced for firms carrying intangible assets and goodwill in their balance sheets. Their evidence confirms that impairment tests for intangible assets, implying the application of the fair value principles and methods, are highly sensitive to management assumptions and are more likely to be manipulated. They also document that these tests are an accounting mechanism explaining a lower level of conditional conservatism. Examining how family ownership affects financial reporting conservatism, Chen and colleagues argue and find that family owners have both the incentives and the ability to implement conservative financial reporting to reduce legal liability and mitigate agency conflicts with other shareholders. The integration of this scattered evidence offers reinforcing arguments that family firm status may positively affect the reliability of the fair value measure used in impairment tests.

Finally, additional arguments can be drawn from studies on the role of real earnings management activities in delaying goodwill loss recognition (Filip et al. 2015). Investigating how managers convince various gatekeepers that recognizing an impairment loss is unnecessary, even if seeming economically justified, Andrej and colleagues find that managers manipulate current cash flows upward to support their choice to avoid reporting an impairment loss, even at the expense of the firm's future performance. However, recent evidence suggests that family firms, compared to non-family firms, treat earnings management activities strategically, avoiding real earnings management activities that inhibit the firm's long-term value (Achleitner et al. 2014). Building on these studies, it could be argued that the lesser propensity of family firms to use real earnings management activities provides an additional argument to suggest that family firm status could positively affect the reliability of the estimates in the context of impairment tests.

In conclusion, based on the converging arguments of these prior theoretical views and empirical evidence, we suggest that the specific set of priorities and preferences of family firms can positively affect the reliability of fair value measurement practices.

Conclusions

This chapter investigates how family firm status may impact fair value accounting use and reliability through comparing the key logics and features of family firms with the fair accounting view and drawing on prior theoretical and empirical studies.

We provide three preliminary insights. First, we acknowledge the possible presence of a lack of cultural fit between family firms and the fair value view. Due to their specific set of priorities and preferences, family owners and managers have a LTO, perceive exit as a failure with respect to the desire to extend family control to the next generation, evaluate assets and groups of assets also considering their impact on non-economic goals, show a deep attachment to the historic roots of the business and typically perceive themselves as stewards of the organization. This approach would appear to be quite inconsistent with some key features of the fair value approach: the 'short-term orientation', the uncontroversial reference to 'exit price', the adoption of a 'market perspective' and the accessory role of stewardship as a distinctive objective of financial statements. In light of such inconsistency of the fair value approach with the logics and values of family firms, we suggest that family firm status may restrict the use of fair value accounting, concurring to discourage the voluntary adoption of international accounting standards for private family firms, and leading public family firms to use the fair value approach only in circumstances where using other accounting methods is not permitted.

A second insight concerns the traditional operating models adopted by family firms and their potential recourse to transactions for which IAS/IFRS mandate the disclosure or recognition of accounting amounts using fair values. Drawing on prior studies, we illustrate that family firms can engage less frequently, compared to non-family firms, in acquisitions; family firms make less recourse to the fair value measurement required by the adoption of equity-based incentive systems; and the perception of exit strategies as a failures rather than a proper portfolio or business decision may lower the likelihood of family firms developing the intention to sell or liquidate non-current assets or group disposal pertaining to the family firm's core business. Existing studies provide conflicting theoretical arguments and empirical evidence on the use of financial leverage, while family firm risk-aversion may lead to refraining from a speculative use of derivatives. Overall, the strategic and financial models of family firms can reduce the number of transactions for which IAS/IFRS mandate the disclosure or the recognition of accounting amounts using fair values.

Finally, we highlight that the potential impact of family firm status on fair value measurement quality has thus far been overlooked in literature. Based on the two alternative views used in accounting literature to examine the impact of family firm status on earnings management and disclosure policies, it could be argued that family firm status may both enhance and reduce the reliability of fair value measurement. However, arguments supporting the potential positive effect of family firm status on fair value measurement can be drawn combining prior studies on the antecedents of the delay in recognizing goodwill impairment and the still-scarce knowledge of the family firm status effect on this indirect application of fair value accounting. Additional arguments in support of the potential existence of a positive effect of family firm status on fair value measurement could be drawn from integrating recent studies on impairment test implementations, and the impact of founding family ownership on accounting conservatism and on real earnings management. Based on the converging arguments of these prior theoretical views and empirical evidence, we suggest that the specific set of priorities and preferences of family firms can positively affect the reliability of fair value measurement practices.

This study has several limitations. We believe this chapter is a first step in the inquiry on fair value accounting and family firms, calling for further development to identify a more comprehensive understanding of the effects of family firm status on fair value accounting and thereby increase the generalizability of our findings. The proposed relationships should then be tested in a subsequent research phase to confirm the existence of the identified effects.

Notes

1 See IFRS 13, § 9.
2 See IFRS 13, § 24.
3 See IFRS 13, §§ 27–30.

References

Abdel-Khalik, AR 2011, "Fair value accounting and stewardship", *Accounting Perspectives*, vol. 9, no. 4, pp. 253–269.
Achleitner, A, Gunther, N, Kaserer, K, & Siciliano, G 2014, "Real earnings management and accrual-based earnings management in family firms", *European Accounting Review*, vol. 23, no. 3, pp. 431–461.
Ali, A, Chen, T, & Radhakrishnan, S 2007, "Corporate disclosures by family firms", *Journal of Accounting and Economics*, vol. 44, no. 1/2, pp. 238–286.

Anderson, RC & Reeb, DM 2003, "Founding-family ownership and firm performance: evidence from the S&P 500", *Journal of Finance*, vol. 58, no. 3, pp. 1301–1328.

André, P, Filip, A & Paugam, L 2015, "The effect of mandatory IFRS adoption on conditional conservatism in Europe", *Journal of Business, Finance & Accounting*, vol. 42, no. 3–4, pp. 482–514.

Astrachan, J, Klein, SB & Smyrnios, KX 2002, "The F-PEC scale of family influence: a proposal for solving the family business definition problem", *Family Business Review*, vol. 16, no. 3, pp. 207–213.

Barth, ME 1994, "Fair value accounting: evidence from investment securities and the market valuation of banks", *The Accounting Review*, vol. 69, pp. 1–25.

Barth, ME & Landsman WR 2010, "How did financial reporting contribute to the financial crisis?", *European Accounting Review*, vol. 19, no. 3, pp. 399–423.

Bertrand, M & Schoar, A 2006, "The role of family in family firms", *Journal of Economic Perspectives*, vol. 20, no. 2, pp. 73–96.

Chen, S, Chen, X & Cheng, Q 2008, "Do family firms provide more or less voluntary disclosure?", *Journal of Accounting Research*, vol. 46, vol. 3, pp. 499–536.

Chen, S, Chen, X & Cheng, Q 2014, "Conservatism and equity ownership of the founding family", *European Accounting Review*, vol. 23, no. 3, pp. 403–430.

Chrisman, JJ, Chua, JH & Sharma, P 2005, "Trends and directions in the development of a strategic management theory of the family firm", *Entrepreneurship Theory and Practice*, vol. 29, no. 5, pp. 555–576.

Christensen, HB, Lee, E & Walker, M 2015, "Incentives or standards: What determines accounting quality changes around IFRS adoption?", *European Accounting Review*, vol. 24, pp. 31–61.

Corbetta, G & Salvato, C 2004, "Self-serving or self-actualizing? Models of man and agency costs in different types of family firms: A commentary on 'Comparing the agency costs of family and non-family firms: conceptual issues and exploratory evidence'", *Entrepreneurship Theory and Practice*, vol. 28, no. 4, pp. 355–362.

Danes, SM, Stafford, K, Haynes, G & Amarapurkar, SS 2009, "Family capital of family firms: bridging human, social, and financial capital", *Family Business Review*, vol. 22, pp. 199–216.

DeTienne, DR & Chirico, F 2013, "Exit strategies in family firms: how socioemotional wealth drives the threshold of performance", *Entrepreneurship Theory and Practice*, vol. 37, pp. 1297–1318.

Fan, J & Wong, T 2002, "*Corporate ownership structure and the informativeness of accounting earnings in East Asia*", *Journal of Accounting and Economics*, vol. 33, pp. 401–425.

Filip, A, Jeanjean, T, & Paugam, L 2015, "Using real activities to avoid goodwill impairment losses: evidence and effect on future performance", *Journal of Business, Finance & Accounting*, vol. 42, no. 3–4, pp. 515–554.

Gomez-Meja, L, Larraza-Kintana, M & Makri, M 2003, "The determinants of executive compensation in family-controlled public corporations", *Academy of Management Journal*, vol. 46, no. 2, pp. 226–237.

Gómez-Mejía, LR, Haynes, KT, Núñez-Nickel, M, Jacobson, KJL & Moyano-Fuentes, J 2007, "Socioemotional wealth and business risks in family-controlled firms: evidence from Spanish olive oil mills", *Administrative Science Quarterly*, vol. 52, no. 1, pp. 106–137.

Gomez-Mejia, LR, Cruz, C & Imperatore, C 2014, "Is all that glitters really gold? Financial reporting and the protection of socioemotional wealth in family controlled firms", *European Accounting Review*, vol. 23, no. 3, pp. 387–402.

Gómez-Mejía, LR, Patel, PC & Zellweger, TM 2015, "In the horns of the dilemma socioemotional wealth, financial wealth, and acquisitions in family firms", *Journal of Management*, doi:10.1177/0149206315614375.

Greco, G, Ferramosca, S & Allegrini, M 2015, "The influence of family ownership on long-lived asset write-offs", *Family Business Review*, vol. 28, no. 4, pp. 355–371.

Habbershon, TG, Williams, M & MacMillan, IC 2003, "A unified systems perspective of family firm performance", *Journal of Business Venturing*, vol. 18, no. 4, pp. 451–465.

Jensen, MC & Meckling, WH 1976, "Theory of the firm: Managerial behavior, agency costs, and ownership structure", *Journal of Financial Economics*, vol. 3, no. 4, pp. 305–360.

Landsman, WR 2007, "Is fair value accounting information relevant and reliable? Evidence from capital market research", *Accounting and Business Research*, vol. 37, no. sup 1, pp. 19–30.

Laux, C & Leuz, C 2010, "Did fair-value accounting contribute to the financial crisis?", *Journal of Economic Perspective*, vol. 24, no. 1, pp. 93–118.

Le Breton-Miller, I & Miller, D 2006, "Why do some family businesses out-compete? Governance, long-term orientations, and sustainable capability", *Entrepreneurship Theory and Practice*, vol. 30, pp. 731–746.

Lennard, A 2018, "Fair value and the conceptual framework", in this handbook.

Lumpkin, GT, Brigham, KH & Moss, T 2010, "Long-term orientation: implications for the entrepreneurial orientation and performance of family businesses", *Entrepreneurship and Regional Development*, vol. 22, no. 3, pp. 241–264.

Magnan, M 2009, "Fair value accounting and the financial crisis: messenger or contributor?", *Accounting Perspectives*, vol. 8, no. 3, pp. 189–213.

Magnan, M & Parbonetti, A 2018, "Fair value accounting: a standard setting perspective", in this handbook.

Miller, D & Le Breton-Miller I 2006, "Family governance and firm performance: agency, stewardship and capabilities, *Family Business Review*, vol. 19, no. 1, pp. 73–87.

Miller, D, Le Breton-Miller, I & Lester, RH 2010, "Family ownership and acquisition behavior in publicly traded companies", *Strategic Management Journal*, vol. 31, no. 2, pp. 201–223.

Naldi, L, Nordqvist, M, Sjöberg, K & Wiklund, J 2007, "Entrepreneurial orientation, risk taking, and performance in family firms", *Family Business Review*, vol. 20, pp. 33–47.

Prencipe, A, Bar-Yosef, S, Mazzola, P & Pozza, L 2011, "Income smoothing in family-controlled companies: evidence from Italy", *Corporate Governance: An International Review*, vol. 19, no. 16, pp. 529–546.

Prencipe, A, Bar-Yosef, S, Dekker, HC 2014, "Accounting research in family firms: theoretical and empirical challenges", *European Accounting Review*, vol. 23, no. 3, pp. 361–385.

Ramanna, K & Watts, RL 2012, "Evidence on the use of unverifiable estimates in required goodwill impairment", *Review of Accounting Studies*, vol. 17, pp. 749–780.

Ronen, J 2008, "To fair value or not to fair value: a broader perspective", *ABACUS*, vol. 44, no. 2, pp. 181–208.

Salvato, C & Moores, K 2010, "Research on accounting in family firms: past accomplishments and future challenges", *Family Business Review*, vol. 23, no. 3, pp. 193–215.

Schulze, WS, Lubatkin, MH & Dino, RN 2003, "Exploring the agency consequences of ownership among the directors of private family firms", *Academy of Management Journal*, vol. 46, no. 2, pp. 179–194.

Sraer, D & Thesmar, D 2007, "Performance and behavior of family firms: evidence from the French stock market", *Journal of the European Economic Association*, vol. 5, no. 4, pp. 709–751.

Steier, L 2003, "Variants of agency contracts in family financed ventures as a continuum of familial altruisitic and market rationalities", *Journal of Business Venturing*, vol. 18, pp. 597–618.

Strebulaev, IA & Yang, B 2013, "The mystery of zero-leverage firms", *Journal of Financial Economics*, vol. 109, pp. 1–23.

Tagiuri, R & Davis, JA 1996, "Bivalent attributes of the family firm", *Family Business Review*, vol. 9, no. 2, pp. 199–208.

Villalonga, B & Amit, R 2006, "How do family ownership, control and management affect firm value?", *Journal of Financial Economics*, vol. 80, no. 2, pp. 385–417.

Wang, D 2006, "Founding family ownership and earnings quality", *Journal of Accounting Research*, vol. 44, pp. 619–656.

Whittington, G 2008, "Fair value and the IASB/FASB conceptual framework project: an alternative view", *ABACUS*, vol. 44, no. 2, pp. 139–168.

Zellweger, T, Eddleston, K & Kellermanns, FW 2010, "Exploring the concept of familiness: Introducing family firm identity", *Journal of Family Business Strategy*, vol. 1, pp. 54–63.

Zellweger, T, Kellermanns, FW, Chrisman, JJ & Chua, J 2012, "Family control and family firm valuation by family CEOs: the importance of intentions for transgenerational control", *Organization Science*, vol. 23, pp. 851–868.

INDEX

For Product Safety Concerns and Information please contact our EU
representative GPSR@taylorandfrancis.com
Taylor & Francis Verlag GmbH, Kaufingerstraße 24, 80331 München, Germany

www.ingramcontent.com/pod-product-compliance
Ingram Content Group UK Ltd.
Pitfield, Milton Keynes, MK11 3LW, UK
UKHW011454240425
457818UK00021B/823